Blended Curriculum in the Inclusive K–3 Classroom
Teaching ALL Young Children

Michelle LaRocque

Florida Atlantic University

Sharon M. Darling

Florida Atlantic University

PEARSON

Boston   New York   San Francisco
Mexico City   Montreal   Toronto   London   Madrid   Munich   Paris
Hong Kong   Singapore   Tokyo   Cape Town   Sydney

Executive Editor: *Virginia Lanigan*
Series Editorial Assistant: *Matt Bucholz*
Marketing Manager: *Kris Ellis-Levy*
Production Editor: *Paula Carroll*
Editorial Production Service: *Publishers' Design and Production Services, Inc.*
Composition Buyer: *Linda Cox*
Manufacturing Buyer: *Linda Morris*
Electronic Composition: *Publishers' Design and Production Services, Inc.*
Interior Design: *Publishers' Design and Production Services, Inc.*
Cover Administrator: *Elena Sidorova*

For related titles and support materials, visit our online catalog at www.ablongman.com.

Between the time website information is gathered and then published, it is not unusual for some sites to have closed. Also, the transcription of URLs can result in typographical errors. The publisher would appreciate notification where these errors occur so that they may be corrected in subsequent editions.

ISBN-10: 0-205-48700-9
ISBN-13: 978-0-205-48700-4

Library of Congress Cataloging-in-Publication Data

LaRocque, Michelle.
    Blended curriculum in the inclusive K–3 classroom : teaching all
young children / Michelle LaRocque, Sharon M. Darling.
        p. cm.
    ISBN-13: 978-0-205-48700-4 (alk. paper)
    ISBN-10: 0-205-48700-9
    1. Inclusive education—United States. 2. Children with disabilities—Education—
Curricula—United States. 3. Education, Primary—Curricula—United States. I. Darling,
Sharon M. II. Title.

    LC1201L.37 2007
    371.9'0460973—dc22   2007020560

Printed in the United States of America
10 9 8 7 6 5 4 3 2 1   11 10 09 08 07

For Olivia, Eliana, and Jude
. . . may your future teachers be prepared to teach ALL children!

Sharon M. Darling, PhD, is an Assistant Professor of Early Childhood Education/Early Childhood Special Education with Florida Atlantic University in Boca Raton, Florida. She prepares preservice, inservice, undergraduate, and graduate students to work effectively with young children birth through third grade who are typically developing and those with delays or disabilities and to particularly attentive to the diversities children bring to the play and learning spaces.

Michelle LaRocque, PhD, is an Associate Professor with Florida Atlantic University in Boca Raton, Florida. Her teaching interests are in areas that affect school and classroom climate, including home–school collaboration, positive behavior support, social skills training, and diversity. Her research interests are in the prevention and remediation of behavioral disorders in early childhood.

Contents

Preface   x

Contributors   xi

chapter **1**   *Rationale for a Blended Education*   **1**
Lynette Chandler and Jennifer Loncola

Practical Application Vignette   2

Overview of Inclusion   2

Rationale for Inclusion or Blended Service Delivery   5

Federal Laws That Support Inclusion   8

Overview of National Organizations' Support for Inclusion   14

Rationale for Blended Teacher Preparation   19

Summary   25

chapter **2**   *Overview of Young Children with Exceptional Needs*   **32**
Sharon M. Darling and Michelle LaRocque

Practical Application Vignettes   33

Young Children with Special Needs in Public Schools   34

Developmental Delay   35

Learning or Behavioral Characteristics   38

High- and Low-Incidence Disabilities   41

Service Delivery Options   42

Referral   45

The IEP Team   45

Implications When Disabilities Coexist with Diversity   54

Changing Roles of Families   55

Changing Needs of Young Children with Disabilities   55

Curricular Implications   55

Summary   58

chapter **3** *Constructivism in Early Childhood* **61**
Nyaradzo Mvududu and Susan B. Gilbert

Practical Application Vignette   62
Components of Constructivist Practice   64
More on Strands of Constructivism   66
Some Theoretical Views on Application   69
What Constructivism Is and What It Is Not   72
Constructivism and Other Pedagogies   74
Classroom Examples   80
Summary   82

chapter **4** *Organizing the Inclusive Classroom for Grades K–3*   **91**
Jack Scott, Debra Leach, and Jessica Bucholz

Practical Application Vignette   92
Introduction to the Inclusive Classroom   92
Assessing the Physical Environment as a Collaborative Team   96
The K–3 Child in the Classroom Environment   96
Organizing Areas within the Class   100
Designing Environments That Will Accommodate a Wide Range of Children   104
The Auditory Environment   107
Creating a Positive Visual Environment in the Inclusive Class   111
Organizing or Optimizing   112
Cultural Diversity   114
Developing Rules and Routines   114
Playground/Recess   119
Scheduling   123
Summary   125

chapter **5** *Positive Behavioral Supports in the Classroom*   **128**
Michelle LaRocque

Practical Application Vignette   129
Why Challenging Behavior May Occur   130
What Can Be Done to Prevent Challenging Behavior   139
When Challenging Behaviors Occur   147

Discipline and IDEA   150

Summary   151

chapter **6**   *Relationships In and Outside the Inclusive Classroom*   **156**
Loury Ollison Floyd and Lisa J. Vernon-Dotson

Practical Application Vignettes   157
Introduction to Relationships   157
Relationships   158
Communication   161
Friendships   161
Social Development   163
Peer-Based Strategies   164
Family Systems   164
Paraeducators   169
Collaboration   173
Special Issues   178
Summary   179

chapter **7**   *Understanding Early Literacy Learning in the*
Inclusive Classroom   **185**
Anne E. Gregory and Jennifer Snow-Gerono

Practical Application Vignette   186
Introduction to Reading   186
Constructing Knowledge in Reading   187
Reading Process Skills   193
Common Views of Literacy Instruction   195
Differentiating Instruction in Reading   197
Principles of Literacy Learning   204
Thinking about Instruction   206
Gathering Information   207
Evaluating Information   215
Teaching   218
Summary   228

c h a p t e r **8** *Understanding Early Writing and Instructional Opportunities in the Inclusive Classroom* **233**
Anne E. Gregory and Carolyn Loffer

Practical Application Vignette   234
Introduction to Writing   235
Constructing Knowledge in Writing   235
Writing Process Skills   236
Integrating Writing throughout the Curriculum   240
Writing Process   248
Differentiating Instruction in Writing   257
The Reading-Writing Connection   273
Summary   274

c h a p t e r **9** *Mathematics in the Inclusive Classroom*   **278**
Jonathan L. Brendefur and Fernanda Morales-Brendefur

Introduction to Math   279
Learning and Teaching Mathematics   279
Mathematical Understanding   281
Math Process Skills   282
Differentiating Instruction in Math   285
Constructing Knowledge in Math   288
Developing Students' Ideas of Measurement   298
Developing Probabilistic and Statistical Thinking   301
Summary   304

c h a p t e r **1 0** *Science in the Inclusive Classroom*   **309**
Greg Conderman and C. Sheldon Woods

Practical Application Vignette   310
Introduction to Science   310
Constructing Knowledge in Science   313
Science Process Skills   315
Integrating Science Throughout the Curriculum   315
Differentiating Instruction in Science   320
Performance-Based Assessments in Science   327

Sample Science Activities with Modifications   328

Summary   342

chapter **11**   *Social Studies in the Inclusive Classroom*   **348**
Ereka R. Williams

Practical Application Vignette   349

Introduction Social Studies   349

Constructing Knowledge in Social Studies   353

Social Studies Process Skills   354

Differentiating Instruction in Social Studies   358

Integrating Social Studies throughout the Curriculum   366

Summary   367

chapter **12**   *Integrating Art and Music in the Inclusive Classroom*   **371**
Susannah Brown and Cathy Smilan

Practical Application Vignette   372

Introduction to the Arts   372

Constructing Knowledge in the Arts   373

Arts Process Skills   375

Multicultural Art and Music Education   375

Integrating the Arts   376

Competencies Taught in an Arts-Based Curriculum   377

Differentiating Instruction in the Arts   380

Summary   403

Index   **407**

Preface

Today's early childhood professionals require many tools to help children develop and become successful learners. Effective educational strategies that reflect the diversity of families and children served in early childhood programs necessitate a dramatically different approach to teacher preparation. This preparation must draw from a wide array of disciplines that integrate information rather than simply add unrelated courses.

Reauthorization of landmark special education legislation, the Individuals With Disabilities Education Improvement Act of 2004 (IDEA) aligns closely to the No Child Left Behind Act, helping to ensure equity, accountability, and excellence in education for *all* children (P.L. 108-446, 2004). Support for teacher preparation programs specializing in the early childhood and primary years has also come from professional organizations. Through a joint position paper and joint guidelines for personnel standards, professional organizations relevant to early childhood and teacher preparation, the Council for Exceptional Children/Division for Early Childhood (CEC/DEC), the National Association for the Education of Young Children (NAEYC), and the Association for Teacher Education (ATE), advocate for the preparation of personnel who are primed to serve the needs of ALL young children in inclusive settings that are natural environments for these young children (ATE, 1994; DEC 1993, 1997; NAEYC, 1994, 1998).

We call for teacher preparation that is designed to prepare teachers to meet the needs of ALL children who are from a variety of backgrounds.

Sharon M. Darling
and
Michelle LaRocque

Contributors

Jonathan L. Brendefur, PhD, is an Associate Professor of Curriculum, Instruction, and Foundational Studies in the College of Education at Boise State University. His research interests lie in mathematics education, teacher beliefs, instructional practices, mathematical discourse, and issues of equity.

Susannah Brown, PhD, is an Assistant Professor and Program Coordinator of Art Education in the Department of Teacher Education, College of Education, at Florida Atlantic University. Her research interests include arts integration, professional development, personal narrative, and visual art.

Jessica Bucholz, EdD, is an Assistant Professor with the University of West Georgia. Her research interests include using social stories for people with mental retardation and inclusion.

Lynette Chandler, PhD, is a Professor in the Department of Teaching and Learning at Northern Illinois University. She teaches courses and conducts research in Early Childhood Special Education, Behavior Analysis/Functional Assessment, and Early Literacy.

Greg Conderman, EdD, is Associate Professor of Teaching and Learning in Special Education at Northern Illinois University in DeKalb. His research interests include instructional methods for students with disabilities and collaboration.

Loury Ollison Floyd, PhD, is an Assistant Professor of Special Education in the Department of Curriculum and Instruction at North Carolina Agricultural and Technical State University. Her research interests include working with families from culturally and linguistically diverse backgrounds, paraeducators, and inclusive education.

Susan B. Gilbert, EdD, is an Assistant Professor of Early Childhood Education at National University in Los Angeles, California.

Anne E. Gregory, PhD, is an Associate Professor of Literacy Education in the Department of Literacy at Boise State University. She researches and teaches courses in early literacy acquisition.

Debra Leach, MEd, is an Assistant Professor at Winthrop University specializing in early intervention for children with autism.

Carolyn Loffer, MEd, is currently a Title One teacher in the Meridian school district in Boise, Idaho. Additionally, she teaches early literacy courses at Boise State University.

Jennifer Loncola, PhD, is an Assistant Professor of Special Education at DePaul University. She teaches courses in Early Childhood Special Education and has expertise in autism.

Fernanda Morales-Brendefur, EdD, is currently the Spanish coordinator and teacher at Foothills School of Arts and Sciences in Boise, Idaho. Her research interests lie in education for social justice, promoting equity, and teaching through a social-constructivist approach.

Nyaradzo Mvududu, EdD, is an Assistant Professor of Curriculum and Instruction at Seattle Pacific University in Washington. Her interests include statistics and research on constructivism.

Jack Scott, PhD, is an Associate Professor in the Department of Exceptional Student Education at Florida Atlantic University. Currently he serves as Director of the Florida Atlantic University Center for Autism and Related Disabilities (CARD).

Cathy Smilan, EdD, is an art integration specialist and teaches art education and curriculum instruction at Florida Atlantic University. Her research and professional development interests include visual arts and literacy integration, museum as classroom, and the arts in early childhood learning.

Jennifer Snow-Gerono, PhD, is currently an Assistant Professor in Curriculum, Instruction, and Foundational Studies at Boise State University. Her scholarly work emphasizes teacher education, professional development, school–university partnerships, and teacher inquiry.

Lisa J. Vernon-Dotson, PhD, was a special educator for over ten years. Her current research includes utilizing school-based leadership teams to promote the use of evidence-based inclusive practices. She is currently an Assistant Professor at Duquesne University in Pittsburgh, Pennsylvania.

Ereka R. Williams, PhD, serves as Coordinator of Elementary Education Programs at North Carolina A&T State University. Her areas of research and focus include social studies, culturally responsive pedagogy, parental perceptions of school, and teacher candidates' perceptions of self, learning, and schooling.

C. Sheldon Woods, PhD, is Assistant Professor of Teaching and Learning in Science Education at Northern Illinois University in DeKalb. His research interests are in science education, service learning, and international education.

Rationale for a Blended Education

Lynette Chandler and Jennifer Loncola

Objectives

After reading this chapter, students will be able to

- Explain the rationale for providing inclusive services to all children.
- Describe federal laws and specific provisions that support inclusion.
- Explain the rationale for providing blended teacher preparation training.
- Identify national early childhood organizations and describe their position statements related to inclusion and blended teacher preparation training.
- Describe recommended practices and standards of national organizations related to inclusive service delivery and blended teacher preparation training.

Key Terms

Inclusion

Division for Early Childhood (DEC) of the Council for Exceptional Children (CEC)

National Association for the Education of Young Children (NAEYC)

Section 504, Americans with Disabilities Act (ADA)

Individuals with Disabilities Education Act (IDEA)

Free and appropriate education (FAPE)

Least restrictive environment (LRE)

Individualized Education Plan (IEP)

Developmentally Appropriate Practice (DAP)

Individually Appropriate Practice (IAP)

Practical Application Vignette

It is the first day of school, and children, parents, and caregivers eagerly line up on the playground, waiting to enter the building. The excitement is palpable as children greet friends they have not seen all summer. As the first bell rings and the children make their way into the school, two friends whisper conspiratorially as they start toward a third-grade classroom. A little girl hugs her mother's leg as they head to the kindergarten classroom for the first time. A group of first graders reluctantly stop an impromptu game of tag and run for the door.

Once inside the school, the kindergartener peers around the classroom and makes a beeline for the play area where she starts stacking blocks; her reluctance no longer evident. The first graders search the room for their desks and excitedly look for their tablemates. The two third graders squeal with delight as they see they will be sitting next to each other.

These children are all happy to be starting school. The shy kindergarten student has autism; one of the first graders has been diagnosed with a developmental delay, and the other first grader is an English language learner; and one of the squealing third graders uses a wheelchair. Despite their differences, all of these children will be successful in the general education classroom. Their teachers have been taught to utilize a blended approach, and each one is prepared to instruct students who are English language learners, students with disabilities, and those who are typically developing. The kindergarten teacher uses a visual schedule for all children in her class to help with transition issues. The first-grade teacher uses a photograph paired with the written name to help the student with a developmental delay identify her desk and has labeled objects and cubbies in her classroom in both Spanish and English. The third-grade teacher has arranged her room with wider aisles to accommodate a wheelchair and placed materials within reach of a child using a wheelchair. These are just a few of the many accommodations these teachers, in collaboration with other team members, have made for their students to help them be successful on the first day of school. As the year progresses, each teacher will continue to modify and adapt the general education curriculum, materials, goals, and instructional environment to ensure that each student, regardless of ability, learning style, linguistic and cultural diversity, and disability status, is successful.

Overview of Inclusion

Definition of Inclusion

The concept of **inclusion,** traditionally defined as educating all children in the same classroom (see below for varying definitions), has been discussed by general and special education teachers and other service providers, administrators, policy makers, researchers, and families since the 1970s. It was not until the 1990s, however, that inclusion became a viable option for young children with disabilities or special needs (Hunt, Soto, Maier, Lioiron, & Bae, 2004; McDonnell, Brownell, & Wolery, 1997; Odom, 2000). Currently, many children with disabilities spend the majority of their day in inclusive settings: those settings that they would be in if they did not have a disability. For example, recent data reported by the U.S. Department of Education indicated that during the 2003/2004 school year approximately 34 percent of the preschool-aged children who received special education and related services were enrolled in inclusive early childhood settings such as Head

Start, community-based programs, and private and public preschool programs. Another 16 percent divided their time between inclusive settings and self-contained special education settings (IDEA-data.org, 2005). The increasing trend for inclusive placement has occurred also for older children. During the 2003/2004 school year, more than 50 percent of the children with disabilities from 6 to 21 years of age spent at least 80 percent of their school day in general education classrooms (National Center for Education Statistics, 2005).

Although we might argue that the percentage of young children currently attending inclusive programs is not at an acceptable level (little more than 50%), we also recognize that the practice of inclusion has increased over time. During and prior to the 1960s and 1970s, children with disabilities who received educational and/or caregiving services most often received those services in segregated, self-contained classrooms or schools or in residential facilities. In addition, many children were denied the opportunity to receive educational services through the public schools, and general education teachers had the right to exclude children with disabilities from their classrooms. Fortunately, the acceptance and practice of inclusion has steadily increased during the past thirty years, and inclusion is now recognized as a major service option for young children and their families from birth to 8 years of age. For example, Miller, Fader, and Vincent (2000) reported that early childhood educators and other early childhood professionals identified inclusion as a preferred and recommended practice for young children with disabilities. Furthermore, the **Division for Early Childhood (DEC) of the Council for Exceptional Children (CEC)** and the **National Association for the Education of Young Children (NAEYC)** have identified inclusion as the preferred service delivery option for all young children with special needs (DEC, 2000).

Although the practice of inclusion is prevalent in schools and communities today, there is considerable variability among classrooms and programs in the variables and practices that are used in inclusive settings. Programs often vary in terms of the ratio of typically developing children to children with special needs, adult–child ratios and staffing patterns, the amount of time and type of activities in which children with disabilities are included, the types of teaching strategies employed and expectations for children with disabilities and typically developing students, the model for delivering special education and related services and the amount of interaction between early childhood educators and early childhood special educators, the roles of special education and general education teachers, and the models of consultation and collaboration between special and general educators (Guralnick, 2001; Schwartz, Sandall, Odom, Horn, & Beckman, 2002).

Differences across inclusive early childhood classrooms and programs may occur because there is no agreed-upon definition of inclusion and no one accepted or recommended model for developing and delivering services in inclusive settings. The concept of inclusion means different things to different individuals, and it is rooted in values, evidence-based practice, community standards, and personal experience.

As discussed by Chandler and Maude (in press), some individuals have adopted a narrow definition of inclusion that focuses primarily on placement, or the type of setting in which the child is enrolled (e.g., general education classroom or segregated special education classroom), the amount of time spent in those settings, or the ratio of children with special needs to typically developing children (Odom, 2000). For instance, Hunt et al. (2004) describe inclusion as situations in which children with disabilities are served in the same classrooms and settings as typically developing peers and receive services to accomplish their goals.

Most individuals agree that physical placement in settings with typically developing children is a necessary first step in developing inclusive programs. This is illustrated by Odom (2000), who wrote, "if we expect that children with disabilities will learn from, interact with, and form relationships with typically developing children, then the children with disabilities need to be around typically developing peers for a substantial part of their day" (p. 22). However, physical placement alone is not sufficient to promote hoped-for outcomes from inclusion. As a result, many have adopted a broad view of inclusion that focuses not only on where services are offered (i.e., placement) but also on how services and supports are provided in those settings (Chandler & Maude, in press). A broader view of inclusion also focuses on variables such as active teaching practices that promote interactions among children during meaningful activities, the use of individualized services and supports, and a focus on social and educational or developmental outcomes for all children (Grisham-Brown, Hemmeter, & Pretti-Frontczak, 2005; Guralnick, 1993; Odom, 2002, Walsh, Rous, & Lutzer, 2000). This broad view has become the current trend in defining inclusion, and it is supported by research, national organizations, and federal and state laws.

Those who adopt a broad view of inclusion recognize that simply placing children in the same environment will not necessarily lead to interactions between typically developing children and children with disabilities or the active participation of children with disabilities in daily activities and routines (Bricker, 2000; Janko, Schwartz, Sandall, Anderson, & Cottman, 1997; McCollum, 2005; Walsh et al., 2000). For instance, Guralnick (2001) states that an essential feature of inclusion is *planned participation* between children with and without disabilities during educational and developmental activities.

The broad perspective of inclusion focuses on children with disabilities and typically developing children sharing the social and learning environment as well as physical environment. In addition, a broad view requires active planning that leads to the participation of children with disabilities in daily activities and routines and the provision of individualized services and support to help them participate and that promotes and supports interaction between children with and without disabilities (Chandler & Dahlquist, 1999; Grisham-Brown et al., 2005; Wickstrom Kane, Goldstein, & Kazmarek, 1999).

An even broader view of inclusion is one that focuses on all children; inclusive programs are able to meet the needs of *all* children: children identified as at-risk, children with disabilities, children with cultural and linguistic diversity, and children who are typically developing (Hyson & Winton, 2005). This broad view of inclusion requires the integration or blending of recommended practices from the fields of early childhood and early childhood special education for serving children who are typically developing and children with disabilities and their families. One example of a practice that reflects a broad view of inclusion and that blends recommended practices from early childhood and early childhood special education is universal theory and design (Council for Exceptional Children, 2005; Odom & Wolery, 2003). Universal design advocates recommend that educators consider the diverse needs of all students and make accommodations for students when developing lesson plans or instructional units, rather than adding them on after students experience difficulties or failure. Universal design is based on the assumptions that there is a continuum of learning abilities and differences within classrooms and that instruction must be flexible and inclusive so that all students are able to progress within the general education curriculum. This may involve providing differentiated instruction, peer tutoring or cooperative learning, multisensory instructional strategies, assistive technology, and adaptations and accommodations to materials, student responses, and instructional delivery (Council for Exceptional Children, 2005). This type of inclusive planning strategy is congruent with Developmentally and Individually Appropriate Practice and other recommended practices for working with all children that are endorsed by NAEYC and DEC. Developmentally and Individually Appropriate Practice will be discussed in more detail later in this chapter.

A broad view of inclusion is applicable to the variety of programs that children may attend, including public school, child care or after-school care, and community programs and the activities that occur within those programs (Guralnick, 2001; Odom, Schwartz, & ECRII Investigators, 2002). A broad view of inclusion is supported by several federal laws that will be discussed in a subsequent section, and by national early childhood and early childhood special education organizations. First, however, we will discuss the rationale for providing inclusive programs and activities.

Rationale for Inclusion or Blended Service Delivery

The current ideas regarding inclusion grew out of discontent with previous terms, beliefs, and practices related to providing services for children with disabilities. In the past, the terms *mainstreaming* and *integration* were used to describe the practice of placing children with disabilities in settings with typically developing peers. For example, mainstreaming has been defined as the placement of children with disabilities in educational settings for and with normally developing children (Odom & McEvoy, 1988) and as students with disabilities participating the general education setting as long as they are able to meet academic demands with minimal supports (Friend & Bursuck, 2006). Integration has been defined as the process of actively mixing children with and without disabilities

(Odom & McEvoy, 1988) and as creating opportunities for children with disabilities to participate with peers in typical classrooms or community settings (Salisbury, 1991). Many individuals have criticized these terms because they focus on the differences between children and they imply that children with disabilities are placed in programs that are developed *for typically developing children* rather than *for all children* (Salisbury, 1991). As such, placement in regular education classrooms was seen as a right that children with disabilities had to earn, and, if they did not meet the same academic and social/behavioral expectations as typically developing peers, they could be placed in segregated special education settings.

The term *inclusion* was adopted to describe a different and broader philosophy regarding the rights of children with disabilities and the importance of inclusion as a value within our educational system. This broader view of inclusion reflects the normalization principle. This principle states that, as much as possible, individuals with disabilities should be treated as, and have the same experiences and opportunities as, individuals without disabilities (Guralnick, 2001; Turnbull, 1990). Children cannot be denied access to programs or services because they have a disability. Programs must be accessible to *all* children. Thus, children with disabilities have the option to attend classes and settings that they would attend if they did not have a disability.

The philosophy underlying inclusion is that children with disabilities are more similar to, than different from, typically developing children. In addition, all classes and settings include children of diverse needs and abilities, and the needs of all children should be accommodated (Miller & Stayton, 1998). Classrooms and activities should be developed for all children, and educators should be able to meet the needs of all children (Council for Exceptional Children, 2005). The focus is on all children being part of the class, creating a community that celebrates diversity and provides supports to enable all children to actively participate and learn (Allen & Cowdery, 2005). Thus, inclusion is seen as a right for all children, not a privilege that is extended to only a few children or only to typically developing children (*Oberti v. Board of Education in Clementon School District,* 1993). This view or rationale for inclusion reflects our values or beliefs about children with disabilities and the educational system. Programs and service providers must be ready for inclusion and provide the supports needed to make inclusion work for all (Odom et al., 2002).

Expected benefits or positive outcomes from inclusion. A second rationale for inclusion is associated with outcomes. Since the early 1970s, advocates for inclusive education (and mainstreaming and integration) have discussed a variety of expected benefits of inclusion for children with special needs. In general, children with disabilities who participated in inclusive programs were expected to make greater academic and preacademic, communication, social, and behavioral gains than children who participated in segregated settings and activities. Expected benefits for other individuals who experienced inclusion also were predicted. For example, in his seminal book on inclusion, Guralnick (1978) discussed positive outcomes from inclusion for children with disabilities, children without disabilities, teachers and other service providers, and families of children with and without disabilities.

Subsequent research has documented many positive outcomes from inclusion, as shown in Table 1.1 (e.g., Buysee & Bailey, 1993; Diamond & Stacey, 2000; Guralnick, 2001; Mortweet et al., 1999; Odom, 2000, 2002; Peck, Odom, & Bricker, 1993; Rea, McLaughlin, & Walther-Thomas, 2002; Stoneman, 2001). This research demonstrates that inclusion affects everyone: children with and without disabilities, families, early childhood educators, early childhood special educators, other service providers, and administrators. The positive outcomes identified in Table 1.1, however, are not guaranteed, and they do not automatically occur when children with disabilities are placed in inclusive classrooms and activities. Rather, there is clear evidence that these positive outcomes occur in high-quality programs that actively plan for inclusion and that employ evidence-based and recommended practices that support learning for all children within inclusive settings (Odom, 2000; Odom & Bailey, 2001; Salisbury & McGregor, 2002).

Hanson and her colleagues point out that positive outcomes from inclusion may be more difficult to achieve for children with diverse linguistic and cultural backgrounds in addition to special needs

Table 1.1 ● Benefits of Participation in High-Quality Inclusive Classrooms and Settings

Children With Disabilities*

● Children attain academic and developmental gains that are equal to or exceed those obtained in segregated, noninclusive settings.

● Many children make greater gains in social, play, behavioral, and communication outcomes than those obtained in segregated, noninclusive settings. Typically, gains in social interaction with peers occur in programs in which teachers actively plan for and support interaction among children.

Typically Developing Children

● Children make academic and developmental gains that are equal to or exceed those that would be expected from maturation alone.

● Children do not develop challenging behaviors.

● Children develop positive attitudes regarding diversity.

Families

● Some families are initially anxious about the effects of their child's participation in inclusive settings and activities and express concerns regarding teacher and other staff expertise, training, and support in inclusive classrooms.

● Most families support inclusion after their child has participated in inclusive settings activities, and their positive attitudes increase over time.

Service Providers

● Practitioners identify increased expertise and confidence in meeting the needs of all children.

● Practitioners develop positive attitudes toward diversity.

● Practitioners generally support inclusion following experience in inclusive settings.

Based on Beckman, Hanson, & Horn, 2002; Bruder, 1993; Buysse & Bailey, 1993; Chandler & Dahlquist; 1999; Diamond & Stacey, 2000; Friend & Bursuck, 2006; Guralnick, 2001; Hunter, 1999; Lamorey & Bricker, 1993; Levine & Antia, 1997; McWilliam, 2000; Mortweet et al., 1999; Odom, 2000, 2002; Odom & Bailey, 2001; Odom & McEvoy, 1988, 1990; Rea et al., 2000; Salisbury, 1991; Stoneman, 2001; and Villa & Colker, 2006).

*The majority of studies that have documented outcomes associated with inclusion have examined outcomes for student with mild disabilities; however, some studies have documented positive outcomes for children with moderate and severe disabilities (e.g., Hunt et al., 2001, 2003, 2004; Hunter, 1999; Kamps et al., 2002; see also Mastropieri, Scruggs, & Hamilton, 1999).

(Hanson, Gutierrez, Morgan, Brennan, & Zercher, 1997). They indicate that the interaction between culture, language, and disability can affect the ability of the child to benefit academically, socially, and linguistically in an inclusive setting. It is especially important to actively plan for these children and to employ evidence-based practices related to inclusion and bilingual education (e.g., small-group cooperative activities, scaffolding, visual supports, exposure to vocabulary throughout the day and in multiple contexts, social or informal and formal opportunities to use and hear English, and guided reading [Cappellini, 2006; Soderman, Gregory, & McCarty, 2005; Young & Hadaway, 2006]).

Numerous studies and publications have described effective strategies, models of teaching and collaboration, and other evidence-based and recommended practices that are associated with successful, high-quality inclusion programs (e.g., Guralnick, 2001; Horn, Leiber, Sandall, & Schwartz, 2001; Odom, 2000, 2002; Peck et al., 1993; Sandall, Hemmeter, McLean, & Smith, 2005). These practices are included in Table 1.2. These evidence-based and recommended practices facilitate the attainment of maximal benefits for children, families, and service providers. When they are not in place, they may serve as barriers to successful inclusion (Chandler & Maude, in press; McWilliam, Wolery, & Odom, 2001). Clearly, it is important for educators to develop high-quality programs and to employ effective practices in order to maximize positive outcomes from participation in inclusive programs for children, families, and educators.

The rationale for inclusion identifies inclusion as (a) a value or right that is available to all children and (b) a practice that produces positive outcomes for children, families, and service providers. Both of these factors have had a profound impact on the development of federal laws regarding the rights of children and other individuals with disabilities to educational and other services in inclusive settings.

Federal Laws That Support Inclusion

We have come a long way from the days in which individuals with disabilities were institutionalized, remained at home with few to no services, or attended classrooms and schools that were separate from those attended by typically developing children. A comprehensive history of inclusion has

Table 1.2 ● Evidence-Based and Recommended Practices Associated With Positive Outcomes for Children, Families, and Service Providers in High-Quality Inclusive Settings

1. Shared philosophy that supports inclusion.
2. Shared approaches and instructional strategies for supporting and teaching children with and without disabilities as well as specialized knowledge within specific positions (e.g., early childhood, early childhood special education, and speech and language pathologist).
3. Individualized and specialized instruction including adaptations and accommodations for children with disabilities.
4. Integrated delivery of services and opportunities to practice skills during meaningful daily activities and routines in the inclusive setting.
5. Collaboration and communication between early childhood and early childhood special educators, and other service providers (e.g., therapists, counselors, school psychologists).
6. Opportunities for family involvement.
7. Administrative support in terms of time, staff training and development, and resources, and administrative leadership in establishing a systems-wide philosophy, fostering positive attitudes among staff and supporting policies and practices that produce positive outcomes for children and families.
8. Planned opportunities and support for peer interaction.

Based on Bruder, 1993; Buysse & Bailey, 1993; Buysse et al., 2001; DEC, 2000; Diamond & Stacey, 2000; Early & Winton, 2001; Frazeur Cross et al., 2004; Horn, Leiber, Sandall, Schwartz, & Wolery, 2002; Hunt, Doering et al. 2001; Hunt, Soto, et al., 2003; Hunter, 1999; Kamps et al., 2002; Lamorey & Bricker, 1993; Leiber et al., 2002; Mastropieri et al., 1999; McWilliam, 2000; McWilliam et al., 2001; Odom & Bailey, 2001; Odom & McEvoy, 1990; Odom et al., 2002; Praisner, 2003; Salisbury & McGregor, 2002; Schwartz et al., 2002; Stoneman, 2001).

been provided elsewhere and is beyond the scope of this chapter (e.g., Allen & Cowdery, 2005; Grisham-Brown et al., 2005; Guralnick, 2001). This chapter will provide a review of major and landmark federal legislation that has addressed the inclusion and the education of young children with disabilities. Before we do this, it may be helpful to have a little background about federal laws.

Federal laws may be identified by a public law number (e.g., P.L. 94-142) as well as by the formal title of the law. The first set of numbers indicates the session of Congress in which the law was passed. The second set of numbers indicates what number the bill was in the sequence of bills that were passed during that Congressional session. For example, The Education for All Handi-capped Act is also referred to as P.L. 94-142. This indicates that the law was passed by the ninety fourth Congress and that it was the 142th bill passed that year. Public laws typically are scheduled for periodic reauthorization. Reauthorization means that the law will no longer be in effect unless Congress approves (i.e., reauthorizes) continuation of the law and establishes yearly funding for the act. Congress also has the opportunity to amend parts of the law during reauthorization.

Federal laws related to the education of children with disabilities provide a general framework that outlines the rights of children and families and the responsibilities and requirements of state agencies. After a law has been passed, it is sent to an agency within the executive branch, and that agency then writes regulations to accompany the law. Regulations provide more in-depth informa-tion and clarification regarding aspects of the law such as definitions of terms, components of edu-cational plans, and timelines and processes to be followed. State agencies are required to comply with federal laws and regulations; however, they may choose to expand on federal requirements as long as they are meeting the minimal requirements of the law. For example, federal law requires schools to provide transition planning to address the needs of students who will exit high school at age 16. Many states begin transition planning at age 14.

Head Start Legislation

Table 1.3 provides a chronological list of major federal legislation regarding children and youth with disabilities. One of the first laws that addressed inclusion of young children with disabilities was initially designed to serve only children considered at-risk. In 1965, the Economic Opportunity Education Act (P.L. 88-452) established Head Start programs in order to address the developmental and physical risks of children who were living in poverty. In 1972, amendments to the Economic Opportunity Act (P.L. 92-424) mandated that Head Start programs reserve 10 percent of their place-ments for children with disabilities. This requirement has been maintained with each reauthorization of the Head Start legislation (Gallagher, 2000).

Civil Rights Legislation

Early civil rights legislation set the stage for inclusion. The civil rights movement and subsequent legislation addressed the issue of racial discrimination in public school education. In 1954, the land-mark *Brown v. Board of Education* case prohibited segregated education on the basis of race. This case found that separate (or segregated) education was not equal and ordered the integration of all children within public school programs. Subsequent court cases such as *PARC v. Pennsylvania* (1971) and *Mills v. the Washington, DC, Board of Education* (1972) extended the right to a public school education to children with disabilities. These and other cases found that the exclusion of children

Table 1.3 ● Landmark Legislation Regarding the Inclusion of Young Children With Disabilities

Year	Number	Title
1972	P.L. 92-424	Economic Opportunity Act
1973	P.L. 93-112	Rehabilitation Act: Section 504
1975	P.L. 94-142	Education for All Handicapped Act
1986	P.L. 99-457	Education for All Handicapped Act Amendments
1990	P.L. 101-476	Individuals With Disabilities Education Act
1990	P.L. 101-336	Americans With Disabilities Act
1997	P.L. 105-17	Individuals With Disabilities Education Act Amendments
2002	P.L. 107-110	No Child Left Behind
2005	P.L. 108-466	Individuals With Disabilities Education Improvement Act

with disabilities from public school education and segregated education was a violation of the four-teenth amendment, which provides for equal protection of all citizens (e.g., *Board of Education v. Rowley,* 1982, *Daniel R. R. v. State Board of Education,* 1989, and *Oberti v. Board of Education,* 1993). For more information on civil rights legislation and case law related to inclusion see www.kidstogether.org/right-ed.html, http://laws.findlaw.com, and www.wrightslaw.com/caselaw.html.

Another important civil rights legislation that supported inclusion was the 1973 the Federal Rehabilitation Act. **Section 504** of this act prohibits discrimination against individuals with disabilities by public and private programs that receive federal funding. This law meant that school programs that received federal funding were required to serve children with disabilities. The Federal Rehabilitation Act was reauthorized in 1990 (P.L. 101-336) and renamed the **Americans With Disabilities Act (ADA)** reflecting the move to use "person-first language" when talking about individuals with disabilities. Person-first language will be discussed in a later section. The ADA continues to protect individuals with disabilities from discrimination and expands that protection to all but the smallest private and public programs and businesses. In addition to public schools, this includes Head Start programs, community-based programs such as preschools and after-school care, and prekindergarten programs. These programs cannot deny enrollment because of a disability, thus enabling many young children with disabilities and their families to participate in neighborhood and community programs (Guralnick, 2001; Odom et al., 2002).

The ADA also requires employers, public agencies and places, and public transportation to provide reasonable accommodations and accessible environments and services to individuals with disabilities. Programs that provide educational services to children with disabilities who are not eligible for special education and related services under federal special education law are required to provide a free and appropriate education and accommodations for those students and to document accommodations on each student's program plan.

The Education for All Handicapped Children Act

The Education for All Handicapped Children Act (P.L. 94-142) was passed in 1975. Many consider this law to be the most significant federal legislation regarding the education and inclusion of children with disabilities in public schools, and it is the core to which subsequent amendments have been added. Prior to this law, many children with disabilities were excluded from public schools. Those who did attend public schools were grouped together, regardless of the type or severity of disability and sometimes regardless of chronological age, and they were segregated from typically developing children and general education settings. It is generally acknowledged that the majority of these children did not receive an education that was appropriate for their needs (Yell, Drasgow, Bradley, & Justesen, 2004).

P.L. 94-142 established eligibility criteria and procedures for determining eligibility for special education and related services. This law required states to provide a free and appropriate public school education for all eligible children with disabilities from 3 to 21 years of age. The **free and appropriate public education,** known as **FAPE,** must be provided in the **least restrictive environment (LRE).** Many individuals interpret the law to mean that all children with disabilities must be placed in inclusive settings for the entire school day. However, LRE should not be interpreted as one specific setting option. Rather, the LRE for each child is to be determined based on his or her individual needs (Yell et al., 2004). Although the law did not specifically identify inclusion as the LRE, the intent of the law was that teams must first consider inclusion in the general education classroom or other community settings when determining the type of program in which the child will be enrolled and what services will be delivered.

The LRE mandate implies that the child should attend the classroom or setting that the child would attend if he or she did not have a disability, unless there are compelling reasons for selecting alternative placement. The decision not to enroll a child full-time in the general education program can be made only after consideration of the child's needs and the use of supplementary aids and services that might facilitate such placement. If the child's team, including parents, decide that full-time placement in the general education program is not appropriate for the child, they may discuss alternative placement options such as dual enrollment in a general education classroom and a self-contained special education classroom or resource room. The regulations for P.L. 94-142 (and subsequent reauthorization amendments) indicate that a continuum of alternative placements options must be available for consideration including, for preschool-aged children, community-based settings (Walsh, Smith, & Taylor, 2000). When alternative placements are selected, teams must explain on the child's **Individualized Education Plan (IEP)** why full-time inclusion in the general education classroom is not appropriate for the child and the extent to which the child will have access to interaction with typically developing peers.

In addition to mandating FAPE and LRE, P.L. 94-142 also mandated the provision of special education and related services (see Table 1.4 for definitions of these terms) and the development of an IEP that specifies educational goals, the type and frequency of special education and related services, settings in which services will be provided, and, as mentioned above, the extent of participation with typically developing peers. P.L. 94-142 also required multidisciplinary and nondiscriminatory assessment and outlined due process procedures for resolving conflicts between schools and families.

Although P.L. 94-142 specified children from 3 to 21 years of age, it included exemptions that allowed states to exclude preschool-aged children with disabilities (as well as students from 18 to 21 years of age). States were not required to serve preschool-aged children with disabilities if they did not also provide educational services to typically developing preschool-aged children. As a result, many young children with disabilities did not receive services through the public schools. This oversight was addressed in a subsequent reauthorization of the law.

Table 1.4 ● Definitions of Special Education and Related Services

Special education is specially designed instruction, at no cost to parents, that meets the unique needs of the child and ensures the child's access to the general education curriculum. Special education may be provided in the classroom, home, hospitals or institutions, or other settings and may include adapting the content, methodology, or delivery of instruction and providing physical education and vocational instruction. Speech-language pathology, travel training, physical education, and vocational instruction or other related services can be identified as special education under State standards if the instruction is specially designed, at no cost to the parents, to meet the unique needs of a child with a disability.

Related services are all the additional aides and supports students need in order to benefit from special education. Some of the most common types of related services include: speech-language pathology and audiology; transportation; psychological services; physical therapy; occupational therapy; recreation including therapeutic recreation; counseling services including rehabilitation counseling; social work services in schools; assistive technology; and parent counseling and training.

The IDEA regulations provide a list of related services. The list is not intended to be exhaustive, however, and could include other related services that are needed to help a child to benefit from special education.

More information about special education and related services can be obtained from the following websites:

    www.nichcy.org   Questions and Answers About IDEA, *News Digest 21 (ND21)*

    http://thomas.loc.gov/cgi-bin/query/F?c108:1:./temp/~c108iEkMmv:e16556   The Library of Congress

    www.cec.sped.org/law_res/doc/law/regulations/glossaryIndex.php   IDEA '97 Laws and Resources

    www.c-c-d.org/IdeaUserGuide.pdf   A user's guide to the 2004 IDEA Reauthorization (P.L. 108-446 and the conference report)

    www.wrightslaw.com/idea/index.htm   Wrightslaw

The Education for All Handicapped Act, P.L. 94-142, was amended in 1986 (P.L. 99-457). This reauthorization extended the age level of mandated education services to include preschoolers with disabilities (Part B of the law), and it provided incentives for states to develop early intervention programs for infants and toddlers with disabilities (Part C). Although discretionary, states that did develop early intervention programs were required to conform to a number of requirements including the provision of services in the natural environment. The term *natural environment* refers to settings in which children with and without disabilities spend time. The child's home often serves as the natural environment for infants and toddlers. Thus, the notion of LRE and inclusion applies to infants and toddlers as well as school-aged children with disabilities (McCollum, 2005).

Individuals With Disabilities Education Act

Public Law 94-142 was again amended in 1990 (P.L. 101-457), and the name was changed to the **Individuals With Disabilities Education Act (IDEA)**. The name was changed to replace the word *handicapped* with *disability* and to reflect the use of person-first language rather than disability-first language. Person-first language is based on the philosophy that people with disabilities are more similar than dissimilar to typically developing people; as such, our language should emphasize the individual first and the disability second (see Table 1.5 for examples of person-first language).

The IDEA was reauthorized in 1997 and, most recently, in 2004. These reauthorizations have maintained and, in some cases, strengthened the LRE requirement, have added new provisions to the

Table 1.5 ● Person-First Language

Words used to describe people with disabilities should emphasize the person or child first and then, if it is necessary, the disability. Person-first language recognizes that people with disabilities are more alike than different from people without disabilities. Person-first language focuses on the person, not the disability. It describes the disability as something the child has, not as what he or she is.

Non-Person-First Language	Person-First Language
Instead of	*Use*
Crippled child	Child with cerebral palsy
Down syndrome boy	Boy with Down syndrome
Autistic girl	Girl who has autism
Wheelchair-bound student	Student who uses a wheelchair
She suffers from epilepsy	She has epilepsy
He is special ed	He receives special education services
He is a victim of retardation	He has mental retardation (or a cognitive disability)
I teach LD or BD kids	I teach students with learning disabilities or behavior disorders
The disabled	People who have disabilities
Handicapped people	People with disabilities
Handicapped parking	Accessible parking

original P.L. 94-142, and have maintained a broad view of inclusion that goes beyond the child's placement or setting in which services are provided. For example, IDEA now requires teams to document on the IEP how the student will have access to the general education curriculum (as well as access to interaction with typically developing peers) and how the team will demonstrate the student's progress in the general education curriculum. It also requires transition planning for children who are exiting early intervention programs for children from 0 to 3 years of age, strengthens collaboration between early intervention and public school programs and families during transition, describes discipline-related procedure requirements, and strengthens family participation in decisions regarding their child's education. In addition, IDEA and the No Child Left Behind legislation have been aligned to include students with disabilities in district and statewide assessments and in current reports regarding adequate yearly progress in reading and math, and assessments expanded to science in the 2007/2008 school year (Friend & Bursuck, 2006).

The 2004 IDEA amendments also include provisions for states to study the use of multiyear IEPs and early intervening educational services, or response-to-treatment, models. *Early intervening services* refers to efforts to provide intervention services to children prior to the initiation of a formal referral process to determine eligibility for special education services. The early intervening, or response-to-treatment, component was added to the IDEA in part as a response to the overrepresentation of minority and linguistically and culturally diverse children receiving special education services (McLaughlin, Schofield, & Hopfengardener Warren, 1999; Yates & Ortiz, 2004) and the increased numbers of children with delayed literacy skills. Early intervening services is one way to address the needs of children whose delays may be a function of linguistic and cultural diversity and/or a lack of explicit instruction in literacy rather than a true learning disability. Although still in the development stage, the early intervening models that are being examined require consultation and collaboration between general education teachers, early childhood special education teachers, and other service providers.

Table 1.6 provides a list of provisions provided by IDEA. More information on IDEA can be obtained from the Council for Exceptional Children (CEC) website (www.cec-sped.org) and from the websites listed on Table 1.7 and from the Federal Register. The final source of support for inclusion comes from national organizations as discussed in the next section.

Overview of National Organizations' Support for Inclusion

Support for inclusion also comes from national organizations including the Division for Early Childhood and the National Association for the Education of Young Children.

National Association for the Education of Young Children

If there is one organization that stands out for its dedication to improving the quality of education for young children it is the **National Association for the Education of Young Children (NAEYC)**. Originally known as the National Association of Nursery Education (NANE), the organization began in the 1920s in an effort to monitor the quality of burgeoning preschool programs. In 1964, NANE was reorganized as the National Association for the Education of Young Children (2005). NAEYC focuses on the early childhood years, defined as 0 to 8 years of age. It publishes the *Young Children* journal and a variety of monographs and books, provides a national accreditation

Table 1.6 ● Provisions of the Individuals With Disabilities Education Act

- Eligibility Determination: Must receive one of the federally defined disability labels and provide evidence that the disability has an adverse impact on the child's education
- Free and Appropriate Education (FAPE)
- Least Restrictive Environment (LRE)
- Individualized Education Plans (IEP)
- Special Education and Related Services
- Multidisciplinary and Nondiscriminatory Assessment
- Document parent or family participation in decision making, consider family concerns, and identify procedures for informing families of their child's progress
- Discipline-related procedures and requirements
- Document participation in state- and districtwide assessments or alternative assessments
- Transition planning
- Due Process procedures
- Early intervening services (to be evaluated through pilot studies)
- Multiyear IEPs (to be evaluated through pilot studies)

Table 1.7 ● Early Childhood, Early Childhood Special Education, and/or Inclusion Websites

Organizations

www.dec-sped.org   Division for Early Childhood
www.naeyc.org   National Association for the Education of Young Children
www.cec-sped.org   Council for Exceptional Children
www2.acf.dhhs.gov/programs/hsb/   Head Start

Linguistic and Cultural Diversity

http://clas.uiuc.edu/   Culturally and Linguistically Appropriate Services
www.ncela.gwu.edu/   National Clearinghouse for English Language Acquisition and Language Instruction Educational Programs
http://gucchd.georgetown.edu//nccc/index.html   National Center for Cultural Competence
www.fpg.unc.edu/~nuestros/pdfs/NNExecSummary.pdf   Addressing the Needs of Latino Children

Information About IDEA

www.nichcy.org   Questions and Answers About IDEA
http://ideapractices.org/   Individuals With Disabilities Education Act Law and Practices
www.wrightslaw.com/idea/index.htm   Wrightslaw
http://thomas.loc.gov/cgi-bin/query/F?c108:1:./temp/~c108iEkMmv:e16556   The Library of Congress
www.cec.sped.org/law_res/doc/law/regulations/glossaryIndex.php   IDEA '97 Laws and Resources
www.c-c-d.org/IdeaUserGuide.pdf   A user's guide to the 2004 IDEA Reauthorization (P.L. 108-446) and the conference report.

Inclusion and Other General Resources and Information

www.nichcy.org   National Dissemination Center for Children with Disabilities
www.inclusion.com   Inclusion.com
http://ericeece.org/   ERIC Clearinghouse on Elementary and Early Childhood Education
www.seriweb.com   Special Education Resources on the Internet
http://kidstogether.org   Kids Together, Inc.
www.fpg.unc.edu/~ecrii   Early Childhood Research Institute on Inclusion
www.circleofinclusion.org   Circle of Inclusion
www.researchtopractice.info   Research and Training Center on Early Childhood Development
www.inclusivepractices.org   Consortium on Inclusive Schooling Practices
www.NECTAC.org/inclusion   National Early Childhood Technical Assistance Center
www.includeme.org/index.org   Connecticut Coalition for Inclusion
www.uni.edu/coe/inclusion/index.html   Inclusive Education
http://rushservices.com/Inclusion/homepage.htm   Inclusion: Yours, Mine, Ours

program, holds several yearly conferences, informs members about policy decisions and changes in federal laws, provides position papers, recommends practices and standards for early learning and standards for personnel preparation, and supports state-level affiliations.

The dedication of NAEYC to all young children is evident in the group's mission and vision statements and associated strategic objectives. Although young children with disabilities are not the primary focus of NAEYC, this organization identifies diversity and inclusion as a core value, and recently, members of NAEYC developed a special interest forum on the NAEYC website for those interested in working with and supporting children with special needs and their families. NAEYC also supports inclusion by providing presentations that address children with disabilities and inclusion during the annual and other conferences. Additional information about NAEYC and the special interest forum can be obtained from their website: www.naeyc.org.

Developmentally Appropriate Practice

One of the most important contributions of NAEYC to the fields of early childhood and early childhood special education is the concept of **Developmentally Appropriate Practice**, often referred to as **DAP**. DAP was developed in response to concerns that preschool and kindergarten classrooms in the 1980s had adopted goals and were employing strategies that were not appropriate for young children (Bredekamp, 1987, 1993; Bredekamp & Copple, 1997). The first definition of DAP indicated that early childhood programs must be designed based on what is known about the development of young children.

Although the guidelines related to DAP were helpful for developing programs to serve typically developing children and children with special needs, many felt that they were not sufficient for addressing the needs of young children with disabilities (e.g., Carta, Atwater, Schwartz, & McConnell, 1993; Mallory, 1992; McLean & Odom, 1993; Wolery, Strain, & Bailey, 1992), and other individuals misinterpreted and misused the concept of DAP (Bredekamp & Copple, 1997). In addition, much was learned about early childhood programs during the 1980s and early 1990s as the composition of children in early childhood programs expanded to include more and more children with disabilities and cultural and linguistic diversity. As a result, NAEYC revised the position statement on DAP in 1996, and in 1997, NAEYC published a revised edition of the book *Developmentally Appropriate Practice in Early Childhood Programs* (Bredekamp & Copple, 1997). A portion of the revised definition of DAP is presented in Table 1.8. The revision of the concept of Developmentally Appropriate Practice highlighted three areas of consideration. In addition to designing programs based on knowledge of child development, the new DAP guidelines indicated that programs should be individually appropriate and culturally appropriate in order to meet the needs of all children.

The revised DAP framework was further described by NAEYC in a recently published book that introduces the concept of DAP to early educators working with preschool-aged children (Copple & Bredekamp, 2006). In this book "DAP refers to teaching decisions that vary with and adapt to the age, experience, interests, and abilities of individual children within a given age range" (p. 7). This book emphasizes the need for teachers to provide early childhood experiences based on (1) their knowledge of child development (Developmentally Appropriate Practice), (2) the individual interests and abilities of children in their programs (Individually Appropriate Practice), and (3) the social and cultural contexts in which children live (Culturally Appropriate Practice). The current

Table 1.8 • NAEYC Position Statement Regarding Developmentally Appropriate Practice

Developmentally appropriate practices result from the process of professionals making decisions about the well-being and education of children based on at least three important kinds of information or knowledge:

1. What is known about child development and learning-knowledge of age-related human characteristics that permits general predictions within an age range about what activities, materials, interactions, or experiences will be safe, healthy, interesting, achievable, and also challenging to children;
2. What is known about the strengths, interests, and needs of each individual child in the group to be able to adapt for and be responsive to inevitable individual variation; and
3. Knowledge of the social and cultural contexts in which children live to ensure that learning experiences are meaningful, relevant, and respectful for the participating children and their families.

Furthermore, each of these dimensions of knowledge—human development and learning, individual characteristics and experiences, and social and cultural contexts—is dynamic and changing, requiring that early childhood teachers remain learners throughout their careers. (Bredekamp & Copple, 1997, pp. 8–9).

conception of DAP is clearly applicable to all children within programs, those with and without disabilities and those who present cultural and linguistic diversity and varying learning styles. The revised guidelines for DAP have become the framework for early childhood and early childhood special educators as they develop early childhood programs, and they are the standard by which early childhood programs are assessed.

Council for Exceptional Children

The Council for Exceptional Children is an international organization focusing on children and youth with disabilities. CEC was developed in the 1920s and has grown to be the largest organization concerned with children with disabilities. CEC publishes two journals (*Exceptional Children* and *Teaching Exceptional Children*) and a variety of newsletters and other publications, provides a yearly conference, is the umbrella organization for seventeen special interest divisions, keeps its members informed of policy decisions and changes to federal laws, advocates at federal and state levels on behalf of students with disabilities, and provides members with information regarding recommended practices and personnel preparation standards.

CEC members are strong advocates of inclusion and the right of children to receive free and appropriate education in the least restrictive environment. Additional information about CEC, including their mission statement and core beliefs about inclusion, can be obtained from their website: www.cec-sped.org.

Division for Early Childhood

Just as NAEYC is considered a leader in early childhood education, the Division for Early Childhood (DEC) is considered a leader in early childhood special education. DEC is one of the seventeen divisions supported by the Council for Exceptional Children. DEC was founded in 1973 as a division to support individuals who work with or on behalf of children with special needs and their families. Like NAEYC, DEC addresses the ages of birth through age 8. DEC currently holds an annual conference and publishes two journals (*Journal for Early Intervention* and *Young Exceptional Children*), position statements and concept papers, monographs, and several books related to recommended practices in early intervention and early childhood special education (Hemmeter, Joseph, Smith, & Sandall, 2001; Sandall, Hemmeter, McLean, & Smith, 2005; Sandall & Ostrosky, 2000; Stayton, Miller, & Dinnebeil, 2003) and supports state subdivisions.

DEC strongly supports the provision of services to young children with special needs in least restrictive environments and natural environments as well as the provision of natural learning opportunities to support development. This can be seen in the DEC mission statement and associated position statements found on their website, www.dec-sped.org, and in *DEC Monograph #2: Natural Environments and Inclusion* (Sandall & Ostrosky, 2000).

DEC also has published a book titled *DEC Recommended Practices: A Comprehensive Guide for Practical Application in Early Intervention/Early Childhood Special Education* (Sandall et al., 2005). The purpose of this book is to "provide guidance on effective practices for attaining our shared goal of improved development and learning outcomes for young children with disabilities and their families" (p. 11). This book includes several chapters related to providing direct services to children and families as well as chapters related to personnel preparation and models of teaming that enable teachers and other service providers to work collaboratively to meet the needs of young children with disabilities and their families. This book can be used when developing early childhood programs and may be used to evaluate the extent to which programs incorporate recommended practices. Recently, DEC published a companion workbook that guides program assessment and the development of program improvement plans based on recommended practices (Hemmeter, Smith, Sandall, & Askew, 2005). In addition to providing recommended practices for early intervention and early childhood special education, DEC provides guidance for personnel preparation through the book *DEC Personnel Preparation in Early Childhood Special Education* (e.g., Stayton, Miller, et al., 2003).

DEC and NAEYC frequently collaborate on publications and activities related to young children with and without disabilities. The two organizations also often endorse each other's position statements and concept papers, and both engage in advocacy related to young children with and without disabilities. The DEC position statement on inclusion is a good example of collaboration between the two organizations. This position statement was developed by DEC and endorsed by NAEYC (Division for Early Childhood, 1993, 2000).

Another example of collaboration is the clarification of the need to attend to the individual needs of children that NAEYC included in the revised position statement on DAP (Bredekamp & Copple, 1997). As stated earlier, many members of DEC and others felt that the initial definition of DAP could be strengthened by reference to the different abilities and needs among children. As a result, the revised guidelines for DAP described Individually Appropriate Practice as a component within the DAP framework. The discussion of **Individually Appropriate Practice (IAP)** stressed the need to recognize and address the individual needs of children. It emphasized that interventions and activities should be individually appropriate in order to meet the needs of children. Individually Appropriate Practices are based on the developmental level and characteristics of each child, including children with developmental delays, children who are English language learners, and those who are gifted. This clarification of IAP makes it clear that educators should make adaptations to meet the individual needs of all children, within a developmentally appropriate framework. DEC endorses DAP as a primary step in developing early childhood programs. The practices provided in the DEC recommended practices book are "designed to be used in the context of developmentally appropriate early childhood environments. . . . they are complimentary to and an essential extension of the NAEYC DAP guidelines" (Hemmeter, Sandall, and Smith, 2005, p. 244).

DEC and NAEYC also have collaborated on issues related to teacher preparation and standards for personnel preparation, as will be discussed in the next section.

Rationale for Blended Teacher Preparation

At the present time, teachers and other school personnel are required to work with an increasingly diverse group of students including students with disabilities, students with cultural and linguistic diversity, and students with diverse learning styles and abilities (Council for Exceptional Children, 2005). For example, in a series of studies, Wolery and his colleagues reported that a majority of early childhood programs enrolled one or more children with disabilities (Wolery, Martin, Schroeder, Huffman, & Venn, 1994; Wolery, Venn, et al., 1994). McDonnell, Brownell, and Wolery (1997) found that approximately 60 percent of the teachers that they surveyed who worked in NAEYC-accredited programs reported that they had one or more children with special needs enrolled in their programs, and nearly 75 percent of the early childhood teachers in public schools had participated in a child's IEP planning meeting. As reported earlier, more than 50 percent of the children with disabilities from 6 to 21 years of age spent at least 80 percent of their school day in general education classrooms in the 2003/2004 school year (National Center for Education Statistics, 2005).

With respect to cultural and linguistic diversity, the prevalence of children and families who present cultural and linguistic diversity in schools is increasing. In 1990, almost 30 percent of children younger than 18 years of age were identified as members of racial or minority groups. In 2003, 42 percent of school-aged children were members of racial or minority groups (National Center for Education Statistics, 2005). The Census Bureau projects that, by the year 2100, 60 percent of the U.S. population will be Hispanic or individuals of color (Center for Disease Control, 2005). Recently, the National Center for Education Statistics (2005) reported that the number of students from 5 to 17 years of age who spoke a language other than English at home more than doubled from 1979 to 2003, to approximately 19 percent. They further reported that 29 percent of those children identified as English language learners were identified as having difficulty in speaking English during the 2003 school year. With data such as these, it is safe to say that most early childhood educators and early elementary teachers will have children with diverse abilities and disabilities in their classrooms and that they must have the dispositions, knowledge, and skills that will enable them to meet the needs of all of the children in their programs.

The move to provide education for students with diverse abilities and disabilities in general education classes has created changing expectations and roles for both early childhood and early childhood special educators. For example, in one common model of inclusion, the early childhood educator is considered the primary teacher for all of the children in his or her classroom, including children with disabilities (Friend & Bursuck, 2006). In another model of inclusion, early childhood and early childhood special educators may coteach a class and share primary responsibility for *all* students in the class (Friend & Cook, 2000). A third model of inclusion, early childhood special educators may address the needs of children with disabilities through consultation with the child's teacher or classroom assistant, rather than by working directly with the child. Each of these inclusion models require early childhood educators to have knowledge about typical development, early childhood practices that support development, and the general education curriculum. They also require early childhood educators to have additional knowledge about atypical development and particular disabilities and to be able to develop and/or implement curricular and instructional adaptations and accommodations for children with disabilities and linguistic diversity.

The role of early childhood special education teachers also may change as they serve children who are enrolled in a number of different classes rather than having a classroom of their own. When this occurs, early childhood special educators may work primarily as a consultant to general education teachers, work directly with children with disabilities in the students' general education classroom for part of the school day, or work with a child or small groups of children for a brief period of time in a resource classroom. They also must collaborate with the general education teacher to identify ways that the general educator can extend learning into additional activities and routines within the general education classroom. These varying roles and models of teaching will require early childhood special educators to have specialized knowledge and skills related to early childhood special education, developmental disabilities, strategies for making adaptations and accommodations, and consultation and collaboration. They also require early childhood special educators to have knowledge of the developmentally appropriate practice approach, effective teaching practices employed by early childhood educators, early childhood standards and the general early childhood education curriculum, and the daily schedule of early childhood classrooms.

Regardless of the type of model adopted, the success of inclusion is dependent in part on the ability of early childhood special education and early childhood education professionals to collaborate and consult with each other and with therapists and other school personnel in making curricular and instructional adaptations. The changing roles and expectations for early childhood and early childhood special education teachers and other service providers have led to changes in teacher training programs that now must focus on preparing teachers to meet the needs of all students in inclusive classrooms (Kilgo & Bruder, 1997; Miller, 1992; Stayton, Miller, et al., 2003; VanLaarhoven et al., 2004). Many preservice or teacher training programs have revised course content as well as the composition of students in classes or programs, and they have changed or expanded the type of degree or certification options that are available. First, we will discuss course content, then the composition of courses or programs.

Course Content

There is a strong link between teacher training and education and early childhood program or classroom quality and between early childhood program or classroom quality and child outcomes (Buysse, Wesley, & Able-Boone, 2001; Catlett & Winton, 2002; Karp, 2006; Miller & Stayton, 2000). There also is a link between prior positive experiences with inclusion and teacher attitudes and support for inclusion. Teacher attitudes also influence the reactions of typically developing children and family support for inclusion (Frazeur Cross, Traub, Hutter-Pishgahi, & Shelton, 2004; Praisner, 2003). The degree to which all children benefit from inclusion then is greatly influenced by teacher's beliefs about inclusion and their knowledge, skills, and willingness to implement effective practices within their programs and to collaborate as members of interdisciplinary teams (Brownell, Adams, Sindelar, Waldron, & Vanhover, 2006). For example, do they believe that all children have a right to participate in the general education classroom, or do they believe that children with disabilities should be segregated from typically developing children? Are they willing and able to make adaptations and accommodations and to individualize scaffolding supports, or do they expect all children to be able to learn from the general education curriculum and activities and lessons provided in the classroom without modifications? Are they willing and able to develop activities that foster interactions between children with and without disabilities, or do they think children with disabilities should be isolated from typically developing children? Are they willing to collaborate with other professionals to make adaptations, or do they feel threatened by sharing information and having additional professionals in their classrooms? The answers to questions such as these will largely determine how a teacher will set up his or her classroom and the teaching practices that he or she employs. This in turn will influence how well children learn and attain the hoped-for benefits from participation in inclusive classrooms. Unfortunately, many programs have not focused on these necessary skills and dispositions; however, recognition of the need to do so is increasing and is changing the face of preservice training.

It is generally acknowledged that traditional early childhood preservice training programs do not include specific instruction in characteristics of disabilities, special education law, collaboration, and assessment and instructional strategies, including adaptations and accommodations for addressing the needs of children with disabilities (Brownell et al., 2006). Many early childhood educators do not have the training needed to serve all children in their classrooms. For example, Early and Winton (2001) and the National Center for Early Development and Learning (2000) reported that, although a majority of early childhood teacher preparation programs identified training students to work with children with special needs as part of their mission statement, only 60 percent of the programs actually offered course work in this area, and almost 40 percent of the programs did not require practicum experiences that included children with disabilities in inclusive settings. They also found that fewer than 50 percent of the teacher preparation programs required students to complete course work that addressed racial and ethnic diversity, and fewer than 15 percent of the programs required students to complete course work on working with children and families with limited English proficiency. In another study, Scott-Little, Kagan, and Frelow (2003) reported that teacher preparation programs provide limited guidance on how to adapt early learning standards for children with disabilities and children with varying characteristics including cultural and linguistic diversity (see also Kagan, Scott-Little, & Frelow, 2003). Brownell and her colleagues (2006) reported that general education teachers often report that they do not feel prepared to serve a primary role in working with students with disabilities.

Many early childhood special education preservice programs, on the other hand, arguably do not provide sufficient instruction in typical child development and developmentally appropriate practice, early childhood curriculum development, early childhood learning standards, theme-based learning, work sampling, and constructivist learning approaches.

Common Core of Knowledge and Skills

Traditionally, early childhood education and early childhood special education were thought of a two separate fields (Bredekamp, 1993; Burton, Higgins Hains, Hanline, McLean, & McCormick, 1992). However, as more and more children with disabilities are served in general education classes and community-based child care settings, the separation between the two fields has blurred (DEC, 1994; 2000). Many individuals and early childhood organizations such as DEC and NAEYC currently agree that early childhood teachers, early childhood special educators, and other service providers must possess a common core of knowledge and skills for working with all young children. They recommend that preservice programs focus on a shared philosophical base, the commonalities across disciplines (e.g., ECE, ECSE, Physical Therapy, Occupational Therapy, and Speech/Language Pathology), and effective practices for meeting the needs of all children (Bailey, 1996; Buysse et al., 2001; DEC, 1998; Fenichel & Eggbeer, 1991; Hyson, 2003; Miller & Stayton, 1998; Salisbury & McGregor, 2002; Stayton, Fiechtl, Rule, Raschke, & Kliewer, 2003; Vauhn, Bos, & Shuman, 2003). Each discipline then can build on the common core by focusing on specific, more in-depth expertise in their particular areas. Many states have developed or are in the process of developing core knowledge, skills, and disposition standards and benchmarks for all early childhood personnel who work with children from birth through 8 years of age (e.g., Illinois, www.ilgateways.com; Kentucky, www.kyepsb.net/teacherprep/iecestandards.asp; Missouri, www.dese.mo.gov/divimprove/fedprog/earlychild/; and Pennsylvania, www.pde.state.pa.us/early_childhood).

The Division for Early Childhood, National Association for the Education of Young Children, and Association for Teacher Educators together developed a concept paper and a shorter position statement that discusses the issue of a common core and provides a set of personnel standards for early education and early intervention (DEC, 1994; 2000). The position statement and concept paper are important for a variety of reasons. First, they identify inclusion as the preferred service delivery model for all children. Second, they underscore the need for all professionals who work with young children to develop supportive relationships with families. Third, they articulate the relationship between early childhood (ECE) and early childhood special educators (ECSE) and emphasize the importance of collaboration among professionals. Fourth, they highlight the importance of all professionals providing services to children and families that are linguistically and culturally competent. Finally, they stress that all individuals who work with young children should share a common core of knowledge and skills that are demonstrated through diverse field experiences. The concept paper further identifies five common core content areas: (1) child development and learning, (2) curriculum development and implementation, (3) family and community relationships, (4) assessment and evaluation, and (5) professionalism. Within these five areas, knowledge and skills might focus on Developmentally Appropriate and Individually Appropriate Practice, intentional teaching, differentiated instruction and scaffolding, a continuum of teaching strategies ranging from child-initiated to teacher-directed instruction, activity-based intervention, the role of the environment, typical and atypical development, cultural and linguistic diversity, the role of different professionals, supporting and working with families, interdisciplinary teaming, and consultation and collaboration among team members (DEC, 1998; Hyson, 2003; Klein and Harris, 2004).

Content Standards for Early Educators and Early Childhood Special Educators

In addition to the standards provided in the DEC, NAEYC, and ATE concept paper, both DEC and NAEYC have developed separate standards related to preparing early childhood and early childhood special education professionals. The National Board for Professional Teaching Standards also has developed standards for early childhood teachers of children from 3 to 8 years of age. NAEYC published each set of standards in the book *Preparing Early Childhood Professionals: NAEYC's*

Standards for Programs (Hyson, 2003). These standards provide guidance to personnel preparation programs regarding the discipline-specific knowledge that teachers should acquire as well as the common core of shared knowledge related to providing services to all children. The areas addressed in each set of standards are listed in Table 1.9.

Table 1.9 ● Core Content Standards of National Association for the Education of Young Children, Division for Early Childhood, and National Board for Professional Teaching Standards

National Association for the Education of Young Children

1. Promoting child development and learning
2. Building family and community relationships
3. Observing, documenting, and assessing to support young children and families
4. Teaching and learning
   a. connecting with children and families
   b. using developmentally effective approaches
   c. understanding content knowledge in early education
   d. building meaningful curriculum
5. Becoming a professional

Division for Early Childhood

1. Foundations
2. Development and characteristics of learners
3. Individual learning differences
4. Instructional strategies
5. Learning environments and social interactions
6. Language
7. Instructional planning
8. Assessment
9. Professional and ethical practice
10. Collaboration

National Board for Professional Teaching Standards

1. Understanding young children
2. Equity, fairness, and diversity
3. Assessment
4. Promoting child development and learning
5. Knowledge of integrated curriculum
6. Multiple teaching strategies for meaningful learning
7. Family and community partnerships
8. Professional partnerships
9. Reflective practice

Composition of Programs

If we expect teachers to have a shared common core of knowledge, skills, and dispositions and to collaborate to meet the needs of students with disabilities, it only makes sense that we focus on this during preservice training through courses and clinical experiences that provide multiple and varied opportunities for interaction and collaboration between ECE and ECSE and other service providers who may work with children enrolled in inclusive programs (Kilgo & Bruder, 1997; Miller & Stayton, 2000; Salisbury & McGregor, 2002; Stayton & Miller, 1993; Vauhn et al., 2003). This view is supported by the U.S. Department of Education (2000), which identified interdisciplinary personnel preparation to prepare teachers to work in diverse early childhood settings as an important challenge and goal for the field.

The goal of teaching a shared common core of knowledge and skills has led many colleges and university programs to change the composition of classes and programs (Miller & Stayton, 1998). Some colleges and universities currently offer blended programs that lead to a combined early childhood and early childhood special education degrees or certification. Other preservice programs provide separate ECE and ECSE certifications but also provide one or more courses that students from a variety of disciplines complete together. These courses may address the common core of shared knowledge across disciplines, provide in-class activities during which students work as interdisciplinary teams, and/or provide clinical or field experiences in inclusion settings. McCollum and Catlett (1997) identified four levels of learning that may be addressed within the common core and discipline specific training of blended preservice courses and programs. These levels are (1) awareness, (2) knowledge, (3) skill, and (4) disposition. Each of these levels contribute to teachers' ability to develop effective inclusion programs that produce positive outcomes for all children.

There are many potential benefits for college and university students, faculty, and ultimately, the children enrolled in inclusive programs and their families from interdisciplinary or blended teacher training programs (Kilgo & Bruder, 1997; Miller & Stayton, 1998). Shared training may have a positive impact on teachers' dispositions or attitudes regarding disability, inclusion, and collaboration (VanLaarhoven et al., 2004). For example, students who collaborate with students from other disciplines during preservice training are more likely to collaborate with team members in providing interdisciplinary services to children (Winton & Mellin, 1997, reported in Stayton, Feichtl, et al., 2003).

Blended preservice training also can have a positive impact on teachers' knowledge and skills related to (a) making curricular and instructional adaptations and accommodations, (b) collaborating with other professionals, (c) providing positive behavioral support, (d) working with families, (e) linking IEP goals to general education learning standards, and (f) scheduling integrated therapy (Buysse et al., 2001; Kilgo & Bruder, 1997; VanLaarhoven et al., 2004). Brownell and colleagues (2006) reported that elementary school teachers who had a strong base of prior knowledge were more able to address the needs of individual students within their general education classrooms and to implement new strategies that were presented during inservice or professional development training. Miller and Stayton (1998) stated that positive outcomes for children enrolled in inclusive programs are more likely when educators have received blended or shared training at the preservice level and when the training has been offered by faculty from multiple disciplines.

Shared preparation also can have benefits in preparing teachers to teach *all* children. Early childhood special educators acknowledge that many of the features of early childhood classrooms and teaching strategies that produce learning in typically developing children, such as developmentally appropriate practice, meaningful experiences, centers-based learning, effective environments, child-initiated learning, and the project approach or theme-based teaching, also will benefit children with disabilities. (Hyson & Winton, 2005; Odom & Wolery, 2003). Likewise, many of the recommended practices that are advocated by early childhood special educators also will produce positive outcomes for typically developing children, including individualized instruction and adaptations, scaffolding, ecobehavioral analysis, and specialized teaching strategies such as milieu teaching, social skills training, prompting and natural reinforcement strategies, peer mediation or peer tutoring, and functional assessment and positive behavioral support strategies (Chandler & Maude, in press; Kamps et al., 2002; Mortweet et al., 1999; Odom & Wolery, 2003).

Finally, blended training programs and courses can produce positive outcomes for faculty. Miller and Stayton (1998) surveyed faculty who provided blended interdisciplinary teacher training programs in twenty states. They reported that faculty providing these programs identified three types of benefits developing blended interdisciplinary programs. These benefits included an increase in their own knowledge and skills, decreased separation between disciplines, increased communication and collaboration with faculty from diverse disciplines, and a more comprehensive teacher training program curriculum that intentionally focused on inclusion and diversity. Miller and Stayton also identified concerns or barriers to developing blended teacher training programs and recommendations for addressing these concerns.

Summary

If children with and without disabilities are to benefit from being educated together in inclusive classrooms, it is imperative that all early childhood educators have the skills and dispositions necessary to provide for the needs of the diverse children in their classrooms. This need is supported by the National Association for the Education of Young Children, the Division for Early Childhood, and the U.S. Department of Education. These skills and dispositions should be central to preservice training programs.

Educators need to understand the critical components of successful inclusion programs and must be able to identify the "implications for practice," or how they might apply those components to their own programs now or in the future. It is one thing to buy into a philosophy or to say, "Yes, I support inclusion"; it is another thing to be able to plan for how that might work in an elementary school classroom. Blended training that addresses a core curriculum and then focuses on discipline specific content is an important step in achieving this goal. Table 1.7 provides a list of websites that provide additional information and resources related to early childhood organizations, the Individuals With Disabilities Education Act, cultural and linguistic diversity, and inclusion and other general information. The remaining chapters in this book provide information about the core content that is needed by early childhood and early childhood education teachers and strategies for making adaptations and accommodations in order to support families and meet the social, emotional, and academic needs of children with linguistic and cultural diversity and special needs in inclusive early childhood classrooms.

Thinking It Through

1. What factors have influenced early childhood inclusion?

2. Describe the Individuals With Disabilities Education Act and how it influenced they way young children with disabilities receive services.

3. Describe what is meant by common core of knowledge. Describe why blended teacher preparation programs lead to the best student outcomes.

4. Define the following acronyms: NAEYC, CEC, DEC. How have each of these organizations influenced the field of early childhood special education?

5. Describe the role of the family in early childhood special education as envisioned by DEC.

References

Allen, K. E., & Cowdery, G. E. (2005). *The exceptional child: Inclusion in early childhood education.* Clifton Park, NY: Thompson Delmar Learning.

Beckman, P. J., Hanson, M. J., & Horn, E. (2002). Family perceptions of inclusion. In S. L. Odom (Ed.), *Widening the circle: Including children with disabilities in preschool programs* (pp. 98–108). New York: Teacher's College Press.

Bredekamp, S. (1987). *Developmentally appropriate practice in early childhood programs serving children from birth through age 8.* Washington, DC: NAEYC.

Bredekamp, S. (1993). The relationship between early childhood education and early childhood special education: Healthy marriage or family feud? *Topics in Early Childhood Special Education, 13,* 258–273.

Bredekamp, S., & Copple, C. (Eds.). (1997). *Developmentally appropriate practice in early childhood programs* (Rev. ed.). Washington, DC: NAEYC.

Bricker, D. (2000). Inclusion: How the scene has changed. *Topics in Early Childhood Special Education, 20,* 114–119.

Brownell, M., Adams, A., Sindelar, P., Waldron, N., & Vanhover, S. (2006). Learning from collaboration: The role of teacher qualities. *Exceptional Children, 72*(2), 169–185.

Bruder, M. B. (1993). The provision of early intervention and early childhood special education within community early childhood programs: Characteristics of effective service delivery. *Topics in Early Childhood Special Education, 13,* 19–37.

Burton, C., Higgins Hains, A., Hanline, M. F., McLean, M., & McCormick, K. (1992). Early childhood intervention and education: The urgency for professional unification. *Topics in Early Childhood Special Education, 11,* 53–69.

Buysse, V., & Bailey, D. B. (1993). Behavioral and developmental outcomes in young children with disabilities in integrated and segregated settings: A review of comparative studies. *Journal of Special Education, 26,* 434–461.

Buysse, V., Wesley, P. W., & Able-Boone, H. (2001). Innovations in professional development: Creating communities of practice to support inclusion. In M. J. Guralnick (Ed.), *Early Childhood Inclusion: Focus on Change* (pp. 179–202). Baltimore: Paul H. Brookes.

Cappellini, M. (2006). Balancing reading and language learning. Portland, ME: Stenhouse.

Carta, J. J., Atwater, J. B., Schwartz, I., & McConnell, S. R. (1993). Developmentally appropriate practices and early childhood special education: A reaction to Johnson and McChesney-Johnson. *Topics in Early Childhood Special Education, 13,* 243–254.

Catlett, C., & Winton, P. (2002). *What have we learned about preparing personnel to serve all infants, toddlers, young children and families?* Chapel Hill, NC: Frank Porter Graham Child Development Center, University of North Carolina.

Centers for Disease Control *Learn the signs, act early.* Retrieved October 31, 2006, from www.cdc.gov/omb/populations/populations.htm

Chandler, L. K., & Dahlquist, C. M. (1999). Integration in the preschool for children with mild or moderate disabilities. In M. J. Coutinho & A. C. Repp (Eds.), *Inclusion: The integration of students with disabilities* (pp. 206–235). Boston: Wadsworth.

Chandler, L. K., & Maude, S. (in press). Teaching about inclusive settings and natural learning environments. To be published in P. Winton, J. McCollum, & C. Catlett (Eds.), *Preparing effective professionals: Evidence and applications in early childhood and early intervention.* Washington, DC: Zero to Three.

Copple, C., & Bredekamp, S. (2006). *Basics of developmentally appropriate practice: An introduction for teachers of children 3 to 6.* Washington, DC: NAEYC.

Council for Exceptional Children. (2005). *Universal design for learning: A guide for teachers and educational professionals.* Reston, VA: Author.

Diamond, K. E., & Stacey, S. (2000). The other children at preschool: Experiences of typically developing children in inclusive programs. Young Exceptional Children Monograph No. 2: *Natural environments and inclusion* (pp. 59–68). Longmont, CO: Sopris West.

Division for Early Childhood (1993; 1998). *Personnel standards for early education and early intervention: A position of the Association of Teacher Educators, the Division for Early Childhood, and the National Association for the Education of Young Children.* Retrieved September 17, 2006, from www.dec-sped.org

Division for Early Childhood. (1993; 2000). *Position on inclusion.* Reston, VA: Council for Exceptional Children.

Division for Early Childhood. (1994; 2000). *Personnel standards for early education and early interventions: Guidelines for Licensure in Early Childhood Special Education. Recommendations of: the Division for Early Childhood, Council for Exceptional Children, the National Association for the Education of Young Children, and the Association of Teacher Educators.* Retrieved November 9, 2006, from www.dec-sped.org

Division for Early Childhood. (2002). *DEC Position on responsiveness to family cultures, values, and languages.* Retrieved November 9, 2006, from www.dec-sped.org

Early, D. M., & Winton, P. J. (2001). Preparing the workforce: Early childhood teacher preparation at 2- and 4-year institutions of higher education. *Early Childhood Research Quarterly, 16,* 185–306.

Fenichel, E. S., & Eggbeer, L. (1991). Preparing practitioners to work with infants, toddlers, and their families: Four essential elements of training. *Infants and Young Children, 4,* 56–62.

Frazeur Cross, A., Traub, E. K., Hutter-Pishgahi, L., & Shelton, G. (2004). Elements of successful inclusion for children with significant disabilities. *Topics in Early Childhood Special Education, 24,* 169–183.

Friend, M., & Bursuck, W. D. (2006). *Including students with special needs: A practical guide for classroom teachers* (4th ed.). Baltimore: Paul H. Brookes.

Friend, M., & Cook, L. (2000). *Interactions: Collaboration skills for school professionals* (3rd ed.). New York: Longman.

Gallagher, J. J. (2000). The beginnings of federal help for young children with disabilities. *Topics in Early Childhood Special Education, 20,* 3–6.

Grisham-Brown, J., Hemmeter, M. L., & Pretti-Frontczak, K. (2005). *Blended practices for teaching young children in inclusive settings.* Baltimore: Paul H. Brookes.

Guralnick, M. J. (Ed.). (1978). *Early intervention and the integration of handicapped and nonhandicapped children.* Baltimore: University Park Press.

Guralnick, M. J. (1993). Developmentally appropriate practice in the assessment and intervention of children's peer relations. *Topics in Early Childhood Special Education, 13,* 344–371.

Guralnick, M. J. (2001). A framework for change in early childhood inclusion. In M. J. Guralnick (Ed.), *Early childhood inclusion: Focus on change* (pp. 3–38). Baltimore: Paul H. Brookes.

Guralnick, M. J., Connor, R. T., Hammond, M. A., Gottman, J. M., & Kinnish, K. (1996). Immediate effects of mainstreamed settings on the social interactions and social integration of preschool children. *American Journal on Mental Retardation, 100,* 359–377.

Hanson, M. J., Gutierrez, S., Morgan, M., Brennan, E. L., & Zercher, C. (1997). Language, culture, and disability: Interacting influences on preschool inclusion. *Topics in Early Childhood Special Education, 17,* 307–336.

Hemmeter, M. L., Joseph, G., Smith, B. J., & Sandall, S. (2001). *DEC recommended practices program assessment: Improving practices for young children with special needs and their families.* Longmont, CO: Sopris West.

Hemmeter, M. L., Sandall, S., & Smith, B. J. (2005). Using the DEC recommended practices for program assessment and improvement. In S. Sandall, M. L. Hemmeter, B. J. Smith, & M. E. McLean (Eds.), *DEC recommended practices: A comprehensive guide for practical application in early intervention/early childhood special education.* Longmont, CO: Sopris West.

Hemmeter, M. L., Smith, B., Sandall, S., & Askew, L. (2005). *DEC recommended practices: A program assessment workbook.* Longmont, CO: Sopris West.

Horn, E., Leiber, J., Sandall, S., & Schwartz, I. (2001). Embedding learning opportunities as an instructions strategy for supporting children's learning in inclusive programs. Young Exceptional Children's Monograph No. 3: *Teaching strategies: What to do to support young children's development* (pp. 59–70). Longmont, CO: Sopris West.

Horn, E., Lieber, J., Sandall, S., Schwartz, I., & Wolery, M. (2002). Classroom models of individualized instruction. In S. L. Odom (Ed.), *Widening the circle: Including children with disabilities in preschool programs* (pp. 154–174). New York: Teacher's College Press.

Hunt, P., Doering, K., Hirose-Hatae, A., Maier, J., & Goetz, L. (2001). Across-program collaboration to support students with and without disabilities in a general education classroom. *Journal for the Association for Persons with Severe Handicaps, 26,* 240–256.

Hunt, P., Soto, G., Maier, J., & Doering, K. (2003). Collaborative teaming to support students-at-risk and students with severe disabilities in general education classrooms. *Exceptional Children, 69,* 315–332.

Hunt, P., Soto, G., Maier, J., Lioiron, N., & Bae, S. (2004). Collaborative teaming to support preschoolers with severe disabilities who are placed in general education early childhood programs. *Topics in Early Childhood Special Education, 24,* 123–142.

Hunter, D. (1999). Integration in the elementary school for students with severe disabilities. In M. J. Coutinho & A. C. Repp (Eds.), *Inclusion: The integration of students with disabilities* (pp. 278–311). Boston: Wadsworth.

Hyson, M. (Ed.). (2003). *Preparing early childhood professionals: NAEYC's standards for programs.* Washington, DC: NAEYC.

Hyson, M., & Winton, P. J. (2005). Forward. In J. Grisham-Brown, M. L. Hemmeter, & K. Pretti-Frontczak, *Blended practices for teaching young children in inclusive settings* (pp. ix–xiii) Baltimore: Paul H. Brookes.

IDEAdata.org. (2005). Individuals with Disabilities Education Act Amendments of 2004. Retrieved September 6, 2005, from www.ideadata.org/tables27th/ar_ab1.htm

Janko, S., Schwartz, I., Sandall, S., Anderson, K., & Cottman, C. (1997). Beyond microsystems: Unanticipated lessons about the meaning of inclusion. *Topics in Early Childhood Special Education, 17,* 286–306.

Kagan, S. L., Scott-Little, C., & Frelow, V. S. (2003). Early learning standards for young children: A survey of the states. *Young Children, 58*(4), 58–76.

Kamps, D., Royer, J., Dugan, E., Kravits, T., Gonzalez-Lopez, A., Garcia, J., Carnazzo, K., Morrision, L., & Garrison

Kane, L. (2002). Peer training to facilitate social interaction for elementary students with autism and their peers. *Exceptional Children, 68,* 173–187.

Karp, N. (2006). Designing models for professional development at the local, state, and national levels. In M. Zaslow & I. Martinez-Beck (Eds.), *Critical issues in early childhood professional development* (pp. 225–230). Baltimore: Paul H. Brookes.

Kilgo, J. L., & Bruder, M. B. (1997). Interdisciplinary approaches to personnel preparation in early intervention. In P. J. Winton, J. A. McCollum, & C. Catlett (Eds.), *Reforming personnel preparation in early intervention: Issues, models, and practical strategies* (pp. 81–102). Baltimore: Paul H. Brookes.

Klein, M. D., & Harris, K. C. (2004). Considerations in the personnel preparation of itinerant early childhood special education consultants. *Journal of Educational and Psychological Consultation, 15*(2), 151–165.

Lamorey, S., & Bricker, D. D. (1993). Integrated programs: Effects on young children and their parents. In C. A. Peck, S. L. Odom, & D. D. Bricker (Eds.), *Integrating young children with disabilities into community programs: Ecological perspectives on research and implementation* (pp. 249–269). Baltimore: Paul H. Brookes.

Leiber, J., Wolery, R. A., Horn, E., Tschantz, J., Beckman, P. J., & Hanson, M. J. (2002). Collaborative relationships among adults in inclusive preschool programs. In S. L. Odom (Ed.), *Widening the circle: Including children with disabilities in preschool programs* (pp. 81–97). New York: Teacher's College Press.

Levine, L. M., & Antia, S. D. (1997). The effects of partner hearing status on social and cognitive play. *Journal of Early Intervention, 21,* 21–35.

Mallory, B. (1992). Is it always appropriate to be developmental? Convergent models for early intervention practice. *Topics in Early Childhood Special Education, 11,* 1–12.

Mastropieri, M. A., Scruggs, T. E., & Hamilton, S. L. (1999). Integration in the elementary school for students with moderate disabilities. In M. J. Coutinho & A. C. Repp (Eds.), *Inclusion: The integration of students with disabilities* (pp. 264–277). Boston: Wadsworth.

McCollum, J. (2005). *One of us: Access and equity for all.* Springfield: Illinois State Board of Education.

McCollum, J. A., & Catlett, C. (1997). Designing effective personnel preparation for early intervention: Theoretical frameworks. In P. J. Winton, J. A. McCollum, & C. Catlett (Eds.), *Reforming personnel preparation in early intervention: Issues, models, and practical strategies* (pp. 105–126). Baltimore: Paul H. Brookes.

McDonnell, A. P., Brownell, K., & Wolery, M. (1997). Teaching experience and specialist support: A survey of preschool teachers employed in programs accredited by NAEYC. *Topics in Early Childhood Special Education, 17*, 263–285.

McLaughlin, M. J., Schofield, P. F., & Hopfengardener Warren, S. (1999). Educational reform: Issues for the inclusion of students with disabilities. In M. J. Coutinho & A.C. Repp (Eds.), *Inclusion: The integration of students with disabilities* (pp. 37–60). Boston: Wadsworth.

McLean, M., & Odom, S. L. (1993). Practices for young children with and without disabilities: A comparison of DEC and NAEYC identified practices. *Topics in Early Childhood Special Education, 13*, 274–292.

McWilliam, R. A. (2000). It's only natural . . . to have early intervention in the environments where it's needed. Young Exceptional Children Monograph No. 2: *Natural environments and inclusion* (pp. 17–26). Longmont, CO: Sopris West.

McWilliam, R. A., Wolery, M., & Odom, S. L. (2001). Instructional perspectives in inclusive preschool classrooms. In M. J. Guralnick (Ed.), *Early childhood inclusion: Focus on change* (pp. 503–530). Baltimore: Paul H. Brookes.

Miller, P. S. (1992). Segregated programs of teacher education in early childhood: Immoral and inefficient practice. *Topics in Early Childhood Special Education, 11*(4), 39–52.

Miller, P., Fader, L., & Vincent, L. J. (2000). Preparing early childhood educators to work with families who have exceptional needs. In *New teachers for a new century: The future of early childhood professional preparation*. Washington, DC: National Institute on early childhood development and education, U.S. Department of Education.

Miller, P. S., & Stayton, V. D. (1998). Blended interdisciplinary teacher preparation in early education and intervention: A national study. *Topics in Early Childhood Special Education, 18*(1), 49–58.

Miller, P. S., & Stayton, V. D. (2000). Recommended practices in personnel preparation. In S. Sandall, M. E. McLean, & B. J. Smith (Eds.), *DEC recommended practices in early intervention/early childhood special education* (pp. 77–106). Longmont, CO: Sopris West.

Miller, P. S., & Stayton, V. D. (2005). DEC recommended practices: Personnel Preparation. In S. Sandall, M. L. Hemmeter, B. J. Smith, & M. E. McLean (Eds.), *DEC*

Recommended practices: A comprehensive guide for practical application in early intervention and early childhood special education (pp. 189–219). Longmont, CO: Sopris West.

Mortweet, S. L., Utley, C. A., Walker, D., Dawson, H. L., Delquadri, J. C., Reddy, S. S., Greenwood, C. R., Hamilton, S., & Ledford, D. (1999). Classwide peer tutoring: Teaching students with mild mental retardation in inclusive classrooms. *Exceptional Children, 65*, 524–536.

National Association for the Education of Young Children (NAEYC) (2006). *About NAEYC*. Retrieved August 24, 2006, from http://naeyc.org/about/

National Center for Early Development and Learning. (2000, November). *Spotlight #28: Teacher prep and diversity*. Chapel Hill, NC: Author. Retrieved November 10, 2005, from www.fpg.unc.edu/~ncedl/PAGES/project_summary.cmf?studyid=21

National Center for Education Statistics. (2005a). *Fast Facts*. Retrieved October 10, 2006, from http://nces.ed.gov/fastfacts/display.asp?id=96

National Center for Education Statistics. (2005b). Program Indicators. Retrieved October 10, 2006, from http://nces.ed.gov/programs/coe/2005/section1/indicators05.asp

National Center for Education Statistics. (2005c). Program Indicators. Retrieved October 10, 2006, from http://nces.ed.gov/programs/coe/2005/section4/indicators27.asp

Oberti v. Board of Education in Clementon School District, 995 F. 2d. 204 (1993).

Odom, S. L. (2000). Preschool inclusion: What we know and where we go from here. *Topics in Early Childhood Special Education, 20*, 20–27.

Odom, S. L. (Ed.). (2002). *Widening the circle: Including children with disabilities in preschool programs.* New York: Teacher's College Press.

Odom, S. L., & Bailey, D. B. (2001). Inclusive preschool programs: Classroom ecology and child outcomes. In M. J. Guralnick (Ed.), *Early childhood inclusion: Focus on change* (pp. 253–276). Baltimore: Paul H. Brookes.

Odom, S. L., & McEvoy, M. (1988). Integration of young children with handicaps and normally developing children. In S. Odom & M. Karnes (Eds.), *Early intervention for infants and children with handicaps: An empirical base* (pp. 241–248). Baltimore: Paul H. Brookes.

Odom, S. L., & McEvoy, M. A. (1990). Mainstreaming at the preschool level: Potential barriers and tasks for the field.

Topics in Early Childhood Special Education, 10(2), 48–61.

Odom, S. L., Schwartz, I., & ECRII Investigators. (2002). So what do we know from all this? Synthesis points of research on preschool inclusion. In S. L. Odom (Ed.), *Widening the circle: Including children with disabilities in preschool programs* (pp. 154–174). New York: Teacher's College Press.

Odom, S. L., & Wolery, M. (2003). A unified theory of practice in early intervention/early childhood special education: Evidence-based practice. *Journal of Special Education, 37*(3), 164–173.

Peck, C. A., Odom, S. L., & Bricker, D. (1993). *Integrating young children with disabilities into community programs: Ecological perspectives on research and implementation.* Baltimore: Paul H. Brookes.

Praisner, C. L. (2003). Attitudes of elementary school principals toward the inclusion of students with disabilities. *Exceptional Children, 69*, 135–146.

Rea, P. J., McLaughlin, V. L., & Walther-Thomas, C. (2000). Outcomes for students with learning disabilities in inclusive and pull out programs. *Exceptional Children, 68*, 203–222.

Salisbury, C. L. (1991). Mainstreaming during the early childhood years. *Exceptional Children, 58*, 146–155.

Salisbury, C. L., & McGregor, G. (2002). The administrative climate and context of inclusive elementary schools. *Exceptional Children, 68*, 259–274.

Sandall, S., & Ostrosky, M. (Eds.). (2000). DEC Monograph #2: *Natural environments and inclusion.* Longmont, CO: Sopris West.

Sandall, S., Hemmeter, M. L., McLean, M. D., & Smith, B. J. (Eds.). (2005). *DEC recommended practices: A comprehensive guide for practical application in early intervention/early childhood special education.* Longmont, CO: Sopris.

Schwartz, I. S., Sandall, S. R., Odom, S. L., Horn, E., & Beckman, P. J. (2002). "I know it when I see it": In search of a common definition of inclusion. In S. L. Odom (Ed.), *Widening the circle: Including children with disabilities in preschool programs* (pp. 10–24). New York: Teacher's College Press.

Scott-Little, C., Kagan, S. L., & Frelow, V. S. (2003). Series Study of Early Learning Standards. Retrieved on November 8, 2005, from http://www.upkcouncil.org/docs/products_07232003cscottlittle.pdf

Stayton, V., Fiechtl, B., Rule, S., Raschke, D., & Kliewer, C. (2003). Interdisciplinary and interagency collaboration in personnel preparation. In V. Stayton, P. S. Miller, & L. A. Dinnebeil (Eds.), *DEC personnel preparation in early childhood special education: Implementing the DEC recommended practices* (pp. 37–59). Longmont, CO: Sopris.

Stayton, V. D., & Miller, P. S. (1993). Combining general and special early childhood education standards in personnel preparation programs: Experiences from two states. *Topics in Early Childhood Special Education, 12*, 372–387.

Stayton, V. D., Miller, P. S., & Dinnebeil, L. A. (2003). *DEC personnel preparation in early childhood special education: Implementing the DEC recommended practices.* Longmont, CO: Sopris.

Stoneman, Z. (2001). Attitudes and beliefs of parents of typically developing children: Effects on early childhood inclusion. In M. J. Guralnick (Ed.), *Early childhood inclusion: Focus on change* (pp. 101–126). Baltimore: Paul H. Brookes.

Turnbull, H. R. (1990). *Free appropriate public education: The law and children with disabilities* (3rd ed.). Denver, CO: Love.

U.S. Department of Education. (2000). *New teachers for a new century: The future of early childhood education.* Washington, DC: Author.

VanLaarhoven, T., Munk, D., Lynch, K., Dorsch, N., Bosma, J., & Rouse, J. (2004). *Project ACCEPT: Preparing preservice special and general educators for inclusive education.* Manuscript submitted for review.

Vaughn, S., Bos, C. S., & Shuman, J. J. (2003). *Teaching exceptional, diverse, and at-risk students in the general education classroom.* Boston: Allyn and Bacon.

Villa, J., & Colker, L. (2006, January). Making inclusion work: A personal story. *Young Children*, 96–100.

Walsh, S., Rous, B., & Lutzer, C. (2000). The federal IDEA natural environments provisions. *Young Exceptional Children, 2*, 3–15.

Walsh, S. Smith, B. J., & Taylor, R. C. (2000). *IDEA requirements for preschoolers with disabilities: IDEA early childhood policy and practice guide.* Arlington, VA: Council for Exceptional Children.

Wickstrom Kane, S., Goldstein, H., & Kazmarek, L. (1999). Integration in the preschool for children with severe disabilities. In M. J. Coutinho & A. C. Repp (Eds.), *Inclusion: The integration of students with disabilities* (pp. 236–263). Boston: Wadsworth.

Winton, P. J., & Mellin, A. (1997, December). The "ammunition" (data and strategies) you need to promote interdisciplinary preservice training. Paper presented at the Division for Early Childhood Conference, New Orleans, LA. Reported in V. Stayton, B. Fiechtl, S. Rule, D. Raschke, & C. Kliewer (2003), Interdisciplinary and interagency collaboration in personnel preparation. In V. Stayton, P. S. Miller, & L. A. Dinnebeil (Eds.), *DEC personnel preparation in early childhood special education: Implementing the DEC recommended practices* (pp. 37–59). Longmont, CO: Sopris.

Wolery, M., Martin, C. G., Schroeder, C., Huffman, K., & Venn, M. L. (1994). Employment of educators in preschool mainstreaming: A survey of general educators. *Journal of Early Intervention, 18*, 64–77.

Wolery, M., Strain, P. S., & Bailey, D. B. (1992). Reaching potentials of children with special needs. In S. Bredekamp & T. Rosengrant (Eds.), *Reaching potentials: Appropriate curriculum and assessment for young children* (pp. 92–111). Washington, DC: NAEYC.

Wolery, M., Venn, M. L., Holcombe, A., Brookfield, J., Martin, C. G., Huffman, K., Schroeder, C., & Fleming, L. A. (1994). Employment of related services personnel in preschool programs: A survey of general early educators. *Exceptional Children, 61*, 25–39.

Yates, J., & Ortiz, A. (2004). Classification issues in special education for English language learners. In A. McCray Sorrels, H. J. Reith, & P. T. Sindelar (Eds.), *Critical issues in special education: Access, diversity, and accountability* (pp. 38–56). Boston: Pearson/Allyn and Bacon.

Yell, M. L., Drasgow, E., Bradley, R., & Justesen, R. (2004). Contemporary legal issues in special education. In A. McCray Sorrels, H. J. Reith, & P. T. Sindelar (Eds.), *Critical issues in special education: Access, diversity, and accountability* (pp. 16–37). Boston: Pearson/Allyn and Bacon.

Overview of Young Children with Exceptional Needs

Sharon M. Darling and Michelle LaRocque

Objectives

After reading this chapter, students will be able to

- Define "young children with exceptional needs."
- Summarize how young children with disabilities are similar and how they are different from their typically developing peers.
- Explain the learning and behavioral characteristics of young children with special needs.
- Summarize the service delivery options for young children with special needs, continuum of services.
- Explain how these learning and behavioral characteristics can be addressed in the inclusive environment.
- Explain why and how curriculum should be modified to address diversity of needs.

Key Terms

Special needs/disability

Exceptional needs

At risk

Developmental delay

Learning characteristics

Behavioral characteristics

Natural environments

Inclusive environments

Primary settings

Curriculum

Curricular approaches

Practical Application Vignettes

The following vignettes provide mere snapshots into the lives of two very different families. These vignettes will assist with understanding and applying the ideas and concepts discussed in this chapter.

Cameron

Cameron was a full-term baby boy born to Mary, a single teenaged mother. His mother reports that his father is not involved with Cameron and that they split up shortly before Cameron was born. Cameron lives with his mother, Mary, and his grandmother Willa. There were no issues to report about the pregnancy and delivery. His mother received prenatal care at the neighborhood clinic. Cameron is now age 5, but at the age of 2 he was diagnosed with a significant developmental delay. His pediatrician referred him to the early intervention program (Part C) for evaluation when he was not meeting his developmental milestones. There were concerns about Cameron's development in the areas of cognitive, social-emotional, and self-help (adaptive) development. His mother, Mary, was 18 years old when Cameron was born. With little knowledge about "areas of development," Mary was not much of a contributor to the implementation of services recommended for her child. She worked full-time and often was not present when the early interventionist visited her mother's home to interact with Cameron. Cameron's grandmother, his primary caregiver during the day, was elderly and also was not very involved with the early intervention service delivery for Cameron. Services were provided to Cameron in an isolated fashion, with little input from family members and caregivers and not within the context of his typical routines. Upon his third birthday, Cameron was transitioned to the Part B preschool special education classroom in a school that was over ten miles from his home.

Cameron rode the bus to school and received special education services in a segregated preschool special education classroom. There was little to no parental involvement in the educational decisions that were made for Cameron. Cameron continues to exhibit delays in the areas of cognitive, social emotional, and adaptive development. Additionally, now at the age of 5, he exhibits a delay in speech and language. Educational decisions about where these services will be provided when he transitions to kindergarten are being discussed among his current teacher and therapists. They are considering the continuum of service options that are available to Cameron within the context of the school system where he currently attends. They are leaning toward providing these services in a self-contained (segregated) classroom for young children with mild disabilities. By law, they have discussed the extent to which Cameron will participate in general education and have decided that he will participate for the curriculum areas of art, music, physical education, assemblies, and special programs. By the time he gets to kindergarten and beyond, Cameron will have received all of his special education services within isolated or segregated settings. He will not have had many opportunities to interact with his typically developing peers. His services and service delivery options were not decided in conjunction with his parent and caregivers.

Dynella

Dynella (Nelly) is a 7-year-old girl who was born at 33 weeks gestation to her mother Ella. Ella was 35 years old at the time of Dynella's birth. Ella reports that besides morning sickness in the beginning, the pregnancy was without concern. She also reports "missing a few" prenatal visits because "everything was fine." Ella and Dynella's father are no longer together, but he visits with Dynella "occasionally." Dynella arrived five weeks early, but her weight and APGAR scores were within normal limits, causing no concern for her pediatrician and mother. By age 2, Dynella started to exhibit delays in the areas of cognitive and physical development. Upon the urging of her child care providers, Ella contacted the early intervention program, which evaluated Nelly and found her to be experiencing significant delays in these areas. Ella expressed her concerns and priorities and contributed to the drafting of Nelly's individualized family service plan. She indicated that she wanted the early intervention services to be provided within Nelly's routines at the child care center and at her Mommy and Me classes. They reached a mutually agreeable plan for Nelly's services, which began immediately. Ella and Dynella's early interventionist stayed in constant communication via phone calls and logs. Ella followed through on suggestions made by the interventionist and inquired about his practices when she had questions. The child care provider, Nelly's mother, and the early interventionist viewed themselves as a team in providing services for Nelly. The early interventionist visited Nelly's child care center twice a week, providing services within the context of the center's routines and involving her typically developing peers.

The team planned for her transition at age 3, writing an individualized education program (IEP) with the provision for an itinerant special educator to continue the services to Nelly at her child care center. At the time of her third birthday, the itinerant special educator took the place of her early interventionist, providing similar services to Nelly and her family. Based on the relationship that Ella developed with her early interventionist, she came to expect and ensured a similar relationship with the special education preschool itinerant teacher. This type of service delivery continued until age 5, when Nelly began kindergarten with her cousins at her neighborhood school. Her IEP was written to provide collaborative special education services within the context of her general education kindergarten class. The special educator worked with her general education kindergarten teacher to modify the curriculum to meets Nelly's needs. When physical adaptations were necessary to meet the fine and gross motor delays that she was experiencing, consultation with the occupational therapist provided recommendations that both her teacher and her mother could implement.

Dynella is now in second grade and receives her education at her neighborhood school with her typically developing peers, including her extended family. She has required less and less special education services and hours, as she has made excellent progress in her development and achievement. Her mother continues to be involved in Dynella's education, working with her classroom teacher and her special education personnel. Her mother reports that Dynella is a happy, well-adjusted child who loves school and all of her teachers.

Young Children with Special Needs in Public Schools

Special needs is the term used to describe children who exhibit learning or behavioral needs based on a delay in development or disabling condition. This could also include children who are at risk for developing a delay or disability. This term is often interchanged with **disability** or **exceptional**

needs. Early childhood will be used to describe the period between birth and 8 years old; this is a standard and accepted definition used by the National Association for the Education of Young Children (NAEYC), the nation's largest professional organization of early childhood educators (NAEYC, 2006). "Young children" is the moniker used to describe children who are within the developmental period or early childhood years. As children grow and develop, they will encounter a number of education and care settings and systems. In some states, if a child is deemed **at risk** for developing a delay or disability based on environmental or medical conditions, he or she is also eligible for special education services. During this developmental period of birth to age 8, if a child is in need of special services, he or she could be a part of two different systems. These are the early intervention, or Part C, program and the preschool and primary special education programs, or Part B. The letters, *B* and *C*, are use to designate the section of Individuals With Disabilities Education Improvement Act of 2004 (IDEA, 2004) that describes the special education services as they are pertinent to each age group (P.L. 108-446, 2004). In some states, these systems have different agencies as their "lead." In all states, the Part B program's lead agency is the Department of Education; however, the Part C program's lead agency can be different agencies as listed in the Lead State Agencies for IDEA, Part C (see Table 2.1). The mandate is that children with special needs or exceptional learning and behavioral needs are required to receive a free appropriate public education.

The educational/service settings for children who are birth to 8 years old spans a number of education and care systems. For children who are typically developing, the education and care systems to which they are exposed during these developmental years may include one or more of the following: parental/family care, family/home child care, group child care, preschool, four-year-old prekindergarten, and elementary school (kindergarten and primary school years). For children who have special learning, behavior needs, or exceptional needs, they become a party of the above systems and additionally may receive education and care services through hospital settings, clinics, and early intervention services as mandated by The Education of the Handicapped Act Amendments of 1986 (P.L. 99-457, 1986). With the extension of services to birth, children/students birth through 21 are mandated to receive special education services if they have a delay or disability (Colarusso & O'Rourke, 1999).

Developmental Delay

When children who are younger than age 5 are deemed to have a delay or disability, they are often categorized as having a **developmental delay**. This terminology is often used as to not "label" a child early on or if the etiology of the disability is unknown. In the initial special education legislation, P.L. 94-142 (1975), services were initially mandated for children as young as age 3, and then

Table 2.1 • Lead Agencies for Part C by State

State/Jurisdiction [1,2]	Lead Agency
Alabama	Rehabilitation Services
Alaska	Health and Social Services
American Samoa	Health
Arizona	Economic Security
Arkansas	Department of Health and Human Services
California	Developmental Services
Colorado	Human Services/Developmental Disabilities
Commonwealth of Northern Mariana Islands	Education
Connecticut	Mental Retardation
Delaware	Health and Social Services
District of Columbia	Human Services
Florida	Health (Children's Medical Services)
Georgia	Human Resources/Division of Public Health
Guam	Education
Hawaii	Health
Idaho	Health and Welfare/Developmental Disabilities
Illinois	Human Services
Indiana	Family and Social Services
Iowa	Education
Kansas	Health and Environment
Kentucky	Health Services
Louisiana	Health and Hospitals
Maine	Education
Maryland	Education
Massachusetts	Public Health
Michigan	Education
Minnesota	Education
Mississippi	Health
Missouri	Education
Montana	Public Health and Human Services
Nebraska	Education and Health and Human Services (co-lead)

Table 2.1 • *(Continued)*

State/Jurisdiction [1,2]	Lead Agency
Nevada	Human Resources/Health
New Hampshire	Health and Human Services
New Jersey	Health and Senior Services
New Mexico	Health
New York	Health
North Carolina	Health and Human Services
North Dakota	Human Services
Ohio	Health
Oklahoma	Education
Oregon	Education
Pennsylvania	Public Welfare
Puerto Rico	Health
Rhode Island	Human Services
South Carolina	Health and Environmental Control
South Dakota	Education
Tennessee	Education
Texas	Assistive and Rehabilitative Services
Utah	Health
Vermont	Education and Human Services (co-lead)
Virgin Islands	Health
Virginia	Mental Health, Mental Retardation and Substance Abuse Services
Washington	Social and Health Services
West Virginia	Health and Human Resources
Wisconsin	Health and Family Services
Wyoming	Health

• The Federated States of Micronesia, Republic of Marshall Islands, and Republic of Palau are not currently eligible for this federal program.

• The Department of the Interior (DOI) receives allocation from the U.S. Department of Education, which then is distributed by DOI to tribes.

Source: National Early Childhood Technical Assistance System (NECTAS), Chapel Hill, NC. Retrieved October 12, 2006, from www.nectac.org/partc/ptclead.asp?text=1

Developmental Delay

later legislation, P.L. 99-457 (1986), suggested services for children starting at birth. In the reauthorization of 1997, states were given the option of being able to extend this label of developmental delay up to age 8 (IDEA '97, 1997). There are people who both oppose and support this possible extension to age 8 for developmental delay. Supporters of this extension put forth argument that it is a natural extension, as the developmental period goes to age 8, that sometimes at age 5 it is still too early to "label" a child with a specific disability label, and, lastly, that the label of developmental delay allows for the possibility of more inclusive service delivery. Opponents of this extension of the developmental delay label say that it allows the delay of more appropriate services for the youngest children who may be in need of additional or different types of services than they are currently receiving, that funding is often contingent upon a specific label, and giving a specific name to describe differences in a child's learning, behavior, or appearance may make professionals more tolerant of diversity among children (Fiedler & Simpson, 1987; Hallahan & Kauffman, 2003).

Young children with special or exceptional needs, disabilities, or developmental delays will be in need of special education and related services. If the special needs are diagnosed before age 3, they are served in the Part C program, upon their third birthday; they are served by the educational system of Part B. By age 5, school systems can choose to continue the label of developmental delay or reevaluate to determine if the student is eligible for one of the other categories of disability served under IDEA. Under IDEA, a child may not be identified as a "child with a disability" just because he or she speaks a language other than English and does not speak or understand English well. A child may not be identified as having a disability just because he or she has not had enough instruction in math or reading.

Learning or Behavioral Characteristics

IDEA identifies thirteen categories of disability. These categories as reported by the National Dissemination Center for Children with Disabilities (NICHCY, 2002), and their associated **learning** or **behavioral characteristics** are as follows:

1. Autism . . .
   . . . means a developmental disability significantly affecting verbal and nonverbal communication and social interaction, generally evident before age 3, and adversely affects educational performance. Characteristics often associated with autism are engaging in repetitive activities and stereotyped movements, resistance to changes in daily routines or the environment, and unusual responses to sensory experiences. The term *autism* does not apply if the child's educational performance is adversely affected primarily because the child has emotional disturbance, as defined in item number 5. A child who shows the characteristics of autism after age 3 could be diagnosed as having autism if the criteria above are satisfied.

   Within the primary classroom setting, these students will have difficulty working collaboratively, communicating their needs, making and maintaining eye contact, and grasping concepts initially. Subject areas that require verbal (and nonverbal) communication can be affected. When designing activities that require cooperative learning, students with autism will need significant coaching in order to participate.

2. Deaf-blindness (DB) . . .

   . . . means concomitant [simultaneous] hearing and visual impairments, the combination of which causes such severe communication and other developmental and educational needs that they cannot be accommodated in special education programs solely for children with deafness or for children with blindness. Children who are deaf-blind tend to have difficulty with participating in activities that require vision or hearing abilities. Adaptations and modifications need to be made to compensate for the lack of hearing and sight. Children who are deaf-blind require reliance on tactile stimulation.

3. Deafness . . .

   . . . means a hearing impairment so severe that a child is impaired in processing linguistic information through hearing, with or without amplification, which adversely affects a child's educational performance. Children who are deaf have difficulty hearing verbal instructions, directions, praise, etc., so these need to be presented in alternative nonauditory, means for children who are deaf to understand. Verbal or sounds need to be paired with tactile and visual to accommodate the learning needs of children who are deaf. Children are often taught alternative means of communicating, such as sign language.

4. Emotional disturbance (ED) . . .

   . . . means a condition exhibiting one or more of the following characteristics over a long period of time and to a marked degree that adversely affects a child's educational performance: (a) an inability to learn that cannot be explained by intellectual, sensory, or health factors, (b) an inability to build or maintain satisfactory interpersonal relationships with peers and teachers, (c) inappropriate types of behavior or feelings under normal circumstances, (d) a general pervasive mood of unhappiness or depression, and (e) a tendency to develop physical symptoms or fears associated with personal or school problems. The term includes schizophrenia. The term does not apply to children who are socially maladjusted, unless it is determined that they have an emotional disturbance.

   Children with emotional disturbance tend to have difficulty with learning because so often their behavioral issues interfere with learning environment and stimulation. Behaviors need to be specifically addressed outside the context of the subject area as well as within the context of the subject area. Systems/programs for modifying and managing behavior should be an integral part of the learning environment.

5. Hearing impairment (HI) . . .

   . . . means an impairment in hearing, whether permanent or fluctuating, that adversely affects a child's educational performance but is not included under the definition of "deafness." Children with a hearing impairment tend to have difficulty hearing, but this can be ameliorated with the aid of amplification and other devices. Children are often taught alternative means of communicating, such as sign language. Verbal or sounds need to be paired with visual aids in order to assist comprehension.

6. Mental retardation (MR) . . .

   . . . means significantly subaverage general intellectual functioning, existing concurrently with (i.e., at the same time as) deficits in adaptive behavior and manifested during the developmental period, that adversely affects a child's educational performance.

Due to their level of intellectual functioning, children with mental retardation tend to have difficulty with all academic areas as well as socialization. Children with mental retardation are generally not on grade level, nor are they developmentally appropriate in social situations. Instruction should be based on the child's mental (according to present level of functioning) age rather than on the child's chronological age (according to birth date).

7. Multiple disabilities . . .

   . . . means concomitant [simultaneous] impairments (such as mental retardation–blindness, mental retardation–orthopedic impairment, etc.), the combination of which causes such severe educational needs that they cannot be accommodated in a special education program solely for one of the impairments. The term does not include deaf-blindness. Children with multiple disabilities tend to have difficulty with all academic areas and may include and require accommodations based on physical needs as well. The manifestations of multiple disabilies are reliant upon the types and combinations of needs. Accommodations and modifications should be based on the types and combinations of needs.

8. Orthopedic impairment (OI) . . .

   . . . means a severe orthopedic impairment that adversely affects a child's educational performance. The term includes impairments caused by a congenital anomaly (e.g., clubfoot, absence of some member, etc.), impairments caused by disease (e.g., poliomyelitis, bone tuberculosis, etc.), and impairments from other causes (e.g., cerebral palsy, amputations, and fractures or burns that cause contractures). Children with orthopedic impairments tend to have difficulty with physical activities. In order to qualify for services under the disability category of orthopedic impairment, the child must not have any mental impairment. Learning and behavioral needs consist of making the appropriate environmental adjustments in order to address issues of mobility and participation in activities.

9. Other health impairment (OHI) . . .

   . . . means having limited strength, vitality, or alertness, including a heightened alertness to environmental stimuli, that (a) results in limited alertness with respect to the educational environment; (b) is due to chronic or acute health problems such as asthma, attention deficit disorder or attention-deficit/hyperactivity disorder, diabetes, epilepsy, a heart condition, hemophilia, lead poisoning, leukemia, nephritis, rheumatic fever, and sickle cell anemia; and (c) adversely affects a child's educational performance. Children with other health impairments may have difficulty with academic, social, and physical participation due to the specific nature of the impairment. Learning and behavioral needs would be based on the individual child's impairment.

10. Specific learning disability (LD) . . .

    . . . means a disorder in one or more of the basic psychological processes involved in understanding or in using language, spoken or written, that may manifest itself in an imperfect ability to listen, think, speak, read, write, spell, or to do mathematical calculations. The term includes such conditions as perceptual disabilities, brain injury, minimal brain dysfunction, dyslexia, and developmental aphasia. The term does not include learning problems that are primarily the result of visual, hearing, or motor disabilities; of mental retardation; of emotional disturbance; or of environmental, cultural, or economic disadvantage. Children with specific learning disabilities by definition have difficulty with ability to listen, think, speak, read, write, spell, or to do mathematical calculations. These difficulties can affect all academic areas, but not necessarily all. It is possible that a child can have a learning disability in one academic area, such as reading and language arts, but is at the same time gifted in another academic area, such as mathematics.

11. Speech or language impairment . . .

. . . means a communication disorder such as stuttering, impaired articulation, a language impairment, or a voice impairment that adversely affects a child's educational performance. Children with speech or language impairments tend to have difficulty with academic areas and activities that require speech or language participation. The manifestation is dependent upon the nature of the speech or language impairment. Children who have issues with stuttering, articulation, or voice impairment may shy away from participating in activities that require vocalizations and sharing in groups. Alternative methods of sharing may be needed.

12. Traumatic brain injury (TBI) . . .

. . . means an acquired injury to the brain caused by an external physical force, resulting in total or partial functional disability or psychosocial impairment, or both, that adversely affects a child's educational performance. The term applies to open or closed head injuries resulting in impairments in one or more areas, such as cognition; language; memory; attention; reasoning; abstract thinking; judgment; problem solving; sensory, perceptual, and motor abilities; psychosocial behavior; physical functions; information processing; and speech. The term does not include brain injuries that are congenital or degenerative or brain injuries induced by birth trauma. Children with traumatic brain injury can exhibit a wide range of learning or behavioral characteristics. Brain injuries are manifested uniquely in different patients. Based on these possible issues with cognition; language; memory; attention; reasoning; abstract thinking; judgment; problem-solving; sensory, perceptual, and motor abilities; psychosocial behavior; physical functions; information processing; and speech, all academic areas can be affected as well as physical functioning. These would require attending to the specific needs exhibited by the child.

13. Visual impairment including blindness (VI) . . .

. . . means an impairment in vision that, even with correction, adversely affects a child's educational performance. The term includes both partial sight and blindness. Children with visual impairments have difficulty seeing, which affects academic areas as well as mobility. Learning needs require that accommodations and modifications are made to ensure that the child is able to understand using alternate modalities as well as altering the environmental to accommodate the mobility issues.

High- and Low-Incidence Disabilities

High-incidence disabilities are those disability categories that are most prevalent in special education. Approximately 90 percent of students with disabilities are classified as having learning disabilities, mental retardation, emotional disabilities, or communication disorders. (Mastropieri & Scruggs, 2003). Students with learning disabilities are the largest group of students with disabilities served in the schools and comprise about half of students with disabilities. These students may exhibit specific problems in understanding or using language which may be present in any curricular area.

Students with mental retardation exhibit deficits in intellectual functioning and adaptive behavior. These students also may exhibit learning problems related to language, social behavior, attention, and the ability to solve problems. Students with communication disorders may exhibit problems with speech or language. Speech is the production of sounds, and disorders may exist as voice, articulation, or fluency disorders. Language disorders are those involving difficulties with phonology, morphology, syntax, semantics, or pragmatics of language use. Students with emotional disturbance may exhibit problems in classroom behavior, social relationships, or may exhibit internalizing behaviors, such as anxiety or depression.

Most students with higher incidence disabilities are served in the general education classroom (Mastropieri & Scruggs, 2003). In many instances, the causes of high-incidence disabilities are unknown; however, a variety of biological and environmental explanations has been suggested. There are numerous accommodations and adaptations in the classroom environment and instruction that can make the general education classroom a positive learning environment for students with higher incidence disabilities.

Low-incidence disabilities are those disabilities which are represented in lower numbers in special education. These include the disability categories of visual impairments, hearing impairments, physical disabilities and other health impairments, severe and multiple disabilities, and autism. Students with low-incidence disabilities are more difficult to serve in public schools because none of the low-incidence categories alone can form a group large enough to support full-time highly specialized personnel, except perhaps in very large school districts. Therefore, students with low-incidence disabilities are more likely to be served in less inclusive settings (such as in special classes, separate schools, and residential facilities) than are students with high-incidence disabilities. Smaller schools that try to serve these students in more inclusive environments typically utilize the expertise of itinerant personnel, often teachers/consultants who travel from school to school as needed. Many times these professionals work in many districts to serve the needs of students with low-incidence disabilities.

Service Delivery Options

Current recommended practices are that young children with exceptional needs are to be served within inclusive settings; this is congruent with the federal mandate that children are served in the least restrictive environment (Sandall, Hemmeter, McLean, & Smith, 2005). Inclusive placements, where young children have the opportunity to be educated alongside their typically developing peers are most preferred. In these inclusive settings, children have the opportunity to interact with and learn from and to be models for their non-disabled peers. Children who are educated within inclusive settings make similar developmental gains as in segregated placements (Lewis & Doorlag, 1999). Vygotsky speaks of cognitive and social development being increased when children have the opportunity for their learning to be scaffolded by their more advanced peers. This scaffolding allows for the children to interact with and learn from each other (Vygotsky, 1978).

Natural/Least Restrictive Environment

The law dictates that special educations services are just that, services, not necessarily a specific place. The law goes further to say that, for the youngest children, these services should be provided within the natural environments to the greatest extent possible. **Natural environments** can be most readily described as "where children live, learn, and play" (McWilliam, 2000). For children over age 3, namely in primary grades, kindergarten through third grade, that law states that children should be educated within the least restrictive environment. Least restrictive environment may or may not be the general education classroom. Service delivery options for students with special needs can be within a continuum, ranging from most to least restrictive. See Figure 2.1 for continuum of services for children in primary grades.

Service delivery placement decisions should be jointly decided by the educational agency and the parents or caregivers of the child. Within the birth-to-3 early intervention system, services are based on family needs and priorities, and, though not as strongly in the preschool and primary grades, parental involvement in the process is strongly encouraged by the federal law. Systems must document when and how caregivers are involved in the processes of referral, evaluation, placement, and service delivery.

From the earliest years, the mandate is to strive for family-centered service delivery, because it recognized that children are not isolated beings. Instead, they are a part of many concentric circles and systems (Bronfrenbrenner, 1979; Turnbull & Turnbull, 2001). With the recognition of the many systems that affect a child's life and the validation that caregivers are with a child for her or his lifetime while teachers are in their lives a relatively short time, striving for family centered services somewhat ensures an extension of the services being provided today. For children and families who are in their primary years of schooling, obtaining family-centered practice, though not required by the fall, is still recommended practice. Schools can be family centered by creating learning environments that parents and caregivers are enlisted to support the common goal of educating all children. Family participation and involvement is highly correlated with student success (Turnbull & Turnbull, 2001). Some strategies for encouraging family participation and involvement include the following:

1. Be specific about goals and value of involvement.
2. Invite families (including fathers) into the classroom as often as possible.
3. Value the diversity of all families and family members.
4. Plan convenient times for families to participate in conferences and school activities.
5. Encourage communication through the use of various methods (e.g., telephone, email, notebooks, and websites).
6. Provide ideas and materials for activities parents can do at home and in the community with their children.

With the provision of services within natural and least restrictive environments, it is logical to consider services within inclusive environments. **Inclusive environments** are places (educational, recreational, etc.) where children of varying abilities coexist, learn together, play together, etc. Children with disabilities fare as well or better in environments that include their typically developing peers (Odom, 2002). Arguments for inclusive service delivery were put forth in Chapter 1, but it warrants being mentioned here as well. If we are to prepare children to function appropriately in the greater society, then they will better learn this within environments that include persons of varying abilities and disabilities. Segregated settings used to be the norm in service delivery for children

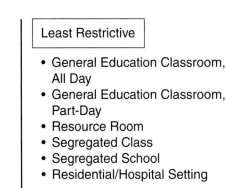

Figure 2.1 • Continuum of service delivery.

with disabilities, but, according to the U.S. Department of Education (2006), more than 48 percent of children with disabilities are being educated with their peers who are typically developing within inclusive environments for more than 75 percent of the day. In 2002, 96 percent of students with disabilities were educated in typical school buildings. However, the time they spent in typical classrooms varied. As more children are being educated within inclusive environments, this will often mean the general education classroom for children in kindergarten through third grades, or **primary settings**.

In the public school setting, children are served via a continuum of services that range from full inclusion to special education schools that may or may not be residential (Smith, 2006). Young children who are ages 5 to 8 years old are considered to be in their primary years (Frost, Wortham, & Reifal, 2001). If they are on grade level, they are served in kindergarten first-, second-, or third-grade classes. According to IDEA, children in need of special education services are to be placed within the least restrictive environment (LRE). This includes, but is not limited to, the general education classroom. The definition of LRE according to IDEA is, "To the maximum extent appropriate, children with disabilities, including children in public or private institutions or other care facilities, are (1) educated with children who are not disabled, and (2) special classes, separate schooling, or other removal of children with disabilities from the regular educational environment occurs only when the nature or severity of the disability of a child is such that education in regular classes with the use of supplementary aids and services cannot be achieved satisfactorily" (IDEA, 2004). Where a student is placed is part of the IEP process under IDEA and determines the educational services provided to students with disabilities.

Since the IEP delineates the school's obligation of special education and related services provided to eligible students, it is critical that teachers have a clear understanding of what it entails. Specifically, every eligible student must have an IEP in effect before special education and related services can be provided by the school, and the IEP must be reviewed and revised at least annually. For students who have undergone a first-time evaluation for special education eligibility, parents must consent to the student's placement in special education before an IEP meeting can be held and an IEP for the student developed.

Referral

Before an evaluation can take place, a child who has not been identified under Part C but who is suspected to have a disability is referred for an evaluation. A referral can be made by parents/family members, teachers, or other professionals. Usually, the referral goes to the school's multidisciplinary team that coordinates the evaluation process. Once data from the evaluations are collected and interpreted, the team determines whether the child qualifies for services under IDEA. If the student is eligible and requires services, then these services are provided under IDEA. The multidisciplinary team then meets to develop the IEP (Drascow, Yell, & Robinson, 2001).

The IEP Team

The multidisciplinary team and the IEP team may or may not be made up of the same members, but the IEP team is responsible for the development of the IEP, reviews it at least annually, and makes any revisions that are needed. IDEA requires that the IEP team consist of (1) the child's parents, (2) at least one general education teacher if the child will or will possibly be participating in general education, (3) a representative from the local education agency (LEA), (4) an individual who can interpret the instructional implications of test results (this may be one of the teachers or LEA representatives), (5) any individuals who have knowledge or special expertise regarding the child, including related services personnel, (6) when appropriate, the child him- or herself.

The LEA is usually the school district. The LEA representative should be one who is qualified to provide, or supervise the provision of, specially designed instruction; is knowledgeable about the general education curriculum; and is knowledgeable about the availability of district resources.

The IEP

IDEA clearly specifies that the IEP document must include the following:

1. A statement of the student's *present levels of academic achievement and functional performance.* This also includes a statement describing how the student's disability impacts his or her involvement and progress in general education and a description of the student's performance in skill areas affected by the disability. This information is derived from the student's most recent assessments and information contributed by the team.

2. A statement of *measurable annual goals* and, for students who complete alternate assessments, *benchmarks or short-term objectives* that align to alternate achievement standards. These statements must be related to meeting the student's needs in order to help her or him be involved and progress in the general education curriculum in addition to meeting other educational needs related to the specific disability. The 2004 reauthorization removed the requirement that all IEP's include short-term objectives for two reasons: (1) to reduce paperwork, and (2) some perceived short-term goals to be a barrier to accessing general education (Gartin & Murdock, 2005).

3. Statements of the *special education and related services* to be provided and program modifications or supports for school personnel (1) to advance toward attaining annual goals, (2) to be

involved and progress in the general education curriculum, (3) to participate in extracurricular and other nonacademic activities, and (4) to be educated and participate with other students with and without disabilities. IDEA defines special education as specially designed instruction to meet the unique needs of a student with a disability. It includes instruction in classrooms, homes, hospitals, institutions, and other settings. IDEA defines related services as developmental, corrective, and other supportive services needed to assist a student with a disability to benefit from special education. Specific services listed under idea include (1) transportation, (2) speech-language pathology and audiology, (3) psychological services, (4) physical therapy, (5) occupational therapy, (6) recreation, (7) therapeutic recreation, (8) social work services, (9) counseling services, (10) rehabilitation counseling, (11) orientation and mobility, (12) medical services (for diagnostic and evaluation purposes only), and (13) early identification and assessment of disabling conditions.

4. An explanation of the *extent, if any, to which the student will not participate with children without disabilities in the general education class.*

5. A statement of any individual m *odifications in the administration of state- or districtwide assessments* in order for the student to participate in such assessments. If the IEP team determines that the student will not participate, the IEP must include a statement describing why that assessment is inappropriate for the student and what alternate assessment will be used.

6. The *projected date services* will be initiated and the frequency, location, and duration of those services.

7. Beginning at least by age 16, appropriate *measurable postsecondary goals* related to training, education, employment, and, where appropriate, independent living skills and the transition services needed to reach those goals. This should be completed at least one year before the student reaches the age of majority under state law. A statement must be included that the student has been informed of his or her rights that will transfer at age of majority.

8. A statement of *how student progress will be measured and how the parents will be regularly informed of student progress.*

Finally, when developing the IEP, there are several factors that must be considered.

- For a child whose behavior impedes the child's learning or that of others, the team must consider the use of positive behavioral interventions, supports, and other strategies to address that behavior.
- For a child with limited English proficiency, the team must consider the language needs of the child.
- For a child who is blind or visually impaired, the team must consider instruction in Braille.
- For a child who is deaf or hard of hearing, the team must consider language and communication needs.
- For all children, the team must consider the need for assistive technology devices and services.

See Figure 2.2 for the State of Massachusetts's sample IEP form.

Figure 2.2 ● Sample Massachusetts IEP Form

School District Name:

School District Address:

School District Contact Person/Phone #:

Individualized Education Program

IEP Dates: from   to

Student Name: _____ DOB: _____ ID#: _____ Grade/Level: _____

Parent and/or Student Concerns

What concern(s) does the parent and/or student want to see addressed in this IEP to enhance the student's education?

Student Strengths and Key Evaluation Results Summary

What are the student's educational strengths, interest areas, significant personal attributes, and personal accomplishments?

What is the student's type of disability(ies), general education performance including MCAS/district test results, achievement toward goals, and lack of expected progress, if any?

Vision Statement: What is the vision for this student?

Consider the next 1- to 5-year period when developing this statement. Beginning no later than age 14, the statement should be based on the student's preferences and interest, and should include desired outcomes in adult living, postsecondary, and working environments.

Present Levels of Educational Performance

A: General Curriculum

Check all that apply.

General curriculum area(s) affected by this student's disability(ies):

☐ English Language Arts   Consider the language, composition, literature (including reading), and media strands.

☐ History and Social Sciences   Consider the history, geography, economic, and civics and government strands.

☐ Science and Technology   Consider the inquiry, domains of science, technology, and science, technology, and human affairs strand.

(Continued)

The IEP Team

Figure 2.2 • *(Continued)*

| ☐ Mathematics | Consider the number sense, patterns, relations and functions, geometry and measurement, and statistics and probability strands. |
| ☐ Other Curriculum Areas | Specify: |

How does the disability(ies) affect progress in the curriculum area(s)?

What type(s) of accommodation, *if any*, **is necessary for the student to make effective progress?**

What type(s) of specially designed instruction, *if any*, **is necessary for the student to make effective progress?**
Check the necessary instructional modification(s) and describe how such modification(s) will be made.

☐ Content:

☐ Methodology/Delivery of Instruction:

☐ Performance Criteria:

Present Levels of Educational Performance

B: Other Educational Needs

Check all that apply.

General Considerations

☐ Adapted physical education

☐ Braille needs (blind/visually impaired)

☐ Extra curriculum activities

☐ Social/emotional needs

☐ Assistive tech devices/services

☐ Communication (all students)

☐ Language needs (LEP students)

☐ Travel training

☐ Behavior

☐ Communication (deaf/hard of hearing students)

☐ Nonacademic activities

☐ Skill development related to vocational preparation or experience

☐ Other _____

Age-Specific Considerations

☐ For children ages 3 to 5 — participation in appropriate activities

☐ For children ages 14+ (or younger if appropriate) — student's course of study

☐ For children ages 16 (or younger if appropriate) to 22 — transition to postschool activities including community experiences, employment objectives, other postschool adult living and, if appropriate, daily living skills

Figure 2.2 ● *(Continued)*

How does the disability(ies) affect progress in the indicated area(s) of other educational needs?

What type(s) of accommodation, *if any*, is necessary for the student to make effective progress?

What type(s) of specially designed instruction, *if any*, is necessary for the student to make effective progress?

Check the necessary instructional modification(s) and describe how such modification(s) will be made.

☐ Content:

☐ Methodology/Delivery of Instruction:

☐ Performance Criteria:

Current Performance Levels/Measurable Annual Goals

Goal #   Specific Goal Focus:

Current Performance Level: What can the student currently do?

Measurable Annual Goal: What challenging, yet attainable, goal can we expect the student to meet by the end of this IEP period? How will we know that the student has reached this goal?

Benchmark/Objectives: What will the student need to do to complete this goal?

Goal #   Specific Goal Focus:

Current Performance Level: What can the student currently do?

Measurable Annual Goal: What challenging, yet attainable, goal can we expect the student to meet by the end of this IEP period? How will we know that the student has reached this goal?

Benchmark/Objectives: What will the student need to do to complete this goal?

Progress Reports are required to be sent to parents at least as often as parents are informed of their nondisabled children's progress.

Each progress report most describe the student's progress toward meeting each annual goal.

1. What is the student's progress toward the annual goal?

2. Is the progress sufficient to enable the student to achieve the annual goal by the end of the IEP period?

(Continued)

The IEP Team

● ....

50

Figure 2.2 ● *(Continued)*

Service Delivery

What are the total service delivery needs of this student?

Include services, related services, program modifications and supports (including positive behavioral supports, school personnel and/or parent training/supports). Services should assist the student in reaching IEP goals, to be involved and progress in the general curriculum, to participate in extracurricular/nonacademic activities, and to allow the student to participate with nondisabled students while working toward IEP goals.

School District Cycle: ☐ 5 day cycle ☐ 6 day cycle ☐ 10 day cycle ☐ other:

A. Consultation (Indirect Services to School Personnel and Parents)

Focus on Goal #	Type of Service	Type of Personnel	Frequency and Duration/Per Cycle	Start Date	End Date

B. Special Education and Related Services in General Education Classroom (Direct Service)

Focus on Goal #	Type of Service	Type of Personnel	Frequency and Duration/Per Cycle	Start Date	End Date

C. Special Education and Related Services in Other Settings (Direct Service)

Focus on Goal #	Type of Service	Type of Personnel	Frequency and Duration/Per Cycle	Start Date	End Date

Figure 2.2 ● *(Continued)*

Nonparticipation Justification

Is the student removed from the general education classroom at any time? (Refer to IEP 5—Service Delivery, Section C.)

☐ No ☐ Yes   If yes, why is removal considered critical to the student's program?

IDEA 2004 Regulation 20 U.S.C. §612 (a) (5).550: ". . . removal of children with disabilities from the regular educational environment occurs ***only when*** the nature or severity of the disability of a child is such that education in regular classes with the use of supplementary aids and services cannot be achieved satisfactorily." (Emphasis added.)

Schedule Modification

Shorter: Does this student require a *shorter school day or shorter school year?*

☐ No ☐ Yes — shorter day ☐ Yes — shorter year   If yes, answer the questions below.

Longer: Does this student require a longer school day or a longer school year to prevent substantial loss of previously learned skills and/or substantial difficulty in relearning skills?

☐ No ☐ Yes — longer day ☐ Yes — longer year   If yes, answer the questions below.

How will the student's schedule be modified? Why is this schedule modification being recommended? If a longer day or year is recommended, how will the school district coordinate services across program components?

Transportation Services

Does the student require transportation as a result of the disability(ies)?

☐ No Regular transportation will be provided in the same manner as it would be provided for students without disabilities. If the child is placed away from the local school, transportation will be provided.

☐ Yes Special transportation will be provided in the following manner:

  ☐ on a regular transportation vehicle with the following modifications and/or specialized equipment and precautions:

  ☐ on a special transportation vehicle with the following modifications and/or specialized equipment and precautions:

After the team makes a transportation decision and after a placement decision has been made, a parent may choose to provide transportation and may be eligible for reimbursement under certain circumstances. Any parent who plans to transport his or her child to school should notify the school district contact person.

(Continued)

The IEP Team

Figure 2.2 • *(Continued)*

State- or Districtwide Assessment

Identify state- or districtwide assessments planned during this IEP period:

Fill out the table below. Consider any state- or districtwide assessment to be administered during the time span covered by this IEP. For each content area, identify the student's assessment participation status by putting an "X" in the corresponding box for column 1,2, or 3.

CONTENT AREAS	1. Assessment participation: Student partici-pates in on-demand testing under routine conditions in this content area. COLUMN 1	2. Assessment participation: Student partici-pates in on-demand testing with accommo-dations in this content area. (See 1 below) COLUMN 2	3. Assessment participation: Student partici-pates in alternate assessment in this content area. (See 2 below) COLUMN 3
English Language Arts	☐	☐	☐
History and Social Sciences	☐	☐	☐
Mathematics	☐	☐	☐
Science and Technology	☐	☐	☐
Reading	☐	☐	☐

1. For each content area identified by an X in the column 2 above: note, in the space below, the content area and describe the accommodations necessary for participation in the on-demand testing. Any accommodations used for assessment purposes should be closely modeled on the accommodations that are provided to the student as part of his/her instructional program.

2. For each content area identified by an X in column 3 above: note, in the space below, the content area, why the on-demand assessment is not appropriate, and how that content area will be alternately assessed. Make sure to include the learning standards that will be addressed in each content area, the recommended assessment method(s) and the recommended evaluation and reporting method(s) for the student's performance on the alternate assessment.

NOTE: When state model(s) for alternate assessment are adopted, the district may enter use of state model(s) for how content area(s) will be assessed.

Additional Information

☐ Include the following transition information: the anticipated graduation date; a statement of interagency responsibilities or needed linkages; the discussion of transfer of rights at least one year before age of majority; and a recommendation for Chapter 688 Referral.

Figure 2.2 • *(Continued)*

☐ Document efforts to obtain participation if a parent and if student did not attend meeting or provide input.

☐ Record other relevant IEP information not previously stated.

Response Section

School Assurance

I certify that the goals in this IEP are those recommended by the Team and that the indicated services will be provided.

Signature and Role of LEA Representative   Date

Parent Options / Responses

It is important that the district knows your decision as soon as possible. Please indicate your response by checking at least one (1) box and returning a signed copy to the district. Thank you.

☐ I accept the IEP as developed.   ☐ I reject the IEP as developed.

☐ I reject the following portions of the IEP with the understanding that any portion(s) that I do not reject will be considered accepted and implemented immediately. Rejected portions are as follows:

_____

_____

_____

_____

☐ I request a meeting to discuss the rejected IEP or rejected portion(s).

_____

Signature of Parent, Guardian, Educational Surrogate Parent, Student 18 and Over*   Date

*Required signature once a student reaches 18 unless there is a court-appointed guardian.

Parent Comment: I would like to make the following comment(s) but realize any comment(s) made that suggest changes to the proposed IEP will not be implemented unless the IEP is amended.

_____

_____

_____

_____

_____

(Continued)

The IEP Team

Figure 2.2 ● *(Continued)*

Parent and/or Student Concerns

What concern(s) does the parent and/or student want to see addressed in this IEP to enhance the student's education?

_____

_____

Student Strengths and Key Evaluation Results Summary

What are the student's educational strengths, interest areas, significant personal attributes and personal accomplishments?

What is the student's type of disability(ies), general education performance including MCAS/district test results, achievement toward goals and lack of expected progress, if any?

Vision Statement: What is the vision for this student?

Consider the next 1- to 5-year period when developing this statement. Beginning no later than age 14, the statement should be based on the student's preferences and interest, and should include desired outcomes in adult living, postsecondary and working environments.

Implications When Disabilities Coexist With Diversity

As the cultural, linguistic, ethnic, and socioeconomic composition of the society changes, this impacts all areas of society; the educational system is not exempt. More children whose primary language is not English, who are from a cultural or ethnic group that is not White/Caucasian, and whose family lives at or below the poverty line are starting school and are becoming a part of the

educational system as well as special education. These attributes represent the diversity that is present in classrooms today. When these facets are paired with that child having a disability or delay, there are specific implications. Sometimes these same facets of diversity may put a child "at risk" for a delay or disability. Different cultures view disabilities differently and, therefore, how that disability should be acknowledged or treated differently. What may be interpreted as indifference by one culture may be the standard reaction in another culture. How educators respond to the family's response to a diagnosis and the provision of services for a child with a disability or delay will directly impact the success of said provision. Regardless of the cultural/ethnic, socioeconomic, linguistic, and other diversity that a child brings to the educational setting, inclusion of the family in every step of the process and beyond tends to positively influence the education of that child.

Changing Roles of Families

Changing Format of Families

The birth or diagnosis of a child with a disability is typically not an expected event in any family. Reactions may differ markedly depending on the family's level of preparedness for the news, familiarity with the disability, severity of the disability, onset of the disability, and family strengths and weaknesses that were already present (Turnbull, Turnbull, Erwin, & Soodak, 2006). Each family has existing supports and needs that exist whether or not there is a child with a disability in the family.

Typically, the family is the key stakeholder in the education of young children with or without disabilities. Yet children live in diverse family arrangements that reflect the many choices of their parents including marriage and divorce. Significant numbers of children today are born out of wedlock and raised by single parents or spend a large portion of their lives with other relatives or stepparents. Many of these findings are described in *America's Children: Key National Indicators of Well-Being* (2005), the U.S. government's nineth annual monitoring report on the well-being of the nation's children and youth. The report was compiled by the Federal Interagency Forum on Child and Family Statistics and presents a comprehensive look at critical areas of child well-being, including health status, behavior and social environment, economic security, and education.

This report clearly stresses that the image of the American family as a married couple with children living in the same household is no longer true. In 2004, 68 percent of children ages birth to 17 lived with two married parents, down from 77 percent in 1980. At the same time, the rate of childbearing by unmarried women rose sharply for women of all ages, with the exception being the adolescent birth rate. This decrease is critical, as infants born to teen mothers are more likely to be of low birth weight, which increases their chances for infant death and for blindness, deafness, mental retardation, mental illness, and cerebral palsy.

The racial and ethnic diversity of children in the United States continues to increase. In 2003, 60 percent of U.S. children were White, non-Hispanic, 16 percent were Black, and 4 percent were Asian. The proportion of Hispanic children has increased faster than any other racial or ethnic group, growing from 9 percent of the child population in 1980 to 19 percent in 2003.

Changing Needs of Young Children with Disabilities

As children enter the primary years of schooling, learning and behavioral requirements change; often these environments become more regimented and stringent. If the child has a disability or delay that changes learning or behavioral needs, these learning environments present many challenges. If these children were served in inclusive settings prior to the primary years, there is an expectation for the same type of inclusive service delivery. If they were not served in inclusive settings prior, the expectation is that it is time to consider this service delivery option as the children transition to this next level of their education. Either way, inclusive service delivery is warranted and expected.

Curricular Implications

Is it possible to achieve a curriculum that will be appropriate for *all* children, regardless of ability/disability, diversity, status? The answer is a resounding yes. Curriculum that is appropriate for all children does not mean that all children should have the same curriculum. Curriculum in the primary grades should be composed of a number of salient features: (1) philosophical framework, (2) scope and sequence, (3) national-, state-, and district-mandated content, (4) instructional methods, (5) activities and experiences, (6) attention to the environment, (7) adaptations, and (8) data collection and use.

Philosophical Framework

The philosophical framework for a curriculum or curricular approach should be grounded with a solid theory of child growth and development. Theoretical approaches such as Maturational, Psychoanalytic, Behaviorist, Social Learning, and Cognitive Developmental Theory/Constructivism are often the basis for early childhood curricula and curricular approaches (Frost, Wortham, & Reifel, 2001). These theories and the associated theorists are influential in the development and design of appropriate programs for children in primary grades.

Scope and Sequence

Scope and sequence of curricula and curricular approaches should be clear before implementation of a chosen curriculum. Knowing where to begin and where to end and how it all fits together is critical to success in curriculum implementation within primary grades. The scope and sequence of curricula and curricular approaches should be informed by the children's developmental levels and abilities. The suggested pace of instruction should be appropriate for the child's level of functioning within the parameters of their abilities or disabilities. The suggested scope and sequence should also be congruent with the chosen time frame for implementation.

National-, State-, and District-Mandated Content

National-, state-, and district-mandated content should be reflected in the content of the curricula and curricular approaches. National standards are usually determined by professional organizations, such as NAEYC's *Developmentally Appropriate Practice* or the Division for Early Childhood of the Council for Exceptional Children's *Recommended Practices*, or content-area professional organizations such as the Nation Council for Teachers of Mathematics (NCTM) or the International Reading Association (IRA). State- and district-mandated content are decided by individual states and school districts. These content standards are either inclusive of or in addition to the National Standards. Chosen curricula or curricular approaches should be amenable to the national-, state-, and distinct-mandated content.

Instructional Methods

Instructional methods describe the manner in which the content is taught and usually falls into two categories; learner directed or teacher directed. There is no single method or one combination of methods that can successfully teach all children everything they need to know. Consequently, teachers must be familiar with a wide range of instructional methods and have strong knowledge of the individual children in their classrooms in order to provide the most appropriate instruction for all learners. Instructional methods of the chosen curriculum must take into account the developmental levels of the students in the primary-age classroom. Instructional methods typically fall into either teacher-directed approaches, such as direct instruction, drill and practice, and large-group activities, or learner-directed approaches such as cooperative learning groups, experiential learning, and computer-assisted instruction.

Activities and Experiences

Good teaching and explicit learning objectives should guide the choice of activities and experiences to be used in the classroom to support the curriculum. A skilled teacher will align curriculum with student's developmental and learning styles. This will support both academic and social skills. It is important that the teacher allow for both planned and unplanned experiences that are developmentally appropriate, significant, and challenging for all the children in the classroom. This includes providing activities and experiences that help children to label and control their emotions and behavior, develop problem-solving skills, develop literacy skills, develop numeracy skills, develop adaptive skills, and develop social skills. This is best done by allowing children to actively explore materials, objects, and events through all of their senses.

Attention to the Environment

Attention to the environment is critical to the social and academic success of students. Classroom environments have a number of characteristics which influence student growth, development, and achievement. Classrooms that are perceived as safe, warm, supportive, and nonthreatening encourage work and promote a sense of enjoyment and accomplishment (Charles, 2002). In addition to affective influences, classroom climate is also related to student achievement (Murphy, Weil, & McGreal, 1986). Fraser and Walberg (1991) suggest that altering the classroom environment to make it more congruent with that favored by students is likely to enhance student outcomes. Classroom environments in the primary grades should encourage exploration and experiential learning and be accessible to students of all abilities.

Adaptations

Adapting the curriculum modifies the delivery of the instructional methods or goals of the student performance. Adaptation does not change the content but may adapt slightly the difficulty of the curriculum. Another way to think about adaptations in the inclusive classroom is differentiating instruction. For example, where most students may have ten spelling words and some students may have five, most students will complete a journal entry and drawing, and some students will complete only the drawing. Adaptations usually require more teacher effort and time than simply changing instructional methods because, before teachers can adapt the curriculum, teachers must identify the individual goals for the specific student. Sometimes adaptations require the use of adapted or different instructional materials and activities for individual students.

Data Collection and Use

Deciding what to measure to evaluate the impact of the curriculum depends upon the goals of the curriculum. For some students in the inclusive classroom, this may depend upon the IEP, which will delineate goals and objectives for individual students. Data collection should be consistent and use techniques that reflect the skills of the teachers. Typically, data collection in the classroom will include observation reports, interviews, document review, and checklists. Teachers can use assessment and data to group students for instruction, to improve their teaching strategies, to evaluate the curriculum, and make changes accordingly.

Critiquing Curricula

Meeting the needs of all children in one classroom can seem like a daunting task and may require the use of more than one curriculum. Critiquing a curriculum requires the teacher to ask several questions to determine if it best meets the needs of the students in the classroom.

1. Is the curriculum developmentally appropriate and appropriate for diverse learners?
2. Does the curriculum have relevance to the lives of the children?
3. Do the materials actively engage the students?
4. Does the curriculum include formal and informal assessment activities?

Summary

Early years truly are learning years, and the importance of the first years of children's lives cannot be overstated. Young children with special needs require extra efforts to ensure that their developmental trajectory mirrors, as closely as possible, their peers without special needs. This is best accomplished by providing a learning environment that incorporates the individual needs of the child and the family, led by highly qualified professionals. Today's professionals who work with young children require many tools to help all children develop and become successful learners. Effective educational strategies that reflect the diversity of families and children served necessitate knowledge of many different systems, approaches, and resources. It is critical that professionals provide best practices that are evidence based to ensure that all children reach their maximum potential.

Thinking It Through

1. Role-play a situation in which you will describe to a parent how his child with a learning disability will be accommodated in your second-grade classroom. Be sure to describe explain the learning/behavioral characteristics as well as how the curriculum will be adapted to meet the child's needs.

2. Find your state's department of education website. Explore their section on students with disabilities. Does your state have a standard IEP form? How is it similar to or different from the one used in the book?

3. Design an activity that will include family in the delivery of services to children in second grade.

4. Discuss the implications for early intervention services when the parent's concerns and priorities are expressed and honored.

5. Dynella's vignette describes special and general educators working collaboratively at the primary-age grade level to provide inclusive services for Dynella and her family. How does this relate to what is described in the Individuals With Disabilities Education Improvement Act of 2004 (IDEA)?

Resources

National Early Childhood Technical Assistance Center (NECTAC)

Campus Box 8040, UNC-CH
Chapel Hill, NC 27599-8040
(919) 962-2001
(919) 843-3269 (TDD)
(919) 966-7463 (fax)
nectac@unc.edu

The National Early Childhood Technical Assistance Center supports the implementation of the early childhood provisions of the Individuals With Disabilities Education Act (IDEA). Their mission is to strengthen service systems to ensure that children with disabilities (birth through 5) and their families receive and benefit from high-quality, culturally appropriate, and family-centered supports and services.

Clearinghouse on Disability Information

Office of Special Education and Rehabilitative Services (OSERS)
Switzer Building, Room 3006
330 C Street SW
Washington, DC 20202-2500
(202) 205-5465
(202) 205-5465 (TTY)
www.ed.gov/offices/OSERS/

The Clearinghouse provides information to people with disabilities, or anyone requesting information, by doing research and providing documents in response to inquiries. Information provided includes areas of federal funding for disability-related programs. Clearinghouse staff is trained to refer requests to other sources of disability-related information, if necessary.

National Information Center for Children and Youth With Disabilities

PO Box 1492
Washington, DC 20013
1-800-695-0285 (Voice/TTY)
(202) 884-8200 (Voice/TTY)
nichcy@aed.org
www.nichcy.org

The National Information Center for Children and Youth With Disabilities serves the nation as a central source of information on

- disabilities in infants, toddlers, children, and youth,
- IDEA, which is the law authorizing special education,
- No Child Left Behind (as it relates to children with disabilities), and
- research-based information on effective educational practices.

Council for Exceptional Children

1110 North Glebe Road, Suite 300
Arlington, VA 22201
(703) 620-3660
(866) 915-5000 (TTY)
(703) 264-9494 (fax)
service@cec.sped.org
www.cec.sped.org

The Council for Exceptional Children (CEC) is the largest international professional organization dedicated to improving educational outcomes for individuals with exceptionalities, students with disabilities, and/or the gifted. CEC advocates for appropriate governmental policies, sets professional standards, provides continual professional development, advocates for newly and historically underserved individuals with exceptionalities, and helps professionals obtain conditions and resources necessary for effective professional practice.

Division of Early Childhood of the Council for Exceptional Children

27 Fort Missoula Road
Suite 2
Missoula, MT 59804
(406) 543-0872
(406) 543-0887 (fax)
dec@dec-sped.org

The Division for Early Childhood (DEC) is one of seventeen divisions of the Council for Exceptional Children (CEC), the largest international professional organization dedicated to improving educational outcomes for individuals with exceptionalities, students with disabilities, and/or the gifted.

DEC is especially for individuals who work with or on behalf of children with special needs, birth through age 8, and their families. Founded in 1973, the Division is dedicated to promoting policies and practices that support families and enhance the optimal development of children. Children with special needs include those who have disabilities, developmental delays, are gifted/talented, or are at risk of future developmental problems.

References

America's Children: Key National Indicators of Well-Being. (2005). Retrieved June 27, 2006, from www.childstats.gov/americaschildren/index.asp

Bronfenbrenner, U. (1979). *The ecology of human development.* Cambridge, MA: Harvard University Press.

Charles, C. M. (2002). *Building classroom discipline* (7th ed.). Boston: Allyn and Bacon.

Colarusso, R., & O'Rourke, C. (Eds.). (1999). *Special Education for all teachers* (2nd ed.). Dubuque, IA: Kendall/Hunt.

Drascow, E., Yell, M. L., & Robinson, T. R. (2001). Developing legally correct and educationally appropriate IEPs. *Remedial and Special Education, 22,* 359–373.

Education for All Handicapped Children Act of 1975. 20 U.S.C. 1401 (P.L. 94-142).

Education of the Handicapped Act Amendments of 1986. 20 U.S.C. 1400 (P.L. 99-457).

Fiedler, C. R., & Simpson, R. L. (1987). Modifying the attitudes of nonhandicapped high school students toward handicapped peers. *Exceptional Children, 53,* 342–349.

Fraser, B., & Walberg, H. (Eds.). (1991). *Educational environments: Evaluation, antecedents, and consequences.* New York: Pergamon Press.

Frost, J. L., Wortham, S., & Reifel, S. (2001). *Play and child development.* Upper Saddle River, NJ: Merrill/Prentice Hall.

Gartin, B. C., & Murdock, N. L. (2005). IDEA 2004: The IEP. *Remedial and Special Education, 26,* 327–331.

Hallahan, D. P., & Kauffman, J. M. (2003) *Exceptional learners: Introduction to special education.* Boston: Allyn and Bacon.

Individuals With Disabilities Education Act. Amendments of 1997. P.L.105-117. 20.U.S.C./1415 (b)-(d) 34 C.R.F.300.506-300.513.

Individuals With Disabilities Education Improvement Act of 2004. P.L. 108-446. H.R. 1350.

Koga, N., & Hall, T. (2004). *Curriculum modification.* Wakefield, MA: National Center on Accessing the General Curriculum. Retrieved October 15, 2006, from www.cast.org/publications/ncac/ncac_curriculummod.html

Lewis, R., & Doorlag, D. (1999). *Teaching special students in general education.* Upper Saddle River, NJ: Prentice-Hall.

Mastropieri, M., & Scruggs, T. (2003). *The Inclusive Classroom: Strategies for Effective Instruction* (2nd ed.). Upper Saddle River, NJ: Merrill/Prentice Hall.

McWilliam, R. A. (2000). It's only natural . . . to have early intervention in the environments where it's needed. Young Exceptional Children Monograph No. 2: *Natural environments and inclusion* (pp. 17–26). Longmont, CO: Sopris West.

Murphy, J., Weil, M., & McGreal, T. (1986). The basic practice model of instruction. *The Elementary School Journal, 87,* 83–95.

National Association for the Education of Young Children. (2006). About NAEYC. Retrieved August 10, 2006, from http://naeyc.org/about/

National Dissemination Center for Children with Disabilities. (2002). *General information about disabilities: Disabilities that qualify infants, toddlers, children, and youth for services under the IDEA.* Retrieved June 1, 2006, from www.nichcy.org

Odom, S. L. (Ed.). (2002). *Widening the circle: Including children with disabilities in preschool programs.* New York: Teacher's College Press.

Sandall, S., Hemmeter, M. L., McLean, M. D., & Smith, B. J. (Eds.). (2005). *DEC recommended practices: A comprehensive guide for practical application in early intervention/early childhood special education.* Longmont, CO: Sopris.

Smith, D. D. (2006). Introduction to special education: Teaching in an age of opportunity (5th ed.). Boston: Allyn and Bacon.

Turnbull, A. P., & Turnbull, H. R. (2001). *Families, professionals, and exceptionality: Collaborating for Empowerment* (4th ed.). Upper Saddle River, NJ: Merrill/Prentice Hall.

Turnbull, A. P., Turnbull, H. R., Erwin, E., & Soodak, L. (2006). *Families, professionals, and exceptionality: Positive outcomes through partnerships and trust.* Upper Saddle River, NJ: Pearson/Merrill/Prentice Hall.

United States Department of Education, Office of Special Education and Rehabilitative Services, Office of Special Education Programs (2006). *26th annual report to Congress on the implementation of the Individuals With Disabilities Education Act, 2004.* Washington, DC: Author.

Vygotsky, L. S. (1978). *Mind and society: The development of higher mental processes.* Cambridge: Harvard University Press.

Constructivism in Early Childhood

Nyaradzo Mvududu and Susan B. Gilbert

Objectives

After reading this chapter, students will be able to

- Understand the basic principles of constructivist theory.
- Differentiate between constructivist theory and practice.
- Clearly identify the components of constructivist practice.
- Understand the implications of constructivist practice, particularly for students with diverse needs.
- Develop some teaching strategies consistent with constructivist principles.
- Appreciate the challenges and benefits of using a constructivist approach to teaching.

Key Terms

Constructivism
Learner-centered instruction
Differentiated instruction
Explicit instruction
Problem-based learning
Anchored instruction

Practical Application Vignette

The children were busy in the block corner, constructing an elaborate city bus. Working as a team, they had created a driver's seat, using a frisbee for the steering wheel. Aside from the driver's seat, there were eight passenger seats, each equipped with a bell from the music center and a basket from the home center became a fare box. Some of the children had even made up fare tickets. When the bus was officially declared done, the play began. Tommy, one of the children in the classroom, had recently begun to enter the children's play, however only as an animal. Tommy had been officially identified as having some special needs with a diagnosis of delays in the communication area.

The children immediately protested. "No, no, no, Tommy! No animals on the bus!" Tommy was crushed and began to cry. The teacher stepped in and asked the children if they could think of any animals that were allowed on the bus. There was a long pause. One child spoke up that he had seen someone on the bus with a guide dog. Someone asked what a guide dog was and the child explained that the bus rider could not see and so he had a dog. A short discussion followed. The teacher wondered aloud, "Would it be okay for Tommy to come on the bus if he were a guide dog?" The children agreed. The teacher then asked Tommy if he would be willing to be a guide dog and he agreed. The bus departed for Bell and Main Street with great enthusiasm.

The way in which knowledge is conceived and acquired, the types of knowledge, skills and activities emphasized, the role of the learner and the teacher, how goals are established—all of these factors are articulated differently in the constructivist perspective (compared to the objectivist perspective, for example).

Constructivism has its roots in a number of fields such as philosophy, psychology, sociology, architecture, and education. **Constructivism** is a learning theory, when applied in the classroom values developmentally appropriate teacher-supported learning that is initiated and directed by the

student. The domain of constructivism can be delineated by two radically different poles (Phillips, 2000). The first end of the pole embodies a thesis about the discipline or bodies on knowledge built up during the course of human history. Human constructs are determined by such things as politics, ideologies, values, the exertion of power and the preservation of status, religious beliefs, and economic self-interest. This view denies that constructs can be objective reflections of the "external world." This broad area is termed social constructivism (Gergen, 1997). Vygotsky's (1978) theories are considered a precursor to social constructivism.

The second pole takes the view that constructivism refers to a set of views about how an individual learns (and about how those who help them learn ought to teach). Learners construct their own sets of meanings and understandings. Knowledge is not a mere copy of the external world, nor is it acquired by passive absorption or by simple transference from one person to another. In other words, knowledge is built not acquired. This area is termed *psychological constructivism.*

In brief, we may say that one foundational premise of constructivism is that children actively construct their knowledge. Rather than simply absorbing ideas spoken at them by teachers, or somehow adopting them through endless, mechanical repetition, constructivism posits that children actually invent their ideas (Heylighen, 1997; Murphy, 1997; Piaget, 1926; von Glasersfeld, 1995; von Glasersfeld & Steffe, 1991; Vygotsky, 1978).

As a philosophy of learning, constructivism can be traced at least to the eighteenth century and the work of the Neapolitan philosopher Giambattista Vico, who held that humans can only clearly understand what they have themselves constructed (Gruender, 1996). Many others worked with these ideas, but the first major contemporaries to develop a clear idea of constructivism as applied to classrooms and childhood development were Jean Piaget and John Dewey.

For Dewey (1916), education depended on action. Knowledge and ideas emerged only from a situation in which learners had to draw them out of meaningful and important experiences in their view. These situations had to occur in a social context, such as a classroom, where students joined in manipulating materials and thus created a community of learners who built their knowledge together.

Piaget's (1973) constructivism is based on his view of the psychological development of children. A biologist by training, Piaget believed that every healthy child was capable of these constructive processes (Beilin, 1992). From his former discipline, he borrowed the concept of homeostasis, the tendency of an organism to maintain internal balance by adjusting its physiological processes, and applied it to psychology, calling the process *equilibration.* Thus, whenever someone is presented with new information, the individual loses cognitive balance. The person is biologically motivated to return to equilibrium, and can accomplish this by either assimilating or accommodating the new material. According to Piaget and Inhelder (1969), an important point to note is that development is not governed by internal maturation or external teaching. It is an active construction process in which people, through their own activities, build increasingly differentiated and comprehensive cognitive structures.

In a short summation of their educational thoughts, Piaget and Inhelder (1969) called for teachers to understand the steps in the development of the child's mind. The fundamental basis of learning, they believed, was discovery. To reach an understanding of basic phenomena, according to Piaget, children have to go through stages in which they accept ideas they may later regard as not truthful. In autonomous activity, children must discover relationships and ideas in classroom situations that involve activities of interest to them. Understanding is built up gradually through active involvement.

Vygotsky is also important to constructivism, although his ideas have not always been clear to the English-reading public both because of political constraints and problems inherent in translations. Vygotsky (1978) believed that children learn scientific concepts out of a "tension" between their everyday notions and adult concepts. He viewed cognitive development primarily as a function of cultural, historical, and social interaction rather than of individual construction. Vygotsky (1978) suggested that people create psychological tools to master their behavior, the most important of these being language. Once the child acquires language, it mediates cognition: "This produces new relations with the environment in addition to the new organization of behavior itself" (p. 25). Thus, Vygotsky assumed that mental processes occur between people (Wertsch & Tulviste, 1992). As a result, Vygotsky (1978) contended that what children can do with the assistance of others might be more indicative of their intellectual development than what they can do on their own. This is the basic premise behind the Zone of Proximal Development, defined by Vygotsky (1978) as "the distance between the actual developmental level as determined by independent problem solving and the level of potential development as determined through problem solving under adult guidance or in collaboration with more capable peers" (p. 86). Therefore, teachers were empowered to be both guides and instructors of their students, adding a stronger social perspective to developmental psychology.

Presented with a preformed concept from the adult world, the child will only memorize what the adult says about the idea. To make it her property the child must use the concept and link it to the idea as first presented to her. In Vygotsky's (1978) view, the relation between everyday notions and scientific concepts, say, is not a linear development. Instead the prior conceptions and the introduced scientific concepts are interwoven. They influence each other as the child works out her own ideas from the generalizations that she had already and that have been introduced to her.

Components of Constructivist Practice

While different perspectives of constructivism each have their particular emphases, Ernest (1995) derives a set of theoretical underpinnings common to most. He states that most perspectives perceive knowledge as a whole, including mathematical knowledge and logic, to be complex; it includes not just the learner's subjective knowledge but also subject matter. According to constructivists, methodological approaches should be much more circumspect and reflexive because there is no one way to truth or near truth. The focus of concern is not just the learner's cognitions but the learner's cognitive abilities, beliefs, and conceptions of knowledge. Furthermore, the focus of concern with the teacher and in teacher education is not just with the teacher's knowledge of subject matter and diagnostic skills, but with the teacher's belief, conceptions, and personal theories about subject matter, teaching, and learning. Such an awareness of the social construction of knowledge suggests a pedagogical emphasis on discussion, collaboration, negotiation, and shared meanings.

Multiple perspectives, authentic activities, real-world environments—these are just some of the themes that are frequently associated with constructivist learning and teaching. No doubt there are many teachers who, without knowledge of the term, without having been informed of the theory, without following a prescriptive design, are providing the students in their care with opportunities for constructivist learning. As von Glasersfeld (1995) comments:

> Constructivism does not claim to have made earth-shaking inventions in the area of education; it merely claims to provide a solid conceptual basis for some of the things that, until now, inspired teachers had to do without theoretical foundation.

Educators often adopt a particular approach or method without necessarily having purposely considered the theory or philosophy that underpins the approach. Intuition, successful experiences, and observations—these factors play an important role in influencing the behavior of teachers and, no doubt, often dictate their practice.

The fact that practice can relate to theory but not be directly or knowingly guided by it is evidence of the complexity of the relationship between the two. It is likely that the more general the theory, the more easily it may translate either directly or indirectly into practice. In this sense, constructivism lends itself well to practice. It has been interpreted, refashioned and reformulated into at least seven different forms (see Table 3.1).

Becoming a constructivist teacher may prove a difficult transformation because most instructors were prepared for teaching in the traditional, objectivist manner. It "requires a paradigm shift" and "requires the willing abandonment of familiar perspectives and practices and the adoption of new ones" (Brooks & Brooks, 1993, p. 25).

- The first objective in a constructivist lesson is to engage student interest on a topic that has a broad concept. This may be accomplished by doing a demonstration, presenting data, or showing a short film.
- Second, ask open-ended questions that probe the students' understanding of or personal experiences relative to the topic.
- Next, present some information or data that does not fit with their existing understanding. Let the students take the bull by the horns. Have students break into small groups to formulate their own hypotheses and experiments that will reconcile their previous understanding with the discrepant information.
- The role of the teacher during the small-group interaction time is to circulate around the classroom to be a resource or to ask probing questions that aid the students in coming to an understanding of the principle being studied.
- After sufficient time for experimentation, the small groups share their ideas and conclusions with the rest of the class, which will try to come to a consensus about what they learned.

Assessment can be done traditionally using a standard paper-and-pencil test, but there are other suggestions for evaluation. Each small group can study/review together for an evaluation, but one person is chosen at random from a group to take the quiz for the entire group. The idea is that peer interaction is paramount when learners are constructing meaning for themselves, hence what one individual in the group has learned should be the same as that learned by another individual (Lord,

Table 3.1 ● Common Components of Constructivist Practice

Common Components of Constructivist Practice

1. Methods should be more reflective
2. Focus on cognitive abilities as well as beliefs and conceptions of knowledge
3. Use discussion, collaboration, negotiation, and shared meanings
4. Multiple perspectives
5. Authentic, "real-world" environments

Components of Constructivist Practice

1994). The teacher could also evaluate each small group as a unit to assess what they have learned. Clearly, a lesson based on constructivism differs greatly from the traditional "teacher as lecturer" class type.

More on Strands of Constructivism

As mentioned earlier, there are various types of constructivism that have been put forward. One might say there are as many strands of constructivism as there are researchers on the topic. We have discussed the strands largely attributed to Piaget and Vygotsky. Let us take a brief look at some other strands of constructivism presented by other theorists.

Trivial Constructivism

The simplest idea in constructivism is what von Glasersfeld calls *trivial constructivism,* also known as personal constructivism. This idea is the root of all the other shades of constructivism discussed in this section. The principle has been credited to Jean Piaget, a pioneer of constructivist thought, and can be summed up by the following statement:

> Knowledge is actively constructed by the learner, not passively received from the environment.

This counters other epistemologies promoting simplistic models of communication as simple transmission of meanings from one person to another. The prior knowledge of the learner is deemed essential to be able to "actively" construct new knowledge.

Learning is work, and effective learning requires concentration. There are some things you have to learn before you learn others. The education system has always been built on a progression of ideas from simple to complex. This is not a new concept, which may explain von Glasersfeld's characterization of the idea as "trivial."

Questions arise, however. What is "the environment"? What is "knowledge"? What is the relation of knowledge to "the environment"? What environments are better for learning? Trivial constructivism alone says nothing about these issues, and these are the shortcomings that the other faces of constructivism attempt to address.

Radical Constructivism

Radical constructivism adds a second principle to trivial constructivism, which can be expressed like this:

> Coming to know is a process of dynamic adaptation toward viable interpretations of experience. The knower does not necessarily construct knowledge of a "real" world.

What is there to stop an individual from developing any "reality" they like? When taken to extremes we would all be living in our own dream worlds, unable to communicate with other people or do anything for ourselves. It is true that to some extent, we do all create our own realities. Radical constructivism does not deny an objective reality, but simply states that we have no way of knowing what that reality might be. Mental constructs, constructed from past experience, help to impose order on one's flow of continuing experience. However, when they fail to work, because of external or internal constraints, thus causing a problem, the constructs change to try and accommodate the new experience.

Within the constraints that limit our construction there is room for an infinite number of viable alternatives. "Truth" in traditional epistemologies is replaced by *viability,* bounded by social and physical constraints. The large diversity of flourishing public opinions in today's society on nearly every conceivable topic is evidence that a range of viable constructs are possible to allow survival and growth in the world.

This idea raises the question of how communication can occur between people with different worldviews. From a radical constructivist perspective, communication need not involve identically shared meanings between participants. It is sufficient for their meanings to be compatible (Hardy and Taylor, 1997). If neither of the parties does anything completely unexpected to the other, then their illusions of identically shared meaning are maintained (von Glasersfeld, 1989).

The emphasis here is still clearly on the individual learner as a constructor. Neither trivial nor radical constructivism look closely at the extent to which the human environment affects learning: It is regarded as part of the total environment. Social, cultural, and critical constructivism tend to focus on these issues in more detail.

Social Constructivism

The social world of a learner includes the people that directly affect that person, including teachers, friends, students, administrators, and participants in all forms of activity. This takes into account the social nature of both the local processes in collaborative learning and in the discussion of wider social collaboration in a given subject.

Many of the authors that identify with social constructivism trace their ideas back to Vygotsky. Cobb (1994) examines whether the "mind" is located in the head or in social action, and argues that both perspectives should be used in concert, as they are equally useful. What is seen from one perspective as reasoning of a collection of individuals mutually adapting to each other's actions can be seen in another as the norms and practices of a classroom community (Cobb, 1998).

This dialectic is examined in more detail in a strong paper by Salomon and Perkins (1998), who suggest ways that these "acquisition" and "participation" metaphors of learning interrelate and interact in synergistic ways. They model the social entity as a learner (for example, a football team, a business or a family), compare it with the learning of an individual in a social setting, and identify three main types of relations:

- Individual learning can be less or more socially mediated learning.
- Individuals can participate in the learning of a collective, sometimes with what is learned distributed throughout the collective more than in the mind of any one individual.
- Individuals and social aspects of learning, in both of these senses, can interact over time to strengthen one another in a "reciprocal spiral relationship."

Teaching strategies using social constructivism as a referent include teaching in contexts that might be personally meaningful to students, negotiating taken-as-shared meanings with students, class discussion, small-group collaboration, and valuing meaningful activity over correct answers

(Wood et al., 1995). In math education Cobb (1994) contrasts the approach of delivering mathematics as "content" against the technique of fostering the emergence of mathematical ideas from the collective practices of the classroom community. Emphasis is growing on the teacher's use of multiple epistemologies, to maintain dialectic tension between teacher guidance and student-initiated exploration as well as between social learning and individual learning. Constructivism-related strategies such as these are starting to be used more often in science and mathematics classrooms but, perhaps not surprisingly, have been common for a longer time in humanities subjects like social studies and communication.

It's interesting to observe the construction process of the wide community of intellectual publishers: liberal quoting of each other's ideas, combining, arguing, extending, and recombining them in order to construct our social and cultural understanding of thought, understanding, and, ultimately, human nature.

Cultural Constructivism

Beyond the immediate social environment of a learning situation are the wider context of cultural influences, including custom, religion, biology, tools, and language. For example, the *format* of books can affect learning by promoting views about the organization, accessibility, and status of the information they contain.

> [What we need] is a new conception of the mind, not as an individual information processor, but as a biological, developing system that exists equally well within an individual brain and in the tools, artefacts, and symbolic systems used to facilitate social and cultural interaction. (Vosniadou, 1996)

The tools that we use affect the way we think. These tools include language and other symbolic systems as well as physical tools. Salomon and Perkins (1998) identify two effects of tools on the learning mind. First, they redistribute the cognitive load of a task between people and the tool while being used. For example, a label can save long explanations, and using a telephone can change the nature of a conversation. Second, the use of a tool can affect the mind beyond actual use by changing skills, perspectives, and ways of representing the world. For example, computers carry an entire philosophy of knowledge construction, symbol manipulation, design, and exploration, which, if used in schools, can subversively promote changes in curricula, assessment, and other changes in teaching and learning.

Critical Constructivism

Critical constructivism looks at constructivism within a social and cultural environment but adds a critical dimension aimed at reforming these environments in order to improve the success of constructivism applied as a referent. Taylor (1996) describes critical constructivism as a social epistemology that addresses the socio-cultural context of knowledge construction and serves as a point of reference for cultural reform. It confirms the relativism of radical constructivism and also identifies the learner as being suspended in semiotic systems similar to those identified in social and cultural constructivism. To these, critical constructivism adds a greater emphasis on the actions for change of a learning teacher. It is a framework using the critical theory of Jurgen Habermas to help make potentially disempowering cultural myths more visible and hence more open to question through conversation and critical self-reflection.

An important part of that framework is the promotion of *communicative ethics,* that is, conditions for establishing dialogue oriented toward achieving mutual understanding (Taylor, 1998). The conditions include a primary concern for maintaining empathetic, caring, and trusting relationships; a commitment to dialogue that aims to achieve reciprocal understanding of goals, interests, and standards; and concern for and critical awareness of the often invisible rules of the classroom, including social and cultural myths. This allows rational examination of the often implicit "claims to rightness" of the participants, especially those derived from social institutions and history (Taylor, 1996). According to Taylor (1996), cultural myths that are prevalent in today's education systems include

> The rationalist myth of **cold reason**—where knowledge is seen as discovery of an external truth. This can lead to the picture of the teacher in a central role as transmitter of objective truths to students. This philosophy does not promote clarifying relevance to the lives of students, but instead promotes a curriculum to be delivered.
>
> The myth of **hard control**—which renders the teacher's classroom role as controller, and "locks teachers and students into grossly asymmetrical power relationships designed to reproduce, rather than challenge, the established culture." (p. 2)

Together these myths produce a culture that portrays classroom teaching and learning as "a journey through a pre-constructed landscape" (Taylor, 1996). Modification of such entrenched environments to reduce these myths and promote approaches based on constructivism can be problematic because of the self-reinforcing nature of administration and the effects of wider culture. To address this challenge, teachers need to work collegially toward reconstructing the culture of education together rather than heroically on their own.

Constructionism

Constructionism asserts that constructivism occurs especially well when the learner is engaged in constructing something for others to see. One of the most important processes in developing one's own knowledge is by explaining and exploring ideas in conversation with fellow students. Gergen (1995) explores the use of the metaphor of dialogue to evaluate a number of educational practices. Particularly, he views knowledge as fragments of dialogue or "knowledgeable tellings" at a given time within an ongoing relationship. This relationship can be between learners, between a learner and a teacher, or between a learner and an environment experienced by the learner. Gergen describes a lecture as a conversation where, because the lecturer has already set the content, the student enters partway through the dialogue and finds he or she has have no voice within it.

Steier (1990) looks into this dialogue process in more detail. Unlike the communicative ethics of Taylor (1998), which also suggest ways to set up a discursive environment, Steier highlights the circularity of reflective thinking in social research and presents a number of ways mirroring occurs between learners (like two mirrors facing each other) where each reciprocator affects the other. Awareness of such issues can help "frame" the dialogue used to communicate more effectively.

Some Theoretical Views on Application

Given the various definitions of constructivism, moving from constructivist philosophy, psychology, and epistemology to the characterization of constructivist learning environments presents the challenge of synthesizing a large spectrum of somewhat distinct concepts. An appropriate analogy for the way in which constructivist concepts have evolved is that of a prism with many facets. While the facets reflect the same light and form one part of a whole, they nonetheless each present distinct and finely defined boundaries.

Situated cognition, *anchored instruction,* apprenticeship learning, *problem-based learning,* generative learning, constructionism, exploratory learning—these approaches to learning are grounded in and derived from constructivist epistemology. Each approach clearly communicates how the theory should be applied in practice to facilitate learning.

Evidently, within constructivism itself, authors, researchers, and theorists articulate differently the constructivist perspective by emphasizing different components. Nonetheless, there is some agreement on a large number of issues, for example, on the role of the teacher and learner. A number of researchers and theorists have suggested ways to link constructivist theory and practice. They provide the beginnings of an orienting framework for a constructivist approach to design, teaching, or learning.

Jonassen (1991a) noted that many educators and cognitive psychologists have applied constructivism to the development of learning environments. From these applications, he has isolated a number of design principles:

- Teachers should strive to create real-world environments that employ the context in which learning is relevant.
- The focus should be on realistic approaches to solving real-world problems. In such a setting the teacher is a coach and analyzer of the strategies used by the students to solve these problems.
- The role of the teacher is to stress conceptual interrelatedness, providing multiple representations or perspectives on the content. Additionally, the teacher is to provide tools and environments that help learners interpret the multiple perspectives of the world.
- When the instructional goals and objectives are negotiated and not imposed, there is greater likelihood that the students will be engaged in the learning process.
- The learning should be internally controlled and mediated by the learner so that evaluation serves as a self-analysis tool.

Jonassen (1994) summarizes what he refers to as "the implications of constructivism for instructional design." He put forward additional principles that illustrate how knowledge construction can be facilitated. The focus is on knowledge construction, not reproduction. This is easier to do when students are presented with authentic tasks so that instruction is contextualized. Teachers should enable both context- and content-dependent knowledge construction. Teachers can support collaborative construction of knowledge through social negotiation and fostering reflective practice.

Wilson and Cole (1991) provide a description of cognitive teaching models that "embody" constructivist concepts. From these descriptions, we can isolate more concepts central to constructivist design, teaching, and learning. Like other researchers, they suggest embedding learning in a rich authentic problem-solving environment and providing for authentic versus academic contexts for learning. They assert that errors that students make should be used as a mechanism to provide feedback on learners' understanding.

Paul Ernest (1995) in his description of the many schools of thought of constructivism suggests the following implications of constructivism, which derive from both the radical and social perspectives. Teachers should exhibit sensitivity toward and attentiveness to the learner's previous constructions. They should use diagnostic teaching in an attempt to remedy learner errors and misconceptions. This requires attention to metacognition and strategic self-regulation by learners.

Honebein (1996) describes seven goals for the design of constructivist learning environments:

1. Provide experience with the knowledge construction process;
2. Provide experience in and appreciation for multiple perspectives;
3. Embed learning in realistic and relevant contexts;
4. Encourage ownership and voice in the learning process;
5. Embed learning in social experience;
6. Encourage the use of multiple modes of representation;
7. Encourage self-awareness in the knowledge construction process. (p. 11)

From these theorists some common characteristics of constructivism emerge: Social interaction is the basis for all learning, some form of dissonance is necessary, and prior knowledge/personal experience plays a key role.

Definition of Constructivism for Current Discussion

On an epistemological continuum, objectivism and constructivism would represent opposite extremes. As previously discussed, various types of constructivism have emerged. We can distinguish between radical, social, physical, evolutionary, postmodern constructivism, social constructionism, information-processing constructivism, and cybernetic systems to name but some types more commonly referred to (Heylighen, 1993; Steffe & Gale, 1995).

Psychologist Ernst von Glasersfeld, whose thinking has been profoundly influenced by the theories of Piaget, is typically associated with radical constructivism—radical "because it breaks with convention and develops a theory of knowledge in which knowledge does not reflect an objective, ontological reality but exclusively an ordering and organization of a world constituted by our experience" (von Glasersfeld, 1984, p. 24). Von Glasersfeld defines radical constructivism according to the conceptions of knowledge. He sees knowledge as being actively received either through the senses or by way of communication. It is actively constructed by the cognizing subject. Cognition is adaptive and allows one to organize the experiential world, not to discover an objective reality (von Glasersfeld, 1989).

In contrast to von Glaserfled's position of radical constructivism, for many, social constructivism has emerged as a more palatable form of the philosophy. Heylighen (1993) explains that social constructivism "sees consensus between different subjects as the ultimate criterion to judge knowledge. 'Truth' or 'reality' will be accorded only to those constructions on which most people of a social group agree" (p. 2). So, while the differences between objectivism and constructivism can be clearly delineated, such is not the case for the differences between the varying perspectives on constructivism. Derry (1992) points out that constructivism has been claimed by "various epistemological camps" that do not consider each another "theoretical comrades." There is considerable debate amongst philosophers, researchers, and psychologists about which brand of constructivism is valid.

The current chapter uses the psychosocial framework of constructivism. Phillips (1995) called this *psychological constructivism,* based upon the framework of Piaget and of Vygotsky. Although individuals have to construct their own meaning of a new idea, the process of constructing meaning always is embedded in a particular social setting of which the individual is part.

Constructivism, as a theory, proposes that knowledge construction is unavoidable if students attend to the learning task. Any and all relevant student experiences result in the construction of knowledge. The issue, then, is whether educators should let students construct on their own in spite of their classroom experiences, or whether they should do whatever is in their power to encourage and facilitate constructivism through experiences specifically designed to promote the making of knowledge (Zahotik, 1995). However, according to Gruender (1996), knowing that to learn anything requires the creation of internal constructs does not tell us what the best methods for the creation of such constructs might be. Nevertheless, this knowledge has important implications for teaching (Clements, 1997). Instructors with a constructivist orientation attempt to find effective techniques for helping students harness their own vitality, energy, curiosity, excitement, and wonder in the difficult and sometimes painful tasks of learning what they will need to know.

What Constructivism Is and What It Is Not

Some feel that constructivism excludes any type of *explicit instruction.* For those that believe *explicit instruction* is necessary, particularly for students with special needs, an important aspect of learning is neglected. For those that believe that the teacher should only "guide" instruction, eschewing *explicit instruction* can have devastating results for at-risk students.

Two important notions orbit around the simple idea of constructed knowledge (Hoover, 1996). The first is that learners construct new understandings using what they already know. There is no *tabula rasa,* or blank slate, on which new knowledge is imprinted. Rather, learners come to learning situations with knowledge gained from previous experience, and that prior knowledge impacts what new or modified knowledge they will construct from new learning experiences.

The second notion is that learning is active rather than passive (Hoover, 1996). Learners contend with their understanding in light of what they encounter in the new learning situation. If what learners encounter is inconsistent with their current understanding, their understanding can change to accommodate new experience. Learners remain active throughout this process: They apply current understandings, note relevant elements in new learning experiences, judge the consistency of prior and emerging knowledge, and, based on that judgment, they can modify knowledge.

Constructivism, therefore, has important implications for teaching (Hoover, 1996). First, teaching cannot be viewed as the transmission of knowledge from the informed to uninformed; constructivist teachers do not take the role of the "sage on the stage." Rather, teachers act as "guides on the side," who provide students with opportunities to test the correctness of their current understandings.

Second, if learning is based on prior knowledge, then teachers must note that knowledge and provide learning environments that exploit inconsistencies between learners' current understandings and the new experiences before them (Clements, 1997; Hoover, 1996). This is a challenge for teachers, because they cannot assume that all children understand something in the same way. Further, children may need different experiences to advance to different levels of understanding.

Third, if students must apply their current understandings in new situations in order to build new knowledge, then teachers must engage students in learning, bringing students' current understandings to the forefront (Hoover, 1996). Teachers can ensure that learning experiences incorporate problems that are important to students, not those that are primarily important to teachers and the educational system. Teachers can also encourage group interaction, where the interplay among participants helps individual students become explicit about their own understanding by comparing it to that of their peers.

Fourth, if new knowledge is actively built, then time is needed to build it. Ample time facilitates student reflection about new experiences, how those experiences line up against current understandings, and how a different understanding might provide students with an improved (not "correct") view of the world.

Misconceptions

Confusion about what constructivism does and does not mean has engendered a number of myths and misconceptions. One of these is cooperative learning. Cooperative and collaborative teaching methods provide the opportunity for more competent students to scaffold tasks as they interact with less competent students. Scaffolding occurs when others assist learners in constructing knowledge (Wood, Bruner, & Ross, 1976). This is a natural setting for Vygotsky's (1978) theory of proximal development, which poses that learners gain knowledge through interaction with more knowledgeable others. From a Vygotskian (1978) viewpoint, the aim of education is to increase the control and responsibility of learners. The challenge for educators is to find a way to communicate that enables students to view the content as meaningful and useful knowledge that promotes their development and helps them tackle complex issues in modern society. It is important to note that just using cooperative groups does not necessarily make teaching more "constructivist." Students can work in groups in different ways, many of which are consistent with the constructivist views of learning. Some approaches to cooperative learning, however, are based on an absorption view.

Another misconception about constructivist teaching that needs to be dispelled pertains to "active learning." Teaching with manipulatives is not necessarily "teaching constructively." Having students work with manipulatives and on projects is consistent with constructivism but not unique to it. Constructivism does not mean that students should always be actively and reflectively constructing. There are times for many different types of constructing: time for "experiencing," for "intuitive" learning, for learning by listening, for practice, and for conscious reflective thinking. During all these activities, students construct valuable, but different, kinds of knowledge. Instructors need to balance these times to meet the goals for the students (Clements, 1997).

The key is to understand and to build on students' thinking. No matter how ineffective or inefficient students' ideas and methods might seem, they must be the starting points for instruction (Steffe & Cobb, 1988). "Constructing their own knowledge" does not mean that students construct their ideas in isolation. Every student may have valid reasons for his or her own solution, but the goal should be building solutions that make sense within the system of the content area that is socially constructed by the class and the wider community. Thus, everybody's effort can be reflected without abandoning the notion that some solutions are better than others and that some just don't make sense (Clements, 1997). A constructivist-oriented teacher must be skilled in structuring the social climate of the classroom such that students discuss, reflect on, and make sense of learning tasks in a safe and respectful environment.

For Whom Is Constructivism?

First, recognize that construction in learning is not just the domain of children but of learners, all learners. All people benefit from approaches to learning that draw upon what they already know or an area of interest or personal relevance. Constructivist professional development gives teachers time to make explicit their understandings of learning (e.g., Is it a constructive process?), of teaching (e.g., Is a teacher an orator or a facilitator, and what is the teacher's understanding of content?), and of professional development (e.g., Is a teacher's own learning best approached through a constructivist orientation?). Furthermore, such professional development provides opportunities for teachers to test their understandings and build new ones (Hoover, 1996). Training that affects student-centered teaching cannot come in one-day workshops. Systematic, long-term development that allows practice—and reflection on that practice—is required.

It is also useful to remember the educator's maxim: Teachers teach as they are taught, not as they are told to teach. Thus, trainers in constructivist professional development sessions model learning activities that teachers can apply in their own classrooms. It is not enough for trainers to describe new ways of teaching and expect teachers to translate from talk to action; it is more effective to engage teachers in activities that will lead to new actions in classrooms.

If our efforts in reforming education for all students are to succeed, then we must focus on students. To date, a focus on student-centered learning may well be the most important contribution of constructivism. As Phillips (2000) noted, "it seems possible for a person who accepts constructivism as a philosophy to adopt a variety of educational practices or for a teacher who uses constructivist classroom practices to justify doing so in a variety of ways, some of which might not philosophically be constructivist at all" (p. 18). This may mean that the best of constructivist pedagogy can be had without constructivist epistemology.

Constructivism and Other Pedagogies

This section will provide more details on the key terms that are used in the application of constructivist approaches to teaching.

Developmentally Appropriate Practice (DAP)

The National Association of Education for Young Children (NAEYC) took the lead in attempting to define developmentally appropriate practice (DAP) in the late 1980s with the understanding that the definition would evolve with new knowledge of child development and learning (Copple & Bredekamp, 2006). The most current definition from NAEYC defines DAP as "meeting children where they are . . . to help them reach challenging and achievable goals that contribute to his or her ongoing development and learning" (p. 3).

Many definitions of DAP are simplistic, indicating "instruction that is in alignment with the student's developmental level" (Schunk, 2004, p. 481). The danger in such definitions is the justification of a maturational view of learning that limits the type and timing of instruction that young children receive in school. For review, a maturational view of learning purports that it is futile to "teach" a child something until she or he is "ready." This view led researchers in search of the right time. The most well-known work from this endeavor is the "reading readiness" belief that children are ready to read at 6 years, 6 months, and exposure to books prior to this age would interfere with learning. We now know that this is simply not true, but the tendency to believe that a child uninterested in letters and sounds is simply "not ready" endures, often with disastrous results.

Developmentally appropriate practice is much more complex and far more difficult to deliver than implied by definition. DAP includes, but is not limited to, knowledge of child development. In 1996, Curtis and Carter referred to DAP as a process that considered the child's cultural context as part of their development. In 1997, the National Association of Education for Young Children's (NAEYC) revised position statement on DAP included knowledge of child development and learning (Copple & Bredekamp, 2006). In 2004, the North Central Regional Educational Laboratory noted that DAP included teaching strategies based upon how people learn. In the past twenty years, we have learned a lot about how people learn.

What have we learned? The literature available is exhaustive and beyond the scope of this text; however, the National Research Council (NRC) attempted to synthesize this research in 1999. Portions of these findings are discussed in greater detail in the following section. In general, there is evidence to suggest that we tend to learn best when information is meaningful and connected to our personal experiences. When new information bumps up against existing information, we play with that information and make decisions as to how the new information fits with existing information. Do we change what we know, or do we make the new information fit with what know? How we manipulate this information is influenced by development and the learning supports in the environment.

The relationship between development and learning is complex and reciprocal. While development overall may proceed sequentially, the amount of time an individual spends in a particular phase of development varies considerably. The interplay among the physical environment, biological processes, and early experiences informs each and may promote or delay development and learning (Bredekamp & Copple, 1997). Complicating the matter is the finding that no single approach to teaching is effective for all children.

For example, Snow (1998) reported that children's experiences with oral language influenced early literacy development. This was an unexpected and surprising result. Specifically, it was children's experience with oral, decontextualized language, or the kind of language used to communicate with others unfamiliar with the circumstances. A very simple example is the very young child that might use a shortened, cryptic, or familiar and funny variation of a word at home, but in order to be understood outside the home needs to use more formal language. Thus environment plays a potent role in the early experiences of the child. Some children come to school with a great deal of this experience, typically coming from families that "teach" their children to talk (e.g., B, ba ba ba, ball) and encourage explanation and "big" words. In essence, this approach gives children a frame for talking about language as something abstract, a distinct advantage when beginning the reading process. Children that come to school without these kinds of experience face a daunting task, especially when the typical school curriculum often fails to recognize the power of these experiences and is not geared to provide opportunity for this kind of "talk."

While all students benefit from what has become commonly referred to as "productive" talk or talk "on task" in school, the need for some students to spend more time consciously developing their language skills is not universal. As more and more is known about the way people learn, the need for differentiated instruction has become more critical.

Differentiated Instruction

Differentiated instruction is a belief that emphasizes the need for instruction to be modified to meet the needs of individual learners as opposed to expecting the learner to adapt to the instruction (Hall, 2002). This belief stems from Piaget's perspective that human development is not a continuous process but rather a process of discontinuity (Schunk, 2004). Learners move through various stages of development at their own pace. The implications for learning and instruction are paramount.

In fact, much has been learned about how people learn in the last decade. In 1999, the National Research Council (NRC) synthesized this research and implications for instruction. A key finding of the NRC (1999) was that

> Students come to the classroom with preconceptions about how the world works. If their initial understanding is not engaged, they may fail to grasp the new concepts and information that are taught, or they may learn them for purposes of a test but revert to their preconceptions outside the classroom. (http://books.nap.edu/html/howpeople2/ch2.html)

This strong relationship between the students' environment and their understanding of how the world works is support for the constructivist view that social mediation plays a central role in learning (Schunk, 2004). It calls for learning material in deeper and more meaningful ways. This approach emphasizes the need for higher level thinking skills. Given the unique nature of students' experiences prior to the start of school, it stands to reason that a "one size fits all" approach to instruction will fail to engage all students.

Differentiating instruction is both a challenge and a necessity in the inclusive classroom. The call to teach deeply conflicts with the traditional approach to instruction, particularly for students with special needs. Jewett (1998) noted that, when faced with challenging situations, it is important to take the time to both reflect and reframe. This process is painful, fraught with regret, and tough work but is also full of promise and reward (Jewett, 1998).

A constructivist approach to teaching requires teachers to rethink their beliefs about their students, their expectations, and approaches to instruction. A hallmark of both constructivist practice and differentiated instruction is that it is student centered, not teacher centered. Teachers, especially teachers in inclusive classrooms, are reluctant to give up their traditional roles for fear of short changing their students. In fact, the opposite may be true.

Diane Miller Parker (1998) poignantly shares her experience working with students that have mild mental disabilities:

> One weekend when my husband and I took students on a trip to a big city, I saw them in a different way. . . . One evening, for example, one of the boys wanted to shower and stayed in the bathroom for quite some time. When we knocked and asked if he was OK, he replied that he didn't know how to turn on the shower. The same night a girl put her dress on a hanger, stood in front of the closet, but didn't know where to hang it.
>
> I became painfully aware that my students did not have many of the skills they needed to be independent; instead, they were very dependent on me. In my pursuit of teaching them the right way to do

things, I had not allowed them to experience, test and err, and problem solve. I had taught them to be compliant and fit into a general education classroom but had been sabotaging their ability to function outside the safety of my classroom. Why did it take me so long to think about all of this?

. . . No longer would I think about [school] as a *place*—a place where students didn't have to solve problems, where I didn't set high expectations. (pp. 111–112)

Parker (1998) went on to become instrumental in working toward inclusive placements for young children in Indiana.

Content Area Methods

In part, because differentiated instruction and constructivist theory focus on higher level thinking skills, there is a tendency to generalize or use common approaches to problem solving across the curriculum. Research has shown that while some aspects of the learning process do apply across content areas (e.g., reading, writing, math, science, and social studies), each of these content areas also features unique processes (Schunk, 2004). These processes are commonly referred to as domain-specific and add another level of complexity to the task of differentiating instruction.

The teaching of reading provides some clear examples of the dilemma faced by educators. A traditional approach to reading would focus on what is commonly referred to as bottom-up processing, or "pattern recognition of visual stimuli that proceeds from analysis of features to building a meaningful representation" (Schunk, 2004, p. 479). An example of this would be students learning to read by first learning to decode using phonetics in conjunction with a set of word recognition strategies. This approach does not utilize the students' personal experiences or prior knowledge as an instructional technique.

On the other hand, top-down processing, or "pattern recognition of stimuli that occurs by forming a meaningful representation of the context, developing expectations of what will occur, and comparing features of stimuli to expectations to confirm or disconfirm one's expectation" (Schunk, 2004, p. 488), does take students' prior knowledge into account, almost exclusively. Good readers tend to be top-down processors (Schunk, 2004).

Each of these approaches provides *all* students, regardless of ability, with important reading skills (National Reading Panel, 2000). However, there is a tendency to think that high-risk or marginalized students benefit more from a strictly bottom-up approach to reading. The high number of children commonly referred to as "word callers" tend to be students that have the technical skills to read but do not understand what they are reading. If the goal of literacy is to read for understanding and write for communication (Hiebert & Rapheal, 1998), these children are clearly at risk.

Good readers tend to be top-down processors, and, while all readers benefit from utilizing this approach, there are pitfalls. Simply activating prior knowledge and drawing on personal experience does not guarantee that children will make the connection. Edwards and Davis (1997) conducted a study that highlights the potential pitfalls of a top-down approach. In their study, they found that teachers, in their desire to honor their students by taking a nonauthoritarian, child-centered approach to instruction, eschewed any form of direct or explicit instruction and opted, instead, to use open-ended questions geared toward personal experience. When many students failed to make the connection between their own experiences and the text, the teachers assumed the students were the problem. As part of the study, student responses to question-and-answer routines were analyzed. The results revealed that, while 56 percent of the teachers heard or predicted their students' answers to be incorrect, less than 1 percent of the students actually gave an unrelated response (Edwards & Davis, 1997).

Explicit Instruction

Explicit instruction is defined as an approach to practice that is rooted in the merger of effective schools research and behavior analysis, described as essential to ensure student success in school (Hall, 2002). Features of this approach to instruction include big ideas or concepts, conspicuous strategies or content methods, mediated scaffolding, strategic integration or conditional knowledge, judicious review or opportunities for reflection, and primed background knowledge (Hall, 2002). Key are high levels of teacher–student interaction.

At the beginning of the Edwards and Davis (1997) study, the student literacy scores were among the lowest in the system. As a result of the study, the teachers rethought their reluctance to explicit instruction and opted to use more mediated scaffolding and modify their questions to more clearly identify what they were looking for, while at the same time listening more carefully to their students' responses, discovering a depth they had not previously heard (Edwards & Davis, 1997). In a postscript to the study, 90 percent of the students in this school were at or above grade level in literacy (Edwards & Davis, 1997).

Educator understanding of theory and practice is a powerful tool. In the above case, the consequences that grew out of a misunderstanding of theory and practice were devastating. Earlier, we talked about some of the misconceptions of constructivist teaching, noting that the challenge to educators is to find a way to communicate or deliver information that enables students to view the content as meaningful and useful knowledge. Constructivist teaching does not preclude the need for direct, explicit instruction. In fact, there are times when it demands it, particularly in the inclusive classroom.

Delpit (1996) noted there are significant political and racial overtones to the debate between skills instruction and the more progressive, child-centered approach to teaching. A strict adherence

to "isolated, meaningless, drilled sub-skills" (p. 18) maintains oppression, particularly of black and minority children whom tend to be both overrepresented in special education classrooms and on the receiving end of this type of instruction. By advocating for "skills instruction within the context of critical and creative thinking" (Delpit, 1996, p. 19), a case is made both for explicit instruction and for the judicious application of constructivist teaching in the classroom.

Problem-Based Learning

Stepien and Gallagher (1993) define problem-based learning and the type of instruction that begins with a real-world problem. That is, the problem is one that would be faced by someone working in the relevant field. Students learn through their engagement with the problem and the teacher provides guidance and resources. While the problems do not test the skills, students develop both problem-solving skills and the content knowledge base by actively seeking answers to the problem.

By shifting the focus from the teaching to learning, **problem-based learning** (PBL) is an approach that is student centered. Students develop expertise through engagement in progressive problem solving, and the teacher serves as a facilitator and a coach in that process. He or she provides guidelines for the students to follow, but there is no one formula that students are required to use. Characteristics of PBL include the fact that

- Learning takes place within the contexts of authentic tasks, issues, and problems that are aligned with real-world concerns.
- In a PBL course, students and the instructor become colearners, coplanners, coproducers, and coevaluators as they design, implement, and continually refine their curricula.
- The PBL approach is grounded in solid academic research on learning and on the best practices that promote it. This approach stimulates students to take responsibility for their own learning, since there are few lectures, no structured sequence of assigned readings, and so on.
- PBL is unique in that it fosters collaboration among students, stresses the development of problem-solving skills within the context of professional practice, promotes effective reasoning and self-directed learning, and is aimed at increasing motivation for lifelong learning.

Anchored Instruction

Anchored instruction is considered part of the social constructivist paradigm. It is a combination of "goal-based scenario" model and problem-based learning, and is closely related to the Situated Learning and Cognitive Flexibility Theory (Kearsley, 1994–2004).

As the name suggests, anchored instruction involves anchoring instruction in a problem-based situation. Anchored instruction is based on two principles:

- "Learning and teaching activities should be designed around an "anchor" which should be some sort of case-study or problem situation.
- Curriculum materials should allow exploration by the learner (e.g., interactive videodisc programs)." (Kearsley, 1994–2004)

The teacher facilitates and coaches the students through the process of investigating the problem, identifying gaps to their knowledge, researching the information needed to solve the problem, and developing solutions. The premise is that, when the problem is a realistic task or event, anchored or focused, students take ownership. It is relevant to them, and they develop knowledge structures that are highly transferable to other situations. The complex content is solved through

---

The list of characteristics is adapted from Stepien, W. J., and Gallagher, S. A. (1993). Problem-based learning: As authentic as it gets. *Educational Leadership, 50(7)* 25–8; and Barrows, H. (1985). *How to design a problem-based curriculum for the preclinical years.* New York: Springer.

interconnectedness of subproblems, multiple scenarios presented, and problems presented in a narrative format, a story with embedded data. The learning context is generative in that students identify with problem and become actively involved in generating solution.

An example of this approach is a teacher preparing a story-based lesson on why saving energy can reduce air pollution. Another example can be a lesson on volcanoes, in which students take on the roles of various scientists investigating a given problem related to a volcano. The teacher can use stories are from various realistic settings that focus on exploration, problem solving, and critical-thinking skills. Within a typical problem-solving story line, there is a complex problem that has about a dozen steps learners will take to solve it. The teacher can use his or her discretion with regards to the complexity of the activity based on the developmental level of the students. The activity could be as simple as gathering information about the volcano and the region, just as "real" scientists would do. For more challenge an investigation of the impact of the volcano on the community can be included, as well as the development of a strategy for addressing evacuation problems. The Internet can be use as a resource in this lesson.

Classroom Examples

What does constructivist practice look like in the classroom? The following table describes teachers' beliefs with regard to the constructivist approach in contrast to the traditional approach based on the results of a national survey of teachers' underlying philosophies of teaching (www.crito.uci.edu/tlc/FINDINGS/special3/page8.htm) (see Table 3.2).

Vivian Gussin Paley (1981) provided some wonderful vignettes that illustrate the delicate balance between *explicit instruction* and constructivist teaching in her book, *Wally's Stories: Conversations in the Kindergarten.* "Rulers" allows us to see inside the logical thinking of young children, to see their preconceived notions and understandings of the world and the importance of both exploring their thinking and at the same time presenting children with a new big idea or concept.

Rulers

Wally and Eddie disagreed about the relative size of our two rugs.

Wally: The big rug is the giant's castle. The small one is Jack's house.
Eddie: Both rugs are the same.
Wally: They can't be the same. Watch me. I'll walk around the rug. Now watch—walk, walk, walk, walk, walk, walk, walk, walk, walk—count all these walks. Okay. Now count the other rug. Walk, walk, walk, walk. See? That one has more walks.
Eddie: No fair, you cheated. You walked faster.

(After much discussion, Wally and Eddie decide that, instead of a ruler, deemed "too short," they will use people's bodies. Wally announces tryouts for "rug measurers." All is well until the following day when Warren, one of the rug measurers, is not in school. A protracted discussion relative to size and age begins. The teacher enters the conversation.)

Teacher: Is there a way to measure the rug so we don't have to worry about people's sizes?
Kenny: Use short people.
Teacher: And if the short people aren't in school?

> *Rose:* Use big people.
> *Eddie:* Some people are too big.
> *Teacher:* Maybe using people is the problem.
> *Fred:* Use 3-year-olds.
> *Teacher:* There aren't any 3-year-olds in our class.
> *Deana:* Use rulers. Get all the rules in the room. I'll get the box of rulers.

(The students attempt to cover the rug with ALL the rulers. There aren't enough rulers to cover the rug.)

> *Teacher:* . . . Here's something we can do. We can use one of the rulers over again, this way.
> *Eddie:* Now you made another empty space.
> *Teacher:* Eddie, you mentioned a tape measure before. I have one here.

(We stretch the tape along the edge of the rug, and I show the children that the rug is 156 inches long. The lesson is done. The next day, Warren is back in school.)

> *Wally:* Here's Warren. Now we can really measure the rug.
> *Teacher:* Didn't we really measure the rug with the ruler?
> *Wally:* Well, rulers aren't really real, are they? (Paley, 1981, pp. 13–16)

Table 3.2 ● Paired Comparisons Measuring Contrasting Teacher Beliefs

Constructivist Perspective		Traditional Transmission Perspective
"I mainly see my role as a facilitator. I try to provide opportunities and resources for my students to discover or construct concepts for themselves."	Vs.	"That's all nice, but students really won't learn the subject unless you go over the material in a structured way. It's my job to explain, to show students how to do the work, and to assign specific practice."
"It is a good idea to have all sorts of activities going on in the classroom. Some students might produce a scene from a play they read. Others might create a miniature version of the set. It's hard to get the logistics right, but the successes are so much more important than the failures."	Vs.	"It's more practical to give the whole class the same assignment, one that has clear directions, and one that can be done in short intervals that match students' attention spans and the daily class schedule."
"The most important part of instruction is that it encourage 'sense-making,' or thinking, among students. Content is secondary."	Vs.	"The most important part of instruction is the content of the curriculum. That content is the community's judgment about what children need to be able to know and do."
"It is critical for students to become interested in doing academic work—interest and effort are more important than the particular subject matter they are working on."	Vs.	"While student motivation is certainly useful, it should not drive what students study. It is more important that students learn the history, science, math, and language skills in their textbooks."

Classroom Examples

Did the teacher fail her students because they did not grasp the big idea or concept of a standard measure? Were the teacher's efforts in vain? No. In fact, the teacher's efforts are in keeping with what we know from the research about how people learn. By actively listening to the children's conversations, the teacher learned a great deal about her students. She chose to introduce the big idea at a time that was meaningful: How would they be able to measure the rug without Warren? Despite her best efforts, the children are not ready to let go of their preconceived ideas; however, we know that within a relatively short period time, with continued opportunities to test their beliefs, they will conclude that a ruler or standard measure is preferable to people. Not only that, but when they do, they will do so with a much deeper understanding of a standard measure.

The vignette also illustrates the importance of understanding student personal beliefs and thinking as a means of assessment that is not possible with drill and practice type activities. Children's ability to reiterate facts and figures is no guarantee that they have acquired knowledge. That is not to say that facts and figures are not important aspects of learning. Facts and figures or declarative knowledge along with the "how to," or procedural, knowledge are important factors in the ability to know how and when to use knowledge or employ conditional knowledge. However, it is conditional knowledge that is somewhat synonymous with higher level thinking skills and directly related to student success.

While recognizing that time constraints and class size limit the practicality of approaching all subject matter from a constructivist approach, ALL students benefit from judicious opportunities to participate in these types of activities.

Summary

Clearly the concept of constructivism is not a simple one. Constructivism has been termed post-epistemological, meaning that it is not another epistemology, or a way of knowing. For instance, it cannot replace objectivism. Rather, constructivism is a way of thinking about knowing, a referent for building models of teaching, learning, and curriculum (Tobin & Tippins, 1993). In this sense it is a philosophy.

Constructivism also can be used to indicate a theory of communication. When you send a message through something you say or information you provide, and you have no knowledge of the recipient of that message, then you have no idea as to what message was received, and you can not unequivocally interpret the response.

Viewed in this way, teaching becomes the establishment and maintenance of a language and a means of communication between the teacher and students, as well as among students. Simply presenting material, giving out problems, and accepting answers back is not a refined enough process of communication for efficient learning.

Some of the tenets of constructivism in pedagogical terms include the following:

- Students come to class with an established worldview, formed by years of prior experience and learning.
- Even as it evolves, a student's worldview filters all experiences and affects their interpretation of observations.
- For students to change their worldview requires work.

- Students learn from each other as well as the teacher.
- Students learn better by doing.
- Allowing and creating opportunities for all to have a voice promotes the construction of new ideas.

A constructivist perspective views learners as actively engaged in making meaning, and teaching with that approach looks for what students can analyze, investigate, collaborate, share, build, and generate based on what they already know, rather than what facts, skills, and processes they can parrot. To do this effectively, teachers need to be learners and a researchers—to strive for greater awareness of the environments and the participants in a given teaching situation in order to continually adjust their actions to engage students in learning, using constructivism as a referent.

Fosnot (1996) has put forward four assumptions that are the basis of what we refer to as "constructivist learning":

1. Knowledge is physically constructed by learners who are involved in active learning.
2. Knowledge is symbolically constructed by learners who are making their own representations of action.
3. Knowledge is socially constructed by learners who convey their meaning making to others.
4. Knowledge is theoretically constructed by learners who try to explain things they don't completely understand.

Von Glasersfeld's musings remind us that theory and practice exhibit a curious interplay that is oftentimes unpredictable and, sometimes, unexplainable. His comments remind us as well that constructivism is more than a theory of learning. It is a way of looking at the world that is broad enough to allow for multiple interpretations and yet is defined sufficiently to allow for a perspective that can explain complex and abstract phenomenon and that can guide our actions. We tend to take for granted and accept unquestioningly the use of terms such as "true," "real," and "worlds." Consideration of the complexities behind these everyday words seems far removed from the daily practice of the classroom and more like the fodder of philosophers such as Socrates.

Constructivism reminds us that these are not only important philosophical notions. On the contrary, they can significantly affect how we see the world and, more important, how we behave in it. Perhaps an important challenge for educational reform is to begin to question and come to a greater understanding of the philosophy, theory, and epistemology that presently informs educational practice.

Regardless of what type of constructive teaching method an instructor may choose, there are potential challenges to implementation inherent in the classroom setting that must be addressed if implementation is to occur successfully (Zahotik, 1995). The first is the student's expectations. In constructivist teaching, the role of the students is to willingly engage in activities, share thoughts in dialogue and journals, and in other ways to pursue topics in depth. While hands-on activities exist in most classrooms, students are more accustomed to teacher control and direction and an emphasis on correct answers. An abrupt change from this type of teaching to a constructivist approach may not be realistic. The teacher can incrementally substitute constructivist practices for traditional practices, then students can learn to assume the role.

Summary

The second challenge concerns content coverage. In constructivist teaching, as in more conventional teaching, the content and processes that experts in the various disciplines have constructed over time are of central importance. However, in a constructivist classroom it is the students' careful interpretation and deep understanding of the content and processes—in contrast to the ability to reproduce them—that is of concern. Constructing knowledge by fitting new content into existing structures or by adjusting existing structures usually cannot be done quickly nor can it be easily contained in arbitrary boundaries. Yet the content from curriculum guides and textbooks that teachers are expected to use consists of facts, concepts, and skills in separate subject areas. However, the expectations of content coverage in each of the subject areas need not preclude the use of constructivist teaching. The constructivist teacher needs to search the content for the most powerful and generative ideas as Bruner (1960) advised, and to make them the main objects of attention. The ideas will embody a large amount of facts, which will result in a degree of content coverage. Because of their breadth, they will also flow into other content areas.

The third concern is testing and evaluation. Although portfolios are gaining a foothold in many classrooms, the most prevalent achievement tests are standardized tests. Generally, these tests are criticized for requiring students to reproduce facts and abilities they have acquired. If one engages in constructivist teaching and learning, and if one can emphasize thinking and understanding, lower test scores on standardized achievement tests are not inevitable. On the contrary, it is reasonable to believe that, if one has a deep understanding of a concept or skill, he or she should score well on a test even though the test emphasizes recall of facts or display of skill segments. However, the question of actually evaluating constructivist thinking remains. Portfolio assessment is a step in the right direction if the focus is on interpretation and understanding (Garfield, 1994).

Other challenges to the implementation of constructivist teaching practices, according to Zahotik (1995), include class periods that are too short for extensive thought, supervision practices that reward more nonconstructivist teaching, school disciplinary practices that support behaviorist ideology, and bulging class enrollments. Be that as it may, they do not prevent the use of constructivist teaching in some form for teachers who are persistent and creative. The degree of constructivism in the classroom may vary from classroom to classroom depending on the factors discussed.

To reiterate, constructivist principles are associated with psychological-cognitive theories. For example, learners possess inaccurate but persistent conceptions of how the world works, and these influence how they respond to formal instruction (Driver & Easley, 1978).

There have been some suggestions for implementing constructivist instruction. Teachers need to try to find where the students are intellectually before instruction. They should then monitor how the students are making sense of the subject matter during instruction. The role of the teacher is to provide students with early experiences that are relevant to the subject matter rather than starting with explanations. Students need to have frequent opportunities to engage in problems or inquiry-based activities. Such problems should be meaningful to the students and should not be oversimplified or taken out of context. In this way, students learn to work collaboratively and are encouraged to engage in dialogue. This gives them various avenues to express what they know to their peers and to the teacher.

Using constructivist principles places more demands on the teacher. Not only should the teacher be familiar with the principles underlying the topic of study, he or she must be prepared for the variety of ways these principles can be explored by students. The question is not what technique to use but how to use a technique to compliment rather than dominate students' thinking. Constructivism cannot appear as a set of isolated instructional methods grafted onto otherwise traditional teaching techniques. It is a culture, a set of beliefs, norms, and practices (Windschilt, 1997). It seems, therefore, that to become a constructivist teacher requires a paradigm shift.

Becoming a constructivist teacher may prove a difficult transformation, since most instructors were prepared for teaching in the traditional, objectivist manner. It "requires a paradigm shift" and "requires the willing abandonment of familiar perspectives and practices and the adoption of new ones" (Brooks & Brooks, 1993, p. 25). The following represent a summary of some suggested characteristics of a constructivist teacher (Brooks & Brooks, 1993):

1. Become one of many resources that the student may learn from, not the primary source of information.
2. Engage students in experiences that challenge previous conceptions of their existing knowledge.
3. Allow student responses to drive lessons and seek elaboration of students' initial responses. Allow student some thinking time after posing questions.
4. Encourage the spirit of questioning by asking thoughtful, open-ended questions. Encourage thoughtful discussion among students.
5. Use cognitive terminology such as "classify," "analyze," and "create" when framing tasks.
6. Encourage and accept student autonomy and initiative. Be willing to let go of classroom control.
7. Use raw data and primary sources, along with manipulative, interactive physical materials.
8. Don't separate knowing from the process of finding out.
9. Insist on clear expression from students. When students can communicate their understanding, then they have truly learned.

Activities

George W. Gagnon, Jr., and Michelle Collay (2005) suggest six elements to consider when designing a lesson that follows constructivist principles. They provide an overview of each of these elements and explain how they are incorporated in the design of a class.

1. Situation—This refers to the tasks set forth for the students to explain. They suggest giving this task a title. Included in the situation should be what you expect the students to do and how they are to construct their own knowledge.
2. Groupings—Refers to how students and materials are grouped for cooperative learning. This will depend on the situation that the students have to address.
3. Bridge—Refers to linking students' prior knowledge and what they might learn. Prior knowledge may be ascertained by an exercise at the beginning of the class, generating a list of terms prior to the lesson or having a class discussion.
4. Questions—These include guiding questions to keep students actively learning and to encourage reflection or they may be questions you anticipate students will ask.
5. Exhibit—This involves some sort of presentation by the students of what they have learned. Learning will be enhanced if students can provide explanations for others to understand.

6. Reflections—This encourages students to reflect on their thought processes as they were constructing knowledge either through explaining to others or through the explanations of others.

These elements are useful to keep in mind when teachers develop activities for the classroom. An example from an article by Schifter (1996) provides an illustration of how these elements can be incorporated in a math lesson. This was a measurement activity concerning Thanksgiving. The teacher used a model of the Mayflower for her lesson. Using masking tape, she taped it to the floor in the center of the room. She then prepared a scroll for the students to read. The edict on the scroll stated that the boat could not sail until the king was told how large it was. The teacher then waited for the students to figure out how they would measure the boat so they could set sail. Following is her description of what happened after the reading of the scroll.

"Well, what should we do? Who has an idea?" I asked. Thus our discussion of measurement began . . . or I thought it would begin. But there was a period of silence—a long period of silence.

What do young children know about measurement? Is there anything already present in their life experiences to which they could relate this problem? I watched as they looked from one to another, and I could see that they had no idea where to begin. Surely, I thought, there must be something they could use as a point of reference to expand on. Someone always has an idea. But the silence was long as the children looked again from one to another, to Zeb, and to me.

After some confusion about the word Edict on the scroll (some students thought the boat was three feet long because the E in edict looked like a three) the following interaction occurred:

I felt we were back to square one again with more silence, until Tom raised his hand and said, "Mrs. Hendry, I know it can't be three feet because the nurse just measured me last week and said that I was four feet, and this boat is much bigger than me!"

From Tom's initial observation, our discussion on measurement was basically off the ground. Hands immediately went up. The children now realized that they knew a little about measurement, especially in relationship to their own size and how tall they were.

"Let's see how many times Tom can fit in the boat," someone suggested. Tom got down and up several times along the length of the boat: The children decided that the boat was four "Toms" long.

"How can we tell that to the King, since he does not know Tom?" I asked. "Send Tom to the King," was their easy solution, while others protested that they wanted Tom to stay on the boat for the trip. I was really hoping that they would relate to the information Tom had already given us about his size. I thought someone might add four feet, four times, presenting us with a quick solution to the problem. But this was not the route they decided to take.

Mark raised his hand and suggested that we could measure the boat with our hands like they do with horses. His neighbor had a horse that was 15 hands. "Then we could tell the King how many 'hands' long the boat was." The children agreed that this might be a better idea.

"All right," I said. "Since it was Mark's idea, he can measure the length of the boat with his hands." Mark was also the biggest child in the class.

At first, Mark randomly placed his hands on the tape from one end to the other, but when he double-checked, he came out with a different answer. The children were puzzled for a while as to why this happened. It took several more tries and much discussion before they came to an important conclusion. The children decided that it was necessary for Mark to make sure that he began exactly at the beginning of the boat and did not leave any gaps in between his palms and his fingers as he placed them on the tape. Measuring this way, he discovered the boat was 36 hands long.

Great! We decided to tell the King this, but just to be sure, I suggested we have Sue, the smallest child in the class, measure the other side. She did and related to the class that her side was 44 hands long. Now there was confusion.

"Why are they different?" I asked. "Can we use hands to measure?" "No," the children decided, this would not work either, since everyone's hands were not the same size.

Al suggested using feet. We tried this, but once again, when someone else double-checked with their feet, we found two different measurements. The children at this time began to digress a little to compare each other's hands and feet to discover whose were the biggest and smallest.

Finally, our original discussion continued, while the children explored various concepts and ideas. Joan sat holding a ruler but, for some reason, did not suggest using it. Perhaps, I thought, it might be that her experience with a ruler was limited, and she may not have been quite sure how to use it.

Our dilemma continued into the next day when the children assembled again to discuss the problem with some new insights. One child suggested that since Zeb knew the King, and everyone knew Zeb, that we should use his foot. "Measure it out on a piece of paper and measure everything in Zeb's foot." Using this form of measurement, the children related to the King that the boat was 24 "Zeb's foot" long and 9 "Zeb's foot" wide.

Curiosity began to get the best of them, and the children continued to explore this form of measurement by deciding to measure each other, our classroom, their desks, and the rug using "Zeb's foot." I let them investigate this idea for the remainder of the math period.

On the third day of our exploration, I asked the children why they thought it was important to develop a standard form of measurement (or in words understandable to a first grader, a measurement that would always be the same size) such as using only "Zeb's foot" to measure everything. Through the discussions over the past several days, the children were able to internalize and verbalize the need or importance for everyone to measure using the same instrument. They saw the confusion of using different hands, bodies, or feet because of the inconsistency of size. (Hendry, 1996)

Mrs. Hendry does not follow the traditional approach of giving directions followed by explanations. Instead she questions the students, allowing the students reflect on what they already know and make connections to the current learning. It should be noted that the questions sometimes lead to confusion, and it is tempting to offer explanations to clear such confusion. With careful prodding, students can be guided to find solutions for themselves and make the learning more meaningful.

Thinking It Through

1. Explain Vygotsky's zone of proximal development. Discuss how you might apply this in the classroom.

2. "Learners construct their own sets of meanings and understandings." What are the classroom implications of this statement?

3. How might the classroom environment hinder or foster successful implementation of constructivist methods?

4. Consider the potential challenges in implementing constructivist methods in the classrooms. Suggest some ways to address these challenges.

Resources

Association for Supervision and Curriculum Development (ASCD): www.ascd.org

Center for Applied Science Technology (CAST): www.cast.org

International Reading Association (IRA): www.reading.org

Concept to Classroom: www.thirteen.org/edonline/concept2class/constructivism/index.html

The following article contains a particularly good listing of links:

Hall, T. (2002). Differentiated instruction. Retrieved September 9, 2006 from www.cast.org/publications/ncac/ncac_diffinstruc.html

References

Barrows, H. S. (1985). *How to design a problem-based curriculum for the preclinical years.* New York: Springer.

Beilin, H. (1992). Piaget's enduring contribution to developmental psychology. *Developmental Psychology, 28,* 191–204.

Bredekamp, S., & Copple, C. (1997). *Developmentally appropriate practice in early childhood programs.* Washington, DC: National Association for the Education of Young Children.

Brooks, J. G., & Brooks, M. G. (1993). *In Search of understanding: The case for constructivist classrooms.* Alexandria, VA: Association for Supervision and Curriculum Development.

Bruner, J. (1960). *The process of education.* Cambridge, MA: Harvard University Press.

Clements, D. H. (1997). (Mis?)Constructing constructivism. *Teaching children mathematics, 4*(4), 198–200.

Cobb, P. (1994). Where is the mind? Constructivist and sociocultural perspectives on mathematical development. *Educational Researcher, 23*(7), 13–20.

Cobb, P. (1998). *Analyzing the mathematical learning of the classroom community: The case of statistical data analysis.* Proceedings of the 22nd Conference of the International Group for the Psychology of Mathematics Education 1, pp. 33–48, University of Stellenbosch, South Africa.

Copple, C., & Bredekamp, S. (2006). *Basics of developmentally appropriate practice: An introduction for teachers of children 3 to 6.* Washington, DC: NAEYC.

Curtis, D., & Carter, M. (1996). *Reflecting children's lives: A handbook for planning child-centered curriculum.* St. Paul, MN: Redleaf Press.

Delpit, L. (1996). Other *people's children: Cultural conflict in the classroom.* New York: New Press.

Dewey, J. (1916). *Democracy and education: An introduction to the philosophy of education.* New York: Macmillan.

Driver, R., & Easley, J. (1978). Pupils and paradigms: A review of literature related to concept development in adolescent science students. *Studies in Science Education, 5,* 61–84.

Edwards, B., & Davis, B. (1997). Learning from classroom questions and answers: Teachers' uncertainties about children's language. *Journal of Literacy Research, 29*(4), 471–505.

Ernest, P. (1995). The one and the many. In L. Steffe & J. Gale (Eds.), *Constructivism in education* (pp.459–486). New Jersey: Lawrence Erlbaum Associates.

Fosnot, C. T. (1996). Constructivism: A psychological theory of learning. In C. Fosnot (Ed.), *Constructivism: Theory, perspectives and practice.* New York: Teacher's College Press.

Gagnon, G. W., & Collay, M. (2005). *Constructivist learning design.* Thousand Oaks, CA: Corwin Press.

Garfield, J. B. (1994). Beyond testing and grading: Using assessment to improve student learning. *Journal of Statistics Education, 2*(1), 17–25.

Gergen, K. J. (1997). Constructing constructionism: Pedagogical potentials. *Issues in Education, 3*(2), 195–201.

Gergen, K. J. (1995). Social construction and the educational process. In L. P. Steffe & J. Gale (Eds.), *Constructivism in education* (pp. 17–39). Hillsdale, NJ: Lawrence Erlbaum Associates.

Gruender, C. D. (1996). Constructivism and learning: A philosophical appraisal. *Educational Technology, 36*(3), 21–29.

Hall, T. (2002). *Differentiated instruction.* Wakefield, MA: National Center on Accessing the General Curriculum. Retrieved September 26, 2005, from www.cast.org/publications/ncac/ncac_diffinstruc.html

Hardy, M. D., & Taylor, P. C. (1997). Von Glasersfeld's radical constructivism: A critical review. *Science and Education, 6*(1–2), 135–50.

Hendry, G. D. (1996). Constructivism and educational practice. *Australian Journal of Education, 40*(1), 19–45.

Heylighen, F. (1993). *Epistemology, introduction.* Retrieved October 19, 2006, from Principia Cybernetica http://pespmc1.vub.ac.be/EPISTEMI.html

Heylighen, F. (1997). *Epistemological constructivism.* Retrieved August 11, 2006, from http://pespmcl.vub.ac.be/CONSTRUC.html

Hiebert, E. H., & Raphael, T. E. (1998). *Early literacy instruction.* Orland, FL: Holt, Rinehart & Winston.

Honebein, P. (1996). Seven goals for the design of constructivist learning environments. *Constructivist Learning Environments, 17*–24.

Hoover, W. A. (1996). The practice implications of constructivism. *SEDLetter 9*(3), 74–87.

Jewett, F. (1998). *Course restructuring and the instructional development initiative at Virginia Polytechnic Institute and State University: A benefit cost study.* Paper presented at the Case Studies in Evaluating the Costs and Benefits of Mediated Instruction and Distributed Learning. Virginia Polytechnic Institute and State University (California State University, 1998), California State University.

Jonassen, D. (1991a). Evaluating constructivist learning. *Educational Technology, 36*(9), 28–33.

Jonassen, D. (1991b). Objectivism vs. constructivism. *Educational Technology Research and Development, 39*(3), 5–14.

Jonassen, D. H. (1994). Thinking technology: Towards a constructivist design model. *Educational Technology, 3*(4), 34–37.

Kearsley, G. (1994–2004). *Theory into practice database.* Retrieved January 17, 2006, from http://tip.psychology.org/lave.html

Lord, T. R. (1994). Using constructivism to enhance student learning in college biology. *Journal of College Science Teaching, 23*(6), 346–349.

Murphy, E. (1997). *Constructivist epistemology.* Retrieved July 30, 2006, from www.stemnetnf.ca/~elmurphy/emurphy/cle2.html.

National Reading Panel. (2000). *Teaching children to read: An evidence-based assessment of the scientific research literature on reading and its implications for reading instruction: Reports of the subgroups.* Washington, DC: National Institute of Child Health and Development.

National Research Council (1999). *How people learn: Brain, mind, experience and school.* Committee on Developments in Science of Learning. J. D. Bransford, A. L. Brown & R. R. Cocking (Eds.), Commission on Behavioral and Social Sciences and Education. Washington, DC: National Academy Press.

National Research Council (2000). *How people learn: Bridging research and practice.* Committee on Developments in Science of Learning. M. S. Donovan, J. D. Bransford, & W. Pellegrino (Eds.), Commission on Behavioral and Social Sciences and Education. Washington, DC: National Academy Press.

Paley, V. G. (1981). *Walley's stories: Conversations in the kindergarten.* Cambridge: Harvard University Press.

Phillips, D. C. (1995). The good, the bad, and the ugly: The may faces of constructivism. *Educational Researcher, 24*(7), 5–12.

Phillips, D. C. (2000). *Constructivism in education: Opinions and second opinions on controversial issues.* Chicago: Ninety-Ninth Yearbook of the National Society for the study of Education, Part I.

Piaget, J. (1926). *The language and thought of the child.* New York: Harcourt, Brace, Jovanovich.

Piaget, J. (1973). The affective unconscious and the cognitive unconscious. *Journal of the American Psychoanalytic Association, 21,* 249–261.

Piaget, J., & Inhelder, B. (1969). *The psychology of the child.* New York: Basic Books.

Rand, M. K. (2000). *Giving it some thought: Cases for early childhood practice.* Washington, DC: NAEYC.

Saloman, G., & Perkins, D. (1998). Individual and social aspects of learning. *Review of Research in Education, 23*(1), 9–19.

Schifter, D. (1996). A constructivist perspective on teaching and learning mathematics. In C. Fosnot (Ed.), *Constructivism: Theory, perspectives and practice.* New York: Teacher's College Press.

Schunk, D. H. (2004). *Learning theories: An educational perspective* (4th ed.). Upper Saddle River, NJ: Pearson.

Snow, M. A. (1998). Trends and issues in content-based instruction. *Annual Review of Applied Linguistics, 18,* 243–267.

Steffe, L., & Cobb, P. (Eds.). (1988). *Construction of arithmetical meanings and strategies.* New York: Springer-Verlag.

Steffe, L. P., & Gale, J. E. (Eds.). (1995). *Constructivism in education* (pp. 3–16). Hillsdale, NJ: Lawrence Erlbaum Associates.

Steier, F. (1995). From universing to conversing: An ecological constructionist approach to learning and multiple description. In L. P. Steffe & J. E. Gale (Eds.), *Constructivism in education.* Hillsdale, NJ: Lawrence Erlbaum Associates.

Stepien, W. J., & Gallagher, S. A. (1993). Problem-based learning: As authentic as it gets. *Educational Leadership, 50*(7), 25–28.

Taylor, P. (1996). Mythmaking and mythbreaking in the mathematics classroom. *Educational Studies in Mathematics, 31,* pp. 151–173.

Taylor, P. (1998). Constructivism: Value added. In B. Fraser & K. Tobin (Eds.), *The international handbook of science education.* Dordrecht, The Netherlands: Kluwer Academic.

Tertell, E., Klein, S., & Jewett, J. (1998). *When teachers reflect: Journeys toward effective inclusive practice.* Washington, DC: NAEYC.

Tobin, K., & Tippins, D. (1993). Constructivism as a referent for teaching and learning. In K. Tobin (Ed.), *The practice of constructivism in science education* (pp. 3–21). Hillsdale, NJ: Lawrence Erlbaum Associates.

von Glasersfeld, E. (1984). An introduction to radical constructivism. In P. Watzlawick (Ed.), *The invented reality* (pp. 17–40). New York: W.W. Norton.

von Glasersfeld, E. (1989). Constructivism in education. In T. Husen & N. Postlewaite (Eds.), *International encyclopedia of education* [Suppl.] (pp. 162–163). Oxford, England: Pergamon Press.

von Glasersfeld, E. (1995). A constructivist approach to teaching. In L. P. Steffe & J. E. Gale (Eds.), *Constructivism in education* (pp. 3–16). Hillsdale, NJ: Lawrence Erlbaum Associates.

von Glasersfeld, E., & Steffe, L. P. (1991). Conceptual models in educational research and practice. *Journal of Educational Thought, 25*(2), 91–103.

Vosniadou, S. (1996). Towards a revised cognitive psychology for new advances in learning and instruction. *Learning and Instruction, 6(2),* 95–109.

Vygotsky, L. S. (1978). *Mind in society.* Cambridge: Harvard University Press.

Wertsch, J. V., & Tulviste, P. (1992). L. S. Vygotsky and contemporary developmental psychology. *Developmental Psychology, 28,* pp. 548–557.

Wilson, B., & Cole, P. (1991). A review of cognitive teaching models. *Educational Technology Research and Development, 39*(4), 47–64.

Windschilt, M. (1997). *The pedagogical, cultural and political challenges of creating a constructivist classroom.* Paper presented at the International Congress of Personal Construct Psychology, Seattle, WA. (ERIC Document Reproduction Service No. ED421473)

Wood, D., Bruner, J. S., & Ross, G. (1976). The role of tutoring in problem-solving. *Journal of Child Psychology and Psychiatry, 17,* pp. 89–100.

Wood, T., Cobb, P., & Yackel, E. (1995). Reflections on learning and teaching mathematics in elementary school. *Constructivism in Education,* 401–422.

Zahotik, J. A. (1995). *Constructivist teaching.* Fastback 396 Phi Delta Kappa, Bloomington, IN. (ERIC Document Reproduction Service No. ED406367)

Organizing the Inclusive Classroom for Grades K–3

Jack Scott, Debra Leach, and Jessica Bucholz

Beauty from order springs.

English poet William King, 1663–1712

The organizational design of the classroom should be an environmental accommodation to maximize children's educational and instructional development.

Tiegerman-Farber & Radziewicz (1998)

Objectives

After reading this chapter, a student will be able to

- Describe the teacher's role and the role of the collaborative inclusive team in organizing a learning environment in which all children will learn.
- Discuss how teacher priorities are expressed in classroom organization.
- Describe specific ways to organize the physical space of the classroom.
- Describe way to organize the use of indoor and outdoor play space to foster inclusion.
- Discuss the interplay between rules and routines with other systems to enhance classroom organization.
- List ways to make the visual and auditory environment more conducive to learning for all children.
- Discuss the need for the teacher and all members of the inclusion team to be safety conscious and work for a healthy and comfortable class and school.

Key Terms

Universal design

Design for all children

Play space

Shared space

Personal space

Equitable curriculum

Barriers

Classroom acoustics

Reverberation time

Routines

PRACTICAL APPLICATION VIGNETTE

A Teacher Holds Her Ground

I was supervising a graduate intern at an elementary school; a child in this inclusive class had a visual impairment and used a large magnification device to view her work. The child was grouped with several classmates into a cluster of four tables. The student with the visual impairment and teacher invited the other children to use her magnifier when they wished. The student and the device fit right into the classroom. To the other children it was just the piece of equipment Ruthie needed to see words. For the other children it was also a cool device for looking at things in a really different way.

I happened to be observing on the day the electricians from the district came to survey the job they would have to do in order to make a safe and permanent installation of the magnifier. They would have to run wiring to power the device. It was rigged in what appeared to be a very substantial manner but not apparently fully up to the standards of the district and county. The electrician, seeing that the job was going to call for sawing the concrete slab floor, breaking into the wall, and a complicated fix on the flooring, was not happy. Simply moving the child's desk over to the wall was, in the electrician's estimation, the easy way to do this job. He began to explain the "problem" for the teacher. He explained how they would have to cut into the floor and break the walls. The teacher knew full well that this child had a spot in this classroom and with her peers. It was right where she was in that cluster of tables. The teacher listened patiently to the electrician. Then she clearly and emphatically told him that the child was established in her spot and that they should make whatever arrangements they needed to make to install the needed wiring. This went on for some time, but the teacher held her ground. The child stayed with her peers. The permanent wiring was installed.

Introduction to the Inclusive Classroom

The Inclusive Classroom

Among the first decisions a teacher must make when beginning the school year is the organization of the classroom. For the teacher of an inclusive classroom, all the elements of a well-organized classroom in addition to some special features must be considered. But the teacher is not making the decisions on how the classroom will be organized alone but rather as a part of a collaborative team. This important difference makes organizing the K–3 inclusive classroom a team effort.

Organization is critical and, in light of the multiple demands on teachers, not optional. A good classroom is one that allows the teacher and other adults in the class to be efficient, and for this to happen it must be carefully organized. Organization is critical to how children will perceive the classroom. Just as teaching methods will foster cooperation and acceptance, so should the environment. And just as the children are partners in helping all be truly included, they must be partners in helping to maintain the order established by the teacher and inclusion team. The systems you establish will be child-friendly and easy for all children to understand. For example, the place for paste and crayons and wet sponges must not rely on spur-of-the-moment thinking. Instead, the children will know were things go and how they can help in keeping things arranged.

The inclusive team faces many important decisions in organizing the classroom. They must decide how the classroom space will be utilized. The arrangement of student desks and other furniture must be carefully considered in light of the overall inclusive goals. The placement of the desk for the teacher or teachers—or even if teacher desks will be used—constitutes an important decision. The traffic pattern is another choice. Children must be able to move about, but, perhaps more important, teachers have to be able to efficiently get around to all children. Beyond use of floor space the team must consider the sensory and special needs of the children who will call the class their own. Too many visuals may distract some children; too much noise may create a challenge for others. Additionally, the tone of the room can be changed by the use of lighting and wall color and even the addition of classroom pets. A classroom is a place for active learning, and this requires lots of supplies and materials. Materials must be put in tubs or bins, and these containers will typically go on shelves or in storage areas. The class and school must also be a healthy place. The federal No Child Left Behind Act of 2001 calls for funding of studies of to consider "the health and learning impacts of environmentally unhealthy public school buildings on students and teachers." This is in recognition of the fact that too many classrooms are not healthy places for children or adults. Teachers must be careful that the actions they take to deal with one issue, such as adding carpeting to reduce noise, do not create another problems of another sort, such as mold or harmful fumes. The safety of the environment must be a concern for K–3 inclusive teachers.

A good K–3 class will have many materials for a wide variety of learning activities. These have to easy accessible to the children, and children must be able to help put things back in the correct locations. Storage areas and a variety of containers will be used. It is not enough to have determined how containers will be used. The inclusive teaching team must determine the routines that will allow the children to smoothly and efficiently help in obtaining and putting away materials. Students must be taught routines for moving their desks so that the classroom space can serve many purposes. Good classroom organization is a natural ally of good routine. For an inclusive class, the classroom space is not the only space requiring team attention. Play space out of the class must be considered. These spaces must be easily accessible to all and viewed by the children as fun places.

Introduction to the Inclusive Classroom

Accommodations and modifications will be called for in a limited number of circumstances to meet the needs of some children. But the trend in classroom organization is to create learning environments in which all can learn and that are designed for all children, known as **universal design**. The bathroom that is thoughtfully designed for the child who uses a wheelchair will work for all other children. And it is easer to design the bathroom for all children originally rather than have to consider expensive renovations to make it work once it is built. **Design for all children**, an extension of universal design, is natural fit for the K–3 inclusive classroom, just as it may soon, hopefully, be natural for all classrooms.

The inclusive classroom is a teacher's blank canvas. The teachers' ideas of how to teach and how children should interact are brought to life by the things a teacher does to make the classroom function. Ideas about what the class will look like and how children and adults will function in this place are put together and formed into the placement of furniture, the position of shelves and tables, and plans for who will do what and where they will do it. Consider this definition of the term *organize* from Samuel Johnson's 1755 dictionary: "To construct so as that one part co-operates with another: to form organically." Teachers construct their classrooms, and in so doing their ideas are given an organic or living quality.

Look at any standard textbook, and the chapter on classroom organization will feature an array of techniques for making the class and positive and efficient place (Jonson, 2002; Kronowitz, 1999; McNary, Glasgow, & Hicks, 2005). Emphasis will be placed on the teacher's choices for room arrangement, use of space, materials storage, placement of desk, etc. These things are important. But for an inclusive classroom, the process of organizing the classroom should be consistent with the modes of planning and working that guide the other elements of the program. The teacher must be prepared to work with a team to help decide how the classroom will be organized. Just as they plan for the instructional program together with others at school, teachers of inclusive classrooms will gather multiple perspectives on how to organize the class.

Collaborative Planning for Classroom Organization

Like most areas of teacher practice, in the past the organization of the classroom was likely to be a very individual decision. Teacher preference and the goals of the teacher would help guide the organizational effort. The choice of students in rows or students in cluttered desks was solely at the discretion of the teacher. The position of bookshelves, bins for materials and toys, the location of the teacher's desk—these and countless other organizational decisions fell to the teacher and the teacher alone. Further, the teacher faces decisions on whether to have pets in the room or plants or areas for group work and perhaps even a time-out area.

While the teacher or teachers in an inclusive K–3 classroom may have primary responsibility for all these organizational elements and much more, a new style is necessary. Just as instructional decisions for students with disabilities will be made collaboratively, so too, decisions on the use of space in the class and the organization of the class should be made in a collaborative manner. While this may not yet be the norm, it is the trend. Fortunately, K–3 inclusive teachers need not know everything about structuring the classroom. They should be able to call upon most of the members of their collaborative team to assist them.

Tiegerman-Farber and Radziewicz (1998) write: "To include children with disabilities within the general education classroom, parents, teacher, and administrators must discuss modifications in all of the variables that influence classroom decision-making. The child diversity will require adaptations in physical space, equipment arrangement, child seating, class size, teacher relationships, and teacher–parent partnerships . . . academic and training differences create a new learning environment for all children" (p. 134).

This collaborative partnership will consider the ages and developmental levels of all the children, the types and degree of disability, the need for certain types of modifications and accommodations. They will examine the formats of instruction likely to be most beneficial and they may rule out some formats of instruction. Competitive games, for example, may be deemphasized or eliminated entirely.

Individual consideration must be given to each child with a disability. The child who uses a wheelchair will require a bit more space to ensure access to his or her desk and work areas. A child with a visual impairment may require that walkways be larger and better defined. Importantly, the socialization goals for many students may dictate that desks be clustered and not arranged in rows. In an effort to foster a sense of acceptance, a decision may be made that areas for isolating children for disciplinary reasons will not be used in the class.

The need for a collaborative style is addressed in other chapters at some length. But it is useful to review the definition of collaboration and some key characteristics of collaboration in relation to classroom organization. Friend and Cook (2003) offer the following definition: "Interpersonal collaboration is a style for directing interactions between at least two co-equal parties engaging in shared decision making as they work toward a common goal." They go on to note, "It can only occur when it is used by people who are engaged in a specific process, task, or activity" (p. 204). Here we see a style of relating and working together toward a common goal. In our context, this common goal is the inclusion of young children with disabilities in regular classes while assuring the success of all children in the class.

Friend and Cook (2003) note six defining characteristics of collaboration:

1. *Collaboration is voluntary.* Educators and others cannot be forced to collaborate. Administrative mandates may insist on cooperation, but collaboration occurs only when participation is voluntary.

2. *Collaboration requires parity among participants.* Here we see the need for each educator's contribution being equally valued with each one having equal power when decisions are made. Certainly, persons from different fields such as speech-language pathology and mobility specialization may have unique skills and experience. But decision making when done collaboratively does not automatically defer to the person with a specific role or title.

3. *Collaboration is based on mutual goals.* Friend and Cook (2003) write, "Individuals who collaborate must share at least one goal" (p. 8). And for our purposes this must be the success of all children in this inclusive class. Without this commitment real collaboration is simply not possible.

4. *Collaboration depends on shared responsibility for participation and decision making.* Collaborators assume responsibility for being involved in the decision making and for sharing responsibility for the outcomes of these decisions. They all must agree to share ideas, voice concerns, and tackle and resolve barriers to success.

5. *Individuals who collaborate share resources.* Collaborators bring many different kinds of resources to the table. Some will be skilled working with families, others will know how to

design work stations for children who use walkers, while others will have long-term experience in the curricular needs of the children at a given grade level. Sharing these talents and other resources is expected.

6. *Individuals who collaborate share accountability for outcomes.* If the end product of the collaboration is good or bad, all members of the team share accountability for the results. This applies not just to gains on summative evaluations but for pitching in when things don't go exactly as planned. Finger pointing and blaming, obviously, have not place in real collaboration.

These characteristics are seen throughout the collaborative process. Refer to Table 4.1 for specific examples of each element within the context of organizing the inclusive K–3 classroom.

Assessing the Physical Environment as a Collaborative Team

The inclusive team will typically concentrate first on the instructional and social elements of child's inclusive program. But in order for these plans to be successful, the child must be comfortable within the environment. At least five areas must be assessed including the classroom, the bathroom, lunchroom (or arrangement for in-class lunch), playground, and other settings such as specials or assemblies that the child will have throughout the year. The Environmental Assessment produced by the Circle of Inclusion Project at the University of Kansas is a useful assessment in this regard. It is shown as Figure 4.1. This simple one-page form poses several questions for each of the areas noted above. For example, in relation to bathrooms, the assessment calls for consideration of height of sinks, toilet size, access to soap and paper towels, supplies such as wipes, gloves, and bags, and disposal of waste. Many children with disabilities may have needs that directly parallel those of children without disabilities. Others will require special assistance, accommodations, facilities mod- ifications, or other forms of support in several areas. For these children, an occupational therapist or physical therapist, or perhaps an adaptive physical education teacher, along with the parents and teachers will want to complete and consider an assessment such as the environmental assessment as part of their collaborative teaming process.

The tradition had been for the teacher to single-handedly organize the classroom. This is nei- ther desirable nor feasible in the K–3 inclusive classroom. The scope of special needs, the range of types of disabilities and degree of impairment, the diversity of child, and family factors all dictate that no one teacher could possibly know it all. Just as other members of the collaborative team are brought together for instructional and social program development, they must be brought together for both individual-child- and group-focused planning for classroom organization.

The K–3 Child in the Classroom Environment

Children read environments differently than adults. Adults tend to understand the purpose of the activity or function of a setting. The way the setting is organized, its ambience, decoration, and climate becomes secondary to an adult's understanding of the total purpose served by the place. Children, on the other hand, are much more heavily impacted by the environment. For many chil- dren, the environment takes on very special meaning. It is not the background for activities, as an

Table 4.1 ● Collaboration in the Context of a K–3 Inclusive Classroom Organization

Characteristic of Collaboration (based on Friend & Cook, 2003)	Examples in the Context of K–3 Inclusive Classroom Organization
Collaboration is voluntary.	• Teachers are given information regarding the set up of an inclusive classroom and given the option to participate or not participate in a collaborative team. • It is important that all team members have the desire to work together to meet the needs of all children.
Collaboration requires parity among participants.	• Suggestions for seating arrangements for a child with spina bifida are offered as suggestions not presented as mandates. • When discussing reading strategies, all teachers offer suggestions to come up with a comprehensive approach to reading instruction.
Collaboration is based on mutual goals.	• Teachers agree that all children should learn to work cooperatively. • Teachers agree that a particular student requires intervention strategies to promote organizational skills.
Collaboration depends on shared responsibility for participation and decision making.	• Members of the inclusive team discuss who will cover specific subject material, what role each teacher will play during instructional lessons, etc. • The inclusive team will create classroom rules and routines, design daily schedules, create assessment criteria, etc.
Individuals who collaborate share resources.	• Collaborative team members may come to the inclusive class on teacher work days prior to start of school year to help set up the class. • Collaborative team members may share knowledge and materials related to different approaches to teaching number concepts.
Individuals who collaborate share accountability for outcomes.	• Members of the inclusive team may appear in class photo. • Members of the collaborative team will analyze standardized test results and make educational decisions based on those results together.

Figure 4.1 • Environmental assessment: Circle of Inclusion Project.

ENVIRONMENTAL ASSESSMENT

CLASSROOM: teacher–student ratio _____

table and chair size _____

toys and materials _____

general philosophy _____

furniture arrangement _____

accessibility to outside _____

floor space _____

accessibility into the classroom _____

bed for naps _____

BATHROOM: height of sinks _____

toilet size _____

access to soap and paper towels _____

changing table _____

supplies such as wipes, gloves, bags _____

_____

disposal of waste _____

LUNCHROOM: lunch routine such as passing out food _____

_____

_____

table and chair size _____

utensils, cups, and plates _____

_____

types of food _____

routes around tables _____

number of children per table _____

space at table per child _____

wheelchair accessible _____

PLAYGROUND: surfaces _____

playground equipment such as slides, swings, etc.

_____

_____

sand toys, balls, riding toys, etc. _____

_____

_____

OTHER: _____

_____

_____

www.circleofinclusion.org

Circle of Inclusion, University of Kansas, Department of Special Education, 521 J R Pearson, 1122 W Campus Rd., Lawrence, KS 66045-3101, (785) 864-0685.

adult might perceive it. Children are sensitive to the many messages they can find in the setting. Does it seem friendly and inviting? Do desks in neat rows signify a high degree of separateness? Do prominent rule or point posters or other management materials suggest that a strict behavior régime is in place? Do the colors and decorations help the child feel comfortable? Does the presence of a classroom pet convey a caring and accepting attitude on the part of the manager of this learning space: the teacher?

Children tend not to understand the rules of expectations in a setting until they know the purpose of the setting. This statement from Maria Montessori says it perfectly, "Only in an environment known as a whole, it is possible for them [the children] to orient themselves and act with purpose." The child with special needs—indeed all young children—will need help in gaining this broader perspective. The teacher must take time to explain why things are organized the way they are: why it is necessary to move desks to a new position for class meetings, for example, and to put them back again in a predetermined place. The teacher must explain why materials will be placed back in marked containers, and that the scissors go with the scissors and the marker pens go with the marker pens. If they are not put away correctly, they cannot be found the next time the class needs to use them. Others students or teachers may not be able to find them. The teacher might order new materials wastefully and deprive the class of some needed supplies.

Consistency is another factor. Children need a high degree of consistency, and environments with these higher levels of consistency foster better learning. A teacher who may have a poorly organized class and inefficient systems for storing materials and weak routines will find it hard to try to impose order on the children. A teacher may be content in his or her own learning world with a low degree of organization. However, the children cannot be asked to adhere to a disorganized set of systems. But for optimum learning in the classroom the children need to be able to participate in the system. They must know the reason for their participation and be helped to support the systems with their good behavior.

Consistency and high levels of support from teachers and the organization of the environment are important in another way. Children usually process or take in the entire environment at one time. Unlike adults they tend not to filter their perception of the setting. This can become chaotic for some children and is more likely to be a problem with children with disabilities. Many suggest that chaos is the natural mode of child perception, or their conceptualization of the world. When a child does make sense of this chaotic jumble, it is by means of relationships among what they see, what is taking place, and what they themselves do. A well-organized class provides the structure for this maturing and developing perception of the classroom and for understanding other settings as well. The function of classroom organization is to be a strong part of the matrix for these relationships to develop within the child.

This should never be confused with harsh attempts to control or overstructure children. Children do request structure and order but only so far as they can relate to it and they believe it helps them function more effectively. However, adults can easily work to overdo this. Indeed, Montessori vigorously opposed the regimentation of young children so common in her time. She was a critic of the tyranny of the stationary school desk and the manner in which it forced conformity to a coerced form of desired student posture. We are long past this, but vestiges linger. Making children walk in the halls with their hands clasped behind their backs is one of the modern equivalents of the stationary desk. On a classroom level, some children will find that it is easier for them to stand while working. Certainly, children need to learn that for many tasks they must be seated. But when we can allow the child to follow his or her own lead to make the setting work, we encourage the development of real understanding of how to behave in different settings at different times. As learning is promoted, everyone benefits. Consider this another way. If we explain to the children that some children require a special positioning device so they can learn best, and at the same time refuse to allow another child to use his or her own accommodation for learning in the form of standing at the desk, for example, we confuse the child and can perpetuate chaotic thinking on the part of the child. The inclusive K–3 classroom is a classroom in which each child can learn how he or she learns best in interaction with the organization established by the inclusive team and managed by the teacher.

Play is an essential part of learning for children. The value of play in the lives of children is highlighted in the Association for Childhood Education (ACEI) 1988 position statement, *Play: A Necessity for All Children* (see Figure 4.2). Play and the spaces and materials and other supports needed for play are key elements of the classroom for young children. The cognitive, social emotional, physical, and other benefits of play for young children are obvious to most early childhood educators. Classroom space is often not sufficient to allow for all of the play activities hoped for. **Play space**, designated areas for play, may be in **shared space** (or common) within the class. In some cases play may require that children reposition their **personal spaces**—their desks and chairs—in order to make more play space.

Most children with special needs do not need special equipment in the classroom. Of those who do, most of that equipment does not require special installation. For those few children who need special equipment requiring special installation, the teacher must be prepared to educate everyone involved, from the principal to the electrician, on the importance of keeping the child with his or her peers in the most normal way possible.

Organizing Areas within the Class

Teachers and the inclusion team face the task of arranging the classroom so that it fulfills their vision and hopefully meets their objectives for inclusive teaching. It is at this juncture were philosophy meets reality. Child desks are arranged one way or another. Centers are used, not used, or used to a very slight degree. And just as teachers and collaborate inclusive teams are emergent and still learning as they progress, the classroom will be a changing and developing place. Yet teachers will appreciate some starting points. This section will offer some starting points for arranging desks and

Figure 4.2 • ACEI position statement on play: *Play: A Necessity for All Children.*

ACEI POSITION: The Association for Childhood Education International (ACEI) recognizes the need for children of all ages to play and affirms the essential role of play in children's lives. ACEI believes that, as today's children continue to experience pressure to succeed in all areas, the necessity for play becomes even more critical. ACEI supports all adults who respect, understand, and advocate legitimizing play as an essential pathway to learning for all populations of children. When working with children, adults should use their knowledge about play to guide their practice.

ACEI/Isenberg & Quisenberry, 1988.

other furniture and floor space, as well as ideas on storage and use of dividers and shelves. Then we will provide some guidance on the environment in relation to the visual, the auditory, and even the sensory aspects of the setting.

What we will not do is offer definitive rules for how things should be done. This, while popular in some books aimed at teachers, seems to not fully value the judgment of teachers and in other cases to be potentially contrary to good inclusive practices. Consider, for example, advice by Wong and Wong (1998): They recommend that children be seated, initially in rows, and that, even if changed later, they should be oriented so that all children face the board. They note, "Desks do not have to be in traditional rows, but all chairs should face forward so that all eyes are focused on you [the teacher]" (p. 95). Desks set in rows becomes the reasonable manner to meet these directives. They cite as advantages the fact that all children are oriented toward the teacher and that peer-to-peer inter-action is minimized. This is, in some ways, the modern equivalent of the stationary desk, which Maria Montessori complained about so strongly one hundred years ago. If an educator sees his or her job as simply imparting information to a child, then this may be useful advice. But the early child-hood class and certainly the early childhood inclusive class cannot be based on his model of teaching. Rather, teachers are facilitators of interaction—interaction of children with other children and chil-dren with learning materials. When, in preparation for a specific instructional activity, children are required to face the board, they can, regardless of the orientation of their seat, reposition so as to see the teacher. Further, the children can be helped to understand the importance of repositioning their seats so that they can face the teacher and thereby pay careful attention to what she or he is saying.

Teachers at the early elementary level must be able to accommodate many different formats for instruction. Evans, Evans, Gable, and Schmid (1991) identified instructional formats likely to be found in classrooms. These included large-group areas, small-group areas, individual student areas, paraprofessional area, recreation space, audiovisual area, and miscellaneous space. Updating this list would call for adding a computer area as well. Many classes will not have enough room to meet all these formats all the time. Jones (2000) suggests that children can be easily coached in moving their desks quickly and efficiently. He recommends the use of small paper dots to indicate the home-base position of each child's desk. As these begin to wear out, the children can help replace them. The teacher can teach the children how to move their desks in the same way that other content is taught. The restoration of all the desks to their original positions will be a confirmation of success and naturally reinforcing for most children. Children can, if necessary, provide special assistance to those children with vision or mobility impairments or help develop creative ways to reposition their desks and chairs.

Seating Arrangements

It is fairly well established that for maximizing student-to-teacher interaction in a traditional class-room layout students should be seated *front and center*. (Adams, 1969; Adams & Biddle, 1970). But with teachers of K–3 children increasingly cruising the classroom, such preferential seating in no longer has the same relevance. Teaching at the early grades clearly reflects the deemphasis on teacher directedness. The children are far more likely to be grouped into clusters. These smaller groups become the focus of many activities.

Doyle (1986), among those who helped popularize the use of clusters and circular arrange-ments, noted that these seating formats encouraged more child-to-child interaction and promoted independent learning. The use of clustered and semicircular arrangements are now far more common in contrast to row arrangements. A survey study by Patton, Snell, Knight, Willis, and Gerken (2001) illustrates just how common is the use of cluster arrangements. They found that 94 percent of surveyed teachers used this arrangement for some teaching and that this was the standard room arrangement for 76 percent of observed classrooms. For the K–3 grades it was, in general, more frequently used. When clusters or perimeter (U-shaped) arrangements were combined in the Patton et al. study, we find that for kindergarten it was used by 15 of 15 teachers (100%), in first grade by 82 percent, in second by 72 percent, and by 85 percent of teachers at third grade. Patton et al. (2001) suggest, "Small group cluster designs were now used pervasively . . . because many contemporary teachers believe that this type of seating arrangement contributes directly to students' educational growth through the effects of socially facilitated learning" (p. 1). The teachers in this study offered the following advantages for cluster arrangement: (1) supports cooperative/collaborative/shared learning processes, (2) provides best use of room space, (3) promotes students' learning of cooperation skills, and (4) builds classroom "community" (p. 8). Interestingly, teachers focused less on social factors in rating the benefits of row arrangements. The top advantages were the following: (1) minimizes room distractions, (2) supports appropriate visual orientation toward instruction, and (3) supports the learning of appropriate class behaviors (p. 8). Here the focus was on good behavior and attending to the teacher.

To the elements cited in the Patton's study can be added these advantages of the cluster arrangement for the K–3 inclusive classes (Patton et al., 2001):

1. Children can engage in cooperative learning activities without repositioning or moving their seats.
2. Children have peers next to them and across from them to solicit information on directions and to give and get help.
3. Children are grouped in a natural work team, a working arrangement that prepares them for future teamwork activities in school and in the workplace.

Clustering children's desks in groups of four or six is the most natural arrangement in the K–3 inclusive class. The advantages are many and the disadvantages few. This arrangement offers the ideal spirit for the inclusive class and may in many ways set the tone for cooperation, friendship, and mutual support.

Room Format

The actual room layout is best determined by the collaborative team. In general, the class should be designed so that is easy for children and adults to move from one area to another. It will be important for the teacher to see all the children and all of the activities taking place from virtually any spot in the room. There must be some division of areas within the room with separation of quiet work areas from play and activity areas. Storage of materials must be relatively close to where the children will be using the materials but should not bring them back and forth across the quiet work areas. A designated area should be established for group activities if space permits. Using small carpet squares that can be replaced when frayed or soiled offers real advantages over larger carpeted areas. The class should be one that a child or adult would want to be in, with inviting visuals and a sense of productivity. Welcoming messages should greet those who come to the doorway. It should be visually obvious to any visitor where children should leave their backpacks, lunch packs, coats, and other items. Ideally, the room should have abundant natural light and be free of unnecessary noise and distraction. If the class is to be a good inclusive class, there should be a high degree of structure or predictability. Children should be doing what their teachers are asking them to do. And teachers and other adults should be asking the children to do things based on plans that structure the behavior of the adults. Within this overall environment, children with disabilities, including those with more severe disabilities, can be successfully included.

An important factor is the degree to which teachers and other adults in the room can easily move around and quickly get to each child. Jones (2000) urges teachers to be cautious of the "custodial" room arrangement, a layout optimized by the custodian to make cleaning most efficient. Jones further suggests that teachers make their walkways large and desk arrangements compact so they do not constitute a barrier to moving from one side of the class to the other. These large walkways, which Jones (2000) likens to classroom *boulevards,* are fashioned into loops. These loops permit easy teacher movement and allow sufficient room for children who use wheelchairs and walkers to move and maneuver. Keep in mind that for a child to turn his or her wheelchair around takes more space that the mere width of the chair. Additionally, a child may be less skilled in comparison to an adult in using a wheelchair and require proportionally more space.

The objective of such an arrangement is to allow the teacher to move efficiently from child to child. These walkway loops allow for teacher mobility, but teachers should stay toward the center of the loop, as a general practice, when supervising regular class activities. This gives them an "inside track," with less travel required, in which to operate. Time spent moving from one end of the class to the other is potentially wasted teaching time. The U-shaped arrangement can offer the teacher the advantage of a central area in the middle of the U from which to quickly move from child to child. Moving out of the U to the other side of the class, should this be necessary is, however, less efficient. The U shape does give most children a buddy to the right and left (except for the children at the ends of the U). While some K–3 teachers use the U-shaped arrangement, it is less often used in comparison to clustered desks. Other types of class activities may call for other layouts.

The four-desk cluster seems to be the format most favored in inclusive settings. The clustered arrangements, as has been noted, provide obvious advantages. Socialization and, with it, the opportunities for cooperation are maximized. Small-group projects can be worked on while the children are at their own desks. And with no repositioning, they can work at their desks on individual assignments. The teacher can strategically place three other children with a child with disabilities to provide positive models for behavior and assistance with instruction should this be needed. A disadvantage to the use of clustered tables is that some children will not naturally be facing the board or screen for some teacher-directed activities. This can be addressed by simply having these children move their chairs and, if necessary, their desks to face the teacher's presentation. The teacher should consider children who may be more able to make this switch easily and quickly and position them so that they make this quick change in position. A second disadvantage, and this is more of a problem at the upper elementary grades, is that children may find it easier to talk to each other when they should be working silently and independently. The benefits offered by the clustered arrangement for fostering social development more than make up for this potential barrier in the K–3 grades.

The collaborative team may decide to change the arrangement, and in the upper grades experimentation is common. But for the early grades frequent rearrangements can cause several issues. Younger children have a harder time adapting to routines. Switching their table assignments demands that the children establish new relationships with peers in their cluster. Too much changing may result in poorly formed relationships. Important for an inclusive class, the typically developing children will require some period of time in which to refine their strategies for helping the children with special needs. While it is good for all children in the class to learn how they can help one another, the special help that may be called for in some cases may take time to become most effective. For these reasons, very careful consideration should be given to seating arrangements early in the school year. This can minimize the disruptions that can come from frequent switching. But if unproductive patterns emerge that are not amenable to simple correction, the team will, of course, want to consider rearrangements.

Balancing groups will require the careful attention of the entire team. Knowing which children will work best together calls for consideration of a wide range of factors, with disability being only one of these factors. One method is to use a teacher rating of the social capacity of children and to then place a high-rated child at each cluster of tables. Similarly, this can be balanced out with a child who is rated lowest in social capacity. The group is then filled in with children who are neither high nor low in social ability. A child with disabilities who may require special assistance, perhaps in the form of a peer buddy who can help with instructions, may require a very capable student, one who is an especially good listener and helper. Here teacher and collaborative team member assessment of the capacity of each child becomes critical.

In the old model of teaching, the positioning of the teacher's desk prominently at the front of the room was the obvious choice. The recommendation we wish to offer is just the reverse of this. Move the desk to the side and out of the way. We know that teachers are rarely sitting at their desks when the children are in the room. They are circulating and assisting on an almost constant basis. The desk does provide a hub for teacher activities but is now rarely used as a hub for students. Many teachers place their desk in the least conspicuous place possible, helping to keep it out of the flow of traffic.

Designing Environments That Will Accommodate a Wide Range of Children

In the past, special schools had to be well prepared to meet the most specialized needs of children with disabilities. Today, children with disabilities are being taught next to their peers who do not have disabilities. The environmental accommodations formerly needed in the special setting may have to be available in these inclusive settings. The trend of making all settings available to persons with a wide range of abilities is, of course, not limited to early childhood. As a society we are seeing a wonderful trend of making sure the design of environments and, to an increasing degree, the nature of the requirements we place on people allow the widest range of individuals to fully participate. Architecture was perhaps the first profession to deal comprehensively with these issues. Faced with developing new standards for accessibility, standards that would allow persons with physical and cognitive disabilities to have easy access, architects crafted what is now referred to as principles of Universal Design (UD). Scott, McGuire, and Foley (2003) have perhaps the best delineation of the principles of universal design. Their primary focus is on the transition of students with disabilities from high school to postsecondary education. However, their nine principles are applicable to any level of instruction:

1. *Equitable use.* Instruction is designed to be accessible to students with diverse abilities.
2. *Flexibility in use.* Multimodal instruction provides for student choice.
3. *Simple and intuitive.* Instruction is designed in a predictable manner with unnecessary complexity eliminated.
4. *Perceptible information.* Instruction is communicated effectively to each student regardless of student's sensory abilities.
5. *Tolerance for error.* Instruction anticipated variation in student pace and skills.
6. *Low physical effort.* Minimize nonessential physical effort.
7. *Size and space appropriate for use.* Instruction considers a student's body, size, posture, mobility, and communication needs.
8. *A community of learners.* Instruction promotes interaction and communication between students.
9. *Instructional climate.* The climate is welcoming and inclusive with high expectations for all students.

These principles have had considerable impact on architectural designs and the planning for public and private buildings. These principles have also influenced the way designers and engineers think about any product or services to make it more accessible. The impact is wide, ranging from Web page designs to the nature of instructions for using products to the placement and function of buttons on appliances, computers, and televisions. Universal Design is a significant movement in respecting the role of persons with diverse needs in society. The relevance of these principles to learning is obvious and has been made explicit in recent publications. These principles have been applied to learning by Mason, Orkwis, and Scott (2005) (see Table 4.2). Movement toward an **equitable curriculum**, curriculum that is designed to engage all students, is what we strive toward.

Recently these principles have been directly applied to early childhood education. Conn-Powers, Cross, Traub, and Hutter-Pishgahi (2006) offer a framework for universal design for early childhood program with specific reference to the physical environment, health and safety components, the social-emotional environment, the teaching environment, individual assessment and program evaluation practices, and family involvement practices. For example, in relation to the physical environment they write that using principles of universal design, "enable[s] all children to have access and equitable opportunities for full participation in all program activities. This includes structures, permanent and movable equipment and furnishings, storage and materials" (p. 4).

The inclusive early elementary teacher should become familiar with the principles and practices of Universal Design for both general societal applications and specifically to education and learning. Here we have a sound framework for making the society ever friendlier to and accepting of children with disabilities. While the readers of this book will likely be focused on their own classroom, they should be looking at their roles in school- and communitywide forums to help reduce **barriers**, or impediments to participation for persons with disabilities, and open opportunities for those with special needs. Consider that Universal Design provides a great framework for the suggestions you will be offering.

Designing Environments That Will Accommodate a Wide Range of Children

Table 4.2 ● Universal Design Principles Applied to Learning

Equitable curriculum Instruction uses a single curriculum that is accessible to student with widely diverse abilities: Curriculum does not unnecessarily segregate students or call undue attention to their "differences." Curriculum is designed to engage all students.

Flexible curriculum The curriculum is designed to be presented flexibly to accommodate a range of individual abilities and preferences; it considers physical and sensory-motor disabilities as well as varied learning preferences and paces.

Simple and intuitive instruction Instruction is straightforward, provided in the mode most accessible to students; language, learning levels, and complexity of presentation can be adjusted; student progress is monitored on an ongoing basis to reset goals and instructional methods as needed.

Multiple means of presentation Curriculum provides multiple means of presentation to teach student in ways that will most effectively reach them, regardless of sensory ability, level of understanding, or attention; presentation can be altered to meet recognition patterns of individual students.

Success-oriented curriculum The teacher encourages engagement with curriculum by eliminating unnecessary barriers to engagement; the teacher provides a supportive learning environment through ongoing assistance, applying principles of effective curriculum design as needed: e.g., teaching Big Ideas, priming background knowledge, scaffolding instruction, and so on.

Appropriate level of student effort The overall classroom environment provides ease of access to curricular materials, promotes comfort, addresses motivation, and encourages student engagement by accommodating varied means of student response; assessment is ongoing, measuring performance; instruction may change based on results of assessment.

Appropriate environment for learning Classroom environment and the organization of curricular materials allows for variations in physical and cognitive access by students as well as for variations in instructional methods; classroom environment allows for varied student groupings; classroom space encourages learning.

From "Instructional Theories Supporting Universal Design for Learning—Teaching to Individual Learners" in *Universal Design for Learning: A Guide for Teachers and Education Professionals* (p. 23), by C. Mason, R. Orkwis, & R. Scott (Eds.), 2005, Upper Saddle River, NJ: Prentice Hall. Copyright 2005 by the Council for Exceptional Children.

Creating a solution for a child with a disability should not come at the expense of a full educational experience for other children. Rather, good design of child environments should enhance the experiences of all children. Stoecklin (1999) has used the term *Design for All Children* in relation to this concept. Stoecklin (1999), an expert on design for children's environments, writes of a faulty solution to the problem of children with disabilities accessing a sand play area: raising it as a sand table. Here none of the children could get into the sand, and no correct height for such a table was likely to be found in any case. Stoecklin then discusses solutions to a problem of access to a water play area that included the use of multiheight tables that allowed for side access for some and under-table access for wheelchairs. The variety of heights permitted the children to select the best arrangement for themselves. Here the elimination of barriers for some children probably resulted in the creation of a more exciting play area for all the children. This is also the goal of universal design. Let this be the goal for your accommodations and modifications in your classroom.

The Auditory Environment

The **classroom acoustics**, or the quality of the sound environment, will have a large impact on what children can hear and how they will learn from what they hear. If a child cannot hear what a teacher or peer is saying or cannot hear it efficiently, she or he may well not attend to the message. If a teacher cannot hear a child's response, valuable feedback to the child could be compromised. Noisy classrooms can be hard on the health of teachers. Speaking at higher volumes to overcome ambient or background noise leads to voice strain, which can predispose teachers to respiratory and other infections. Teachers have control over noisy classrooms to some degree. Some factors, such as loud air conditioners or outside noise, may require that teachers advocate for administrative support to address the issues.

Parents and advocates of many children with disabilities are often highly critical of the auditory environments for their children. They may offer recommendations that may be difficult or impossible to accommodate in an inclusive classroom without negatively impacting the naturalness of the setting. But special accommodations may only rarely be needed if the auditory environment is of good quality or can be brought up to a satisfactory level.

In a booklet by the Acoustical Society of America (Seep, Glosemeyer, Hulce, Linn, & Aytar 2000) we see that "In many classrooms in the United States, the speech intelligibility rating is 75 percent or less. That means that, in speech intelligibility tests, listeners with normal hearing can understand only 75 percent of the words read from a list" (p. 1). For young children this is an even more critical problem. "Another group for whom learning is especially dependent on good acoustics is young children, who are unable to *predict from context*" (p. 2). This source suggests that it is not lack of funds but rather lack of awareness of the problem and awareness of solutions that prevent effective remedial action. Building new schools with good acoustics is offered as the best and most cost-effective solution, as renovation of older schools is often problematic and expensive. When we consider that the average school in the United States is 43 years old, it is not surprising that many schools have compromised acoustic characteristics. Noise can come from outside sources that are transmitted into the classroom, or it can be an issue of reflection or diffusion of sound within the classroom. An important measure is the **reverberation time** or (RT60), and it is used to estimate how rapidly sounds fade within a given room or space. Large rooms have longer reverberation times and can tend to sound "boomy," while smaller rooms are less reverberant (Seep et al., 2000). The long reverberation times of the common classroom constitute the major factor to the poor acoustic environment. One way to deal with this problem is to reduce the volume of the room, something not easily accomplished by the inclusive team. But when classrooms for children in primary grades are being renovated or being planned, all aspects of the environment, especially the acoustic environment, should be considered. Dropping the ceiling height is one common way to accomplish this while keeping adequate floor space. A second way to reduce reverberation is to add sound-absorbing tiles or panels on the walls. While acoustic consultants might also recommend carpeting, the potential health risks with carpeting may argue against it. The use of fabric wall hangings, plants, and soft-textured bulletin board materials can all help reduce the reverberation in the classroom. The use of fabric wall panels can play a major role in reducing excessive cafeteria noise, a likely source of sound stress for many children with disabilities. See Figure 4.3 for suggestions from a clinical audiologist on how classroom teachers can deal with some of these issues.

In addition, teachers will want to explore a number of ways to generally reduce the noise in the classroom. Installing tennis balls on the legs of chairs and desks can help reduce classroom noise. A helpful set of suggestions for using these readily available items is featured in Figure 4.4. Recycled tennis balls on chair legs can be one of the easiest and certainly the most cost-effective noise reduction measures a teacher can take.

Figure 4.3 ● Ten tips for reducing the noise in your K–3 inclusive class.

Unwanted sounds, noise, can impose an additional challenge for most learners. For some children, such as those children with autism, or those with auditory processing disorders, competing noise in the classroom or poor acoustical environment can make learning very difficult. There are three factors that can influence speech intelligibility in a classroom. These include signal-to-noise ratio, reverberation time, and distance. An ideal classroom will have a signal-to-noise ratio of 12 dB. This means that the teacher's voice is 12 dB louder than the background noise. A less reverberant classroom is perfect for better speech intelligibility. A class with a .4-second reverberation time is excellent. Here are some solutions you can do to make your classroom less noisy.

Signal-to-Noise Ratio (S/N): It is the difference in dB between the signal of interest (i.e., speech or teacher's voice) and unwanted noise (i.e., background noise).

Reverberation Time (RT): It is the amount of time in seconds that takes for sound to drop by 60 dB below its original level.

1. Close the windows.
2. Classrooms should be away from the playground.
3. Locate the teacher's desk in the middle of the room in front of the blackboard.
4. Consider a surround-sound system with loudspeakers.
5. Consider carpeting the classroom floor (with hard-floor rooms consider using tennis balls on chair legs and table legs to muffle their sounds).
6. Improve reverberation time by carpeting the floor or by using acoustic tile ceilings.
7. Increase signal-to-noise ratio by using a personal voice enhancer/amplifier.
8. Reduce your distance from the students.
9. Allow illumination of your face for better visual cues.
10. Do not walk away while talking to a child with hearing problems.
11. Plan on installing sound-field speakers in the room.

Ali A. Danesh, PhD, Clinical Audiologist.

Dr. Danesh is an associate professor of audiology in the Department of Communication Sciences and Disorders at Florida Atlantic University in Boca Raton, Florida.

Figure 4.4 ● Tennis Balls Increase Children's Attention

Tennis Balls Increase Children's Attention *By Carolyn Edwards*

Children hear more poorly than adults in noisy situations. Although there is a gradual improvement through the elementary years, children are thirteen to fifteen years of age before they can cope in noise as well as adults do. Children with recurrent ear infections, language disorders, English as a second language, hearing loss in one ear, and any degree of hearing loss in both ears have even more difficulty understanding speech in noise than their peers.

Classrooms are noisy places and the noise is primarily generated by children talking and chairs moving on uncarpeted floors. To give you an idea of sound levels, teachers' voices are often at a loudness level of 65 dB. During activity times, loudness levels range from 70 to 85 dB. The sound of one chair scraping on the floor of a portable classroom was measured at 85 dB. (The sound of a motorcycle or a jackhammer is about 100 dB.)

Noise interferes with children's comprehension of speech. Studies have consistently shown decreases of 35% to 40% in children's speech recognition from a fairly quiet room to the typical noise levels experienced in today's classroom.

Tennis balls are an inexpensive solution to decrease chair noise in the classroom. Take an X-Acto knife and cut an X in the top of each tennis ball. The X should be just large enough to insert the metal leg of the chair. Each chair requires four tennis balls.

CONSUMER INFORMATION

Durability: Tennis balls have lasted two to three years in a classroom before losing their effectiveness.

Sound Reduction: Sound from chairs moving is reduced to a minimum.

Price: Varies with source.

Color: Ranges from fluorescent yellow to pink.

Where to Obtain: In addition to purchase, some teachers have approached local tennis clubs for donations of used tennis balls. Of course there are always the tennis balls from the roof of the school. Some teachers have put a box at the front of the school for donations from students and staff. Finally, some communities now include tennis balls as an item for recycling.

Teacher Comments: When teachers on the second floor have used the tennis balls on chair legs, the teacher underneath on the first floor has been delighted with the reduction in noise. Paradoxically, the elimination of noise has made the children more aware of noise, and communication has been easier in the classroom.

Children's Comments: They don't want to remove the tennis balls once the balls have been installed. Children say it is easier to hear other children, and easier to pay attention in the classroom.

Try it—one of the easiest improvements to the classroom!

This helpful suggestion comes from the Hands and Voices website: www.handsandvoices.org/articles/education/ed/tennis_balls.html.

Even with all that a teacher and team can do to adjust the physical environment (see Figure 4.5), accommodations and changes may still be required to allow the auditory environment to be comfortable for some children. The program for a child with autism, for example, may require careful attention to sound (Kluth, 2003; Quill, 2000). Kluth (2003) offers the following suggestions for children with autism spectrum disorders (ASD), but they may be relevant to any child with sound issues:

1. Once a disturbing sound has been discovered, helping the student can be as simple as moving him or her as far away as possible for the sound source.
2. Use a soft voice when possible. Instead of shouting to get a student's attention, try whispering.
3. Try earplugs or headphones for some activities or for use in some parts of the school building (e.g., gymnasium).
4. Reduce classroom noise. Echoes and noise can be reduced by using carpeting. Carpet remnants can sometimes be obtained from a carpet store at a low cost. Some teachers cut tennis balls open and

Figure 4.5 ● Make the classroom fit the children's bodies.

Make the Classroom Fit the Children's Bodies

By Marlynn K. Clayton with Mary Beth Forton

Too many times I have watched students struggle with attention and behavior problems that were clearly the result of being in spaces that were too small, too crowded, or otherwise unsuited to their physical size. So, before you even meet the students, estimate the range of sizes based on what's typical for that age. Use this estimate to:

1. Choose desks, tables, and chairs that fit the children. Check out school furniture catalogues that offer standard height and width calculations based on grade ranges. Also, consider making modifications to the furniture you currently have.
2. Select and arrange bookcases and shelves. In general, children should be able to see and be seen over any shelves. Taller shelves should be placed along the perimeter.
3. Determine where to locate display areas. Displays meant for children should be at their eye level whenever possible.
4. Plan the amount of space needed for class meetings. When children are sitting in a circle, there should be approximately three inches between children.
5. Plan enough space for table work. Keep in mind that, when children sit at a table to work, they need "elbow room" and space to spread out materials.
6. Plan enough space for the children to line up at the exit door. For comfort and safety, it's best to allow about nine inches between children.
7. Plan passageways—the aisles children use to move about the room. In general, a passageway should allow two children to walk past each other comfortably.

After students arrive, observe how they use the room. Make necessary adjustments and invite the students to be part of the design process whenever possible. This gives children a sense of ownership and increases their investment in making the design work.

From *Classroom Spaces That Work,* by Marlynn K. Clayton with Mary Beth Forton (2001) place them on the bottoms of the chair or desk legs; this adaptation muffles the scraping sound created when furniture is shuffled around.

5. Change the sound, if possible. For instance, if a student cringes when he hears clapping, students could develop another system of appreciation for student presentations, birthday celebrations, and assemblies.

6. Prepared the student for the sound. If you know the school bell is about to ring, cue the student to plug his or her ears or simply tell the student to get ready.

7. In noisy or chaotic environments, allow students to listen to soft music using headsets or play soft music (e.g., classical, environmental) for all students. (p. 80)

When considering changes such as those offered by Kluth, consider gathering direct observation data on the behavior of the child who will benefit from the change. This will allow the team to determine if the change has, in fact, made a difference in the child's behavior. Analysis of the data may suggest that further changes are needed, or it may indicate that a change made no difference. Such analysis can help strengthen the decisions being made and reduce the likelihood of arbitrary changes that may have an adverse impact on the total classroom environment.

Skillful use of partitions can help reduce noise in the room. Teachers have long used partitions and furniture such as shelves to divide space within a classroom. Shelves both offer the advantage of storage and display options and can serve as room dividers. Place taller shelves against walls so they do not block the line of sight necessary for the teacher to monitor the class. Shelves that children can look over, generally these will be low shelves, can be used as dividers. The children can see what is taking place in other parts of the room and, importantly, so can the teachers. Avoid placing heavy objects on high shelves, as these could be a danger if they were to fall. All shelf units need to correctly installed. In some cases this may call for fasteners to secure the shelf to a wall. The back of a shelf can be used to display student work and could be covered with fabric to reduce noise in the class. Shelf backs or sides often serve as a great location for visual schedules or permanent prompts or other posted information for children who may need them.

In addition, new and very flexible options are now available for dividing room space. Among these are the Angeles Baseline Quiet Divider (Angeles Group, Pacific, Missouri: www.angeles-group.com). These lightweight dividers are made to be easily repositioned, and, by clever use of magnetic connectors, they are very safe. These are perhaps most frequently used in pre-K settings, but they have much to offer in K–3 settings. Importantly, they are designed to absorb sound, thereby reducing noise both in divided areas and in the total classroom. The textured surface readily accepts hook-and-loop fasteners so that schedules or learning materials can be temporarily positioned. The Quiet Divider is just one example of an array of new options available to teachers for truly customizing their classrooms.

Creating a Positive Visual Environment in the Inclusive Class

Classrooms can have a dazzling array of creative materials. We expect the typically developing children to respond to these multiple visual stimuli in a positive manner. But children with disabilities, especially neurological disabilities such as autism or Asperger's disorder, can find the visuals in a classroom to be a problem. While teachers will want to keep their classroom attractive and full of appealing and information displays, they should also consider how they could adapt their class to help all children. The following steps will help make the visual aspect of the class more conducive for all learners.

Mask or cover those items that can easily be distracting. Why one visual may distract a child or complicate his or her learning is not merely a factor of the visual itself. In many cases, the anticipated use in the context can contribute to problems. The presence of a television in the classroom is a perfect example. Many teachers are now fortunate to have larger TV sets in their rooms on a permanent basis. The mere presence of the TV may cause many children to attend to it, perhaps in the hope that they will be watching something of interest. Covering the screen with a cloth can easily reduce or eliminate the visual distraction. Removing the cloth for an instructional activity then provides a clear message for the child to get ready to watch something on the screen.

In some cases, the teacher may wish to remove the visual presence of a classroom items for a specific activity. For example, covering a fish tank or pet cage during test time may reduce the distraction potential. Mobiles or other hanging items can constitute a visual challenge for some children. Low-hanging mobiles present an obvious problem for children with visual impairments. Mobiles by their very nature are moving and offer strong distraction potential for children with attention issues. Carefully consider the placement of such items, perhaps putting them in less used sections of the class and limiting how long they are displayed.

Bulletin boards are a prominent visual in the classroom. Reduce the changes for a bulletin board to become a distraction by having it feature useful information for the students. An excellent idea for the theme of one classroom bulletin board is a classroom motto. Clark (2006) writes of using the motto *Carpe Diem* (seize the day) with his students. Mottos that reflect the inclusive character of the class could feature "Growing and Learning Together." These classroom mottos can provide a daily reminder of important positive messages. They can help unify the spirit of the classroom, a spirit that naturally includes all children.

The spirit of the classroom is impossible to pin down. But it is what teachers strive for and must strive for when they have an inclusive K–3 classroom. The room must be efficiently set up, probably with clustered desks with wide boulevards for the teacher to circulate. Noise, to the degree the teacher can control it, is kept down, and the visual space is free of too much distraction and clutter. But beyond this each teacher will want to stamp her or his room with unique attributes. We are seeing a trend toward incorporating more homelike features in classes, with greater use of lamps with incandescent lights, decorative plants, pets, and perhaps some comfortable chairs. Soft music during reading and independent work time may also help make the classroom a more comfortable place for all. The message sent to children with disabilities is a very positive one: This is a comfortable and inviting place—a place in which I feel safe and in which I will have fun learning with my classmates and friends.

Organizing or Optimizing

In computer-speak, the term *optimizing* means that a hard disk not only is organized to deal with the data it must store but is organized in the most efficient manner possible. It is possible to consider this analogy in relation to the early elementary inclusive classroom. Certainly the teacher wants the room to be well organized. But beyond this it should be as efficient as possible in meeting the many purposes that must be served if a teacher is having all children learning at an optimal level. It may be that terminology will change or is now in the process of changing. Teachers should strive to optimize their classrooms. And, just as with computers, this is something done both on a maintenance basis and, occasionally, on a full-scale basis. With computer hard drives it is relatively easy to click on a disk-optimizing program. It takes more work for teachers to do this. But the results are the same in many ways: less wear and tear and greater speed and efficiency in fulfilling important tasks teaching and learning tasks. Teachers can make this a cooperative adventure with the children by scheduling time for everyone to pitch in and discard unneeded papers and items and to make adjustments that make the class an even more inviting place in which to learn and work (Clayton & Forton, 2001).

The room the teacher sets up the first day of school will undergo many changes and challenges to organizational capacities as time goes by. Keeping things organized is an ongoing process. Involve the students to the greatest degree possible in keeping things organized. However you do it, each teacher will need to be on alert to keep his or her classroom organized, or it will get out of control.

Set aside a brief period of time each day, five or ten minutes should be sufficient, for all members of the class to help keep things organized. Check that all classroom jobs have been completed, ask students to remove unneeded papers or other materials from their desks and dispose of them. Have students help put any stray materials back in their designated places. You may want to use proximity control to bring attention to areas that present a special organizational challenge. Stand in that area and by your presence hope to encourage students to see the organizational challenges as you see them. While the emphasis here is on organization within the classroom, the same can be applied to each child's individual desk and their backpack. These may need weekly reorganizing opportunities. In the daily classroom organization check, you may want to develop a poster or individual check sheet with elements such as those offered by Nations and Boyett (2002, p. 55), seen here in Figure 4.6.

Figure 4.6 ● Classroom organization check.

At the end of the day

Student: Did I . . .	Teacher: Did I . . .
● Check my desk or workspace?	● Check my desk or workspace?
● Write down my homework assignment?	● Prepare by lesson plans?
● Prepare my supplies for tomorrow?	● Gather supplies I will need to teach tomorrow?
● Complete my classroom job?	● Complete my schoolwide jobs/responsibilities?
● Help check the room?	● Put only the things I need in my tote bag, including papers to grade?
● Put only the things I need in my backpack, including any papers I need?	

Expect to teach your students how to help keep things organized. For students who are not yet able to read, a checklist or poster could feature pictures, symbols, or rebuses of the tasks. Such as checklist could be used as part of a point system. Many children, both those with disabilities and those who are now typically developing, may have few chores to do at home. There may be few or no real expectations that a child routinely assist in keeping his or her room and family living areas organized. Plan to teach them how to help, and do not be surprised that this may be something with which they have no experience, except perhaps from school. A useful short book filled with creative approaches to dealing with the challenges of clutter in an elementary classroom is *So Much Stuff, So Little Space* by Nations and Boyett (2002).

In addition to classroom organizing times, set aside a time each week for students to organize their backpacks. Many students will do this without special instruction or prompting. Perhaps their parents do this for them. But many students with disabilities will be less likely to keep their packs organized without specific direction and support.

Cultural Diversity

It is important to consider the cultural diversity among the students in a classroom when setting up the classroom environment. Learning about the culture of the children in your class can be done by conducting interviews, which may be oral or written, meeting with family members, and simply spending time with children informally to understand each child as an individual. Once you learn about the culture of the children, it is important to arrange the classroom, plan instruction, and develop rules and routines that are sensitive to the needs of all children. For example, the cultural structures of many ethnic groups are holistic, group centered, and collaborative. Thus, students from these groups are more likely to prefer cooperative learning arrangements and active and affective interaction within classroom activities (Diaz, 2001, p. 37). Cooperative group and pair arrangements for learning should occur often as opposed to the occasional exception. The format of learning activities should be varied to incorporate more affective responses and movement.

The importance of establishing clear expectations for classroom behavior was discussed earlier in the chapter. This is critical in culturally diverse classrooms because different cultures hold different views about appropriate behavior. For example, a teacher may expect students to sit quietly and listen when someone is talking, but some African American students may be accustomed to more active participation. To avoid confusion or misunderstanding, the teacher needs to engage students in discussions about behavioral expectations, model the expected behavior, and provide opportunities for students to practice (Weinstein, Curran, & Tomlinson-Clarke, 2003).

Developing Rules and Routines

Developing efficient rules and routines assists in creating effective classrooms (Levin & Nolan, 1991). At the core of a well-managed classroom will be a comprehensive management system consisting of rules and routines that are clearly defined, explicitly taught, and continually reinforced. This section will discuss methods for creating and teaching rules and routines in the primary grades to create a foundation for a structured, nurturing, and organized classroom in which all children can learn and grow.

Rules

Creating classroom rules that will enhance the learning environment requires careful consideration and a structured plan for implementation. Simply creating a teacher-generated list of rules and posting it in the classroom will not promote student understanding and meaningful interpretation of the rules and how they impact everyday classroom activities. It is essential to use research-based practices in creating rules, teaching the rules, and reinforcing students who follow the rules.

Creating classroom rules.   When creating classroom rules it is important to involve the students in the process (Charles, 1989). The participation of students in developing classroom rules helps create a feeling of community as well as ownership. Although the teacher should guide the discussion, student involvement is essential. When students are involved in creating the classroom rules, the teacher alone does not create the rationale for each rule.

Once the teacher and students select the behaviors that are critical to building a structured, safe, and nurturing environment, there are several guidelines that should be followed when writing the actual list of rules.

Most important, the rules should be positively stated (Brophy, 1988). This means that the rules indicate what the children are expected to do, as opposed to what they shouldn't do. For example, instead of stating a rule as "No hitting or kicking," state the rule as "Always keep your hands and feet to yourself."

There should also be a limited number of classroom rules. Large numbers of rules are difficult for students to remember—and difficult for teachers to remember as well. The actual number of rules should depend on the developmental level of the students and should include only as many rules as are necessary to foster a positive classroom environment (Emmer, Everston, Sanford, Clements, & Worsham, 1989). Typically, there should be five items or fewer on a list of classroom rules (Walker & Shea, 1991). Since it is important to have a small number of rules, they should be broad enough so that they let students know what behaviors are expected in the classroom at all times throughout the day (Canter, 1989).

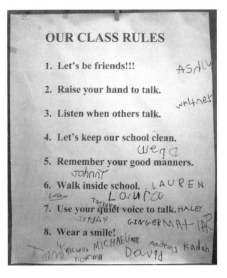

Another consideration for selecting classroom rules is that they should be observable and measurable. Vague rules are difficult for children to understand and difficult for teachers to enforce. For example, a rule such as "Be respectful to others" may be too abstract for children in the primary grades. Instead a rule may state, "Use polite words when talking to others." Because you can observe a child using polite language, it would be quite simple for a teacher to measure whether the student is following the rule. However, measuring whether a child is being "respectful to others" can be much more subjective.

Finally, when choosing classroom rules, be sure they apply to behavior only. Rules should not address academic or homework issues. The purpose of classroom rules is to create the foundation for classroom behavior. Teachers themselves must know how they want their students to behave and then communicate those expectations clearly to the students (Canter & Canter, 1992).

Teaching classroom rules. Teachers cannot assume that students will automatically understand the rules and have the innate ability to comply with the rules. There must be a structured plan for teaching the rules just as there are structured plans for teaching academics. During the first two weeks of school, it is key to provide intensive instruction related to following the classroom rules.

Rules must be explicitly taught to the students. This involves defining the rules and giving examples and nonexamples. If one of the classroom rules states, "If you need help, raise your hand and wait quietly for the teacher," the teacher will need to define what that means. The students will be instructed on the meaning of needing help. For example, needing help may mean a student does not understand the directions for an assignment, a student cannot locate the materials needed, the student is stuck on a particular part of the assignment, etc. The students will also need to be instructed on what "raise your hand and wait quietly for teacher" means. The teacher may tell the students that they should raise their hand straight up in the air without waving it around, look directly at the teacher, and wait for the teacher to come without saying any words.

Once the rule is clearly defined, the teacher can then give examples and nonexamples. Sometimes using humor is effective when giving nonexamples. For example, the teacher may raise her hand, wildly shouting out, "I need help!" to show the students what not to do. Then immediately following the nonexample give the correct example and have students practice the model. The students should not be given the opportunity to practice the nonexample to discourage them from displaying the inappropriate behavior to get laughs from others.

After the rules are defined and examples and nonexamples given, the students should then be given opportunities to demonstrate following the rules. This can be done through role-plays in which the teacher creates scenarios that require the students to use the required behaviors. It is important for the teacher to provide positive reinforcement when the students display the expected behavior. Positive reinforcement will increase the likelihood that a behavior will continue or increase. This can be in the form of specific praise, smiles, high-fives, tokens, etc. It is equally important to provide positive redirection to students not meeting the behavioral expectations. Positive redirection involves helping the child display the appropriate behavior in a supportive manner. This can be a gentle verbal reminder of what is expected ("Remember to keep your hands and feet to yourself"), physical assistance (gently assisting the child to raise his or her hand straight up), or gestural cues (the teacher holds up two fingers to remind the child of rule number two).

In addition to role-plays, the teacher can also provide repeated practice to ensure all students understand the rules and know how to comply. Again, it is important to provide positive feedback for those meeting the expectations and positive redirection for those not meeting the expectations to increase the likelihood that the children will continue to follow the rules.

Art activities are also beneficial in helping students understand the classroom rules. Having students draw pictures or create clay figures or any other artistic representations of themselves following the rules can help children internalize and remember the rules.

Once the children have demonstrated their ability to follow the rules through structured lessons, the teacher must be sure to positively reinforce the students following the rules throughout the course of the day during naturally occurring activities (and positively redirect when necessary). While the teacher should provide intensive instruction for rule following during the first two weeks of school, it is necessary to provide continual feedback to students related to following the rules throughout all of the school days. Sometimes the teacher may need to schedule some "booster sessions" if behaviors seem to be declining. Logically it makes sense to do so after students are on vacation or after long weekends, but structured lessons on the rules may need to be delivered throughout the course of the year as needed.

It is vital not to display anger or deliver intensive negative consequences when students have difficulty following rules. Punishment accompanied with anger creates stress among students and increases the likelihood that the inappropriate behaviors will continue (Henley, 2005). Instead, the teacher may have to schedule another lesson to teach a specific rule, provide more positive redirection, and be sure to acknowledge the students meeting the behavioral expectations. Students who meet the expectations after being positively redirected should be given immediate positive reinforcement.

Once the rules are established, the teacher should ensure the parents of the students are informed about the rules. This can be done through a letter to parents, a classroom newsletter, parent night (open house), weekly behavior checklists, etc. The rules should certainly be posted visibly in the classroom as reminders for students, parents, and any other adults that enter the classroom.

Rules outside of the classroom. In addition to classroom rules, teachers will need to teach rules for various environments within the school. This may include rules for the cafeteria, hallway, and the playground. For example, young children will need to explicit teaching related to going through the line in the cafeteria, maintaining appropriate volume while eating, and procedures for throwing garbage away. Additionally, they will need to learn the expectations for walking through the hallway, which may include hands at their sides, silent voices, staying on the designated painted lines, and stopping at corners. Young children will also need explicit instruction related to playground and recess. They may learn about the amount of children permitted to be on the equipment at one time, the physical boundaries for other physical games, acceptable contact during game playing, and the cues to attend to for lining up to go back into the classroom. Regardless of the environment in which the rules are applied, the teacher must still explicitly teach the behavioral expectations just as is necessary for classroom rules.

Routines

While classroom rules inform the students of general behavioral expectations, clearly defined routines are also essential to create classrooms that are productive, orderly, and pleasant. **Routines** are procedures for participating in daily classroom activities. Establishing specific routines for managing materials, transitioning between activities, various instructional formats, and other special situations helps increase instructional time and student involvement in appropriate learning activities (Brophy & Good, 1986; Mercer & Mercer, 1993).

Examples of instructional formats in K–3 classrooms include circle time, centers, small-group instruction, whole-group instruction, and cooperative learning groups. Clearly established routines for these various formats will help young children understand the different behavioral and academic expectations. For example, during circle time the children may be permitted to participate in choral responding, but in whole-group instruction children may be required to answer only after the teacher calls their names.

Transitions in the K–3 classroom may include changing from one instructional format to another, going to the bathroom, getting a drink, lining up to leave the classroom, and rotating through different centers. Without clearly established routines for transitions such as these, young children may have difficulty transitioning smoothly, which may result in longer transition periods and potentially disruptive behaviors. Similarly, teaching routines for managing materials, such as sharpening pencils, retrieving and returning supplies, and turning in assignments, will minimize classroom disruptions and increase time children are engaged in academic activities.

In addition to instructional formats, transitions, and managing materials, other special situations will arise that require clearly established routines. For example, if the children are going on a field trip to the theater, behavioral expectations will need to be discussed related to riding on the bus, attending during the presentation, and eating a picnic lunch off school grounds. Other special situations may include going to the nurse, arriving to school late, leaving school early, fire drills, and school assemblies.

The format used for teaching classroom rules should also be used for teaching routines. A rationale for the routine should be discussed. For example, students may learn that a routine for center time is necessary so that all students get the opportunity to visit each center and the materials are handled properly. The teacher should then explicitly teach the routine. Each step needs to be defined and demonstrated. Students should be given many opportunities to practice the routine, receiving positive reinforcement when meeting the expectations and positive redirection when they do not. It is important to be consistent with expecting students to follow the routines and provide structured review lessons when necessary. Table 4.3 shows examples of routines that may be part of a classroom for children in the primary grades. In general, routines help create a classroom environment that is predictable, safe, and well managed. Ms. Bonino, a former special teacher and district ESE supervisor, is the principal of the only primary school in Palm Beach County. Her inclusive school has grades kindergarten through second grade and nearly 1,000 students. Ms. Bonino provides advice aimed at new teachers on how to organize their inclusive early elementary classroom,

Table 4.3 • Routines

Instructional Routines	Transitions	Managing Materials	Special Situations
Circle time	Between instructional activities	Storing/retrieving personal materials	Going to the nurse
Small-group instruction	Leaving the classroom for lunch, specials, etc.	Accessing/returning shared materials	Leaving school early
Whole-group instruction	Using the bathroom/getting a drink	Turning in assignments	Attending assemblies
Cooperative learning	Entering the class in the morning	Sharpening pencils	Attending field trips
Centers	Packing up in the afternoon		Fire drills
			Having a guest in the classroom

and in Table 4.4 Ms. Bonino gives suggestions aimed at meeting the needs of children with special needs in inclusive classrooms.

Finally, a teacher needs to plan for behavioral considerations in an inclusive classroom. Rules should be simply stated and clear. A behavior management system should be written, explained, practiced, and monitored consistently. A weekly/daily behavior communication tool should be implemented so that the students' parents are getting timely and accurate information about their children's behavior. It is also important that teachers provide frequent, short breaks during instruction so as to minimize inappropriate off-task behavior. While it is impossible to provide an exhaustive list of all the items one needs to consider when setting up an inclusive classroom, the measures described here would be beneficial for all students.

Playground/Recess

Outside playtime is often considered to be less important than indoor academic activities in light of the pressure for students to pass high-stakes tests and perform higher academically at younger and younger ages. Teachers are focusing more and more of their time on direct instruction and preparing

Table 4.4 ● Meeting the Needs of Children With Special Needs in Inclusive Classrooms

Lesson Presentation	Instructional Tasks/ Assignments	Test-Taking	Behavior
Have student face presentation area	Teacher should stand near student when giving directions	Allow open books/notes	Simply stated rules
Provide pre/post organizers	Check for understanding of oral directions	Allow tape-recorded answers	Weekly/daily behavior communication tool
Break lessons into smaller segments	Allow extra time to complete assignments	Give oral exams	Provide frequent, short breaks during instruction
Utilize several modalities	Provide flexibility in grading	Allow extra time for test-taking	
Write key points on board/ overhead	Allow tape-recorded or computer-printed assignments	Allow flexible setting/ grouping for exam	
Pre-teach vocabulary	Provide a "study buddy"	Allow transcription (scribe)	
Seat student near a positive role model	Show a completed model of finished products	Allow student to respond on a computer	
		Provide a modified format for the test	

Source: Lori Bonino, principal, Lighthouse Elementary School, Jupiter, Florida.

for tests. As a result there is less time for physical activity or creative play (Hennger, 1993). This emphasis on academic achievement often leads to teachers and administrators overlooking the benefits of outside playtime. According to Wellhousen (2002), "Today, the basic need to play outdoors is largely overlooked and the multitude of opportunities to learn from the outdoors is underestimated in most early childhood programs serving children from infancy through third grade" (p. 2). Playing outside offers children many opportunities to enhance physical development and foster positive social skills. When children play outside they interact with one another as well as with different types of nature through the use of play materials such as sand, water, grass, and trees. Outside play provides children with the opportunities to develop gross motor, cooperative, and communicative skills while at the same time developing their imaginations through pretend play.

It is necessary for school administrators, teachers, and parents to create outside playground environments for children to use. Children need a safe and well-planned outside environment in which to play, exercise, explore nature, and interact with one another, and develop friendships. The school playground should be accessible to all children, those with and without disabilities. Playgrounds should have curb cuts, wide gates, and walkways. Surface materials should be shock absorbent yet provide a solid surface to accommodate wheelchairs, strollers, walkers, or canes. Braille markers and audible cues that are associated with certain play areas are beneficial for students with visual impairments. Adapted swings, prone standers, and larger balls are just a few items that can facilitate playtime for children with physical disabilities. Frisbee, basketball, parachute games, hopscotch, and tether ball are all activities that use a number of different senses and might appeal to a student with a hearing impairment (Kieff & Flynn, 2005).

Additional Playground Materials

One way that children learn is by interacting with and trying to change their environment. While most indoor play equipment such as blocks, costumes, and puzzles can be manipulated by children, outside play equipment does not usually offer children such opportunities. Teachers can easily change this by adding manipulative equipment to the outside play environment. Dramatic play props such as costumes, dishes, a telephone, baby dolls, and strollers can be added to a playground playhouse. The addition of props can help children who have special needs engage in pretend play activities (Klein, Cook, & Richardson-Gibbs, 2001). Hennger (1993) suggests the idea of creating a camp area for dramatic play. Setting up a tent, adding sleeping bags, cooking equipment, and a fire pit (without the fire) will allow the children to pretend to be anything from Cub or Girl Scouts to explorers of ancient civilizations.

Safety Issues

The United States Consumer Products Safety Commission (1997) has written guidelines for public playground equipment, including child care facilities and schools. These guidelines include recommendations for supervision, surface materials, and use zones for equipment.

The first concern identified by the United States Consumer Products Safety commission (USCPSC) is the safety of children when using playground equipment. Children will often use playground equipment in ways that are unintended and/or unexpected, and therefore it is recommended that there always be adult supervision on a playground. In order to properly supervise playground use, adults need to be able to see all areas of the playground from where they are standing.

Fences are an important safety feature of a playground. Fences can prevent children from leaving a play area without adult permission or supervision. They can prevent a child from inadvertently running into a street without looking while chasing a ball or toy. Furthermore, fences can help prevent strangers from entering the playground area.

In the handbook by the USCPSC there are recommendations for the surface materials used under and around the playground equipment. The more shock-absorbing a surface can be the less likely there is to be a serious injury from a fall. There are two types of acceptable surface material: unitary and loose-fill. Unitary materials are generally rubber mats or a combination of rubberlike materials that are held together by a binder such as polyurethane. Examples of loose-fill materials include sand, shredded wood products, and shredded tires. Loose materials can have adequate shock absorbency when installed and maintained to be a sufficient depth. The handbook includes a chart providing the minimum depth for each type of loose material. These types of materials should never be installed over concrete or asphalt, although concrete or asphalt can be used as a base for a unitary material.

There are a number of unsuitable materials for use under or around playground equipment. These materials include concrete, asphalt, hard-packed soil, and hard-packed dirt. Grass and turf are also not recommended because, unless they are properly maintained, the wear and tear can significantly reduce their shock absorbency.

When planning the layout of a playground, it is essential to consider each piece of equipment's use zone. The use zone is the area under and around a piece of playground equipment where surface material is required and activity and movement can be expected. The use zone for stationary equipment, with the exception of a slide, should extend a minimum of six feet in all directions around the perimeter of the equipment. The handbook provides specific guidelines on use zones for slides, swings, merry-go-rounds, and spring rockers. To summarize these guidelines, there must be adequate space provided for a child to swing with his or her legs stretched out, exit a slide, or run around a merry-go-round. Use zones for all pieces of equipment should not overlap.

Playground equipment should be organized into different areas to prevent injuries. Physical activity areas should be set away from less active areas such as sandboxes. Adequate space should be maintained between types of equipment to avoid over crowding in one area due to heavy use of one particular piece of equipment. Focusing the exit area of a slide toward a vacant area will help to prevent accidents.

The USCPSC has developed a public playground safety checklist with ten important tips to help ensure playground safety:

1. Make sure surfaces around playground equipment have at least 12 inches of wood chips, mulch, sand, or pea gravel, or are mats made of safety-tested rubber or rubber-like materials.
2. Check that protective surfacing extends at least 6 feet in all directions from play equipment. For swings, be sure surfacing extends in back and front, twice the height of the suspending bar.
3. Make sure play structures more than 30 inches high are spaced at least 9 feet apart.
4. Check for dangerous hardware, like open "S" hooks or protruding bold ends.
5. Make sure spaces that could trap children, such as openings in guardrails or between ladder rungs, measure less than 3.5 inches or more than 9 inches.

Playground/Recess

6. Check for sharp points or edges in equipment.
7. Look out for tripping hazards, like exposed concrete footing, tree stumps, and rocks.
8. Make sure elevated surfaces, like platforms and ramps, have guardrails to prevent falls.
9. Check playground regularly to see that equipment and surfacing are in good condition.
10. Carefully supervise children on playgrounds to make sure they're safe (USCPSC, 1997).

Social Skills and Social Interactions on the Playground

Playground and outside playtime offer wonderful opportunities for all children to develop social skills. Children must practice turn-taking skills while waiting for a swing or a turn on the slide. They learn negotiating skills when creating and playing games. Sharing skills are learned when children use toys, balls, buckets, shovels, and other equipment on the playground. Children practice cooperation skills when playing on a team or digging in a sandbox.

Teachers can do a number of things to increase the interaction of children with and without disabilities while on the playground. To begin, teachers should not allow children to spend their recess time with the adults. These children need to be encouraged to interact with their peers. A teacher can facilitate this interaction by arranging for a buddy system, arranging in advance for buddies who will play together on the playground. In order to help some children with disabilities interact on the playground, the teacher may need to have the peer buddy participate in an activity that the child enjoys and is comfortable with rather than encouraging the child with a disability to try a new activity (Beninghof, 1997).

Teachers need to emphasize the importance of play as a social activity within their classes. One way for teachers to do this is to play with their students. Teachers can help to organize a game of catch or Frisbee or have tea with a group of children playing house. Doing so models appropriate play and social skills for children who may have difficulty with these activities. Teachers should be aware of the need to create organized activities for children who are unable to create activities independently. Teachers should also talk with their students about the types of play activities they participate in outside of school. Learning about the types of activities children enjoy at home will allow the teacher to incorporate those activities into recess at school.

One way for a teacher to support the importance of play is to bring outside play into the classroom. Teachers can display photographs of children playing kickball, the block structures children have created, or children playing house on the playground (Brewer, 2004). They can have children write essays or stories about what they enjoy about playing outside or their favorite playground game.

Playground Rules

Playground or recess time should be considered an extension of the classroom environment, and therefore rules that are put into place in the classroom should apply to the playground as well. At the beginning of the school year it will be important to review these rules with the class before going to recess. In addition, the teacher would be wise to include safety rules for use of the playground. These safety rules should include information on how to avoid being hit by someone on a swing, the importance of only sliding down the slide one person at a time, and not throwing a ball directly at someone's head.

Scheduling

Schedules help to make sure that the goals and objectives of each school day are met in an organized and timely fashion. They allow students to know what subjects will be taught and activities will be accomplished during the day. Many students, those with and without special needs, will benefit from the structure a daily schedule provides. Creating a schedule with pictures and words makes the schedule accessible to most students. Scheduling may involve two types of schedules, one for the entire day and one for a specific lesson or activity (Smith, Polloway, Patton, & Dowdy, 2004).

Thoughtful and well-planned daily scheduling can ensure that adequate class time has been allocated to teach the various subject areas. Preparing a schedule in advance helps the teacher to alternate highly preferred activities with less preferred activities. For example, if show-and-tell is a preferred activity and social studies is not, schedule social studies first and show and tell after (Mercer & Mercer, 1993). Scheduling in advance allows the teacher to alternate hands-on, or kinesthetic, activities with ones requiring more focus and less activity. This might involve scheduling a physically active task, for instance physical education class, after an activity that involves a great deal of thought, such as a math lesson.

When planning the day's schedule it is also important for the teacher to take into account each type of activity planned for the day. Examples of activities that occur in most classrooms every day include teacher-directed lessons, cooperative learning groups, independent assignments, and physically active tasks. Varying these types of activities throughout the day will help to keep students actively engaged and enthusiastic about learning. For example, if the social studies lesson for the day will require the students to listen to a lecture and then complete an independent reading and writing assignment, it may be wise to schedule a task that requires movement or cooperative learning, such as science, after the social studies lesson.

When developing the daily schedule the teacher is advised to consider the needs of individual children. While it is not always possible to plan for each individual child, thoughtful planning can help to prevent some behavior and learning problems in the classroom. For example, if you have a student who has a behavioral disorder and consistently has difficulty during math in the afternoon, you might consider moving math to the morning, when this child is fresh, rested, and more prone to learning.

Teachers of primary-aged students are generally responsible for the majority of the instruction that occurs during the school day. With the exception of lunch and specials such as physical education, music, art, or library, the elementary classroom teacher is usually responsible for instruction in all subject areas. This requires a great deal of planning, from beginning of the school day activities to preparing to go home at the end of the day (Mercer & Mercer, 1993).

A daily schedule must be broken down into all the tasks and activities that must be accomplished over the course of a school day. Starting with the beginning of the school day, there are many tasks that must be accomplished. These tasks may include unpacking for the day, taking attendance, collecting lunch money, turning in homework assignments, listening to morning announcements, saluting the flag, reading notes from parents, and delivering the attendance and lunch count to the front office. Scheduling an independent activity during this time period can help to ensure that all morning tasks are accomplished in a timely and organized manner. Examples of independent tasks may include silent reading, buddy reading, solving a math challenge problem, working on a crossword puzzle or completing a class job. Class jobs allow students to learn responsibility while providing them with a sense of belonging within the class. Class jobs may include taking attendance, collecting homework assignments, watering plants, helping classmates unpack for the day, or changing the class calendar.

The majority of time within the school day will be spent teaching the specific curriculum areas. Careful planning of these periods will help to efficiently use the time and ensure that students are actively engaged in learning. Furthermore, within each subject area lesson there is contained a number of components including the transition from one lesson or activity, grabbing student attention, teacher presentation of material, guided and independent practice, and closure. Planning for transitions, providing visual reminders, minimizing the amount of time in which students are not academically engaged, and encouraging students to complete one task before moving on to another will help to ensure that each lesson schedule runs smoothly (Smith, Polloway, Patton, & Dowdy, 2004).

Sample Schedule for Third Grade

8:00–8:15	Get ready for school day, unpack, turn in homework, attendance, lunch count, independent activity (e.g., math challenge problem on board)
8:15–10:15	Reading/language arts
10:15–10:30	Snack/bathroom break
10:30–11:30	Math
11:30–12:20	Lunch/recess
12:20–12:40	Silent reading time
12:40–1:30	Science
1:30–2:00	Special (PE: Tuesday & Thursday; Art: Monday; Computer Lab: Wednesday; Music: Friday)
2:00–3:00	Social studies
3:00–3:30	Center time
3:30–3:45	Pack-up/dismissal

Sample Schedule for Kindergarten

8:00–8:20	Unpack, lunch count, attendance, independent morning work
8:20–8:45	Circle time/morning meeting
8:45–9:45	Reading/language arts
9:45–10:00	Bathroom break
10:00–10:45	Snack/center time
10:45–11:45	Math
11:45–12:45	Lunch/recess
12:45–1:00	Bathroom break/story time
1:00–1:15	Show and tell
1:15–2:00	Science

2:00–2:30	Special (Art: Tuesdays; PE: Monday and Wednesday; Computer Lab: Friday; Music: Thursday)
2:30–3:00	Social studies
3:00–3:30	Center time
3:30–3:45	Clean-up/pack-up/dismissal

Summary

For the instructional and social elements of an inclusive classroom to be successful, a well-planned and well-organized environment is essential. Classroom organization must accommodate different types of instruction and activities, including large-group instruction, small-group instruction, individual instruction, cooperative learning, and centers. In the inclusive K–3 classroom, this organization should be done as part of a collaborative team rather than as an individual process by one teacher.

Organization includes decisions on how the space will be utilized. Arrangement of student desks, storage of materials, creation of work and play areas, and traffic flow patterns must be considered. Clustered seating provides many advantages including supporting a shared learning process, engagement in cooperative learning, promoting the learning of cooperation skills, and building a sense of a classroom "community." Thoughtful seating arrangements are important, because frequently rearranging a classroom can be difficult for young children who have a hard time adjusting to a change in routine.

Classroom organization is more than just the organization of the class space. Good organization includes classroom rules and routines. Rules and routines that are clearly defined, explicitly taught, and continually reinforced are essential in an effective classroom. Organization extends outside of the classroom. Playtime is often considered to be less important than academic activities; however, playtime offers children many opportunities to enhance physical development and increase positive social skills. Teachers must provide structure, rules, and routines for environments such as the lunch room or playground to ensure their safe and appropriate use.

Thinking It Through

1. Margot is a first grader who has autism. Currently Margot's desk is located near the classroom teacher's desk. The current room arrangement consists of student desks being placed in pairs, with Margot's "partner" being the classroom teacher. Margot is progressing academically in this setting. However, her social skills remain below those of her peers. Using the information from the text, design a classroom layout to help her increase the number of positive interactions Margot has with her peers.

2. Create a list of classroom rules. Describe how you will explain and teach these rules to your class. This could include modeling, guided practice, role-play, etc.

3. Brainstorm a list of times throughout a school day in which your class and students will go through a transition. This might include arriving at school, preparing to go to lunch, or turning in a completed assignment. Select two of these necessary transitions, and develop a routine to teach your students to make this transition go smoothly.

4. Consider the idea of adding materials to the playground environment that was discussed in this chapter. Design an activity that would foster social interaction and inclusion of all students at recess by adding props or materials. What materials or props would you add? What activity would you have students engage in?

5. Explain why it is important in a collaborative environment to work together when designing the physical space of the classroom, including wall space, furniture, and materials.

References

Adams, R. S. (1969). Location as a feature of instructional interaction. *Merrill Palmer Quarterly, 15*(4), 309–321.

Adams, R. S., & Biddle, B. (1970). *Realities of teaching: Exploration with videotape.* New York: Hold, Rinehart, and Winston.

Beninghof, A. M. (1997). *Ideas for inclusion: The classroom teacher's guide to integrating students with severe disabilities.* Longmont, CO: Sopris West.

Berg, F. S. (1993). *Acoustics and sound systems in schools.* San Diego: Singular.

Brewer, J. A. (2004). *Introduction to early childhood education: Preschool through primary grades.* Boston: Pearson Education.

Brophy, J. (1988). Educating teachers about managing classrooms and students. *Teaching and Teacher Education, 4*(1), 1–18.

Brophy, J. E., & Good, T. L. (1986). Teacher behavior and student achievement. In M. D. Wikttrock (Ed.), *Handbook of research on teaching* (3rd ed., pp. 328–375). New York: Macmillan.

Canter, L. (1989). Assertive discipline: More than names on the board and marbles in a jar. *Phi Delta Kappan, 71,* 57–61.

Canter, L., & Canter, M. (1992). *Assertive discipline: Positive behavior for today's classroom.* Santa Monica, CA: Lee Canter.

Charles, C. (1989). *Building classroom discipline: From models to practice* (3rd ed.). New York: Longman.

Clark, R. (2006, January/February). Getting kids to go for it. *Instructor,* p. 34.

Clayton, M. K., & Forton, M. B. (2001). *Classroom spaces that work.* Turners Falls, MA: Northeast Foundation for Children.

Conn-Powers, M., Cross, A. F., Traub, E. K., & Hutter-Pishgahi, L. (2006, September). The Universal Design of early education: Moving forward for all children.

Journal of the National Association for the Education of Young Children, pp. 1–7.

Diaz, C. F. (2001). *Multicultural education for the 21st century.* New York: Addison Wesley Longman.

Doyle, W. (1986). Classroom organization and management. In M. C. Wittrock (Ed.), *Handbook of research on teaching* (3rd ed., pp. 392–431). New York: Macmillian.

Emmer, E. T., Everston, C., Sanford, J., Clements, B., & Worsham, M. (1989). *Classroom management for secondary teachers* (2nd ed.). Englewood Cliffs, NJ: Prentice-Hall.

Evans, W. H., Evans, S. S., Gable, R. A., & Schmid, R. E. (1991). Instructional management for detecting and correcting special problems. Boston: Allyn and Bacon.

Friend, M., & Cook, L. (2003). *Interactions: Collaborative skills for school professionals* (4th ed.). Boston: Allyn and Bacon.

Henley, M. (2005). *Classroom management: A proactive approach.* Columbus, OH: Merrill/Prentice Hall.

Hennger, M. L. (1993). Enriching the outdoor play experience. *Childhood Education, 70*(2), 87–91.

Isenberg, J. P., & Quisenberry, N. (1988). *Play: A necessity for all children.* Retrieved October 30, 2006, from www.acei.org/playpaper.htm

Johnson, S. (1967). *A dictionary of the English language. Vol. II.* New York: AMS Press. (Original work published 1755, London: Strahan)

Jones, F. H. (2000). *Tools for teaching.* Hong Kong: Fred H. Jones & Associates.

Jonson, K. F. (2002) *The new elementary teacher's handbook* (2nd ed.). Thousand Oaks, CA: Corwin Press.

Kieff, J., & Flynn, L. (2005). Including students with special needs in outdoor play. In K. G. Gurrias & B. F. Boyd (Eds.), *Outdoor learning and play ages 8–12* (pp. 27–35). Olney, MD: ACEI.

Klein, M. D., Cook, R. E., & Richardson-Gibbs, A. M. (2001).

Strategies for including children with special needs in early childhood settings. Albany, NY: Delmar.

Kluth, P. (2003). *You're going to love this kid.* Baltimore: Paul H. Brookes.

Kronowitz, E. L. (1999) *Your first year of teaching and beyond* (3rd ed.). New York: Longman.

Levin, J., & Nolan, J. (1991). *Principles of classroom management: A hierarchical approach.* Englewood Cliffs, NJ: Prentice-Hall.

Mason, C., Orkwis, R., & Scott, R. (2005). Instructional theories supporting universal design for learning-teaching to individual learners. In Council for Exceptional Children and Merrill Education (Eds.), *Universal design for learning: A guide for teachers and education professionals.* Upper Saddle River, NJ: Prentice Hall.

McIntosh, K., Herman, K., Sanford, A., McGraw, K., & Florence, K. (2004). Teaching transitions: Techniques for promoting success between lessons. *Teaching Exceptional Children, 37*(2), 32–38.

McNary, S. J., Glasgow, N. A., & Kicks, C. D. (2005). *What successful teachers do in inclusive classrooms.* Thousand Oaks, CA: Corwin Press.

Mercer, C. D., & Mercer, A. R. (1993). *Teaching students with learning problems* (7th ed.). Upper Saddle River, NJ: Pearson.

Montessori, M. (1912). *The Montessori method.* Anne Everett George, Trans. New York: Frederick A. Stokes.

Nations, S., & Boyett, S. (2002). *So much stuff, so little space: Creating and managing the learner-centered classroom.* Gainesville, FL: Maupin House.

No Child Left Behind Act of 2001 (ESEA), Healthy and High Performance Schools. P. L. 107-110

Patton, J. E., Snell, J., Knight, W., Willis, R., & Gerken, K. (2001). A survey study of elementary classroom seating designs. (ERIC Document 454–194)

Quill, K. A. (2000). *Do-watch-listen-say: Social and communication intervention for children with autism.* Baltimore: Paul H. Brookes.

Rydeen, J. (2002). A positive environment. *American School and University, 75*(2), 36, 38–39.

Schrenko, L. (1994). *Structuring a learner-centered school.* Palatine, IL: IRI/Skylight Publishing.

Scott, S. S., McGuire, J. M., & Foley, T. (2003). Universal Design for Instruction: A framework for anticipating and responding to disability and other diverse learning needs in the college classroom. *Equity & Excellence in Education, 36,* pp. 40–49.

Seep, B., Glosemeyer, R., Hulce, E., Linn, M., & Aytar, P. (2000). *Classroom acoustics: A resource for creating learning environments with desirable listening conditions.* Melville, NY: Acoustical Society of America.

Siebein, G. W., & Gold, M. A. (2000). Ten ways to provide a high-quality acoustical environment in schools. *Language, Speech, and Hearing Services in Schools, 31,* pp. 376–384.

Smith, T. E. C., Polloway, E., Patton, J. R., & Dowdy, C. A. (2004). *Teaching students with special needs in inclusive settings.* Boston: Pearson Education.

Stoecklin, V. L. (1999). *Designing for all children.* Kansas City, MO: White Hutchinson Group.

Strohmer, J. C., & Carhart, C. (1997). *Time-saving tips for teachers.* Thousand Oaks, CA: Corwin Press.

Tiegerman-Farber, E., & Radziewicz, C. (1998). *Collaborative decision-making: Pathway to inclusion.* Upper Saddle River, NJ: Merrill.

Walker, J., & Shea, T. (1991). *Behavior management: A practical approach for educators* (5th ed.). New York: Macmillan.

Warner, J., & Bryan, C. (1995). The unauthorized teacher's survival guide. Indianapolis, IN: JIST Works.

Watkins, D. E. (2005). Maximizing learning for student with special needs. *Kappa Delta Pi Record, 41*(4), 154–158.

Weinstein, C., Curran, M. & Tomlinson-Clarke, S. (2003). Culturally responsive classroom management: Awareness into action. *Theory Into Practice, 42*(4), 269–275.

Wellhousen, K. (2002). *Outdoor play every day: Innovative play concepts for early childhood.* Albany, NY: Delmar Thomson Learning.

Wilke, R. L. (2003). *The first days of class: A practical guide for the beginning teacher.* Thousand Oaks, CA: Corwin Press.

Wong, H. K., & Wong, R. T. (1998). *How to be an effective teacher: The first days of school.* Mountain View, CA: Harry K. Wong.

Positive Behavioral Supports in the Classroom

Michelle LaRocque

Objectives

After reading this chapter, the student will be able to

- Describe the rationale for an environment in a blended classroom that organizes space, time, and materials to ensure students safety and addresses children's age, background, and exceptionality.

- Identify and demonstrate the appropriate use of instructional materials and resources to create a climate conducive to developing prosocial and academic skills.

- Describe theories, models, laws, and strategies associated with the behavior of young children with and without exceptionalities.

- Identify developmentally appropriate cultural and individual differences in conflict issues and strategies.

- Demonstrate sensitivity to diverse children and families and identify strategies to provide for their needs.

- Identify and apply skills that contribute to the development of social, emotional, and self-advocacy skills.

- Identify and apply skills that contribute to their development as ethical, reflective, and responsive practitioners.

Key Terms

Challenging behavior	Positive behavior support
Prosocial skills	Functional behavioral assessment
Modeling	Social competence

Practical Application Vignette

Ms. Mathews has been teaching first grade at Oak Park Elementary School for two years. Though she loves her job and the children, she often goes home frustrated and feeling as though she did not accomplish everything she had hoped for. Today was a perfect example. She thought her students would enjoy using M & M's for their math lesson but couldn't believe how difficult it had been. In particular, Doug and Jose argued over who received more M & M's (she had given each student the same amount), who received better colors (!), and whether and when they could eat them. Ms. Mathews's attempts to calm them down by explaining they all received the same amount, the color combinations were random, and she would let them know when they could eat them proved futile. Their arguing soon escalated into grabbing one another's candy. The remaining students in their cluster of four soon got into the act, and everyone began shouting and shoving. Ms. Mathews tried to gather up all the remaining M & M's while separating students, asking others to pick some off of the floor, and trying to make sure that the remaining students at other groups did not emulate this behavior. Ms. Mathews was heartbroken. She thought that the use of what she believed was a motivating element (candy) would reduce misbehavior and that everyone would learn in a fun environment. She prided herself on being an excellent classroom manager but left the school in tears that day.

As Ms. Mathews is realizing, supporting children in the inclusive classroom offers teachers many opportunities and challenges. The opportunity to be responsive to the needs of a variety of children is a chance for teachers to demonstrate the full range of their knowledge and skills. However, one of the greatest tests to meeting the needs of all children is children who exhibit challenging behavior. **Challenging behavior** can get in the way of teachers teaching and students learning. Challenging behavior is just that. It is any behavior that challenges children's ability to safely learn, develop, and/or play. It may be harmful to the child, other children, or adults and does not lend itself to a warm classroom climate.

Creating a climate that is conducive to learning is critical, and teachers need knowledge of several things: (1) why challenging behavior is occurring, (2) what can be done to prevent it, (3) how to encourage more appropriate behavior, and (4) what to do when challenging behavior occurs.

Many textbooks on student behavior begin with frightening statistics on how dangerous the classroom has become before they go on to list strategies for containing these troublesome students. The focus of intervention is the student and what can be done to the student to get him or her to behave. Often titles contain references to "managing," "controlling," or "changing" students rather than teaching or interacting with them. What is often overlooked is the idea that behavior can be

affected by many things, including where we are, why we are there, who we are with, and what we are doing.

Directing attention toward one aspect of behavior and ignoring other elements is not likely to be a successful or pleasant experience for the teacher or the student. While classrooms need to be orderly places where students can learn, academic learning is not the only learning that takes place in the classroom. Classrooms are also important places that can facilitate the development of socially desirable behaviors that will lead to positive interactions with peers, teachers, family members, and other adults.

The National Association for the Education of Young Children (NAEYC) provides guidelines for practices in the classroom that are developmentally appropriate and take into account individual student needs and the context in which they live (Bredekamp, 1987; Bredekamp & Copple, 1997). The Division of Early Childhood (DEC) of the Council for Exceptional Children (CEC) also supports strategies that are comprehensive, individualized, and positive (DEC, 1999). Specifically, behavioral goals in the classroom emphasize self-esteem, self-control, and concern for others. To further these goals, NAEYC and DEC define the teacher's role as one of acceptance, support, and promotion of desirable behavior through prevention, redirection, and collaboration. This chapter will help you identify strategies to meet these goals.

Why Challenging Behavior May Occur

Biological

New information about infants' and young children's brain development is influencing the way educators view this critical time period. Knowledge of how the brain develops and what factors influence its optimal growth can help adults respond effectively to the needs of children. From the beginning of life a child's genetic influences are working together with factors from his or her environment. Biological factors are rarely the only cause of challenging behavior, but there is a complex interplay between biology and environment. For example, while there are traits associated with aggressive behavior, generally the interaction with the environment results in specific behavior problems. Other factors that may interact with the environment include the following:

1. ***Pregnancy complications, prenatal stress, and/or prematurity.*** Research is beginning to uncover the neuropsychological effects of numerous factors during pregnancy. For example, prematurity predisposes a baby to brain injury and may deprive it of the nourishment it needs (Shonkoff & Phillips, 2000). The result is that premature and low-birth-weight babies are more likely to incur problems associated with the development of aggression such as speech and language disorders, perceptual difficulties, and problems with balance and coordination.

2. ***Mother's drug, alcohol, or tobacco use during pregnancy.*** Substance abuse can reduce the growth and development of babies developing nervous system during pregnancy. The amount of harm depends on various factors including the stage of development and how long the exposure occurs. The overall health of the mother and the fetus also seems to play a role, as does the mother's behavior after birth (Shonkoff & Phillips, 2000). Maternal depression is associated with poor developmental outcomes. For optimal development, mothers should have regular prenatal doctor visits and refrain from substances that may harm their babies.

3. ***Developmental delays.*** On December 3, 2004, President George Bush signed the Individuals with Disabilities Education Improvement Act of 2004 (IDEA), a reauthorization of the nation's law that works to improve results for infants, toddlers, children and youth with disabilities. For children aged 3 through 9 under IDEA, states and local educational agencies (LEAs) are allowed to use the term "developmental delay" with children rather than one of the thirteen disability categories listed below. This means that, if they choose, states and LEAs do not have to say that a child has a specific disability. For children aged 3 through 9, a state and LEA may choose to include as an eligible "child with a disability" a child who is experiencing developmental delays in one or more of the following areas:

- Physical development
- Cognitive development
- Communication development
- Social or emotional development
- Adaptive development

. . . and who, because of the developmental delays, needs special education and related services.

"Developmental delays" are defined by the state and must be measured by appropriate diagnostic instruments and procedures. However, some children with more specific disabilities may have been identified using one of the thirteen disability categories.

The IDEA lists thirteen different disability categories under which 3- through 21-year-olds may be eligible for services. For a child to be eligible for services, the disability must affect the child's educational performance. Table 5.1 lists the disability categories and *possible* behavioral areas of concern, and the accommodation and modification recommendations provide some basic information for teachers.

It is important to note that across all disabilities categories there exists interindividual variation and intraindividual variation. Interindividual variation refers to the idea that children, even children with the same disability may not be exactly alike. Intraindividual variation means that even within the same child, a great deal of variation may exist. For example, the child who has great social skills and behavior at school may wreak havoc at home. So while motivational difficulties and learned helplessness may be traits found in *some* young children, by no means does it encompass *all* children with or without disabilities.

4. ***Gender/age.*** There is no denying the fact that girls and boys do have many different social and emotional characteristics, but the majority of studies have not found *consistent* gender difference in how they respond to others. Gender may play a role in challenging behavior, but it is

not clear whether this is a matter of biology or environment. In some studies, boys rated higher than girls on *physical* aggression in every age group, but aggressive behavior in girls can take many forms and may be more covert. Unfortunately, aggression in females is becoming more common. How children are raised seems to have more of an impact than gender. In families and cultures where aggressive behavior is more tolerated, boys are at greater risk for aggressive behavior than girls (Berk, 2000).

Regardless of gender, age does seem to play a role in challenging behavior. While parents frequently report that their children display problematic behavior during the toddler and early child-hood years, most behavior problems are transient. At a young age, as children become more adept at controlling their environment, they may use aggression to obtain and maintain their activities and possessions. The National Longitudinal Survey of Children and Youth (Tremblay et al., 1996) found that the use of physical aggression peaks between the ages of 27 and 29 months. Age or biological maturity is often considered a factor in the development of prosocial behavior, caring behavior that is intended to help another person. As children mature and encounter socializing experiences, they develop more prosocial strategies to obtain what they want. From the age of 30 months on, physical aggression declines. This is important, as the longer a child continues to use aggressive behavior, the more it becomes imbedded in her or his repertoire and is more difficult to change.

5. ***Temperament.*** Babies are born with a set of physical characteristics that make them unique from any other individual. Babies are also born with their own patterns of behaviors or temperament that set them apart from others. Temperament is the manner in which a person responds to experiences and is generally observable in earliest infancy. We have often heard of "easy" or "fussy" babies, and these labels show how temperament has implications for the child's future social and emotional development, because children view themselves based on how others respond to their behavior. While some infants are "easy," others are irritable and cry more and for longer periods of time. Easy babies are more pleasant to care for, and they may receive (and give back) affection and positive attention. The fussy, feisty child may scream and thrash when given attention. As a result, the fussy child may feel less inviting to the caregiver and may receive less nurturance and affection.

Thomas and Chess (1977) developed a developmental theory of temperament resulting form their research in the New York Longitudinal Study and characterized infants as "easy," "difficult," and "slow-to-warm-up." Others have used "fearful," "flexible," or "feisty" to name different temperament styles. General characteristics associated with temperament include the intensity and duration of reactions, activity level, approach to new things, adaptability, mood, perseverance, and distractibility. How we get our temperaments is debatable. Some researchers believe we are born a certain way, predetermined by genetics. Others believe that a child's temperament is the interplay between inheritance and multiple factors including mental, emotional, physical, and environmental ones (Greenspan, 1997).

Variations in temperament occur in all children, with or without disabilities. The expectation that children with Down's syndrome have easy temperaments is a stereotype that is not supported by research (Pelco & Reed-Victor, 2003). A basic understanding of temperament is necessary to understand behavior. Thomas and Chess (1977) discuss the notion of a "goodness of fit" between an individual's temperament and the environment. With this understanding, adults can create environments that are more comfortable for each child and help children to develop strategies for environments that are not suitable for their temperaments.

Table 5.1 • Disabilities and Behavior

Disabilities and Behavior

IDEA Disability Category	Possible Areas of Concern	Accommodation/Modification
Autism	Communication problems (e.g., using and understanding language) Difficulty in relating to people, objects, and events Unusual play with toys and other objects Difficulty with changes in routine or familiar surroundings Repetitive body movements or behavior patterns	• Functional communication training • Augmentative communication devices • Social skills groups • Peer tutoring • Peer buddy
Deaf-Blindness	Aggression Self-injury tantrums	• Functional communication training • Reduce frustrating tasks • Peer tutor/buddy
Deafness	Social withdrawal/isolation Lack of communication	• Be clear as to topic discussed • Expect and encourage participation • Clearly identify who is speaking or asking a question (pointing is OK) • Develop procedures so the student who is hearing impaired can express his/her communication needs to others • Sit in a horseshoe or circle • Repeat or summarize most relevant classroom questions, answers, discussions • Initiate communication • Gain student's attention (e.g., tapping gently on the shoulder or arm, or using a visual signal) • Seat the student with his/her "better" ear toward the class
Emotional Disturbance	Immaturity Social withdrawal Self-injurious behavior Excessive fear or anxiety	• Model/reinforce appropriate behavior • Teach self-management • Behavior contract

(Continued)

Why Challenging Behavior May Occur

Table 5.1 • *(Continued)*

Disabilities and Behavior

IDEA Disability Category	Possible Areas of Concern	Accommodation/Modification
Hearing Impairment	*See* deafness	
Mental Retardation	Self-regulation Making and keeping friends Inattention Disruptive behaviors	• Systematic instruction • Real-life settings with real materials • Time delays
Multiple Disabilities	Self-stimulation Tantrums Aggression Self-injury	• Teach more effective, efficient ways to communicate • Reduce frustrating activities • Select functional curricula • Precorrection (e.g., teacher suggests what to do when upset)
Orthopedic Impairment	Moodiness Depression Pain	• Make sure student has a way to communicate • Reinforce participation
Other Health Impairment (e.g., ADHD)	Inattention Impulsivity	• Reduce stimuli • Structure with emphasis on teacher-directed activities • Self-monitoring
Specific Learning Disability	Social rejection Poor self-concepts Misread social cues/emotions Distractibility Social withdrawal	• Model appropriate behavior • Reinforce social interactions • Structure group activities
Speech or Language Impairment	Anxiety Isolation Easily frustrated	• Social skills instruction • Provide opportunities for interaction

Table 5.1 ● *(Continued)*

Disabilities and Behavior

IDEA Disability Category	Possible Areas of Concern	Accommodation/Modification
Traumatic Brain Injury	Sudden mood changes Anxiety Depression Trouble relating to others Lack of control over emotions Easily tired	• Give directions one step at a time • Have consistent routines. If the routine is going to change, provide warnings • Check to make sure that the student has actually learned the new skill. Give the student lots of opportunities to practice the new skill • Let the student rest as needed • Reduce distractions • Keep in touch with the student's parents • Be flexible about expectations • Be patient • Maximize the student's chances for success
Visual Impairments	Imitating social behavior Understanding nonverbal cues Independence Listening skills Communication	• Use technology • Interdisciplinary approach

Environmental

Social-emotional development. Children need nurturing environments that are conducive to learning and the development of social and emotional skills. Developing and maintaining high-quality experiences for children is a cost-effective way for society to prepare its citizens and work force as it reduces the amount of money needed for special education, welfare, and prison. Relationships are the building blocks for social emotional development, and positive early relationships can greatly influence children's abilities to achieve success in school and in life. Environmental factors play a large role in the prevention, development, and intervention of challenging behavior. Creating thoughtful, mutually beneficial relationships can go a long way in preventing problems from occurring.

Why Challenging Behavior May Occur

Erik Erikson (1963) examined development over the entire lifespan and developed a well-respected framework for understanding children's social-emotional development. Erikson's theory is unique in that it encompasses the entire life cycle and recognizes the impact of society, history, and culture on personality. Erikson's theory consists of eight stages of development. Each stage is characterized by a different conflict that must be resolved by the individual. When the environment makes new demands on people, the conflicts arise. Individuals are then forced to choose between two ways of coping with each crisis: one that is adaptive and one that is maladaptive. Only when each crisis is resolved can the person effectively deal with the next stage of development. If a person is unable to resolve a conflict at a particular stage, he or she will confront and struggle with it later in life. The eight stages are described in the summary Table 5.2.

According to Erikson, during the first stage of development, infants learn to either trust or mistrust their environment. If they are fed when they are hungry, changed when they are wet/soiled, and comforted when they are upset, they learn that the world is a place they can trust. This sense of trust gives them the security to venture out and explore the world. During the second stage of life,

Table 5.2 ● Erikson's Eight Stages of Development

Stage	Ages	Basic Conflict	Summary
Oral-Sensory	Birth to 12–18 months	Trust vs. Mistrust	The infant must form a loving, trusting relationship with the caregiver or develops a sense of mistrust: "I'm not safe here, I can't depend on you."
Muscular-Anal	18 months to 3 years	Autonomy vs. Shame/Doubt	The child's energies are directed toward the development of physical skills. May develop shame and doubt if not handled well: "I can't do it; I don't make good choices."
Locomotor	3 to 6 years	Initiative vs. Guilt	The child continues to become more assertive and to take more initiative but may be too forceful, leading to guilt: "I'm doing it wrong, I'd better not try."
Latency	6 to 12 years	Industry vs. Inferiority	The child must deal with demands to learn new skills or risk a sense of inferiority, failure, and incompetence: "I can't do anything; I'm scared of trying new things."
Adolescents	12 to 18 years	Peer relationships	Achievement of a sense of identity about politics, religion, occupation, gender roles
Young Adulthood	19 to 40 years	Love relationships	The development of intimate relationships or risk of isolation
Middle Adulthood	40 to 65 years	Parenting	Way to satisfy and sustain the next generation
Maturity	65 to death	Reflection and accepting one's life	Sense of self and fulfillment with one's self and choices

toddlers are learning about self-control and independence. If adults are accepting and encourage their emerging sense of self, toddlers develop autonomy. During the early childhood years, children are interested in exploring, creating, and expressing their natural curiosity. Adults can help children resolve these important issues successfully, or they can hamper their development.

Erikson's theories are relevant with both typically developing children and children who have special needs. Children who have special needs will in most cases pass through the same stages as typical children but may take longer and may have greater physical and sensory difficulty depending on the nature and severity of their disability. Educators must strive to recognize and attend to all children's social and emotional development, recognizing where they are and where they may need assistance.

Parents are the first people a child has a relationship with and play a critical role in childrens' development. A stable attachment to an adult is critical to solid emotional development. Parenting requires many skills, and there are several factors within families that can put children at risk, including poverty, a parent who is abusing alcohol or drugs, a parent with antisocial or criminal behavior, maternal depression, parents with little education, parents who had their children very young, and a large number of children in the family. Children are taught to initiate interactions with others, communicate their needs, develop friendships, express their feelings, and respond to others in a way that matches the behavioral norms expected by their family. These will be different for different families and may be influenced by a variety of factors including, but not limited to, ethnicity, race, gender, socioeconomic status, religion, culture, and culture. It is important to remember that family perspectives and values about behavior may be very different from an educator, or recommended practices in early childhood. Teachers should be aware of these differences and cultivate relationships with families to identify specific outcomes and strategies for addressing social and emotional goals.

Sociocultural

Today's children live in an increasingly diverse society, and often teachers and students are not from the same cultural groups. Cultural differences may affect whether a teacher considers a child's behavior as appropriate or inappropriate. Since classrooms may consist of children from many cultures speaking many languages, teachers who are knowledgeable about differences among and within cultural groups and understand the impact on children of different backgrounds are better able to provide positive social experiences and promote collaboration and friendships among classmates. It is important that teachers be aware of the diverse composition of an ethnic group and also not make assumptions regarding students' language capabilities based on their ethnic background. For example, being from a non-American ethnic group does not necessarily mean limited English proficiency, and being born in the United States does not ensure English proficiency. Language and behavior are interwoven and easily misunderstood. Behavior is communicative (LaRocque, Brown, & Johnson, 2001), and a lack of language skills may result in inappropriate behavior. Similarly, behavior problems can interfere with language learning and reflect common deficits (e.g., social skills, maturity, etc.).

Some of the areas behavior may be influenced by cultural factors include cooperation, sharing, waiting, and expressing one's feelings. Below are some tips to consider when teaching a diverse group of students:

- Pay equal attention to *all* students.
- Monitor students' comments to avert any inappropriate comments and deal with them directly.
- Do not allow preconceived notions and attitudes about *any* students' ability to perform, high or low.
- Do not assume that there is a "collective identity" students share.
- Do not assume the identity or racial affiliation of a student based on physical appearances.
- Do not single out a student to "represent" her or his country, racial group, gender, or linguistic group.

Academic–Behavior Connection

Mr. White was passing out materials for the next assignment and approached Owen's desk with dread. Lately, every time they began a new project, Owen would become hostile and verbally abusive. Once, he even crumpled up his paper and threw it on the ground. Although he was labeled as having attention-deficit/hyperactivity disorder, Mr. White was fairly certain Owen could do the work and was just acting this way to assert control and "push his buttons."

It is fairly common for people to think of behavior as a reaction to certain nonacademic events and not the subject matter itself. However, not having the skill to successfully complete an activity or task can sometimes result in inappropriate behavior. Schools with low academic achievement are those where students spend less time on task and have more behavior problems. The result is that teachers spend less time on preparation and communication, and there are fewer instances of positive reinforcement. This does not let itself well to a warm, friendly classroom climate. Effective instruction can reduce student misbehavior, and schools can improve students' academic performance and reduce problem behavior at the same time.

The increasingly diverse needs of students require that teachers examine curriculum and teaching strategies as possible causes for student misbehavior. Factors such as the use of groups, group composition, cultural and language barriers, and the lack of prerequisite skills may hinder the acquisition of content. Likewise, a mismatch between the instructional style of the teacher and the learning style of the student may also result in misbehavior.

Teachers can remedy some of these problems by identifying whether the problem is motivationally, style, or skill based. For motivationally based problems, teachers need to make sure that concepts are being taught with clearly delineated relationships between skills and how these skills fit into the bigger picture of the student's lives. For "goodness of fit" stylistic differences that occur, the teacher should examine their teaching strategies to make sure that there is enough variation to capture a variety of student interests. For example, are all modalities being used? We all know of the teacher who only lectures, or just provides materials in print. We also know that this teacher may quickly lose the interest of some students. Students who are not engaged have more time to get into trouble! If the teacher discovers that the cause of the misbehavior may be the student's lack of prerequisite skills, teachers can use task analysis to teach skills. A task analysis involves breaking down a task into smaller, manageable pieces. Each piece is then taught sequentially until the student has mastered all steps. Think of a simple, everyday task such as tooth brushing or putting on your coat and the many steps that are involved. Now think of an academic task and how difficult it may be for the student to master each of these steps. Using a task analysis ensures more opportunities for student success and takes away some of stress associated with an overwhelming task. As you can see, teachers will often have to differentiate instruction to meet the needs of all children and reduce the likelihood of off-task or disruptive behavior.

What Can Be Done to Prevent Challenging Behavior

A Supportive Classroom Environment

Classroom environments have a number of characteristics that influence student growth, development, and achievement. Classrooms that are perceived as safe, warm, supportive, and nonthreatening encourage work and promote a sense of enjoyment and accomplishment. In addition to affective influences, classroom climate is also related to student achievement (LaRocque, Brown, & Johnson, 2001). Research suggests that altering the classroom environment to make it more congruent with that favored by students is likely to enhance student outcomes and reduce problem behavior. This occurs because how students feel about school, their relationships in school, and how this makes them feel about themselves influence their behavior emotionally and academically.

Students thrive in environments where they feel accepted and trust their teachers to make good decisions that meet their developmental needs. Teachers who carefully plan and evaluate the various aspects of the classroom setting can construct classrooms that meet the needs of all students.

The schedule of activities and curriculum. Scheduling tells a student who does what, when they do it, and where they do it. As in most areas relating to behavior, consistency is key. Maintaining a consistent schedule helps students understand what the behavioral expectations are and can reduce the frequency of behavioral problems. Knowing the routines associated with events in the curriculum can help students feel secure and add to the predictability of the environment. Researchers have documented that this positively affects students' social and emotional growth. This can be enhanced by giving students choices within the daily schedule that individualize their activities. This shows that the teacher values each student's individual interests and abilities and does not expect all students to be able or want to do the same activities at the same time. In addition, this allows teachers to plan for activities that meet the individual cultural, linguistic, and educational needs of each student.

At the start of the school year, teachers should teach students the routines and post schedules for students to become familiar with. Teachers should consider the balance of activities (e.g., a difficult activity followed by a rewarding one), at what times students are most alert, the number of adults available in the classroom (e.g., paraprofessionals), and other events that may be occurring in the classroom. Teachers should review the schedule at the beginning of the day to assist students in understanding expectations and any changes.

Grouping.   Researchers report that students learn best when they are actively involved in the learning process. Students who are actively involved in learning have less need to exhibit inappropriate behaviors. Students working in small groups tend to learn more of what is taught and remember it longer than when the same information is presented in other instructional formats.

How students are grouped may have an impact on their achievement and their behavior. Heterogeneous ability groups allow students to be with their same-age peers and have access to the general curriculum. This ensures that teachers have high expectations for all students and allows for individual strengths to shine. In some instances, students who are generally viewed as less able to participate may have strengths that the group needs. As previously mentioned, some behaviors have academic functions, and heterogeneous grouping may allow students to work toward their strengths.

In order for grouping to be successful, the teacher must consider several things. Below are some questions a teacher should ask when planning and implementing group work:

1. Am I thoughtful about group composition, considering gender, ability, personality, etc.?
2. Have I created a task that requires genuine collaboration?
3. Do students understand the task and their individual role?
4. Have I presented clear guidelines of what constitutes quality work in terms of process and product?
5. Am I incorporating strategies for encouraging cooperation?
6. Do students understand the rules and responsibilities of group work?
7. Have I presented clear timelines?

In the inclusive classroom, there will be a variety of activities that may be well suited to group work. Generally, groups work best when there is a clear understanding of what to do, how to do it, and what the expectations are (Tomlinson, 2001). Many classrooms have a set routine that they follow for every group activity.

Routines.   All of us like to know what our daily schedule is going to be and what we are required to do within that daily schedules. Clear routines in academic and nonacademic settings can reduce or prevent many behavior problems by providing consistent classroom activities. For example, a change of schedule due to a fire drill can cause increased behavior problems. Having routines for beginning the day, classroom meeting time, center time, etc., helps students stay on schedule and know what your expectations are. Scheduling a particular activity at the same time every day (e.g., snack) or the same day every week (e.g., art) is helpful for students who need the stability of knowing what their day or week will entail.

Transitions.   Transitions occur throughout the classroom day, and often children spend a great deal of time waiting to move or begin the next activity. For example, students may have to wait until *everyone* has cleaned up before the teacher moves on to the next subject. Transitions must be planned for by the teacher so that students are more likely to have incident-free, independent transitions. When thinking of transitions, consider the following questions:

1. How do I prepare students to move from one activity or setting to another?
2. Do I consider transitions when planning my schedule?
3. Do I plan what the children and staff will do during transitions?
4. Do I plan for students who may require more support during transitions with, for example, a picture schedule, an auditory signal, etc.?
5. Do I have too many transitions during the school day?
6. Do students have enough time to finish an activity?
7. Do I teach, model, practice, and reinforce appropriate behavior during transitions?

Strategies that support smooth transitions between activities include verbal cues such as verbal reminders before transitions (e.g., "5 minutes before snack time," "it's almost lunch time") and praise after successful transitions.

Engaging Parents

The value of strengthening parent and teacher collaboration to promote positive outcomes for children is supported by the literature on best practices and by knowledge about teaching this. This collaboration contributes to the behavior and support needed by families and schools to create environments that are proactive, positive, and responsive to the needs of children. By involving parents, we better meet the needs of the child by developing good working relationships that serve as the medium for effective intervention. Frequent and open communication builds strong relationships and is vital to working effectively with parents. Listen and hear what parents concerns and strengths are regarding their children, and make sure they understand any concerns and strengths you have identified. As an educator, you are in an ideal position to assist and advocate for children and their families. Use the Teacher/Family Assessment in Table 5.3 to evaluate your family friendliness.

Teaching Prosocial Skills

Social competence is the ability to interpret and respond appropriately to social situations to get one's needs met. Being socially competent is critical to success in school and life and is composed of **prosocial skills**. These skills allow us to know the appropriate things to say and do in a variety of different situations. The degree to which children have good prosocial skills can influence their academic performance, their behavior, and their relationships with peers, teachers, and family. Teachers should not assume that students will walk in the door with a full repertoire of social skills. It is critical that teachers spend time and energy teaching and reinforcing social skills in the same manner in which they teach and reinforce academic skills.

While many children do learn prosocial skills through natural interactions with adults and peers, many also pick up negative skills that might hinder development, friendships, or safety. Teachers must reinforce prosocial skills while replacing negative behaviors with more positive ones.

Table 5.3 • Teacher/Family Assessment

	Not Yet	Almost There	Done Consistently
Have and use an established communication system			
Involve parents in classroom activities			
Create activities for fathers/other caregivers			
Schedule meetings at mutually convenient times			
Possess and distribute community resources			
Reflect the diversity of culture and family experiences			
Involve parents in decision making			
Inform parents in advance about instructional activities			
Use a translator when necessary for oral and written communication			

Schools should not rely solely on families to teach prosocial skills and may have to teach them directly and indirectly. This is necessary to maintain positive classroom and school environments and to promote the healthy social and emotional development of all children. Students who have good, well-developed social skills have the tools to make choices that will strengthen their interpersonal relationships and facilitate friendships and success at school. They will be able to engage others in positive interactions and seek appropriate resolution or assistance for frustrating and stressful occurrences. This will assist in developing resiliency, which is necessary to protect children from risk factors they may encounter in their lives.

Students with poor social skills often experience difficulties in interpersonal relationships with their parents, teachers, and peers that will lead to negative experiences at home and at school. These include peer rejection (which has been associated with school violence) and poor academic performance. Lack of success with others often contributes to depression and anxiety. Another unfortunate side effect of poor social skills is that without positive interactions it becomes more difficult to learn how to respond appropriately, particularly when we consider how much children learn from their peers.

While there are a vast number of important social skills for students to learn, we can organize them into specific skill areas to make it easier to identify and determine appropriate interventions. For example, Table 5.4 contains a social skills chart that organizes skills into four areas.

Many children never learned the acceptable behavior for different social situations, so it is important to understand what the student can and cannot do before attempting any interventions. Using a simple chart like the one above or assessment instruments found in many of the commercially prepared social skills packages (e.g., Skillstreaming the Elementary School Child) or formal assessment instruments (e.g., The Social Skills Rating System, SSRS) will allow you to better assess and clarify types of social skill deficits in order to devise and implement the most appropri-

Table 5.4 ● Social Skills

Social Skill	Examples
Skills Used in the Classroom	<ul><li>Listening</li><li>Following directions</li><li>Asking for help</li><li>Completing assignments</li><li>Attending to task</li></ul>
Skills for Developing and Maintaining Positive Relationships	<ul><li>Sharing</li><li>Turn taking</li><li>Joining/leaving an activity</li><li>Making/keeping friends</li><li>Positive interactions with others</li></ul>
Skills for Solving Problems	<ul><li>Self-control</li><li>Deciding what to do</li><li>Accepting consequences</li><li>Learning an internal dialogue</li><li>Waiting before reacting</li><li>Negotiating</li></ul>
Skills for Managing Conflicts Peacefully	<ul><li>Dealing with peer pressure</li><li>Dealing with embarrassment</li><li>Dealing with being left out</li><li>Using words instead of physical contact</li><li>Seeking the assistance of an adult</li></ul>

What Can Be Done to Prevent Challenging Behavior

ate intervention. Some of the reasons children may experience difficulty with social skills include the following:

1. ***Knowledge:*** We cannot assume that children enter the classroom with the necessary social skills. Remember that expectations are different at home and in different classrooms. In some cases, the child does not know the necessary social skills. For example, a child will grab the ball at recess because he does not know how to join a group.

2. ***Implementation:*** Sometimes children *know* social skills in theory but do not use them consistently or appropriately. For example, the child who knows about sharing and turntaking may do a good job in class but may not know these skills apply to games at recess.

3. ***Reinforcement:*** In this instance, the child knows how to perform the skill but does so inadequately because he or she does not have the opportunity to practice or receive any feedback on the skill. Sometimes, the skill may *not* be reinforced at home, causing confusion for the student. For example, the child may know how to resist peer pressure but may be encouraged to go along with siblings at home. Furthermore, the teacher is not always present during instances of peer pressure and does not have the opportunity to praise or correct this skill.

4. ***Behavior:*** Although skills have been taught and learned, there are internal and external factors that can interfere with social skills. For example, anxiety can cause a student to blurt out an answer even though she knows that one must raise one's hand before speaking. Likewise, anger can get in the way of conflict management.

Teaching Social Skills

Before planning to teach specific social skills, it is a good idea to include parents and other teachers. They can assist you in developing and selecting interventions and also to reinforce the strategies and skills taught in other environments. This will be important for the K–3 populations, as often they are not included in social skills interventions on the belief that they will "grow out of it." Including others in the planning and implementation helps ensure that they will support your efforts and reinforce the child/children.

Effective social skills programs and the teachers using them understand that social behavior can be taught effectively using the same principles and techniques for teaching academic concepts. As with academic instruction, there will be a range of how much systematic social skills instruction an individual student needs, and it is important to adapt interventions to meet the individual needs of the student or group. Almost all aggressive students will benefit from social skills instruction, and students who speak English as a second language may need more intensive instruction because cultures vary widely in what is considered appropriate social skills. Additionally, students in nearly all recognized categories of disability have some deficits in their social skills and may need adapted curriculum or materials to assist them. Finally, typically developing children often have at least one area in which they need improvement (e.g., asking for assistance). Figure 5.1 helps us to think about this concept.

It is important to remember that, regardless of how much intervention takes place, the emphasis must be on teaching and reinforcing the skill and not punishing inappropriate behavior. One informal way teachers can do this is through incidental learning, in which naturally occurring behaviors or events are used to teach and reinforce appropriate social behavior. Adults can reinforce

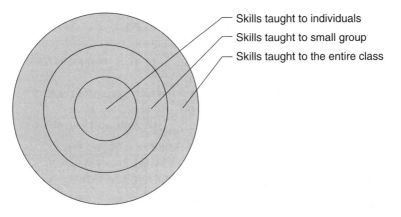

Skills taught to individuals
Skills taught to small group
Skills taught to the entire class

Figure 5.1 ● Social skills and the classroom.

demonstrated positive social skills by praising children when they demonstrate appropriate behavior, or offer more appropriate choices to poor decisions to teach the more socially competent behavior. It will be necessary to constantly look for situations to praise children who have particular difficulty when they are doing the right thing. Additionally, you can "create" situations in which students may naturally make the right choice so you have the opportunity to "catch them being good."

While the teacher can "create" positive situations, she or he can also prevent negative ones. Often the environment is to blame for the child experiencing difficulty demonstrating a particular skill. Think about the following questions as they pertain to social skills.

1. Do you have a method for students to ask for help? Do you respond quickly? consistently?

2. Are your classroom routines in place? Entering class? Homework? Group activities? Requesting the bathroom?

3. Do students know what your behavioral expectations are? Noise level?

Most students will need reminders of these items throughout the school year, and new challenges will arise that will require teachers to refocus their efforts and teach new desirable behavior.

Teaching specific behavior requires all of the attention and skills that educators place into teaching academics. You will want students to learn the skill, perform the skill, generalize the skill, and maintain the skill. As with academics, you will need to provide students with immediate feedback regarding their performance. Learning the skill requires you **modeling** what is expected, that is, actually performing the desired skill so that students have the opportunity to see it performed correctly. Then students can perform the skill through role-playing while you coach them through more difficult components. That way as they are practicing, you can make sure they are learning it correctly. Teaching students to generalize a behavior is often difficult and requires that you provide practice opportunities in a wide range of settings with different groups and individuals in order to encourage students to generalize new skills to multiple, real-life situations. This is important because students need the opportunity to address naturally occurring causes, triggers, consequences, etc.

What Can Be Done to Prevent Challenging Behavior

Table 5.5 • The Teacher's Classroom Behavior Self-Assessment

	Yes	No	Sometimes
Environment			
Clear physical boundaries			
Unnecessary materials out of sight/reach			
Materials organized for ease of use			
Visual schedules, rules, procedures			
Routines			
Consistent and predictable schedule			
Visual schedule			
Balance of indoor/outdoor, small/large group, quiet/active activities			
Minimize transitions, provide warnings, and explain what happens next			
Consistent group routines			
Practice rituals for arrival and departure			
Eliminate excessive waiting/sitting for long periods			
Adjust schedule as needed to respond to children/circumstances			
Strategies			
Model behavior you want children to follow			
Reinforce appropriate behavior			
Offer choices to children			
Ignore nondisruptive inappropriate behavior			
Redirect and offer acceptable solutions			
Make requests and give directions respectfully			
Social Skills			
Model/demonstrate turn-taking behavior			
Plan activities to teach specific social skills in small/large groups (i.e., initiating play)			
Encourage children to explore and express their emotions			
Teach/practice relaxation and calming down techniques			
Problem Solving			
Teach problem solving using role play, puppets, books			
Involve children in decision making and problem solving in the classroom			
Guide child through steps in actual conflict situations			
Other items I could be working on:			

When Challenging Behaviors Occur

Positive Behavior Support

Fortunate for the teacher, most students respond well to the teachers' prevention and intervention strategies. The teacher's use of social skills instruction, teaching classroom expectations, and arranging the environment to meet the needs of all students are typical strategies that even students with challenging behavior respond to. Before moving on to more intensive interventions, review the chart in Table 5.5 and ask yourself whether you do the items listed. This will also assist you in identifying areas where you can be more consistent in providing support.

There are a small number of students who do not respond to typical strategies teachers use in the classroom. For these students, **positive behavior support** (PBS) is an effective method of reducing challenging behaviors and encouraging more prosocial behavior. PBS is a process that can assist both teachers and families in understanding and addressing persistent challenging behavior that interferes with learning and social opportunities.

Defining PBS. PBS is not a process you need for every student with challenging behaviors. It is for the child whose challenging behavior continues after you have tried prevention approaches and developmentally appropriate procedures. PBS was developed from the science of applied behavior analysis *and* the values of child-centered approaches to teaching and learning. In the past, strategies for addressing challenging behaviors were often reactive and punitive. PBS uses proactive strategies that are individualized and *teaches* the students appropriate replacement behavior to optimize long-term success.

PBS is not a prepackaged curriculum created in a vacuum by one person. Because students communicate in a variety of ways for a variety of purposes, a team approach is necessary to provide information and identify the goals of any intervention. Members of the team should include individuals from all environments in which the child interacts. The team should include individuals with special areas of expertise (e.g., speech therapists, occupational therapists, school counselors) and individuals who know the child well and have a vested interest in obtaining positive results for the child. Finally, team members should include individuals who are knowledgeable about existing supports and barriers and have the authority to allocate personnel, money, or resources to address them. Potential team members include family members, teachers, paraprofessionals, therapists, and administrative staff. Once a team has been established, a functional behavior assessment can be conducted.

Functional Behavior Assessment

Proactive classroom management represents a philosophical shift in the way educators look at behavior from one that focuses on consequences and punishment to one that recognizes that behavior serves a function. Recognizing that behavior is communicative can shift the problem from simply being the child's to one that can be environmental and *prevented.* Identifying the function of behavior allows the teacher to describe and analyze children's interactions within their environment and create environments that are more conducive to learning. Problem behavior often serves as the most efficient method for children to get their needs met. The behavior has probably worked for the student in the past, and will likely continue to be used in the future to meet the student's needs unless conditions change. **Functional behavioral assessment** (FBA) is an attempt to understand what those needs are and assist children in developing positive alternatives for meeting them. Identifying the function of behavior cannot occur simply by describing the actions of children. For example, describing the crying of a child does not identify the conditions that control crying. A child may be screaming in pain, for attention, or to avoid an undesirable activity. Functional behavioral assessment is generally considered to be a process for identifying the function of student problem behavior. It relies on a variety of techniques and strategies to identify the purposes of specific behavior and to help educators select interventions to directly address the problem behavior.

A functional behavioral assessment looks beyond the behavior itself. The focus when conducting a functional behavioral assessment is on identifying significant, student-specific social, emotional, cognitive, and/or environmental factors associated with behavior. This broader perspective offers a better understanding of the function or purpose behind student behavior. Resulting behavioral intervention plans based on an understanding of "why" a student misbehaves are extremely useful in addressing a wide range of problem behaviors.

Functional behavioral assessments are an essential component of PBS. There is no one correct way of completing one, because it is a *process* for understanding the function of a behavior and how the behavior is influenced by environmental events. The first step in conducting an FBA is collecting information. Essentially, you are looking for situations that predict the occurrence or absence of that behavior. For example, if there is a teacher or adult who claims, "That never happens with me!" you might observe that situation to identify what is being done in that situation. Observations are used with interviews to provide evidence or data on the factors that predict or maintain challenging behavior. A popular and easy way to observe is by using ABC analysis.

Antecedent (A) = Watch the student and write down the events immediately before the behavior.

Behavior (B) = Describe the behavior using observable and measurable terms.

Consequence (C) = Write down what happens immediately after the behavior.

While it may be difficult to collect this information while teaching, you can jot down information on an index card or clipboard and compile it later.

Interviews are another way to gather this information in different settings with individuals who are very familiar with the students. Interviews help in the process by including multiple settings from the perspectives of multiple people. It is important to create simple, user-friendly items (e.g., forms, checklists, rating scales, etc.) to collect this information and that the individuals using them understand how to use them. Reviewing existing records can also assist in this process, as some of this information may have been previously collected and can give you an idea of how long the problem has persisted and what has been tried before.

Once all of the information is collected, the information is analyzed by the team to determine the purpose of the challenging behavior. In most students, it occurs in order to obtain something (e.g., attention, an item, an activity) or to avoid something (e.g., difficult demands). At this point a hypothesis or "best guess" statement describing the function of the behavior is necessary to guide intervention. For example, when faced with a demand she finds difficult (structured writing activities), Olivia avoids the activity by resisting or withdrawing. If pushed to participate, Olivia will throw objects or scream. When this occurs, teachers allow her to discontinue participating in the activity.

These hypotheses statements allow you to see the behavior more clearly and manipulate the antecedents (what happens before the behavior) or the consequences (what happens after the behavior).

Managing All Students

Unfortunately, no matter how well organized and prepared you are, challenging behavior is still going to occur in the inclusive classroom for students without disabilities and students with disabilities. In most instances, classroom teachers can use the same techniques to manage the challenging behavior of students with disabilities that they use to manage the behavior of those without disabilities. Much of the behavior exhibited by both groups is similar in nature. The differences, however, may originate in the teacher's selection of the particular behavioral strategy. When selecting interventions for a student with disabilities, teachers should ensure that the strategies are developmentally appropriate and take into consideration the student's disability and due process rights.

Before tackling specific requirements for students identified with disabilities, let's review some basic principles. For all students, it is important to hold and communicate high behavioral expectations that are reinforced with clear rules and procedures that instruct students in how to follow them. It is critical that students are aware of the reinforcers and consequences of their behavior and that classroom rules are enforced promptly, consistently, and fairly from the very first day of school. For the teacher, it is important to maintain a motivating instructional pace that has smooth transitions between activities. The teacher must monitor all classroom activities and make sure that students are given feedback regarding their academic and behavioral performance. Finally, the teacher must create a classroom environment that builds self-discipline, social skills, and a sense of community and belonging.

For many behaviors, your intervention should be hierarchical in nature. That is, start from the least intrusive intervention and move up the continuum to more intrusive. For many children, nonverbal cues such as a finger to the lips, raised eyebrows, a head shake, or a hand signal are enough to get them to stop what it is they are doing. Getting closer to students while using these nonverbal cues can halt inappropriate behavior without interrupting what you or the student is doing. Finally, redirecting or reminding the entire group of what they *should* be doing can sometimes work wonders to redirect students back to the task at hand even if only one or two students are misbehaving. For example, "Everyone should have their eyes on me" or "Everyone should have their scissors and paper on top of their desks" can remind off-task students about what the group activity is.

Managing behavior will require that you use a variety of techniques and strategies. A useful strategy for bring it all together is to remember that management does not require physical exertion, but it does require mental sweat.

S—Stay positive and focused.

W—Welcome parents and other family members.

E—Engage children in one-to-one and face-to-face interactions.

A—Acknowledge progress, not perfection.

T—Teach social skills alongside academic skills.

Discipline and IDEA

While teachers can in many instances use the same discipline strategies for students with disabilities as those used for students without disabilities, they should be aware of instances where this may not be appropriate. All students deserve schools that are safe and provide an environment conducive to learning. The Goals 2000: Educate America Act considers safety and discipline as goal seven of the nation's eight primary goals for education (National Education Goals Panel, 1999). At times, the behavior of individual students seems at odds with this goal. Before the passage of Public Law 94-142 (Education of All Handicapped Children Act, EAHCA) in 1975, approximately one million students with disabilities were excluded from public elementary and secondary schools based on their disability (U.S. Department of Education, 1999). In *Honig v. Doe* (1988), the Supreme Court stated that, in passing this law, "Congress very much meant to strip schools of the unilateral author-ity they had traditionally employed to exclude disabled students, particularly emotionally disturbed students, from school." Today, when students with disabilities break school rules, implementation of school discipline policies has been perceived as confusing because of laws designed to protect these students' rights (U.S. Department of Education, 1999).

Current law stipulates the manner in which schools must address problem behavior and still provide a free, appropriate, public education (FAPE) to students with disabilities. The reauthoriza-tion of the Individuals with Disabilities Education Act (IDEA, 2004) (previously EAHCA) yield a number of provisions concerning the assessment, placement, instruction, and discipline of students with disabilities who present problem behaviors. Congress delineated procedural rules that schools must follow to respond to problem behavior exhibited by students while still providing FAPE. Con-gress sought to protect the rights of students with disabilities and those suspected of having disabili-ties without imposing excessive requirements on schools. In addition, by promoting the use of appropriate behavioral assessments and interventions, Congress expected that schools could increase the probability of student success and school completion (Hartwig & Reusch, 2000).

Discipline and children with disabilities were a contentions issue during the 1997 reauthoriza-tion and remained so in the 2004 reauthorization. Schools have argued that the discipline provisions for students with disabilities under IDEA created too much paperwork and that they should be the same as those for children without disabilities. Advocates for children with disabilities have argued that these children should not be punished for behavior that was caused by their disability and that certain due process procedures are necessary to ensure that schools are not denying services to children with disabilities. Below is a brief description of key provisions.

1. *Manifest Determination:* A manifest determination is based upon the premise that, when behavior is caused by a disability, the school must respond differently than when behavior is not related to the disability. The 2004 reauthorization provides that, within ten days of a decision to change the placement of a child with a disability because of a violation of a code of student conduct, steps must be taken to determine if the conduct was caused by or had a direct and considerable relationship to the disability or if it was a result of a failure to implement the Individualized Educa-tion Program (IEP). If it is determined that the conduct was a manifestation of the child's disability, the IEP team must conduct a functional behavior assessment (FBA) and implement a behavior inter-vention plan (BIP) for the child if it has not been done before. If there is a BIP, is must be reviewed and modified as necessary to address the behavior (§615[k][5]).

2. *When Conduct Is Not a Manifestation of Disability:* School personnel may consider on a case-by-case basis any unique circumstances when determining whether to change placement for a child with a disability for a child who violates a code of student conduct (§615[k][1][A]). In addition, school personnel may remove a child to another placement or suspend her or him for more than ten school days. In essence, when conduct is not a manifestation of disability, school personnel may apply the same disciplinary procedures to children with disabilities as to those without disabilities, except educational services must continue, even if in an interim alternative educational setting (§615[k][1][C]).

3. *Educational Services:* Children with disabilities must continue to receive educational services that enable the child to continue to participate in the general education curriculum and to progress toward meeting his or her IEP goals during the period in which he or she is in an interim alternative education setting.

4. *Interim Alternative Educational Settings:* School personnel may remove a student with a disability to an interim alternative education setting regardless of whether the behavior is a manifestation of the disability in certain circumstances and for a limited amount of time, not more than forty-five school days. The IEP team determines the interim alternative educational setting if a child carries to or possesses a weapon at school or a school function; if a child knowingly possesses or uses illegal drugs or sells or solicits the sale of a controlled substance while at school or on school premises or at a school function; or if a child has inflicted serious bodily injury upon another person while at school, on school premises, or at a school function.

5. *Children Not Yet Eligible for Special Education and Related Services:* There are certain protections afforded to students who have not yet been identified as needing special education and related services. Generally, it is deemed that a Local Education Agency (LEA) is said to have knowledge that a child is a child with a disability if, before the behavior that precipitated the disciplinary action,

1. the parent of the child expressed concern, in writing, to supervisory or administrative personnel of the LEA or the child's teacher that the child is in need of special education and related services,
2. the parent has requested an evaluation, or
3. the teacher of the child or other LEA personnel has expressed specific concerns about a pattern of behavior directly to the director of special education or other supervisory personnel ($615[k][5]).

For all children, it is important that learning take place in an environment that is safe and conducive to learning. For students with disabilities, it is important that the teacher be aware of procedural and due process requirements.

Summary

In addition to preparing students to meet the academic challenges of schools, teachers teaching in the inclusive classrooms also prepare students to meet social and behavioral challenges. All students benefit from classrooms that are warm and caring and allow them to experience positive interactions with peers and adults. While there are many things the teacher can't control outside of the classroom, there are many things teachers can do within the classroom to contribute to the success of all children. First, teachers must assess their own instruction to ensure that it is differentiated, engaging, and motivating. Second, teachers must assess the academic and social skills of the students and provide accommodations, supports, and instructions where needed.

Review Questions

1. What factors inhibit the development of social skills?

2. What are academic strategies teachers can use to reduce the likelihood of challenging behavior?

3. How does PBS differ from traditional behavioral techniques?

4. What can teachers do to encourage parent participation and true involvement?

5. Describe the key discipline provisions of IDEA.

Thinking It Through

1. The environment of the classroom can support the development of trust, autonomy, and initiative. Identify some of the ways the physical and social environment can convey the messages we want children to receive.

2. Write a letter to future families explaining your classroom management policy. Make sure to include reinforcers and consequences for behavior and how you will consider children's individual differences in ability, culture, and language.

3. Describe techniques to handle the following potentially disruptive situations:

    a. Transition times between activities

    b. Fire drills

    c. Schedule changes

    d. Students called from class or leaving early

4. Children from the same culture or ethnic group often like to be together. How do you feel about this? What will you do in your classroom to encourage children to interact beyond cooperative grouping?

Appendix: Position Statement on Interventions for Challenging Behavior

Adopted: April 1998
Reaffirmed: June 2001

Many young children engage in challenging behavior in the course of early development. The majority of these children respond to developmentally appropriate management techniques.

Every parent, including parents of young children with disabilities, wants his or her child to attend schools, child-care centers, or community-based programs that are nurturing and safe. Many young children engage in challenging behavior at various times during their early development. Typically, this behavior is short-term and decreases with age and use of appropriate guidance strategies. However, for some children these incidences of challenging behavior may become more consistent despite increased adult vigilance and use of appropriate guidance strategies. For these children, the challenging behavior may result in injury to themselves or others, cause damage to the physical environment, interfere with the acquisition of new skills, and/or socially isolate the child (Doss & Reichle, 1991). Additional intervention efforts may be required for these children.

DEC believes strongly that many types of services and intervention strategies are available to address challenging behavior.

Given the developmental nature of most challenging behavior, we believe that there is a vast array of supplemental services that can be added to the home and education environment to increase the likelihood that children will learn appropriate behavior. A variety of intervention strategies can be implemented with either formal or informal support. Services and strategies could include, but are not limited to: (a) designing environments and activities to prevent challenging behavior and to help all children develop appropriate behavior; (b) utilizing effective behavioral interventions that are positive and address both form and function of a young child's challenging behavior, (c) adopting curricular modification and accommodation strategies designed to help young children learn behaviors appropriate to their settings; and (d) providing external consultation and technical assistance or additional staff support. In addition, all professionals who work with children in implementing IEPs or IFSPs must have opportunities to acquire knowledge and skills necessary for effective implementation of prevention and intervention programs.

DEC believes strongly that families play a critical role in designing and carrying out effective interventions for challenging behavior.

Given the family-focused nature of early childhood education, we acknowledge the critical role that families play in addressing challenging behavior. Often times, challenging behavior occurs across places, people and time, thus families are critical members of the intervention team. A coordinated effort between family members and professionals is needed to assure that interventions are effective and efficient and address both child and family needs and strengths.

All decisions regarding the identification of a challenging behavior, possible interventions, placement, and ongoing evaluation must be made in accordance with the family through the IEP, IFSP, or other team decision-making processes.

Reference

Doss, L. S., & Reichle, J. (1991). Replacing excess behavior with an initial communicative repertoire. In J. Reichle, J. York, & J. Sigafoos (Eds.), *Implementing augmentative and alternative communication: Strategies for learners with serve disabilities.* Baltimore: Brooks Publishing Co.

This DEC position endorsed by the following organizations: NAEYC, NABE, NACCRRA, NBCDI, and NHSA.

Division for Early Childhood
27 Fort Missoula Road, Suite 2
Missoula, Montana 59804
Phone: (406)543-0872
Fax: (406) 543-0887
Email: dec@dec-sped.org
www.dec-sped.org

Further Reading

Brady, K., Forton M. B., Porter, D., & Wood, C. (2003). *Rules in school.* Greenfield, MA: Northeast Foundation for Children.

Charney, R. S. (2002). *Teaching children to care: Classroom management for ethical and academic growth, K–8.* Greenfield, MA: Northeast Foundation for Children.

Close, N. (2002). *Listening to children: Talking with children about difficult issues.* Boston: Allyn and Bacon.

Faber, A., & Maazlish, E. (1999). *How to talk so kids will listen and listen so kids will talk* (20th anniversary ed.). New York: Avon.

Gartrell, D. (2001). Replacing time-out: Part one. Using guidance to build an encouraging classroom. *Young Children, 56*(6), 8–16.

Gartrell, D. (2002). Replacing time-out: Part two. Using guidance to maintain an encouraging classroom. *Young Children, 57*(2), 36–43.

Katz, L. G., & McClellan, D. E. (1997). *Fostering children's social competence: The teacher's role.* Washington, DC: NAEYC.

Kreidler, W. J. (1984). *Creative conflict resolution: More than 200 activities for keeping peace in the classroom.* Goodyear Education Series. Santa Monica, CA: Goodyear.

Levin, D. E. (2002). *Teaching young children in violent times: Building a peaceable classroom* (2nd ed.). Cambridge, MA: Educators for Social Responsibility.

National Association for the Education of Young Children (NAEYC). (1998). *Helping children learn self-control: A guide to discipline.* Brochure. Washington, DC: Author.

O'Neill, R. E., Horner, R. H., Albin, R. W., Sprague, J. R., Storey, K., & Newton, J. S. (1997). *Functional assessment and program development for problem behavior.* Pacific Grove, CA: Brookes/Cole.

Paley, V. (1993). *You can't say you can't play.* Cambridge: Harvard University Press.

Shonkoff, J. P., & Phillips, D. (Eds.). (2000). *From neurons to neighborhoods: The science of early childhood development.* Washington, DC: National Research Council.

Webster-Straton, C., & Herbert, M. (1994). *Troubled families—problem children. Working with parents: A collaborative process.* Chinchester, England: John Wiley.

Weinstein, C. S. (1999). Reflections of best practices and promising programs: Beyond assertive classroom discipline. In H. J. Freiberg (Ed.), *Beyond behaviorism: Changing the classroom management paradigm* (pp. 147–63). Boston: Allyn and Bacon.

Resources

Center for Evidence-Based Practice: Young Children With Challenging Behavior

Florida Mental Health Institute
University of South Florida
13301 Bruce B. Downs Boulevard
Tampa, FL 33612-3807
(813) 974-4602
http://challengingbehavior.fmhi.usf.edu/index.html

The Center for Evidence-Based Practice: Young Children With Challenging Behavior is funded by the U.S. Department of Education, Office of Special Education Programs to raise the awareness and implementation of positive, evidence-based practices, and to build an enhanced and more accessible database to support those practices. The Center engages in a comprehensive and collaborative process for identifying evidence-based practices; develops partnerships with national early childhood organizations and other dissemination networks to ensure a widespread campaign of awareness and system enhancement; develops materials and implementation strategies to impact personnel preparation; and implements a national research program to address critical issues for young children and their families affected by challenging behavior.

Center on the Social and Emotional Foundations for Early Learning (CSEFEL)

University of Illinois at Urbana–Champaign
Children's Research Center
51 Gerty Drive
Champaign, IL 61820-7469
(877) 275-3227
http://csefel.uiuc.edu

CSEFEL is a national center focused on strengthening the capacity of child care and Head Start to improve the social and emotional outcomes of young children. The Center develops and disseminates evidence-based, user-friendly information to help early childhood educators meet the needs of the growing number of children with challenging behaviors and mental health needs in child care and Head Start programs. It focuses on promoting the social and emotional development of children as a means of preventing challenging behaviors.

National Technical Assistance Center on Positive Behavioral Interventions and Supports (PBIS)

www.pbis.org

The Center has been established by the Office of Special Education Programs, U.S. Department of Education, to give schools capacity-building information and technical assistance for identifying, adapting, and sustaining effective schoolwide disciplinary practices.

Association for Positive Behavior Support

PO Box 328
Bloomsburg, PA 17815
(570) 389-4081
(570) 389-3980 (fax)
www.apbs.org

The Association for Positive Behavior Support is an international organization dedicated to the advancement of positive behavior support. APBS strives to expand application of this approach with children, adolescents, and adults with problem behavior.

Center for Effective Collaboration and Practice

http://cecp.air.org/

It is the mission of the Center for Effective Collaboration and Practice to support and promote a reoriented national preparedness to foster the development and the adjustment of children with or at risk of developing serious emotional disturbance. To achieve that goal, the Center is dedicated to a policy of collaboration at federal, state, and local levels that contributes to and facilitates the production, exchange, and use of knowledge about effective practices.

The Collaborative for Academic, Social, and Emotional Learning (CASEL)

Department of Psychology (M/C 285)
University of Illinois at Chicago

1007 W. Harrison Street
Chicago, IL 60607-7137
(312) 413-1008
(312) 355-4480 (fax)
www.casel.org

CASEL's mission is to enhance children's success in school and life by promoting coordinated, evidence-based social, emotional, and academic learning as an essential part of education from preschool though high school.

References

Berk, L. E. (2000). *Child development* (5th ed.). Boston: Allyn and Bacon.

Bredekamp, S. (Ed.). (1987). *Developmentally appropriate practice in early childhood programs serving children from birth through age 8.* Washington, DC: NAEYC.

Bredekamp, S., & Copple, C. (Eds.). (1997). *Developmentally appropriate practice in early childhood programs* (Rev. ed.). Washington, DC: NAEYC.

Division for Early Childhood of the Council for Exceptional Children. (1999). Position statement on interventions for challenging behavior. In S. Sandall & M. Ostrosky (Eds.), *Young Exceptional Children Monograph Series No.1:* Practical ideas for addressing challenging behaviors (pp. 3–4). Sopris West Longmont, CA.

Erikson, E. (1963). *Childhood and society.* New York: W. W. Norton.

Greenspan, S. I. (1997). *The growth of the mind and the endangered origins of intelligence.* Reading, MA: Addison-Wesley.

Hartwig, E. P., & Reusch, G. M. (2000). Disciplining students in special education. *Journal of Special Education, 33* (4), 240–248.

Honig v. Doe. (1988). 484 U.S. 305.

Individuals with Disabilities Improvement Act. (2004). PL 108–446.

LaRocque, M., Brown, S., & Johnson, K. L. (2001). Functional behavioral assessments and intervention plans in early intervention. *Infants and Young Children, 13*(3), 59–68.

National Education Goals Panel. (1999). *The National Education Goals Report: Building a nation of learners.* Washington, DC: U.S. Government Printing Office.

Pelco, A., & Reed-Victor, E. (2003). Understanding and supporting differences in child temperament: Strategies for early childhood environments. *Young Exceptional Children, 6*(3), 2–11.

Shonkoff, J. P., & Phillips, D. A. (Eds.). (2000). *From neurons to neighborhoods: The science of early childhood development.* National Research Council and Institute of Medicine, Committee on Integrating the Science of Early Childhood Development, Board on Children, Youth, and Families, Commission on Behavioral and Social Sciences and Education. Washington, DC: National Academy Press.

Thomas, A., & Chess, S. (1977) *Temperament and development.* New York: Brimer/Mazel.

Tomlinson, C. A. (2001). *How to differentiate in mixed-ability classrooms* (2nd ed.) Columbus, OH: Merrill/Prentice Hall.

Tremblay, R. E., Boulerice, B., Harden, P. W., McDuff, P., Perusse, D., & Pihl, R. O. (1996). Do children in Canada become more aggressive as they approach adolescence? In *Growing up in Canada: National Longitudinal Survey of Children and Youth* (pp. 127–137). Ottawa, ON: Human Resources Development Canada and Statistics Canada.

U.S. Department of Education. (1999). To assure the free appropriate public education of all children with disabilities: Twenty-first annual report to Congress on the implementation of the Individuals with Disabilities Education Act. Washington, DC: Office of Special Education Programs.

Zurkowski, J. K., & Kelly, P. S. (1998). Discipline and IDEA 1997: Instituting a new balance. *Intervention in School & Clinic, 34,* 1, 3–9. Washington, DC: Author.

Relationships In and Outside the Inclusive Classroom

Lorry Ollison Floyd and Lisa J. Vernon-Dotson

Objectives

After reading this chapter, students will be able to

- Describe how teacher attitudes and expectations foster a friendly and collaborative classroom environment.
- Discuss the importance of establishing effective interactions within and outside the classroom setting.
- Describe how ones own cultural background can influence interaction with students, parents/caregivers, colleagues, and other professionals.
- Discuss how to assist parents/caregivers in using home learning activities as an extension to their child's education.

Key Terms

Paraeducator

Social development

Family systems

Collaboration

Trust

Cultural and linguistic diversity

Sibshops

Practical Application Vignettes

The following vignettes provide mere snapshots into the lives of two very different families. These vignettes will assist with understanding and applying the ideas and concepts discussed in this chapter.

Aaron Clark

Aaron was just 5 years old when his family moved to Delaware. Mr. and Mrs. Clark struggled with adjusting to a new location and worked to find housing immediately. Understandably, this was the family's primary concern and took precedence over Aaron's speech therapy, which had been interrupted quite abruptly over two weeks ago. One week later, Aaron's family was finally able to secure housing and began living in a converted garage apartment in a neighborhood known for its gang-related activities, illegal drugs, and a high unemployment rate. Aaron's mother went to school to get him registered and hoped to resume speech therapy services right away. Initially, she was not able to meet with Mrs. Giles, Aaron's teacher. They were able to meet three days later. That was some time ago, and it is time for a parent conference. To no avail Mrs. Giles attempted to schedule several appointments with Aaron's parents to discuss his behavior because she is really concerned about Aaron's progress in school.

Yomara Gonzalez

Maria Gonzalez is a single mother of two, Carlos and Yomara. Carlos is the oldest and is enrolled in the local middle school. Yomara is 5 and just enrolled in kindergarten. Ms. Gonzalez lives with her sister Theresa. Neither Maria nor Theresa speaks English, only Spanish. Ms. Gonzales finds communicating with Yomara's school to be extremely difficult. She has to rely on neighbors, relatives, children, or another teacher as a translator. Ms. Gonzalez believes that teachers seldom listen to her because she does not speak English. Ms. Gonzalez is concerned about Yomara and agreed that she could be making more progress if she spoke English and were able to review with her at home in the evenings on a consistent basis. However, right now taking English classes is not her chief concern. Ms. Gonzalez must find work. Her sister can not afford to continue to take care of them. Until then, Ms. Gonzalez must make finding employment the priority while her sister works double shifts to make ends meet. Mr. Allan, Yomara's kindergarten teacher, is concerned about Yomara's social and emotional development. She does not seem to be the happy little girl she was when the school year began.

Introduction to Relationships

The need to build relationships both in and outside the classroom is imperative. This chapter describes how teacher attitudes and expectations foster a friendly and collaborative classroom environment. The importance of establishing effective interactions within and outside the educational setting is also discussed. Additionally, a description of how ones own cultural background can influence, encourage, and support positive interaction with students, parents/caregivers, colleagues, and other professionals is also incorporated. Furthermore, this chapter provides strategies that encourage teachers to assist parents/caregivers in using home learning activities as an extension to their children's education.

The success of an inclusive classroom is highly dependent upon the attitudes of the stakeholders directly involved in providing services for young children. Teachers, parents/caregivers, and support personnel must genuinely believe in the inclusive process and the positive impact the program can and will have on all the children in the classroom. Adults who exhibit negative attitudes and/or behaviors will ultimately consciously or subconsciously suppress the efforts of those around them, further influencing pessimism and unhealthy classroom environments. Professionals who demonstrate these behaviors should be counseled to leave the setting and/or profession.

As high, attainable expectations are set for students in K–3 classrooms, the expectations for the teachers, parents/caregivers, and other support staff should be set even higher. Stakeholders are expected to collaborate and communicate effectively while keeping the educational, social, and emotional welfare of all children at the forefront of professional conversations. Parents/caregivers are expected to be actively involved in their children's education; likewise, teachers, **paraeducators** (paid educational assistants), administrators, and other support staff are responsible for opening the doors and encouraging ongoing relationship building opportunities.

Children, with and without disabilities, benefit from adults who work together in a professional, mature manner. Positive attitudes, high expectations, effective collaboration, and open communication build the foundation for relationships needed to support successful inclusive education settings.

Children First

It cannot be stated enough that children with special needs are children first. Professionalism, political correctness, and common sense lay emphasis on the importance of using person-first language when discussing students with disabilities. These are the same children who have the characteristics and needs comparable to their "typical" peer counterparts. All young children, no matter how significantly challenged or disabled, will benefit from best practices that create supportive and nurturing environments for all young children. This chapter was grounded and written with this belief in mind.

Relationships

In this section, the importance of relationships is explored. Effective relationship building on many different levels is imperative in an inclusive education program. Positive relationships are grounded in communication that is genuine, continuous, and, most important, effectual. Teachers must understand the important roles that these relationships play in a successful educational environment. This includes those social interactions that occur between children as well as professional interactions with parents/caregivers, paraeducators, volunteers, school administrators, related service providers, and other support personnel.

Student–Teacher Relationships

Once a child begins school, teachers often become the most influential adults, in addition to parents, in that child's life. Research shows that the quality of children's early relationships with teachers during the first years of school is crucial in shaping children's school success over time (Pianta, 1999; Stormont, 2007). Establishing such relationships should begin with creating a positive classroom environment. This can be described as a community where the student and teacher interact in a manner that reflects caring about one another (Jones & Jones, 2001; Stormont, 2007). This section describes research that reveals the importance of children's relationships with teachers.

Students tend to be more responsive to teachers if they have a supportive and caring relationship with them (Jones & Jones, 2001). Stormont (2007) emphasis three considerations for building positive student–teacher relationships: (1) know each student; (2) communicate caring and model kindness; and (3) share personally. Table 6.1 provides suggestions that might assist teachers in building relationships.

Researchers (Jones & Jones, 2001; Ortiz & Flanagan, 2002; Pianta, 1999) in education and psychology have assessed the teacher–student relationship in numerous ways. However, much of the research on this topic has used Robert Pianta's (1999) Student–Teacher Relationship Scale (STRS). This scale assesses three dimensions of a teacher's perception of his or her relationship with a student: closeness, conflict, and dependency. Table 6.2 provides sample statements used to asses each area.

Table 6.1 ● Positive Student–Teacher Relationships

Know Each Student	Learn the names of all students (including preferred nicknames and the correct pronunciation and spelling of each name).
	Understand individual supports needed.
	Spend time with students outside of the classroom setting (Watson & Ecken, 2003).
Communicate Caring and Model Kindness	Greet students when they enter the classroom each day. Bid farewell to each student at the end of the school day.
	Develop classroom activities that children view as special, and that are not contingent on good behavior.
	Ensure (whenever possible) that all children participate in classroom activities.
Share Personally	Model the sharing of information by volunteering to go first.
	Personally respond to children's journal entries.
	Ask students to write a letter to the teacher every Monday about what they did over the weekend (Stormont, 2007).

Certainly teachers will be influenced by a child's readiness for school. The National Center for Early Development and Learning conducted a survey of over 3,500 kindergarten teachers. The center found teachers reported that, on average, nearly half (48%) of their students were not prepared for the transition to kindergarten and experienced a difficult adjustment to school. Teachers identified several areas in which students were most likely to be below expectations. In particular, students were most likely to be underprepared in areas such as following directions, working independently, working in groups, and communicating.

Positive teacher–student relationships are particularly important for children with disabilities, who are "at risk" because they are less likely to have these basic school skills and are more likely to start school with behavior problems, cognitive difficulties, or social problems. For these children, a positive teacher–student relationship during kindergarten to grade three can change the course of school experiences, setting them on the track to positive school adjustment and academic success.

Peer Relationships

A positive classroom community supports not only student–teacher relationships but also relationships among children. This extends beyond concern about supporting young students in building positive peer relationships within the educational setting, but also in making meaningful and ongoing friendships that continue outside the environment as well. Teachers and other education personnel must be vigilant about creating settings that promote and thrive on positive peer relationships. Programs and classrooms must be environments that set up students who typically have difficulty building friendships for success. These young children must be taught valuable friendship making skills and given the appropriate means, tools, and opportunities to practice those skills in a safe, nurturing, and supportive environment.

Table 6.2 ● Assessing the Teacher–Student Relationship

Closeness	Conflict	Dependency
"I share an affectionate, warm relationship with this child."	"This child and I always seem to be struggling with one another."	"This child asks for my help when he/she does not really need help."
"If upset, this child will seek comfort from me."	"This child easily becomes angry with me."	

Communication

The serious and critical role that communication and language play in the cognitive development of children in the early years has been emphasized by the likes of both Piaget (1926) and Vygotsky (1962), in addition to others who function under the principles of constructivism. Language and the ability to communicate are essential to developing a child's social and emotional skills. Educators who focus on language development may benefit the children who have disabilities affecting their communicative growth. Without adequate supports, personnel, and resources, children with disabilities and those at risk for school failure tend to form socially segregated subgroups within an inclusive setting. They may not interact with peers without disabilities because of developmental delays, language differences, or social and emotional deficits (Hanson, Gutierrez, Morgan, Brennan, & Zercher, 1997).

Many children who come from families who do not speak English in their homes and communities are likely to experience communication and social dilemmas. Teachers must encourage and teach appropriate social interactions to all students. Because of the high rates of expressive language deficits in many children identified with disabilities, programs must concentrate on the cognitive and linguistic needs of the students, as well as their social and emotional development, which may be impacted by their deficits (Hanson et al., 1997).

Friendships

Peer interactions are particularly important at the during the first years of school. Promoting positive social interactions among young children both within and outside the classroom setting is essential. Young children with disabilities may have extreme difficulty recognizing, making, and maintaining the healthy friendships that are imperative for adequate social and emotional development. Strategies that support these positive relationships among children in the classroom are discussed in the next section of this chapter. It is crucial to remember that social relationships do not occur spontaneously, and, more important, teachers and school personnel can make a difference in how positive (or negative, unfortunately) relationships are initiated, generalized, and maintained throughout and beyond the learning environment. The role of the teacher is merely to create opportunities, nurture support and friendship, and provide positive role models for one underlying goal: getting students to understand, appreciate, support, and interact respectfully (Turnbull, Pereira, & Blue-Banning, 2000).

Special Friends and *Circle of Friends* are two activities that nurture and support friendships. With the primary objective of building friendships, Special Friends creates opportunities for children with disabilities to learn how to communicate, interact, and play with their peers or adults without disabilities. This type of relationship provides for a positive social experience, affording an opportunity for "the child to grow in confidence, to feel more bonded to their school, and to cope better with their peers" (Autism Network, 1999, ¶ 3). Teachers unite "special" friends to socialize and nurture each other in interactive social functions both within and outside the learning setting. Although this relationship is typically formed using older volunteers from the community (e.g., local high school students, retirees, members of religious organizations or social clubs), it has been found extremely effective with age-appropriate peers at various grade levels.

With adult assistance, young students can develop a social map of their Circle of Friends (Pearpoint & Hollands, 2001). The purpose of this activity is to help young children increase their awareness of the different levels of friendships and to assist teachers in being proactive in recognizing those students who may be at risk for social isolation by eliciting peer mentors (OASIS, n.d.). The Circle of Friends social map is typically demonstrated to a whole class or small group prior to being completed individually. In an activity using concentric circles (see Figure 6.1), the student places his or her picture or name inside the inner circle. At the next level, the student is assisted with recognizing immediate support people. The people identified in this ring are those who bring unconditional love and nurtured encouragement or support for the child and will include the parents/caregivers, sisters or brothers, godparents, and possibly extended family members or other important friends of the family. The next ring is composed of those persons who are advocates of the child. These are people who provide the young person with various care tasks and assistance. Teachers, doctors, tutors, and neighbors would typically be listed at this level. The outermost ring is reserved for the student's friends, classmates, and playmates. Once the map is completed by the child experiencing some social or emotional concerns in the classroom setting, the teacher encourages others to volunteer to be a part of that student's Circle of Friends. Although many variations and purposes of this activity exist, the ultimate goal is for the student to recognize the different types of friends and the many roles these persons play throughout that child's life.

Positive role models for students come in various forms. Teachers, parents/caregivers, and other professionals are role models by default. Whether constant or ever-changing, they are the people who are easily identifiable to the child. Positive role models can also be triggered by cross-age and peer tutoring. In peer tutoring, students at the same chronological age level work together, while cross-age tutoring involves tutors who are two or more years older than the tutee (Kalkowski, 1995). Both tutoring types have the specific goal of helping each other learn through the process of teaching each other and assisting one another with specific skills. Cross-age and peer tutoring facili-

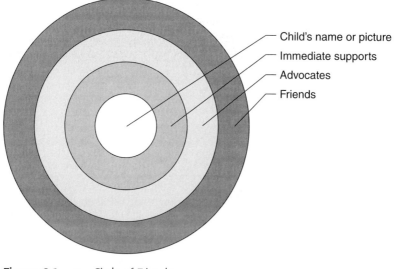

Child's name or picture
Immediate supports
Advocates
Friends

Figure 6.1 ● Circle of Friends.
OASIS, n.d.

Figure 6.2 • Tips for training tutors for peer or cross-age tutoring.

Topics to Address When Training Tutors

- *Sensitivity to others' feelings.* Tutors should be aware of person-first language and confidentiality issues when working with students with various needs.
- *Ways to develop positive relationships.* Tutors would benefit from conversation starters and interest inventories. One way to develop a rapport is to begin the first session with a "getting to know each other" activity instead of an academic session.
- *Effective communication and interaction skills.* Tutors should use effective turn-taking techniques and conversation skills. Additionally, they would benefit from a list of guiding questions created and distributed by the teacher.
- *Tutoring procedures and guidelines.* The tutor and tutee must be advised of the "dos and don'ts" of tutoring. For example, the tutor may read the questions on the test, but may not provide hints for the answers to the tutee.
- *Procedures for gathering data on progress.* Both the tutor and the tutee should submit a completed rubric on progress. This could be as simple as circling a smiley or sad face. Additionally, checklists and charts provide data for completion of tasks.
- *Resolving problems.* Problem-solving resolutions should be mapped out in advance. Tutors and tutees should be required to follow certain outlined procedures prior to adult interventions.
- *Schedule and commitment.* Tutors must be aware of and agree to the scheduling of the tutoring session. A formal contract outlining time constraints and responsibilities of tutors is helpful.

tates increased social interactions and academic gains for both the tutor and tutee. This relationship will contribute to the development of social behaviors, decreased classroom discipline problems, and the enhancement of peer relations. Additionally, the tutoring may contribute to students who are not liked becoming more socially accepted by their peers. (For tips and topics for training peer and cross-age tutees, refer to Figure 6.2)

Social Development

The attempt to provide quality programs for many diverse enthusiastic students is challenging enough; nevertheless, that diversity is compounded when students with disabilities are added to the classroom making it an inclusive setting. When responsible for the instruction of students with disabilities, teachers must consider all the cognitive, social, emotional, and behavioral issues that come with them.

Children's **social development** is characterized by their experiences. Their social and emotional skills are a result of many interactive experiences throughout their lives, along with the engagement and interactions between themselves and their family members. These skills may be progressed by properly planned activities and learning materials. Parents and educators must "set the stage" for learning by working together to increase the opportunity for social and emotional development.

John Dewey (1973) said, "Children learn by doing." One interpretation of this is that children learn by playing. Play provides children with natural, repeated, opportunities for critical learning (Heward, 2005). This is how children explore the world and discover their own capabilities and interests. Play becomes increasingly complex over time and, if adequately supported, will lead to the development of social skills, in addition to gross and fine motor skills (Morrison, 1999; Weber, Behl, & Summers, 1994). Some agree that play is the work of a child. If this is so, then toys are the instruments children use to accomplish their work. Toys should provide meaningful, motivating activities that serve as a precursor to more complex intentional learning (Brewer & Krieff, 1996, Mann, 1996; Perlmutter & Burrell, 1995).

Parents/caregivers and educators alike must be especially diligent when selecting toys for children with disabilities. The National Lekotek Center is a nationwide, nonprofit network for play centers, toy lending libraries, and computer loan programs that is dedicated to making play accessible for children with disabilities and to those living in poverty. The planning and information officer at Lekotek recommends keeping ten things in mind when selecting toys for young children with disabilities (see Table 6.3).

Peer-Based Strategies

Five-year-old Joshua and 6-year-old Rashawn have been best friends since they were in preschool together two years ago. Rashawn recently moved on to kindergarten, and now Joshua feels really sad.

Joshua asked his mom, "Will I ever see Rashawn again?" Joshua's mother spoke about this with the preschool teacher, who suggested she read *Frog and Toad Are Friends* by Arnold Lobel. Joshua enjoyed reading about the adventures of two best friends.

As a part of social development, 5 year olds like Joshua began to form deeper attachments to buddies, especially those of the same sex. For Joshua this makes losing his friend Rashawn particularly stressful. Children who have developed competence in social skills share toys, take turns, cooperate with others, and resolve conflicts. Children should feel good about themselves and know how to express their emotions and feelings.

Family Systems

Families play a vital role in the education of their children. Certainly, the role of the family is critical in the education of young children, due to the fact that they are usually a child's first and most invested teachers. Families create conditions that support and maximize the child's behavior and achievement at school. Consequently, in order to meet the needs of young students, teachers should

Table 6.3 ● Considerations for Selecting Toys for Young Children With Disabilities

Characteristic	Questions to Consider
1. Child's Individual Interest	Does the toy provide activities that reflect both developmental and chronological ages?
	Does it reflect the child's interest?
2. Multisensory Appeal	Does the toy respond with lights, sounds, or movements?
	Are there contrasting colors?
	Does it have a scent?
	Does it have texture?
3. Method of Activation	Will the toy provide a challenge without frustration?
	What force is required to activate it?
	What are the number and complexity of steps required?
4. Adjustability	Does the toy have adjustable height, sound, volume, speed, or level of difficulty?
5. Opportunities for Success	Can play be open-ended, with no definite right or wrong way?
6. Self-Expression	Does the toy allow for creativity and choice making?
	Will it give the child experience with a variety of media?
7. Potential for Interaction	Will the child be an active participant during use?
	Will the toy encourage social and language engagement with others?
8. Safety and Durability	Are the toy and its parts sized appropriately given the child's size and strength?
	Can it be washed and cleaned?
	Is it moisture resistant?
9. Use of Toy	Will the toy be easy to store?
	Is there space in the home?
	Can the toy be used in variety of positions?
10. Current Popularity	Is it a toy almost any child would like?
	Does it tie in with popular books, TV programs, or movies?

understand the various family systems and how to communicate with diverse family structures in order to facilitate supportive relationships. Positive relationships with the parents/caregivers may include understanding the importance of home learning activities, as well as recognizing the significance of involving fathers in students' education. Additionally, teachers must embrace the role that the families' cultural backgrounds play in this relationship-building process.

The traditional definition of family as a nuclear construct is insufficient; rather, a family is composed of parents or any other family or nonfamily members who have an important caregiving responsibility for a child (Healy, Keesee, & Smith, 1989). Simply stated, this definition is consistent with the **family systems** model, which acknowledges all important influences on individuals within families. The family systems model provides a framework for understanding what a family is and how it functions. Educators should embrace the family systems model and consider and respect the fact that family configurations include foster families, adoptive families, nuclear biological families, single-parent families, extended families, and same-gender-parents families.

Three of the most significant assumptions of the family systems model are (1) the input/output configuration of systems, (2) the concepts of wholeness and subsystems, and (3) the role of boundaries in defining systems (Whitechurch & Constantine, 1993). This model focuses mainly on what happens to the input as it is processed by the system on its way to becoming an output. Inputs consist of family characteristics. Think back to both Yomara's and Aaron's families and their inputs. How do family characteristics listed influence how these families interact within and outside the family? (See Table 6.4.)

The second assumption focuses on wholeness. This operates from the premise that the family system is one unit. It must be understood as a whole and cannot be understood by examining individual parts. For example, in order to begin to teach Yomara, you must understand her family and how it works. There are key interacting pieces surrounding siblings, extended family, and parents that must be considered.

Boundaries describes the third assumption. Family systems are separated from everything else by boundaries. These boundaries are created by the family and defined by the family's interaction with one another and those outside the family unit. Families vary in the degree to which their boundaries are open or closed to nonfamily members such as school personnel. The openness of boundaries affects the degree to which families will collaborate with educators (Turnbull & Turnbull, 2001).

A working knowledge and understanding of who families are is imperative. Once steps have been made in this direction, teachers and school personnel can begin to build collaborative relationships. This will assist in defining steps toward family involvement in their child's education.

Parents/caregivers should be viewed as partners or collaborative team members in the decision making and treatment of their children. Recently, all education legislation passed by Congress has strengthened a commitment to collaboration (Dettmer, Dyck, & Thurston, 1999). The Beach Center on Families and Disability (1999) identified eight components important for family-centered practice. The first component focuses on the parent/caregiver, not just the child. Family is an important part of a child's life and should be considered as educational plans are developed. The second component places an emphasis on mutual respect and teamwork. Respecting and valuing one another's opinions and inputs solidifies the relationships among stakeholders. By working together

Table 6.4 • Family Characteristics

Inputs—Family Characteristics	Outputs—Family Functions	
Characteristics of the family	Affection	Daily care
Personal characteristics	Self-esteem	Socialization
Special challenges	Spiritual	Recreation
	Economics	Education

for the benefit of the child, parents/caregivers and teachers reinforce the learning, maintenance, and generalization of skills across several settings.

The third component focuses on providing organized assistance according to individual parent/caregiver needs. The provision of organized assistance prevents the delivery of fragmented services. The fourth element emphasizes a need for consideration of parent/caregiver strengths, talents, resources, attributes, and aspirations. Certainly families as complex as they are come with their own unique talents and attributes. Resources are sometimes available within the extended family unit. This includes aunts, uncles, cousins, and members of the community. The fifth component speaks to a need for service providers to exhibit actions that address parent/caregiver needs holistically. Such holistic practices begin not only to focus on one member of the family, the student, but to consider the needs of the entire family.

The sixth element outlined by the Beach Center for Families and Disability details the need to provide information to families in a supportive manner. This certainly includes the need to extend appropriate resources and supports. Knowledge of the community is an important key here. The seventh component recognizes that there are similar parent/caregiver reactions to exceptional circumstances. Finally, the eighth and element explores the desire to establish an infrastructure that will encourage delivery of services, which are accessible for families without undue disruption of the families integrity and routines.

In order to fully appreciate student differences, teachers need support from parents/caregivers whose ethnic and cultural backgrounds differ from their own. Educators of young children must be sensitive to cultural differences that may be of concern to specific culturally diverse groups (Heward, 2005). For example, it is important to recognize cultural influences on childrearing practices.

Regardless of cultural differences among various cultural or ethnic groups, one must always be aware that each family comes with its own unique experiences and vary as far as their distance from traditional norms, values, beliefs, and practices. Attitudes regarding childrearing vary in many ways and can lead to conflict between families and professionals. A family's educational level, socioeconomic status, history within the mainstream culture, and geographic location will make a difference in how closely or differently they mirror a particular cultural profile (Harry, 2002).

Some families, especially those with monetary resources, usually have the opportunity to exercise choice. For example, many families have choices as to where their children will be educated and where their families will live. Often families from culturally and linguistically diverse backgrounds do not have such opportunities unless financial means are available. Donato (2005) recommends systemic reform in educational policy, which includes funding (allocating personnel and funding on a per-pupil or as-needed basis). There is clearly a need for a substantial investment in those schools that educate our impecunious children. Additionally, incentives should be provided for those highly qualified individuals who choose to teach in our schools within the neediest neighborhoods.

Considerations for the Culturally Competent Educator

Classrooms in the United States are becoming more ethnically diverse, and this diversity can present challenges for educators (Johnson, 2003). The culturally competent educator is one who has moved from being culturally unaware to being aware and sensitive to his or her own cultural heritage and to valuing and respecting differences. This educator is aware of their own values and biases and how these biases affect people from various culturally and linguistically diverse backgrounds. A culturally competent educator is sensitive to circumstances (personal biases, stages of ethnic identity, socio-political influences, etc.) that may indicate that others may need to talk about concerns with people of their own race or culture.

The culturally competent educators have a thorough understanding of the socio-political system's operation in the United States with respect to treatment of those who fall within the minority (i.e., people of color, women, individuals with disabilities, etc). These teachers strive to gain specific knowledge and information about the particular group(s) whom they serve. Think back to the discussion of Yomara and her family earlier in the chapter. A culturally competent educator is comfortable with differences that exist between the teacher and students and families in terms of race, culture, and beliefs (Kea, Campbell-Whatley, & Richards, 2004; Ortiz & Flanagan, 2002).

Two-way communication between educators and parents/caregivers not only is critical for the success of students but is also the foundation for an effective partnerships. An effective relationship with parents/caregivers is grounded in good communication. Although not always easy, communication with parents/caregivers does not have to be a difficult task. It is imperative that educators inform parents/caregivers about the program in general and, specifically, the progress of the students. Regular and clear communication regarding student progress, curricular objectives, standards of the program, and assessment procedures and learning outcomes builds these strong partnerships that have affirmative impacts on student learning and socialization.

Respect for the home language means respect for the students and their culture (Au, 2005). This type of respect allows teachers to build on the strengths that certain aspects of the home language generate. It is also important to integrate good multicultural literature, that is, literature portraying people from the students' cultures and ethnic backgrounds in a variety of positive life experiences. It must be authentic and from an emic perspective—an insider's view of the culture. Care should be given to communication effectively with non-English-speaking parents/caregivers, as well. Providing copies of materials in their native language, employing translators at meetings, or eliciting community group members to assist with relationship building are other means of encouraging participation and building relationships with parents/caregivers who speak and understand no or very limited English (NCPIE, n.d.).

Involvement of Fathers

Judah Edwards is the father of three children. His children are 6 years old, 3 years old, and 9 months old. Mr. Edwards is also a single parent who recently lost his wife in a traumatic automobile accident. After eight years of marriage he found himself as, not only the primary caregiver, but also the primary wage earner of his family. The 6-year-old is in first grade, while the 3 year old attends an early childhood special education program, and the 9-month-old is taken care of in a home daycare in their neighborhood. Mr. Edwards worked hard to embrace each new challenge but still needed a great deal of support. This father felt overwhelmed and isolated. He began to wonder whether there were other men in similar situations. He began by asking about a support group that might be available. While there was no such group currently available, the social worker at his child's elementary school assisted Mr. Edwards with starting a support group for fathers who are primary caregivers or single parents.

A father's involvement is a key component of a child's education. Statistics support that a father's involvement in a child's schooling has an astounding affect on the overall educational success of the child. In a study conducted by Nord and West (2001), when fathers, regardless if living with or apart from their children, had some involvement in their children's education, the students were likely to get better grades and less likely to be retained at any grade level. Additionally, the fathers' involvement contributed to fewer severe disciplinary actions including suspensions and expulsions than among those students whose fathers were not involved in some aspect of their education.

It is imperative that teachers make a concerted, sincere effort to involve fathers. Activities that encourage fathers to attend school functions may include bring-your-father-to-school day, breakfast with daddy, after-school athletic events, weekend or evening family fun events, or any other affair or fund-raiser that would support family and father involvement. The key is to be creative and flexible. Teachers can make telephone calls to fathers asking them to volunteer or generate ideas for events held at times convenient for working parents/caregivers. The teachers can have students create invitations to mail directly to the father (or other significant male in the child's life). Some fathers may not know how to participate, so it is up to the educators within those programs to lay the groundwork. Surveys or interviews on what contributions these important family members can do for the program are one way to accomplish a positive relationship and encourage more fathers to be involved.

Parent–Professional Collaboration

There are several strategies that can be used to promote parent/caregiver empowerment. These include finding ways to involve parents/caregivers in developing plans to address critical needs, as well as personalizing contacts between assistants and parents/caregivers to build mutual trust and support. Helping establish a network with other parents/caregivers will aid in problem solving and enrichment, as well as break through feelings of isolation. Other strategies to empower consist of enabling action through provision of services such as child care and transportation and offering a variety of meaningful activities, such as home visits, group meetings, and individual conferences. Focusing on the prevention of risk factors and advocating for collaborative community services (Howard, Willis, & Lepper, 2005) are also excellent approaches.

Paraeducators

Researchers are discussing the teachers' utilization of paraeducators in the classroom, with an emphasis being placed on inclusive setting. This section will discuss the paraeducator's role in the general classroom setting and provide suggestions for effective use of this powerful human resource.

The prefix *para-* is defined as "at the side of, beside, alongside of." A "paraeducator," therefore, is a person who works alongside of the teachers, specialists, and administrators in a school. This section will highlight the importance of establishing effective connections with paraeducators, who so often have to work within the classroom setting along with the teacher. Paraeducators are likely the most valuable human resource in our schools today (Morgan & Ashbaker, 2001a). Paraeducators can be referred to as school employees

> whose position is either instructional in nature or who deliver other direct or indirect services to students and/or parents; and who work under the supervision of a teacher or other professional staff member who

is responsible for the overall conduct of the class, the design and implementation of individualized educational programs, and the assessment of the effect of the programs on the student progress. (Pickett, 1988)

A pareducator should be considered as an extension of the teacher. Vigilant planning on the part of the teacher and with the paraeducator will establish a relationship built on respect that will contribute to increased capacity to meet the needs of all students—both with and without disabilities. Paraeducators should be permitted and encouraged to assist with the instructional process and daily routines.

In recent years, as more children with special needs are integrated into programs originally designed for those students without disabilities, the role of paraeducators has grown. The inclusive service delivery model has increased the need to support both the students and teachers, thus paraeducators have been hired to assist with behavioral and physical challenges of children with special needs.

Principles Versus Preferences

Several researchers (Morgan & Ashbaker, 2001b; Pickett, 1988; Pickett & Gerlach, 1997) discuss ideas that may help prevent problems in the classroom. Most people have principles that govern the actions we take; likewise, most have preferences also. Principles can be looked at as truths, laws, or moral standards that we will not compromise, whereas preferences are the things that we choose to do or prefer to do as the most desirable among various choices (Morgan & Ashbaker, 2001a). Teachers should be aware of the paraeducators' strengths and preferences. For example, some paraeducators prefer to have things written down. The paraeducator may not say this, but the teacher may notice that tasks do not get done unless they are written down. Other paraeducators may need to have instructions explained several times. It is important for the teacher to express her or his needs and preferences to the paraeducator so that the strengths of each person can be respected. It is important for both the teacher and paraeducator to recognize the significance of principles and preferences and the difference between the two. Communicating about what is important may prevent working relationship problems. Figure 6.3 (Virginia Department of Education, 2002) lists some items that may assist with pinpointing areas of focus for continued improvement.

Supervision

Effective use of paraeducators in the inclusive classroom should include adequate supervision. The teacher as supervisor is an evolving role. This involves supervisory functions such as role clarifying, planning, directing or delegating, monitoring, mentoring, and evaluating.

> *Role clarifying.* Roles should be discussed and clarified for paraeducators. When designing roles and responsibilities, teachers should consider "experience, training, comfort level, time constraints, and knowledge level of paraeducators (Picket & Gerlash, 1997). Teachers should also consider assigning roles incrementally to correspond to the paraeducators' increasing skills, which is similar to the instructional practice teachers use with students, adding to their knowledge base after carefully determining that they have a sound understanding on which to build (Morgan & Ashbaker, 2001a).

Figure 6.3 ● Self-evaluation checklist for working with paraeducators.

Self-Evaluation Checklist for Working With Paraeducators

Key

1 = No problem	I have done this or do it regularly
2 = Minor problem	I could improve on this
3 = Major problem	This definitely needs attention

Activity	Rating 1–3	How can I improve in this area?
I have a clearly defined role for my paraeducator.		
I have checked that my paraeducator understands this role.		
My paraeducator(s) knows the school district and state guidelines regarding the paraeducator roles.		
I have clear priorities for student learning.		
I have communicated these to my paraeducator(s).		
I understand my paraeducator's preferred work style.		
I have clear priorities for student learning and have communicated these to my paraeducator(s).		
I set aside regular time to meet and plan with my paraeducator(s).		

Virginia Department of Education, 2002

Planning work assignments. Planning work assignments includes providing written plans for the paraeducator to follow (Chissom, 2002; Dover, 2001; Floyd, 2004, French, 1998). Designing the instructional environment and making decisions about the goals, objectives, activities, and evaluations of instruction are tasks not within the paraeducator's scope of responsibility. Whether planning is formal or informal, it remains the responsibility of the teacher.

Directing or delegating tasks. Directing or providing direct assistance is accomplished through ongoing contact to observe and assist the paraeducator with classroom instruction (Glickman, Gordon, & Ross-Gordon 2001), whereas delegating is the assignment of certain tasks to others to allow the leader or supervisor to focus on more critical tasks at hand. Delegation is an informal involvement tactic used by open and effective leaders (Blasé & Kirby, 2000). Responsible delegation can assist paraeducators in gaining new skills and initiative.

Monitoring performance. Monitoring the quality of a paraeducator's work is a supervisory function that may come naturally to some teachers. Performance monitoring has been seen as adding an extra burden to a teacher's already full schedule of duties (Floyd, 2004), but it is essential to ensure that the paraeducator is performing his or her duties responsibly. Even informal assessment of paraeducator performance can be time-consuming. However, the opportunity to reinforce positive behaviors through observation should not be overlooked (Blasé & Kirby, 2000).

Mentoring and on-the-job training. Systematic on-the-job training and mentoring are supervisory techniques teachers can use to encourage paraeducators to perform their delegated tasks to the best of their abilities. Teachers can provide on-the-job training in numerous ways, which include meeting formally or informally, modeling, providing feedback, and coaching paraeducators through various situations.

Evaluating. This kind of supervision is best suited for the classroom teacher, yet teachers are often unprepared and uncomfortable when asked to supervise paraeducators (French, 1998; Frith & Lindsey, 1982; Scruggs & Mastropieri, 1996). While monitoring performance includes the informal observation of task, evaluating performance focuses on ensuring the fulfillment of job descriptions, providing constructive feedback, and issuing reprimands when needed (Dover, 2001). Observation is also a method for evaluating the performance of paraeducators.

A considerable amount of literature offers information pertaining to the preparation, training, and duties of paraeducators (Cramer, 1997; Hoover, 1999; Mueller, 1997; Werts, 1998), but their supervision has not been given significant attention. There are a few recent studies that help clarify what teacher supervision of paraeducators should entail. To some degree, outcomes or common elements that emerged from these studies relate to the six key supervisory functions for teachers working with paraeducators. The importance of communication and collaboration between the supervising teacher and paraeducator has been well documented as an important link in inclusive classrooms (Chissom, 2002; Prigge, 1996; Rose, 2000).

Classroom Application Tips for Working With Paraeducators

The following strategies can assist in building productive relationships with paraeducators.

- Meet at a regularly scheduled time to plan. Situations may change, so the planning that was done and the roles that were assigned at the beginning of the school year may need to be adapted to new student needs or changes in schedule.
- Identify legal limits of roles and responsibilities.
- Communicate what to do, how to do it, and why it is being done.
- Have a "teamwork party," where both the teacher and the paraeducator can see each other's strengths in a different setting.
- Be honest with the paraeducator. If you have concerns about the way something was done, then discuss it. Share with the paraeducator when something is done that you like.

- Remember that the students' best interests come first. All of the decisions made with and in regard to paraeducators work should be based on whether or not they will generate student success. (Morgan & Ashbaker, 2001b; Virginia Department of Education, 2002)

Paraeducators are recognized today as a major means of support to programs and students with special needs. When assigning tasks to paraeducators, teachers need to consider students and personnel, as well as the competencies and skills of the paraeducator (French, 1999a). Students benefit from having the teacher and paraeducator work together as a team and sense this "oneness of purpose" between the teacher and paraeducator. Such unity assures students that the team's first priority is their learning and well-being. Pickett and Gerlach (1997) recommend that school officials ensure that teachers and paraeducators have time to meet on a regular basis to plan activities and exchange information. The regular communication of teachers and paraeducators can lead to a positive impact on student achievement.

Other Professionals

Related service personnel, if utilized effectively, can serve as a natural extension to your classroom. When teachers suspects a student's home life may be troubled, they rely not only on the support of support staff and related service personnel employed by the school system but also on social service agencies and community personnel to help them find the appropriate assistance. Teachers need support from other teachers and service providers who specialize in areas outside their own expertise and disciplines.

Collaboration

Collaboration involves more than simple two-way communication. The major key to effective programs is collaboration. One may have communication without collaboration; however, it is impossible to have collaboration without communication. **Collaboration** is an interactive process where "interactions throughout the process are characterized by mutual respect, trust, and open communication" (Welch, 1998, p. 28). Collaboration is a process whereby people come together in order to meet a common, agreed-upon goal. Increasing collaboration in settings serving young children requires structures and processes whereby every member of the group is working together toward a shared, common purpose (DuFour, 1997; Pinchot, 1998).

The start of the new millennium initiated a collaboration movement and a major shift in the thinking for education professionals. Educators and researchers now focus their attention on "how" and "what" to teach students with disabilities instead of where to teach them. The general education setting, as opposed to more segregated settings, has become the preferred placement for students with disabilities—especially in the early years of schooling. More than ever before, students with disabilities are being educated in inclusive settings alongside their peers without disabilities—a movement that educators foresee as only getting stronger. As with all school settings, this generated a trend toward more collaborative practices within educational programs.

As more and more students with disabilities are participating in the general education setting, effective restructuring of education must incorporate professional collaboration (Hourcade & Bauwens, 2001). Teacher assistance teams, coteaching, and collaborative consultation and are just three examples of educational models brought about by inclusive practices that are based on high quantities of effective, quality collaboration.

Characteristics

Collaboration in the inclusive educational setting involves two or more people with different expertise planning, implementing, and evaluating the progress of all students. In the inclusive classroom, collaboration occurs on many levels and has many variations. Proponents of more inclusive practices argue that the collaboration taking place in general education environments reinforces the progress of students with disabilities "because they are held to higher expectations, exposed to more challenging content, and inspired by the example of their nondisabled peers" (Willis, 1994, p. 2).

A critical collaborative skill is effective communication. In order to appropriately and successfully communicate, teachers must have time for planning. This requires the support of program administrators. Many times, administrators must be creative in finding this time for planning. This may include splitting schedules for teachers, utilizing roving aides, paraeducators, and volunteers to assist in covering classes, or even providing financial incentives for collaborators to meet on their own time (Walther-Thomas, Korinek, McLaughlin, & Williams, 2000). It is important for all stakeholders to devote adequate time for this planning process. This investment of time entails all involved in the process wanting to be an active, participant on the collaborative team. Hence, true collaboration is voluntary.

When working in collaborative teams, certain personal and professional characteristics also come into play. Team members need to be flexible and open to new ideas. They must respect each others thoughts and contributions, remembering that everyone is working toward the same purpose. Each team member must be knowledgeable and proficient in their discipline so to ensure that contributions are reliable and viable. Additionally, they must have a vested interest in professional growth—keeping up with emerging best practices in their fields.

With all that successful collaboration entails, organizational skills on the part of its members are absolutely necessary for the team to be effectual. In addition to keeping up with the agendas, meetings, program schedules and progress, team members are responsible for an even more important task—the welfare and education of the students in the classroom. While having experience working on teams may assist in these tasks, it is not mandatory. These professionals must stay "on their toes" and maintain positive attitudes about the work they are doing.

Collaboration allows for acquisition of new information and skills. It is an ongoing problem-solving process with the specific, expressed purpose of solving the learning and behavior problems exhibited by young children. In review, researchers and literature support that stakeholders must possess several essential characteristics in order for collaboration to be successful (Bauwans & Hourcade, 1995; Friend & Cook, 2000; Turnbull & Turnbull, 2001; Walther-Thomas et al., 2000). Table 6.5 presents a compiled list of characteristics gleaned from research that are necessary for effective collaboration.

Once an adequate collaborative environment is up and running, focus must shift toward maintaining effective collaboration. Team members must embrace a constant vigilance of the collaborative process through ongoing reevaluation of the operating procedures. During this time, the use of problem-solving sessions is essential to handling situations that may have become problematic. Flexibility contributes to long-term success of the collaborative process.

Table 6.5 ● Eleven Essential Characteristics for Successful Collaboration

Characteristic	Suggestions for Practice
1. *Effective communication and problem-solving skills*	● Establish guidelines for communication early ● Create steps for a problem-solving process
2. *Dedication to planning regularly with a partner*	● Schedule meetings at the same time every week
3. *Willingness to invest time (including extra time) in the process*	● Share personal and other professional responsibilities with the team
4. *Voluntary participation in the collaborative process*	● Encourage perspective members to participate by being honest about the positive aspects of the team ● Avoid "mandating" participation or appointing members
5. *Personal and professional confidence*	● Believe in team members' abilities to contribute both personally and professionally ● Acknowledge efforts and suggestions of others on the team
6. *Flexibility and openness to new ideas*	● Listen to others ● Be willing to investigate new thoughts, strategies, or ideas
7. *Respect for colleagues' contributions and skills*	● Believe in presuming positive intent—all are on the team for the same purpose ● Know that others have different skills and backgrounds and view situations differently
8. *Professional competence*	● Investigate and ask questions ● Stay up-to-date on the latest emerging best practices in your area of expertise
9. *Efficient organizational skills*	● Invest in a calendar or daily planner (and use it) ● Create agendas for meetings and timelines for activities (and follow them as closely as possible)
10. *Professional passion for the cause*	● Leave the team (politely) if not interested in the purpose or overarching goals
11. *Previous experience working as a group member*	● "Practice makes perfect" (although helpful, not necessary) ● Remember the positive aspects of prior teaming experiences and relate them to new one

Collaborative Models

As the number of students with disabilities in public school programs increase, more and more collaborative teaming takes place. Collaboration can take many forms. Collaborative consultation, aid services, and coteaching are the most commonly used models in the inclusive setting.

Collaborative consultation is a model that emphasizes a close working relationship between general and special educators. According to Walther-Thomas and her colleagues (2000), collaborative consultation as a support service is rooted in consultation models used in many other professional fields (e.g., medicine, mental health, behavior psychology). Described as indirect collaboration (Hourcade & Bauwens, 2001), it is considered a support service that is indirect because the teacher receives assistance outside the classroom from consultants who typically do not interact with the students (Walther-Thomas et al., 2000). This model elicits little direct service to students with disabilities by special education teachers except in assessment, observation, and planning meetings. The new IDEA Improvement Act of 2004 makes clear statements about the role of consultation in inclusive programs, especially as it applies to working with teachers who have students at risk for learning disabilities or emotional and behavior disorders:

> [T]he term "consultative services" means services that adjust the learning environment, instructional methods, adapt curricula, use positive behavioral supports and interventions, and select and implement appropriate accommodations to meet the needs of individual children. (U.S. Department of Education [USDOE], 2004, H.R. 1350, Sec. 602[10])

Collaborative consultation requires a strong trust and an effective, organized communication system. The most critical piece to the collaborative-consultation model is the coplanning time. This is when stakeholders determine what specific adaptations and modifications that are needed to support student learning, behavior, and socialization. Special education service providers may offer additional instructional materials but typically do not provide service directly to students.

Benefits of this type of collaboration are that it facilitates the ongoing planning, evaluation, and modifications necessary to ensure the success of students in inclusive placements. It also enables school personnel to meet the needs of students with and without disabilities by providing the personnel support of highly skilled colleagues. A collaborative-consultation process results in personal and professional growth for all involved and helps teachers identify ways to access the skills, knowledge, and expertise of others in the field.

The success of paraeducator services depends on professional abilities of these assistants. It also greatly depends on the ability of the teachers—both general and special educators—to collaborate and communicate with the paraeducators. In a classroom with one to four students with disabilities paraeducators are able to check student's progress, provide individual or small-group tutoring assistance, directly assist the classroom teacher, and report back to special education teacher (Elliott & McKenney, 1998).

Collaborative teaching, cooperative teaching, and team teaching are all more commonly known as coteaching. Coteaching refers to two or more professionals possessing distinct sets of knowledge and skills, teaching together on an ongoing basis for at least a portion of the day (Hourcade & Bauwens, 2001; Vernon, 2003; Walther-Thomas et al., 2000). Typically, these educators consist of a general education teacher who is primarily responsible for content and a special educator with strengths in teaching strategies, modifications, and accommodations. This affords coteachers more flexibility as well as ongoing evaluation and monitoring of all students in the inclusive setting. Pugach and Johnson (1995) refer to coteaching as "one of the most powerful manifestations of professional collaboration" (p. 193) because it removes teachers from isolated classroom settings, therefore promoting collaboration as an integral part of the daily classroom routine.

Some challenges to a coteaching environment may include lack of autonomy, some pedagogical differences, loss of space (sharing one room or setting), and, according to Pugach and Johnson (1995), professionals may be uncomfortable because they tend to feel that someone is watching them and possibly judging them on a regular basis—a situation that is very unfamiliar to most veteran teachers. As the responsibility for educating students with disabilities extends beyond special education to a schoolwide or programwide function, general education teachers are held accountable for educating more diverse populations than ever before. Coteaching precludes the "your" students and "my" students effect. All students are the responsibility of both educators.

Several authors and researchers outline benefits collaborative environments (Lipsky & Gartner, 1997; McLaughlin & Verstegen, 1998; Stainback & Stainback, 1996; Vernon, 2003; Walther-Thomas et al., 2000). However, Sage (1997) summed it up best when stating that effective collaboration creates inclusive opportunities that

- help all students feel welcome and feel a sense of belonging,
- help students to become aware that everyone has strengths and weaknesses,
- ensure that students form an appreciation of diversity in relation to individual differences,
- present opportunities for students to observe and model positive social interactions, and
- result in greater availability of adults to facilitate educational development of all students. (p. 219)

Moreover, support for students with disabilities in an inclusive education setting could lead to better ways of meeting the needs of other students considered at risk for school failure, such as those with lower-than-average cognitive ability or delayed social skills or who are second-language learners. Thus, the role of the special educators in inclusive education is expanded to provide support to classroom teachers for any child with problems, not just students labeled as having disabilities (Pugach & Johnson, 1995).

Collaborative consultation, aide services, and coteaching are not new concepts in education; they have recently resurfaced as a means to meet the needs of students with disabilities within the inclusive setting. These examples of collaborative models provide support for the notion that collaboration is "the foundation of successful inclusive education" (Hourcade & Bauwens, 2001, p. 242). In turn, inclusive practices cannot exist without appropriate collaboration and effective communication.

Trust

Relationships in and outside of the classroom are built on trust. Trust contributes to organization, program, and partnership effectiveness and is a required element for both cooperation and collaboration in school settings (Tschannen-Moran, 2001). **Trust** is the extent to which one person allows themselves to be vulnerable to another. Such vulnerability is based on confidence in several facets important in building trust, including reliability, competence, openness, and honesty (Hoy & Tschannen-Moran, 1999). Trust takes dedication and time to build, yet a trusting relationship can be destroyed in a mere instance.

In their extensive studies on teams and teamwork, Yeatts and Hyten (1998) found that, when trust was reported as being high, team members spent less time and energy worrying about what others were thinking or doing and more time and energy on actually doing the work. Trust directly contributes to the success of collaborative teaching models as well. The effectiveness of collaborative consultation, aide services, and coteaching is grounded in trusting relationships. Trust is a required element effective collaboration in school programs and is embedded in collaborative practices.

Special Issues

Cultural and Linguistic Diversity

Cultural and linguistic diversity is represented by people from varied cultural and/or linguistic backgrounds coexisting in the society. The rich diversity of today's population challenges conventional patterns of involvement and communication between teachers and families. Such diversity requires sensitivity when considering regular methods of contacting all parents or caregivers. Educators are challenged to become personally aware and to use culturally responsive interaction practices. The vignette at the beginning of the chapter mentioned the challenge of the teacher, Mrs. Giles, reaching Aaron's parents for a conference. Regardless of the family's background or cultural difference, the teacher must remain professional and committed to establishing trust with the parents/caregivers.

Siblings

Siblings of children with special needs can have their specific needs addressed as well. This can be done via a series of workshops designed just for them, called Sibshops. **Sibshops** are described as opportunities for brothers and sisters of children with special health and developmental needs to obtain peer support and education within a recreational context (Meyer & Vadasy, 1994). These workshops reflect a commitment to the well-being of the sibling, the family member who is most likely to have the longest-lasting relationship with the person with special needs. The Sibshops model provides the sibling without a disability with opportunities for unique peer support. Emphasis is primarily placed on school-age children.

Creators of Sibshops carefully note that the workshops are not therapy, group or otherwise. However, it is important to note that the effects of Sibshops have been known to have therapeutic effects for some children in attendance (Meyer & Vadasy, 1994). Facilitators of Sibshops are trained to use a wellness approach.

There are five goals of the Sibshop model. Sibshops will provide

1. Brothers and sisters of children with special needs and opportunity to meet other siblings in a relaxed, recreational setting.
2. Brothers and sisters with opportunities to discuss common joys and concerns with other siblings of children with special needs.
3. Siblings with an opportunity to lean how others handle situations commonly experienced by siblings of children with special needs.
4. Siblings with an opportunity to learn more about the implications of their siblings special needs.
5. Parents and other professionals with opportunities to learn more about the concerns and opportunities frequently experienced by brothers and sisters of people with special needs.

Summary

This chapter provided a discussion of relationships in and outside the classroom. A wide range of topics have been introduced as well as suggestions and strategies for use in the classroom. Certainly, the focus has been on the provision of support to young children with and without disabilities. Central to building and maintaining effective relationships is communication along with the concepts of collaboration, consultation, and teaming. The role of paraeducators and the need for appropriate supervision of these personnel has expanded in recent years. Paraeducators are key in extending the teacher's care and development of young children. The degree to which this potential is tapped into depends on how the teacher communicates and works to build a collegial working relationship with the paraeducator.

The importance of family involvement in any program is essential; however, it is most imperative when considering the education of young children with special needs. Educators must reflect on reasons for wanting to involve parents/caregivers, then be prepared think creatively when doing so. Teachers must create "father-friendly" environments. Fathers too need help and encouragement as they develop nurturing relationships with their children (Lue, Smalley, & Seaton, 1998). Family involvement also includes embracing the diverse backgrounds of the students and their families. It is important that teachers communicate not only their commitment to the child they are the teaching but also respect to the families, like those of Aaron and Yomara, whom they serve.

Thinking It Through

1. In a coteaching model of inclusion support, what are some strategies to ensure that both teachers share equal responsibility for *all* children in the class?

2. What are some various ways in which paraeducators can serve students with disabilities in the inclusive classroom?

3. Develop a set of questions you would ask potential volunteers in your classroom. Questions should delve into determining how the volunteer will fit into your classroom environment and assist with daily activities.

4. What can you do to begin to build relationships with families from culturally and linguistically diverse backgrounds? Develop an action plan to outline what steps you will take; be sure to include resources needed to complete each step.

5. Brainstorm a list of ways you can work to involve fathers in your program. Focus on fathers from culturally and linguistically diverse backgrounds.

6. How do the culture, values, language, and resources of Yomara's family enter into the interactions between the classroom teacher and Yomara?

7. In what ways can having a child with disabilities affect the family system?

8. According to Attwood (1998), Circle of Friends can also be used to explain to the child with a disability appropriateness of social contact. Using the same descriptions from above, with the family being in the innermost circle and strangers being in the outermost circle, this method can be used to explain appropriate behaviors. For example, hugs and kisses would be appropriate for the immediate family and close friends, but not for those in the outer circles. Create a Circle of Friends map using pictures as visual aids that indicate appropriate behaviors for each "level" of relationship. Discuss the strengths and challenges of using this type of activity in an inclusive education setting.

9. In this chapter, the importance of family involvement in a child's education was discussed. You are a kindergarten teacher in a very diverse school. You have a good relationship with a few members of the parent-teacher organization who volunteer in your classroom every week. All of the volunteers are White mothers. Design a plan to get a more diverse crew to volunteer. How will your plan include family members from other cultural and ethnic backgrounds? How will you get fathers involved?

10. Paraeducators are extremely beneficial in assisting students with disabilities as well as teachers. Identify five instructional or supervisory responsibilities and roles of paraeductors to assist students in the inclusive classroom.

11. This chapter has dealt with a variety to topics pertinent to relationships in and outside of the classroom, including siblings. Think about Aaron and his family, review the five goals of Sibshops, and visit the website listed in the Resources section. You will need to determine which of the five goals will benefit Aaron's family. Then move on to sponsor a Sibshop for not only Aaron's family but all the families of children in your school. Develop your invitation and a sample Sibshop schedule of activities. Your invitation should include an explanation of Sibshops.

12. In this chapter you were introduced to Mr. Edwards, a father of three small children. Mr. Edwards is also a single parent. Review the vignette about his family situation, consider what supports are needed, then research your local area to find three support groups that might be appropriate for Mr. Edwards. Evaluate these support groups using the following criteria, and prepare to share the information with him during an upcoming conference.

Organization Name:
Contact Person:
Phone Number:
Cost:
Service Provided:
Areas/Goal Addressed:
Benefits for the Exceptional Student:
Benefits for the Exceptional Parent:
Benefits for the General and Special Educator:
Agency Recommendation:

★★★★ Superior (strongly recommend)

★★★ Above Average (recommend)

★★ Average (recommend with reservation)

★ Below Average (do not recommend)

Resources

Parent/Caregiver

The Beach Center on Families and Disability

www.beachcenter.org

The Beach Center on Disability consists of a rehabilitation research and training center on policies and families funded by the National Institute on Disability and Rehabilitation Research, U.S. Department of Education; doctoral training programs and research initiatives funded by the Office of Special Education, U.S. Department of Education; and a research center on the ethical, legal, and social implications of the Human Genome Project, funded by the National Human Genome Project Institute, National Institutes of Health.

PACER Center

www.pacer.org

The mission of PACER Center is to expand opportunities and enhance the quality of life of children and young adults with disabilities and their families, based on the concept of parents helping parents. PACER offers assistance to individual families, workshops, materials for parents and professionals, and leadership in securing a free and appropriate public education for all children.

National Center on Fathering

www.fathers.com

Created by the National Center for Fathering, fathers.com provides research-based training, practical tips, and resources to help men be the involved fathers, grandfathers, and father figures their children need.

National Parent Information Network

www.npin.org

The National Parent Information Network offers educational software and services for middle school, high school, and college students. A selection of creative, innovative, and interactive products to empower students of all ages is also available.

The National Information Center for Children and Youth With Disabilities (NICHCY)

www.nichcy.org

The NICHCY website serves as a source of information on disabilities, laws, and research-based educational practices. It includes a number of features, such as frequently asked questions (FAQ) and an In Spanish (En Espanol) feature, that increase its effectiveness.

Collaboration

The Power of 2

www.powerof2.org

A website dedicated to the collaboration of parents and teachers to successfully include children with special needs in the general education classroom.

Project PARA

www.para.unl.edu

Project PARA is a committed to offering training beneficial to both paraeducators and the teachers who supervise them. It offers two Study programs; one Paraeducator Self-Study Program, and two Supervisors of Paraeducators Self-Study programs. It is an online, flexible, and creditable training program.

American Federation of Teachers, Paraprofessional and School-Related Personnel Division

www.aft.org/psrp/

The American Federation of Teachers (AFT) believes that a strong partnership between schools and parents is essential to the academic well-being of students. Information is presented on topics that parents frequently ask about, as well as ideas about how families can help their children be successful in school.

National Resource Center for Paraprofessionals in Education and Related Services

www.NRCpara.org

This site is the National Resource Center for paraprofessionals. It provides information on, and links to, materials used in their conferences. NRCpara is also a convenient way to keep up with related news and Para community events.

Siblings

Sibling Support Project

6512 23rd Avenue NW #213
Seattle, WA 98117
(206) 297-6368
www.thearc.org/siblingsupport

The Sibling Support Project was founded on the belief that disabilities, illness, and mental health issues affect the lives of *all* family members. The project seeks to increase the peer support and information opportunities for brothers and sisters of people with special needs and to increase parents' and providers' understanding of sibling issues.

References

Ashbaker, B. Y., & Morgan, J. (1999, March). *The "S" in ASCD: Teachers supervising paraeducators for professional development.* Paper presented at the 54th ASCD Annual Conference, San Francisco, CA. (ERIC Document Reproduction Service No. ED432561)

Attwood, T. (1998). *Asperger's syndrome: A guide for parents and professionals.* London: Jessica Kingsley.

Au, K. (2005). What research tells us about improving the literacy achievement of students of diverse backgrounds. Presentation at LASER (Linking Academic Scholars to Educational Research) Research Conference, University of South Florida, Tampa, FL.

Autism Network. (1999). Circle of friends. Retrieved July 14, 2005, from www.autismnetwork.org/modules/social/circle/index.html

Bauwens, J., & Hourcade, J. J. (1995). *Cooperative teaching: Rebuilding the schoolhouse for all students.* Austin, TX: Pro-Ed.

Beach Center on Families and Disability. (1999). *Quality indicators of exemplary family-centered legislation.*

Retrieved August 9, 2005, from www.lsi.ukans.edu/beach/html/17.htm

Blasé, J., & Kirby, P. C. (2000). *Bringing out the best in teachers: What effective principals do* (2nd ed.) Thousand Oaks, CA: Corwin Press.

Brewer, J., & Kieff, J. (1996). Fostering mutual respect for play at home and school. *Childhood Education, 7,* pp. 92–96.

Chissom, J. (2002). *Supervising paraprofessionals in middle school classrooms: A descriptive case study.* Unpublished doctoral dissertation, Virginia Polytechnic Institute and State University, Blacksburg, VA.

Cook, R., Klein, M. D., & Tessier, A. (2004). Adapting early childhood curricula for children in inclusive settings (6th ed.). Upper Saddle River, NJ: Prentice Hall.

Cramer, M. M. (1997). *Factors influencing the tasks performed by paraprofessionals in elementary school classrooms* (Doctoral dissertation, Virginia Polytechnic Institute and State University, 1997). ETD-82597-22506.

Dettmer, P., Dyke, N., & Thurston, L. P. (1999). *Consultation, collaboration, and teamwork* (3rd ed.). Boston: Allyn and Bacon.

Dewey, J. (1973). *Experience and education.* New York: Colliet Press.

Donato, R. (2005). *Mexican American education: Learning from the past, prospects for the future.* Presentation at LASER Research Conference—Raising the Roof: Higher visions for research in urban schools and communities, University of South Florida, Tampa, FL.

Dover, W. (2001). The instructional management of paraeducators in inclusive settings. Unpublished doctoral dissertation, Kansas State University.

Doyle, M. (1997). *The paraprofessional's guide to the inclusive classroom: Working as a team.* Baltimore: Brookes.

DuFour, R. P. (1997). The school as a learning organization: Recommendations for school improvement. *National Association of Secondary School Principals, 81*(588), 81–87.

Elliott, D., & McKenney, M. (1998 March/April). Four inclusion models that work. *Teaching Exceptional Children,* pp. 54–58.

Epstein, J. L. (1990). School and family connections: Theory, research, and implications for integrating sociologies of education and family. *Marriage & Family Review, 15,* pp. 99–126.

Floyd, L. (2004). *Supervision of paraeducators: Perceptions of special education teachers* (Doctoral Dissertation, The College of William & Mary, 2004). *Dissertation Ab-stracts International.* A: The humanities and social sciences.

French, N. K. (1998). Working together: Resource teachers and paraeducators. *Remedial and Special Education, 19*(6), 357–368.

French, N. K. (1999a). Paraeducators and teachers: Shifting roles. *Teaching Exceptional Children, 32*(2), 59–73.

French, N. (1999b). Supervising paraeducators: What every teacher should know. *CEC Today, 6*(2). Available online at www.cec.sped.org/bk/cectoday/1999/parasup-sept99.html

Friend, M., & Bursuck, W. D. (1996). *Including students with special needs: A practical guide for classroom teachers.* Boston: Allyn and Bacon.

Friend, M., & Cook, L. (2000). *Interactions: Collaboration skills for school professionals* (3rd ed.). New York: Addison Wesley Longman.

Frith, G. H., & Lindsey, J. D. (1982). Certification, training and other programming variables affecting special education and the paraprofessional concept. *The Journal of Special Education, 16,* 229–236.

Funkhouser, J. E., & Gonzales, M. R. (1997). *Family involvement in children's education: Successful local approaches.* Idea Book Series. Washington DC: Office of Educational Research and Improvement, National Institute on the Education of At-Risk Students. Retrieved July 26, 2005, from www.ed.gov/PDFDocs/97-7022.pdf

Glickman, C. D., Gordon, S. P., & Ross-Gordon, J. M. (2001). *Supervision and instructional leadership* (5th ed.). Boston: Allyn and Bacon.

Hanson, M. J., Gutierrez, S., Morgan, M., Brennan, E. L., & Zercher, C. (1997). Language, culture, and disability: Interacting influences on preschool inclusion. *Topics in Early Childhood Special Education, 17*(3), 307–336.

Harry, B. (2002). Trends and issues in serving culturally diverse families of children with disabilities. *The Journal of Special Education, 36*(3), 131–138.

Healy, A., Keesee, P. D., & Smith, B. S. (1989). *Early services for children with special needs: Transactions for family support.* Baltimore: Paul H. Brookes.

Heward, W. L. (2005). *Exceptional Children* (8th ed.) Upper Saddle River, NJ: Pearson/Merrill/Prentice Hall.

Hoover, J. H. (1999, March). *The roles of paraeducators in a rural-remote state: Views of administrators, teachers, and paras.* Rural Special Education for the New Millennium Conference Proceedings of the American Council on Rural Special Education (ACRES), Albuquerque, NM.

Hourcade, J. J., & Bauwens, J. (2001). Cooperative teaching: The renewal of teachers. *The Clearing House, 74*(5), 242–247.

Howard, V. F., Willis, B. F., & Lepper, C. (2005). *Very young children with special needs: A formative approach for today's children* (3rd ed.) Upper Saddle River, NJ: Pearson Merrill/Prentice Hall.

Hoy, W. K., & Tschannen-Moran, M. (1999). Five faces of trust: An empirical confirmation in urban elementary schools. *Journal of School Leadership, 9,* 184–208.

Johnson, L. M. (2003). What we know about: Culture and learning. Arlington, VA: Education Research Service.

Jones, V., & Jones, L. V. (2001). *Comprehensive classroom management: Creating communities of support and solving problems* (6th ed.). Boston: Pearson Education.

Kalkowski, P. (1995). Peer and cross-age tutoring. *School Improvement Research Series #18.* Available from Northwest Regional Education Laboratory at www.nwrel.org/scpd/sirs/9/c018.html

Kea, C. D., Campbell-Whatley, G. D., & Richards, H. V. (2004). Becoming culturally responsive educators: Rethinking teacher education pedagogy. Retrieved Oct. 14, 2006 from http:.//www.ncrest.org/Briefs/reacher_Ed.pdf

Levine, J. A. (1993). Involving fathers in head start: A framework for public policy and program development. *Families in Society, 74*(1), 4–19.

Lipsky, D. K., & Gartner, A. (1997). *Inclusion and school reform: Transforming America's classrooms.* Baltimore: Paul H. Brookes.

Lue, M. S., Smalley, B. S., & Seaton, G. (1998). African-American fathers with their preschool children. *The Educational Forum, 62*(4), 300–305.

Mann, D. (1996). Serious play. *Teachers College Record, 97*(3), 447–469.

McLaughlin, M. J., & Verstegen, D. A. (1998). Increasing regulatory flexibility in special education programs: Problems and promising strategies. *Exceptional Children, 64,* pp. 371–384.

Meyer, D. J., & Vadasy, P. F. (1994). *Sibshops:* Workshops for siblings of children with special needs. Boston: Paul H. Brookes.

Morgan, J., & Ashbaker, B. (2001a). *A teacher's guide to working with paraeducators and other classroom aides.* Richmond, VA: Association for Supervision and Curriculum Development.

Morgan, J., & Ashbaker, B. (2001b). 20 ways to work more

effectively with your paraeducator. *Intervention in School and Clinic, 36*(4), 230–231.

Morrison, R. S. (1999). Effects of correspondence training with photographic activity schedules on toy play by young children with pervasive developmental disorders. Unpublished doctoral dissertation, The Ohio State University, Columbus.

Mueller, P. H. (1997). A study of the roles, training needs, and support needs of Vermont's paraeducators. (Doctoral dissertation the University of Vermont: 1358). *Dissertation Abstracts International, 61,* 04-A.

National Coalition for Parent Involvement in Education (NCPIE). (n.d.). *A framework for family involvement.* Retrieved July 26, 2005, from www.ncpie.org/DevelopingPartnerships/

Nord, C. W., & West, J. (2001, May). *Fathers' and mothers' involvement in their children's schools by family type and resident status* (NCES 2001032). Washington DC: National Center for Educational Statistics. Retrieved July 26, 2005, from http://nces.ed.gov/pubs2001/2001032.pdf

Online Aspergers Syndrome Information and Support (OASIS). (n.d.). *Circle of friends.* Available at: www.udel.edu/bkirby/asperger/socialcircle.html

Ortiz, S. O., & Flanagan, D. P. (2002). Best practices in working with culturally diverse children and families. In A. Thomas & J. Grimes (Series Eds.), *Best practices in school psychology* IV (Vol. 1, pp. 337–351). Bethesda, MD: The National Association of School Psychologists.

Pearpoint, J., & Hollands, C. (2001). Common sense tools: MAPS and CIRCLES for inclusive education. *In Inclusion papers: Strategies to make inclusion work* (pp. 40–56). Toronto, ON: Inclusion Press.

Perlmutter, J., & Burrell, L. (1995, January). Learning through play as well as work. *Young Children,* pp. 14–21.

Piaget, J. (1926). *The language and thought of the child.* New York: Harcourt, Brace, Jovanovich.

Pianta, R. C. (1999). *Enhancing relationships between children and teachers:* School psychology book series. Washington, DC: American Psychological Association.

Pickett, A. L. (1988). *The employment and training of paraprofessional personnel: A technical assistance manual for administrators and staff developers.* New York: City University of New York, National Resource Center for Paraprofessionals in Education and Related Services, Center for Advanced Study in Education.

Pickett, A. L., & Gerlach, K. (Eds.). (1997). *Supervising*

paraeducators in school settings: A team approach.
Austin, TX: Pro-Ed.

Pinchot, G. (1998). Building community in the workplace. In
F. Hesselbein, M. Goldsmith, R. Beckhard, & R. F.
Shubert (Eds.), *The community of the future* (pp.
125–138). San Francisco: Jossey-Bass.

Prigge, D. J. (1996). Supervising the special education paraprofessional in inclusionary Settings (Doctoral dissertation University of Washington: 3893). *Dissertation
Abstracts International, 57,* 09A.

Pugach, M. C., & Johnson, L. J. (1995). Unlocking expertise
among classroom teachers through structures dialogue:
Extending research on peer collaboration. *Exceptional
Children, 62,* 101–110.

Robertson, J., Green, K., Alper, S., Schloss, P. J., & Kohler, F.
(2003). Using a peer-mediated intervention to facilitate
children's participation in inclusive childcare activities.
Education and Treatment of Children, 26(2), pp.
187–197.

Rogers, R. (1996). *Making friends.* New York: The Putnam &
Grosset Group.

Rose, R. (2000). Using classroom support in a primary school.
British Journal of Education, 27(4), 191–196.

Sage, D. D. (Ed.). (1997). *Inclusion in secondary schools:
Bold initiatives challenging change.* Port Chester, NY:
National Professional Resources.

Scruggs, T. E., & Mastropieri, M. A. (1996). Teacher perceptions of mainstreaming/inclusion 1958–1995: A research
synthesis. *Exceptional Children, 63,* pp. 59–74.

Stainback, W., & Stainback, S. (Eds.). (1996). *Controversial
issues confronting special education: Divergent perspectives* (2nd ed.). Boston: Allyn and Bacon.

Stormont, M. (2007). Fostering resilience in young children at
risk for failure: Strategies for grades K–3. Upper Saddle
River, NJ: Merrill/Prentice Hall.

Tab, E. D. (2005, May). *Parent involvement in education:
2002–2003* (NCES 2005043). Washington, DC: National
Center for Education Statistics. Retrieved July 26, 2005,
from http://nces.ed.gov/pubs2005/2005043.pdf

Tschannen-Moran, M. (2001). Collaboration and the need for
trust. *Journal of Educational Administration, 34*(4),
308–331.

Turnbull, A. P., Pereira, L., & Blue-Banning, M. J. (2000).
Teachers as friendship facilitators. *Teaching Exceptional
Children, 32*(5), 66–70.

Turnbull, A. P., & Turnbull, H. R. (2001). *Families, professionals, and exceptionality: Collaborating for empowerment*
(4th ed.). Upper Saddle River, NJ: Merrill/Prentice Hall.

U.S. Department of Education. (2004). *Individuals With Disabilities Education Improvement Act,* P.L. 108–446. H.R.
§§ 1350.

Vernon, L. J. (2003). Collaborative practices in schools: The
impact of school-based leadership teams on inclusive
education (Doctoral Dissertation, The College of
William & Mary, 2003). *Dissertation Abstract International, 64,* 02. UMI Number 3080232.

Virginia Department of Education. (2002). Get on the team!
Improving the working relationship between teachers
and paraprofessionals. Richmond, VA: Author.

Vygotsky, L. S. (1962). *Thought and language.* Cambridge:
MIT Press.

Walther-Thomas, C., Korinek, L., McLaughlin, V. L., &
Williams, B. T. (2000). *Collaboration for inclusive
education: Developing successful programs.* Needham
Heights, MA: Allyn and Bacon.

Watson, M., & Ecken, L. (2003). *Learning to trust: Transforming difficult elementary classrooms through developmental discipline.* San Francisco: Jossey-Bass.

Weber, C., Behl, D., & Summers, M. (1994). Watch them
play—watch them learn. *Teaching Exceptional Children,
27*(1), 30–35.

Welch, M. (1998). Collaboration: Staying on the bandwagon.
Journal of Teacher Education, 49(1), 26–36. Retrieved
July 9, 2002, from Info Trac OneFile database.

Werts, M. G. (1998). Child academic engagement related to
proximity of paraprofessionals (Doctoral dissertation,
University of Pittsburgh; 3407). *Dissertation Abstracts
International, 59,* 09-A.

Whitechurch, G. G., & Constantine, L. L. (1993). Subsystems
theory. In P. G. Boss, W. J. Doherty, R. LaRossa, W. R.
Schumm, & S. K. Steinmetz (Eds.), *Sourcebook of
family theories and methods: A contextual approach* (pp.
325–352). New York: Plenum.

Willis, S. (1994). Making schools more inclusive: Teaching
children with disabilities in regular classrooms. *ASCD
Curriculum Update,* 1–8.

Yeatts, D. E., & Hyten, C. (1998). *High-performing self-
managed work teams: A comparison of theory to practice.* Thousand Oaks, CA: Sage.

Understanding Early Literacy Learning in the Inclusive Classroom

Anne E. Gregory and Jennifer Snow-Gerono

Objectives

After you have read this chapter, you should be able to

- Identify the dimensions of literacy.
- Explain the importance of teachers developing a set of beliefs and the role they play in literacy learning and instruction.
- Describe how young children learn about language and literacy and the connection between language and early literacy learning.
- Elaborate upon the nature of emergent literacy (i.e., that oral language, reading, writing, etc., are developmental and vary across individuals and over time).
- Define and explain the purpose(s), use(s), and modification(s) necessary to use instructional approaches to meet the learners' needs found within the classroom.
- Discuss the value of supporting children's literacy learning at multiple levels.

Key Terms

Vocabulary

Phonics

Comprehensive literacy instruction

Concepts about print (CAP)

Phonological awareness

Alphabetic principle

Graphophonic relationships

Reading aloud, shared reading, guided reading, independent reading, dialogic reading

Language experience approach (LEA)

Practical Application Vignette

Underlying Aspects of Literacy Learning

Ms. Balance walked into her first-grade classroom at Literacy Elementary School and glanced around before the room filled with children and their accompanying noises, including excitement and distress. She smiled when she noticed the word wall with Natasha's additions from the previous day. Natasha had been writing a story and needed assistance with words to describe her story setting. Thankfully, Ian had helped her script "gloomy" and "gros" for adjectives to describe her basement before the family cleaning.

As Ms. Balance walked to a back corner of the room to set her lunch on her desk, she perused the student-written books on the top of the library bookshelves to select one with which she could begin the morning meeting. It was Carter's turn to read aloud to the class, so she carried his book over to the author's chair. She then made sure that her literacy wheel was pointing to the proper centers for different literacy groups. Today's groups would focus on blending sounds from flashcards for making words, guided reading with the teacher, shared reading at the student teacher's center and the listening center, and preferred choice activities. She made a mental note to have the students remind each other of appropriate free choice activities during morning meeting. She did not want Kassie to have to listen to teasing about choosing to create letters from clay rather than engage in independent reading with friends.

Ms. Balance smiled as she straightened some pillows in the reading corner and walked to the outside door to greet her students as they entered their first-grade learning community. She had a morning message on the board and watched as the students completed their morning duties, including lunch count, weather report, and practicing reading the message. Upon an auditory signal, the students joined her on the carpet in the front of the room, and the small group in charge of reading the morning message and sharing a new vocabulary word began their leadership of the morning meeting.

After students worked through greetings and sharing, Ms. Balance pointed to the literacy centers chart and dismissed students by the vowel sounds in their names. She smiled as she sat with four students engaging in a picture walk of their story for the day and made sure she had her running records notebook nearby for any independent reading opportunities with students. Who says you cannot effectively teach all students?

Introduction to Reading

Literacy learning is often viewed as a complex, dynamic, and transactive process where literacy refers to the interrelatedness of language—speaking, listening, reading, writing, and viewing. As a process, we know that it begins long before children enter a classroom or school. Like learning to speak and listen, learning about print and those things associated with it begins at home starting from birth when parents read or tell stories, when songs are sung and nursery rhymes chanted, when scribbles on a page are seen and understood to have some meaning.

Literacy teachers and scholars currently have a fairly well-developed understanding of how young children become aware of print (Teale & Sulzby, 1989) and begin their entry into the literacy club (Smith, 2005). Studies of children as young as 2 demonstrate they are able to identify signs, labels, and logos that are familiar to them (Goodman, 1986; Hiebert, 1981). Correspondingly, home-based case studies conducted with children under the age of 3 found that children are extensively

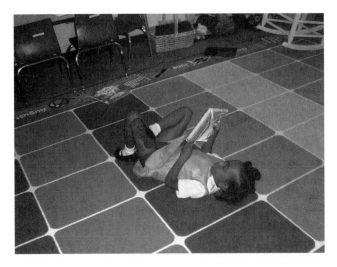

aware of the practical functions for writing: creating a list to aid memory, writing signs to control behaviors (e.g., stop signs), and writing to communicate (Heath, 1983; Taylor & Strickland, 1986).

These early understandings of literacy are often referred to by the term *emergent literacy* (Teale, 1986). Emergent literacy suggests that the development of literacy is taking place within the child. It is a gradual process and will take place over time. Emergent literacy focuses on two aspects: (1) how and when children begin to construct knowledge about reading and writing and (2) how parents and early childhood educators could most effectively support young children's ongoing literacy development (Morrow, 2001).

Constructing Knowledge in Reading

Language as a Process: The Centrality of Oral Language

Entrée into the language process begins with birth as a child seeks to have her or his needs met through differentiated crying (i.e., crying that varies in sound, depending on the stimulus: tiredness, hunger, or wetness) and through cooing, babbling, and one-word sentences. This is the beginning of language development and use—the beginning of literacy learning. Learning to use language is almost universally accomplished without formal instruction before children enter school. How do children learn the intricacies of language and its use? And, if all of this happens before school, then what do teachers need to know about the process of language learning?

Here, language is defined as a human-designed system used as a means of communicating with others either through oral or sign production. All languages are rule governed, arbitrary, and dynamic. To be rule governed simply means that languages follow rules that have been agreed upon by different social groups. For example, there are rules related to types of words that can be used and rules related to the order of words to express thoughts or ideas in every language. The arbitrariness is found in the relation of sounds to the symbols used to represent them and the labels given to objects. For example, we call a four-legged animal that barks, has a tail, and fur typically *dog*, but there is nothing about the actual animal to suggest its identifier should be "dog" other than the fact that we have all agreed to do so. Language is always changing as new words are created and old words are discarded.

Language Learning

Most children engage in language learning, learning about language, and learning through language simultaneously (Genishi, 1987; Halliday, 1975). Essentially, language learning is a social endeavor in which language is both received and expressed by the individual learning. We use specialized terminology to refer to this process: *receptive language* and *expressive language*. Receptive language is children learning how to listen and understand the language spoken around them. Expressive language is connected to receptive as children are learning to speak and use language (see Table 7.1).

Table 7.1 ● Typical Receptive and Expressive Language Development

Age of Child	Receptive Language	Expressive Language
Birth to 3 months	• Turns when someone speaks • Quiets and smiles when they *recognize* a familiar voice • Stops activity and attends to unfamiliar voice • Responds to comforting tones even from an unfamiliar voice	• Smiles when someone familiar comes into view • Cries are "differentiated"; cries differently for different needs • Makes pleasure and familiar sounds repeatedly (cooing, gooing when content)
4 to 6 months	• Moves eyes in direction of sounds • Responds to changes in tone of voice, especially the word "no" • Enjoys music and toys that make sounds	• Engages in vocal play when playing with self or primary caregiver • Babbling appears at times to sound more speechlike; includes many sounds like *p, b,* and *m* • Communicates with sounds and gestures that he wants or needs something from you
7 months to 1 year	• Obviously listens when spoken to, turning and looking when called by name • Engages and enjoys games like peek-a-boo and pat-a-cake • Names are recognized for familiar objects ("Mommy," "cup," "doggy") • Begins to respond to requests and questions ("More juice?" "Come here")	• Sound of babbling changes; includes more consonants and both short and long vowel sounds; imitates many different speech sounds • Uses speech and other noncrying forms of communication to gain the attention of others and hold on to it • First words have appeared although they may not be clear ("MaMa," "Doggie," "Bye Bye")
1 to 2 years	• Points to objects/pictures in books when named by another, and some body parts • Follows simple commands and understands simple questions ("Roll the ball," "Where's Daddy?")	• Vocabulary is increasing every month • Asks two-word questions (Go bye-bye?) • Combines two words in other ways to make simple sentences ("More milk," Mommy book")
2 to 3 years	• Understands two-stage commands ("Get your toy bunny and put it in the basket.") • Understands contrasting concepts or meanings (hot–cold, up–down, big–little)	• Rapid vocabulary growth; appears to have a word for almost everything • Speech is understood by familiar listeners and consists of one-, two-, and three-word utterances • Asks for or draws attention by naming, drawing attention to an attribute, or commenting ("Elephant!" "Big!" "Wow!")

Table 7.1 ● *(Continued)*

Age of Child	Receptive Language	Expressive Language
3 to 4 years	• Understands simple "Who?" "What?" "Why?" and "Where?" questions • Hears when called from another room	• Talks about things that have happened away from home—those that occurred at preschool, with friends, on outings, or other interesting things • Most utterances consist of sentences with four or more words • Speech is generally clear, fluent, and easily understood by "others"
4 to 5 years	• Enjoys stories and is able to answer questions about her • Understands nearly everything that is said to her	• Is able to tell long and involved stories that remain on topic and incorporate "adultlike" syntax • Sentences used include details • Uses syntax of the family • Communicates easily with both children and adults • May tell "tall stories" or fantastic ones to engage in conversation
6 to 8 years	• Understands all that is said to him, even as more complex and varied vocabulary is introduced (content-specific vocabulary)	• Speech is completely intelligible and useful in social situations • Able to construct stories about pictures or objects where relationships are identifiable • Understands terms like *alike, different, beginning, end*, etc. • Able to tell time to the quarter • Able to read and write • Complex and compound sentences used easily with few lapses in grammatical constrictions (tense, pronouns, plurals, etc.) • Understanding of pragmatic functions of language present as rate, pitch, volume are controlled appropriately; able to carry on conversations at a very adult level

Adapted from the works of Bowen, 1998, and Genishi, 1987.

However, the interactive, social dance of language development can be derailed. There are many reasons for language delays (e.g., hearing loss, autism, brain injury, mental retardation, etc.), and special attention from a speech pathologist, school nurse, or others may be warranted to determine the cause. Recent research suggests that the most common derailment in language delay is hearing loss. Research indicates that early services to develop language (spoken and/or signed) may create language learning similar to hearing peers (American Speech-Language-Hearing Association, 2005).

Supporting language learning. Because language learning is primarily a social endeavor (i.e., used to communicate needs of an individual to others), teachers can promote language development by providing environments full of language growth opportunities. General guidelines for teachers, parents, and other caregivers include the following:

- Understand that every child's language or dialect is worthy of respect as a legitimate system for communication that reflects the identities, values, and experiences of the child and the child's family and community.
- Think of all children as if they are conversationalists, even if they are not talking yet. This helps children from a very early age learn how conversations work (i.e., taking turns, looking attentively, using facial expressions, etc.).
- Encourage and support interactions among children, keeping in mind that play and repetition are prerequisite to early speech and language development.
- Peer learning and balance between individual activities and those that nurture collaboration and discussion, such as dramatic play, block building, book sharing, or carpentry should be provided.
- Keep in mind that adults in the child's life are chief resources of language development. The primary conversationalists in the child's life act as questioners, listeners, responders, and sustainers of language development and growth.
- Maintain and encourage children's interactions with others as they continue to learn about written language. In the primary grades, children can continue to develop oral abilities and skills by consulting with each other, raising questions, and providing information in a variety of settings. All areas of the curriculum benefit and are enhanced through language, where classrooms full of active learners are hardly ever silent. (Genishi, 1987)

Learning about language. Children learn the systems of language (linguistic components) as well as when to use certain kinds of language and to whom to speak about what (meaning constructing components) as they are attending to and relating sounds to meaning. For example, the child that says, "I goed to the store" instead of "I went to the store" is overgeneralizing a linguistic rule that he has learned about making a verb past tense (the English rule of adding *-ed*). He will eventually learn the conventional form of *went*, sorting out for himself the rules of English syntax, but it will not likely occur because he has constant correction. Rather, it will occur after a period of time in which he applies *-ed* to all forms of verbs and checks these hypotheses of "past tense" with other resources around him (e.g., books, peers, adults). Learning to talk takes time. To learn about any language children must come to understand the systems of language: phonology, morphology, semantics, syntax, and pragmatics. Each system has principles that determine how they operate in both oral and written language.

Phonology. Phonology relates to sounds used in a language. It is one of the first systems that a child comes to understand in learning language. All human children are born with the ability to produce the sounds found in any human language; however, early on children learn to recognize and produce only those sounds and tones used in their native language. It is through the use of these sounds and tones as they are babbling that young children initiate and participate in "conversations" with others around them. In English, most linguists estimate the number of sounds to be at or around forty-four. The convention for signifying a sound is the use of two forward slash marks around the sound (/s/).

The principle that governs this system of language is the social convention for how sounds and patterns of stress and pitch can be put together to form words. In English, for example, ending a sentence with a rising intonation signals to the listener that a question is being asked and that an answer must be provided. In Chinese, however, tones are associated with individual words so that if a word is pronounced with one tone it means one thing and with a different tone another (e.g., the word *ma* can be /má/, hemp; /mà/, to scold; /mā/, mother; or /mǎ/, horse). As children continue to refine their understandings of spoken language, they are able to distinguish the difference between *phonemes*—the smallest units of sound in a language—and the patterns of intonation that signal different meanings in the language of their home and community. The understanding of rhyme (detecting and generating rhymes), the syllabication of words, the blending of sounds into words, the segmenting of words into composite sounds, and *phonemic awareness* comprise an area of learning typically referred to as *phonological awareness*. Phonemic awareness is seen as the ability to manipulate, delete, or insert a phoneme found within a word.

Morphology. In any language the smallest unit of meaning is called a *morpheme*. Words can either be single morphemes or combinations of morphemes. For example the word *dog* is a single, free morpheme; it means something by itself. However, when we add an *s* to the end of the word *dog* to become *dogs*, the meaning has changed. The *s* in this case is a bound morpheme; it only has meaning or influence on meaning when attached to another morpheme. So, the word *dogs* means more than one dog and is made up of two morphemes: a free morpheme — *dog*—and a bound morpheme—*s*. The principles that govern this system consist of forming possessives, plurals, and past tense.

Semantics. Semantics refers to the construction of meaning at the word, sentence and text level. **Vocabulary** (words) and meaning are essential to the understanding of this system. Initially, children overgeneralize word labels used by adults. For example, a child might call any four-legged animal *doggie*. However, as her semantic system is refined and *schemata*—a mental set or representation for an object, event, or idea—continue to develop, this and other labels for various four-legged animals are used and replace the use of *doggie*. Now these animals are called *cow, cat, horse, deer*, etc.

Language learners have to determine which meaning of a word is indicated by the context. Now the child has to consider more than the possible meanings for an individual word; she or he has to consider who is speaking, the occasion, and what is happening in a moment in time. Look at the following sentence: "It was raining cats and dogs." Does this mean that cats and dogs are falling from the sky, or does it mean that it is raining fairly steadily? To determine the appropriate meaning the child has to consider what she knows to be true about the world: that dogs and cats do not typically fall from the sky. She also must take into consideration what is happening around her, that it is indeed raining. Additionally, she must think about her experiences with these words in other contexts to see how they fit together within the current framework.

Finally, vocabulary learning plays a continued role of importance at any level of language learning. There are specialized vocabularies for various professions, and being part of that profession means understanding and using the appropriate terminology. For example, when discussing sounds in words with others, most teachers would use the term *phonemes* rather than repeatedly state the "sounds found within the words" and might continue the discussion to include the words *phonological awareness* and *blending*. The governing principle of this system is that context and experience account for what makes most of what we hear and read comprehensible.

Syntax. In all languages there are rules for how words may be combined with others to form phrases and sentences and for how those sentences may be transformed into other sentences. Word order, governed by rules, influences the meaning that a person can convey or construct with words. Try this: How many ways can you put the following words in a sentence that makes sense (follows sense making of English)? *A can dog I black see.* Did you get the following?

I can see a black dog.

Can I see a black dog?

Why could we not have said the following?

A black can I dog.

Dog can I a black.

The rules for determining order, grammatical constructions, are commonly and socially shared. We could not say the last two because they do not fit the rules of our social group (English). Principles governing this system are learning to construct negatives, questions, compound sentences, passives, imperatives, and complex with embedded forms.

Pragmatics. Perhaps the most extensive system of language, *pragmatics* deals with the use of language in social settings. Social uses include rules for politeness and the degree of formality in any given social situation. In French, pragmatics determines the use of *vous*, the formal, or *tu*, the informal form of the word *you*. Pragmatics determines the use of language appropriate for use with our closest friend and that which is appropriate for our teachers. Basic rules for language use in social contexts are often a determining factor in deciding whether an individual is competent in the use of that language.

In school, when teachers ask children to use their "inside voices" instead of their "outside voices," they are engaging in pragmatics. This, along with helping children to understand the changes in language necessary for speaking with a visitor or the principal as opposed to a friend, is part of the conversational skill that children develop throughout school years and into adulthood (Hulit & Howard, 2002). Pragmatics includes the ability of an individual to initiate a topic, maintain that topic, end that topic, make eye contact, and maintain appropriate proximity to another speaker, etc., as he or she engages with this person in language use. It is conversational competence that serves as the governing principle for this system.

Clay (1991) suggests that oral language is a child's first self-extending system of strategies by which she or he comes to understand and communicate with those around her or him. Every sentence a child produces is a hypothesis. If it is understood, then the child's hypothesis is confirmed and the child learns that one can say it that way. If, however, the listener is puzzled, then the hypothesis is rejected and the idea must be expressed in a different manner. This puzzling out of how language works provides the foundation for later interactions with print (Sulzby, 1996).

As theory builders and hypothesis testers, children are actively engaging with their environment through the use of language to construct rules and understandings not only for their immediate world but also for the world of both spoken and written language. These understandings serve as the means by which other processes that are necessitated by literacy learning come to be understood and incorporated with a child's worldview. In the next section we will examine some of the processes that influence literacy learning.

Reading Process Skills

Cognitive Processes

Psychologists have distinguished between two kinds of processes: bottom-up processes and top-down processes. Supporters of bottom-up processing see the act of reading as originating with some form of stimuli—letters or words—and the processing of that information, giving little attention to the higher level knowledge that an individual might bring to the task. The focus here rests primarily in how readers extract information from the printed page, where readers are seen to deal with letters and words in a systematic and complete fashion (Gough & Tunmer, 1986) From this perspective, a child reading the sentence "The weekend begins tomorrow, so tomorrow must be . . ." would use the letters found in the next word, "Friday," to read it.

Supporters of top-down processing, on the other hand, believe that reading is guided by an individual's prior knowledge and expectations. Here the reader is judged to generate hypotheses about which words they will encounter and take in only enough visual information to test their hypotheses (Goodman, 1970; Smith, 2005). Readers following this perspective would read the earlier sentence, providing the word "Friday" based on their understandings of the world. They would further confirm their hypotheses by checking that the word does begin with the letter "F," concluding that their prediction was correct, and no further examination of the letters in the word is necessary. "In most situations, bottom-up and top-down processes work together to ensure the accurate and rapid processing of information" (Treiman, 2001, pp. 664–665). Theories of literacy learning vary in the amount of emphases placed on the two processes.

Affective Processes

Affective processes related to literacy learning typically are found in the literature related to student motivation. Motivation is influenced by internal and external factors that can start, sustain, intensify, or discourage behavior. Unfortunately, most traditional school reading and literacy programs can lead to negative attitudes toward reading, writing, listening, and speaking. In these programs, the purpose for *tasks* assigned in the name of reading are not made readily apparent. Notice here the word *tasks* is used, because oftentimes children are asked to do "things" other than reading as part of reading. Usually these things come in the form of worksheets, workbooks, or other activities where connections between tasks assigned and real reading and writing are not made clear. However, in classrooms where children are given frequent opportunities to select, read, and discuss books of interest to them, motivation increases.

Hickman (1995) identified characteristics of classrooms where children like books and read extensively. The teachers in these classrooms are readers themselves, and the children mirror the teachers' enthusiasm for reading. The teachers are able to recommend appropriate literature for students' varied levels of literacy learning, and frequently share, promote, and recommend books to the whole class or individuals within it. Additionally, the teachers in these classrooms read books aloud to students everyday. Their classrooms are well stocked with carefully selected books that are easily accessible and displayed in pleasing arrangements. Children in these classrooms are provided with time to browse, choose, and read. And finally, books are shared and discussed and often serve as the basis for further reading and writing activities (Hickman, 1995).

To further this point, work by Allington (1994) suggests that children read so little in school because there is not much time to do so. Little time is coupled with the limited variety of current books in schools. Libraries may have many copies of a single title versus single copies of multiple titles. Easy, interesting titles are typically in short supply, thus providing children with few experiences of real reading (Allington, 2001).

Sociocultural Processes

The sociocultural perspective views literacy learning as being more than a set of processing skills; instead, it is viewed as a process embedded in social interaction and culture (Gee, 2001). As children interact within various social contexts, they learn the social languages (rap, classrooms, etc.) and the ways of being, doing, and acting within these various contexts. Children learn how to act, speak, and behave within communities of practice, creating "identity kits" and frameworks for what they can expect from texts and from themselves. This perspective acknowledges that meaning and identities are both socially constructed (Halliday, 1975).

This perspective suggests that second-language learners bring to the classroom context culture, understandings for interactions that occur within social spaces, as well as a developed home language. They have an "identity kit" framed upon the language that is spoken in the home. When this "identity kit" is disallowed or ignored in favor of the rapid acquisition of the second language (i.e., English), the child loses the ability to know what to expect from him- or herself and the texts found in the secondary language context.

Emerging Processes

This notion of literacy posits that children acquire knowledge about reading, writing, and oral language prior to entering school. Learning to read is not a matter of being "ready," but is naturally embedded and integrated in social exchanges with literate others that a child engages in from birth (Lonigan & Whitehurst, 1998).

A child, for example, is taught much about reading and the language used in texts (i.e., literate register) long before she or he is able to read. This happens as adults read aloud and engage children in stories. As a child participates in these shared readings of books, she or he learns more about the complexity of language and may acquire some understandings of letter forms and names, and perhaps some understandings of the phonemes associated with these forms (Wilkinson & Silliman, 2000). The hallmark of this perspective is that children enter school with understandings about literacy, and that the job of the teacher is to recognize these understandings and support them for further development.

Common Views of Literacy Instruction

There are many views on how literacy learning should occur and what teaching should look like. An important consideration is how your instruction aligns with your beliefs about the processes children engage in as they read, write, and speak. As Delpit (1995) suggests, "We do not really see through our eyes or hear through our ears, but through our beliefs" (p. 46). In the sections that follow, we describe four theories of reading instruction: (a) skills-based, (b) holistic, (c) interactive, and (d) transactional. By making the connection between theory and practice more explicit, you, as a teacher, will be better able to define for yourself and others the theories that underlie your literacy beliefs.

Skills-Based Theory

This theory of literacy learning proposes that children learn the *parts* of language (letters) first and then proceed to understanding the *whole* (meaning). Supported by the work of Gough and Tunmer (1986) and other "bottom-up theorists," in which reading is seen as a serial process involving the translation of letters in speech sounds, with these sounds then translated into words and eventually meaning, this perspective involves explicit instruction in the subskills of reading (sound–symbol relationships) with efficient decoding leading directly to comprehension (words to meaning). It is assumed that children who experience difficulties with reading have an inability to decode. **Phonics** instruction, in which children are taught the letters of the alphabet and the sounds they represent before they begin to read books independently, serves as the foundation for literacy learning.

Instruction proceeds from learning letter names (all twenty-six) to the learning of the sounds represented by the letters (approximately forty-four sounds). Once associations are learned between sounds and symbols—the alphabetic principle—children are taught to blend together the sounds represented by the letters to form words from left to right and "sound out" phonically regular words—this means that the sound–symbol relationships are clearly connected—as in the words *cat* or *dog*. Additionally, a limited number of sight words are taught, and the children read texts that use carefully controlled words that are either known sight words or are phonically regular. As more phonics patterns, rules, and generalizations are taught and learned, texts are controlled so that these understandings can be applied. Traditionally, following sound–symbol correspondences, children taught with this approach learn phonograms. *Phonograms*, repeated patterns of sounds and symbols, are typically found in word families. For example, the phonogram -*ack* is found in the words: **back**,

cl**ack**, sh**ack**. Gradually, the control of text is released, and phonically irregular words are introduced and incorporated. Because comprehension is seen as a direct outgrowth of decoding and the ability to pronounce words, children who are able to read the words are seen as being able to understand what they have read.

Holistic Theory

Literacy learning here imagines that literacy learning processes begin with language developed from the whole to the parts. Influenced by "top-down" theorists, learning to read, as with any aspect of literacy, is seen to be larger than summing the parts to form the whole, and children are immersed in print-rich and language-rich environments. Comprehension is viewed as the driving force behind the development of literate understandings as children learn how to read stories that are authentic and of interest initially so that they can then learn about the code. Advocates of this approach support the systematic building of an increasingly large body of words that children are able to identify or read by sight so that further analysis is not needed.

Instruction begins during children's engagement in an abundance of stories and books read aloud, demonstrating how good readers sound as they read and increasing children's oral language base. Guessing the identity of a word based upon pictures, context, or first-letter clues is supported and encouraged so that large amounts of attention are available for meaning making. Children are encouraged to learn words by sight without further decoding or analysis, and patterned books and authentic children's stories are used. Practicing reading a story again and again is encouraged so that children begin to internalize the language, structure, and meaning for a story. It is believed that the use of letter sounds to unlock unknown words is a strategy of last resort, as oftentimes words do not follow strict sound–symbol correspondences.

Interactive Theory

Proponents of interactive theory suggest that readers must draw upon their background knowledge as well as process an array of information found in print (e.g., context, sentences, sounding out unknown words) to understand the author's message. These theories suggest readers use only what is necessary to make sense of the text. Readers are viewed as active constructors of meaning where learning to read is accomplished through the balance of instruction in three skill areas: decoding, vocabulary, and comprehension (Weaver, 1994).

Instruction focuses in all three skill areas in isolated lessons. Children begin in the skill area of decoding by learning the twenty-six letters and the forty-four sounds associated with them. In vocabulary, children learn high-frequency sight words in list form (e.g., the, me, look, and). Initial comprehension instruction includes listening to stories read aloud for main idea, details, and sequence. Where decoding includes the letter–sound relationships and blending these together to form words, vocabulary continues to include new sight words, with attention to conceptual knowledge and meaning categories and simple comprehension skills (main idea and supporting details) focused on the short stories found in the teacher's edition. The student's anthology of stories is incorporated, and instruction continues in the three areas throughout the elementary years. Vocabulary instruction focuses on multiple meanings and unfamiliar words, and decoding involves the structural analysis of words as relates to meaning making (prefixes, suffixes, etc.).

Transactional Theory

Transactional theory continues and elaborates upon the understandings of interactive theories. In this theory, readers construct meaning for texts using language, their own experiences, and knowledge that is conditioned by their intentions, purposes, and the context of the situation. In other words, what children bring to a text and their goal or purpose for reading it suggest how they will construct meaning for it. Reading, then, is seen as an event conditioned by the *cueing systems* of text: the relationship between symbols and sounds (*graphophonic*), syntax, and semantics found in the text; the people engaged with the text; the physical environment; the cultural expectations of the situation; and each individual's experiences, knowledge, skills, and strategies for processing text. The interpretation or meanings assigned to a text by an individual are uniquely his or her own following this line of thought.

Instruction found coinciding with transactional theory is often termed **comprehensive literacy instruction** (Reutzal & Cooter, 2003) or *best practice* (Gambrell & Mazzoni, 1999). The following list, generated by Gambrell and Mazzoni (1999), includes ten research-based practices to use in literacy instruction:

1. Teach reading for authentic meaning-making literacy experiences, for pleasure, to be informed, and to perform a task.
2. Use high-quality literature.
3. Integrate a comprehensive word study-phonics program into reading/writing instruction.
4. Use multiple texts that link and expand concepts.
5. Balance teacher- and student-led discussions.
6. Build a whole class community that emphasizes important concepts and builds background knowledge.
7. Work with students in small groups while other students read and write about what they have read.
8. Give students plenty of time to read in class.
9. Give students direct instruction in decoding and comprehension strategies that promote independent reading. Balance direct instruction, guided instruction, and independent instruction.
10. Use a variety of assessment techniques to inform instruction. (p. 14)

Differentiating Instruction in Reading

Instruction focuses on teaching children oral language; phonemic awareness; letter recognition and the conventions associated with it; **concepts about print (CAP)**, or the ways in which books work (directionality, return sweep, concepts of word and letter, punctuation); phonics; spelling; writing conventions; vocabulary; comprehension; and fluency through the use of a variety of text types and levels of difficulty. With instruction focusing on the end goal of meaning construction, all instructional activities are based on best practices that have been confirmed in reading research (e.g., interactive read aloud, shared reading, guided reading, independent reading, shared writing, interactive writing, guided writing, and independent writing). Integral to this approach is the environment of the classroom; it should be one that is print-rich, well organized, and active. In this environment, children would be engaging in language learning workshops including varied literacy tools, books, and print. Interactions and lively conversations about and around these resources would form an integral part of a child's day. See Table 7.2 for differentiating instruction in reading in accordance with the Individuals with Disabilities Education Act disability categories.

What Is Reading?

Reading, as part of literacy learning, is seen as a complex set of behaviors that requires individuals to create meaning from symbols. A child must employ knowledge of print and other symbols, knowledge of the potential or possible meanings for such symbols, and knowledge of the world to create meaning for a text. It, therefore, is a problem-solving activity (Clay, 1991) in which the reader transacts with the text (Rosenblatt, 1994) to construct meaning. If a child reads the words on the page but does not understand what he or she has read, then the child is not reading.

Think about it this way: A reader looks at text and makes an informed prediction about what it will say. She then samples the text to confirm her predictions, and, if she believes meaning has been achieved, it is integrated into what she knows and uses to make predictions, inferences, and samplings of the text. If she does not make meaning, she must go back to the text to gather more information and samples and rethink original inferences and predictions (Goodman, Watson, & Burke, 1996). What is amazing is that this process occurs on a mostly unconscious level, with conscious attention being used or called for primarily when confirmation of predictions is not attained.

Stages of Development

Literacy learning is a continuum in which all children are continually in the process of becoming literate (Teale & Sulzby, 1986). Hence, children begin the literacy learning process long before entering schools and classrooms. They engage and develop literate understandings beginning with birth. Our work as teachers, then, is to help children to move along the continuum, becoming skilled readers who continue to read, grow, and learn long after school is finished.

There is some predictability to the way that children move through stages of development in reading (Chall, 1983). As children grow and develop their literate understandings, their performances differ qualitatively from their performances at other stages. Children's responses, behaviors, and performances differ as a result of interactions with their environment. And, as Chall (1983) suggests, reading at each stage involves problem-solving behavior that depends on full engagement with text.

Chall's (1983) stages are as follows:

Stage 0: Prereading, birth to age 6

Stage 1: Initial Reading, or Decoding: grades 1–2, ages 6–7

Stage 2: Confirmation, Fluency, Ungluing From Print: grades 2–3, ages 7–8

Stage 3: Reading for Learning the New—A First Step: grades 4–8, ages 9–13

Table 7.2 • Differentiating Instruction Across IDEA Categories

IDEA Disability Category	Reading and Language Arts			
	Concept	Accommodation/Modification	Concept	Accommodation/Modification
Autism	Early Print Awareness	• Use of predictable text with repetitive, "natural" language patterns • Large print/format books for shared reading (Big Books) • Familiar texts read aloud often during period of time (same book shared for five or more days) • Language Experience Approach • Labeling of familiar areas and activities • Talk and opportunity to respond to texts in multiple ways	Phonics	• Use of manipulatives (letter forms) • Hands-on exploration of letter–sound relationships • Use of predictable text with repetitive language patterns • Nursery rhymes, songs, poems with movement as well as large-text formatting • Concept sorts
Deaf-Blindness	Early Print Awareness	• Use of predictable text with repetitive, "natural" language patterns • Large print/format books for shared reading (Big Books) • Familiar texts read aloud often during period of time (same book shared for five or more days) • Language Experience Approach • Labeling of familiar areas and activities in braille and large print • ASL story language and patterning • Talk and opportunity to respond to texts in multiple ways	Phonics	• Use of manipulatives (letter forms) • Hands-on exploration of letter–sound relationships • Concept sorts • Kinesthetic and tactile movements with letters in conjunction with letter representation and sound • Interactive writing
Deafness	Early Print Awareness	• ASL story language and patterning • Use of predictable text with repetitive, "natural" language patterns • Large print/format books for shared reading (Big Books)	Phonics	• Use of manipulatives (letter forms) • Hands-on exploration of letter–sound relationships

(Continued)

Table 7.2 ● (Continued)

IDEA Disability Category	Concept	Accommodation/Modification	Concept	Accommodation/Modification
		• Familiar texts read aloud often during period of time (same book shared for five or more days) • Language Experience Approach • Labeling of familiar areas and activities • Talk and opportunity to respond to texts in multiple ways	Phonics	• Nursery rhymes, songs, poems with movement as well as large-text formatting • Elkonin Boxes used in conjunction with mirror for visual recognition of mouth movements • Interactive writing
Emotional Disturbance	Early Print Awareness	• Use of predictable, high-interest text with repetitive, "natural" language patterns • Large print/format books for shared reading (Big Books) • Familiar texts read aloud often during period of time (same book shared for five or more days) • Language Experience Approach • Labeling of familiar areas and activities • Shorter periods of time for activities, with increased number of activities addressing concept–predictable pattern to activity • Talk and opportunity to respond to texts in multiple ways	Phonics	• Use of manipulatives (letter forms) • Hands-on exploration of letter–sound relationships • Use of predictable text with repetitive language patterns • Nursery rhymes, songs, poems with movement as well as large-text formatting • Concept sorts • Interactive writing • Elkonin Boxes
Hearing Impairment	Early Print Awareness	• ASL story language and patterning • Use of predictable text with repetitive, "natural" language patterns • Large print/format books for shared reading (Big Books) • Familiar texts read aloud often during period of time (same book shared for five or more days) • Language Experience Approach • Labeling of familiar areas and activities • Talk and opportunity to respond to texts in multiple ways	Phonics	• Use of manipulatives (letter forms) • Hands-on exploration of letter–sound relationships • Use of predictable text with repetitive language patterns • Nursery rhymes, songs, poems with movement as well as large-text formatting • Interactive writing

Disability	Skill Area	Strategies
Mental Retardation	Early Print Awareness	• Concept sorts • Language Experience Approach • Labeling of familiar areas and activities • Use of predictable text with repetitive language patterns • Large print/format books for shared reading (Big Books) • Familiar texts read aloud often during period of time (same book shared for five or more days) • Predictable pattern to activity • Talk and opportunity to respond to texts in multiple ways
	Phonics	• Use of manipulatives (letter forms) • Hands-on exploration of letter–sound relationships • Use of predictable text with repetitive, "natural" language patterns • Nursery rhymes, songs, poems with movement as well as large-text formatting • Interactive writing
Multiple Disabilities	Early Print Awareness	• Use of predictable text with repetitive, "natural" language patterns • Large print/format books for shared reading (Big Books) • Familiar texts read aloud often during period of time (same book shared for five or more days) • Language Experience Approach • Labeling of familiar areas and activities • Shorter periods of time for activities, with increased number of activities addressing concept–predictable pattern to activity • Talk and opportunity to respond to texts in multiple ways
	Phonics	• Use of manipulatives (letter forms) • Hands-on exploration of letter–sound relationships • Use of predictable text with repetitive language patterns • Nursery rhymes, songs, poems with movement as well as large-text formatting • Concept sorts • Interactive writing • Elkonin Boxes
Orthopedic Impairment	Early Print Awareness	• Use of predictable text with repetitive, "natural" language patterns • Large print/format books for shared reading (Big Books) • Familiar texts read aloud often during period of time (same book shared for five or more days) • Language Experience Approach • Labeling of familiar areas and activities • Talk and opportunity to respond to texts in multiple ways
	Phonics	• Use of manipulatives (letter forms) • Hands-on exploration of letter–sound relationships • Use of predictable text with repetitive language patterns • Nursery rhymes, songs, poems with movement as well as large-text formatting • Concept sorts • Interactive writing • Elkonin Boxes

(Continued)

Table 7.2 ● *(Continued)*

IDEA Disability Category	Concept	Accommodation/Modification	Concept	Accommodation/Modification
Other Health Impairment	Early Print Awareness	• Use of predictable text with repetitive, "natural" language patterns • Large print/format books for shared reading (Big Books) • Familiar texts read aloud often during period of time (same book shared for five or more days) • Language Experience Approach • Labeling of familiar areas and activities • Talk and opportunity to respond to texts in multiple ways	Phonics	• Use of manipulatives (letter forms) • Hands-on exploration of letter–sound relationships • Use of predictable text with repetitive language patterns • Nursery rhymes, songs, poems with movement as well as large-text formatting • Concept sorts • Interactive writing • Elkonin Boxes
Specific Learning Disability	Early Print Awareness	• Use of predictable text with repetitive, "natural" language patterns • Large print/format books for shared reading (Big Books) • Familiar texts read aloud often during period of time (same book shared for five or more days) • Language Experience Approach • Labeling of familiar areas and activities • Talk and opportunity to respond to texts in multiple ways	Phonics	• Use of manipulatives (letter forms) • Hands-on exploration of letter–sound relationships • Use of predictable text with repetitive language patterns • Nursery rhymes, songs, poems with movement as well as large-text formatting • Concept sorts • Interactive writing • Elkonin Boxes
Speech or Language Impairment	Early Print Awareness	• Use of predictable text with repetitive, "natural" language patterns • Large print/format books for shared reading (Big Books) • Familiar texts read aloud often during period of time (same book shared for five or more days) • Language Experience Approach • Labeling of familiar areas and activities • Talk and opportunity to respond to texts in multiple ways	Phonics	• Use of manipulatives (letter forms) • Hands-on exploration of letter–sound relationships • Use of predictable text with repetitive language patterns • Nursery rhymes, songs, poems with movement as well as large-text formatting • Concept sorts • Interactive writing • Elkonin Boxes

Traumatic Brain Injury	Early Print Awareness	• Use of predictable text with repetitive, "natural" language patterns • Large print/format books for shared reading (Big Books) • Familiar texts read aloud often during period of time (same book shared for five or more days) • Language Experience Approach • Labeling of familiar areas and activities • Shorter periods of time for activities, with increased number of activities addressing concept–predictable pattern to activity • Talk and opportunity to respond to texts in multiple ways
	Phonics	• Use of manipulatives (letter forms) • Hands-on exploration of letter–sound relationships • Use of predictable text with repetitive language patterns • Nursery rhymes, songs, poems with movement as well as large-text formatting • Concept sorts • Interactive writing • Elkonin Boxes
Visual Impairment Including Blindness	Early Print Awareness	• Use of predictable text with repetitive, "natural" language patterns • Large print/format books for shared reading (Big Books) • Familiar texts read aloud often during period of time (same book shared for five or more days) • Language Experience Approach • Labeling of familiar areas and activities in braille and large print • Talk and opportunity to respond to texts in multiple ways
	Phonics	• Use of manipulatives (letter forms) • Hands-on exploration of letter–sound relationships • Use of predictable text with repetitive language patterns • Nursery rhymes, songs, poems with movement as well as large-text formatting • Concept sorts • Interactive writing • Elkonin Boxes

Stage 4: Multiple Viewpoints: high school, ages 14–18

Stage 5: Construction and Reconstruction—A World View: college, ages 18 and above (pp. 13–23)

The prereading stage can be seen as a time when children learn about letters, words, and books. This is a time of tremendous value and importance, for it is here that the foundation is established upon which later literacy learning will occur. A hallmark of this stage is a child's pretend reading.

The initial reading period is seen as a time when children are learning the correspondence between letters and sounds. Central to this stage for Chall (1983) was print and children working to "break the code." She believes readers at this stage were unable to focus on meaning, as more mature readers were able to do, because of the centrality of print. During the reading for learning the new stage, readers are able to begin to learn as much from reading as they previously could only do from listening and watching. However, many teachers of early readers would suggest that they are learning from print from the beginning of reading as they engage and interact with nonfiction or information texts in their early reading experiences.

Additionally, even though the final stages of reading development are beyond the scope of this chapter, it is good to keep in mind how literacy learning continues to evolve and expand for children. These stages should not be viewed as precise because all children are unique and different. Rather, think of these as guideposts for the possibilities of what is to come next in a child's literacy development.

Principles of Literacy Learning

With an idea for how progression along the literacy continuum may occur, it is now important that we begin to examine principles that motivate the literacy learning of young children. Fountas and Pinnell (1998) suggest eight principles that should be considered and incorporated into the learning opportunities developed for young children:

1. Children need to understand the purposes of literacy so they can fully appreciate and enjoy literacy in their lives.
2. Children need to hear written language so they can learn its structure and take in new information and ideas.
3. Children need to become aware of the sounds of language, to enjoy those sounds, and to use this knowledge as a tool in becoming literate.
4. Children need to have many experiences working with written symbols so they can learn how to look at letters and use information to read and write.
5. Children need to explore words and learn how words work so they can use this information effectively and efficiently in reading and writing.
6. Children need to learn the conventions of print and how books work so they can use this knowledge as readers and writers.
7. Children need to read and write continuous text so they can use and expand their knowledge about letters, sounds, words, and language.
8. Children need to develop flexibility and fluency to enhance comprehension and enjoyment. (p. 3)

The first principle suggests that children need to become aware of the purpose for literacy, its relevance to their lives, and the enjoyment it can create for them. It is through engagement in literate activities that are meaningful and authentic that children will want to continue their participation in such activities. For example, the child who sees her mother writing a list of errands to do for the day, and the use of this list as the errands are completed (i.e., checked off), is more likely to see the literate task of list making as one that is meaningful and holds value in her life.

The second principle speaks to the development of a literate register in children. This is a pragmatic function of language in which children learn that the language in books is often different than that spoken in everyday settings. The ability to adapt language use for specific purposes enables children to make better predictions and inferences for texts.

The third principle relates to children's understandings of the elements of phonological awareness or understanding rhyme, the breaking of words into syllables, blending sounds together to form words, segmenting words into constituent parts, and manipulating individual sounds (phonemic awareness). By engaging in these activities, children begin to form an understanding for the constituent aspects of language. No longer is what is spoken one long stream of ideas. It can be written down and thought to be comprised of individual words, which are in turn comprised of individual sounds. All of this information can be used to write new words and ideas when a child is ready to do so. For example, a child is writing the sentence "I like candy." She quickly writes the first two words, "I" and "like," but sits for a minute before writing the word "candy." You see that she appears to be clapping the parts in the word, /can/ and /de/, before she writes "cande" on his paper. Though her attempt is not fully conventional, this example illustrates the point of this principle.

Phonics instruction and word study instruction are embodied in the fourth and fifth principles. These principles suggest that children use information found within words to assist them in further reading and writing. Such is the case in the following example: A child comes to the word "that" in a book and stops. Instead of telling him what the word is directly, his teacher asks him to find parts in the word he knows. The child isolates the "th," saying that is like the word "the" he knows and then isolates the "at" and says it is the word "at" he knows. The teacher suggests that he now blend those two parts together to make a word. The child says "that" and continues reading. This is an example of effective and efficient use of information found in print and demonstrates that the child is developing an understanding for the *generative principle* of words, which suggests that by knowing one word he is able to know many words. By learning about the conventions of print, the sixth principle, children learn how another pragmatic function of language fits together with reading. The print conventions found in texts assist readers in reading text with appropriate expression, intonation, pitch, and rate so that meaning is effectively conveyed. As we do in oral language, in reading we modulate these aspects to improve our meaning construction and conveyance of message.

Principle seven suggests that all literacy learning activities occur in meaningful and authentic ways. Continuous texts are texts that tell a story or convey an idea in which the thoughts are connected. Examples include most children's literature stories, most expository texts, and poems. Worksheets and activities that address skills in isolation are neither seen as containing continuous texts nor authentic. For example, a teacher has determined that his students need further work in short vowel sounds. He has the option of using a worksheet on the short vowel sounds or to share a book with his students that has words in it that have short vowel patterning. If he goes with the worksheet, he is not using a continuous text, and his students are less likely to make the connections between the short vowel sound work done on the worksheet and what they read and write. If, however, he shares the story and they engage in finding words within it that contained the short vowel sounds, he would be using continuous texts, and the children would be more likely to connect this learning to that which they engage in as they read and write.

The final principle suggests that fluidity and flexibility with how children use literate understandings is a goal for which to strive. A child able to adapt her or his knowledge use to different contexts and settings is one who has developed a self-extending system for getting better at reading and writing every time she or he engages in it (Clay, 1991).

Thinking about Instruction

We support the use of the analytic process as means for preparing instruction. Gipe (2006) suggests that the analytic process is a "systematic way to help teachers observe and assess aspects of literacy learning in their students, identify areas of strength and need for individual students, and provide instruction for specific literacy domains" (p. 17). The process can be viewed as a cycle in which the teacher analyzes information, forms hypotheses, teaches based upon these hypotheses, and then engages in more analyses: of the teaching event, children's understandings, or changes that are needed (see Figure 7.1.)

A reflective means for thinking and teaching, the analytic process fits nicely with teacher inquiry. Teacher inquiry is a systematic examination undertaken by teachers into their teaching practices to gather information about how their methods affect student learning. It allows you to view instructional models as ideas to be adapted rather than rules to be followed (Duffy, 1998). As such, the connection to differentiated instruction becomes clear, as both are guided by similar principles. The principles for both differentiated and analytic instruction are that teachers should

1. Focus on essential concepts, principles, and skills or an area;
2. Attend to student differences;
3. View assessment and instruction as inseparable;
4. Modify content, process, products, and the learning environment;
5. Arrange for opportunities in which students participate in respectful work;
6. Collaborate with students in learning;
7. Balance group and individual norms; and
8. Work with students in a flexible manner.

Initiating the Analytic Cycle

Perhaps the most common question asked about instruction is, "What strategies and lessons should I plan to help all levels of students?" To answer this question, we must first gather some information on the students we are to teach. This is a demonstration of the inherent connection between assessment and instruction, and, although we are here discussing the initiation of instruction, it should be understood that assessment—the gathering of information—is an ongoing process that occurs throughout teaching and learning. This means that information needs to be analyzed to determine what the strengths and needs of individual children are. In doing so, you will be able to attend to the differences of children, make necessary modifications, and balance expectations for individuals and groups. Following this analysis, you will generate hypotheses about what instructional activities and

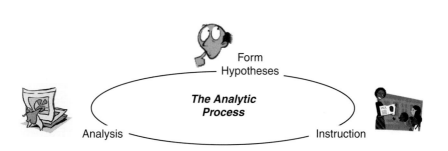

Figure 7.1 ● The analytic process.

opportunities should be provided. Once learning opportunities for the children have been planned, you will implement them. As you instruct, you will monitor children's understandings, make adjustments to requirements, and further fine-tune explanations and clarifications based upon the feedback you receive from the children.

Gathering Information

There are many published assessments that you might use to gain information about early and emergent readers. This section identifies some of these assessments as well as informal ones that can be created to determine strengths and needs of children.

Oral Language Checklist

Through observations of a child in interactions with peers, classroom settings, interactions with adults, etc., you are able to make a determination of oral language use. As you observe, notation should be made about use of both receptive and oral language. A sample oral language assessment can be found in Table 7.3.

Anecdotal records

Put simply, anecdotal records are the recordings of teacher observations of children in the classroom. The value of these observations is the documentation of what is observed, which can later be analyzed for patterns that support other findings. It is typically most useful to consider what literacy behaviors (i.e., those associated with oral language, listening, reading, and writing) one is looking for from children. In this instance, you might be observing for how a child forms or writes the letters; uses slow articulation (does he say the word slowly to hear the sounds within it?) to assist in writing words; matches the sounds he or she hears with symbols; uses space to delineate words he or she is writing; or writes words automatically (writing quickly and with minimal attention to details or letters of the word).

Phonological Awareness Inventory

An inventory can easily be created that will assess the elements of **phonological awareness**— the awareness of the structure of spoken language. In doing so, you must be sure that you move from the larger units of sound to smaller ones—words to phonemes. As a rule, rhyme (recognition

Table 7.3 ● Sample Oral Language Assessment

Name:

Criteria	Little Evidence	Some Evidence	Strong Evidence
1. Converses easily Comments:	_____	_____	_____
2. Is extending oral vocabulary Comments:	_____	_____	_____
3. Uses appropriate sentence structures Comments:	_____	_____	_____
4. Relaxes when speaking in or to a group Comments:	_____	_____	_____
5. Shares and supports ideas, thoughts, feelings, and opinions Comments:	_____	_____	_____
6. Demonstrates a sense of narrative Comments:	_____	_____	_____

Adapted from Malloch & Malloch, 1986.

precedes generation) tends to be one of the easier phonological concepts, followed by syllabication (hearing "breaks" in words), then blending (combining of sounds to form words) and segmenting (breaking a word into smaller sounds), and finally phonemic awareness (manipulating sounds within words). Phonological awareness is seen as a precursor to learning about the **alphabetic principle**—that one or more letters can represent each sound spoken (see Table 7.4)

Concepts About Print

Commonly known as CAP, *concepts about print* refers to a child's understandings for our system of print (i.e., writing and reading). Concepts typically assessed with this measure include directionality (left-to-right movement across the page and where to go at the end of a line of print—return sweep); knowledge that print and not pictures carries the message; word-by-word pointing (the correspondence of one spoken word to one printed one); letter, word, sentence, first and last part (of word, sentence, story); knowledge that letter order in words is important (there are first and last letters in words); knowledge that different punctuation marks have meaning; and the differing purposes for upper- and lowercase letters. To best determine a child's concepts about print, you will want to sit with the child in a quiet place and use a short picture book from the classroom. When selecting the book be sure that the print is large enough and the words spaced far enough apart so that you will be able to see where the child is pointing, and that it contains a variety of punctuation marks. A sample Observation Form adapted from Marie Clay's (1993) concepts about print (CAP) follows (see Table 7.5).

Table 7.4 ● Sample of Phonological Awareness Inventory

Phonological Skill	Description
Rhyme Recognition	This task is asking children to recognize words that rhyme or sound similar at the end. To assess this you might say, **"Do these words rhyme? Mat, cat"** or **"Which of these words rhyme? Dog, door, log"**
Rhyme Generation	A subtle, yet more complex, form of rhyme is the ability to provide a word that matches the rime pattern—the part of the words making them rhyme. To assess this you might say, **"What is a word that rhymes with** *can?"*
Syllabication	Following rhyme, syllables are the next speech sound unit for children to orally segment. To assess this you might say, **"Clap the parts you hear in the following words:** *window.* **(window) Now, try** *butterfly.* **(but-ter-fly) How about** *stop*? **(stop)"** or **"How many parts do you hear in the word** *window*? **(2)** *butterfly*? **(3)** *stop*? **(1)"**
Blending	Blending requires that children blend together smaller units of sound (syllables, onsets-rimes, and phonemes) to form naturally spoken words. To assess this you begin by asking the children to blend together first syllables, then move to onsets-rimes, and finally individual phonemes. The following are examples for what you might say to do this:
	"I'll say a word broken apart. You say it normally. Cow—boy" Child says: **"Cowboy."** (blending syllables/initial level)
	"I'll say a word broken apart. You say it normally. /m/—/at/" Child says: **"mat"** (blending onsets-rimes/intermediate level)
	"I'll say a word broken apart. You say it normally. /d/—/o/—/g/" Child says: **"dog."** (blending individual phonemes/advanced level)
Segmenting	Segmenting is the reverse skill of blending. Children are asked to take a word and break it into its smaller sound units (i.e., syllables, onset-rimes, and individual phonemes). Again, what follows is a progression in the level of sophistication of the development of this skill.
	"Say only the larger parts or syllables you hear in the word *hippo"* Child says: **"hip—po"** (segmenting syllables/initial level)
	"Say just the first part of the word *tree"* Child says: **"/tr/"** (segmenting onset-rimes/intermediate level)
	"Say all the sounds you hear in the word *cap"* Child says: **"/c/—/a/—/p/"** (segmenting individual phonemes/advanced level)
Phonemic Awareness	As the most sophisticated level of **phonological awareness**, phonemic awareness involves the manipulation of phonemes found within words. This understanding is a necessary forerunner to letter-by-letter sounding out in phonic instruction. The four tasks typically considered parts of phonemic awareness and arranged in order of the level of sophistication are categorization and identity; deletion; addition; and substitution. Following are examples of how you might assess these areas.

(Continued)

Gathering Information

Table 7.4 • (Continued)

Phonological Skill	Description
	Show the child four pictures and say, **"Which of these pictures begin with the same sound?"** Child says: "Map, mitten, and moon start with /m/"
	Say, **"What sound is the same in** *boy, bake,* **and** *butter?***"** Child says: "The first sound /b/ is the same."
	"Which word doesn't belong? Run, rabbit, truck." Child says: "Truck, it begins with /t/" (categorization and identity/initial level)
	"If I take away the sound /p/ in the word *play,* **what word is left?"** Child says: "lay" (phoneme deletion/intermediate level)
	"If I add the sound /b/ to the beginning of *rat,* **what word do I have?"** Child says: "brat"
	"If I add the sound /s/ to the end of *car,* **what new word would I have?"** Child says: **"cars"** (phoneme addition/intermediate level)
	"The word is *pat.* **Change the /t/ to /n/. What's the new word?"** Child says: "pan"
	"The word is *bar.* **Change the /b/ to /f/. What's the new word?** Child says: "far"
	"The word is *cat.* **Change the /ă/ to /ŭ/. What's the new word?"** Child says: "cut" (phoneme substitution/advanced level)

Alphabet Inventory

Essential in early reading instruction is knowledge of the alphabet, because it provides teachers and children with a common language for talking about graphophonic relationships. **Graphophonic relationships** are the relationships between sounds and the symbols that are used to represent them in print. Alphabet knowledge should be assessed in two contexts: identifying letters in isolation and letter production.

To begin, you will create a random list of letters displayed on a sheet of paper. You will then ask a child to sit next to you and explain that you want to find out which letters of the alphabet she can name as you point to them on the page. You begin by pointing at the top letter and moving left to right down the page, keeping the letters below the line of focus covered with a blank sheet of paper. Record the child's responses on a photocopy of the display sheet, marking which letters she identified correctly and how she identified those that were incorrect. Following the child's naming of the letters, use the same display sheet and ask the child to point to the letters you name in the display. Record this information. Most children will identify at least half of the letters correctly (see Figure 7.2).

Unlike letter identification, assessing a child's understandings of letter production requires that he or she be able to produce letters from memory. This task is determined to see what letters a child knows and can write. Create a list of ten letters drawn randomly from the alphabet, being sure to include at least three vowels (see Figure 7.3). Provide the child with a piece of paper and a pencil and ask him to write down any letters he may know. After he has written a letter, ask him to name it

Table 7.5 ● Concepts About Print Observation Form

Print Concept	How to Assess	Child's Response/Observation
Print carries message	Open book to first page with a picture, and say, **"I'm going to read you this story, but I need your help. Show me where to start reading."**	Child receives credit if he points to the words on the page. Pay special attention to where on the line of print he points, being sure to note if it is at the beginning of the line of print.
Directionality and return sweep	On the next page, say, **"Point to where I start reading. Which way do I go? After that?"**	Child receives credit if she points at the first word, moves left to right across the page, and returns to the bottom left when she gets at the end of the line.
One-to-one correspondence	On the following page, say, **"Point to the words as I read them."**	Child receives credit if he matches his pointing to your voice—pointing to a word for every word you say.
Letter, word, sentence	Turn to the next page and say, **"Show me a sentence. Show me a word. Show me a letter."**	Child receives credit for each if he frames the entire sentence with her fingers; frames one word with her fingers; and frames only one letter.
First and last part	On the following page, say, **"Show me the first part of the story. Show me the last part of the story."**	The child receives credit if he points out any of the following combinations: • first and last words on a line • first and last words in a sentence • first and last words on a page • first and last words in the book
First and last letters in words	Turn the page and after reading it say, **"Now, show me the first letter of _____. Show me the last letter of _____."**	The child receives credit for framing the designated letter in each of the words. Be sure to note if she is only able to do one of the concepts.
Upper- and lowercase letters	On the next page point to an uppercase letter and ask, **"What do you call this kind of letter?"** Point to a lowercase letter and ask, **"What about this one?"**	The child receives credit for naming the letter as *uppercase* or *capital*, but not for naming it *big*. The same is true for the next. The child receives credit for naming the letter as *lowercase*, but not *little*.
Meaning of a variety of punctuation marks (? and .)	Pointing to a question mark in text, say, **"What is this for?"** Pointing to a period in text, say, **"What is this for?"**	Child receives credit if he says, **"Question mark"** or **"When you ask something."** Child receives credit is he says, **"Period"** or **"When you get to the end of a sentence."**

```
        B

      T   e

    I  M  o  s

  A  n  X  P  I

    y  w  K  C

      H  u

        J
```

Figure 7.2 ● Alphabet letter display.

for you. Then, invite him to write the letters you name from the random list you created. Be sure to record the child's responses and attempts at letter writing on a copy of the random letter list you created (see Figure 7.3).

Interests and Attitude Surveys

We know that interest in materials provided increases a child's motivation to read and engage with those materials. The literature also suggests that motivation works to increase a child's understanding for materials, concepts, and ideas. To determine what is of interest, you might interview a child using questions designed by Strickland, Ganske, and Monroe (2002):

1. What are your favorite types of books?
2. Who are your favorite authors?
3. What do you like to read other than books (for example, magazines, comics, newspapers, encyclopedias)?
4. What are you working on to improve in your reading?
5. What do you like least about reading?
6. What are your favorite hobbies, activities, and/or sports?

```
1. m      6. o
2. a      7. t
3. s      8. I
4. f      9. p
5. h     10. i
```

Figure 7.3 ● Random letter list.

7. What do you know a lot about?
8. Where do you usually get your reading materials?
9. How do you decide which books or materials to read?
10. When and where do you like to read? (p. 202)

Or, you could use the Garfield Reading Survey (McKenna & Kear, 1990) consisting of twenty simply worded statements about reading followed by four pictures of Garfield. Four poses are designed to depict different emotional states ranging from very positive to very negative. The child simply circles her or his response to the statement that has been read.

Running Record

Running records (Clay, 1993) allow you to determine two things about a child's literacy understandings. A child's reading level can be established by calculating the percentage of words read correctly by the child. Second, you can determine "in-the-head" problem solving strategies and sources of information (cues from the semantic, syntactic, or graphophonic systems) a child is using as she or he reads a book.

Administering a running record requires working one-on-one with a child. There is great flexibility with running records in that they can be administered on any type of texts that a child is reading at anytime. The child reads a book as you record any miscues (insertions of words, skipped words, substitutions of new words for those found in texts), repeated phrases or words, decoding behaviors (sounding or chunking of words), and/or self-corrections the child makes as he or she reads. This is accomplished through an established coding system and is typically recorded on any type of paper. Following the reading of the text, you can calculate the percentage of words read accurately by dividing the total number of words read correctly by the total number of words and multiplying by 100. An accuracy rate of 95 percent or higher is a child's *independent* or *easy level* of text. An accuracy rate of 90 to 94 percent is considered a child's *instructional level* of text, and this is where instruction should be pitched. An accuracy rate of 89 percent or lower is considered a child's *frustration level*. Texts here should be avoided for instruction.

Additionally, miscues can be further analyzed to determine the sources of information children use when they make a miscue. There are patterns that can be found in children's reading behaviors. By looking for these patterns, you are better able to determine what the child next needs instructionally. To do this, you ask yourself a series of questions for each miscue. To determine if the child is using meaning, or semantic information (M), you ask yourself, "Does it make sense to say_____ in this story?" To determine if the child is using the structure of English to guide her or his prediction, or syntactical information (S), you ask yourself, "Can we say it that way in English?" To determine if the child is using the graphophonic, or visual information (V) found in words and the letters of words, you ask yourself, "Does this word look like the word in the book?" Again, you are looking for a pattern of behaviors. Take a look at the sample running record to see how another teacher analyzed this child's reading behaviors, looking for patterns (see Figure 7.4).

Retellings

Retellings, or having children tell about what they have just read or heard read, are effective ways for determining what a child understands about what he or she has just read or heard. Usually,

Reading Accuracy: 90%	Text Level: 4 (early emergent)
Title: *Dan the Flying Man*	
	Information Used

p. 2	✓	✓	✓	✓	<u>boy</u>			MS
	I	am	Dan	the	man			
p. 3	✓	✓		✓	✓	✓	✓ ✓	
	catch	me		catch	me	if	you can	
p. 4	<u>up</u>	<u>above</u>	✓	✓				MS
	---	over	a	house				MS
p. 5	✓	✓	✓	<u>car</u>				V
	and	over	a	crane				

Figure 7.4 • Child's running record of reading.

retellings are conducted in individual conferences with children where you are able to ask them about their books. During this time, it is often good practice to have the book available, to scan the front and back covers, read the page the child is on, etc. Ultimately, it is most beneficial to have read the story, but realistically this may be difficult when children select texts from large classroom libraries.

This assessment may begin by prompting, "Tell me what this is about." When the child appears to be finished you might continue, "What else can you remember?" If the book is a narrative, you can base your questions on the text's structure (setting, characters, problem, events, and solution). If it is informational (expository text), then your questions can be geared to the specific content of the book ("Tell me, what have you learned about dinosaurs?"). For specific prompts for narrative and expository texts, see Table 7.6.

Assessing Sight Vocabulary

Common to most of us, sight words fit into two categories: (1) *high-frequency words*, or words that are found often in most sentences and texts and include words such as *a, for, the, like, can, have, and said*, and (2) words that do not follow regular phonic patterns or "rules" and so must simply be known, since decoding them will not work, such as *was, because, some, come*, and *of*. Research suggests that a child's recognition of words that are familiar accounts for about 95 percent of a child's ability to recognize unfamiliar or unknown words (Moustafa, 1995).

To assess a child's sight vocabulary, construct a list of high-frequency and/or phonically irregular words and record the child's performance. You are looking for words known automatically—those that appear to be almost known when sound–symbol relationships are used to decode them and those that are completely unknown—a child makes no attempts to read them. Useful in construction of such an assessment might be Dolch (1948) or Fry (2000) word lists. See Table 7.7 for an example of this assessment.

Table 7.6 ● Narrative and Expository Texts Retelling Prompts

Narrative Text Structure	Sample Prompt(s)
Setting	Where did this story take place?
Characters	Who were the characters in this story?
	Who was the main character?
	How did you know _____ was the main character?
Problem	What were the characters trying to do in this story?
Events	What important things happened in this story?
Solution	How was the problem solved?
Theme	What was the author trying to tell us in this story?

Expository Texts Retelling Prompts

What were some of the main points or ideas in the text?

How did you know this?

Tell me something that you have learned that you find interesting.

Are there any confusing parts in this text? Show me.

What do you think other people will learn from this book? or What was the most important idea of this book?

Table 7.7 ● Dolch Word-First Word List

the	I	was	for
to	you	said	on
and	it	his	they
he	of	that	but
a	in	she	had

Dolch, 1948.

Evaluating Information

Once information has been collected, it is important to evaluate it and determine what it says or means. In other words, the information alone does not benefit your instruction unless you analyze it for patterns. To ascertain these patterns, begin to ask yourself questions based upon the information gathered. Gipe (2006) suggests three levels of analysis: (1) lack of literacy learning, (2) where difficulty might lie in a broad sense, and (3) where difficulty might lie more specifically. The following are questions to pose to yourself as you move through each level of analysis with the information you have gathered.

Level 1: Determining lack of literacy learning

1. Is the child experiencing a lack of success in literacy? If so, where is this occurring (i.e., in what situations)?

Level 2: Determining where difficulty may lies in a broad sense

1. Does the child demonstrate underdeveloped oral and/or written language ability? What are examples of this?
2. Does the child have difficulty with word recognition? letter recognition? What does she know about words? What does she know about letters?
3. Does the child have difficulty with understanding narrative texts? Expository texts? Where does understanding appear to break down for this learner?

Level 3: Determining where the difficulty may lie more specifically

1. *Oral and written language*
   a. Does the child demonstrate underdeveloped oral (speaking and/or listening) and/or written language ability needed for the particular reading or writing task? Is it only in one area or in many? What is it that you notice when the child engages in these tasks?

2. *Word recognition*
   a. Does the child have a limited sight vocabulary? What words does he know automatically?
   b. Does he have a word recognition strategy? In other words, what does he do when he comes to a word with which he is unfamiliar?
   c. Does the child have difficulty in the area of word analysis (i.e., visual analysis and decoding)?
   d. Can he blend word parts that have been visually or auditorially analyzed?
   e. Does the child have knowledge of word morphology (i.e., structural analysis)?
   f. Does he have difficulty using context clues?

3. *Reading comprehension and strategic reading for narrative/expository text*
   Specifically, does the child appear to construct meaning using the following strategies:
   a. activate relevant, prior knowledge before, during and after reading text?
   b. create visual and other sensory images from text during and after reading?
   c. draw inferences from the text to form conclusions, make critical judgments, and create individual interpretations?
   d. ask questions of herself, the author(s), and texts as she reads?
   e. determine the most important ideas and themes in text?
   f. synthesize what she read?

(Adapted from Gipe, 2006, level of analysis questions and proficient reader research synthesized by Pearson, Dole, Duffy, & Roehler, 1992)

Generating Hypotheses

Once you have evaluated the information gathered, determining both the strengths and needs of a child, you need to consider how to provide learning opportunities and assistance. Essentially, you are attempting to create a tentative instructional focus based upon what a child needs and what his or her strengths are.

Rachel

Rachel is 5 and has just entered school. When assessed on her knowledge of letters, she was able to identify the following letters as "in my name" but appeared to be unaware of the names associated with the symbols or the sounds related to them: *r, h, l, a*. When her phonological awareness was measured, Rachel appeared to be able to identify rhyming pairs, especially when given pictures from which to select options. However, she appeared unable to generate rhyming pairs. On the concepts about print task, she pointed to the picture to indicate where meaning was, identified the front of the book, and that the left page is read before the right one. From observations of Rachel in the classroom, it appeared that she understood one-step directions by the teacher, and she often responded in one- or two-word utterances to requests from adults or peers. When read a story aloud, she appeared able to follow the story and would comment on pictures following the one- or two-word utterance pattern observed in her oral language use.

From the information gathered, the following appear to be Rachel's strengths: rhyme generation; she knows and makes connections with some of the letters that represent her name; she appears to have some additional awareness of print and how it functions in books; she appears to engage with stories, interacting with the pictures in doing so; she can identify rhyming pairs; and she communicates in one- and two-word utterances or sentences. The following are a list of needs for Rachel based upon this information: She appears to need help in learning to expand her vocabulary and sentence structure use; she appears to need to develop a fuller understanding for how her name can be represented (i.e., letters in her name); her awareness of rhyme needs to develop more fully so that she can begin to generate rhyming pairs; and she appears to need continued exposure to books to gain more understandings for how print functions within them as well as to develop narrative structures for use in her oral communication.

Hypotheses. To begin instruction for Rachel, we first need to generate hypotheses about what this information tells us about her understandings for literacy. A natural starting point is to look at Rachel's oral language. It appears she is communicating in an incomplete manner. If we were to work to develop her vocabulary, her use of this vocabulary, and expose her to more comprehensive ways for communicating (sentence structures different from one- and two-word utterances), then Rachel would be better able to express herself and communicate with others. Since she appears to have some understanding of rhyme, rhyme identification, it makes sense to build on this understanding. We could begin with the pictures, since this appeared to make the task easier for her, and talk about what makes words rhyme. We could include discussion of pictures in the stories we read and rhyming pairs found in classroom songs and poems. Through the use of varied and multiple forms of texts accompanied by rich, meaning-centered discussions involving all children in the classroom, we are able to introduce and incorporate multiple and varied sentence structures in classroom talk.

Teaching

Fountas and Pinnell (1996) suggest a framework for literacy that provides children with opportunities to use language, learn through language use, and experience new ways for using it. They propose there is flexibility in the framework so teachers may respond to classroom needs and activity.

Types of Reading

The four types of reading include reading aloud, shared reading, guided reading, and independent reading. There is flexibility for the level of support and scaffolding provided by the teacher.

Reading aloud.   Beginning with the first day of school, **reading aloud** serves as the starting point for early literacy learning experiences. The teacher purposefully selects texts for variety and text types so that children experience a sense of pleasure for reading; see that reading has a purpose; begin to develop a sense of story and an understanding for written language syntax; be supported in making connections between the story and themselves, between the story and other texts, and between the story and the world (Keene & Zimmerman, 1997); and further expand and develop their oral language. To do this, the teacher selects and reads a book or other text to children. As she reads, the teacher provides full support for the children in accessing the text through questions that she poses ("Where do you think the bears are going?"), by making her thoughts clear ("I'm wondering who broke that chair?"), or demonstrating the connections she is making ("That makes me think of my brother's little chair. He has one just like that"). Children respond to the pictures, the meaning, and the language used in the text. These responses may not at first be unclear to the teacher ("I have a dog" when the book is about camping), but with some further probing and input from others the connections can be made clearer. Typically, texts that are rich in meaning or language as well as those that are class favorites are read over and over again. Time spent engaging with the same text encourages language use and may allow children to begin to analyze and compare texts.

Shared reading.   When conducting a **shared reading** with children, it is necessary the children see the text and its print features so they can engage in the group reading process. To do this, use Big Books, a poem, or any enlarged texts (texts used on an overhead projector, enlarged versions of retellings, products of interactive writing, etc.). As the book is read aloud, the teacher or another student directs the reading by pointing to the words on the page with a pointer. Over a period of days the book is read again and again, and, as children gain familiarity with the language structure for the text, they begin to "join in," reading in unison the refrain or highly repetitive patterns found in the text, and then read most of the story by the last day. Initially, children are asked to engage with print in incidental ways as the teacher is reading the story. Since the print and features of the text are visible to the children, they are able to see how print and books work (i.e., left-to-right movement across the text, etc.). However, as familiarity with the text develops, more explicit direction is given as the teacher draws the children's attention to print and to model reading behaviors (word-by-word matching, use of sight words, etc.).

Shared reading provides children with opportunities to behave and participate like readers. Children build upon their previous knowledge for story structure and sense, use a social system for learning about reading and problem solving, and come to understand early strategies for reading (e.g., left-to-right movement across text, word-by-word matching). It also provides children with a body of known texts that they can use to read independently, for writing and creating their own texts, and for the study of words and understanding of sound–symbol relationships in a meaningful context.

Guided reading.   **Guided reading** places children in a more formal instructional reading setting as the teacher works with small, flexible groups of children with similar literacy needs. The decision to place a child in guided reading rests on teacher observations of what occurs as the child explores books independently and participates in shared reading (e.g., is he trying to emulate the word-by-word pointing of shared reading). If it is your goal to fully use this framework for literacy learning for children earlier in their development, a small-group shared reading may be an appropriate substitution for guided reading. Here the teacher would select and introduce a new book, read it aloud to support the children in developing text familiarity, with the book being read in unison on subsequent days and attention given to different features of print and text.

For children in first grade and above, guided reading should serve as the foundational element of the literacy curriculum that sustains a child's forward progress. Typically, a child participates in guided reading three to five days per week, with a new book introduced and read every time. Here the teacher introduces the book and asks the children to read the whole text themselves. If support from the teacher is needed, he or she provides it in the form of prompts (e.g., "Read that again and think what would make sense."). The idea is children learn to problem-solve and extend their use of strategies.

It should be understood that, as children develop in their understandings for literacy, the focus of guided reading would naturally change. Usually, for early readers the focus is on learning about the code of printed language, conventions of print, and problem-solving strategies. However, as children further develop and refine their understandings, the purpose and form of guided reading could be to analyze characters in texts, learn text structures and how they can be used to guide or set the purpose for reading, or learn to read in a variety of genres or how to get information from texts. An idea behind guided reading is that children develop in different ways, at different times, and different rates. Therefore, children do not read the same sequence or sets of books. Teachers select books so they afford maximum learning opportunities for a particular group of children. Groups are flexible and dynamic, so when a child's understandings change, so too does the child's placement, as he or she is moved to be with a group of children to whom he or she is more similar.

Independent reading.   All children should engage in **independent reading** every day. Here they are reading not just books but all of the written materials found in the classroom. It is through the reading and rereading that young children are supported in their literacy development. This is an opportunity for every child to act and behave like a good reader. To do this, children may read on their own or with a partner from a wide range of material. These materials might include Big Books from shared reading, name charts, large charts of nursery rhymes and poems, word walls, pocket charts, interactive writing, class-published books, books from guided reading, menus and recipes, etc.

Instructional Activities

Oral language.   Children need a variety of daily opportunities to talk in classrooms. These should be opportunities to use talk to socialize with classmates, play with language, to ask questions, and to participate in discussions and share information (Fountas & Pinnell, 1996). The following some examples of oral language presentations that may be used to foster children's use and development of both expressive and receptive oral language.

Show and tell.   As part of most children's early experiences, show and tell involves sharing a favorite or familiar object with classmates. Oftentimes, a child may not know exactly what to say about the object. To assist the child here, you may begin the show-and-tell process by modeling for the children how to select an object and share about it.

Three types of oral presentations.   The first type of oral presentation that a child may engage in is a *picture report*. In this report, the child shares a picture he has drawn to illustrate an important fact or idea. As he talks about the picture, the teacher encourages the child to use content-related words when appropriate and to articulate important facts. Another easy oral presentation to give is the *question-and-answer* report. For this report, children and teachers begin by generating a long list of questions related to a unit of study or a book that is being read. The child then develops a report to answer the questions that have been asked. A third type of oral presentation that a child may give is called the *three-things-I-know* report. In this type of presentation the child selects a topic and develops three things she knows that she wants to share about it.

Modified dialogic reading.   **Dialogic reading** is a technique used by researchers to study development of oral language skills through shared storybooks (Whitehurst & Lonigan, 2001). This approach is one that has been used when working with individual children, placing them in the active role of a storyteller. In the initial stage of the dialogic reading intervention, children are encouraged to connect texts with their experiences, previous knowledge, and other information contained within the pictures and story (e.g., "What is that?" or "I wonder why that is in the picture?"). The responses children make are then evaluated, with praise and encouragement being given to extend an intentional, ongoing invitation to actively respond and interact with the reading of the story ("I like the way you are thinking about_____. What do you think will happen next?"). Children's responses are further expanded through the teacher's use of additional words and restatements (the child says, "boy shirt red." The teacher responds, "Oh, the boy is wearing a red shirt. Good noticing!"). Then, the child is asked to repeat the adult's response.

The second stage of dialogic reading employs more questions that are open-ended and calls for expansion on what a child has said (Hargrave & Senechal, 2000). Some of the question types that might be used include

1. *Complete prompts*, with a word or phrase that has been omitted (e.g., "The little girl was going to_____").

2. *Recalling prompts*, where children are asked to think about what has happened already in the story ("Where did Goldilocks go first?).

3. *Open-ended prompts*, asking a child to respond to the story in his or her own words ("I wonder if there is anything that you know that is like that . . .").

4. *Wh-prompts*, where the adult asks *what, where, when, why, who, which,* and *how* questions ("What is it that Goldilocks was eating?").

Through this activity, the adult assumes the role of active listener, asking questions, adding information, and prompting for more information (Whitehurst & Lonigan, 2001).

Language Experience Approach (LEA).   The Language Experience Approach (LEA) to reading begins with children engaging and sharing in an experience. This experience may be the reading of a story, a fieldtrip, or a walk around the school. After engaging in this experience, the teacher and children meet and discuss it. This discussion helps children determine what it is they want to write about. Children are encouraged to first draw about what they want to write and then dictate to the teacher the story they want to share. The teacher acts as scribe, transcribing verbatim the story the child dictates. The purpose of verbatim transcription is so the child may be able to read this text later. These experiences increase a child's use and understanding of oral language.

Learning about print.   Learning about and developing further literacy understandings requires that children gain an awareness of aspects of print. Print awareness here includes *graphic principles, concepts about print*, and *orthographic knowledge*.

Graphic Principles.   Clay (1975) identified graphic principles that emerge as children engage and experiment in writing. The first to appear is that of the *recurring principle*. The recurring principle is one in which the same mark or graphic feature is repeated in a linear arrangement. The second principle, the *generative principle*, occurs when children realize that they can add some variety to their writing. The understanding gained at this point is that a few marks can be combined or recombined in different orders to produce a whole page or more of writing. This usually occurs when a child has learned or almost learned the letters that spell her or his name and then uses these same symbols to write or label other items and pictures. The *flexibility principle* is when the child has developed the awareness that print often assumes different forms (e.g., different typefaces) and begins to experiment with the forms of letters, oftentimes producing original forms. The *directionality principle* is when the child has an awareness that directional principles have to do with learning to associate the identity of letters with their direction. To foster the development of the understandings of these principles in children, it is necessary for children to have many opportunities in which they interact with text. Writing for many and varied purposes is perhaps the best way. You may have children write their names to sign in to class, to write letters to others, or to label their areas in the classroom.

Concepts about print.   It is through experiences that children learn that print carries meaning and that reading and writing are used for a variety of purposes. To demonstrate these purposes and to provide opportunities for children to experiment with written language, teachers might do the following:

- Post signs throughout the room
- Write morning messages
- Record questions and information on a chart
- Write notes to parents and children
- Sing and read songs and poems from charts
- Write in journals
- Make a list of classroom rules
- Make posters for favorite books

Environmental print—the words and logos that children see in the world around them—in classrooms also offers children opportunities to learn about concepts associated with print. For example, a child is encouraged to write a story about her favorite place. She draws the golden arches of McDonald's and says, "McDonald's" when asked to later share her drawing with the class. These symbols allow children to develop relationships between the meaning associated with the symbol and the concepts of written language.

Literacy play centers afford children with many opportunities to learn about the concepts of print. When children are encouraged to write and tape signs on their building projects, write grocery lists as they play in housekeeping, write receipts and make notations for hair appointments in the beauty salon, or play teacher and read aloud stories to others, they are using reading and writing for a variety of purposes and, in doing so, learning more about how print works and functions in their everyday lives.

Orthographic Knowledge

Orthographic knowledge refers to a child's knowledge of letters and understandings of how these symbols correspond to the sounds of oral language. Children need to have opportunities to learn about letters: the name of the symbol, the features of it, and the forms in upper- and lowercase writing. Using the names of the young children with whom you work is a good way to help them begin to develop these understandings for letters. For example, a teacher might point to a chart in the classroom and discuss that Cole and Callay begin with the letter C, or that Grace's name begins like Goldilocks. The alphabet song can also be useful in providing children with a strategy for determining the name of an unknown letter. They locate the letter on the alphabet chart and then sing the song, pointing to each letter until they reach their finger. An activity to help children attend to the featured letters is the *letter sort*. Children are asked to sort magnetic letters to match upper- and lowercase letters, find all the *t*'s and *o*'s, find the letters with circles, sort the tall letters and the short letters, sort the letters by color, find the letters in their name, put the letters in alphabetical order, etc. You might extend this activity to one including sound, where the children sort the letters by the sounds associated with them ("Put all the /s/ letters here and all the /m/ letters here."). Encouraging the use of inventive spelling is another way to help children extend their understandings for letter and sound relationships.

Phonological Awareness.   As stated earlier, phonological awareness deals with the sounds heard in spoken language and deals primarily with rhyme, syllabication, blending, segmenting, and phonemic awareness. Activities related to each of these areas will be shared here.

Rhyme.   Books, songs, and poems often contain examples of rhyming and alliterative words that may be used to teach these concepts. After using a poem, song, or book for shared reading, you might create a rhyming-word list in which you and the children identify and list the words that rhyme. Another activity that fosters further understandings of alliteration is to use a song like "Zippity-doo-dah" replacing the initial sound with another. For example, replacing the /z/ with an /m/. The song would sound something like this, "mippity-moo-mah, mippity-may, my oh my what a wonderful day, plenty of sunshine coming my way, mippity-moo-mah, mippity-may." Fitzpatrick (1997) provides many activities related to the development of phonological awareness including "Rhyme Away" and "Draw a Rhyme." In Rhyme Away, the teacher starts by drawing a simple picture on the board and tells the children they are going to make the picture disappear by erasing it a little at a time. The teacher then reads aloud the Rhyme Away story, and the children orally complete the sentences using clues found in the picture. That part of the picture is then erased until the entire picture has disappeared. For the Draw a Rhyme activity, children are asked to help you draw a monster by completing the missing rhyming words of the story. The teacher reads each rhyme aloud, omitting the rhyming word. The children are asked to complete the rhyme orally, with a volunteer coming to the board to draw the corresponding rhyme.

Syllabication.   Syllabication has to do with the hearing of larger parts within words, syllables. You might ask children to count, clap, or tap the number of syllables they hear in words found in a story, poem, or song that is being shared. You might ask children to engage in a *picture sort* in which they sort a selection of pictures into groups based upon the numbers of syllables they contain. A version of the game "I Spy" could also be used to help children understand syllables. To play this game, children would use the syllables in another child's name as what was spied. For example, a child might say, "I spy with my little eye, a name that has two parts." Another child would guess, "Is it Callay?" and the first child would respond indicating if the guess was correct. If so, then that child would give a number of syllables for a name of someone in the room.

Blending.   Blending refers to the ability to join syllables or sounds together to form words. An activity involves the use of pictures that could be blended together to form larger words. For example, the picture of a cow and a boy would be put together to form the word *cowboy*. Another activity for blending is called "Pop-up People" (Fitzpatrick, 1997). Children are selected to come to the front of the room. The number of children selected relates to the number of sounds found in a word. For example, the word *top* has three sounds, so three children would come to the front of the room and sit in chairs. The teacher would then whisper a sound in each of the children's ear. The teacher would tap each child on the shoulder, and each would "pop up" and say his or her sound: /t/—/o/—/p/. The rest of the class would blend the sounds together to form the word "top."

Segmenting.   Segmenting involves children isolating sounds in spoken words. A word stretch, or rubber-banding, in which the children are given a rubber band or slinky and stretch it for every sound they hear and say in a word, are examples. Yopp (1992) suggests a song set to the tune of "Twinkle, Twinkle Little Star" for this purpose:

Listen, listen
To my word
Tell me all the sounds you heard: *tree (this word is pronounced very slowly)*
/t/ is one sound
/r/ is two
/ee/ is last in *tree*
It's true.

After several times through, in which other words are segmented, the song ends this way:

Thanks for listening
To my words
And telling all the sounds you heard! (p. 702)

Children's understandings and abilities to segment words relates directly to the their developing understandings for how letters and sounds are connected.

Elkonin boxes (1963) are an activity to use with children so that they can begin to hear and mark all of the sounds spoken in words. A teacher uses a picture card, a card with boxes for each sound, and something with which to mark the sounds (i.e., pennies or tokens). The teacher says the word slowly, pushing one counter into the box for each sound heard, as it is heard (/ddddd/. . ./ooooo/. . ./gggg/). Phonemic awareness also includes a child's ability to manipulate sounds found within words. As children play with words and create nonsense words, they add and substitute sounds. Children can substitute sounds in refrains of songs (Yopp, 1992). For example, "Ee-igh, ee-igh, oh!" in "Old MacDonald Had a Farm" can be changed to "Bee-bigh, bee-bigh, boh!" to focus on the initial /b/ sound. Another activity is the "Change the Name Game." You start by saying to the children, "Say *man*." The children say, "man." Then, you say, "Now change the /m/ in man to a /t/. What do you get?" The children say, "tan" (see Figure 7.5).

Phonics

Phonics instruction emphasizes how spellings are related to speech sounds in systematic and predictable ways (Burns, Griffin, & Snow, 1999). Letter-sound cards are intended to help children make connections between a sound and letter or letter combinations (i.e., digraphs and blends) that have already been introduced. Children are provided with their own word cards on which they have written a key letter sound or sounds on one side and a word on the other. Another activity asks children make groups of words with different kinds of letters (e.g., magnetic letters, tile letters, or foam letters). Fountas and Pinnell (1996) suggest the following possibilities:

Words from a set of letters (c, n, t, a, p); words with the same first letter (box, bat); words with the same final letter (up, hop); words one of which is included in the other (but, butter); words with the same letters in them (once, twice); words with a particular letter sequence (sh, ch); words with a letter cluster at the beginning (stop, clay); words with a letter cluster at the end (sand, rust); words with e in them (egg, clean, tree); words with a letter that makes a particular sound (the s in sun or bus, was, or treasure); words with the same root but varied endings (looking, looks, looked); words with a letter that makes no sound (here, meat, make); one-,two-, or three-letter words; or words in a category or theme (colors, animals, names). (p. 174)

Figure 7.5 ● Elkonin boxes for marking sounds.

Such activities enable children to apply their understanding of letter–sound relationships to the creation of words. Word sorts are another effective way for children to come to understand about patterning in words (Bear, Invernizzi,Templeton, & Johnston, 2000; Fountas & Pinnell, 1996). Some possible categories of sorts include words that rhyme (cat/sat, go/no); words with inflectional endings (playing, jumping); words with the same vowel sound but different spelling patterns (sky/shine, play/weigh); and words with similar letters that have different sounds (took/food/flood, cow/snow).

Word Recognition

A child's ability to recognize words while at the same time understanding what is being read should advance together. Research suggests that children who are able to recognize words rapidly and efficiently have an easier time understanding the meaning of what they read, because the efficient recognition frees the mind to concentrate on the message (Stanovich, 1986). Again, word sorts and word-making activities are effective in helping children learn more about words. For example, a teacher might ask a child to sort words according to the concepts they represent—*a concept sort*. So, the children place all the words related to weather in one pile (e.g., sunny, rainy, snowy) and those related to cooking in another (e.g., stove, bowl, spoon). To make the task easier, the teacher repeats the lesson several times before asking the children to work with word cards, or she or he works with only one set of words at a time. To make the task more challenging, the teacher may introduce blends, digraphs, and mixed sorts (e.g., different short vowels, blends, and digraphs sorts). Children use spelling patterns in known words to generate new words (e.g., use what they know in the word *cat* to make the word *flat* or *hat*—this is called the *generative value of words*). Word hunts are another way to help children make the connection between spelling words and reading them. To do this, the teacher uses the book, poem, or song from shared reading and asks the children, "What do you notice about some of these words?" Some suggest that there are words that rhyme in the text. The teacher says, "Now I'm going on a word hunt. I'm looking for words that rhyme as I read." As the teacher reads she notes aloud both words that rhyme and do not, creating lists from text. Word walls provide a strong support for children's learning. The word wall consists of words children are learning and are arranged alphabetically. Typically, these are high-utility, high-frequency, or sight words children encounter in many contexts. As an interactive tool, word walls are made and used by the teacher and children in their reading and writing (Cunningham, 1995). For more information about word walls, see Cunningham's (1995) *Phonics They Use: Words for Reading and Writing*.

Meaning Making With Texts

The ultimate goal in the complex process of reading is the construction of meaning. Every time a child engages in reading, he or she goes through the recursive process of *sampling, predicting, confirming or disconfirming,* and *monitoring or self-correcting.* Essentially, reading is a two-faceted activity: It involves the alphabetic code used to determine words and thinking about those words as a reader constructs meaning. In this section, we look at activities that help readers to "interact more completely with their reading, bringing themselves to the text to engage in a richer, deeper, more thoughtful reading experience" (Harvey & Goudvis, 2000, p. 1). In particular we will examine: *making connections, asking questions, visualizing, drawing inferences, determining importance, synthesizing information, and repairing understandings* (Harvey & Goudvis, 2000; Keene & Zimmerman, 1997; Miller, 2002).

Making connections.   Readers naturally make connections between texts and their own lives. It is our job as teachers to help them to understand the types of connections they are making to enable them to move from making connections close to home (text-to-self), to broader ones (text-to-text), and finally to include more expansive issues beyond home and community to that of the larger world (text-to-world). It is easiest to start this process by connecting with stories that are close to the children's lives and experiences.

The activity of "That reminds me of . . ." proves to be a valuable starting point. As you are reading a story aloud to children, you simply engage in a think-aloud process of the connections that you are making related to your life, experiences, and background knowledge. During the reading of *Cinderella*, you might say, "The cleaning that Cinderella is always doing reminds me of my mom at my house. She is always cleaning." As you make more connections, the children will begin to share in the process. You might list the connections that the children make in two columns, *what the story is about* and *what it reminds me of,* to make connections explicit.

When considering how to help children make connections with other texts, start by thinking about the characters, story events and plot lines, and different versions of stories with which children have familiarity. Oftentimes, connections made with other texts with young readers are difficult to determine simply, because we, as adults, do not have the same familiarity of references. We suggest using a set of different versions of the same story to begin this process. Read aloud each story on different days, and ask the children to think about the characters or the elements of the story in the different versions. You might say, "What is the troll like in the book we read yesterday? Is the troll in this book the same? Different? How?"

For early learners to make text-to-world connections, background knowledge will most likely need to be built. You may need to help children understand a place, like Africa, before they can begin to make connections. You may need to find and read a lot of books about Africa aloud to the children so they will be able to engage and discuss pictures and photographs as well as to ask questions. These questions can be sorted into categories, and children can start to explain and discuss what they learned that was memorable. All connections, however, are not equal. We should strive to help children think about connections in terms of their use in understanding the story or text being read.

Questioning.   Questions are what establish the purpose for reading a text. By asking questions, children are propelled into reading. Questions, therefore, can be seen as the "master key to understanding" (Harvey & Goudvis, 2000, p. 81). As proficient readers we use questions to clarify confusion, stimulate inquiry, and take us deeper into meaning. As you are reading aloud to children, you can model the process of question asking through the use of sticky notes that you place in the text as questions arise. You should note and discuss whether or not the questions you asked were answered later in the story or not. In doing this, the teacher is demonstrating that some questions are not always answered. To begin this process, you may simply share the questions you have before, during, and after reading and talk about them. Listing questions help make the process more explicit and help children to see that not all questions are answered in the text.

Visualizing and inferring.   Visualization is the process of creating "movies in the mind"; it is the aspect of reading that brings joy. Each of the movies generated is unique to the person creating it. You might begin this process through the use of wordless picture books. Children use visualization to create or fill in the missing information. In doing so, children are taking clues revealed in the illustrations and combining them with background knowledge to fill in the gaps in the pictures they have created in their minds to make meaning. For example, when sharing *Good Dog Carl* by Alexandra Day, children often erupt in laughter. To get at what they are visualizing, you might ask, "What do you think is happening between this picture and the next?" or "What makes this so funny? What do you think happened?" Visualizing helps children build meaning.

Inferring is essentially "reading between the lines" of text. We use inferring in many contexts other than reading (reading our boss's mood, the quivering lips of a child, etc.). To help students understand about inferential thinking, we might use pictures of different expressions (happy, angry, frightened, etc.) and ask them what they mean. If they mention something like scared or frightened, then we can talk about the accurate inference they are making and what helped them to make it (the way the expression communicates that meaning). Another activity that might help children understand inference is to have a child stand in the middle of a circle with a feeling card (e.g., happy) on her back and have the other children give her clues as to how they feel when they are that card to help her guess what the word/feeling is. This could then be extended to texts that contain pictures where the teacher and children generate a list of the *quote or picture from the text* and the *inference* that was made.

Determining importance.   The idea behind this strategy is to help children sort through the information present in texts to know which they should retain and which should be discarded. As a central aspect of making sense of reading, it is often easier to begin instruction in this strategy with nonfiction text. An activity that you can use to do this is for children to claim to be a specialist on a favorite topic, choose what is important to include in a piece of writing, and then share it with others. To begin, a definition for what a specialist is must be given. From this definition, children are then able to generate a list of several topics that they know something about and love. Then, the children create a way of representing their understandings and what they know.

Synthesizing information.   To synthesize information, we take individual pieces of information and combine them without prior knowledge to create a new picture or idea. As a means of demonstrating and introducing this concept to learners, you might start by making brownies with the children. The brownies represent the whole that is synthesized from the parts, the ingredients necessary to make it. As you go, say something like, "All the different parts that we mixed together became a whole new thing, the brownies. When you read and listen to stories, there are a lot of different parts and characters, but in the end all of the parts go together to make up the whole story, just like the brownies we made." Miller (2002) suggests a basic framework that is used when readers synthesize: They remember what is important, tell it in ways that make sense, and try not to tell the entire story. This framework proves useful when helping young children with synthesizing. After the teacher finishes reading a story with children, she or he shows them how to synthesize the story using the basic framework. Sometimes the synthesis can be written on chart paper or sticky notes. Other times it can simply be a discussion.

Repairing understanding. In all of the activities mentioned here for strategy instruction, the tracking of children's and adult's thinking is recorded. There are many reasons for meaning to break down: insufficient background knowledge, a focus on details rather than important ideas or information, the maintenance of misconceptions in the face of more accurate information, and simply losing track of meaning as they read. Therefore, we need to teach children to monitor and repair their understandings when they go awry. To do this, we begin by teaching them to track their thinking, to notice when they lose focus, to reread to enhance meaning, to identify what is confusing, to question, and to match the problem with the strategy that will solve it (Harvey & Goudvis, 2000).

Summary

As this chapter has demonstrated, literacy learning is a complex, dynamic, and transactive process that begins long before children enter a classroom or school. Language learning, learning about language, and learning through language often occur simultaneously (Genishi, 1987; Halliday, 1975) as children engage in and with the world around them. The initial social endeavors of the child in knowing his or her world provide the foundation for the later print and literacy understandings that he or she will develop. These understandings serve as the means by which other processes that are necessitated by literacy learning come to be understood and incorporated with a child's worldview.

How teachers understand children's use of language, the processes involved in literacy learning, and the various theoretical perspectives of literacy instruction serves as the basis for the instructional decisions that will be made. When considering the needs of children with disabilities, even more consideration is required for determining how literacy learning opportunities can and will be provided.

Thinking It Through

1. Write a personal literacy narrative, examining how you developed literacy skills and experience. Connect your personal experiences to what you learned in this chapter and how that will influence your role as a literacy teacher.

2. Collect resources and materials that will guide your teaching of varied dimensions of literacy.

3. Define early emergent literacy and connect oral language, CAP, and the development of enjoyment for reading and literacy activities.

4. Identify an instructional strategy for literacy and explain why you would prefer to use it with specific children.

5. Describe how differentiated instruction may look in literacy learning environments and how such strategies meet learners' needs.

6. Create a plan for supporting children's literacy learning at multiple levels.

Children's Literature in Reading

Alliterations

Faint Frogs Feeling Feverish by Lilian Obligado (Viking)
Alfred's Alphabet Walk by Victoria Chess (Greenwillow)
Alligators All Around by Maurice Sendak (HarperCollins)
Have you Ever Seen . . . ? by Beau Gardner (Dodd)
Six Sick Sheep: 101 Tongue Twisters by Joanna Cole (Morrow)

Rhymes

Goodnight Moon by Margaret Wise Brown (Harper)
Jamberry by Bruce Degen (Harper)
Is Your Mama a Llama? by Deborah Guarino (Scholastic)
I Wish That I Had Duck Feet by Theo LeSieg (Random House)
The Shape of Me and Other Stuff by Dr. Seuss (Random House)
Street Rhymes Around the World by Jane Yolen (Wordsong)
More Spaghetti, I Say! by Rita Gelman (Scholastic)
Pickles Have Pimples and Other Silly Statements by Judi Barrett (Antheneum)

Songs and Chants

Arroz con Leche: Popular Songs and Rhymes from Latin America by Lulu Delacre (Scholastic)
Baby Beluga by Raffi (Crown)

I Know and Old Lady Who Swallowed a Fly by Nadine Westcott (Little, Brown)
Oh, A-Hunting We Will Go by John Langstaff (Atheneum)
Shimmy Shimmy Coke-Ca-Pop! by John and Carol Langstaff (Doubleday)
Tingalayo by Raffi (Crown)
The Wheels on the Bus by Harriet Ziefert (Random House)

Repetitive Sentences

The Very Hungry Caterpillar by Eric Carle (Philomel)
Where's Spot? by Eric Hill (Putnam)
We're Going on a Bear Hunt by M. Rosen (Macmillan)
The Lady With the Alligator Purse by N. B. Westcott (Little, Brown)
I Went Walking by S. Williams (Harcourt Brace Janovich)

Sequential Patterns

One, Two, Three, Going to Sea by Alain (Scholastic)
Over in the Meadow by Ezra Jack Keats (Scholastic)
If You Give a Mouse a Cookie by L. J. Numeroff (HarperCollins)
The Napping House by Audry Wood (Harcourt Brace Janovich)

Further Reading

Brown, R. A. (1973). *First language: The early stages*. Cambridge: Harvard University Press.

Cazden, C. B. (Ed.). (1981). *Language in early childhood education*. Washington, DC: NAEYC.

Fletcher, P., & Garman, M. (Eds.). (1986). *Language acquisition* (2nd ed.). New York: Cambridge.

Genishi, C. (1988, November). Children's language: Learning words from experience. *Young Children, 44*, pp. 16–23.

Genishi, C., & Haas Dyson, A. (1984). Language assessment in the early years. Norwood, NJ: Ablex.

Heath, S. B. (1983). Ways with words: Language, life, and work in communities and classrooms. New York: Cambridge.

Hough, R. A., Nurss, J. R., & Wood, D. (1987, November). Tell me a story: Making opportunities for elaborated language in early childhood classrooms. *Young Children, 43*, pp. 6–12.

Lindfors, J. W. (1987). Children's language and learning (2nd ed.). Englewood Cliffs, NJ: Prentice Hall.

Wells, G. (1986). The meaning makers: Children learning language and using language. Portsmouth, NH: Heinemann.

Young Children's Oral Language Development. (1988). *ERIC Digest:* (ERIC Document Reproduction Service No. ED301361) http://ericae.net/

Resources

www.childdevelopmentinfo.com/development/language_devel opment.shtml Provides information about language development in children

www.reading.org/ International Reading Association's website www.ed.gov/pubs/TeachersGuide/index.html U.S. Department of Education website

www.ala.org/ala/alsc/alscresources/borntoread/bornread.htm American Library Association website

www.cliontheweb.org/ Children's Literacy Initiative

www.ldonline.org/ General information on learning disabilities and ADHD

www.nationalreadingpanel.org/ National Reading Panel

www.readingrockets.org/ Reading Rockets: Launching Young Readers

www.ciera.org/ Center for the Improvement of Early Reading Achievement

References

Allington, R. (1994). The schools we have. The schools we need. *The Reading Teacher, 48*, pp. 14–29.

Allington, R. L. (2001). *What really matters for struggling readers: Designing research-based programs.* New York: Longman.

American Speech-Language Hearing Association (ASHA). (2005). How does your child hear and talk? Retrieved on October 6, 2005, from www.asha.org/public/speech/ development/child_hear_talk.htm

Bear, D., Invernizzi, M., Templeton, S., & Johnston, F. (2000). *Words their way: Word study for phonics, vocabulary, and spelling instruction.* Upper Saddle River, NJ: Merrill.

Bowen, C. (1998). *Developmental phonological disorders: A practical guide for families and teachers.* Camberwell, Australia: ACER Press.

Burns, M.S, Griffin, P., & Snow, C.E. (Eds.). (1999). *Starting out right: A guide to promoting children's reading success.* Washington, DC: National Academy Press.

Chall, J. (1983). *Stages of reading development.* New York: McGraw-Hill.

Clay, M. (1975). *What did I write? Beginning writing behavior.* Portsmouth, NH: Heinemann.

Clay, M. (1991). *Becoming literate.* Portsmouth, NH: Heinemann.

Clay, M. (1993). *Reading recovery: A guidebook for teachers in training.* Portsmouth, NH: Heinemann.

Cunningham, P. M. (1995). *Phonics they use: Words for reading and writing.* New York: Longman.

Delpit, L. (1995). *Other people's children: Cultural conflict in the classroom.* New York: The New Press.

Dolch, E. W. (1948). *Problems in reading.* Champaign, IL: Garrard Press.

Duffy, G. G. (1998). Powerful models or powerful teachers? An argument for teacher as entrepreneur. In S. Stahl and D. Hayes (Eds.), *Instructional models in reading.* Mahwah, NJ: Lawrence Erlbaum Associates.

Elkonin, D. B. (1963). The psychology of mastering the elements of reading. In B. Simon & J. Simon (Eds.), *Educational psychology in the U.S.S.R.* Stanford, CA: Stanford University Press.

Fitzpatrick, J. (1997). *Phonemic awareness: Playing with sounds to strengthen beginning reading skills.* Huntington Beach, CA: Creative Teaching Press.

Fountas, I. C., & Pinnell G. S. (1996). *Guided reading: Good first learning for all children.* Portsmouth NH: Heinemann.

Fountas, I., & Pinnell, G. S. (1996). *Guided reading: Good first teaching for all children.* Portsmouth, NH: Heinemann.

Fountas, I., & Pinnell, G. S. (1998). *Matching books to readers: Using leveled texts in guided reading, K–3.* Portsmouth, NH: Heinemann.

Fry, E. (2000). *How to teach reading.* Chicago: Contemporary Books.

Gambrell, L., & Mazzoni, S. (1999). Principals of best practice: Finding the common ground. In L. Gambrell, S. Morrow, S. Neuman, & M. Pressley (Eds.), *Best practices in literacy instruction* (pp. 11–21). New York: Guilford Press.

Gee, J. P. (2001). A sociocultural perspective on early literacy development. In S. B. Neuman & D. K. Dickinson (Eds.), *Handbook on research in early literacy* (pp. 30–42). New York: Guilford Press.

Genishi, C. (1987). Acquiring oral language and communicative competence. In C. Seefeldt (Ed.), *The early childhood curriculum: A review of current research* (pp. 75–106). New York: Teacher's College Press.

Gipe, J. P. (2006). *Multiple paths to literacy: Assessment and differentiated instruction for diverse learners, K–12* (6th ed.). Upper Saddle River, NJ: Prentice Hall.

Goodman, K. (1970). Reading: A psycholinguistic guessing game. In H. Singer & R. Ruddell (Eds.), *Theoretical models and processes of reading* (pp. 259–271). Newark, DE: International Reading Association.

Goodman, K. (1986). Children coming to know literacy. In W. Teale & E. Sulzby (Eds.), *Emergent literacy: Writing and reading* (pp. 1–14). Norwood, NJ: Ablex.

Goodman, Y., Watson, D., & Burke, C. (1987). *Reading miscue inventory: Alternative procedures.* Katonah, NY: Richard C. Owen.

Gough, P. B., & Tunmer, W. E. (1986). Decoding, reading, and reading disability. *Remedial and Special Education, 7,* pp. 6–10.

Halliday, M. A. K. (1975). *Learning how to mean: Exploration in the development of language.* London: Edward Arnold.

Hargrave, A. C., & Senechal, M. (2000). A book reading intervention with preschool children who have limited vocabularies: The benefits of regular and dialogic reading. *Early Childhood Research Quarterly, 15,* 75–90.

Harvey, S., & Goudvis, A. (2000). *Strategies that work: Teaching comprehension to enhance understanding.* Portland, ME: Stenhouse.

Heath, S. (1983). *Ways with words.* Cambridge, England: Cambridge University Press.

Hickman, J. (1995). Not by chance: Creating classrooms that invite responses to literature. In N. Roser & M. Martinez (Eds.), *Book talk and beyond: Children and teachers respond to literature.* Newark, DE: International Reading Association.

Hiebert, E. (1981). Developmental patterns and interrelationships of preschool children's print awareness. *Reading Research Quarterly, 16,* pp. 236–260.

Hulit, L., & Howard, M. (2002). *Born to talk: An introduction to speech and language development* (3rd ed.). Boston: Allyn and Bacon.

Keene, E. O., & Zimmerman, S. (1997). *Mosaic of thought: Teaching comprehension in a reader's workshop.* Portsmouth, NH: Heinemann.

Lonigan, C., & Whitehurst, G. (1998). Relative efficiency of parent and teacher involvement in a shared-reading intervention for preschool children from low-income backgrounds. *Early Childhood Research Quarterly, 23,* pp. 263–290.

Malloch, J., & Malloch, I. (1986). *Books alive: Teacher's guide 4.* Toronto, ON: Doubleday Canada.

McKenna, M., & Kear, D. (1990). Measuring attitude toward reading: A new tool for teachers. *Reading Teacher, 43*(9), 626–639.

Miller, D. (2002). *Reading with meaning: Teaching comprehension in the primary grades.* Portland, ME: Stenhouse.

Morrow, L. (2001). *Literacy development in the early years: Helping children read and write* (4th ed.). Boston: Allyn and Bacon.

Moustafa, M. (1995). Children's productive phonological recoding. *Reading Research Quarterly, 30*(3), 464–476.

Pearson, P. D., Dole, J. A., Duffy, G. G., & Roehler, L. R. (1992). Developing expertise in reading comprehension: What should be taught and how should it be taught? In J. Farstrup & S. J. Samuels (Eds.), *What research has to say to the teacher of reading* (2nd ed.). Newark, DE: International Reading Association.

Reutzel, D. R., & Cooter, R. B. (2003). *Strategies for reading assessment and instruction: Helping every child to succeed.* Upper Saddle River, NJ: Merrill/Prentice Hall.

Rosenblatt, L. M. (1994). The transactional theory of reading and writing. In R. B. Ruddell, M. R. Ruddell, & H. Singer (Eds.), *Theoretical models and processes of reading* (4th ed.). Newark, DE: International Reading Association.

Smith, F. (2005). *Understanding reading* (6th ed.). Hillsdale, NJ: Lawrence Erlbaum Associates.

Stanovich, K. (1986). Matthew effects in reading: Some consequences of individual differences in the acquisition of literacy. *Reading Research Quarterly, 21,* pp. 360–407.

Strickland, D. S., Ganske, K., & Monroe, J. K. (2002). Improving reading comprehension. In *Supporting struggling readers and writers: Strategies for classroom intervention 3–6* (pp. 141–154). Portland, ME: Stenhouse.

Sulzby, E. (1996). Roles of oral and written language as children approach conventional literacy. In C. Pontecorvo, M. Orsolini, B. Burge, & L. Resnick (Eds.), *Children's early text construction* (pp. 25–46). Mahwah, NJ: Lawrence Erlbaum Associates.

Taylor, D., & Strickland, D. (1986). *Family storybook reading.* Portsmouth, NH: Heinemann.

Teale, W. (1986). The beginnings of reading and writing: Written language development during the preschool and kindergarten years. In M. Sampson (Ed.), *The pursuit of literacy: Early reading and writing* (pp. 173–205). Dubuque, IA: Kendall Hunt.

Teale, W., & Sulzby, E. (1986). Emergent literacy as a perspective for examining how young children become writers and readers. In W. Teale & E. Sulzby (Eds.), *Emergent literacy: Writing and reading* (pp. vii–xxv). Norwood, NJ: Ablex.

Teale, W., & Sulzby, E. (1989). Emergent literacy: New perspectives. In D. S. Strickland & L. M. Morrow (Eds.), Emerging literacy: Young children learn to read and write (pp. 1–15). Newark, DE: International Reading Association.

Treiman, R. (2001). Reading. In M. Aronoff and J. Rees-Miller (Eds.), *Handbook of linguistics* (pp. 664–672). Oxford, England: Blackwell.

Weaver, C. (1994). *Reading process and practice: From sociopsycholinguistics to whole language.* Portsmouth, NH: Heinemann.

Whitehurst, G. J., & Lonigan, C. J. (2001). Emergent literacy: Development from prereaders to readers. In S. B. Neuman & D. K. Dickinson (Eds.), *Handbook of early literacy research.* New York: Guilford Press.

Wilkinson, L. C., & Silliman, E. R. (2000). Classroom language and literacy learning. In M. L. Kamil, P. B. Mosenthal, P. D. Pearson, & R. Barr (Eds.), *Handbook of reading research, Vol. III* (pp. 337–360). Mahwah, NJ: Lawrence Erlbaum Associates.

Yopp, H. (1992). Developing phonemic awareness in young children. *Reading Teacher, 45,* pp. 696–703.

Understanding Early Writing and Instructional Opportunities in the Inclusive Classroom

Anne E. Gregory and Carolyn Loffer

Objectives

After you have read this chapter, you should be able to

- Identify perspectives on early literacy as related to writing.
- Describe the connection between how young children learn about language and writing.
- Elaborate upon the processes involved in writing.
- Define and explain the purpose(s), use(s), and modification(s) necessary for use of instructional approaches to meet the learners found within the classroom.
- Discuss the value of supporting children in their writing on multiple levels.

Key Terms

Emergent literacy

Schema

Invented/developmental spelling

Conventions of print

Emergent writing

Genres

Phonological awareness

Practical Application Vignette

Perspectives on Early Literacy

Mrs. L. Rich surveyed the scene before her and couldn't help smiling. Scattered on the floor, huddled under tables, lounging on pillows and seated in chairs were dyads of children, one from her kindergarten class and one from the first-grade buddy classroom. Younger children were reading published pieces they had penned, then finishing with the facial beam that comes only from the feelings of ownership and pride. The observations only further validated the efforts of the past few days. Mrs. Rich reflected on those . . .

It began as so many writing endeavors do, with a shared experience that generated curiosity, enthusiasm, or wonder. In this case, it was the upcoming field trip to the beach to explore life in tide pools. The class began by making lists. The whole group generated a list of things to take on their field trip. Mrs. Rich transcribed the items as the brainstorming progressed. She purposely suspended the process in mid-brainstorm by distributing small squares of paper and asking children to write one idea on each of the squares. Some children represented their list items with sophisticated orthography, like Morgan, who felt strongly that he and his classmates must bring "sunskn," to prevent sunburns. Others followed the lead of Shayla, who drew elaborate pictures of things like notebooks, lunches, and sandals. Jude attempted a blending of both strategies by labeling his picture of a camera with a large K. Always resourceful, Ben visited the classroom library, found the small card with the environmental print label, and copied the conventional spelling of *book* onto his card. After this concerted classwide effort (they believed this list to be paramount to the success of the field trip) they reconvened on the floor to compile the list by reading each item.

The following day found the class dictating a letter to their families inviting any and all who could attend the field trip. As Mrs. Rich transcribed the eloquent words of the children, she made some fascinating observations. Clearly many children were seeing connections between the conventions of their own shared pen writing and those in the literature read lately, such as *A Letter for Amy* by Ezra Jack Keats, *Love, Lizzie* by Lisa Tucker McElroy and Diane Paterson, and *The Jolly Postman* by Janet and Alan Ahlberg.

After returning from the field trip, the children's desire to record their adventure was palpable. A class meeting yielded the suggestion to share their experiences through stories with their first-grade buddies. Thus, an audience and purpose were established. Due to the authentic nature of both, enthusiasm and engagement levels were high.

Transcription, word collections, topical books, sentence stems, and a word wall helped to scaffold the writing process for these young authors. Writing workshop was a daily flurry of activity as children sought ways to communicate their ideas. Some pieces appeared expository, while others developed a narrative voice and form. Some were developed with two or more sentences, others just a thought or a word. As writers moved into publishing, their mindset became that of an award-winning author. Mrs. Rich signaled the end of buddy time with the soothing sounds of her rain stick, a nonverbal signal to return to the home classroom. She was eager to get back to her language-rich learning community, where more writing opportunities waited—the class butterflies were due to hatch any time.

Introduction to Writing

Most children enter schools believing they are writers. They have the expectation that print, especially the print that they make and use, will be meaningful (Harste, Woodward, & Burke, 1984). This understanding is commonly observed when they question the adults around them about their writing, saying things like, "What did I write?" or "What does this say?"

Children in these instances are creating and constructing meaning, and they are communicating  these meanings through their explorations with print. Writing for these early literates is not about conforming to adult models of correctness, but is rather a process of experimentation. As they engage with print, initially using scribbles and soon marks that look something like letters, then writing strings of letters; they are hypothesizing and checking their hypotheses on what print is and how it can and does function in their lives.

It is the role of the teacher to confirm when their hypotheses about print are correct and to support these young writers in this process. But how does a teacher of young children do this? This chapter offers some explanation of this early process and provides some instructional strategies that you might use to scaffold the writing of young children.

Constructing Knowledge in Writing

Where Are Children? The Origins of Writing

When considering where to begin instruction in writing, we must first understand a little bit about where children are. Long before children enter school, similar to learning to talk and listen, children learn about reading and writing. Their early literacy begins when they encounter books and other printed materials in their own social, cultural environments. It is within a natural environment that children learn that written texts can be used to get things done, what written texts are, how they can be used, and what is in reading and writing for them (Pappas, Kiefer, & Levstik, 1995).

Additionally, it is important to keep in mind that children's development of literacy behaviors changes over time in ways that are qualitatively different (Adams, 1990; Chall, 1983; Snow, Burns & Griffin, 1998; Sulzby & Teale, 1991). These developmental changes are gradual, but are thought to occur in a predictable manner. The developmental differences are often identified as follows:

- Emergent (birth through early-first-grade reading level)
- Developing (early/middle first grade through early-third-grade level)
- Transitional (early-third-grade through sixth-grade reading levels)

Constructing Knowledge in Writing

For the purpose of this chapter, we will look at the emergent and developing levels of literacy learning as related to writing.

Writing Process Skills

Emergent Literacy

During the emergent stage children begin to

- Internalize purposes of print and understand that print is used to communicate and make meaning.
- Develop knowledge about and appreciation of different types of text through repeated exposures.
- Show increasing interest in reading and writing independently.
- Develop concepts about print, including book-handling skills and an understanding of the permanence and directionality of print.
- Develop concepts about words including distinguishing letter shapes, letter names, and the sounds represented.
- Develop basic levels of phonological awareness (sounds in language), including the concept that words are composed of strings of sounds that can be manipulated to make other words.
- Make meaning from simple books but rely heavily on memory of familiar words, illustrations, story contexts, and selected letter cues.
- Recognize that printed English moves from left to right and top to bottom on a page.
- Recognize that the same letter shapes reoccur from word to word and can appear in different places within words.
- Recognize that a particular ordering of letters stands for a particular object and is called a word.
- Recognize that there is a relationship between the sounds in words and the letters that we use to represent those sounds.
- Recognize that words in writing are shown by making spaces between groupings of letters. (Combs, 2006, p. 27).

Emergent literacy is the stage of development at which children begin formal instruction in reading and writing. It typically refers to the gradual development of literacy behaviors in children from birth to about age 5 (Clay, 1966; Sulzby & Teale, 1991). It is during this time that children are becoming aware of and learning about print (Brown, 1999/2000).

During the emergent stage, a child is just beginning to explore and work with print. It is throughout this stage that children develop an awareness of sounds spoken in language as well as awareness that those sounds can be represented with letters of the alphabet. Additionally, they become aware that these sounds can be manipulated to form many words.

An emergent literacy perspective assumes that oral and written languages develop simultaneously, each supporting the development of the other. Moreover, this perspective posits that literacy need not be taught or instructed in specific ways. Here it is thought that children learn about written language by interacting with adults in reading and writing situations, by exploring print on their own, and through observations of adults using written language for their communicative needs.

Early in the emergent stage, children learn that the meaning in their head can be transferred to the page and that the movement of a pen on paper accomplishes this. Writing initially is found in the form of scribbles and shapes. And as children have more experiences with print and as fine motor capabilities are refined, these scribbles give way to more letter- and numberlike forms. And, with even more added print experiences, their writing becomes strings of letters that have no relationship to sound and no spacing to indicate the beginning or ending of words (i.e., word boundaries). Children with disabilities that limit their fine motor skills often require additional support through the use of hand-over-hand writing, technology (i.e., computers and assistive technology), or teacher as scribe so that they understand that concepts and ideas can be written to the page. Oftentimes the letters used in these writing attempts are those that are important to the child, those found in her or his name or the names of other important people in the child's life. Finally, the child begins to use letters to represent the sounds found in words. This usually begins as the use of one letter, typically the first, to represent an entire word. For example, the child may write *c* to represent the word *cat*. By the time children transition to the next developing stage, they are able to represent beginning and ending consonant sounds in words fairly consistently, and middle vowels are beginning to be represented though not accurately.

Early in the developing stage, children are seen to be intent on generalizing their concepts about words and print and letter-sound patterns to words. They are learning to break the code (Brown, 1999/2000) and engage in word-to-word print matching (Holdoway, 1980). As writers, children in this stage of development are gaining control over conventional spelling of one-syllable words, especially predictable vowel patterns. They are also gaining control over how to represent accurately the second and third syllables in longer words. Throughout this stage of development, children need guidance in refining their understandings about how words are formed in English. This is especially true in the experiences that they have with letters and letter patterns that are likely to occur in English (i.e., phonic generalizations). It is from these phonic generalizations that they will be best able to make predictions for the pronunciation and representation of unfamiliar words. We will explore the importance of learning about words in a later section.

Developing Schema

We all possess categories that help us to make sense of and interpret the world around us. These categories, or **schema**, help us to organize our experiences in relational ways and create networks of concepts and procedures. It is these networks that enable us to access knowledge and ideas in different contexts, to make sense of new experiences, and to predict what might happen next (Shanklin, 1982).

Over time children add new information about writing to their "writing" schema by "filing" new information with similar concepts and/or procedures that exist in their framework. If a schema does not include an appropriate place to "file" new information, the brain must create a new schema or adapt an already existing file within the learner's framework. As learners, we can add to, change, or create a new schema.

Children's schemata (plural for *schema*) for oral and written language are changing continuously over time. Learning experiences must be planned consistent with the schemata children have for particular topics, events, and so on so that children may engage in activities that are understandable and meaningful. As children transition from oral to written language, important changes that they make are in developing understandings for concepts about print and learning about words.

Concepts About Print

The distinction between print and pictures is one of the first concepts that children learn. For most 3-year-olds, when asked to draw a picture and write their names, the markings they make for the picture and their names are distinctively different. It is this distinction that helps to establish an identity separate for print and allows for the learning of its functions and structure (Christie, Enz, & Vukelich, 2003).

Knowledge of print follows a loose developmental sequence (Lomax & McGee, 1987):

1. Concepts that print has purpose and function
2. Graphic awareness
3. Phonemic awareness
4. Letter–sound relationships

Purpose and function of print.   As mentioned earlier in this chapter, one of the earliest understandings children develop for print is that it has meaning (Harste, Woodward, & Burke, 1984). This means that from very early in their experiences with print, children develop an expectation that not only what others write (e.g., books, signs, etc.) but what they write has meaning and can be understood.

In addition to viewing print as having meaning, they also determine very early on that it has a function. With this understanding, children see that print can be used to get things done. This knowledge of the practical uses of print grows considerably during the preschool years as children explore writing during their dramatic play experiences (i.e., writing down phone messages, writing checks, looking up recipes in cookbooks, making shopping lists, etc.) (Neuman & Roskos, 1997).

Graphic awareness.   Environmental print, the print that occurs in real-life contexts, is something that children begin to recognize at a very early age. Lomax and McGee (1987) have shown that many 3- and 4-year-olds can recognize and know the meanings of product labels (Cheerios, Coca Cola), restaurant signs (McDonald's), and street signs (stop).

When recognizing environmental print, children are logographic reading. They are attending to the entire context that the sign or symbol is embedded within rather than just the print (Masonheimer, Drum, & Ehri, 1984). It is around this time that children are also beginning to recognize the letters of the alphabet. McGee and Richgels (1996) found that interest appears to be a key factor in determining the specific letters that children learn first, although the names of the children as well as environmental print features are often the source for initial letter learning.

Phonemic awareness.   For most children, awareness of the phonological or sound system in spoken English develops during their preschool years. Phonological awareness is a broad term that refers to both the explicit and implicit knowledge of the sounds in language. It includes the ability to identify and generate rhymes, hear syllables in words, hear the parts of words (onsets and rimes), alliteration, blending, and segmenting of sounds in words, and hear individual sounds in words. For example, young children are often observed rhyming words (e.g., cat, hat, mat, fat) or manipulating/playing with sounds (e.g., butterfly, flutterby, pufferhy).

Phonemic awareness is one kind of phonological awareness. It refers to the ability to identify, isolate, and manipulate individual sounds (i.e., phonemes) in words. It is a fairly sophisticated ability. In other words, a child who is phonemically aware would be able to replace the /m/ sound in the word *man* with the sounds /p/ and /l/ and say the word *plan,* and then add to that word the sound /t/ at the end and say the word *plant.* This is a challenging task for most children, since there are few clues in oral language that indicate the different or separate phonemes that make up a word (Ehri, 1997).

While research suggests that a child's level of phonemic awareness on entry to school is one of the strongest predictors of success in learning to read (Adams, 1990), there is substantial argument over how best to teach this skill.

Letter–sound relationships. Also known as phonics, an understanding for letter–sound relationships is part of concepts about print. Building upon a child's phonological awareness, in particular his or her phonemic awareness, letters help the child bridge between the sounds heard in spoken language and the ways in which they may be represented. Learning the connections between letters and sounds, as well as letter clusters and sounds, is basic to understanding written language (Pinnell & Fountas, 2002). Children's independent attempts at writing, especially their use of **invented/developmental spelling**, where they make up the spelling of words they do not know how to spell, help us to know what their understandings for letter–sound relationships are.

Conventions of Print

To be a successful participant with print, children must develop an understanding for the rules or conventions that surround written language (Clay, 1979). The **conventions of print**, the rules surrounding print concepts, that are most beneficial for early readers and writers are

- permanence of print,
- directionality of print,
- concept of word, and
- language to talk about print.

Permanence of print. For young children, the realization that print in storybooks is permanent is central to their use of past readings to predict words or events in a text. By developing an expectation that stories and words in books remain the same from reading to reading allows print to become predictable. It is this predictability that allows children to begin to focus or notice other details and patterns found in print that help to distinguish letters and words from one another.

Directionality of print. Essential to success in reading and writing are concepts of directionality that develop through many experiences with print over time (Clay, 1979). We often model concepts of directionality as we track print with a pointer or our finger in a left-to-right movement across the page. They are also seen as we write with children.

Concepts of directionality include the following:

- Books have fronts and backs; we read a book from front to back.
- We read print, not pictures.
- There is a right-side-up to print.
- We read the left page before the right page when text is on both pages.
- We read left to right, top to bottom on a page.
- When we finish one line of print we make a return sweep, returning to the left side of the page and dropping down one line to continue reading.
- Words in a sentence must be arranged in a certain left-to-right order, or syntax, to make sense in English language (e.g., "here is a cat" and "cat is here a" do not communicate the same ideas). (Combs, 2006, p. 30)

It is through many interactions with print, both reading and writing with children, that we help to support children's developing understandings for the rules of written language. These interactions need to be meaningful.

Concept of word. Understanding that words and letters differ is a conceptual leap made by most kindergarten students. Underlying the need for this understanding is that, once children have an awareness of sounds spoken in English and some awareness for letters, representing ideas becomes a bit more complex. Now, children must learn that letters or groupings of letters can be used to represent ideas and that these ideas are composed of words. When writing or reading, words are indicated by the space that is left before and after the word. In other words, it is the spaces in print that signal to the reader and the writer that a word is complete. The spaces mark where the word begins and ends; letters are used to write or record the word for others to see.

Language to talk about print. We use a specific form of language when we talk about reading and writing with children. As we demonstrate writing, we talk about our demonstrations to help clarify and call attention to certain behaviors that might not be noticed. We use language that talks about *spacing, left, right, line, beginning, end, sentence, word, letter, capital letter, period, question mark,* etc. To understand what we are referring to as we write, a child needs to develop an understanding for this academic language. By knowing the language used to talk about print, children gain more control over their thinking about print (Combs, 2006).

Integrating Writing throughout the Curriculum

Developing Literacy

Children in the developing levels of literacy learning are consolidating their growing reading and writing expertise as well as exploring new genres. It is during this time period that children begin to transition from learning the code of reading and writing to learning how to learn and understand through the use of reading and writing.

At this point in development, children have a foundational understanding of the literacy processes requisite necessary for constructing of meaning. To construct meaning the learner is required to activate background knowledge (i.e., schema) and to relate new information to prior knowledge. This meaning making involves critical thinking, prediction, inferring, and problem solving, among other processes. Skills include the use of language, context cues, and phonics for reading; the use of visual and spelling patterns in writing; and the use of conventions (e.g., grammar, usage, capitalization) in writing and speaking. Strategies, which are cognitive, include establishing purposes for reading and writing, predicting what will come next, self-questioning about meaning, and summarizing to think about the sense of the story that they are hearing or constructing. For these reasons, teachers will see children enter their classrooms with a variety of literacy skills and confidence levels.

Written Language Principles

Written speech is not just oral speech on paper but represents a higher level of thinking. It has a profound influence on development because

1. it makes thinking more explicit
2. it makes thinking and the use of symbols more deliberate
3. it makes the child aware of the elements of language (Bodrova & Leong, 1996, p. 102)

This suggests that written ideas, like spoken ones, are forced into a sequence only because you can write or say only one idea at a time. Writing allows the child as she learns to write to take on the role of reader, to see her thoughts for the first time. It enables her to see gaps in her thinking and understandings. Writing becomes a much more deliberative process than speaking; children must choose symbols and record them according to the rules of syntax and the decontextualized nature of writing (there is no one present to give the writer an indication that what she is saying doesn't make sense). Additionally, writing helps a child to develop awareness of the elements of language (e.g., sound–symbol relationships, etc.). Metalinguistic awareness, or the ability to think about and reflect on the language being used, develops as children engage in meaningful writing experiences.

As children engage in wide-ranging experiences with written language, Clay (1975) found that they demonstrate a developing understanding of the principles that govern print. Developing over time, these understandings and features of the following principles were found to be evident in their writing:

- Recurring principle
- Generative principle
- Sign concept
- Flexibility principle
- Directionality

Recurring principle. The recurring principle refers to a child's growing perception of similar shapes that occur repeatedly in English words. A child demonstrates this awareness when he or she includes one or two shapes (e.g., a hump, loop, or a cross) over and over again to fill pages of paper.

Sometimes the writing during this period of awareness shares features that are similar to those found in texts that are written in cursive handwriting.

Generative principle. The generative principle is found when children use several letters or letterlike forms repeatedly to express a meaning. Usually these will be the letters of the child's name; however, the combination and variation of the patterning and use of these letter and letterlike symbols will vary. In such use, children are demonstrating an understanding that a variety of letter arrangements can be used to create or generate words and convey meaning.

Sign concept. Simply put, children must develop an understanding for their social and cultural group referents, or meanings, and the signs that are associated with them. For example, in English we agree that *t-r-e-e* stands for a type of plant that has woody outer coverings and usually broad, green leafy shapes in the summer that can grow rather tall, etc. Although there are variations and specific names or signs associated with this plant, we would all recognize them as belonging to a similar category, or schema, representing trees that we have developed through our membership in this group. The sign for this, *t-r-e-e,* while arbitrary, is one that other members of our group of English speakers agree to let represent these objects. As a picture of a tree would represent or show it, so too does the word *t-r-e-e,* our shared sign for that object.

Flexibility principle. As children's awareness for print increases, their exploration of the boundaries for what constitutes letters and what does not begins. The familiarity that children have developed with print enables them to detect that some letters share similar lines or shapes, while others do not. In their experimentation with letters, they may try to add more lines when writing an uppercase *E* than are necessary. Or, they may try flipping or sliding letters along the vertical and horizontal axes to see if they remain constant (e.g., a *W* becomes and *M* when flipped on the horizontal axis, it becomes an *E* when turned on the vertical, and flipped once again it can be a 3). As they explore and manipulate letter forms, children are learning what letters share in common with each other and what differentiates them from one another. They are also learning about the effect of font on print and the differences between cursive and manuscript, upper- and lowercase forms.

Directionality. Another concept that young children become aware of as they work with print is the concept of directionality. English is written in a linear form. We start at the top, left-hand side of a page and move left to right across, progressing toward the bottom. Words and letters in relation to one another are important aspects of print that children need to discover, for it is this concept that enables children to notice that, for writing to make sense, there must be order—order not only on the page, but also order within words. In other words, letters must be arranged in specific ways to make words, and the orientation of these letters may change the word because the letter itself has changed. For example, when writing the word *boy,* a child must know that the letters of the word are *b-o-y* and that if you orient the *b* incorrectly you will have the letter *d,* which then produces a word different than the word one is trying to communicate.

Early Attempts at Writing

Building on the earlier work of Marie Clay (1975) and Emilia Ferreiro and Ana Teberosky (1982), Elizabeth Sulzby asked preschool children to write and read what they had written. This was an attempt to capture **emergent writing**, the earliest forms of writing and use of writing principles. From this research, she was able to develop seven broad categories of early writing: drawing as writing, scribble writing, letterlike units, nonphonetic letter strings, copying from environmental print, invented spelling, and conventional writing (Sulzby, 1990). While these categories should not be seen as hierarchy, there is a general movement from less mature forms to more conventional forms as children compose texts. It has also been determined that children appear to adjust their form of writing to the task that they are undertaking. For example, kindergartners tend to use invented spelling when attempting to write single words, but, when writing longer pieces of text, they shift to less mature forms, such as nonphonetic letter strings or scribbles, that require less time and effort (Sulzby & Teale, 1991).

Drawing as writing.   In this early awareness of print, a child uses pictures to represent the meaning or message that they wish to convey. Examples of this can be found in shopping lists that children write in housekeeping. Here, instead of writing the words to represent the object, the child draws a picture for the item she or he wishes to buy.

Scribble writing.   Similar to the recurring principle mentioned earlier, in this early form of writing a child uses continuous wavy lines to represent a message. This form of writing, which mimics cursive writing, is usually undertaken with a flourish.

Letterlike units.   In this form of writing, the child makes a series of separate marks that have some letterlike characteristics. The marks may be a series of lines with others that cross over them (similar to the letters t or x) or a series of circles and loops (similar to letters e and o) or a combination of the two. The features of letters that the child represents in his or her writing are the ones that are the most salient or obvious to him or her at this time.

Nonphonetic letter strings.   Characteristics that were found in Clay's (1975) generative principle can be found in children's attempts at writing here. A child's writing that falls within this category includes the use of real letter forms but does not indicate any evidence of an awareness of letter–sound relationships. Often the letters used are the ones found in the child's name, and the patterns vary, with random groupings of letters or repeated clusters of letters used to represent a child's intended message.

Copying from environmental print.   The writing in this category consists of print that includes copies of print found in the environment. Often there is an indication of word boundaries (i.e., spacing between the words), as the words or letters copied come from sources where they are grouped together. For example, a child writes on his paper "door window" and reads it as "My house." He is using the print available around her to write the message she intends to convey.

Invented spelling.   In writing where invented spelling is used, we see a child using her or his understandings of letter names and letter–sound relationships to write or spell an unknown word. This can range from a child's use of one letter to represent every word to using a letter for every sound in each of the words she or he is writing. For example, when spelling the word *dinosaurs* a child wrote "dinososs." In this example, the child in some way represented most of the sounds found or heard in the word.

Conventional spelling.   The writing found in this category typically has the correct spelling for most words. This writing is easy to read and understand because other print conventions are also present (i.e., spacing, left-to-right movement across the page, etc.).

While some research suggests that invented spelling is a common occurrence among 4- and 5-year-olds, Sulzby and Teale's (1991) research suggests that the use of invented spelling does not arrive until late kindergarten for some and not until the end of first grade for others. Whatever the timeline for development and use of invented spelling, it is an aspect that is typical of early learners.

Authentic Writing

Authentic writing is writing that serves a purpose for the writer, that focuses on a real audience, and that uses life experiences. For young children, the criteria for authentic writing also include the role of print and communicating this message. To develop these ideas, opportunities for writing and learning about writing should center on writing for real audiences and build upon the lived experiences of the children. As children engage in opportunities where they are asked to write for audiences and purposes that are real to them, they will begin to develop an understanding for the multiple purpose or functions of writing. They will come to understand why we write.

Why do we write?   Oftentimes, we write to signify or identify important things. For most children, one of the first things they learn to write is their name. Names serve as powerful tools for the child. They allow her to indicate her spot, to signal to others that she is part of the group, to identify and label things that belong to her. We can assist children in learning their names by asking them to label their work and belongings, by creating name charts and games where children are asked to match names of their classmates to photos, and through the use of magnetic letters for the making and remaking of their name. As the opportunities are provided, we should also be sure to include the language of talking about the things (i.e., letters) that make up the child's name, using the names of the letters that make up these words so that these soon become identifiable and useful in talking about writing and words for the child.

We also write to communicate with others. Throughout this chapter we have discussed this idea of communicating messages, expressing ideas and thoughts. Aside from the ideas that have already been presented, teachers might support this purpose for writing by having children make cards for different occasions, to write or dictate letters, to draw and annotate pictures that show what is important to them, or to make lists of things. We might also write to record events (e.g., diaries or autobiographies), to explain (e.g., create charts, recipes, brochures, instructions, captions), to persuade (e.g., applications, advertisements, arguments), to invite a response (e.g., complaints, requests, want ads), to predict (e.g., horoscopes, forecasts, timetables, graphs), to entertain (e.g., bumper stickers, graffiti, stories), to find out (e.g., questionnaires, surveys, observations), or to summarize (e.g., postcards, reports, verdicts, signs). All of these activities provide children with opportunities to write in meaningful ways and for an audience.

Additionally, the purposes for writing can be communicated and developed with children through the offering of numerous opportunities for children to observe, explore, and experiment with writing. Seeing adults writing in order to accomplish a real task communicates and helps the child learn the function and value of writing. This may be done through the use of notes written to parents or listing the foods that will be eaten tomorrow during snack time. Writing materials should be available to capture these opportunities as they occur.

Meaningful Opportunities

Perhaps the greatest impacts on writing are the opportunities that are provided or afforded the children. These opportunities begin with the environment of the classroom. There should be writing opportunities within all classroom areas as well as out-of-door ones. To do this, teachers can establish an area near the door where children can sign in or out each day. There can be a writing area established where writing materials and resources are located and used on a regular basis. Teachers can include writing materials and tools in the dramatic play area. Materials to include here may be pads of paper for making shopping lists, writing prescriptions, or parking and speeding tickets. As children create artwork, they should be asked to dictate or write stories that go along with their artwork. Teachers can use journals for recording observations that occur in the science area or for writing problems and solutions in the math area. Alphabet letters and magnetic letters along with charts and books can be used as reference tools as long as they are displayed where children can easily see and reach them.

For encouraging writing outside the classroom, teachers can use colored chalk and other writing materials outside. When going on nature walks or field trips, include journals so that children may record what they are observing learning about the world around them. Additionally, teachers should encourage children to sign out their own books from the classroom library, which they will take and share at home.

Additionally, the variety of materials that you use and provide for use by children can serve as a means for motivating children. Toward this end teachers will want to provide materials that the children they are working with respond to. Some students enjoy crayons and markers, while others are more willing to challenge themselves with letters and words when they have the chance to use paint, sand, or shaving cream. Teachers should also provide different kinds of paper, such as construction paper, lined paper, envelopes, stationery, index cards, textured paper, paper with raised lines, and colored paper. Additionally, teachers may want to include stencils, stamps, scissors, hole punches, staplers, and anything else that might be motivating and encouraging for a child to participate in writing activities.

Letter and Word Study

A natural aspect of writing is learning about the code that is used to record and communicate messages. As children have many opportunities to encounter words in a variety of contexts, they use many words, become flexible as word solvers, and build the vocabularies they need to for quick, automatic reading and writing (Fountas & Pinnell, 1998).

Instruction in phonics, or letter–sound relationships, is a natural outgrowth of writing. It is through writing that instruction in letter–sound relationships, how speech sounds can be connected with letters that can be used to represent ideas and form words, is contextualized and made meaningful for children. Typically, most instruction in phonics, or learning about the code, begins by working with children in learning the names of letters. As we mentioned earlier, the letters of a

child's name serve as an initial starting point in this process. Simply put, the purpose for learning about letter names is so that we have a way to talk about how words are written. An *A* is called *A* only because we have agreed that it is so. Since we have agree to this (on some societal level), then we can all use the language or term *A* to communicate with others that we are talking about letter forms A and a and the sounds /ā/, /ă/, /â/, /á/, and /à/.

Letters. Letter learning typically begins with consonants (letters that are not vowels), since they generally have a firm sound (e.g., b, c, d, f, g). Some instructional practices used to teach letters of the alphabet letter of the day or letter of the week. Teachers using these approaches attempt to make letter learning meaningful to children by having them engage in activities that focus on the letter being learned. For example, on the day that they are learning about the letter *B,* children might be asked to bring in something from home that begins with the letter *B* and place it in a box labeled with a *B.* As a class, the children are encouraged to participate in naming the objects selected and placed in the box. For the rest of the day, the children look for the letter *B* in the reading and writing activities that they do. The activities for these days are playful and build on what children know and can do, for example, alphabet puzzles, letter sorts in ice cube trays, use of ink-stamp pads with letter stamps, painting letters, etc.

Another common letter-learning activity is for children to create their own alphabet books. These books can then be used later as references for the children as they are writing. Children make their own alphabet books by using pictures cut from magazines or phonic workbooks to represent the letters.

Words. Again, names form the foundation for children's word learning. Ample opportunities should be afforded them to engage and manipulate not only the letters and sounds in their names but also those of their classmates. The next area of word learning that children typically enter is that of sight or high-frequency words. These are words that are so familiar to readers and used so often by writers that they become recognized instantly and automatically. Teachers work hard with early writers to develop their writing vocabulary, a bank of words that they know and can write without much conscious attention. Word walls or even small word charts taped to children's desks can facilitate this process.

Additionally, teachers use prompting for word solving as children are writing to help them further develop and refine their understandings for how words, letters, and sounds all work together. During brief interactions with children, teachers may ask the child to

a. clap the parts they hear,
b. listen for the parts of the word,

c. listen for the sound they hear in the first part, or

d. say the word slowly (slow articulation) and think about what they hear.

Teachers also teach for visual analysis of words. They may prompt the child in the following ways during such instruction:

a. Does it look right?

b. What would look right there?

c. It's almost right. Add the ending.

d. You're nearly right. Add a letter to make it look right.

e. It looks like (another word they know). (McCarrier, Fountas, & Pinnell, 1999)

These word-solving strategies encourage independent problem solving at the word level on the part of the child. They also encourage the child to use developmental or invented spelling. Developmental spelling, also called invented spelling, is a temporary stage in a child's development as a speller and writer. During this stage, children record writing the way they believe it to be. It is also during this time that we are able to see evidence of what children understand about our written language and its written representations.

Letter and word activities. While it is not recommended that word and letter work be undertaken in isolation, the activities discussed here represent ways for drawing children's attention to letter and words that can be beneficial to early literacy learning.

Word walls. Cunningham (1995) provides excellent information on how to begin, create, and use word walls with children. Words selected for inclusion on the word wall tend to be either high-frequency or sight words: These are the words that are frequently encountered by children as the read and write. The wall is set up in an area of the room to which all children have ready access. It is organized using large letters of the alphabet under which the high-frequency or sight words will be placed as they are learned. These walls of words provide an excellent resource for children in their reading and writing.

ABC or word center. This is an area of the classroom where many opportunities for exploring and working with letters and words. Included in this center are magnetic letters, wikki sticks, salt trays, etc., that encourage children to manipulate and write letters and words as they are learning them. The activities included in this center should be ones that facilitate children's explorations. They often require focus lessons in which the teacher demonstrates the activity and process before children are able to engage in independent work here. For example, a teacher might include an alphabet linking chart that provides a clear letter–sound link to key words, and children are to read and write letters with those on the chart. Another idea might be for children to make their own individual letter books. These are books that focus on one letter that the child is learning and in which the child selects pictures of objects that can be used that begin with the letter be studied. Matching and sorting letters is another activity that might be undertaken in this center. There are many other activities that might be part of this center area; the idea is that whatever you are asking children to do here should facilitate their developing awareness for sounds, letters, and words.

Writing Process

What Is Writing?

"Writing is not so much one skill as it is a bundle of skills that includes sequencing, spelling, reread-ing, and supporting big ideas with examples" (Fletcher & Portalupi, 2001, p. 1). Writing begins early in a child's literacy development as she or he seeks to communicate, express, question, per-suade, synthesize, teach others. It is a process.

The focus in the writing process is on what children think and do as they write. Typically, this process is considered to involve the five recursive stages of prewriting, drafting, revising, editing, and publishing. As children engage in writing, they engage in these stages in recurring cycles; we label them here simply as a means for identifying and discussing writing activities. In classrooms, however, it should be understood that these stages merge and recur throughout the time a child is writing.

How Does the Writing Process Work With Younger Children?

Often the writing process as it has been outlined here needs to be adapted to better meet the needs of younger writers. Typically, the revising and editing steps are abbreviated for young children. Ini-tially, teachers accept children's writing as it is written and focus on the message. It is only as they gain more experiences with writing and print that children are encouraged to "fix" more and more of their errors. Figure 8.1 presents some guidelines for adapting the writing process to emergent and beginning writers.

Further Examining the Writing Process

Prewriting.   Perhaps one of the most crucial stages of the writing process is prewriting. It is dur-ing this stage that writers begin to tentatively talk, read, and write about an idea to see in what direc-tion they want to go. Murray (1982) suggests that at least 70 percent of writing time be spent in prewriting, for it is during this stage that children will choose a topic, consider purpose, audience, and form, and gather, and organize ideas for writing.

Choosing a topic.   Children need to choose their own writing topics. Simply supplying children with topics often forces children to write about topics they know little about or are not interested in. For children who find generating topics difficult, teachers can help them brainstorm a list of three, four, or five topics and identify the one they are the most interested in and know the most about. Through various prewriting activities, children talk, draw, read, and even write to further develop information about their topics (Tompkins, 2003).

Purpose of writing.   Additionally, children need to determine the purpose for their writing. Are they writing to entertain? inform? persuade? Whatever the purpose for the writing, the determination of it influences the decisions that children will make about form and audience.

Audience.   Primarily, children write for themselves as they consider how to express and clarify their own ideas and feelings. Sometimes, they may write for others (i.e., classmates, younger chil-

Figure 8.1 ● Adapting the writing process for emergent and beginning writers.

1. Prewriting

Prewriting is as important to young children as it is to other writers. Children write about topics they know well and for which they have the necessary vocabulary. Topics include personal experiences, classroom activities, stories students have heard read aloud or have read independently, and thematic unit topics. Children use drawing to gather and organize ideas before writing. Children often talk about the topic or dramatize it before beginning to write.

2. Drafting

Young children usually write single-draft compositions. They add words to accompany drawings they have already made. The emphasis is on expressing ideas, not on handwriting skills or conventional spelling. Often children write in small booklets of paper, and they write equally well on lined or unlined paper.

3. Revising

Teachers downplay this stage until children have learned the importance of revising to meet the needs of their readers. At first, children reread their writings to see that they have included everything that they wanted to say, and they make very few changes. As they gain experience, they begin to make changes to make their writing clearer and add more information to make their writing complete.

4. Editing

Like revising, this stage is deemphasized until children have learned conventional spellings for some words and have gained control over rules for capitalizing words and adding punctuation marks. To introduce editing, teacher help children make one or two corrections by erasing the error and writing the correction in pencil on the child's writing. Teachers do not circle errors on a child's paper with a red pen. As children become more fluent writers, teachers help them make more corrections.

5. Publishing

Children read their writings to their classmates and share their drawings. Through sharing, children develop a concept of audience and learn new ways of writing from their classmates. Kindergartners and first graders usually do not recopy their writings, but sometimes the teacher or an aide types the final copy, changing the child's writing into conventional form. Unless there is a good reason for converting the kid writing to adult writing, adults should refrain from recopying young children's writing, because this sends the message that the children's writing is inadequate.

Tompkins, 2003, p. 320

dren, parents, pen pals, etc.). Whomever the audience, an influence is seen on the writing that the children actually do; in other words, children adapt their writing to fit the needs of their audience just as they adjust their speech to meet the needs of the people listening to them.

Form.   Form deals exclusively with the style the writing will take. Will it be a story? a letter? a poem? a journal entry? There is a wide variety of **genres** or writing forms that children learn.

Table 8.1 presents six of these genres from Tompkins (2003). Children, even in the classrooms of very young children, need to experiment with a wide variety of writing forms and explore the potential for each of these formats.

Typically, children experience and develop a strong sense of these genres and how they are structured through reading and writing. Decisions about function, audience, and form influence each other (see Table 8.1).

Gathering and organizing ideas.   Commonly referred to as "rehearsal activities" (Graves, 1983), these help children prepare to write. While these activities may take many forms, some of the most common ones follow:

Drawing.   For young children, drawing is a way to gather and organize ideas. It is through drawing that many young children are able to determine what it is they want to write. For these children, drawing serves a tool for gathering and organizing their thoughts. By seeing what they have drawn, they come to understand what it is they wish to write (Dyson, 1986).

Clustering.   Also referred to as concept maps or webs, clusters provide another way for children to gather and organize information about what they want to write. Clustering begins by having children record in the center of a piece of paper the idea or topic about which they wish to write. Then, the children add details and other information on rays coming out of the main idea or topic. This type of prewriting activity often works well for use with children, as it is nonlinear and enables children to flexibly add information or move information from one area to another.

Talking.   When children talk with their classmates, they learn how to share ideas about possible writing topics. This discussion with a peer helps them try out different ways to express the idea as well as to ask questions of their peers about the topic. It serves as a means for determining audience and the appropriateness of how they are talking about their ideas before they write to communicate it with others.

Reading.   Reading provides a venue for exploration of ideas and topics as well as the various forms that children may use to convey their message. To do this, children may read to find information to include in their writing. For example, they may read to find out more about dinosaurs and use this information in their writing about where a dinosaur lived and what it might have looked like. Children may also read to extend or retell a story that they are familiar with. In doing so, they are learning more about the features and characteristics of the particular story that they are working with as well as the features of written language and how to express ideas with print.

Drafting.   The next stage found in the writing process is that of drafting. In drafting, children write and refine their writing through a series of drafts. While the focus of the previous stage was generating ideas and organizing them, the focus of this stage is the refinement and development of these ideas through a series of drafts of the form of writing. Here the children are focusing on getting the idea down; little attention and concern should be given to spelling, punctuation, or other conventions of print—the focus is on content.

Table 8.1 ● Writing Genres

Genre	Purpose	Activities
Descriptive Writing	Children become careful observers and choose precise language when they make description. They take notice of sensory details and learn to make comparisons (metaphors and similes) in order to make their writing more powerful.	Comparisons Descriptive paragraphs Descriptive sentences Five-senses poems Found poems Observations
Informational Writing	Children collect and synthesize information for writing. This writing is objective, with reports being the most common type of informational writing. In this form, children may give directions, sequence steps, compare one thing to another, explain causes and effects, or describe problems and solutions.	Alphabet books Autobiographies Biographies Data charts Dictionaries Directions Interviews Posters Reports Summaries
Journals and Letters	In this type of writing, children write to express themselves to specific, known audiences. Their writing here is personal and often less formal than other genres. They share news, explore new ideas, and record notes. Letters and envelopes require special formatting, and children typically learn these formats during the primary grades.	Business letters Courtesy letters Email messages Friendly letters Learning logs Personal journals Postcards Reading logs
Narrative Writing	Narratives, or stories, are written as children retell familiar stories, develop sequels for stories they have read, write stories called personal narratives about events in their own lives, and create original stories. Narratives include a beginning, middle, and an end. In the beginning, the children introduce the characters, identify the problem, and interest readers in the story. In the middle, the problem becomes worse, or additional roadblocks are set up to thwart the main character as he or she attempts to solve the problem. In the end, the problem is resolved.	Original short stories Personal narratives Retellings of stories Sequels to stories Scripts of stories

(Continued)

Table 8.1 ● *(Continued)*

Genre	Purpose	Activities
Persuasive Writing	Persuasion is winning someone to your viewpoint or cause. The three ways that people are persuaded are by appeals to (1) logic, (2) moral character, and (3) emotion. In this form of writing, children present their position clearly and then support it with examples and evidence.	Advertisements Book and movie reviews Persuasive letters Persuasive posters
Poetry Writing	As children create poems, they create word pictures and play with rhyme and other stylistic devices. It is through experimenting with poems that they learn that poetic language is vivid and powerful while at the same time concise, and that poems can be arranged in different ways on a page.	Acrostic poems Cinquain poems Color poems Diamante poems Five-senses poems Found poems Free verse Haiku "I am" poems "If I were . . ." poems "I wish . . ." poems Riddles

Tompkins, 2003, p. 309

It is during the drafting stage that children may need to modify decisions they made earlier about audience, form, and purpose for the writing. The idea is that, whatever the modifications are that are made to the draft document, they are made to help the children in communicating more effectively.

Revising. Revising is the process by which writers refine their writing. It typically begins as part of the drafting phase. What is different is that in the revising stage children solicit others for reactions and revise their drafts on the basis of the comments they receive. It is erroneous to consider revising simply a polishing phase. Instead, it should be thought of as a means for children to better meet the needs of their audience (i.e., readers) by adding, substituting, deleting, and rearranging material. This is the process of "seeing again" the text with the help of classmates. To do this, writers typically engage in three activities during the revising stage: rereading the rough draft, sharing the rough draft with others in a small group, and revising based on feedback from the group.

Rereading the rough draft. After a short period time following the completion of a rough draft (a day or two typically), the writer comes back to the text to reread it from a fresh perspective—that of reader. As he or she is rereading, the child may make changes—adding, substituting, deleting, and moving—or placing question marks by sections that need work. These actions and any areas that the writer perceives as needing more attention are then discussed with his or her writing group.

Sharing the rough draft with others.   Following his or her initial rereading and revising of the text, the child meets with a small group of classmates to share their writing. In these groups, the children share their writings with each other and make suggestions about possible revisions.

Writing groups can be formed in a variety of ways. They can form spontaneously when four or five children have finished their writing, or they can be assigned. However the format works in the classroom, the idea is that, when children have their rough drafts completed, they meet to listen and respond, offering compliments and suggestions for revision to their classmates.

Revising what has been written.   As stated previously, children typically make four types of changes to their rough drafts: additions, substitutions, deletions, and moves (Faigley & Witte, 1981). To do so they may use colored pens, skip every other line on the page, add words, delete paragraphs, substitute sentences, etc. In this way the teacher is able to see the revisions that the children have made when she or he examines their rough drafts. The types and numbers of revisions a child makes indicate growth in his or her writing.

Editing.   Considered to be the fourth stage of the writing process, editing is when a child puts a piece of writing into its final form. Up until this point, the focus of writing has been on content—the child's message or meaning. In this stage, the focus changes to the mechanics or conventions of writing. The goal here is to make the writing "optimally readable" (Smith, 1982, p. 127).

Conventions of writing are also referred to as the mechanics of written Standard English. They include capitalization, punctuation, spelling, sentence structure, usage, and any formatting considerations necessary for specific forms of writing (i.e., poems, letters, scripts, etc.). Conventions of print are what make the print accessible to readers.

Additionally, research suggests that teaching mechanical skills as part of the writing process is more effective than teaching them through practice exercises (Calkins, 1980; Graves, 1983). It is through editing a piece of writing that they have written and that will be shared with an audience that children will become more interested in using mechanical skills correctly so they can communicate more effectively.

Three activities typically found in the editing stage of the writing process are getting distance from a piece of writing, proofreading to locate errors, and correcting errors.

Distancing.   As in the revision stage, children need to get distance from a piece of writing by putting it aside for a few days before working on editing it. This time allows the familiarity with the writing to subside and the children to gain a fresh perspective necessary for editing the piece.

Locating errors.   As a unique form of reading, proofreading requires that children read their own writing slowly, word by word, hunting for errors rather than reading for meaning (King, 1985). Often errors are overlooked because our natural inclination is to read for meaning, and, if an error does not interfere with meaning making, it can go unnoticed. Therefore, it is important to demonstrate and take time to explain proofreading to children.

Correcting errors.   After having proofread their writing and located as many errors as they can, children use colored pens to correct the errors individually or with an editor's assistant. It is unrealistic to expect children to locate and correct all of their mechanical errors. Editing is complete when the children meet with their editors or the teacher to conference for final editing.

Publishing.   The final stage of the writing process is publishing. This is when the children's writings are brought to life as final copies are written and shared with an appropriate audience. It is through this sharing that children come to see themselves as writers and authors.

Making books.   Perhaps the most popular way to share a piece of writing is by making books. Simple books can be made by stapling sheets of writing paper together with construction paper for the front and back.

Sharing writing.   Some ways that Tompkins (2003) suggests for sharing children's writing are the following:

- Submit the piece to writing contests
- Display the writing as a mobile
- Contribute to a class anthology
- Contribute to the local or school newspaper
- Make a shape book
- Record the writing on a cassette tape
- Submit it to a literary magazine
- Read it at a school assembly
- Share it at a read-aloud party
- Share it with parents and siblings
- Display poetry on a "poet-tree"
- Send it to a pen pal
- Display it on a bulletin board
- Make a Big Book
- Design a poster about the writing
- Read it to foster grandparents
- Share it as a puppet show
- Display it at a public event (i.e., open house, parent conferences, etc.)
- Read it to children in other classes (p. 316)

What Makes a Piece of Writing Good?

This is not an easy question to answer, because what is taken into consideration for what makes something good is different in different contexts and at different times. While there is no formula or program that can be used to write well, there are certain qualities found in writing that is effective in communicating its message. These qualities can be summarized as the six traits of effective writing (Spandel, 2004). The six traits are ideas, voice, organization, sentence fluency, word choice, and conventions. Table 8.2 provides a description of these.

For emerging writers, developing awareness for the six traits is part of instruction. However, it is unrealistic to expect that all of these traits be present in their writing at all times. Children are gradually developing into the processes involved in writing, and need to have ample opportunities that will enable them to attend and engage with texts that explore these traits to further refine their hypotheses about written language.

Table 8.2 ● Six Traits of Writing

Trait	What It Is	To Support
Ideas	As children begin to write, they need to generate ideas. It is from these ideas that the rest of their writing will flow.	Use of picture books to illustrate what it is an author is trying to say can help children understand the importance of expressing an idea clearly. Ask questions to help writers think about their own writing: "What do you want to say?" or "What else can you tell me about that?"
Voice	This is the "sound" of the writer found in his or her writing. It is the way the author comes through communicating his or her style and personality.	Picture books are a great way to begin to help children learn about voice. Kevin Henkes's book *Chrysanthemum* provides a rich example of voice and how it is used to make his message even clearer.
Organization	This is the form and structure that is used to put ideas together so they make sense. For early writers, organization often begins with how to translate the ideas in their heads to ones on paper that make sense.	Begin at the level of the sentence. Concepts like beginning, middle, and end are part of learning about organization.
Sentence Fluency	Writing that is fluent has a rhythm; this is sentence fluency.	This can best be seen through the use and writing of songs and poetry in the classroom. Picture books like Bill Martin's *Chicka Chicka Boom Boom* also provide great examples of fluency in writing and can be used to introduce and define this idea for young children. When working on developing the idea of sentence fluency, emphasis should be given to the enjoyment of reading writing like this aloud.

(Continued)

Table 8.2 • *(Continued)*

Trait	What It Is	To Support
Word Choice	The words used to express and convey a message are word choice. It is the painting of a picture for the reader with words that is necessary when writing for others.	Word choice aids in the pleasure and enjoyment for reading someone else's writing. *Piggie Pie!* by Margie Palatini is a great book to share with young children and talk about word choice.
Conventions	Conventions are those characteristics of print that make it accessible for the reader. They include things like grammar, punctuation, spelling, capitalization, etc.	Conventions can be stumbling blocks for many children. To minimize this potential debilitating effect, engagement in the writing process is necessary. Children need to learn that conventions are things that we pay particularly close attention to during the editing stage, but that they are not necessarily that important when drafting and getting our ideas out.

Writing Instruction

Instruction in writing occurs long before children enter classrooms. As children watch their parents, teachers, and other significant people in their lives write, they are forming hypotheses about how writing and drawing work together. To support them in their emergence into writing, teachers can support children learn more about writing and how written language can be used to represent their thoughts. For children to become writers, they need to be immersed in written language (New Zealand Staff Ministry of Education, 1992).

Differentiating Instruction in Writing

Four Kinds of Writing and Four Levels of Support

Fountas and Pinnell (1996) have developed a framework for classroom and reading teachers as a means for thinking about the instruction and the literacy learning opportunities that they provide. In this framework they include elements of both reading and writing. For the purposes of this chapter, we are going to focus only on the elements of writing. They are shared writing, interactive writing, guided writing or writing workshop, and independent writing. These can be seen in Table 8.3. Table 8.4 describes how to differentiate instruction in writing in accordance with the disability categories served under IDEA.

Shared writing.   In shared writing, the teacher and the children collaborate to construct and write messages and stories. This is similar to the language experience approach in which the ideas,

Table 8.3 ● Kinds of Writing and Levels of Support.

Kind of Writing	Levels of Support	Methods Used	Materials
Shared Writing or Language Experience	• Teacher guides children to compose messages and acts as their scribe. The message is reread many times. • Teacher may use a combination of writing for the children and interactive writing being aware of time and pacing. • Teacher may provide additional ways for children to talk or respond (i.e., one-word/one-sign, picture exchange communication system, communication boards, assistive technology, etc.)	• The teacher provides full support. • The teacher models and demonstrates the process of putting children's ideas into written language—how messages are composed.	• Large charts and markers • Materials for making Big Books • Magnadoodle or slate for the teacher • White tape for making corrections • Pointers for reading • Letter chart of letters for modeling letter formation
Interactive Writing	• The teacher guides group writing of a large-print piece, which can be a list, a chart, pages of a book, or another form of writing. As part of this guidance, additional time for responses may need to be afforded, shorter periods of time for working/contributing to the writing may be needed, verbal responses may need to be expanded beyond single words, and	• There is a high level of teacher support, and the teacher models and demonstrates the writing process involving individual children. • The teacher selects letters, words, or other writing actions for individual children to do; the pen is shared. • The message or story is composed by the group and then constructed word by word.	• Large charts and markers • Materials for making Big Books • Magnadoodle or slate for the teacher • White tape for making corrections • Pointers for reading • Letter chart of letters for modeling letter formation

(Continued)

Differentiating Instruction in Writing

Table 8.3 ● *(Continued)*

Kind of Writing	Levels of Support	Methods Used	Materials
	additional ways for responding and engaging with task may be needed (i.e., one-word/one-sign, picture exchange communication system, communication boards, assistive technology, etc.) ● All children participate in the composing and constructing various aspects of the writing. ● The piece of writing is read many times by the group during the process.		
Guided Writing or Writing Workshop	● The teacher has individual conferences with writers, giving selected feedback. ● The teacher may work with the whole class or a small group to provide general guidance and focus lessons on any aspect of writing. ● Additional support may be needed for children with disabilities that impact their fine motor skills (i.e., acting as a scribe, dictating writing into tape recorders for later writing, use of computers, etc.)	● Some teacher support is needed. ● Children generally select their own topics and pieces, but teacher sets the scene and gives specific guidance and/or feedback as needed—either in conferencing or through focus lessons. ● Children problem solve on their own in writing.	● Word wall, dictionaries, or other resources. ● Paper, pencils, markers, staples, premade plain paper books, and art materials. ● Print-rich environment as a resource.

Table 8.3 ● *(Continued)*

Kind of Writing	Levels of Support	Methods Used	Materials
Independent Writing	• Children write their own messages and stories, sometimes helping each other. • Additional support may be needed for children with disabilities which impact their fine motor skills (i.e., acting as a scribe, dictating writing into tape recorders for later writing, use of computers, etc.)	• Little or no teacher support is needed as children compose and write independently. • Children use known words to construct spellings for unknown words. • Children know how to use the resources in the room to get words they cannot write independently.	• Paper, pencils, markers, staples, premade plain paper books, and art materials. • Resources children use on their own, such as the word wall or dictionaries. • Print-rich environment as resource.

Adapted from Fountas & Pinnell, 1996, p. 28

thoughts, and messages of children are used to facilitate the construction of a written piece. As children work with the teacher, they talk and create a message. The teacher then writes the message down exactly how the children communicate it. By acting as a scribe for the children's messages, the teacher enables the children to see how their ideas can be turned into written language. The teacher is also able to demonstrate and model how this process occurs. Since the children have participated in this writing event (i.e., they generated and constructed the messages written), they are also able to read the messages that have been created. Therefore, the written language products created in shared writing events should be displayed and used by the children as resources in their future reading and writing endeavors.

The role of the teacher in shared writing is highly supportive. She or he acts by providing a model and demonstration for how ideas are put into written messages for the children. While the children are working to develop and construct a message, the teacher guides the composition process by supplying words, helping children to reread and restate the message as it is being written. As part of this process, the teacher is "thinking aloud" the steps that she or he is undertaking while writing, saying things like, "What did we want to say next?" or "I better put a period there, because we are all done with our idea." These types of questions and statements encourage further engagement with text, features of the form of writing, and bring to light concepts about print as they occur within the meaningful context of children's writing. The results of shared writing experiences are as follows:

1. Illustrations of how writing works for young children
2. Opportunities to draw attention to features and concepts about print (e.g., letters, words, sounds, etc.)
3. Recordings of children's thoughts, ideas, and messages
4. Resources of written language are created that can and should be displayed within the classroom for later use

Interactive writing. Similar to shared writing, interactive writing differs in the amount of support that is provided by the teacher as well as the level of control of the child. In interactive writing, children are placed in the role of apprentice learning alongside a more expert writer. Learning in interactive writing allows us to language as a tool for learning, to build a community with varied tools for communication (i.e., speaking, reading, writing, drawing), to document the accumulated understanding of a group, to use the print to make messages clear, to use language in the writing process, to develop textual resources for the classroom, and to use written language for a variety of purposes. Figure 8.2 illustrates the web of understandings that are formed through the use of interactive writing.

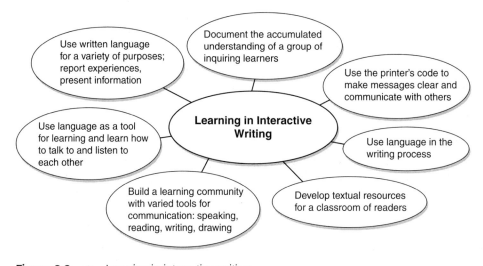

Figure 8.2 • Learning in interactive writing.

For interactive writing to be successful in a classroom, an interactive learning community needs to be created. We want children to be able to engage in conversation within a fairly large group. This means that they will need to learn to take turns, respect one another, and to listen to each other's responses. It is helpful in such instances to establish classroom routines. McCarrier, Fountas, and Pinnell (1999) suggest the following routines:

1. Space is left in front of the easel for the writer or pointer to stand.
2. Children sit on their bottoms and look at the easel and the teacher.
3. Children listen to others during the composition of the text.

Table 8.4 ● Differentiating Instruction in Writing

Writing and Language Arts

IDEA Disability Category	Concept	Accommodation/Modification	Concept	Accommodation/Modification
Autism	Emergent & Early Writing	• Use of predictable text with repetitive, "natural" language patterns to model writing after • Shared and interactive writing: modeling of task • Language Experience Approach • Labeling of familiar areas and activities • Smaller tasks and repetition; extended time • Talk and opportunity to respond in multiple ways (i.e., computer, one-word/one-sign, picture exchange communication system, assistive technology, etc.)	Alphabetic Principle	• Use of manipulatives (letter forms) • Hands-on exploration of letter–sound relationships • Use of predictable text with repetitive language patterns • Nursery rhymes, songs, poems with movement as well as large text formatting • Letter/sound sorts • Increased writing opportunities • Language Experience Approach
Deaf-Blindness	Emergent & Early Writing	• Use of predictable text with repetitive, "natural" language patterns • Familiar texts read aloud often during period of time (same book shared for five or more days) • Shared and interactive writing: modeling of task–explicit verbalization of the experience and process • Increased opportunities to write and for a variety of purposes • Language Experience Approach • Labeling of familiar areas and activities in braille and large print • ASL story language and patterning • Talk and opportunity to respond in multiple ways (i.e., computer, one-word/one-sign, picture exchange communication system, assistive technology, etc.)	Alphabetic Principle	• Use of manipulatives (letter forms) • Hands-on exploration of letter–sound relationships • Kinesthetic and tactile movements with letters in conjunction with letter representation and sound • Interactive writing • Increased writing opportunities • Letter–sound relationships established through use of target or "key" words–like "cat" for the letter–sound relationship /c/ for C • Language Experience Approach

(Continued)

Table 8.4 ● *(Continued)*

		Writing and Language Arts		
IDEA Disability Category	**Concept**	**Accommodation/Modification**	**Concept**	**Accommodation/Modification**
Deafness	Emergent & Early Writing	• ASL story language and patterning • Use of predictable text with repetitive, "natural" language patterns • Familiar texts read aloud often during period of time (same book shared for five or more days) • Shared and Interactive writing: modeling of task • Increased opportunities to write and for a variety of purposes • Language Experience Approach • Labeling of familiar areas and activities • Talk and opportunity to write for real/authentic purposes	Alphabetic Principle	• Use of manipulatives (letter forms) • Hands-on exploration of letter–sound relationships • Nursery rhymes, songs, poems with movement as well as large text formatting • Elkonin boxes used in conjunction with mirror for visual recognition of mouth movements • Interactive writing • Increased writing opportunities • Letter–sound relationships established through use of target or "key" words—like "cat" for the letter–sound relationship /c/ for C • Language Experience Approach
Emotional Disturbance	Emergent & Early Writing	• Use of predictable, high-interest text with repetitive, "natural" language patterns • Familiar texts read aloud often during period of time (same book shared for five or more days) • Shared and interactive writing: modeling of task • Language Experience Approach • Labeling of familiar areas and activities • Shorter periods of time for activities, with increased number of activities addressing concept–predictable pattern to activity • Talk and opportunity to write for real/authentic purposes	Alphabetic Principle	• Use of manipulatives (letter forms) • Hands-on exploration of letter–sound relationships • Use of predictable text with repetitive language patterns • Nursery rhymes, songs, poems with movement as well as large text formatting • Letter–sound sorts • Interactive writing • Elkonin boxes • Language Experience Approach • Increased writing opportunities

		Emergent & Early Writing	Alphabetic Principle
Hearing Impairment	Emergent & Early Writing	• ASL story language and patterning • Use of predictable text with repetitive, "natural" language patterns • Familiar texts read aloud often during period of time (same book shared for five or more days) • Language Experience Approach • Shared and interactive writing: modeling of task • Labeling of familiar areas and activities • Increased opportunities to write and for a variety of purposes • Talk and opportunity to write for real/authentic purposes	• Use of manipulatives (letter forms) • Hands-on exploration of letter–sound relationships • Use of predictable text with repetitive language patterns • Nursery rhymes, songs, poems with movement as well as large text formatting • Interactive writing • Letter–sound relationships established through use of target or "key" words—like "cat" for the letter–sound relationship /c/ for C • Language Experience Approach • Increased writing opportunities
Mental Retardation	Emergent & Early Writing	• Language Experience Approach • Labeling of familiar areas and activities • Use of predictable text with repetitive, "natural" language patterns • Familiar texts read aloud often during period of time (same book shared for five or more days) • Shared and interactive writing: modeling of task • Predictable pattern to activity • Talk and opportunity to respond in multiple ways (i.e., computer, one-word/one-sign, picture exchange communication system, assistive technology, etc.)	• Use of manipulatives (letter forms) • Hands-on exploration of letter–sound relationships • Use of predictable text with repetitive language patterns • Nursery rhymes, songs, poems with movement as well as large text formatting • Interactive writing • Language Experience Approach • Letter–sound relationships established through use of target or "key" words—like "cat" for the letter–sound relationship /c/ for C • Letter/sound sorts • Increased writing opportunities

(Continued)

Table 8.4 ● *(Continued)*

IDEA Disability Category	Writing and Language Arts			
	Concept	Accommodation/Modification	Concept	Accommodation/Modification
Multiple Disabilities	Emergent & Early Writing	• Use of predictable text with repetitive, "natural" language patterns • Familiar texts read aloud often during period of time (same book shared for five or more days) • Language Experience Approach • Shared and interactive writing: modeling of task–verbalization of the experience and process • Labeling of familiar areas and activities • Shorter periods of time for activities, with increased number of activities addressing concept–predictable pattern to activity • Talk and opportunity to respond in multiple ways (i.e., computer, one-word/one-sign, picture exchange communication system, assistive technology, etc.)	Alphabetic Principle	• Use of manipulatives (letter forms) • Hands-on exploration of letter–sound relationships • Use of predictable text with repetitive language patterns • Nursery rhymes, songs, poems with movement as well as large text formatting • Concept sorts • Interactive writing • Elkonin boxes • Letter/sound sorts • Language Experience Approach • Letter–sound relationships established through use of target or "key" words–like "cat" for the letter–sound relationship /c/ for C • Increased writing opportunities
Orthopedic Impairment	Emergent & Early Writing	• Use of predictable text with repetitive, "natural" language patterns • Familiar texts read aloud often during period of time (same book shared for five or more days) • Shared and interactive writing: modeling of task • Language Experience Approach • Labeling of familiar areas and activities • Talk and opportunity to respond in multiple ways (i.e., computer, one-word/one-sign, picture exchange communication system, assistive technology, etc.)	Alphabetic Principle	• Use of manipulatives (letter forms) • Hands-on exploration of letter–sound relationships • Use of predictable text with repetitive language patterns • Nursery rhymes, songs, poems with movement as well as large text formatting • Letter/sound sorts • Interactive writing • Elkonin boxes • Language Experience Approach • Increased writing opportunities

Other Health Impairment	Emergent & Early Writing	• Use of predictable text with repetitive, "natural" language patterns • Familiar texts read aloud often during period of time (same book shared for five or more days) • Shared and Interactive writing: modeling of task • Language Experience Approach • Labeling of familiar areas and activities • Talk and opportunity to respond in multiple ways (i.e., computer, one-word/one-sign, picture exchange communication system, assistive technology, etc.)	Alphabetic Principle	• Use of manipulatives (letter forms) • Hands-on exploration of letter–sound relationships • Use of predictable text with repetitive language patterns • Nursery rhymes, songs, poems with movement as well as large text formatting • Letter/sound sorts • Interactive writing • Language Experience Approach • Elkonin boxes • Increased writing opportunities
Specific Learning Disability	Emergent & Early Writing	• Use of predictable text with repetitive, "natural" language patterns • Familiar texts read aloud often during period of time (same book shared for five or more days) • Shared and interactive writing: modeling of task • Language Experience Approach • Labeling of familiar areas and activities • Talk and opportunity to respond to texts in multiple ways	Alphabetic Principle	• Use of manipulatives (letter forms) • Hands-on exploration of letter–sound relationships • Use of predictable text with repetitive language patterns • Nursery rhymes, songs, poems with movement as well as large text formatting • Letter/sound sorts • Interactive writing • Language Experience Approach • Elkonin Boxes • Increased writing opportunities
Speech or Language Impairment	Emergent & Early Writing	• Use of predictable text with repetitive, "natural" language patterns • Familiar texts read aloud often during period of time (same book shared for five or more days) • Shared and interactive writing: modeling of task • Language Experience Approach • Labeling of familiar areas and activities • Talk and opportunity to respond in multiple ways (i.e., computer, one-word/one-sign, picture exchange communication system, assistive technology, etc.)	Alphabetic Principle	• Use of manipulatives (letter forms) • Hands-on exploration of letter–sound relationships • Use of predictable text with repetitive language patterns • Nursery rhymes, songs, poems with movement as well as large text formatting • Letter/sound sorts • Interactive writing • Language Experience Approach • Elkonin boxes • Increased writing opportunities

(Continued)

Table 8.4 • *(Continued)*

Writing and Language Arts

IDEA Disability Category	Concept	Accommodation/Modification	Concept	Accommodation/Modification
Traumatic Brain Injury	Emergent & Early Writing	• Use of predictable text with repetitive, "natural" language patterns • Familiar texts read aloud often during period of time (same book shared for five or more days) • Shared and interactive writing: modeling of task • Language Experience Approach • Labeling of familiar areas and activities • Shorter periods of time for activities, with increased number of activities addressing concept–predictable pattern to activity • Talk and opportunity to respond in multiple ways (i.e., computer, one-word/one-sign, picture exchange communication system, assistive technology, etc.)	Alphabetic Principle	• Use of manipulatives (letter forms) • Hands-on exploration of letter–sound relationships • Use of predictable text with repetitive language patterns • Nursery rhymes, songs, poems with movement as well as large text formatting • Letter/sound sorts • Interactive writing • Elkonin boxes • Language Experience Approach • Letter–sound relationships established through use of target or "key" words—like "cat" for the letter–sound relationship /c/ for C • Increased writing opportunities
Visual Impairment Including Blindness	Emergent & Early Writing	• Use of predictable text with repetitive, "natural" language patterns • Familiar texts read aloud often during period of time (same book shared for five or more days) • Shared and interactive writing: modeling of task–verbalization of the experience and process • Language Experience Approach • Labeling of familiar areas and activities in braille and large print • Talk and opportunity to respond in multiple ways (i.e., computer, one-word/one-sign, picture exchange communication system, assistive technology, etc.)	Alphabetic Principle	• Use of manipulatives (letter forms) • Hands-on exploration of letter–sound relationships • Use of predictable text with repetitive language patterns • Nursery rhymes, songs, poems with movement as well as large text formatting • Letter/sound sorts • Interactive writing • Language Experience Approach • Letter–sound relationships established through use of target or "key" words—like "cat" for the letter–sound relationship /c/ for C • Elkonin boxes • Increased writing opportunities

4. Children offer ideas during text composition.

5. Children write large enough for others to see.

6. Children say words slowly with the teacher.

7. Children read with the child or teacher who is pointing. (see Figure 8.2)

8. Children refer to resources such as charts while constructing the text.

With a routine established, we now consider how to actually get to writing. A base of active and shared learning experiences is where we will start the process. These experiences may arise from a book that we have read with the children, a play that we have seen, a thank-you note to a visitor, examining the growth of plants, or a nature walk. Once we have shared in the experience, we need to talk about it to establish the purpose for our writing. This purpose will guide us in the next step of composing the text. For young children, it should be understood that a text does not readily equate with a story. Typically, text here should be considered any message that the children can agree upon. The text is then constructed with the children. This is a word-by-word process in which the message is read over and over again so that the words may be written. As the text is being composed in this manner, the teacher may call on specific children to share and contribute to the physical writing of the message. This may range from writing a specific letters or words that they know to "feeling" the spaces in between words, to ending the piece of writing with the appropriate punctuation mark. The message is then reread, revised, and checked (i.e., proofread) for any changes that may need to be made. The text is placed in a location around the room (i.e., hung on the wall) so that it may be revisited by the children and serve as a resource in their future writing endeavors.

What is of central importance in interactive writing is the "children's ownership of and engagement with the text. . . . They must all be active participants in the negotiation so that they see the text as their own rather than something dictated by the teacher" (McCarrier, Fountas, & Pinnell, 1999, p. 85). The purpose is for children to be able to communicate their messages to others; the job of the teacher is to enable the children to use and control conventions of our written language. The goals of interactive writing are to

- Stimulate and guide oral language.
- Guide children's thinking in shaping an appropriate text.
- Help children understand purposes of writing.
- Help children develop a sense of audience.
- Focus children's attention on examples that will help them learn more about written language. (McCarrier, Fountas, & Pinnell, 1999)

The idea here is not just to "do" interactive writing, but for children to learn something during the process. The instructional decisions made during this activity help to determine the opportunities children have to learn new things.

McCarrier, Fountas, and Pinnell (1999) suggest that at least ten decisions are part of the interactive writing process:

1. Select clear examples to bring to children's attention. If you are going to show a particular principle, show it in a clear example instead of a distorted one.

2. Think about level of difficulty in a sequence of learning. Focus on easier concepts before harder concepts. Work on shorter sentences before harder ones. Attend to the regular sound patterns before the irregular sound patterns.

3. Base teaching points on information about children's strengths and needs.

4. Be highly selective in making decisions about children's coming up to the chart to "share the pen."

5. Don't try to teach too much with the whole group or a small group.

6. Decide whether to work with the whole group or a small group.

7. Attend as much to the composition as to the construction. The arrangement of ideas in language is often a neglected aspect of interactive writing.

8. In general, although some individual teaching will occur, select teaching points in relation to the overall patterns of learning evidenced by most of the group.

9. Select points that have potential for children's application of principles in their own writing.

10. Above all, have good reasons, related to research or theory about children's learning, for the decisions you make (p. 192).

The goals of interactive writing are to stimulate and guide oral language development, to facilitate and guide children's thinking in shaping and composing texts, to help children develop an awareness of the purposes of writing and how these guide the way messages are composed, to help children develop a sense of audience, and to focus children's attention on examples that will help them learn more about written language. These goals are accomplished by knowing what individual children's strengths and needs are as writers, knowing characteristics of text, and knowing the writing process and how it is learned well in relationship to reading development.

Guided or writing workshop.   Children in guided writing are constructing their individual pieces of writing. The teacher acts and supports this process by providing guidance, assistance, and feedback. This is usually accomplished in the forms of individual conferences or through the use of focus lessons on an aspect of writing such as generating ideas or how to write or form letters.

To be most effective, Fountas and Pinnell (1996) suggest that this time be structured in a simple and predictable manner. They suggest the following:

● Focus lessons (5–10 minutes)

● Writing and conferring time (20–30 minutes)

● Sharing time (10–15 minutes)

Focus lessons.   Focus lessons are short periods of instruction in which the teacher provides assistance to the writers on what they next need to learn. The teacher gathers information about what to teach from what he or she notices occurring in their writing, observations of their learning and writing in other areas of the day, the conferences he or she holds with them about their writing, and through a review of their writing folders. The topics of for these lessons may be on *procedures, strategies/skills,* or the development of *craft* (Giacobbe, 1981).

Procedural focus lessons deal with helping children learn about the routines or materials to be used so that they may act independently. They typically occur early in the year as children are learning about writing folders and the routines and use of time during writer's workshop. Some examples of focus lessons on procedural elements might include instruction on organizing a workspace or work folder, how to confer with a partner, where to find help when writing an unknown word, or how to use materials like the stapler.

Focus lessons that work on strategies and skills are ones that address the skills used by writers as they write. These include using slow articulation (i.e., saying the word slowly to hear the sounds that comprise it), the use of space to indicate word boundaries, the generative value of words (i.e., that knowing one word can help me know other words that sound and look similar to it), the role of capitalization and punctuation in writing, etc.

Craft lessons are ones in which what writers and illustrators do to communicate their message are the focus. Instruction in the six traits of writing should be considered here, since these are characteristics of writing that are found to be effective in helping the writer communicate her or his message to readers.

Writing and conferring.   During this period of time, all children are engaging at some level in the writing process. They are all writing. One child may be revising a draft, another may be generating ideas, and another may be making her or his own book for publication and sharing. As the children work, the teacher circulates through the room and interacts with children in brief conferences or conversations that facilitate their writing. The teacher may ask the children to talk about their writing, to share their writing with him or her so that he or she can give feedback on what was understood, or work to problem solve on the writing of the word (e.g., use of slow articulation, the word wall, or other resources found in the classroom). The focus of this time is on developing the child as a writer, not just on improving a piece of writing.

Sharing time.   Children need to have the opportunity to share their writing with others. As discussed earlier under publishing in the writing process, there are a variety of ways that children may share their written work. They can read it to the class, create a book, display it for others to see and read, etc. In guided writing, sharing does not have to be only thought of as the completed work, however. It can be the sharing of a something that the child is writing that she or he wants feedback on or help with from others. So, sharing during this time of the day can be any piece of writing that the child selects to share with others.

The goals of guided writing are to engage children in writing a variety of texts so that they develop their voice, learn to use different forms, and are provided with opportunities to learn to be writers. The role of the teacher in this activity is to serve as a guide in the process by providing instruction on focus lessons for what the children need to learn next and using conferences as a means for individualizing instruction to best meet the writer's needs.

Independent writing.   In independent writing, children generate their own pieces of writing. This writing may be in the forms of annotated drawings, charts of songs and poems that have been created, or any writing that they have done. Dictionaries and word walls are present to serve as resources for the child. All of this writing is displayed around the room so that it can be read and reread by the child and others.

Ideas for independent writing are generated in group sessions where children are exposed to the wide variety of writing forms and purposes. This writing occurs across the curriculum as teachers demonstrate how new learning can be used in different ways. The role of the teacher is one of observation. The teacher watches as the children engage in writing on their own or sometimes with the help of others. During this time children know where to find resources that will help them write words that they cannot write independently, and use known words as the compose and read their messages.

The goal of independent writing is provide opportunities for children's independent production of written text, to use writing for different purposes across the curriculum, and increase the writer's abilities to use different forms of writing. This is a period of time in which the teacher watches to see what the child is able to do on her or his own, observing for transfer of information and generalizations of understandings.

Assessment in Writing

To be the most effective at teaching, we must provide instruction on the "cutting edge" of a child's understandings. The way that we know what the writing strengths and needs of an individual are, as well as the patterns of strengths and needs across a classroom, is to conduct assessment. Simply stated, assessment is the act of gathering information upon which instructional decisions can be based. In this section of the chapter, we highlight some means for gathering information about a child, provide criteria for assessing the quality of a child's writing, and provide a list of questions to use when evaluating writing samples. While this is not an exhaustive list for all of the assessments one might conduct, these assessments do provide us with an initial starting point for examining writing with young children.

Writing assessments

Anecdotal records.   Perhaps the easiest place to begin when thinking about children's writing is observation. Observations of children engaging in authentic writing tasks provide information on what the children do as they begin to write. However, most teachers do not collect or organize these observations in a systematic way so that they can be used not only to inform instruction for this child but also to examine patterns of responding across groups of children. To be more systematic about the process of observing, we must record our observations of literacy behaviors. The record of these observations is called an *anecdotal record.* To do this, simply watch a child as she writes and record your observations. Some things that you might observe for are, How does she compose a message? Is this message clear? Is it clear for whom she is writing? and How does she work to actively solve the problems she encounters as she writes?

Writing samples.   Once children have written in journals or engaged in the writing process, their drafts and final products can be evaluated using a checklist like the one found in Figure 8.3. Such a checklist allows you to evaluate the representational features found in a child's writing and can help you to determine where your instruction needs to be.

Interviews.   Interviews with children about writing and the process they engage in as they write can be telling in terms of determining their developing understandings for the writing process as

Figure 8.3 ● Emergent writing checklist.

Child's Name _____

Forms of Writing	Date(s) Observed	Situation
● Uses drawing (might be circular scribbles)	_____	_____
● Uses drawing and writing	_____	_____
● Uses linear scribble	_____	_____
● Uses letterlike shapes	_____	_____
● Uses random letters	_____	_____
● Uses invented spellings	_____	_____
● Uses conventional spellings	_____	_____

Adapted from Sulzby, Barnhart, & Hieshima (1989). Forms of Writing checklist found in Christie, Enz, & Vukelich, 2003, p. 184.

well as purpose for writing. These may be conducted formally or informally and become part of conferences that you have with children.

Self-assessments.   The purpose of self-assessment is to give children an opportunity to reflect upon their individual strengths in writing. Again, this assessment may be used in conjunction with student–teacher writing conferences. To begin this assessment, you would discuss the positive behaviors you see in the child's writing and then ask him or her to fill out a "My Writing" checklist. See Figure 8.4 for an example of this checklist. By discussing and recording what a child knows about his or her own writing, you are able to better determine a focus for the next writing session.

Figure 8.4 ● My writing self-assessment.

I had a message.

It was clear who I was writing to.

It was clear why I was writing.

I wrote letters.

I wrote the first letter of the word.

My illustrations help tell the story.

I like what I wrote.

Figure 8.5 ● Criteria for quality writing.

Writing Element	Criteria
● **The message and its effect**	
● *Purpose and meaning*	Does the writer have a purpose for writing and an audience in mind?
	Does the writing say anything?
	Does it have meaning?
	Is the purpose reflected in the form?
● *Authority*	Can the writer explain the content of the writing?
	Does the writing show that the author knows the topic?
	Is early interest sustained?
	Is there evidence of observations?
	Does the writing reflect personal voice?
	Is the writing honest?
● *Clarity*	Does the writer feel that the content and vocabulary achieve the intended effect?
	Does the writer see the benefits of revision?
	Is the writing clear and informative?
	Is there adequate information?
	Is the information accurate?
	Is there evidence of revision?
● **Design**	
● *Genre and structure*	Did the writer have a plan for how the writing was to be ordered?
	Can the writer identify those characteristics appropriate to the genre used?
	Does the writing have structure, order, and coherence, showing a well-developed sequence of ideas; effective opening, middle, and ending; well-structured paragraphing?
	Does the writing have appropriate form?
● *Title*	Can the writer explain the choice of title and topic?
	Is the title appropriate?
● **Conventions**	
● *Spelling*	Does the writer approximate the spelling of words that are not known?
	Is the spelling accurate, or does the writing show evidence of identifying and/or correcting misspelled words?
● *Vocabulary*	Does the writer feel that he or she can draw on a widening vocabulary?
	Is an appropriate vocabulary used, with aptness and economy?

Dictation.   The purpose for dictation tasks is to determine the specific phonemes or sounds that a child hears and is able to record. This assessment allows you to better understand a child's knowledge of letter–sound relationships and the awareness of spelling that a child is developing. For this assessment you can use any sentences that have a variety of phonemes that you wish to assess. It may be administered whole group, small group, or to individual children. You simply provide each child with a piece of blank paper and slowly and clearly read the sentence you have selected. You ask the children to write what they hear, and you can repeat the entire sentence if necessary.

A sentence you might use is *My dog likes to run at the park.* Through the use of this sentence you would be able to determine how the child responded to the phonemes and spelling patterns found in it: For example, did the child write a letter to represent each sound in a word? Did the child spell any words correctly? Which ones? Did the student write initial sounds, final sounds, vowels, and so on? This information could then be used to help guide your instruction in **phonological awareness**, or letter–sound relationships, activities.

Further analyzing writing samples.   The New Zealand Staff Ministry of Education (1992) provides valuable information for ways to analyze children's writing products that enable you to take into account both the writer in process (i.e., what the child does while he or she writes) as well as writing (i.e., the product of the child's engagement in writing). These criteria are provided in Figure 8.5 to provide you with an additional means for examining children's writing.

As stated previously, assessment is the gathering of information about a child's developing understandings about writing. It should be used to inform the instructional decisions being made within the classroom.

The Reading–Writing Connection

Throughout this chapter we have learned about the characteristics of emergent and beginning writers. The characteristics that we have seen can be seen in both the reading and writing of emergent and beginning readers and writers. Figure 8.6 outlines some of these characteristics.

What can be seen in such a list are the inextricable connections that occur between the reading and writing processes. This means that, when children are learning to read, they are constructing meaning from print; when they are learning to write, they are composing messages using print from which others can construct meanings. In both of these processes, thinking and action on the part of the child are involved.

Reading and writing can be thought to be interrelated; learning in one area makes it easier to learn in the other (Fountas & Pinnell, 1996). Processes in both are constructed and deconstructed as complex series of actions are learned. For young children, it is through writing that they understand, manipulate, and use symbols to create a message. They are learning about how written language works. Fountas and Pinnell (1996) suggest that young children need abundant and ample opportunities to write; there should be writing centers with a wide variety of writing materials; and there should be writing materials in other centers to take notes and keep records, to label pictures, to keep records of books, to write responses or extensions to texts, etc.

In such environments, most young children will learn, notice, and discover what they need to know about how print works (this learning occurs in both home and school settings). It is these early

Figure 8.6 ● Characteristics of emergent readers and writers.

THE WRITER IN THE PROCESS	WRITING—THE PRODUCT
Does the writer consciously select words that are suited to narrative or descriptive writing, or reportage?	Are sentences well linked and varied?
● *Punctuation*	
Does the writer feel that he/she is developing more accurate and effective use of punctuation?	Is punctuation correct and appropriate?
Can examples of this be identified in the writing?	
● *Handwriting*	
Is the writing readable for this stage of the process or development of the learner?	Is the handwriting legible?
● *Attitude*	
Does the writer enjoy writing?	Does the writing show commitment, experimentation with words and ideas, and vitality?
Does the writer enjoy sharing his or her own writing with others and responding to the writing of others?	

New Zealand Staff Ministry of Education, 1992, pp. 118–120

experiences with print and language through talk, books, the environment, and writing opportunities that they form their hypotheses for how print and writing work to mediate the meanings they will construct. "Out of the act of writing, some early readers begin to link what they know in writing to what they know in reading; they discover the reciprocal nature of reading and writing" (Gunderson, 2002, p.2).

Summary

As we have seen in this chapter, the view of many early literates is that they are entering school as writers. They have the expectation that the print that they make and use is meaningful (Harste, Woodward, & Burke, 1984). Children in these are connecting their understandings for language and its use as they create and construct meanings for others.

The teacher assumes the role of guide and facilitator in this process, enabling children to construct hypotheses about print and its functions in their lives and the world around them. To do this effectively, the teacher must be aware of both the purposes and uses for writing as well as the instructional strategies that may be employed to better meet the divergent needs found within the classroom of learners. It is through various levels of instructional support that the teacher scaffolds children's growing understandings of print.

Thinking It Through

1. Make the connection between early writing principles and concepts about print. What are ways that each facilitates the development of the other?

2. Create a model of the writing process. How will you use this with your young learners?

3. Write a personal narrative examining how you developed writing skills and experience. Connect your personal experiences to what you have learned in this chapter and how it will influence your role as a literacy teacher.

4. Collect resources and materials that will guide you teaching of writing.

5. Identify an instructional strategy for writing and explain why you would prefer to use it with specific children.

6. Create a plan for supporting children's writing development at multiple levels.

7. List appropriate scenarios for using the four types of writing: shared writing, interactive writing, guided writing/writing workshop, and independent writing.

8. Write a lesson plan or structure to develop quality writing while exploring a specific writing form.

Children's Literature in Writing

Sequential Patterns

If You Give a Mouse a Cookie by L. J. Numeroff (Harper-Collins)
If You Give a Moose a Muffin by L. J. Numeroff (Harper-Collins)
The Very Hungry Caterpillar by Eric Carle (Collins-World)
The Grouchy Ladybug by Eric Carle (Crowell)
A House for Hermit Crab by Eric Carle (Picture Book Studio)
Busy Monday Morning by J. Domanska (Greenwillow)
10 Bears in My Bed by S. Mack (Pantheon)
The Napping House by Audrey Wood (Harcourt Brace Janovich)

Rhythm and Rhyme

Twinkle, Twinkle, Little Star by J. Messenger (Macmillan)
Chicken Soup With Rice by Maurice Sendak (Harper & Row)
Hop on Pop by Dr. Seuss (Random House)
Green Eggs and Ham by Dr. Seuss (Random House)
Hey Diddle Diddle and Other Mother Goose Rhymes by Tomie de Paola (Putnam)

Repetitive Sentences

Just Like Daddy by F. Asch (Simon & Schuster)
Teeny Tiny by J. Bennett (Putnam)
Millions of Cats by W. Gág (Coward-McCann)
The Little Red Hen by Paul Galdone (Seabury)
The Doorbell Rang by Pat Hutchins (Morrow)
If You're Happy and You Know It by N. Weiss (Viking)
Wheels on the Bus by S. K. Wickstrom (Crown)
I Went Walking by S. Williams (Harcourt Brace Janovich)
Are You My Mother? by P. D. Eastman (Random House)
Brown Bear, Brown Bear, What Do You See? by Bill Martin (Henry Holt)
Polar Bear, Polar Bear, What Do You Hear? by Bill Martin (Henry Holt)
If the Dinosaurs Came Back by B. Most (Harcourt Brace)
Wemberly Worried by Kevin Henkes (Scholastic)
Chrysanthemum by Kevin Henkes (Scholastic)
Lily's Purple, Plastic Purse by Kevin Henkes (Greenwillow)

Further Reading

Bear, D. R., Invernizzi, M., Templeton, S., & Johnston, F. (2004). *Words their way: Words study for phonics, vocabulary, and spelling instruction.* Upper Saddle, NJ: Pearson.

Fountas, I., & Pinnell, G. S. (1996). *Guided reading: Good first teaching for all children.* Portsmouth, NH: Heinemann.
McCarrier, A., Fountas, I., & Pinnell, G. S. (1999). *Interactive*

writing: How language and literacy come together, K–2. Portsmouth, NH: Heinemann.

Pinnell, G. S., & Fountas, I. C. (1998). *Word matters: Teaching phonics and spelling in the reading/writing classroom.* Portsmouth, NH: Heinemann.

Tompkins, G. E., & Colom, S. (2004). *Sharing the pen: Interactive writing with young* children. Upper Saddle, NJ: Pearson.

Resources

Websites for Word Walls

- www.coe.ilstu.edu/portfolios/students/wjmirow/word%2520walls%2520web%252
- www.k111.k12.il.us/lafayette/fourblocks/word_wall_grade_level_lists.htm
- www.wfu.edu/~cunningh/fourblocks/block4.htm

Websites for Poems and Games

- www.bbc.co.uk/education/wordsandpictures/

Websites for Writing with Young Children

- www.readyforlearning.net/html/writing.html
- www.naeyc.org/about/positions/pdf/PSREAD98.PDF
- www.ericdigests.org/pre-9218/encouraging.htm

Websites for Interactive Writing

- www.trcabc.com/interwriting.html
- www.stanswartz.com/IAW%20excerpt.pdf
- http://t4.jordan.k12.ut.us/Balanced_Literacy/Writing/interactive_writing.htm

References

Adams, M. (1990). *Beginning to read: Thinking and learning about print.* Cambridge: MIT Press.

Bodrova, E., & Leong, D. J. (1996). *Tools of the mind: The Vygotskian approach to early childhood education.* Upper Saddle River, NJ: Pearson.

Brown, K. J. (1999/2000). What kind of text—For whom and when? Textual scaffolding for beginning readers. *The Reading Teacher, 53,* pp. 292–307.

Calkins, L. (1980). When children want to punctuate: Basic skills belong in context. *Language Arts, 57,* pp. 567–573.

Chall, J. (1983). *Stages of reading development.* New York: McGraw-Hill.

Christie, J., Enz, B., & Vukelich, C. (2003). *Teaching language and literacy: Preschool through the elementary grades.* Upper Saddle River, NJ: Pearson.

Clay, M. (1966). *Emergent reading behavior.* Unpublished doctoral dissertation, University of Auckland, New Zealand.

Clay, M. (1975). *What did I write? Beginning writing behavior.* Portsmouth, NH: Heinemann.

Clay, M. (1979). *Reading: The patterning of complex behavior.* Portsmouth, NH: Heinemann.

Combs, M. (2006). *Readers and writers in primary grades: A balanced and integrated approach, K–4.* Upper Saddle River, NJ: Pearson.

Cunningham, P. (1995). *Words they use: Words for reading and writing* (2nd ed.). New York: Harper Collins.

Dyson, A. H. (1986). The emergence of visible language: Interrelationships between drawing and early writing. *Visible Language, 6,* pp. 360–381.

Ehri, L. (1997). Phonemic awareness and learning to read. *Literacy Development in Young Children, 4*(2), 2–3.

Faigley, L., & Witte, S. (1981). Analyzing revision. *College compositions and communication, 32,* pp. 400–410.

Ferreiro, E., & Teberosky, A. (1982). *Literacy before schooling.* Exeter, NH: Heinemann.

Fletcher, R., & Portalupi, J. (2001). *Writing workshop: The essential guide.* Portsmouth, NH: Heinemann.

Fountas, I., & Pinnell, G. S. (1996). *Guided reading: Good first teaching for all children.* Portsmouth, NH: Heinemann.

Fountas, I., & Pinnell, G. S. (1998). *Matching books to readers: Using leveled texts in guided reading, K–3.* Portsmouth, NH: Heinemann.

Giacobbe, M. E. (1981). "Who says children can't write the first week?" In R. D. Walshe (Ed.), *Donald Graves in Australia* Rozelle, New South Wales: Primary English Teaching Association.

Graves, D. (1983). *Writing: Teachers and children at work.* Portsmouth, NH: Heinemann.

Gunderson, S. (2002). *The reading/writing connection.* Unpublished manuscript, Purdue University, West Lafayette, IN.

Harste, J., Woodward, V., & Burke, C. (1984). *Language stories and literacy lessons.* Portsmouth, NH: Heinemann.

Holdoway, D. (1980). *Independence in reading.* Gosford, New South Wales: Ashton.

King, M. (1985). Proofreading is not reading. *Teaching English in the Two-Year College, 12,* pp. 108–112.

Lomax, R., & McGee, L. (1987). Young children's concepts about print and reading: Toward a model of word reading acquisition. *Reading Research Quarterly, 22,* pp. 237–256.

Masonheimer, P., Drum, P., & Ehri, L. (1984). Does environmental print identification lead children to word reading? *Journal of Reading Behavior, 16,* pp. 257–271.

McCarrier, A., Fountas, I., & Pinnell, G. S. (1999). *Interactive writing: How language and literacy come together, K–2.* Portsmouth, NH: Heinemann.

McGee, L., & Richgels, D. (1996). *Literacy's beginnings: Supporting young readers and writers* (2nd ed.). Boston: Allyn and Bacon.

Murray, W. S. (1982). *Sentence matching: The influence of meaning and structure.* Unpublished doctoral dissertation, Monash University, Victoria, Australia.

Neuman, S., & Roskos, K. (1997). Literacy knowledge in practice: Contests of participation for young writers and readers. *Reading Research Quarterly, 32,* pp. 10–32.

New Zealand Staff Ministry of Education. (1992). *Dancing with the pen: The learner as writer.* Katonah, NY: Richard C. Owens.

Pappas, C., Kiefer, B., & Levstik, L. (1995). *An integrated language perspective in the elementary school: Theory into action* (2nd ed.). White Plains, NY: Longman.

Pinnell, G. S., & Fountas, I. C. (2002). *Phonics lessons: Letters, sounds, and how words work.* Portsmouth, NH: Heinemann.

Shanklin, N. K. (1982). *Relating reading and writing: Developing a transitional model of the writing process.* Bloomington, IN: Monographs in Teaching and Learning, School of Education, Indiana University.

Smith, F. (1982). *Writing and the writer.* New York: Holt, Rinehart and Winston.

Snow, C. E., Burns, M. S., & Griffin, P. (Eds.). (1998). *Preventing reading difficulties in young children.* Washington, DC: National Academy Press.

Spandel, V. (2004). *Creating writers through 6-trait writing assessment and instruction* (4th ed.). Boston: Allyn and Bacon.

Sulzby, E. (1990). Assessment of emergent writing and children's language while writing. In L. Morrow & J. Smith (Eds.), *Assessment for instruction in early literacy* (pp. 127–200). Englewood Cliffs, NJ: Prentice Hall.

Sulzby, E., Barnhart, J., & Hieshima, J. (1989). Forms of writing and rereading from writing: A preliminary report. In J. Mason (Ed.), *Reading and writing connections* (pp. 31–63). Boston: Allyn and Bacon.

Sulzby, E., & Teale, W. (1991). Emergent literacy. In R. Barr, M. L. Kamil, P. Mosenthal, & P. D. Pearson (Eds.), *Handbook of reading research* (Vol. 2, pp. 727–757). New York: Longman.

Tompkins, G. E. (2003). *Literacy for the 21st century: Teaching reading and writing in pre-kindergarten through grade 4.* Upper Saddle River, NJ: Pearson.

Mathematics in the Inclusive Classroom

Jonathan L. Brendefur and Fernanda Morales-Brendefur

Objectives

After reading this chapter, students will be able to

- Understand more deeply how young children develop mathematical thinking.
- Possess ideas on how to teach mathematics conceptually.
- Know how to reach diverse learners and provide them rich mathematical activities.

Key Terms

Equity
Conceptual understanding
Discourse
Notational System

Introduction to Math

Typically, parents and teachers spend little time helping young children develop mathematical ideas. Some take time to count objects with their toddlers, and even fewer ask them to join objects (add two quantities together) or separate them (subtract out a quantity from another). This chapter focuses on how to best help young children develop mathematical ideas, observe the world through a mathematical lens, and gain mathematical confidence and skills.

In general, many adults, including elementary teachers, have a false notion that young children do not or can not think deeply about mathematics. They believe mathematics should not be introduced or taught in preschool and kindergarten. If they do believe it should be introduced, it usually focuses on counting objects and doing basic calculations. Learning how young children develop mathematical understanding in preschool and through third grade is critical to enabling children, all children, to become mathematically literate. **Equity**, the ability to differentiate and reach all children, then, becomes the underlying principle throughout the chapter. In other words, learning how to develop every child's own mathematical understanding and encouraging them to express their experiences mathematically will enable them to create a foundation that will carry them from elementary school mathematics through algebra.

Learning and Teaching Mathematics

Teaching is viewed by many as a craft in which teachers create learning environments that foster students' intellectual development (Fennema & Franke, 1992). In mathematics, an important aspect of any such environment is an opportunity for students to explore mathematical ideas, to deepen their understanding of these ideas, to make mathematical connections within and outside mathematics (Brown & Borko, 1992; NCTM, 1991, 2000), and to feel safe and empowered to do so (Lampert, 1989).

As indicated in reports regarding the Third International Mathematics and Science Study (TIMSS), the ability of U.S. students to compete with students from other nations has become a national priority (Stigler & Hiebert, 1999). Initiatives have examined, and are currently examining, how mathematics is taught in U.S. schools and how students learn best. These initiatives, sparked by mediocre performances of U.S. students on international achievement tests, have fueled the development of innovative models and programs (as can be seen from the National Science Foundation's [NSF] commitment to fund curricula projects in the mid-nineties).

These national proposals stem, in part, from two events. First, there is a national concern that American students are not learning enough or the right type of mathematics (NCEE, 1983; NCES, 1990, 1996; Stigler & Hiebert, 1999). Second, current research on learning has demonstrated that students understand topics in greater detail and become better problem solvers when they learn mathematics as an interconnected web of knowledge as opposed to one mathematical topic at a time in isolation from real-world or complex events (Hiebert & Carpenter, 1992; Romberg, 1992).

In addition, when serious discussions about curriculum, instruction, and assessment standards for the teaching of mathematics began in the 1980s, mathematics educators also began discussing the possible ramifications of reform on teachers' knowledge of mathematics and their approach to teaching it. To teach to such standards, a teacher needs knowledge of how mathematics is constructed and connected and knowledge of how students might think (informally and formally)

about the mathematics. Unfortunately, after two decades of working within the mathematics reform movement, elementary teachers are still entering the teaching field unprepared to teach mathematics in the way envisioned by these standards (Frykholm, 1996; Zeichner, 1993). In addition, most elementary teachers have not experienced mathematics in this manner (Cohen & Ball, 1990; Knapp & Peterson, 1995). Due to this lack of exposure to rich mathematical experiences, and because it becomes increasingly difficult for teachers to acquire the knowledge, skills, and dispositions to teach in ways aligned with the reform once out in the field (Cuban, 1990; Frykholm, 1996; Richardson, 1990), it becomes critical for elementary teachers to be in situations where they can experience mathematics in the aforementioned ways.

Our concerns lie at the heart of enculturating elementary students into a field of mathematics that uses reasoning to make sense of problems, that moves from informal ideas to more formal and abstract ones, and that uses articulation of one's ideas and conjectures as a focal point to improved understanding. In addition to enculturating students into this type of mathematics, it is equally important that teachers understand the developmental nature and connectedness of students' thinking about mathematics. In other words, teachers must know not only the formalism of mathematics but the informal and generative process of students' mathematical ideas and how to encourage fluid growth of these ideas as well.

Moreover, teachers' existing belief structures regarding the nature of mathematics play a large part in determining not only what mathematics is taught but how it is conveyed. Hence, many teachers who never experienced mathematics conceptually as learners, or who view mathematics as a static, hierarchical field instead of a dynamic, interconnected set of ideas (Thompson, 1992), later resist the adoption of such pedagogical strategies in their own teaching practices (Brendefur, 1999; Frykholm, in press). The goal for primary teachers is to create intellectually rich learning environments for their students.

The Importance of Teacher and Pedagogical Knowledge

Over the last sixteen years, there have been many articles focusing on elementary teachers' content and pedagogical content knowledge (Ball, Lubienski, & Mewborn, 2001; Ball & Mosenthal, 1990; Ma, 1999; McDiarmid & Ball, 1989; Mewborn, 2000; Sowder, Philipp, Armstrong, & Schappelle, 1998). The premise is that, if teachers' develop greater content knowledge, then their mathematics teaching will improve along with their students' performances.

Most elementary teachers enter the teaching force having taken only a few courses with limited mathematics. Typically, they are required to take two college mathematics courses that emphasize arithmetic, basic geometry, and possibly some simple probability and statistics. Few elementary teachers have a major or minor in mathematics. And once out in the field, these teachers rarely receive professional development focusing on the **conceptual understanding** behind the mathematics; instead, typical mathematics professional development focuses on gimmicks, tricks, and only sometimes innovative ways to teach mathematics (Frechtling, Sharp, Carey, & Vaden-Kiernan, 1995). It is critical, then, that elementary teachers have the opportunities to understand both the procedural and conceptual underpinnings of the mathematics they are teaching in order to increase their students' mathematical understanding (Grouws & Cebulla, 2000).

Many researchers have written about the different types of knowledge teachers should have in order to teach for understanding (Ball, 1989; Ball et al., 2001; Fennema & Romberg, 1999; Grossman, Wilson, & Shulman, 1989; McDiarmid, Ball, & Anderson, 1989; Putnam, Heaton, Prawat, & Remillard, 1992). Noticeably, all of these types of knowledge are grounded in Shulman's (1986) three categories of knowledge. First, subject-matter knowledge is the structure of the subject. There are substantive structures organizing the concepts within the subject and syntactic structures categorizing the rules that govern the subject. This describes teachers' procedural and conceptual knowledge. Shulman's second form of knowledge is their pedagogical content knowledge. It is ". . . in a word, the ways of representing and formulating the subject that make it comprehensible to others" (Shulman, 1986). This knowledge enables a teacher to present the mathematics to students in a way that maximizes understanding and minimizes mistakes and misconceptions. The third form of knowledge is curricular knowledge. It involves knowing alternative curricular materials. When we refer to a teacher's knowledge of mathematics, we are referring to her or his knowledge of mathematics: how students develop mathematical knowledge and knowledge of the environment or the types of situations a student should be in to gain a deep foundation of mathematical knowledge. This type of teaching can be described as teaching for understanding.

Mathematical Understanding

Understanding is described as knowing *how* to do something and *why*. Knowing why enables us to use concepts flexibly, extend our knowledge to new situations, and connect it to the world outside of school (Ball, 1989; Hiebert et al., 1997; McDiarmid et al., 1989; NCTM, 2000; Newmann & Associates, 1996; Perkins, 1993). However, conceptual understanding is rarely seen in U.S. mathematics classrooms, and, therefore, content is taught as isolated rules or procedures to be memorized (Ma, 1999; Mewborn, 2000; Stigler & Hiebert, 1999). Teaching conceptually helps students extend their knowledge to new situations (Grouws & Cebulla, 2000; Hiebert & Carpenter, 1992). If mathematical ideas are only seen in isolation, it is unlikely that students will use their previous knowledge in new situations (Ball, 1989; Borko et al., 1992; Ma, 1999; Newmann & Associates, 1996).

Ma (1999) conducted an in-depth study of teachers' mathematical understandings in four main areas: subtraction with regrouping, multidigit multiplication, division by fraction, and area and perimeter. Considering it is the most basic of the four concepts, most people would assume teachers would have a deep understanding of subtraction with regrouping. However, Ma found that 77 percent of the U.S. teachers in her study had only procedural knowledge of the concept. These teachers knew how to subtract with regrouping but could not provide sufficient explanations of why regrouping works. In Mewborn's (2000) analysis of research, she cites many other studies that document teachers who lacked mathematical understanding. "For example, Ball (1988) found that half of the preservice elementary teachers she interviewed thought that zero divided by zero was zero, and an additional 20 percent of the elementary candidates stated they could not remember the rule for division by zero and were unable to answer the question" (Mewborn, 2000).

If teachers have limited knowledge of the mathematical content they teach, it is unlikely they will be able to teach for understanding. Many studies demonstrate that the quality of what and how a teacher teaches is influenced by the teacher's knowledge (Ball et al., 2001; Ball & Mosenthal, 1990; Borko et al., 1992; Grossman et al., 1989; Ma, 1999; McDiarmid & Ball, 1989; Mewborn, 2000; Putnam et al., 1992). In fact, Ma (1999) found that teachers who expected their students to only know mathematical procedures tended to have only procedural knowledge themselves.

Ball (1989; Ball & Wilson, 1990) has illustrated the need for more than just subject-matter knowledge in her studies that compared mathematical knowledge of preservice elementary education majors and preservice secondary mathematics education majors. She found that secondary majors answered more questions correctly but were unable to explain the mathematical reasoning behind the procedures they used to obtain those correct answers. Mewborn (Mewborn, 2000) found that, in over four decades of research on teacher knowledge, all the studies concluded that teachers, in general, lack a conceptual understanding of many elementary mathematics concepts. Therefore, we now turn the discussion to how knowledge is developed and then move to how to create learning environments that best build mathematical ideas.

Math Process Skills

"We construct our knowledge of our world from our perceptions and experiences, which are themselves mediated through our previous knowledge. Learning is the process by which human beings adapt to their experiential world" (Simon, 1995). This opening quote is our focal point for teaching mathematics. All students, at all ages, enter into solving a problem or having a discussion with beliefs about the topic. Some of these ideas might be correct and others may not. Teachers must be able to discern between the two and create instructional spaces that ensure all students learn. Some students will have many more experiences and might have more innate ability to do mathematics, which makes the teacher's work much more difficult. To develop as a teacher in order to really work with all students, it is important to understand how knowledge is acquired and retained over time. There are two critical aspects of understanding that are drawn from a structural and a functional perspective (Hiebert et al., 1996). The ideas below should provide you with reasons for changing your mathematics instruction to become more cognitively structured.

Structural Perspective of Understanding

Cognitive psychologists propose that knowledge is structured with weblike connections, hierarchal connections, or a combination of both. Understanding is then described as "the way information is represented and structured" in the mind and evolves by increasing or strengthening these hierarchal and/or weblike connections (Hiebert & Carpenter, 1992). "More specifically, the mathematics is understood if its mental representation is part of a network of representations" (Hiebert & Carpenter, 1992). Presuming that knowledge is represented by connections of related ideas, understanding can be thought of as a network of strands called *schemata* (Anderson, 1995; Brewer & Nakamura, 1984; Hiebert & Carpenter, 1992). Each network, or schema, holds a number of related pieces of information. The more or stronger the connections (or related pieces of information) are, the more complex the network and the higher degree of understanding there is (Hiebert & Carpenter, 1992). Greater understanding of phenomena occurs by linking a representation of a new fact to an existing network, by forming new connections between networks, by reorganizing existing networks, or by revising or abandoning old erroneous connections.

The last way of increasing understanding, revising or abandoning old erroneous connections, needs further elaboration. Erroneous strands are bits of information that may be true for some circumstances but not others or are altogether false. These strands are usually referred to as misconceptions. Understanding may be weak in an area when a person's network contains erroneous strands or when it has many weak links. For example, some students make a connection that when two numbers are multiplied the product is larger than either of the multiplicands. It should be no surprise when these same students question the answer to the problem, What is three-tenths times three? These students had a valid conception that worked for most of the multiplication cases they had previously encountered. However, when confronted with multiplying a number by a rational number between zero and one, they must reorganize their current schema to include this new case. Students do this by reorganizing their schema in some way (Smith, diSessa, & Roschelle, 1993).

The work of developing constructive conceptions and mitigating misconceptions is the work of primary teachers. It is a view of learning that holds that students actively integrate incoming information with preexisting knowledge that is already structured in some way. Students use this existing knowledge to make sense of incoming ideas. Understanding increases when children continually find or create relationships between the new incoming information and existing schemata. "Without schema into which new information can be assimilated, experience is incomprehensible and therefore, little can be learned from it" (Romberg, 1993). This argument refers to learning isolated pieces of information: The less that knowledge is connected to other knowledge, the more difficult it is for students to make sense of the incoming information and remember it long-term. From this structural position on understanding, instruction aims toward creating situations that assist students in organizing new information so as to build well-connected schemata.

When instruction ignores students' existing knowledge, their understanding might become more localized and restricted in use. For example, Konold (1993) found that, when students' misconceptions about probability were not confronted during a course on probability, they tended to maintain two separate schemas pertaining to probability. One schema held preexisting or informal intuitions about probability, while the other one contained formal probabilistic notions learned in class. He also discovered that students used these separate schemas at different times to solve different problems. Konold hypothesized that new schemas had been formed, but students never created the necessary connections between their informal and formal knowledge. Another possibility is that the students' new connections or reorganized schemas were still too weak relative to their old conceptions to be used effectively to solve the probability problems.

This finding implies that, when there are no connections (or at best, weak connections) that link two or more "supposedly related" schemas, students have difficulty seeing and using the information to solve problems. Thus, if instruction encourages connections to be made, informal schemas could be reorganized into more formal schemas. Consequently, students' understanding improves. In essence, when students' existing knowledge is confronted with new, possibly opposing or problematic ideas, they must be encouraged to restructure or build upon existing schemata. As students enter school at the age of 4 or 5, they enter with initial conceptions about mathematics. Allowing these

Math Process Skills

conceptions to exist in isolation from other related conceptions limits students' ability to understand the mathematics and to form meaningful and useful relationships later on (Hiebert & Carpenter, 1992; Konold, 1991, 1993; Romberg, 1993). The implication for teachers' pedagogical practices is that tasks need to challenge students to mentally organize new information into their existing knowledge. When this occurs, students' understanding of the topic increases.

Students reorganize and strengthen their mathematical schemas when they have opportunities to make connections among topics, ideas, and perspectives within and outside of mathematics. How teachers best give students these opportunities is discussed below.

Functional Perspective of Understanding

From this perspective, understanding is described in pragmatic terms of how students interact and share knowledge with other students and society (Hiebert et al., 1996). It is a social constructivist view of learning that maintains that students need to have the chance to actively integrate incoming information with existing knowledge through social interactions (Wood, 1993). The ways in which students organize the information or the degree of their understanding can be discovered in situations where students are communicating and reasoning about their ideas.

Mathematics teachers can use students' verbalized conceptions to further individualize instruction by adapting situations to fit individual abilities (Carpenter, Fennema, Peterson, Chiange, & Loef, 1989; Fennema et al., 1996). The problems and tasks teachers present should be rich enough for students to reflect and reorganize their own understanding (Shulman, 1986) as well as to reflect on other students' statements. Hiebert et al. (Hiebert et al., 1996) propose that teachers should not debate whether students should be given information or should discover information themselves but that teachers should "select appropriate tasks, [where] the teacher must draw on two resources: knowledge of the subject to select tasks that encourage students to wrestle with key ideas and knowledge of students' thinking, to select tasks that link with students' experience and for which students can use the relevance of ideas and skills they already possess" (p. 16). Instructional practices from an early age should require students to use reflective or interactive dialogue. In fact, this type of instruction suggests that students should be engaged in extended and elaborated conversations with the teacher and other students on central ideas of mathematics that involve the manipulation of ideas (Newmann, Secada, & Wehlage, 1995).

In further support for mathematical communication, Konold (Konold, 1991) found that shared discussions allowed "students [to] explore in greater depth the implications of and interconnections among their own beliefs" (p. 153). However, he found that it takes more than just one discussion to subdue any inconsistencies and to promote wanted outcomes. The schemas students create are very complex and self-consistent (Konold, 1991). In other words, students need to be put in situations where, through articulation, they can reflect on how they solved the problem and constructed relationships. This suggests that, by being in problematic situations where they must communicate to others their understandings, students are more able to construct lasting and coherent schema or understanding of the topic.

Hiebert and Carpenter (Hiebert & Carpenter, 1992) also promote mathematical communication through shared discussion. During this open exchange of ideas, the teacher can carefully monitor and direct the conversation toward desired outcomes, allowing students to reorganize their current schemas—or at least to confront some inadequacies or misconceptions.

Substantive conversation, as promoted in this framework, is supported by previous research. First, students reveal their understanding of the mathematics and their ability to make sense of it through conversations. Second, elaborated communication among students allows them to share their ideas and to see whether they are thinking about the problem or situation in similar ways as their classmates. In both situations, the conversation is used as a learning technique for the teacher and the students.

Beliefs and Knowledge

Beliefs have been defined as "proposition[s], conscious or unconscious, inferred from what a person says or does" (Rokeach, 1969) and as "assumptions about the nature of reality that underlie goal-oriented activity" (Cobb, 1986). Whether assumptions or propositions, beliefs are thoughts that people base action upon. They are a set of ideas that are dependent on specific contexts and are related to certain behaviors.

Furthermore, beliefs are formed by a person's informal and formal experiences (Schoenfeld, 1985). In other words, a person's "beliefs are created through a process of enculturation and social construction" (Pajares, 1992). Hence, mathematics teachers' beliefs about education have been formed, to some degree, by their own K–12 educational experiences, their college content and educational methods courses, life experiences, and their exposure to teaching students (Brown & Borko, 1992). All of these experiences affect teachers' beliefs and, therefore, the decisions they make in the classroom.

The working hypothesis of this chapter is that "beliefs are more influential than knowledge in determining how individuals organize and define tasks and problems and are stronger predictors of behavior" (Pajares, 1992). Typically, beliefs differ from knowledge in that beliefs do not need to be validated by others while knowledge does. Beliefs are more personal and based on one's own experiences and assumptions. Knowledge can be used to form beliefs, but not all beliefs are based on externally verified knowledge. A number of different possibilities can occur. In one case, knowledge can generate or mold beliefs. However, in another case, a person can know something but believe something else. A third possibility is that a person believes something but does not know if it is true or externally validated. In all cases there are interrelationships among beliefs, knowledge, and action.

The more strongly or more centrally a belief is held, the more difficult it is to change (Pajares, 1992). Beliefs are also similar to schemata in that they can be relatively isolated from other beliefs (Rokeach, 1969). When beliefs are distantly connected to other beliefs, people can hold perceivably inconsistent beliefs, and, depending on the context, they can take a higher priority relative to one another. It is essential, then, when teaching young students that misconceptions are not promoted from an early stage. For instance, young children are told that they cannot subtract a larger number from a smaller number. This not the case, and young children can hold this belief for many years and in isolation of others. Language and vocabulary become important for similar reasons. An example here is saying "corner" for *vertex* when discussing geometric shapes.

Differentiating Instruction in Math

"Every learner—bilingual students, students [with disabilities], students of all ethnic groups, students who live in poverty, girls, and boys—can learn mathematics with understanding. In order to do this, each student must have access to learning with understanding" (Hiebert et al., 1997). This opening quote summarizes our major tenet for learning mathematics with understanding. Our work, then, as primary teachers, is to create these types of spaces for all children to learn.

If equity is achieved by promoting understanding, then we must create situations for all students to learn no matter their cognitive, social, ethnic, language or social background. Before continuing we ask the reader to think about her own vision of equity and how it plays out in classroom settings. We believe that teaching for understanding creates equitable situations for students to develop as mathematical thinkers and, as such, encourages mathematical power. Here, a more substantive conversation will ensue regarding equity.

Many elementary teachers do not believe they themselves are mathematical thinkers and, therefore, have an impoverished grasp on the content and its processes. Furthermore, and especially in mathematics, elementary teachers are not comfortable venturing out of the conventional transfer-of-facts mode and, thus, create educational experiences that are not equitable for many marginalized students. The purpose of this section is to highlight theoretically how we build intellectual spaces. We then spend the rest of the chapter demonstrating how to steep students in these types of experiences, promoting equity for all students.

In order to change elementary teachers' instructional practices to enable their own and their students' ability to reason mathematically, to explore, analyze, and debate, it is essential to create situations for our students to feel, think about, and construct mathematical practices—in other words, to empower all students to understand mathematics. The students must become enculturated into an environment of quality learning where they discuss and reflect on the consequences of their mathematical decisions. One key aspect of this is that students should encounter dissonance: It is by being on the edge, by pushing students to a level of understanding that touches the boundaries of knowledge—the grey, soft edges—where understanding truly grows.

In addition to gaining equity by pressing children's knowledge to the border of their understanding, it is also essential to make connections. Students should not walk away from school disassociating mathematics from the real world. Teachers must create a mathematical environment that enables them to make these connections. "One important purpose of mathematics education is to prepare students to incorporate mathematical reasoning and communication into their everyday lives. However, conventional pedagogy has often persuaded students to consider school mathematics as a subject divorced from their everyday experiences and from their attempts to make sense of their world" (Tate, 1994).

By centering the mathematical discussions along the lines of discovery, connections, notations, similarities, differences, strategies, and cognitive conflict, teachers produce students who are not only mathematically literate, but who think mathematically. All students then have the chance to be successful, instead of the few that actually finish algebra in high school. In essence, we are ensuring that students are building a solid foundation for taking and understanding advanced mathematics.

Mathematical Discourse

In an effort to foster teaching practices that focus on how students think about, talk about, and represent mathematics, the NCTM Standards documents (NCTM, 1989, 1991, 2000) strongly recommend mathematical communication as a fundamental element in daily classroom activity. Learners need "extensive experience listening to, reading about, writing about, speaking about, reflecting on, and demonstrating mathematical ideas" (NCTM, 1989). Advocated are activities in which students explore and investigate mathematics, make connections, attempt definitions, and make basic generalizations.

For teaching, there are four levels of communication that should all be encouraged during classroom instruction: *unidirectional, contributive, reflective, and instructive communication* (Brendefur & Frykholm, 2000). *Unidirectional* communication is commonplace in our schools and occurs when teachers dominate discussions by lecturing, asking closed questions, and allowing few opportunities for students to communicate their strategies, ideas, and thinking. This type of communication is obviously needed, but only to a point. If this type of discussion is too commonplace, then students do not construct the big ideas in mathematics (Cooney & Shealy, 1997; Cooney, Shealy, & Arvold, 1998).

Some of the mathematical discussions should include *contributive communication*, in which the conversations move between the teacher and, usually, a student. This type of communication allows for students to provide feedback in the way of explaining how they solved a problem. Typically the conversation is limited to assistance or sharing, with little or no deep thought. For example, teachers may provide opportunities for students to discuss mathematical tasks with one another, to present solution strategies, or to assist each other in the development of solutions and appropriate problem solving strategies. These conversations are typically corrective in nature (e.g., "This is how you do it . . .").

The type of mathematical teaching we support encourages a type of *reflective communication*. It includes some contributive communication like sharing ideas, but goes deeper allowing these initial conversations to be springboards into deeper ideas. This type of dialogue parallels the equity discussion we presented earlier. Students are now encouraged to make various connections and to understand the mathematics at a much broader level. Both students and the teachers become reflective of the mathematics and the processes they are using to make sense of the mathematical situations. This kind of rich, reflective **discourse** often occurs as students attempt to justify or refute conjectures posed by peers (Lampert, 1990).

Instructive communication takes reflective communication one step farther. Teachers are now using students' ideas as the curriculum guide. This type of communication brings together each child's own prior knowledge with the prior knowledge built on a day-to-day experience in the classroom. By doing this, teachers increase the chances of children developing procedural and conceptual understanding or simply the ability to make sense of the mathematics and how to use it. As the thinking of the students is exposed, teachers not only begin to understand the thought processes, strengths, and limitations of particular students, they also begin to shape subsequent instruction (Fennema & Franke, 1992; Steffe & D'Ambrosio, 1995).

Thus far, we have provided the theoretical foundations and reasons for developing children's mathematical thinking. It will take teachers much more effort, time, and patience than before to create this type of classroom. However, the rewards are amazing for both the teacher and the student. The remainder of the chapter focuses on how to build these environments with young children. We discuss the mathematical ideas and the teacher approach for the different mathematical topics.

Constructing Knowledge in Math

How Students Develop Ideas of Number

Developing concepts in number and algebra is viewed by most mathematics educators as the hinge to promoting and understanding all other mathematical ideas. It is for this reason that many elementary teachers and textbooks focus much of their activities on adding, subtracting, multiplying, and dividing. This next section highlights a simple framework to help teachers understand and select or build tasks around number operations and number sense.

In 1986 Carpenter presented a framework of eleven different problem types for addition and subtraction problems and three for multiplication and division problems (Carpenter, Fennema, Franke, Levi, & Empson, 1999). These problem types allow teachers to determine which problems to present to students to build understanding of number and early algebraic ideas. In addition, these problem types become windows into how children develop mathematical ideas.

The basic structure of the eleven addition and subtraction problem types are presented in Table 9.1. Knowing the problem-type structures enable the teacher to either find appropriate problems or create them. It is from these problem types that much of the early childhood mathematics curriculum is built. Notice that each of the problems has three pairs of numbers that can be placed into the blanks of the story. These numbers are chosen with increasing difficulty in size. Once a problem has been solved using the smaller pair of numbers, the student can continue on with the next set. The number pairs can be modified for older students as well. The structure of the problem remains, but the number choices change based on the appropriate developmental stage of the child. For older students the number pairs would include larger numbers than three digits and would include such numbers as fractions, percents, and decimals. Below, we will explain the significance of each type of problem (see Table 9.1).

Join problems. The first row contains three problem types, which are considered join problems. Each of these problem types follows an addition number sentence where the word problem includes an action for the students to model. In all three problems, the first two sentences of the story are written that a person has something, in this case pencils, and then picks up more of them. The joining action in the second sentence is located in the verb "pick." This action provides the child with a verbal clue on how to solve the problem.

The final sentence in each of the problems is a question referring to the unknown quantity. The unknown quantity has three different locations in each of the problems and is what makes each of the problems different. The first problem type is the Join Result Unknown. Here, the student is told how many pencils Allison has and how many she picks up. The unknown quantity is the result of joining the first two quantities. Once children begin to count and have an initial understanding of one-to-one correspondence, they are able to solve this type of problem—typically with manipulatives. (Note that more detailed information regarding students' strategies and development of concepts will be explained in the next section.)

The next problem type, Join Change Unknown, places the unknown in the change location. In our example, the child knows how many pencils Jason has and the total number of pencils he has after the Jason has picked up an unknown amount. Again, young children can solve this problem with manipulatives and tend to do so by counting out 2 pencils and then counting out more pencils

Table 9.1 ● Addition and Subtraction Problem Types

Join Result Unknown	Join Change Unknown	Join Start Unknown
Allison has __ pencils. She picked up __ more pencils. How many pencils does she have now? (3, 1) (5, 8) (17, 24)	Jason has __ pencils. He picked up some more pencils. Now he has __ pencils. How many pencils did he pick up? (2, 5) (4, 9) (11, 24)	Maria has some pencils. She picked up __ more pencils. Now she has __ pencils. How many pencils did she have at the start? (2, 3) (3, 8) (14, 23)

Separate Result Unknown	Separate Change Unknown	Separate Start Unknown
Rachel has __ stickers. She used __ of them. How many stickers does she have now? (3, 1) (8, 5) (24, 17)	Juan has __ stickers. He used some of them. He now has __ stickers. How many stickers does Juan have left? (5, 2) (9, 6) (27, 9)	Isabel has some stickers. She used __ of them. Now she has __ stickers. How many stickers did she have to begin with? (1, 3) (3, 8) (14, 23)

Part-Part-Whole: Whole Unknown		Part-Part-Whole: Part Unknown
Megan has __ brown puppies and __ white puppies. How many puppies does she have altogether? (2, 1) (7, 8) (12, 9)		Tanali has __ puppies. __ of them are brown and the rest are white. How many white puppies does she have? (5, 2) (12, 7) (23, 9)

Compare Difference Unknown	Compare Referent Unknown	Compare Quantity Unknown
Alexander has __ dogs. Rebecca has __ dogs. How many more dogs does Alexander have then Rebecca? (5, 4) (12, 7) (29, 18)	Alexander has __ dogs. He has __ more then Rebecca. How many dogs does Rebecca have? (6, 2) (15, 6) (27, 11)	Alexander has __ dogs. She has __ fewer dogs then Alexander. How many dogs does Rebecca have? (6, 3) (15, 6) (27, 11)

until there are 5. The student then has to determine how many extra pencils were counted out after the initial 2. In order to do so, they must somehow keep this second set separate from the first.

Join Start Unknown problems are the most difficult of the three join problems for very young children to solve. The unknown quantity is at the beginning of the story—Maria has some pencils. Developmentally, young children will grab "some" manipulatives and start with this quantity. They will add 2 more pencils (in this case) and then check to see whether they have the final quantity.

This trial-and-error strategy does not change until children mature and are able to conserve quantity and have temporal sense of past, present, and future.

Separate problems. Separate problems are similar to join problems in that there is an action involved in the story that helps the child solve the problem, and that the unknown quantity can occur in the three locations. Each number sentence for the separate problem types follows a subtraction format (e.g., $3 - 1 = \Box$; $5 - \Box = 2$; $\Box - 1 = 3$).

For Separate Result Unknown problems, the child begins knowing the initial quantity—for instance, Rachel has 3 stickers. The second sentence gives the child the second quantity and information about how to solve the problem. In this case, the child hears that Rachel used 1 sticker and then uses this information to separate out 1 sticker from the original 3.

In the Separate Change Unknown problem, the child is given the initial quantity of 5 stickers, but how that quantity changes is unknown—Juan used some of the stickers. The third sentence gives the final information that Juan now has 2 stickers. Young children using manipulatives count out the original 5 stickers and then remove stickers/manipulatives until there are 2 remaining. The children then count the number of stickers that were used or pulled out of the group of 5 to get the answer of 3 stickers.

The Separate Start Unknown problem is the most difficult for young children to solve for the same reasons listed above for the Join Start Unknown problems. To solve this problem, young children tend to use a trial-and-error method. They pull some manipulatives out of pile to start with and then separate out the number given—in this case, 1 sticker. The child then checks to see whether there are indeed 3 stickers left. If not, the number of original stickers/manipulates pulled out is modified—most often haphazardly.

Part-part-whole problems. Part-part-whole problems are the most universal of all the problem types. Structurally, there are only two unknowns: either one of the parts or the whole. In the example, Megan is given the two parts—brown and white puppies—and then must use this information to find the whole—the number of puppies. This problem type is similar to the Join Result Unknown problem except for two important differences. First, the verbs in the sentences do not give the child any clues on how to solve the problem. In this example, Megan "has" brown and white puppies. The verb "has" does provide a hint on whether to add the puppies together or to separate them. Verbs like "pick" and "used" have the connotation of joining and separating. Second, part-part-whole problems are created using a context where there is something—the whole—and then that something is broken into two or more parts.

When the parts are given and the whole is the unknown, children tend to solve it in a similar way as to the Join Result Unknown problem. When one of the parts is missing, children tend to solve this problem type in a similar way to a Separate Result Unknown problem.

These two problem types, however, can be used to create other problems within and outside the domain of number. Here are a few examples. The child could be asked of what fraction of the whole are brown puppies or white puppies. To get at proportional thinking, you might ask what the ratio is of brown puppies to white puppies. Or, how many brown and white puppies would there be if the proportion stayed the same but there were twice or three times as many total puppies? Furthermore, the child might be asked to predict whether a white puppy or brown puppy might be chosen at random from the litter.

Compare problems. Compare problems are similar to the part-part-whole problems in that there is no action, and the verbs do not necessarily tell the child what to do with the numbers. There are three types of compare problems and all can be used to extend to the domain of graphing. The first compare problem type is the Compare Difference Unknown. Unlike the part-part-whole problem that focuses on one unique set or whole, the compare problems entertain two related but unique sets that can be compared. For instance, Alexander has 5 dogs—a distinct set—and Rebecca has 4 dogs—another distinct set. The child is then asked to provide the difference between the two sets. Commonly, a child is asked to state how many more dogs Alexander has than Rebecca. However, the question, "How many fewer dogs does Rebecca have than Alexander?" is also appropriate. Very young children have a difficult time hearing the phrase "how many more" and instead answer the question as "How many dogs does Alexander have?" instead of "How many more dogs does Alexander have?" Another question that might be substituted for young children would be, "How many more dogs does Rebecca need to have to have the same number of dogs that Alexander has?"

Because there is no action in the problem, children tend to solve it as a join problem and combine the two numbers. Be encouraging children to match the two separate quantities or, in essence, graph them using cubes (or drawings when they are older), children can manipulate or visually observe the pairings and count the ones that are different or do not match.

The other two problem types are Compare Referent Unknown and the Compare Quantity Unknown. These two problems start out the same by giving information about one of the quantities. In our example, the following information is given: Alexander has 6 dogs. Then information is given about the same person in relation to the referent—Alexander has 4 more dogs than Rebecca. Here, Rebecca is the referent, and this information is unknown. For this reason, this type of problem is called Referent Unknown. When the problem starts out the same—Alexander has 6 dogs—but the then information is given about the other person—Rebecca has 4 fewer dogs than Alexander—the problem is labeled Quantity Unknown. In either case, the child has to determine whether to add or subtract from the given amount based on the rest of the clues in the problem.

Developmental Strategies for Solving Addition and Subtraction Problems

There are three classifications for solving addition and subtraction problems: direct modeling, counting, and derived facts (Carpenter et al., 1999). These strategies are developmental in nature, which means a child will first solve the problems by directly modeling the information given. After they mature cognitively, they advance to counting strategies and then derived facts. It is the teacher's role to provide different problems for students to solve and encourage them to solve the problem based on their developmental maturity. This means that a child who directly models a problem may not be able to count on or use derived facts. It is important to encourage students to solve the problem using a method that makes sense to them and then to slowly encourage more advanced and abstract thinking. A cautionary note is to not impose a teacher's strategy. The child may mimic the strategy and solve a similar set of problems, but at a cost to the students' understanding. Once the child begins to mimic the more advanced strategies without conceptual understanding, the child begins to lose number sense and consistent building of ideas.

To describe the three different strategies, the following Join Result Unknown (JRU) problem will be used. Allison has 5 pencils. She picked up 8 more pencils. How many pencils does she have now?

Soon after students begin to count and have one-to-one correspondence they begin solving addition and subtraction problems using a direct modeling technique. A student in this stage will solve the above problem by counting out each set in the problem. Somehow the child must keep track of each set, which is easily accomplished with manipulatives, fingers, tally marks, or some similar technique. In the above problem, a child might do the following:

Push out five cubes: □□□□□, saying "1, 2, 3, 4, 5"

Push out eight cubes: □□□□□□□□ , saying "1, 2, 3, 4, 5, 6, 7, 8"

Join both sets together physically: □□□□□□□□□□□□□ , recounting them all and saying, "1, 2, 3, 4, 5, 6, 7, 8, 9, 10, 11, 12, 13"

The child demonstrates knowledge of one-to-one correspondence for numbers up to 13 and the conceptual understanding of adding two groups together.

As children mature, they move into the counting stage. This occurs around age 6 but is different for every child and is not a trivial matter or one that can be forced. In order for children to move into the counting stage, they must be able to retain or hold a number in their head. Different than in the direct modeling stage, a child does not have to count both sets—only one. In this example, the child might solve the problem by counting on from the first. She would say, "5 pencils, so 6, 7, 8, 9, 10, 11, 12, 13." Here, the child uses fingers or tally marks to keep track of the 8 pencils picked up. In this case, the manipulatives were used as place holders to count up, instead of being used to represent each number in each set as they were used when directly modeling the problem. Furthermore, when children's understanding develops, they will be able to solve the problem by counting on from the larger number. This occurs when a child's sense of temporal placement matures. Here a child can start in the middle of the story, "Allison picks up 8 more pencils" and then go back to the beginning of the story, "Allison has 5 pencils."

The final stage is derived facts. This developmental stage marks the advent of a child's abstract thinking with numbers and the beginning of using and building facts. Once in this stage, a child's thinking and choice of strategies becomes flexible. To be labeled within this stage a child uses multiple facts to derive the answer. Many of the derived fact strategies can be characterized as decomposing strategy or compensating. For instance, when a child says, "I know that 5 and 5 is 10 and 3 more is 13," she has decomposed the 8 into a 5 and 3. She has knowledge of the 5's double and understands that 8 can be broken into other numbers such as a 5 and a 3 to solve this problem. A child could also solve this problem by compensating. He might say, "I know that 5 and 10 is 15. I added 2 to the 8 to get 10, so I have to subtract 2 from 15. The answer is 13." In both cases, each child knows number facts and uses number sense to solve the problem. These two strategies are extremely useful to their construction and comprehensive knowledge of mathematics.

Decomposing, compensating, and notational systems. To be able to understand number means being to be able to understand abstract relationships. Children begin their mathematical journey by counting objects. At first, they count by memorizing the sequence of numbers similarly to memorizing the sequence of letters in the alphabet. When 4-year-olds count objects, it is typical for them to say, "1, 2, 3, 4, 5, 6, 7, 9, 10," skipping 8. After repeating this sequence again and again children finally memorize the correct sequence, but this does not mean that they necessarily under-

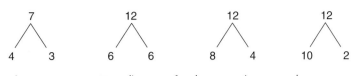

Figure 9.1 • Tree diagrams for decomposing a number.

stand quantity (Kamii, 2000). It is not until later that children understand that counting 1, 2, 3 objects means that there are 3 objects.

After children develop one-to-one correspondence and have an understanding of quantity, they begin to solve addition and subtraction problems through direct modeling, then counting strategies, and finally derived facts. Once in this latter stage, students' thoughts and calculations become more complex. This is when they need to begin using **notational systems**. There are two systems that enable students to build understanding of number and place value: tree diagram and arrow language.

Encouraging children to decompose or break numbers apart is very important to building number sense and place value. In Figure 9.1 there are some examples of decomposing the numbers 7 and 12 using *tree diagrams*. Initially, ask students to decompose numbers into two addends. Students write the number and then draw two branches below it, writing the two addends below. The tree diagram is a simple visual that allows children to observe the relationship between the numbers (see Figure 9.1).

Initially, students should be able to break down any number. For instance, 7 can be broken into a 4 and a 3, and a 12 can be broken down into a 6 and a 6. This can be shown with manipulatives, a picture, or the tree diagram. Asking children to decompose numbers into other combinations is important for developing children's number sense. To extend this activity, you ask students to find all the possible ways to break the number 7 into two numbers. Once students believe they have completed this task, ask them whether they have all the possible combinations and, if so, how they could justify whether they have all the possibilities.

Later, when solving problems, it is important students know how to decompose numbers in a way to use them to solve problems. If the problem is, "There are 12 cookies on a plate. Your mom puts 12 more cookies on the plate. How many cookies do you have all together?" the students can decompose the problem in, at least, two useful ways (see Figure 9.2).

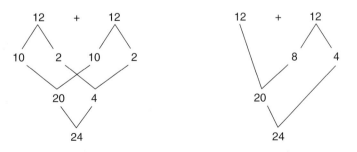

Figure 9.2 • Decomposing strategy using a tree diagram notation.

Figure 9.3 • Decomposing strategy using an arrow language notation.

In the first example in Figure 9.2, the student decomposed both 12s into 10s and 2s. Here, the student is demonstrating an understanding of number sense and place value. The student then puts together the 10s and the 2s to get 20 and 4, and finally 24. In the second example, the student realized that 8 more than 12 would get her to 20. The remaining 4 is easily added to get a sum of 24.

Another notational system that students can use to keep track of their thinking and find the result is *arrow language*. This notation is very useful when decomposing numbers and when a student might have multiple calculations. Using the previous problem, a student's strategy might look like one of the arrow language examples in Figure 9.3.

Both notional strategies help build students' ability to solve problems along with building number sense and a solid understanding of place value (both procedurally and conceptually).

Another strategy for solving problems for children in this developmental stage is *compensation*. Here, students modify one of the numbers to make them "more friendly." For instance, if a student was to add the numbers 28 and 17, she might say, "Well, 28 is close to 30. And 30 and 17 is 47. But I added 2 to 28 to get 30, so I must subtract 2 from 47 to an answer of 45. Compensation is a very useful strategy in many different situations. For instance, asking older students (or adults) to solve 2000 − 999 is very taxing when trying to use the conventional subtraction algorithm. A compensation strategy makes the problem easy. 2000 minus 1000 is 1000. Compensating by taking away the extra 1 (the difference between 999 and 1000) means adding one back, to get 1001.

Multiplication and Division Problems

Besides solving addition and subtraction problems, young children can also solve simple multiplication and division problems. There are three basic problem types that can be written, depending on where the unknown is: multiplication, measurement division, and partitive division (see Table 9.2).

In preschool, students should be encouraged to place objects into equal groups. For instance, place 6 objects on the floor. Ask the student to separate out 2 objects at a time or 3 objects at a time. Then change the larger amount. This task builds ideas of separating out and grouping. This process is the first step toward understanding multiplication.

Multiplication. Similarly to solving addition and subtraction problems, young children approach multiplication and division problems through stages: direct modeling, a version of counting, and derived facts. Young children will solve the first multiplication problem in Table 9.2 using the numbers 2 and 5 by directly modeling. They will typically draw two circles to represent the 2 fish bowls in the story and, then, count out 1 fish/manipulative at a time and place them in the first fish bowl until they reach 5. Then they will repeat the process, placing the second set of 5 in the second bowl. Finally, they will count all the fish, "1, 2, 3, 4, . . . 9, 10. Ten fish!"

To help students in transition between direct modeling and derived facts, have students practice skip counting a few times a week. For younger children have students progress through the numbers 2, 5, and 10. Later, students can practice counting by 3s and 4s, and then finally 6s, 7s, 8s, and 9s.

Table 9.2 ● Multiplication and Division Problem Types

Multiplication	Measurement Division	Partitive Division
Ann has __ fish bowls.	David has __ cups of Fruity cereal.	Marilynn has __ beads.
She has __ fish in each bowl.	He eats __ cups of cereal a day.	She has __ braids.
How many fish does she have altogether? (2, 5) (4, 9) (8, 12)	How many days can he eat cereal? (4, 2) (12, 3) (84, 7)	How many beads will go on each braid, if she puts the same number on each braid? (6, 2) (15, 3) (54, 6)

Ask students to begin counting at 0 to a designated number and then reverse the counting. The reasons for this are explained in the measurement section. As an example, ask the students to count by 2s to 24—0, 2, 4, 6, . . . 24—and then back down, 24, 22, 20, . . . 2, 0. In a classroom situation, ask students to count either in unison, individually in a row, or in popcorn style. In popcorn style, point to a student to say the next number in the sequence. Select students at random, and come back to the same student from time to time. This last way encourages students to pay attention by anticipating being called on (see Figure 9.4).

Strategy 1

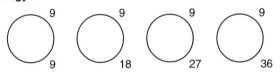

Strategy 2

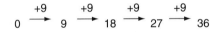

Strategy 3

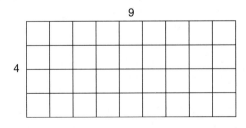

Figure 9.4 ● Arrow language notation for multiplication.

As students develop, they will begin to solve multiplication problems by more advanced strategies. Using the second set of numbers (4, 9) in the multiplication problem, students might solve the problem in the following ways: Some students might draw 4 circles, then place the number 9 in each and count 9, 18, 27, 36 fish. A variation on this strategy is to place the numbers 9, 18, 27, and 36 in the circles. Arrow language notation can be used to depict the students' thought process (see Figure 9.4, strategy 2). Starting with 0 fish, the person adds 9 fish to the first fish bowl, then another 3 more 9s. The arrow language allows the student to keep track of the running total. The third strategy is creating a 4 × 9 area where the students can visually see a geometric representation of the multiplication. Each row represents 9 fish in 1 bowl, or 36 fish in all. Encouraging students to observe and attempt strategies slightly more advanced then their own is one way to promote advanced thinking without sacrificing understanding.

Division.   There are two different types of division problems: measurement division and partitive division. In all division problems the total is known, and either the number of groups or sets or the number of members in each group is missing. In the measurement division problem in Table 9.2, David has 12 cups of cereal and eats 3 cups a day. The total number of cups is known, as is the members. The number of groups is unknown.

Students initially solve the measuring division problem by directly modeling it. As depicted in Figure 9.5, the student will take out 12 manipulatives or draw 12 circles. Then, he will "measure out" 3 cups at a time, saying "1 day, 2 days, 3 days, 4 days." As students' ideas of number become more sophisticated, they begin to use a skip counting strategy and must keep track of each time they skip count. This strategy is similar to the direct modeling strategy, but students do not need to draw a visual. Instead they might keep track with their fingers or tally marks. For more difficult problems or ones using larger numbers, students might use arrow language (see Figure 9.5, strategy 2).

After students' thinking has developed in ways that they can use flexible thinking, they will begin to solve division problems using invented algorithms or derived facts. For instance, if a child was to solve the measurement division problem with the numbers 84 and 7, she might use number facts she already knows (see Figure 9.5, strategy 3). Here she uses the facts of 7 to determine that 12 of them go into 84. This type of flexible problem solving enables students to build conceptual and procedural understanding of division using multiplication ideas (see Figure 9.5).

Partitive division is when the unknown in the problem is the members. In Table 9.2, the first example, Marilynn has 6 beads (the total) and 2 braids (the group). The number of beads on each braid is what students must figure out. Using a direct modeling strategy, students will put out 6 cubes representing the beads and draw 2 circles on a piece of paper. Next, the students will use a dealing-out strategy (similar to dealing out cards) to distribute the beads alternating one at a time into the circles (see Figure 9.6, strategy 1).

As the problems increase in difficulty and the students' ideas advance, they will begin to distribute the cubes into patterns. For instance, using the numbers 15 and 3 in the bead problem, students might distribute 2 beads at a time onto the 3 braids. For instance, a student might say the following: "I put 2, 2, 2 beads on each braid. Six are gone. Then I put 2, 2, 2 beads on each of the braids. I had 3 beads left, so I put 1 bead on each braid. When I counted the number of beads on a braid; it was 2 + 2 + 1 = 5 beads on each braid!" (see Figure 9.6, strategy 2).

It is important to encourage students to use their prior ideas and strategies and to build more sophisticated ideas. After students have experience and success solving the division problems using

Strategy 1

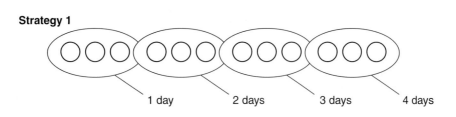

1 day   2 days   3 days   4 days

Strategy 2

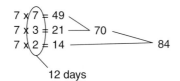

Strategy 3

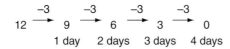

Figure 9.5 ● Measurement division strategies.

Strategy 1

3 beads on each braid

Strategy 2

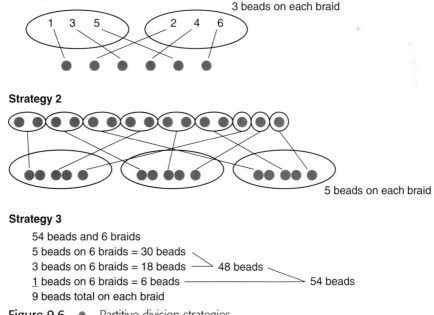

5 beads on each braid

Strategy 3

54 beads and 6 braids
5 beads on 6 braids = 30 beads
3 beads on 6 braids = 18 beads ⟶ 48 beads
<u>1</u> beads on 6 braids = 6 beads ⟶ 54 beads
9 beads total on each braid

Figure 9.6 ● Partitive division strategies.

a variety of ways using manipulatives and drawings, they will begin to move toward or should be encouraged to use number sense and notational systems to be more systematic about solving the problems. Using the numbers 54 and 6 in the bead problem, students will begin to solve it using number facts they know. As mentioned earlier, they should use "friendly numbers" to solve the problem. For example, a student might say, "There are 6 braids. So, I could put 5 beads on each braid. That makes 30 braids—5 $\times$ 6. If I put 3 more beads on each braid, that would be 3 $\times$ 6, or 18 more beads. I've used 48 beads so far. Next, I put 1 bead on each, and all 54 beads were gone. So, there are 9 beads (5 + 3 + 1) on each braid (see Figure 9.6, strategy 3).

This approach of allowing students to solve problems on their own, using their prior knowledge of number and their cognitive ability, has a number of learning benefits for all types of learners. Their number sense is strengthened. Their vocabulary and communication skills increase. Mathematics is seen as a discipline that makes sense and not something that is imposed on them or something to memorize. Their strategies advance as they observe and listen to other students share their ideas. Their procedural and conceptual understanding grows together and forms a strong base for future learning to occur. They make multiple connections to mathematics, language, and context. And, throughout this process, their confidence increases.

Developing Students' Ideas of Measurement

Measurement

One of the initial ideas that underpins measurement is comparing and ordering objects. Measurement is about understanding specific attributes of objects, such as length, weight, and capacity. As children grow in their understanding of measurement, they should learn to collect measurable attributes, understand relationships among these attributes, and focus on becoming more precise. These ideas should be continually expanded over time.

As students begin to develop their understanding of measurement they first begin to compare objects. As described in the number section above, one problem type is the compare problems. In the first problem in Table 9.1, students are asked to compare the number of dogs Rebecca and Alexander have. Which child has more dogs? Which child has fewer? Ask children to describe objects based on opposite attributes such as longer and shorter, heavier or lighter, bigger or smaller, taller or shorter, holds more or holds less. These types of questions encourage students to begin understanding size and help build their mathematical vocabulary.

Advancing the students' ideas of comparing is ordering. Ask children to put five students in order of height, to place five rocks in order of weight, or to place measuring cups in order of how much they hold. Continue to push students' ideas by asking them to state why they ordered them in the way they did. Choose two objects that are close in size and ask them to explain how they can determine why one object is longer, or weighs more or holds more than the other.

Students should also be encouraged to describe relationships using both qualitative change and quantitative change (Joram, Hartman, & Trafton, 2004). For instance, each year students grow taller, which is a qualitative change. To be more specific, Maria grew three inches in one year. This would be a quantitative change.

Once students have had practice comparing and ordering objects and describing most relationships through a qualitative lens, they should begin measuring objects with nonstandard units (and later standard units). When using units, students' must understand that they will describe measurable attributes using a unit and a number. For instance, the length of a pencil might be four paperclips long. The nonstandard unit is a paperclip, and it takes four of them.

As students begin to measure, there are a number of misconceptions that students should be encouraged to address. Using the example above, measuring the length of a pencil with paperclips, students can be confronted with these problematic issues. For instance, if the pencil is just longer than four paperclips, students tend to spread them out so the first and last paperclip meets the ends of the pencil. Gaps are left. Students must be asked whether this okay. This is a good place to have a discussion regarding how humans are constantly inventing instruments to give more and more precise measurements. So, an answer of four paperclips is not okay, but students can be encouraged to say, "The pencil is a little bit more than four paperclips." Then, the teacher can ask, "How much is a little bit more? Is it a half? Is it a fourth? How could we find out? Do we need another tool?" These questions enable students to develop an understanding that measuring is related to the precision of the tool and that we must find appropriate tools to help us measure objects.

A similar misconception is overlaps. If the pencil was just shorter than the four paperclips, students might overlap them to create a similar issue as gaps, above. Teachers should use a similar line of questioning, as above, to address this issue. Another major idea is that zero is arbitrary. Students might be using a standard measuring tool such as an inch-ruler. If the ruler is broken so 0 and 1 cannot be read, then what will students do? For instance, if they are measuring a line and, when the ruler is placed next to it, the 3-inch mark is at the beginning of the line and the 5-inch mark is at the end, then what happens? Most students will say it is 3 inches long, counting the first mark at 3, the mark at 4, and the mark a 5. Other students will say 5 inches, because that is the number where the line ends. The idea that, when we start to measure an object, we must start at zero no matter the measuring tool, is a critical idea. Another way to address that zero is arbitrary is to encourage students to begin counting with zero. We start with nothing and then 1. When we start a race, how many steps have we taken before the race begins? How old is a baby when she is born? Focusing on the idea of zero helps ensure students develop a deep and correct understanding of measurement.

In all, it is critical that teachers have trajectories of students' ideas related to topics and be able to predict their responses to tasks and questions. Knowing that students will form these types of misconceptions in measurement enable teachers to create environments to address them. When this type of teaching occurs, teachers can differentiate their instruction and equitably press students' ideas to ultimately develop procedural and conceptual understanding.

Geometry

Geometric shapes are all around us in the buildings we live and work in, the cars we ride in, even the food we eat. Children recognize these shapes early even if they do not know the technical terms for the different shapes they see. Geometry in the early elementary grades can build on children's informal knowledge by giving them appropriate vocabulary and opportunities to practice identifying geometric shapes in the classroom and the real world. These learning activities help students make connections between what happens in and out of the classroom.

Appropriate activities also help children begin to informally develop their concept of spatial sense through such observations as "close" and "far away." Giving students opportunities to practice developing their spatial sense will increase their awareness and application of geometric concepts in different areas of mathematics and other disciplines, including art, science, and social studies.

Geometry is an exciting part of mathematics for young children. As they are introduced to blocks, they begin their journey to understanding five key geometric dimensions: space, location, transformation, visualization, and justification or proof. One way to begin developing children's understanding of geometry is to provide different types of manipulatives for them to play with.

Blocks are very universal and enable students' to address all of these dimensions and become a large part of children's geometric development. There are many different types of blocks, linking and nonlinking, foam and wooden, small and large. Each type of block affords children different experiences. Initially, children should play with large, nonlinking, foam blocks. With these attributes children are free to experience the physical forces on blocks as they attempt to stack them, usually precariously. In addition, teachers should ask the children a set of questions regarding the blocks and, at the same time, introduce mathematical vocabulary. They might ask children to count the blocks as they stack them (0, 1, 2, . . .), and as they pull the construction apart (4, 3, 2, 1, 0). As stated earlier, when children are asked specific mathematical questions and introduced to mathematical vocabulary as they are playing with the blocks, they begin to construct mathematical ideas that are meaningful to them—thus enhancing long-term memory and deepening understanding.

Shape

Children first begin to explore space in both two and three dimensions. Initially, students are asked to identify shapes such as triangles, squares, rectangles, pyramids, and spheres. However, by only naming the shapes children will not build conceptual understanding. They also need to compare, sort, and describe shapes by focusing on their attributes. Children can create misconceptions unless their ideas are challenged using conjectures and examples and nonexamples. For instance, a cube is not a good choice when discussing a square, even though each face is a square, because students may walk away thinking a square has thickness.

Here is an example to build understanding in geometry and an approach that can be used with other topics. Also note that this lesson builds understanding for the spectrum of students from disadvantaged to gifted students. First, ask children to find or draw all the different types of triangles they can. Next, have the students get up from their desks an do a gallery walk—walking in a continuous fashion around the room and examining what others students have found or drawn. The students can now draw additional triangles that they might not have noted before and edit their older drawings. This initial activity allows you to assess what students know about drawing triangles.

Next, ask the students to produce conjectures based on their drawings. (After looking for patterns in the data—in this case, the different triangles—the students can state or write down what they think are true statements. These statements are called conjectures and are meant to be proven true or false.) For instance, a student might say that "all triangles have a flat bottom," indicating that the base of any triangle must be drawn along an x-axis, or horizontal line. Other students should be asked to justify with examples or nonexamples whether this conjecture is true. By writing, stating, and justifying conjectures, the students learn to use the correct mathematical language, understand that mathematics is a process of argumentation and problem solving, and begin to eliminate misconceptions while deepening their understanding of geometry.

Another activity to get students to develop geometric thinking is called Name That Shape. In this game, you or other students can give attributes of a shape to draw or build. Here is an example: *This shape has four vertices or points connected with straight lines. What is it?* Encourage students to think globally and determine whether there is only one solution or multiple solutions. Ask questions such as, What shape did you make? Explain how you created it. Are there any other solutions? What would happen in two dimensions? What about three dimensions? By asking these types of questions, students might draw different quadrilaterals or even a tetrahedron. The idea is to encourage students to visually understand shape and to be able to manipulate shapes in different ways to analyze the important elements. Allow students to use their own language while providing them with more formal or technical language.

Developing Probabilistic and Statistical Thinking

Probability

Probability and statistics are useful mathematical topics for both students' understanding of the world around them and building their understanding of other mathematical topics. Young children are very attuned to ideas of fairness and chance or the basic ideas of probability. They intuitively know when they get more or less of a cookie than someone else. These initial ideas of fairness should be capitalized on.

In probability children should develop an understanding of both experimental and theoretical probability. For instance, ask children what happens when they flip a coin: "What are the possibilities?" Students will say "heads and tails" or figure this out after flipping a coin a few times. The theoretical probability is one in two, or $\frac{1}{2}$. Ask students to predict how many times a coin will land on heads if the coin is flipped ten times or twenty times. Once students predict, ask them to justify their solution and then try it. When students get answers different than their predictions ask, "What happened? Why did you get a different result?"

As students work more and more with probability, they should experience more challenging events. For instance, you might choose 5 different blocks (2 green, 2 blue, and 1 red) and ask them a series of questions: Which color do you think you will pick first? Why? Which color do you think will come up last? Why? Students should also be asked similar questions with spinners, dice, and cards.

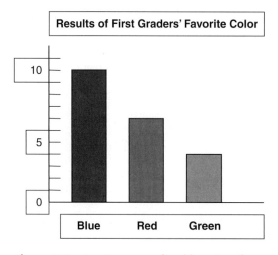

Results of First Graders' Favorite Color

Figure 9.7 • Survey results of favorite color.

Statistics

Statistics are used to describe or summarize a set of data or a lot of information. Conducting surveys and creating graphs or other representations is useful in building students' ideas of number as well as supporting knowledge of statistics and higher order thinking. Unifix cubes can be used to help create three-dimensional graphs. For instance, students can create a survey about something they might want to know about their classmates. They might want to know what each others' favorite color is, what languages they speak, or how many siblings they have. In one class, children found that 11 students liked the color blue, 7 liked red, and 4 liked green. Each child used blue, red, and green Unifix cubes to create a bar graph of the data. Students counted each of the colors to create the graph (see Figure 9.7).

Once students create the graph, then they should be able to describe what the graph is about, make predictions, and answer a series of questions. The students should state that the graph represents a summary or visual picture of their classmates' favorite colors. The bar graph is another way of asking questions related to the compare problem type (see Table 9.1). Here is a series of questions that teachers can choose to ask children or children can ask the classmates: Which color was the most popular? Which was the least favorite? How many more students would have to vote for green to have the same number of red? How many more students voted for blue than red? How many students voted all together? How many students voted for green and red?

In addition, students can be asked to make some predictions. If we surveyed another first-grade classroom, would we find the same results? Why or why not? Would we find similar results? Why or why not? For young children, predicting is a difficult concept. Therefore, students should be asked these types of questions on a regular basis. Many students will say that another class would have different results. If asked which color will be the most popular in another class, students will state their own favorite color. It is important to encourage students to begin examining their ideas against others and seeing other perspectives.

Manipulatives and Games

We encourage parents and teachers to use objects in children's everyday life. Have children, for instance, count objects around them, have them build using materials found inside and outside the house, ask children to describe geometric characteristics in the world around them, both natural and synthetic.

Besides the objects we find in our environment, there are some excellent manipulatives to help build mathematical ideas. We list which manipulatives and games we use most often with young children by content strands below.

Building geometric understanding is very object intensive for young children. We take special attention to describe some useful manipulatives in this topic. Polydrons, Geomags, Tanagrams, Geofixs, and blocks are very useful for play and educational purposes. As stated earlier, blocks are the most universal and enable young children to manipulate their physical world. Plain blocks—ones that do not allow connections—are very useful in building students' fine motor skills, physical properties of solids and gravity, and geometric properties in both two and three dimensions. The other manipulatives are wonderful in extending these geometric ideas, but in more specific ways.

Number
- Cards
- Dice
- Unifix Cubes

Measurement
- Unifix Cubes

Geometry
- Blokus
- Geomags

- GeoFixs
- Unifix Cubes

Probability
- Cards
- Dice
- Spinners
- Unifix Cubes

Statistics
- Unifix Cubes

Summary

Helping young children to develop mathematical ideas, observe the world through a mathematical lens, and gain mathematical confidence and skills forms the basis of effective math instruction. The use of everyday objects, routines, and children's literature is an excellent way to expand mathematical literacy. Learning how to develop *every* child's own mathematical understanding and encouraging them to express their experiences mathematically will enable them to create a foundation that will allow them to use mathematics to best meet their individual needs.

Thinking It Through

1. How do children best develop mathematics ideas?

2. Why promote conceptual understanding over procedural knowledge?

3. How is possible to equitably create a teaching environment that best supports a large range of children's thinking?

4. Why do teachers need to understand mathematics and how children develop mathematical understanding?

5. How and why does mathematical discourse promote a deeper understanding of mathematics?

Children's Literature in Mathematics

Number

Cave, K. (2002). *One child, one seed: A South African counting book.* New York: Henry Holt.

Clements, A. (1992). *Mother Earth's counting book.* Saxonville, MA: Picture Book Studio.

Dee, R. (1988). *Two ways to count to ten: A Liberian folktale.* New York: Henry Holt.

McGrath, B. B. (1999). *The baseball counting book.* Watertown, MA: Charlesbridge.

Murphy, S. J. (2001). *Missing mittens.* New York: HarperCollins.

Murphy, S. J. (2003). *Double the ducks.* New York: HarperCollins.

Pallotta, J. (1992). *The icky bug counting book.* Watertown, MA: Charlesbridge.

Pallotta, J. (2001). *Underwater counting: Even numbers.* Watertown, MA: Charlesbridge.

Shea, P. D., and Weill, C. (2003). *Ten mice for Tet.* San Francisco: Chronicle Books.

Wadsworth, G. (1997). *One on a web.* Watertown, MA: Charlesbridge.

Other Pre-K–2

Burris, P. (2003). *Five green and speckled frogs.* New York: Scholastic.

DeBrunhoff, L. (2003). *Babar's counting book.* Cambridge, MA: Abrams.

Friedman, A. (1994). *The king's commissioners.* New York: Scholastic Press.

Gerth, M. (2000). *Ten little ladybugs.* Santa Monica, CA: Piggy Toes Press.

Giganti, P., Jr. (1988). *How many snails? A counting book.* New York: Scholastic.

Giganti, P., Jr. (1992). *Each orange had 8 slices: A counting book.* New York: Mulberry.

Gill, S., & Tobola, D. (2000). *The big buck adventure.* Watertown, MA: Charlesbridge.

Horacek, P. (2004). *When the moon smiled: A bedtime counting book.* Cambridge, MA: Candlewick Press.

Jenkins, S. (2004). *Actual size.* Boston: Houghton Mifflin Company.

Murphy, S. J. (1996). *Give me half!* New York: Harper Collins.

Murphy, S. J. (1996). *Too many kangaroo things to do!* New York: Harper Collins.

Murphy, S. J. (2003). *Coyotes all around.* New York: HarperCollins.

Olson, K. C. (2004). *Construction countdown.* New York: Henry Holt.

Pallotta, J. (2002). *Apple fractions.* New York: Scholastic.

Pinczes, E. J. (2001). *Inchworm and a half.* Boston: Houghton Mifflin.

Tang, G. (2001). *The grapes of math: Mind-stretching math riddles.* New York: Scholastic Press.

Tang, G. (2003). *Math appeal: Mind-stretching math riddles.* New York: Scholastic Press.

Tang, G. (2003). *Math-terpieces: The art of problem-solving.* New York: Scholastic Press.

Tang, G. (2004). *Math fables: Lessons that count.* New York: Scholastic Press.

Thomas, K. (2004). *The kids guide to money cents.* Tonawanda, NY: Kids Can Press.

Turner, P. (1999). *Among the odds & evens: A tale of adventure.* New York: Farrar Straus Giroux.

Williams, R. L. (2001). *The coin counting book.* Watertown, MA: Charlesbridge.

Yates, P. (2003). Ten little mummies: An Egyptian counting book. New York: Viking Books.

Fractions

Adler, D. (1996). *Fraction fun.* New York: Holiday House.

Froman, R. (1973). *Less than nothing is really something.* New York: Thomas Y. Crowell.

Gifford, S. (2003). *Piece = part = portion: Fraction = decimal = percents.* Berkeley, CA: Tricycle Press.

Hulme, J. N. (1991). *Sea squares.* New York: Hyperion Paperbacks for Children.

Hutchins, P. (1986). *The doorbell rang.* New York: Greenwillow Books.

Murphy, S. J. (2001). *Dinosaur deals.* New York: HarperCollins.

Murphy, S. J. (2003). *Less than zero.* New York: HarperCollins.

Murphy, S. J. (2003). *3 little firefighters.* New York: HarperCollins.

Pinczes, E. J. (1993). *One hundred hungry ants.* Boston: Houghton Mifflin.

Pinczes, E. J. (1995). *A remainder of one.* Boston: Houghton Mifflin.

Pinczes, E. J. (2002). *My full moon is square.* Boston: Houghton Mifflin.

Ross, T. (2002). *Centipede's 100 shoes.* New York: Henry Holt.

Sayre, A. P., & Sayre, J. (2003). *One is a snail, ten is a crab: A counting by feet book.* Cambridge, MA: Candlewick Press.

Tang, G. (2002). *The best of times.* New York: Scholastic Press.

Thompson, L. (2001). *One riddle, one answer.* New York: Scholastic Press.

Schwartz, D. M. (1985). *How much is a million?* New York: Lothrop, Lee & Shepard Books.

Schwartz, D. M. (1999). *If you hopped like a frog.* New York: Scholastic Press.

Schwartz, D. M. (1999). *On beyond a million: An amazing math journey.* New York: Random House.

Ziefert, H. (2003). *You can't buy a dinosaur with a dime.* Brooklyn, NY: Blue Apple Books.

Zimelman, N. (2000). *Sold! A mathematics adventure.* Watertown, MA: Charlesbridge.

Grades 3+

Anno, M. (1983). *Anno's mysterious multiplying jar.* New York: Philomel Books.

Anno, M. (1995). *Anno's magic seeds.* New York: Penguin Putnam Books.

Barry, D. (1994). *The Rajah's rice: A mathematical folktale from India.* New York: W. H. Freeman.

Birch, D. (1998). *The king's chessboard.* New York: Puffin.

Demi. (1997). *One grain of rice.* New York: Scholastic Press.

Tang, G. (2001). *The grapes of math: Mind-stretching math riddles.* New York: Scholastic Press.

Tang, G. (2003). *Math appeal: Mind-stretching math riddles.* New York: Scholastic Press.

Measurement

Pre-K–2

Clement, R. (1991). *Counting on Frank.* Milwaukee, WI: Gareth Stevens.

Myller, R. (1992). *How big is a foot?* New York: Dell Yearling.

Pinczes, E. J. (2001). *Inchworm and a half.* Boston, MA: Houghton Mifflin.

Wells, R. E. (1993). *Is a blue whale the biggest thing there is?* Morton Grove, IL: Albert Whitman.

Grades 3+

Flournoy, V. (1985). *The patchwork quilt.* New York: Dial books for young readers.

Hopkinson, D. (1993). *Sweet Clara and the freedom quilt.* New York: Dragonfly Books.

Murphy, S. J. (1997). *Betcha!* New York: HarperCollins.

Neuschwander, C. (1999). *Sir Cumference and the Dragon of Pi: A math adventure.* Watertown, MA: Charlesbridge.

Neuschwander, C. (2001). *Sir Cumference and the Great Knight of Angleland: A math adventure.* Watertown, MA: Charlesbridge.

Schwartz, D. M. (2003). *Millions to measure.* New York: HarperCollins.

Geometry

Pre-K–2

Adler, D. A. (1998). *Shape up! Fun with triangles and other polygons.* New York: Holiday House.

Burns, M. (1994). *The greedy triangle.* New York: Scholastic Press.

Glasser, H. (2003). *Hello Kitty Hello shapes!* New York: Harry N. Abrams.

Murphy, S. J. (2000). *Let's fly a kite.* New York: HarperCollins.

Grades 3+

Coerr, E. (1977). *Sadako and the thousand paper cranes.* New York: Putnam.

Compestine, Y. C. (2003). *The story of kites.* New York: Holiday House.

Flournoy, V. (1985). *The patchwork quilt.* New York: Dial.

Friedman, A. (1994). *Cloak for the dreamer.* New York: Scholastic Press.

Hopkinson, D. (1993). *Sweet Clara and the freedom quilt.* New York: Dragonfly Books.

Neuschwander, C. (1997). *Sir Cumference and the first round table: A math adventure.* Watertown, MA: Charlesbridge.

Neuschwander, C. (2003). *Sir Cumference and the sword in the cone.* Watertown, MA: Charlesbridge.

Tompert, A. (1990). *Grandfather Tang's Story.* New York: Crown.

Probability and Statistics

Pre-K–2

Murphy, S. J. (1997). *The best vacation ever.* New York: HarperCollins.

Murphy, S. J. (2001). *Probably pistachio.* New York: HarperCollins.

Murphy, S. J. (2003). *3 little firefighters.* New York: HarperCollins.

Grades 3+

Murphy, S. J. (2003). *The sundae scoop.* New York: HarperCollins.

Schwartz, D. M. (1998). *G is for googol: A math alphabet book.* New York: Scholastic Press.

Scieszka, J. (1995). *Math curse.* New York: Viking.

References

Anderson, J. R. (1995). *Cognitive psychology and its implications.* New York: W. H. Freeman.

Ball, D. L. (1988). *Knowledge and reasoning in mathematical pedagogy: Examining what prospective teachers bring to teacher education.* Unpublished doctoral dissertation, Michigan State University, East Lansing, MI.

Ball, D. L. (1989). *Teaching mathematics for understanding: What do teachers need to know about the subject matter?* Paper presented at Competing Visions of Teacher Knowledge, proceedings from an NCRTE seminar for education policy makers, East Lansing MI.

Ball, D. L., Lubienski, S. T., & Mewborn, D. S. (2001). Research on teaching mathematics: The unsolved problem of teachers' mathematical knowledge. In V. Richardson (Ed.), *Handbook of research on teaching* (4th ed., pp. 433–456). Washington DC: American Educational Research Association.

Ball, D. L., & Mosenthal, J. H. (1990). *The construction of new forms of teaching: Subject matter knowledge in inservice teacher education.* East Lansing, MI: National Center for Research on Teacher Learning.

Ball, D. L., & Wilson, S. M. (1990). *Knowing the subject and learning to teach it: Examining assumptions about becoming a mathematics teacher.* East Lansing, MI: National Center for Research on Teacher Learning.

Borko, H., Eisenhart, M., Brown, C. A., Underhill, R. G., Jones, D., & Agard, P. C. (1992). Learning to teach hard mathematics: Do novice teachers and their instructors give up too easily? *Journal for Research in Mathematics Education, 23*(3), 194–222.

Brendefur, J. L. (1999). *High school mathematics teachers' beliefs about learning, pedagogy, and mathematics and their relationship to teaching authentically.* Unpublished dissertation, University of Wisconsin, Madison.

Brendefur, J. L., & Frykholm, J. A. (2000). Promoting mathematical communication in the classroom: Two preservice teachers' conceptions and practices. *Journal of Mathematics Teacher Education, 3*(2), 125–153.

Brewer, W., & Nakamura, G. (1984). The nature and functions of schemas. In R. Wyer & T. Srull (Eds.), *Handbook of social cognition.* Mahwah, NJ: Lawrence Erlbaum Associates.

Brown, C. A., & Borko, H. (1992). Becoming a mathematics teacher. In D. A. Grouws (Ed.), *Handbook of research on mathematics teaching and learning* (pp. 209–242). New York: Macmillian.

Carpenter, T. P., Fennema, E., Franke, M. L., Levi, L., & Empson, S. B. (1999). *Children's mathematics: Cognitively Guided Instruction.* Portsmouth, NH: Heinemann.

Carpenter, T. P., Fennema, E., Peterson, P. L., Chiange, C. P., & Loef, M. (1989). Using knowledge of children's mathematics thinking in classroom teaching: An experimental study. *American Educational Research Journal, 26*(4), 499–531.

Cobb, P. (1986). Contexts, goals, beliefs and learning mathematics. *For the Learning of Mathematics, 6*(2), 2–9.

Cohen, D. K., & Ball, D. L. (1990). Relations between policy and practice: A commentary. *Educational Evaluation and Policy Analysis, 12*, pp. 331–338.

Cooney, T. J., & Shealy, B. (1997). On understanding the structure of teachers' beliefs and their relationship to change. In E. Fennema & B. S. Nelson (Eds.), *Mathematics teachers in transition* (pp. 87–110). Hillside, NJ: Lawrence Erlbaum Associates.

Cooney, T. J., Shealy, B. E., & Arvold, B. (1998). Conceptualizing belief structures of preservice secondary mathematics teachers. *Journal for Research in Mathematics Education, 29*, pp. 306–333.

Cuban, L. (1990). Reforming again, again, and again. *Educational Researcher, 19*(1), 3–13.

Fennema, E., Carpenter, T. P., Franke, M. L., Levi, L., Jacobs, V. R., & Empson, S. B. (1996). A longitudinal study of learning to use children's thinking in mathematics instruction. *Journal for Research in Mathematics Education, 27*(4), 403–434.

Fennema, E., & Franke, M. L. (1992). Teachers' knowledge and its impact. In D. A. Grouws (Ed.), *Handbook of research on mathematics teaching and learning: A project of the National Council of Teachers of Mathematics* (pp. 147–164). New York: MacMillan.

Fennema, E., & Romberg, T. (Eds.). (1999). *Mathematics classrooms that promote understanding*. Mahwah, NJ: Lawrence Erlbaum Associates.

Frechtling, J. A., Sharp, L., Carey, N., & Vaden-Kiernan, N. (1995). *Teacher enhancement programs: A perspective on the last four decades*. Rockville, MD: Westat.

Frykholm, J. A. (1996). *Rethinking supervision: Learning to teach mathematics in community* (Doctoral dissertation). Madison, WI: University of Wisconsin.

Frykholm, J. A. (in press). Struggling with the standards: Preservice teachers in mathematics. *Teaching and Teacher Education*.

Grossman, P., Wilson, S. M., & Shulman, L. (1989). Teachers of substance: Subject matter knowledge for teaching. In M. C. Reynolds (Ed.), *Knowledge base for the beginning teacher* (pp. 23–36). New York: Pergamon Press.

Grouws, D. A., & Cebulla, K. J. (2000). *Improving student achievement in mathematics* (Educational Practices Series-4). Brussels, Belgium: International Academy of Education.

Hiebert, J., & Carpenter, T. P. (1992). Learning and teaching with understanding. In D. A. Grouws (Ed.), *Handbook of research on mathematics teaching and learning* (pp. 65–97). New York: Macmillan.

Hiebert, J., Carpenter, T. P., Fennema, E., Fuson, K. C., Human, P., Murray, H., Olivier, A., & Wearne, D. (1996). Problem solving as a basis for reform in curriculum and instruction: The case of mathematics. *Educational Researcher, 25*(4), 12–21.

Hiebert, J., Carpenter, T. P., Fennema, E., Fuson, K. C., Wearne, D., Murray, H., Olivier, A., & Human, P. (1997). *Making sense: Teaching and learning mathematics with understanding*. Portsmouth, NH: Heinemann.

Joram, E., Hartman, C., & Trafton, P. R. (2004). As people get older, they get taller: An integrated unit on measurement, linear relationships, and data analysis. *Teaching Children Mathematics, 10*(7), 344–357.

Kamii, C. (2000). *Young children reinvent arithmetic: Implications of Piaget's Theory*. New York: Teachers College Press.

Knapp, M. S., & Peterson, P. L. (1995). Teachers' interpretations of "CGI" after four years: Meanings and practice. *Journal for Research in Mathematics Education, 26*(1), 40–65.

Konold, C. (1991). Understanding students' beliefs about probability. In E. v. Glaserfeld (Ed.), *Radical constructivism in mathematics education* (pp. 101–127). Dordrecht: Kluwer.

Konold, C. (1993). Inconsistencies in students' reasoning about probability. *Journal for Research in Mathematics Education, 24*(5), 392–414.

Lampert, M. (1989). Choosing and using mathematical tools in classroom discourse. In J. Brophy (Ed.), *Advances in research on teaching and learning* (pp. 115–126). New York: Macmillian.

Lampert, M. (1990). When the problem is not the question and the solution is not the answer: Mathematical knowing and teaching. *American Educational Research Journal, 27*, pp. 29–63.

Ma, L. (1999). *Knowing and teaching elementary mathematics*. Mahwah, NJ: Lawrence Erlbaum Associates.

McDiarmid, G. W., & Ball, D. L. (1989). *The teacher education and learning to teach study: An occasion for developing a conception of teacher knowledge*. East Lansing, MI: National Center for Research on Teacher Learning.

McDiarmid, G. W., Ball, D. L., & Anderson, C. W. (1989). Why staying one chapter ahead doesn't really work: Subject specific pedagogy. In M. C. Reynolds (Ed.),

Knowledge base for the beginning teacher (pp. 193–205). New York: Pergamon Press.

Mewborn, D. S. (2000). *An analysis of the research on K–8 teachers' mathematical knowledge.* Paper presented at the Annual Meeting of the American Educational Research Association, New Orleans, LA.

National Center for Education Statistics (NCES). (1990). *The state of mathematics education.* Washington, DC: NCES, U.S. Department of Education.

———. (1996). *Pursuing excellence: A study of U.S. eighth grade mathematics and science teaching, learning, curriculum, and achievement in international contexts* (NCES 97 198). Washington, DC: NCES, U.S. Department of Education.

National Commission on Excellence in Education (NCEE). (1983). *A nation at risk.* Washington DC: NCEE. U.S. Government Printing Office.

National Council of Teachers of Mathematics (NCTM). (1989). *Curriculum and evaluation standards for school mathematics.* Reston, VA: Author.

———. (1991). *Professional standards for the teaching of mathematics.* Reston, VA: Author.

———. (2000). *Principles and standards for school mathematics.* Reston, VA: Author.

Newmann, F. M., & Associates. (1996). *Authentic achievement: Restructuring schools for intellectual quality.* San Francisco: Jossey-Bass.

Newmann, F. M., Secada, W. G., & Wehlage, G. G. (1995). *A guide to authentic instruction and assessment: Vision, standards and scoring.* Madison: Wisconsin Center for Education Research, University of Wisconsin.

Pajares, M. F. (1992). Teachers' beliefs and educational research: Cleaning up a messy construct. *Review of Educational Researcher, 62*, pp. 307–332.

Perkins, D. (1993). Teaching for understanding. *American Educator, 17*(3), 28–35.

Putnam, R. T., Heaton, R. M., Prawat, R. S., & Remillard, J. (1992). Teaching mathematics for understanding: Discussing case studies of four fifth-grade teachers. *The Elementary School Journal, 93*(2), 213–228.

Richardson, V. (1990). Significant worthwhile change in teaching practice. *Educational Researcher, 19*(7), 10–18.

Rokeach, M. (1969). *Beliefs, attitudes and values: A theory of organization and change.* San Francisco: Jossey-Bass.

Romberg, T. A. (1992). Assessing mathematics competence and achievement. In H. Berlak, F. M. Newmann, E. Adams, D. A. Archbald, T. Burgess, J. Raven, & T. A. Romberg (Eds.), *Toward a new science of educational testing and assessment* (pp. 23–52). Albany: State University of New York (SUNY) Press.

Romberg, T. A. (1993). How one comes to know: Models and theories of the learning of mathematics. In M. Niss (Ed.), *Investigations into assessment in mathematics education* (pp. 202–217). London: Kluwer.

Schoenfeld, A. H. (1985). *Mathematical problem solving.* San Diego: Academic Press.

Shulman, L. (1986). Those who understand: Knowledge growth in teaching. *Educational Researcher, 15*(2), 4–14.

Simon, M. A. (1995). Reconstructing mathematics pedagogy from a constructivist perspective. *Journal for Research in Mathematics Education, 26*, 114–145.

Smith, J. P., diSessa, A. A., & Roschelle, J. (1993). Misconceptions reconceived: A constructivist analysis of knowledge transition. *The Journal of the Learning Sciences, 3*(2), 115–163.

Sowder, J. T., Philipp, R. A., Armstrong, B. E., & Schappelle, B. P. (1998). *Middle-grade teachers' mathematical knowledge and its relationship to instruction.* Albany: SUNY.

Steffe, L. P., & D'Ambrosio, B. S. (1995). Toward a working model of constructivist teaching: A reaction to Simon. *Journal for Research in Mathematics Education, 26*, pp. 114–145.

Stigler, J., & Hiebert, J. (1999). *The teaching gap: Best ideas from the world's teachers for improving education in the classroom.* London: Freedom Press.

Tate, W. F. (1994). Race, retrenchment, and the reform of school mathematics. *Phi Delta Kappan, 75.*

Thompson, A. G. (1992). Teachers' beliefs and conceptions: A synthesis of the research. In D. A. Grouws (Ed.), *Handbook of research on mathematics teaching and learning* (pp. 127–146). New York: Macmillan.

Wood, T. (1993). Creating an environment for learning mathematics: Social interaction perspectives. *Journal for Research in Mathematics Education, 24*(5), 15–20.

Zeichner, K. (1993). Connecting genuine teacher development to the struggle for social justice. *Journal of Education for Teaching, 19*(1), 5–20.

Science in the Inclusive Classroom

Greg Conderman and C. Sheldon Woods

Objectives

After reading this chapter, students will be able to

- Define science.
- Identify the science standards.
- Identify thematic strands and content knowledge for young children in science.
- Provide a rationale for including science in an elementary curriculum.
- Design ways to integrate science throughout the curriculum.
- Differentiate among the various approaches for teaching science.
- Describe accommodations and modifications in science for students with disabilities.
- Identify resources for teaching science in the elementary classroom.

Key Terms

Process skills
Activity-based approach
Content enhancements
Accommodations
Modifications
Universal design for learning
Planning pyramid
Performance-based assessments

Practical Application Vignette

Celest and JoAnne are two general education first-grade teachers who have both been teaching for nearly ten years in an old urban school. The students in their classrooms are culturally, economically, and academically diverse. Due to recent pressure to raise academic scores in their school, both teachers have been spending extra instructional time on teaching reading and math. Celest and JoAnne have been pleased with the results of "doubling up" on their instruction in these areas as evidenced through improved student test scores. However, their extra instruction in these basic skill areas has come with a price—their students have had considerably less exposure to specials as well as social studies and science concepts. During a recent staff development meeting, these teachers learned that their state will soon be assessing students' knowledge in science along with math and reading. Acknowledging their frustration with raising standards for all children, a low-budget science curriculum, and limited time in the school day to teach all subjects, Celest and JoAnne turn to their colleague, Marcus, the special education teacher, who often coteaches with them. Some of the questions they want to discuss with Marcus include, How can we maintain student growth in the academic skills while addressing the new mandate of teaching science? What methods of teaching science are effective for teaching a diverse class? Do students with disabilities need special accommodations in science? Can students learn from a hands-on approach when they have difficulty with written and oral expression and following directions? Reading from the science text and showing science videos would be easier than developing hands-on activities, but will students really learn from just reading and watching? And . . . how do we get started?

Celest, JoAnne, and Marcus are like many other elementary education teachers who have admittedly placed a low priority on science instruction in response to recent academic accountability demands. Additionally, just like their colleagues, they now realize that they must address the science standards in their first-grade curriculum. Further, they acknowledge their inadequate teacher preparation for teaching science. In light of these issues, this chapter will address the concerns from our first-grade team with regard to what constitutes effective science instruction for young children in diverse educational settings.

Introduction to Science

Science—What Is It?

It is important to note that science is not just a body of facts to be memorized and then repeated on an exam, nor is it just a series of experiments to be performed in a laboratory. Science is a process-oriented, discovery- or inquiry-based approach to answering questions or solving problems. Science can take place indoors and/or outdoors. Science can be conducted alone or in groups. Science in-

volves information about the natural and man-made world as well as the skills in discovering that information. In short, science is a way of knowing. According to Abruscato (2000), science is the body of knowledge people build when they use a group of processes to make discoveries about the natural world.

The National Science Standards

The National Research Council (NRC), in conjunction with the National Academy of Sciences, developed the National Science Education Standards. The standards rest on the premise that science is an active process, not relying solely on hands-on activities, but also incorporating minds-on experiences that facilitate and promote active mental activity, such as brain teasers. The standards call for more than the "science as process" approach in which students learn skills such as observing, inferring, and experimenting. Inquiry is central to science learning (National Research Council, 1996).

The standards do not require or endorse a specific curriculum. The content of the standards can be organized and presented with many different perspectives. In fact, many local districts and state education agencies have used the national science standards to develop their own outcomes and curricula. The ultimate goal of science instruction is to produce scientifically literate citizens.

The Nature of Science

School science is too often taught from a text book and is limited to worksheets and memorization. This has little to do with science, and this approach does not convey to students the nature of science and how scientific knowledge is acquired. The National Science Teachers Association (NSTA), the leading professional organization of teachers, scholars, and researchers responsible for coordinating science education in the United States, adopted the following position on the nature of science (2000):

- Scientific knowledge is simultaneously reliable and tentative. Having confidence in scientific knowledge is reasonable while realizing that such knowledge may be abandoned or modified in light of new evidence or reconceptualization of prior evidence and knowledge.

- Although no single universal step-by-step scientific method captures the complexity of doing science, a number of shared values and perspectives characterize a scientific approach to understanding nature. Among these are a demand for naturalistic explanations supported by empirical evidence that are, at least in principle, testable against the natural world. Other shared elements include observations, rational argument, inference, skepticism, peer review, and replicability of work.

- Creativity is a vital, yet personal, ingredient in the production of scientific knowledge.
- Science, by definition, is limited to naturalistic methods and explanations and, as such, is precluded from using supernatural elements in the production of scientific knowledge.
- A primary goal of science is the formation of theories and laws, which are terms with very specific meanings.
- Laws are generalizations or universal relationships related to the way that some aspect of the natural world behaves under certain conditions.
- Theories are inferred explanations of some aspect of the natural world. Theories do not become laws even with additional evidence; they explain laws. However, not all scientific laws have accompanying explanatory theories.

Well-established laws and theories must

1. be internally consistent and compatible with the best available evidence;
2. be successfully tested against a wide range of applicable phenomena and evidence;
3. possess appropriately broad and demonstrable effectiveness in further research.

- Contributions to science can be made and have been made by people the world over.
- The scientific questions asked, the observations made, and the conclusions in science are to some extent influenced by the existing state of scientific knowledge, the social and cultural context of the researcher, and the observer's experiences and expectations.
- The history of science reveals both evolutionary and revolutionary changes. With new evidence and interpretation, old ideas are replaced or supplemented by newer ones.
- While science and technology do impact each other, basic scientific research is not directly concerned with practical outcomes, but rather with gaining an understanding of the natural world for its own sake. (pp. 1–2)

Scientific knowledge is both reliable and tentative. While this may seem a contradiction, these qualities speak to the developmental nature of science. Scientific knowledge is developmental because it is constantly growing and changing. This development, as well as the changes associated with scientific knowledge, portray a continual process. However, this knowledge is reliable because it is constantly being testing and challenged. For example, as new technology is developed or new information is discovered, better explanations and/or understandings of prior knowledge become known. In these ways, old information or scientific knowledge is under constant scrutiny and viewed in new ways. Each new generation adds to the body of scientific knowledge. Consequently, there are no facts or absolute truths in scientific knowledge, only information that is more acceptable, current, and potentially changeable by future generations who have newer technology or new information.

Similarly, there is no one "scientific method" as often described by school science textbooks. The notion of the "scientific method" is a myth. Scientists use many different creative methods to answer questions and solve problems. Various methods have in common: observation, logical arguments, inference, and healthy skepticism. Peer review of challenges adds replicability. This replicability makes scientific knowledge testable. One of the major tests of scientific knowledge is testability. New discoveries are challenged or tested by other scientists who attempt to duplicate the discovery. If the discovery can be duplicated by several scientists or researchers (skeptics) with the same results, then this new information is accepted into the body of scientific knowledge. This process of testing is important in maintaining the accuracy of scientific knowledge over time. A variety of scientific methods are used to accomplish this.

Science is a creative process. Each scientist, researcher, or individual brings her or his own creative flair to the process. In this aspect, science is a personal process. These creative contributions are made by individuals from all over the world. Science is a field of study that encourages innovation, exploration, and imagination to solve real-world problems. Children naturally do this as they play and develop. They are constantly exploring their worlds and using their imagination and creativity to solve problems or complete tasks.

Science is limited to naturalistic studies and explanations. This excludes supernatural elements in the production of knowledge. Science is amoral; it is neither good nor bad. Science is not ethical. Scientific knowledge can be used to inform ethical decisions, but, in and of itself, it is just knowledge. Scientific knowledge itself cannot be judged as morally good or bad; science is merely a tool. Much like a pencil or crayon can be used on paper or on a wall, it is the manner in which the tool is used that can be judged morally good or bad. Science is often portrayed in the media as being good or bad, but this is inconsistent with the nature of science.

Science is parsimonious. The aim of scientists is to make knowledge simple and easier to understand. At times it appears that the goal of science is to make information more complex and difficult to understand. This often happens because scientists use language or vocabulary specific to their field of study. Outsiders unfamiliar with this vocabulary might find explanations difficult or hard to understand.

Finally, scientific knowledge is unified, in that scientific laws, theories, and concepts are interrelated. Knowledge from one field of study is related or connected to knowledge in another field of study. One of the primary goals of science is to form theories and laws. Theories and laws have specific meanings and uses and are based upon well-established, consistent information using the best evidence available, after having been scrutinized and thoroughly examined.

Constructing Knowledge in Science

The Role of Science Education in the Elementary Classroom

Science plays a vital role in the elementary classroom by providing students opportunities to develop critical and analytical thinking skills. Further, when taught appropriately, science provides students with the critical foundations and experiences in using **process skills**—the tools that scientists and researchers use to conduct the enterprise of science—they will need to function as scientifically literate citizens. However, as noted in the opening vignette, science is often omitted from the elementary curriculum in favor of providing more instructional time for reading, writing, and mathematics. The NSTA (2002) has taken a position on this crucial topic by emphasizing that inquiry science must be a basic in the daily curriculum of every elementary school student at every grade level. NSTA further asserts that the elementary science program must provide opportunities for students to develop skills and understandings necessary to function as problem-solvers in a scientific and technological world (NSTA, 2002).

Science Standard Themes

The National Science Education Standards are divided into eight categories or themes: (1) unifying concepts and processes, (2) science as inquiry, (3) physical science, (4) life science, (5) earth and space science, (6) science in personal and social perspectives, (7) science and technology, and (8) history and nature of science. These themes are broad in their scope and have been used by many states and local districts to write their goals and standards. The first area, unifying concepts and process, is common for all grade levels. The other seven themes have clustered grade-level-specific information.

The *unifying concepts and processes* standard describes some of the interactive schemes that bring together students' many experiences in science education across grade levels. Under this theme are systems, order, and organization; evidence, models, and explanations; change, constancy, and measurement; evolution and equilibrium; and form and function. The standards are written with the intention that these concepts would also be covered under other standards and themes.

The *science as inquiry* standard requires students to combine process skills and scientific knowledge as they use scientific reasoning and critical thinking to develop their understanding of science. For kindergarten through fourth grade the focus of this standard is for students to develop the abilities necessary to engage in and understand scientific inquiry.

The *physical science, life science,* and *earth and space science* standards describe the subject matter using three widely accepted science divisions. Science subject matter focuses on the science facts, concepts, principles, theories, and models important for students to know and use. The *physical science* standard for grades K–4 focuses on properties of objects; position and motion of objects; and light, heat, electricity, and magnetism. The *life science* standard for grades K–4 is concerned with the characteristics of organisms, life cycles of organisms, and organisms and environments. The *earth and space science* standard looks at the properties of earth materials, objects in the sky, and changes in the earth and sky.

The *science in personal and social perspectives* standard provides students with ways to understand and act on personal and social issues and develop decision-making skills. For grades K–4, this standard focuses on personal health, characteristics and changes in populations, types of resources, changes in environments, and using science and technology with local challenges.

The *science and technology* standard establishes connections between the natural and designed world and provides students with opportunities to develop decision-making abilities. This standard does not provide standards for technology but instead emphasizes abilities associated with design and with various linkages of technology with science. In grades K–4, this standard helps children develop the abilities to distinguish between natural objects and objects made by humans, become acquainted with technological design, and understand science and technology.

The *history and nature of science* standard emphasizes that science reflects its history and is an ongoing, changing enterprise. The National Science Education Standards recommends the use of history in school science programs to clarify the different aspects of scientific inquiry, the human aspects of science, and the role that science has played in the development of various cultures and civilizations. For grades K–4, the focus is on science as a human endeavor.

These standards or themes are not a curriculum but rather a guide for what students should learn. How students learn will be up to state and local school boards and you, their teacher.

Science is a mixture of process and product. This mixture changes with the age of the learner. Younger children learn in a variety of settings from naturalistic (at play) settings to a more structured (directed by an adult or teacher) settings. Sometimes learning or play becomes a teachable moment (informal) learning setting (Neuman, 1992). Constructivists believe that learners build or construct their knowledge from their experiences or environment and that knowledge is not transmitted. From a constructivist perspective, knowledge in science is constructed (1) gradually over time, (2) by the learner within a social context, (3) through a series of interactions with the content, and (4) when new information is integrated with old information, which (5) results in an awareness of what is being learned (Barber, 1998).

Science Process Skills

The process skills, presented in Table 10.1, are the tools that scientists and researchers use to conduct the enterprise of science; these skills are central to the work prescribed by the National Science Standards. These process skills allow students to process information through concrete experiences. The skills are progressive; they build on each other. The process skills are divided into two categories, the basic and the integrated. The basic process skills are more appropriate for preschool and primary students; however, the integrated skills should not be ignored at these levels. Each integrated skill is a combination of two or more of the basic process skills.

Integrating Science Throughout the Curriculum

Researchers have shown that when science is integrated with other subjects, especially around a central Science Technology and Society (STS) theme, children learn both science and the other subjects more effectively (Kellough, 1995; Pappas, Kiefer, & Levstick, 1990). Furthermore, integrating science with other disciplines such as language arts, social studies, art, and mathematics has potential for improving both the quantity and quality of science instruction and student learning (Jarrett, 1999).

Science and Language Arts

Evidence suggests that early experience with science helps students develop critical language and logic skills regardless of their socioeconomic status. Kellough (1995) discovered that young children's experiences with natural phenomena in active science programs improved reading readiness and reading skills. Reading and writing skills can be naturally integrated with science. For example, children can read about science from more than their science text. Many trade books have science themes or content and are excellent sources for supporting science activities.

For example, the trade book *A Handful of Dirt* by Raymond Bial (2000) contains colorful photographs and meaningful text that present the nature and importance of soil and the many forms

Table 10.1 ● Science Process Skills

Basic Skill	Example	Adaptation 1	Adaptation 2
Observation Using one or more of the five senses to gather information about an object or event	Describing a lemon as yellow and sour	Preteach vocabulary in categories related to the senses (e.g., various tastes) with hands-on activities. Taste, discuss, and chart foods that are salty, sweet, bitter, etc.	Provide fill-in-the-blank sentences with binary word or picture choices, such as *This feels (rough or soft). This is (big or small). This tastes (sweet or sour.)* Refer to pictorial charts as visual reminders of the vocabulary words.
Inference Making an "educated guess" about an object or event based on previously gathered data or information	Indicating that a person who has muddy shoes walked through mud based on evidence of his or her dirty shoes	Play "detective" story games where the evidence is presented (e.g., Julio's dirty shoes) and provide one obviously true and false statement as to what caused the dirty shoes such as *Julio walked in the mud* OR *Julio walked on clean carpeting*. Children indicate which statement caused the evidence and explain why.	Use a visual flowchart graphic organizer to show the chain of events leading to a final event.
Measurement Using both standard and nonstandard measures to describe the dimensions of an object, distance or event	Using a ruler to determine the length of a pencil in inches or half-inches	Use specially modified materials such as talking measuring sticks or rulers with larger print, color-coded markings, or braille.	Have children measure only to the nearest basic unit, such as inch (rather than half-inch, quarter-inch), etc.
Communication Using words, pictures or graphic symbols to describe an action, object, or event.	Describing the texture, height, weight, and color of a classroom pet	Play "I spy" games based on items in the classroom where children guess what is being described (e.g., I spy something red, white, and blue with stars on it). Children and teacher take turns being the leader.	Provide binary or multiple-choice options for students for their descriptions, such as *Is our classroom pet white or brown? Big or small? Fat or thin?*

Table 10.1 ● *(Continued)*

Basic Skill	Example	Adaptation 1	Adaptation 2
Classification Grouping or ordering objects or events into categories based on properties or criteria	Placing all the similar pattern blocks in to groups	Provide a match-to-sample activity where children match and classify items from a group to their pictorial representations.	Group items based on obvious differences, rather than subtle differences.
Prediction Stating the outcome of a future event based on a pattern of evidence	Predicting the height of a plant in two weeks' time based on a chart of its growth during the previous four weeks	Provide many experiences with predictable patterns using sequenced pictures such as the sequence of the child's day at school. Have children sequence pictures and tell the story.	Use focused questions with embedded information, such as *What was the plant's size when we started? During week 2? 3? 4? What did you notice about the chart? If the plant keeps growing at this rate, what would the chart show next?*

Integrated Process Skill	Example	Adaptation 1	Adaptation 2
Controlling Variables Being able to identify variables that can affect an experimental outcome, keeping most constant while manipulating only the independent variable	Realizing through past experiences that the height of a ramp will affect how fast and far a toy car travels when rolled down that ramp	Pose a problem-based situation, use critical questions, and use a K-W-L chart to guide children's understandings of the variables affecting the car's performance.	Show and discuss various situations involving the variables (e.g., car and ramp) through virtual field trips or technology-based simulations.
Operational Definitions Stating how to measure a variable in an experiment	Stating that distance traveled by the toy car will be measured in centimeters per second	Provide a chart of various standards of measurement with a key example for each.	Preteach critical vocabulary and prefixes (milli, kilo, etc) and provide length, weight, pressure, volume, and/or temperature-conversion charts that show the relationships among and between various measures.

(Continued)

Integrating Science Throughout the Curriculum

Table 10.1 • *(Continued)*

Integrated Process Skill	Example	Adaptation 1	Adaptation 2
Formulating Hypothesis Stating the expected outcome of an experiment	Making a statement such as, "The higher the ramp, the farther the car will travel."	Preteach the relationship, or "rule," between two objects or events, e.g., during a discussion on the human body, teach the rule, "When people run faster, their hearts beat faster."	After teaching the relationship or rule, provide "if-then" scenarios for students to test their understanding of the rule, such as *If Bart raises the height of the ramp, the car will travel (slower, faster). If Rusty lowers the heights of the ramp, the car will travel (slower, faster).*
Data Interpretation Organizing data and drawing conclusions from it	Recording data from the experiment with the distance traveled by the toy car in a data table and forming a conclusion that relates trends in the data variables	Provide scaffolding to help students form conclusions, such as *Was Bart's ramp the highest or lowest? Did Bart's car go the slowest or fastest? Therefore, the (higher, lower) the ramp, the (faster, slower) the car traveled.*	Use technology-based charting and graphing options.
Experimentation Being able to conduct an experiment, including asking an appropriate questions, stating a hypothesis, identifying and controlling variables, operationally defining those variables, designing a "fair" experiment, conducting the experiment, and interpreting the results of the experiment	The entire process of conducting the experiment on the affect of distance traveled by a toy car	Provide an example of each step of the experiment and have children complete individual parts of the experiment in order with specific feedback from the teacher on each step before moving onto the next step. Explicitly teach students the strategy to control one variable at a time.	Assign partners to work together as a team to design and conduct the experiment.
Formulating Models Creating a physical or mental model of a process or event	The model of how the height of a ramp affects the distance traveled by a toy car	Have students demonstrate, role-play, or draw their model rather than writing or talking about it.	Have students listen to true and false statements about the model and indicate if they agree or disagree with the statements.

of life it supports. This work takes the reader on a vivid, down-in-the-dirt tour of one of the Earth's most common but precious resources: soil and its ecology. Another example of a trade book that supports the integration of language arts and science and math is *Tiger Math: Learning to Graph From a Baby Tiger* by Ann Whitehead Nagda and Cindy Bickel. Through the use of text, pictures, and various types of graphs, these authors describe the growth of T. J., an orphaned Siberian tiger cub. NSTA publishes an annual list of science trade books that are linked to the science standards and process skills on its webpage under Teacher Resources (see Resources list at end of chapter for web address).

When teachers utilize trade books and other supplemental reading materials, students learn that science is indeed all around them and a part of their everyday lives. In addition, having students discuss and write about their science investigations improves their oral and written communication skills. In the area of language arts, teachers can have students research, write, and give presentations about famous scientists and scientific discoveries, maintain an ongoing log of the meaning and spelling of science words in their writing portfolio, record observations of their changing environment, and share science-related feature or news stories from newspapers, magazines, the news, or the Internet.

Science and Mathematics

All of the recent science reform movements stress the inclusion or integration of mathematics with science. Many science activities have a number of mathematical components. For example, science can be used to "enlarge" how teachers instruct students to solve problems. Instead of using contrived or made-up problems, real-world science and mathematical problems enrich and expand students' problem-solving skills (Goldberg & Wagreich, 1989). In the area of math, teachers can also present specific thinking and problem-solving strategies that can be used in science; provide instruction on reading and interpreting data from tables, graphs, and charts; introduce vocabulary that is common to both math and science, such as terms used in measurement; and help students use tools such as the calculator, the computer, and other technologies.

Science and Social Studies

Integrating science and social studies fits nicely into the science standards. This integration also provides students with opportunities to develop decision-making skills as they develop a basic working knowledge of science. Science, technology, and society (STS) activities provide experiences that develop an informed citizenry and help to produce scientifically literate citizens. When properly introduced, STS activities provide opportunities for children to explore and investigate both subjects. In social studies, teachers can reinforce inductive and deductive reasoning skills, real-life-based problem-solving skills, and inquiry-based problems and simulations. Students can study the environment, the Earth, and the Earth's systems. Social studies also lends itself well to using many instructional tools common to science such as graphic organizers, concept diagrams, charts, and graphs (Mastropieri & Scruggs, 2004). Further, children of all ages can engage in a variety of service learning opportunities in their home, school, or community (Woods & Conderman, 2005) that relate to science and social studies concepts.

Science and Art

Teachers can also integrate art with science in many ways. For example, bulletin boards, posters, student art work, class collages, and other projects can be used to reinforce science concepts and themes. In art, students can learn about chemicals, mixtures, compounds, light, and light waves. According to Karten (2005), art relates to science as students see how different mediums react and combine with each other by mixing and separating colors and learning how pigments and dyes come from nature. Students can use science elements—such as living and nonliving things—in their art media. Students use their observation skills naturally in art. Finally, many instructional procedures are emphasized both in art and science, such as safety, cleanup, displaying respect for various tools and pieces of equipment, and transporting items for use and display (Mastropieri & Scruggs, 2004).

Science and Music

Music is a part of everyday life. Even very young children hum, dance, whistle, and sing television or radio commercials or songs. As you introduce new topics in your classroom, find music that fits the theme, or have students bring in music. Additionally, students typically are fascinated by musical instruments. They can make their own instrument or have access to real ones which can be used to teach simple science concepts such as vibrations or sound. Music is connected to science as students learn about acoustics and the science of hearing sounds; charting frequencies; intensities; adjusting volumes, pitches, melodies, and harmonies; and learning how instruments are made (Karten, 2005).

Science and Health and Physical Education

Often abstract concepts in science are challenging to teach. Sometimes role playing or engaging in physical games or demonstrations can be effective tools for making abstract concepts more concrete. For example, a game of tag can be used to show predator–prey relationships. Similarly, holding hands and moving can demonstrate how hot and cold particles behave. Weber (1999) described an authentic science lesson that involved having students physically move into correct position to demonstrate the processes of melting, freezing, evaporating, and condensing as well as the physical properties of solid, liquid, and gas. Weber maintained that students remember these concepts when they can act them out, and that providing students with opportunities to demonstrate such terms operationally provides an excellent review before a test. Science, PE, and health share common curricular topics such as body systems, personal hygiene, movement, weight, balance, fitness, sports, and mental and physical well-being.

Differentiating Instruction in Science

In the past, many students with disabilities received little or no science instruction (Cawley, 1994). These students may have received some science instruction in the special education classroom, or they may have been excused from science instruction altogether in an attempt to spend more time remediating their math, reading, and writing skills. When science was taught to students with disabilities, general and special education teachers often used a content-oriented approach that focused on learning vocabulary and factual text-based information through textbooks and

teacher-directed presentations such as lecture and demonstrations (Mastropieri & Scruggs, 1994). Many students with disabilities were unsuccessful with this approach due to the heavy demands on reading, writing, and memorizing. This textbook approach is in sharp contrast to the activity-based approach recommended by the Council for Exceptional Children (CEC) and the National Association of Science Teachers (Brownell & Thomas, 1998). The third approach often used in general and special education science is the combined approach, in which teachers use a mixture of both textbook and activity-based applications.

An **activity-based approach** for teaching science to students with disabilities relies less on textbooks, lectures, vocabulary, and paper-and-pencil tests. Therefore, the language and literacy demands, which typically interfere with learning for students with learning and language-based difficulties, are reduced (Fradd & Lee, 1995). Instead, students are provided with experiences that allow them to discover and experiment with science. An integral part of an activities-based approach is providing hands-on multisensory experiences and materials. Hands-on learning provides students with actual experiences that provide a foundation for understanding abstract concepts and discovering content. In this approach, students spend longer periods of time on a narrower range of topics, so depth of content is covered over breadth (Brownell & Thomas, 1998).

Despite the advantages of an activity-based science curriculum—such as that students learn about the process of science, the activities provide direct interaction with concrete and meaningful materials, and students enjoy and learn from this approach (Shymansky, Kyle, & Alport, 1990)—teachers should also be aware of some of the issues with this instructional approach, especially for students with disabilities. For example, Brownell and Thomas (1998) noted that the activities-based approach required more teacher preparation time, more attention to classroom management issues, and additional guided coaching and extra prompting for students with disabilities through the use of systematic questioning during thinking and problem-solving activities than the textbook approach.

Using a published science curriculum that includes classroom materials with lesson plan suggestions, sharing critical instructional planning responsibilities with a coteacher such as a special education teacher or a paraprofessional, integrating science concepts into other curricular subjects, and developing a long-range plan for implementing the science curriculum rather than "doing a science activity whenever there is time" are suggestions for maximizing teacher preparation time. Classroom management issues can be addressed by positively reinforcing students for displaying appropriate behavior, strictly enforcing laboratory rules, modeling the appropriate use of equipment, providing visual and verbal prompts to students as rule reminders such as providing charts or self-monitoring checklists, developing clear classroom rules, and managing transitions wisely (Magg, 1999). Additionally, in an activities-based classroom involving student group work, teachers need to verify that students with disabilities are active participants in the learning process rather than passive observers. It may be tempting for peers or the paraprofessional to complete the majority of the work (Conderman, 1998).

Students with disabilities often experience difficulty in the activity-based approach with tasks that emphasize problem-solving and reasoning skills because they may lack skills in drawing inferences, attending to the critical features of a concept, and retaining the meaning of vocabulary words. Further, many students with disabilities exhibit outer-directedness, which is the tendency to be overly reliant on others. These challenges can be addressed by redirecting students' attention, enhancing their memory through repetition and elaboration, using carefully guided questions, and accepting and reinforcing divergent responses (Mastropieri & Scruggs, 2004). When using guided questioning, these authors remind teachers to (1) select information that is logically related, and for which students have some prior knowledge to help them, (2) ask follow-up questions that help students activate relevant knowledge when they do not immediately respond to questioning, and (3) provide relevant information in the content of the question if students are still unable to draw relevant conclusions. Finally, Kame'enui, Carnine, Dixon, Simmons, and Coyne (2002) noted that any type of science instruction for students with disabilities should include the following six major principles of effective instruction:

1. *Focus on the big ideas*—highly selected concepts, principles, rules, strategies, or heuristics that facilitate the most efficient and broadest acquisition of knowledge.

2. *Teach conspicuous strategies*—the sequence of teaching events and teacher actions to make the steps in learning explicit. They are made conspicuous by the use of visual maps or models, verbal directions, full explanations, etc.

3. *Provide mediated scaffolding*—temporary support for students to learn new material.

4. *Include strategic integration*—planful consideration and sequencing of instruction in ways that show the commonalities and differences between old and new knowledge.

5. *Access primed background knowledge*—related knowledge, placed effectively in sequence, that students must already possess in order to learn new knowledge.

6. *Provide judicious review*—the sequence and schedule of opportunities learners have to apply and develop facility with new knowledge. The review must be adequate, distributed, cumulative, and varied. (pp. 67–69)

Clearly, an activity-based approach is less structured than a textbook approach. Therefore, many of the suggestions noted above and throughout this chapter provide teachers with ideas for instructional supports that provide additional structure within the context of the lesson. When such structure is present, students with disabilities may require fewer and less dramatic accommodations in science than in any other subject (Choate, 2000).

The textbook approach to teaching science relies primarily on a published text as the source for instruction. Oral and silent reading of the text, class discussions, worksheets, and occasional extending activities are used in this approach. Although relying on a text may be easier for the teacher trio presented at the beginning of the chapter, some issues with this method include the following: (1) The focus tends to emphasize language arts skills (reading, writing, and vocabulary) rather than the science processes; (2) the textbook may provide inaccurate information (Kame'enui et al., 2002); (3)

the textbook may not be written at a reading level suitable for a diverse classroom; or (4) the approach itself may not be developmentally appropriate for students who learn best by doing.

Content enhancements are techniques that help students identify, organize, comprehend, and remember content information (Nolet & McLaughlin, 2005). Content enhancements are often used in the textbook approach to address some of these issues. These authors noted that some frequently used content enhancements include the following:

1. *Advance organizers*—These are preinstructional methods designed to help children connect new information with prior knowledge. Some examples include asking questions prior to a discussion or reading assignment; listing vocabulary words on the board; presenting statements that activate student's prior knowledge; presenting an outline of content; providing necessary background information to the class; motivating students by showing the relevance of the lesson; and stating the lesson objectives or outcomes (Friend & Bursuck, 2006).

2. *Visuals*—These include a variety of displays that portray relationships among and between concepts. Some examples include diagrams, models, videos, digital material, graphic organizers, and concept maps. Another example, concept diagrams, provide the name of the concept, its definition, characteristics that are always, sometimes, and never present, and examples and nonexamples of the concept (Carnine, Silbert, Kame'enui, & Tarver, 2004).

3. *Study guides*—Typically, these are worksheets that include a set of statements or questions that focus the learner's attention on critical information from the text. Some adaptations for students with special needs include including only critical questions, providing the page number of the text where the answer can be located, providing a word bank, writing the study guide at the student's reading level, and allowing for peer teaching situations using the study guide (Friend & Bursuck, 2006).

4. *Peer-mediated instruction*—This group of content enhancements uses peers as instructional agents within the classroom. Some examples of using peers include peer and cross-age tutoring, classwide tutoring, or cooperative learning (Nolet & McLaughlin, 2005).

5. *Mnemonics*—These are strategies that help students store and retrieve information—often for a test or quiz. Mnemonic devices can be written, verbal, or pictorial, and they can be developed by the teacher, the class, or both. Jingles, rhymes, poems, images, acrostics, and sentences are examples of mnemonics (Conderman & Pedersen, 2005). One mnemonic device, used to teach science vocabulary, is called the keyword method. This strategy uses verbal associations and visual imagery to help students remember vocabulary through these steps: (1) The vocabulary word (i.e., drone = a male honeybee) is "changed" (or associated) with another word that is familiar to the students, acoustically similar to the vocabulary word, and something that can be easily illustrated in a interactive image (i.e, bone). This "new word" (bone) is the key word. (2) Students draw the vocabulary word (drone) interacting with the key word (bone). (3) When asked the meaning of the vocabulary word (drone), students recall their interactive image (their picture), and this helps them recall the meaning (Friend & Bursuck, 2006).

Regardless of the chosen instructional approach, students with an Individualized Educational Program (IEP) or a Section 504 Accommodation Plan are entitled to accommodations or modifications. **Accommodations** are services or supports that provide access to the subject matter, instruction, or assessment. Providing the students extra time, putting books or other reading material on tape, allowing oral testing, allowing the student to dictate written responses, and allowing the use of technologies such as a calculator or computer are common classroom accommodations (Wood, 1998). Additionally, teachers can make accommodations in the test or quiz (i.e., allow more time, a quiet environment, the test to be read); in teacher techniques (adjust instruction to student learning styles); and in the format of the content (i.e., use graphic organizers, provide checklists to students, and use task analysis to break assignments into critical steps) (Wood, 1998).

In contrast, **modifications** are changes in the instruction, performance level, or assessment. A student is either taught something different from the rest of the class or taught the same information but at a different level of complexity (Nolet & McLaughlin, 2005). Some examples of modifications include the student writing sentences describing pictures while others are writing a story, a student learning one-digit addition while others are learning two-digit addition, or some students using a science textbook or science materials one or more grade levels below their peers (Nolet & McLaughlin, 2005).

These accommodations and modifications are often part of a concept called **universal design for learning** (UDL), which refers to building in flexibility to accommodate the instructional needs of diverse learners in a classroom (Hitchcock, Meyer, Rose, & Jackson, 2002). The underlying premise of UDL is that products and environments should be usable by the largest number of people possible without the need for additional modifications beyond those incorporated into the original design. When additional adaptations are needed, they should be easily and unobtrusively added. Therefore, UDL requires teachers to consider the critical effects of their instructional decisions on every student in the classroom. A benefit of UDL is that the built-in features that accommodate individuals with disabilities make it easier for everyone else to participate and learn in that environment. This is accomplished by including goals that appropriately challenge all learners, using flexible materials that support transformations between media and multiple representations, incorporating instructional methods that are flexible and diverse, and using assessments that are flexible and accurate (Nolet & McLaughlin, 2005). Ideas based on the principles of universal design are included in Table 10.2.

In addition to UDL in diverse classrooms, such as the one team taught by Celest, JoAnne, and Marcus, teachers can use the planning pyramid to strategically plan instruction. The **planning pyramid** is a framework for planning instruction to enhance the learning of all students. This structure is especially helpful in science and social studies (Schumm, Vaughn, & Harris, 1997). The planning pyramid has three layers. The layer at the base of the pyramid represents what all students will learn, the middle layer represents what most (but not all) students will learn, and the top layer represents what some students will learn. The pyramid is designed to help teachers prioritize curricular components and help students focus on these components. This planning system also enables teachers to be more explicit about their instruction and more proficient in their planning (Schumm et al., 1997). An example of a planning pyramid for a diverse science classroom, which differentiates learning among the three levels, is presented in Figure 10.1.

UDL and the planning pyramid support the recent educational reform movement, which maintains that science instruction is for all students (Kame'eniu et al., 2002). Under No Child Left Behind (NCLB) legislation, states must assess at least 95 percent of all students with disabilities in reading/language arts, mathematics, and science (Nolet & McLaughlin, 2005). Students with

Table 10.2 ● Universal Design Principles in Science

- Provide typed and legible handouts, color-code steps of an activity, underline or highlight important words, provide students with their own set of lab directions, use graph paper with larger grids (Ormsbee & Finson, 2000).

- Use adapted equipment, such as braille-marked materials, talking thermometers and balances, enlarged three-dimensional models, and large-screen videos and microprojectors for students, with physical, sensory, and fine-motor difficulties (Mastropieri & Scruggs, 1995).

- Demonstrate essential aspects of the experiment, team students with disabilities with students without disabilities, provide a checklist of the steps of the activity, and periodically check student progress (Salend, 1998).

- Post, discuss, and review safety features. Use print and tactile substances to label areas and equipment, and have all students wear safety equipment (Kucera, 1993).

- Provide adapted workspaces and specialized equipment for students with physical disabilities, such as work surfaces 30 inches from the floor, accessible equipment controls, flexible connections to water, electricity, or gas lines, light-weight fire extinguishers, and appropriate clearance for leg and aisle space (Kucera, 1993).

- For English-language learners, label parts of the classroom and lab equipment with English and Spanish names; show objects, draw pictures or, demonstrate the meaning of key terms; repeat instructions, actions, or demonstrations as needed; demonstrate procedures and provide clarifying diagrams and illustrations before beginning lab work; strategically assign lab partners; review at the end of each lesson; provide feedback to students regarding their language use; enlist parental support in building students' background knowledge (Short & Echevarria, 2005; Watson, 2004).

- Use instructional technology and multimedia such as computer software, hypertext/hypermedia, computer simulations, videocassettes, videodiscs, captioned television, CD-ROM, virtual reality, liquid crystal display (LCD), and the Internet (Trowbridge & Bybee, 1996).

- When using the textbook, provide study guides and audiotaped texts, prioritize the material the student must learn, and teach students mnemonics to remember important information. For large-group instruction, provide guided notes, response cards, and use cooperative learning groups (Munk, Bruckert, Call, Stoehrmann, & Radandt, 1998).

- Have a "cooling off" place for students who need behavioral support, stabilize science equipment to avoid spills by using Velcro, use large clear labels on all equipment and materials, provide clear directions in a step-by-step process, develop behavioral or academic checklists, and prepare for spills by placing tarps on the floor, having students wear large shirts over their school clothing, and using trays and tubs to hold supplies (Mastropieri & Scruggs, 2004).

- Clearly identify expectations in writing, put reading material on tape, provide students with chapter outlines or handouts that highlight key points in their readings; read aloud material written on the chalkboard or that is presented in handouts or transparencies; provide the student with book summaries, synopses, or digests of major reading assignments to review beforehand; and make downloads for Cliffs Notes available for computer use (and for transformation to tape output) (*Inclusion in Science Education for Students With Disabilities,* 2005).

- Consider various grading options such as changing letter or number grades by adding written comments or symbols; changing the grading criteria or the standard on which the grade is based; using alternatives to letter and number grades such as pass/fail grades and checklists of skill competencies; basing the student's grade on the attainment of individualized goals, personal improvement, or prioritized content; or modifying the weight of different requirements (Friend & Bursuck, 2006).

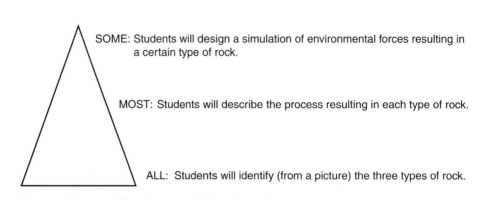

SOME: Students will design a simulation of environmental forces resulting in a certain type of rock.

MOST: Students will describe the process resulting in each type of rock.

ALL: Students will identify (from a picture) the three types of rock.

Figure 10.1 ● Planning pyramid for science lesson.

disabilities receive the bulk of their instruction from their general education teacher or with periodic assistance from a special education teacher or paraprofessionals. Even in cotaught science classes or those where a paraprofessional is present, the general education teacher is responsible for ensuring that students with disabilities learn the same content and concepts as others in the class (Jarrett, 1999). The National Science Teachers Association (2004) has taken a very strong position regarding teaching science to students with disabilities. In 2004, NSTA made the following declarations concerning teaching science to students with special needs:

- Have appropriate assistance, such as paraprofessionals or sign language interpreters, available to students with disabilities, so that they can master the science material. Ensure that paraprofessionals and tutors are competent to help students with disabilities learn science content.

- Ensure that educational aids, such as computers and assistive technologies, are available to help students with disabilities learn the science material.

- Provide literacy and mathematical tools to help students with disabilities access the science resources.

- Ensure that the classroom and work stations are accessible to students with different kinds of disabilities, including physical and sensory disabilities.

- Ensure that the classroom and the work stations are safe for all students by making necessary accommodations, such as modifying counter height, adjusting lab groups as appropriate, and bringing in paraprofessionals on an as-needed basis.

- Ensure that high-stakes assessment tests are not used in a punitive way for students with disabilities and that positive decisions are made as a result of these tests.

- Make every effort to select quality curriculum print materials and multimedia products that promote inclusiveness of people with disabilities through the text, illustrations, and graphics.

- Make every effort to select quality curriculum materials that present culturally diverse people with disabilities as role models working in all disciplines and at all levels of science.

- Ensure that the science materials meet the educational needs of students with a range of learning styles, so that the quality and depth of science investigations are equivalent for all students in the classroom.

Such principles will likely gain importance as the number of students with disabilities receiving their science instruction in the general education classroom continues to rise (Turnbull, Turnbull, Shank, & Smith, 2005), as districts seek to satisfy the demands of having highly qualified teachers under the NCLB legislature, and as states begin assessing students' knowledge and understanding of science. In addition to the principles noted above, Rakes and Choate (2000) provided the following principles for teaching science to learners with special needs:

- Use an activity-based format to teach concepts and skills.
- Choose important survival topics and apply them to everyday life.
- Use realistic and relevant experiments and examples.
- Establish the experiential base for each topic.
- Emphasize and directly teach vocabulary.
- Limit each lesson to the most relevant information.
- Provide generous review activities with each lesson.
- Integrate science with other subjects.
- Carefully structure the content and format of the program.
- Provide response prompts and teach self-monitoring.
- Encourage parents to reinforce the science program.
- Keep up with scientific advances.
- Build interest and enthusiasm.
- Adjust instruction for specific student needs and teach specific skills.

Performance-Based Assessments in Science

Although teachers should use a variety of assessments to measure student skill growth and understanding of concepts, science lends itself particularly well for using performance-based assessments. **Performance-based assessments** provide students with opportunities to demonstrate their mastery of a skill or concept by actually performing a task, rather than taking a traditional paper-and-pencil test (Friend & Bursuck, 2006). Paper-and-pencil assessments typically measure the student's language arts abilities, rather than their level of understanding the science concept or skill (Jarrett, 1999), and many students with disabilities perform poorly on reading, writing, and/or language tasks (Mastropieri & Scruggs, 2004). Therefore, this traditional assessment may not be an accurate or fair assessment to use in science classroom for students with disabilities. For these and other reasons, in 1994, the National Assessment of Educational Progress (NAEP) began including performance tasks, open-ended items, and portfolios as part of its assessment (Hein & Price, 1994). This change is important because most state standards emphasize applied problem solving and authentic knowledge. Further, many of the standards cross subject areas, such as requiring students to apply math concepts and skills in science (Nolet & McLaughlin, 2005).

Performance-based assessments are also sometimes referred to as authentic assessments, or authentic learning tasks, when they can be presented within real-world contexts and lead to real-world outcomes (Friend & Bursuck, 2006). In short, they require students to develop a product or demonstrate an ability or skill based on understanding of concepts and relationships and are especially useful when students are working on long-term projects, as they can show use of a variety of resources and demonstrate mastery of various concepts and principles (Cohen & Spenciner, 1998). It is generally believed that authentic assessments provide a more accurate measure of the academic level of the student than paper-and-pencil tests (Jarrett, 1999). Some examples of performance-based assessments in science include portfolios where students include representative work samples, student-selected best performances, reports from hands-on investigations, notes from a science fair project, and journal entries, including self-evaluation (Wood, 2006); problem-based tasks where students provide information about their use of scientific inquiry and their use of problem solving strategies (Nolet & McLaughlin, 2005); lab activities where students write observations and complete tasks; student drawings or concept maps illustrating a process; prediction activities; original written stories that relate to a science concept; and presentations or exhibits given to the class or a wider audience (Hein & Price, 1994). Performance-based assessments can also be used to determine the extent to which students work cooperatively, are sensitive to others, or use computers, manipulatives, or other resources (Cohen & Spenciner, 1998).

Where more traditional assessments are used, teachers should employ best practices in item construction. Conderman and Koroglanian (2002) offered the following tips for teachers: (1) For true-false items, test one idea, write items without any qualifications, avoid using negatives, avoid items that are obviously true or false, write items of the same length, and write an equal number of true and false items; (2) for multiple-choice items, write direct questions, make the stem longer than the choice, avoid using "all" or "none" choices, avoid clues, avoid negatives, write items of the same length, and scatter the correct choices equally; and (3) for matching items, use homogeneous lists, place longer phrases in the left column, include more responses than premises, arrange responses in a logical order, and restrict the number of matches to ten or fewer. Additional assessment accommodations, for various conditions, are noted in Table 10.3.

Sample Science Activities With Modifications

Table 10.4 provides a sample science activity for each of the National Science Education Standards or themes. Each sample lesson also has the science processes emphasized, as well as possible modifications for students with special needs. These activities, with their suggested adaptations for students with disabilities, provide guidelines for teachers like Celest, JoAnn, and Marcus as they plan for their diverse class of first graders. This team they might also consider the Resources provided at the end of this chapter.

Table 10.3 ● Assessment Accommodations

Disability/Condition	Assessment Accommodations
Visual Impairment	• Provide additional time • Provide a reader • Provide a scribe • Allow testing in a quiet location • Allow frequent breaks • Enlarge test, use braille format, use illumination systems
Hearing Impairment	• Provide assistance *before* the test to teach new forms of test taking • Provide additional time • Assist with interpreting directions • Change test format • Rephrase content
Traumatic Brain Injury	• Use recognition rather than recall test items • Provide a scribe
Physical and Other Health Impairments	• Use computer-based applications • Allow more frequent breaks • Provide a scribe • Allow extended time • Provide physical access to the testing site
Severe and Multiple Disabilities	• Develop alternative assessments based on the student's IEP that are aligned with state standards
Autism	• Provide positive reinforcement • Allow a familiar person to administer the test • Implement methods to reduce test anxiety
Mental Retardation	• Provide a scribe • Allow extended time • Read items orally • Clarify or rephrase test items
AD/HD	• Allow extra breaks • Allow multiple testing periods • Provide a testing environment that does not distract the student
Communication Disorders	• Provide additional time • Paraphrase or simplify questions • Use recognition rather than recall questions • Allow use of technology, per IEP • Provide visual supports • Assess student in most appropriate mode of expression

(Continued)

Sample Science Activities With Modifications

Table 10.3 • *(Continued)*

Disability/Condition	Assessment Accommodations
ED/BD	• Provide extended time • Allow extra breaks • Reduce test anxiety • Administer test individually

Turnbull et al., 2005

Table 10.4 • Science Content and Modifications

	How Are Rocks the Same and Different
NSES	Earth and Space Science
Science Processes	Observation
Materials	3 locally gathered rocks
	3 sheets of white paper
	1 large nail
Questions	Do any of the rocks look or feel like any of the other rocks?
	How can we tell if one rock is harder or softer than the others?
Directions	• Bring to class or take the class outside to find three rocks that look and feel different.
	• Display one rock on each sheet of paper, and have children come forward to make observations. As they do, write their observations on the board.
	• Scratch each rock with the nail, and have children observe that some rocks are harder than others, that some rock particles scrape off, and that the scraped-off particles are different sizes and colors.
Science Content	The earth's crust is made of different types of rocks. Rocks are different because of the materials within them and the ways in which they are formed. Wind, water, and ice break up rock into smaller pieces. Soil is made of small particles of rock as well as other material.
Modification Suggestions	General adaptations: Have students work in partners or teams, provide small containers or bags for groups to collect their rocks, provide guidelines regarding which rocks to collect (no smaller than your thumb and no larger than your hand and light enough so that you alone can carry it), review safety issues (no throwing rocks), have each group search for a certain quality of a rock to share with the class. For students with language issues, preview vocabulary words such as *rough, soft,* and *hard* using a reference chart containing descriptive words with their definitions and an associated visual or picture symbolizing that quality. Allow students with vision impairments to touch and examine rocks and use illumination or

Table 10.4 ● *(Continued)*

magnifying systems to see the rock particles (Cox & Dykes, 2001). Allow such students to feel a specific place on a rock before a scratch test, so they can feel the scratch. The "Big Eye Lamp" (Big Eye Lamp, Inc.) consists of a high-intensity light with a large magnifying lens attached that is helpful for students with low vision (Mastropieri & Scruggs, 2004)

How to Make a Fossil

NSES	Science and Technology
Science Processes	Hypothesizing, Experimenting, Communicating
Materials per Child or Group	Aluminum foil pie plate, plastic spoon, water, Vaseline, plaster of paris, assortment of plant materials, including portions of a carrot, a leaf, and a twig
Motivation	Be sure to have two or three real fossils on hand, if possible, or reference books with pictures of various fossils. Display the fossils or pictures of the fossils, and have students make observations about their characteristics. Encourage the students to discuss how the fossils may have been formed. Inform the students that they will be making their own fossils during the activity.
Directions	• Have students coat each portion of the plants they are using with a thin layer of Vaseline • Have students mix the plaster of paris with water in the bottom of the pie plate until they obtain a thick, smooth mixture. • Have students gently press the plant material into the upper surface of the plaster of paris and set the plaster aside to harden. • Bring the children together for a group discussion. Emphasize that what they have done represents one way in which fossils are formed; that is, plant or animal material falls into sediment, making an imprint. If the sediment then hardens into rock, the imprint will remain even though the organic matter decays.
Science Content	A fossil is any preserved part or trace of something that lived in the past. Leaves, stems, bones, and even footprints have been preserved as fossils. Some fossils are formed when water passing over and through portions of animal or plan remains deposits minerals that replace the original materials. In other cases, animal and plant remains are buried in sediment. An imprint of the shape is left in mud even when the material decays, and if the mud hardens and turns to rock, the imprint is preserved. This type of impression, which the students have replicated in this activity, is known as a mold.
Discussion Questions	Have you ever found and fossils or seen any fossils on display? If so, what were they like and where did you see them? *Answers will vary.* The fossils you made are known as molds. How could a scientist use a mold fossil to make something that looked like the object that formed the mold? *They could use something like clay to press against the mold fossil. They surface of the clay would take the shape of the original material.*

(Continued)

Sample Science Activities With Modifications

Table 10.4 ● (Continued)

Modification Suggestions	General adaptations: Form cooperative learning groups, model the activity first, provide a visual task analysis of each step, have solution(s) premixed, use switches, levers, or other technologies for students with motor challenges to press the material, and review safety and cleanup measures. Activities such as this one can be especially helpful for students with cognitive difficulties understand an abstract concept. Remember to introduce students with visual impairments to materials and equipment before the activity, so they can concentrate on the concepts during the activity rather than the equipment (Cox & Dykes, 2001).

Whose Fault Is It?

NSES	Earth and Space Science
Science Processes	Observing, Inferring
Materials per Child or Group	2 blocks of wood 4 sticks of modeling clay, each a different color
Motivation	Ask the students how you could use clay to make rock layers. Flatten each stick of clay into a strip that is about 1 centimeter (less than $1/2$ inch) thick and 8 to 10 centimeters (about 3 to 4 inches) wide.
Directions	• Place the clay strips on top one another. Ask the students to guess whether the strips represent sedimentary, igneous, or metamorphic rocks. • Gently press the wood blocks against the ends of the clay layers, and have the students observe changes. • Eventually, small cracks will appear on the layers, and the layers will be forced into a hump. Note if the clay is too soft or too warm, the fractures will not occur. Allow the layers to dry or cool for a day before performing this part of the demonstration.
Science Content	Layers of sedimentary rock provide important clues about the relative ages of rocks. Top layers are usually younger than lower layers. Sometimes, however, layers of rocks are turned upside down as a result of the collusion of the crustal plates and the movement of molten rocks beneath the surface.
Discussion Questions	If the clay layers were layers of rock, which layer would probably be the youngest? Why? *The top. The material in it was deposited last.* What causes the bends and breaks in real rock layers? *Answers will vary. Some students may be aware that pushing together of the plates of the earth's crust produces great forces that change and fracture rock layers.* Do you think that breaks in the rocks layers might allow molten rock to move toward the earth's surface? Why? *Yes. The molten rock can flow up through the cracks because there is nothing to hold it back.*

Table 10.4 • *(Continued)*

Modification Suggestions	General adaptations: Review the types of rock before the activity, provide a comparison chart of the different types of rock, use different textures of clay for students with vision issues, show video clips of the development and formation of rocks, use visuals like graphic organizers to illustrate the rock sequence as well as concepts such as cause and effect. Demonstrations or activities such as this are helpful for students with cognitive disabilities to understand abstract concepts. Students with autism may have aversions to certain textures or smells (Friend, 2006), so use caution, allow the use of gloves or other protective materials, or assign such students other responsibilities if they will be conducting this activity.

Is It a Plant or an Animal?

NSES	Life Science
Science Processes	Observation, Classification
Materials per child or group	10 colorful magazine pages that show plants and animals Scissors 3 mailing envelopes
Motivation	Do you see any living things in the pictures? What is the same (different) about all the plants (animals)?
Directions	• Distribute the materials, and ask the children to cut out all of the pictures they find of living things. • Write words *animals* and *plants* on the board, pronounce them, and have the children write each word on one of the envelopes. Tell the children that there is another type of living thing called a protist. • Make a protist envelope and then explain that most protists are too small to see. • Have children sort their pictures into plant and animal envelopes.
Science Content	There are many different ways to group living things. A common classification system uses three categories: plants, animals, and protists. Plants have cell walls that have cellulose and make food through photosynthesis. Animal cells do not have cell walls. Their cells are bounded by cell membranes. Animals take food into their bodies. Bacteria, viruses, protozoa, and slime molds are classified as protists.
Discussion Questions	What are some differences between plants and animals? Are there some plants or animals that we can not see with our eyes? How would we see them? What tools do we use? How do we know they exist? How do plants and animals help us?

(Continued)

Sample Science Activities With Modifications

Table 10.4 ● *(Continued)*

Modification Suggestions	General adaptations: Review safety measures, if scissors will be used; provide several pictures or magazine pages for each child; ask students to discuss their pictures before they sort them; provide an example and nonexample (Carnine et al., 2004) of an animal and a plant before the children begin the sorting activity; and model the activity. For students with physical or sensory challenges, have some pictures precut, provide larger scissors or other, safer cutting adaptive aids, as needed, allow the use of illumination or magnifying devices, have precut pictures labeled in braille, have envelopes prelabeled, provide larger envelopes, provide a visual on the cover of each envelope to accompany the word label.

Are You a Good Animal Detective?

NSES	Science in Personal and Social Perspective
Science Processes	Observation
Materials per Child or Group	Sheet of easel paper Marking pen
Motivation	What animals do you think we will see outside? How many animals do you think we will see?
Directions	• Take the children on a ten-minute walk around the school grounds to identify the animals that live around the school. • On your return to the classroom, prepare a three-column chart and list the children's recollections of the types and quantities of animals seen. Also note where the animals were seen—for example, under a rock.
Science Content	Life is both diverse and widespread. Any lawn, playground, or natural area on or near the school will have an abundance of animals. Depending on your locale and the season, expect to see squirrels, birds, cats, and dogs. Search for insects and other small creatures under rocks and near moist areas such as the ground near a water fountain or a mud puddle as well as on the bark of trees.
Discussion Questions	What other animals have you seen in your neighborhood? On your way to school? Why do we some animals in certain locations and not others? Why do we see some animals only at certain times of the day or night? Do we see some animals only during certain seasons? Why?
Modification Suggestions	General adaptations involving animals in science activities: preteach about respecting animals and nature as some children with disabilities may have negative experiences or fears associated with certain animals. Consider the health needs of children (allergies, asthma, sensitivities, etc.). Remind students of any rules about touching animals and other safety issues. Substitute photographs or videotapes of animals if needed (Dugger-Wadsworth & Knight, 1999).

Table 10.4 ● *(Continued)*

	What Is a Seed?
NSES	Life Science
Science Processes	Predicting, Observing, Communicating, Interpreting Data, and Controlling Variables
Materials per Child or Group	Large cardboard box cut 2 to 4 inches tall and lined with plastic Soil or starting mixture(vermiculite plus soil) Collections of seeds and other small things ("red-hot" candy, marbles, pebbles) Chart paper 1 index card per student
Motivation	Ask students to bring in seeds and other small items for some science experiments. When the candy arrives, tell them they will begin their study of seeds and discover whether candy will grow.
Directions	● Begin by setting out samples of the small things that students brought. Ask students to describe the items while you list their observations on the chart paper. ● Have each group record in pictures and in words the appearance of each item at the start of the experiment. In addition, each group can glue an item to an index card and use the card to record observations. ● Have each group decide how many of each item should be planted and the depth of planting. Explain that the amount of water, light, warmth, and so on should be the same for each item. These things will be easy to control if the samples are planted in the same box. ● Have each group label each row with the name of the item planted. ● Then, set aside a short period of time each day for maintenance and data gathering. Encourage the children to keep a daily log of what they see. Some children may want to peek at the seeds during the experiment. If they do this, they need to think about the number of each item that was planted and how they can make their inspection without disturbing the others. One way to observe the germination without disturbing the seeds is to place moist paper toweling in a glass jar and "plant" the item between the toweling and the glass. Such a jar will allow students to see what is going on in the soil in the boxes, but perhaps it can be kept a secret until the students have dug up a few of their own seeds. ● When the seeds have been growing for awhile, have the children dig up samples of each type of seed. They can make observations, record them, and compare their new observations with the observations they made at the start of the experiment. ● After some items have sprouted, divide the original set of items into growers and nongrowers. With this set to examine, students should begin to investigate where the items come from and develop a general definition of a true seed.

(Continued)

Sample Science Activities With Modifications

Table 10.4 ● *(Continued)*

Science Content	Seeds come in all sizes, from those as small as the period at the end of a sentence to others as big as a walnut. Shape can also vary dramatically, from round and smooth to pyramidlike. Seeds have protective shells (seed coats) that keep the embryonic plant alive. Stored food will provide the energy for the seedling to reach the soil surface and begin producing food of its own. In order to survive, some plants produce great numbers of seeds, and others produce seeds with structures (such as the hooks on burrs and the "wings" on maple seeds) that enable them to be dispersed. Some seeds even look like insects, which discourage seed-eating birds from consuming them.
Discussion Questions	In what ways are all these items alike? *They are small.*
	How many items of each type should be planted? *More than one or two because some might die before they come up and can be seen.* How deeply should they be planted? *Answers will vary based upon gardening experience, but common sense usually prevails.*
	What should be done about amount of water, sunlight, temperature, and so on that the items receive? *They should be kept the same, so that all the seeds have the same chance of living.*
	What is the biggest difference among the items at the end of the experiment? *Some grow and some don't.*
	What did some seeds become? *They grew into new plants.*
Modification Suggestions	General adaptations for activities involving plants: Provide direct instruction and modeling on the planting process; use larger cards, paper, and graph paper for recording observations; use water syringes to help students deliver the exact amount of water needed by a plant; wrap a rubber band around a dowel or pencil to help students plant seeds at a standard depth; and use plants that grow and develop faster to accommodate for students with waning interests or attention spans. Consider using beans, which grow fast, or Wisconsin Fast Plants (available from Carolina Biological Supply Company), which develop much faster than most plants.
	To help students directly observe root structure, grow plants in clear plastic baggies or all water containers. Students with visual impairments can feel the sunlight in relation to the plant and feel the effect of sunlight on the plant's development (Mastropieri & Scruggs, 2004).

Who Goes There?

NSES	Life Science
Science Processes	Observing, Inferring
Materials per Child or Group	Set of pictures of the animals for which you have footprints Set of pictures showing the various environments in which the animals live Set of animal name cards
Motivation	Hand out the animal pictures to each group. Suggest that they pretend they are teams of animal trackers.

Table 10.4 ● *(Continued)*

Directions	● Before beginning this activity, you will need a set of unlabeled animal footprints and a set of pictures illustrating environments in which the animals are likely to be found. Note: A good source of information on is the ESS unit *Animal Tracks,* originally published by McGraw-Hill but now available from Educational Resources Information Center: Clearinghouse for Science, Mathematics, and Environmental Education; Ohio State University, Columbus, OH.
	● Hold up pictures of the animal track and its environment. After some discussion, have the children think of the animal being described. The group members can discuss the possibilities among themselves before the group suggests an animal.
	● When all the teams are ready, have a member of each group hold up the picture of the animal they have selected. Encourage each group to tell why they think their choice is the correct one.
Science Content	Footprints hold clues about the lives and environments of the animals that made them. Very large footprints often belong to large animals or to animals that travel over soft terrain. For example, the relatively large feet of the snowshoe rabbit support its weight on snow, thus allowing it to travel well on terrain that hinders most other animals. Most animals that live on the open range have smaller feet with hooves that allow them to run fast on fairly smooth, hard land. Some footprints show evidence of claws used for defense as well as climbing. Retractable claws are an obvious benefit to animals that must be able to run quickly and silently before catching their prey.
Discussion Questions	Which of the tracks comes from the biggest animal? *Answer will depend on the tracks and the pictures you are using.*
	Which of the tracks comes from the smallest animal? *Answers will vary.*
	Which of the tracks belongs to an animal that can climb trees? *Answers will vary.*
	Hold up the pictures of various environments (e.g., a treetop for squirrels and an open plain with trees in Africa for elephants), and ask which of the animals might be found in them. Ask the students to guess which footprints might be found in most environments. (Be sure to have the teams explain why they decided on the particular footprints.)
Modification Suggestions	General adaptations: As a small-group activity, ensure that students with disabilities are dispersed in groups with students without disabilities, preteach the job of animal trackers, discuss if children have seen their own tracks (shoe, boot), etc., in mud or snow, discuss how detectives use foot tracks, tire tracks, etc., in their investigations, reduce the number of choices for groups to choose from. Students with visual impairments may need the pictures described in more detail, while others may need three-dimensional pictures or pictures with raised features. Use amplification systems such as FM or personal sound-field systems for students with hearing impairments (DiSarno, Schowalter, & Grassa, 2002).

(Continued)

Sample Science Activities With Modifications

Table 10.4 • *(Continued)*

	When Do We Do Things That Keep Us Healthy and Strong?
NSES	Science in Personal and Social Perspectives
Science Processes	Classifying and Sequencing
Materials per Child or Group	1 large clock with hour and minute hands Easel paper and marker
Motivation	What things do you do before, during, and after school that help keep you healthy and strong? What things could you do that you are not doing now?
Directions	• Begin by explaining to the children that they are going to discuss what an imaginary child named Pat might do to stay healthy and strong. Tell them that you are going to make a chart on which you will record their ideas. • Set the hands of the clock to 7:00 am, review time telling, and have the children give their ideas about what Pat might be doing. For example, 7:00 am might be the time for washing, 7:15 am might be the time that Pat eats a healthy breakfast, 7:30 am might be the time that Pat brushes her/his teeth, and 7:45 am might be the time that Pat puts on a seat belt for the bus ride to school. • Carry this through the school day.
Science Content	Children do many things in the course of a day that contribute to their health and well-being. The sequence of activities is relatively constant. By thinking about what more they could do and by trying to fit new ideas into their sequence, children can improve their health.
Discussion Questions	How many of the items listed do you do? How are you like or not like Pat? How can you improve your choices for healthy living?
Modification Suggestions	Some general adaptations: Provide added verbal descriptions and even a picture prompt of the time shown (7:00) such as "when Pat gets up" (show picture of student getting out of bed) to help students who cannot tell time on a standard clock, illustrate student suggestions on the chart along with the word labels, instead of using the clock, chunk the day into segments such as when Pat gets up, as Pat gets ready for school, when Pat is at school, etc. Use different colored markers on the chart to show different kinds of actions (some dealing with food choices, others with exercise, etc.), provide binary choices (if needed) such as "For a snack, should Pat eat an apple or a candy bar?" In its current form, the activity is largely verbal. Supplementing the instruction with visual prompts may be needed for students with language-based disabilities. Consider making a pictorial time line as a handout with you and the students drawing pictures of Pat throughout the day making healthy choices. Students could later make a pictorial time line of healthy choices they can make throughout their day.

Table 10.4 ● *(Continued)*

	The Mystery Bag
NSES	Science and Technology
Science Processes	Observing, Inferring
Materials per Child or Group	Assorted objects, including pencils, erasers, paper clips, rubber bands, wooden blocks, marshmallows, and coins of various sizes boxes or bags for the objects Large paper bags with two holes (large enough for a hand to fit through) cut near the bottom of each bag 2 paper clips to close the tips of the bags
Motivation	Before class begins, place one of the objects in a bag. Explain to the students that they are going to discover how their sense of touch can help them identify things. Begin the activity by placing your hand in one of the holes in the bag to feel the object inside. Describe the object to the children. Have various children come to the front of the room to feel the object in the bag and also describe the object. On the chalkboard or easel pad, record their guesses of the object.
Directions	● Form two-person cooperative learning teams, and give each team a box or bag containing the objects listed for this activity. Have the teams decide who will go first in each team, and have that person close his or her eyes (or use blindfolds). ● At the front of the room, hold up the object for the other team member to place in the container. Have the children who have had their eyes covered put one hand through each hole and feel the mystery object. ● Ask the children to identify the object. If they are unable to name the object, hold up an assortment of objects and have the children vote for the one they think is correct.
Science Content	The skin has the sense receptors that are sensitive to touch, warmth, cold, pain, and pressure. These sense receptors are not evenly distributed. Pressure is felt most accurately by the tip of the nose, the tongue, and the fingers. Sense receptors in our hands give us our awareness of heat, cold, pain, and pressure.
Discussion Questions	What part of the body do we use most to feel things? *The hands.* What are some of the things that the hands can feel? *How hot or cold things are and whether objects are sharp, smooth, rough, soft, hard, and so on.* What are some things that hands can't tell? *The color of an object, and its general physical appearance, and so on.*

(Continued)

Sample Science Activities With Modifications

Table 10.4 •   *(Continued)*

Modification Suggestions	General adaptations: Be mindful of safety issues if you use items that are sharp (even paperclips), as well as items that may cause strong reactions (allergies, etc.), initially use items with which students are quite familiar, gradually introduce more difficult items, provide clues, as needed, for the child to guess the item, allow the student to ask questions about the mystery item (questions which can be answered by yes or no by their partner).

Where Does the Water Go?

NSES	Physical Science
Science Processes	Observing
Materials per Child or Group	1 sponge, paper towels, 1 clean, dry dishcloth, bowel of water, 3 dishes, and pan balance (optional)
Motivation	How will the sponge (paper towel, cloth) change when we dip it in water?
	Where do you think the water goes when something dries?
Directions	• In this demonstration, the students will observe a sponge, paper towel, and cloth when dry and when wet. The students will already know that when they dry themselves after a bath or shower, the towels they use become wet, but they may not have connected this knowledge with the concept that some material can absorb water.
	• Dip the sponge, paper towels, and dishcloth in the bowl of water.
	• Have the children make observations that you record on the board.
	• After wringing out the objects, place them on plates so that further observations can be made. If a pan balance is available, the children can check changes in mass as the objects dry.
Science Content	Many materials are capable of absorbing water. They retain this water as a liquid. The liquid that is in contact with the surrounding air evaporates and enters the air as water vapor.
Discussion Questions	Are some materials more absorbent than others? Why is this finding important? How could you test to see which paper towel is the best to use for large spills in your kitchen?
Modification Suggestions	General adaptations: Using different types of materials for dipping, using modified equipment, and dipping and observing one item at a time. Use simpler and larger balances for weighing materials. The American Printing House for the Blind has a spring scale for use by individuals with visual impairments (Mastropieri & Scruggs, 2004). Have students feel (as well as weigh) the difference between wet and dry items.

Table 10.4 ● *(Continued)*

	What Is Your Squeezing Force?
NSES	Physical Science
Science Processes	Measuring, Interpreting Data
Materials per Child or Group	1 bathroom scale thin enough for children to grip
Motivation	Display the bathroom scale and explain that it provides a measurement of the amount of pull the earth exerts on our bodies. Tell the children that they will use the scale to see how much pushing force they can exert with their hands.
Directions	• Divide the class into groups and have each group member squeeze the top and bottom of a bathroom scale together. The children should use both hands.
	• As each child concentrates on squeezing the scale, another member of the group writes down the reading on the scale's weight display.
	• Have each group make a graph that shows the names of the person and the squeezing force he or she applied.
Science Content	A bathroom scale has a spring system that reacts in response to the pull of gravity on any mass placed on the scale. Some scales include electrical devices that convert the movement of the springs to electrical information that is displays in the form of a digital display.
Discussion Questions	Is the force you used to squeeze the scale a push or pull? *The children should realize they are exerting two pushes with each hand. They are pushing the top of the scale down and the bottom of the scale up.*
	When we weigh ourselves, what is pulling us down on the scale? *The earth is pulling on us.*
Modification Suggestions	General adaptations: Use scales with large numbers or braille numbers, preteach graphing skills, allowing students with poor muscle control to exert force in other ways on the scale. Some of the STC (Science and Technology for Children) curriculum materials, which are available from Carolina Biological Supply Company, contain lessons on teaching preskills in graphing, charting, and recording data. The AIMS materials (Activities for Integrating Math and Science) also include lessons on beginning graphing and recording data.

Source: Abruscato, 2000.

Summary

Science instruction has the potential for meaningful, integrated, hands-on instruction that encourages critical thinking for all students. The science reforms of recent years support and encourage meaningful science instruction for all students. Many resources are available for teachers to integrate science into the curriculum, as well as plan and deliver effective, interesting, and fun science lessons. Children are inquisitive by nature and tapping into this curiosity by using the science processes helps students understand the nature of science while they gain new information. A hands-on approach is essential in making the abstract concepts of science instruction concrete and meaningful. Students with special needs are entitled to accommodations or modifications in their science instruction. Designing lessons that incorporate the principles of universal design allow greater flexibility for all students. The planning pyramid is a tool for layering instruction in a diverse classroom.

With the information from this chapter in mind, teachers such as Celest, JoAnne, and Marcus can begin systematically planning their science instruction. Their road map will include familiarizing themselves with their local and/or state science standards, prioritizing instruction during their day, strategically infusing science concepts and examples throughout their daily curriculum, incorporating authentic, hands-on problem-based activities whenever possible, and ensuring that students with disabilities have full access to the science standards. Viewed in this way, science instruction no longer needs to be a mystery or an "add on" whenever time permits. Rather, science can be an integral and exciting component of the elementary education curriculum.

Thinking It Through

1. Describe and provide an example of three qualities of science.

2. Explain how the textbook/worksheet approach to teaching science violates the goal of elementary science instruction.

3. Provide a rationale and at least three of your own examples of integrating science into other areas of the elementary curriculum.

4. Differentiate between accommodations and modifications and provide an example of each relating to an elementary science lesson.

5. Differentiate between traditional, pencil-and-paper assessment and performance-based assessment as each is used in science.

Children's Literature in Science

Aldrin, B. (2005). *Reaching for the moon.* New York: Harper-Collins.

Carle, E. (1969). *Very hungry caterpillar.* New York: Philomel.

Carle, E. (1988). *Mixed-up chameleon.* New York: Harper-Collins.

Cobb, V. (2004). *I fall down.* New York: HarperCollins.

Cole, H. (2003). *On the way to the beach.* New York: Greenwillow Books.

French, V. (2006). *T. Rex.* Westminster, MA: Candlewick Press.

Llewellyn, C. (2003). *Starting life butterfly.* Minneapolis: Northword Books.

Mastro, J. (2003). *Antarctic ice.* New York: Henry Holt.

Still, C. (2006). *About arachnids: A guide for children.* Atlanta: Peachtree.

Wadsworth, G. (2003). *Benjamin Banneker: Pioneering scientist.* Minneapolis: Carolrhoda Books.

Resources

National Science Teachers Association

www.nsta.org/

The National Science Teachers Association, or NSTA, was founded in 1944 and is the largest organization in the world committed to promoting excellence and innovation in science teaching and learning for all. NSTA's current membership of more than 55,000 includes science teachers, science supervisors, administrators, scientists, business and industry representatives, and others involved in and committed to science education. The website contains many resources for science educators.

National Science Education Standards On Line

www.nap.edu/readingroom/books/nses/html/

This site contains the complete text to the National Science Education Standards. This is in hypertext format and easy to navigate from one part to the other.

American Association for the Advancement of Science

www.aaas.org/

The American Association for the Advancement of Science (AAAS) is a worldwide leader in science education. The organization sponsored Project 2061, a reform movement that lead to the publication of the National Science Education Standards. AAAS (1990) published Project 2061's *Benchmarks for Science Literacy.* The resources for Project 2061 can be found on AAAS's website along with any other science resources. One fundamental premise of Project 2061 is that schools do not need to teach more and more content but rather focus on what is essential to science literacy and to teach it more effectively.

Science Lesson Plans

www.col-ed.org/cur/science.html#sci1

This is a no-frills site that contains a cache of science lesson plans. This site contains no pictures or fancy text, but just the title of the lesson plans along with the appropriate grade level and a link to the lesson plan.

Young Inventors Educational Resources

http://inventors.miningco.com/msub11er.htm

This site contains lesson plans for teaching about inventions and inventors and other science lesson plans for grades K–12. The site includes fun experiments all about inventing, inventions made by children, workshops, courses and summer camps for "kid inventors," and contests children can submit their inventions to.

Assessment Ideas for Elementary Science Classrooms

www.sasked.gov.sk.ca/docs/elemsci/ideass.html

This site contains assessment ideas for the elementary science classroom. It includes templates for assessments, self-check lists, and ideas and links for various types of assessments for the science classroom.

ERIC Clearinghouse on Disabilities and Gifted Education

www.hoagiesgifted.org/eric/

This is a link to what remains of the ERIC Clearinghouse for Disabilities and Gifted Education (ERICEC), which was disbanded by the U.S. government on December 19, 2003. However, the site contained valuable resources and its supporters refused to let it go. This link leads to an archive of the material that was available on the original site at the time it was disbanded. It was created by Hoagies' Gifted Education Page. The site is for general use and is updated with current links wherever possible. The information contained in this archive is in the public domain.

Science for All Americans

www.project2061.org/publications/sfaa/online/sfaatoc.htm?ql

This is a link to the full text of a book from Project 2061. The book written by AAAS (1990), is about science literacy. *Science for All Americans* consists of a set of recommendations regarding what understandings and ways of thinking are essential for all citizens in a world shaped by science and technology. The book provides a rationale for the need for scientific literacy and an easy-to-understand discussion of scientific literacy and themes from Project 2061's *Benchmarks for Science Literacy. Science for All Americans* is based on the belief that the science-literate person is one who is aware that science, mathematics, and technology are interdependent human enterprises with strengths and limitations; understands key concepts and principles of science; is familiar with the natural world and recognizes both its diversity and unity; and uses scientific knowledge and scientific ways of thinking for individual and social purposes.

4000 Years of Women in Science

www.astr.ua.edu/4000ws/4000ws.html

This site is a comprehensive collection of biographies, photographs, and graphics about women scientists and their contributions to the field of science. The site's content is ever growing.

The Faces of Science: African Americans in the Sciences

https://webfiles.uci.edu/mcbrown/display/faces.html

This site profiles African Americans who have made important contributions to science and engineering. It is well organized and lists individuals by categories and serves as a link to biographical information.

Playtime Is Science

www.edequity.org/playtime.php

This website provides information about Playtime Is Science (PS), which is an early childhood, hands-on science program that creates partnerships among school, home, and the community. It encompasses a process where children with and without disabilities are encouraged to wonder, question, and experiment—in short, to start thinking like scientists everyday. Guidelines and practical recommendations for conducting science activities with children with disabilities are included.

LatinoWeb

www.latinoweb.com

This site is currently under construction. This site contains a plethora of information related to strategies and techniques for encouraging youths from minority groups to pursuer careers in science and engineering.

ERIC Website for Science, Mathematics, and Environmental Education

www.ericse.org/ or www.stemworks.org/

This site was formerly an ERIC clearinghouse. It is now being maintained by Educational Realms and has the same information formerly housed on the ERIC site. Go to the site and perform searches on topics in science education to get the latest information.

Center for Research on Education, Diversity, and Excellence (CREDE)

www.cal.org/crede/credeprj.htm

This site contains information on educating children from culturally diverse backgrounds. The center sponsors a variety of educational related projects that include attention to "Instruction in Context," which deals with various subjects, including science, to these students, and "Assessment Programs," which suggests alternative ways of assessing their progress.

Council for Exceptional Children's Teaching Science to Students With Disabilities

http://ericec.org/faq/science.html

This site provides readers with articles, books, and other resources on teaching science to students with disabilities. It is sponsored by the ERIC Clearinghouse on Disabilities and Gifted Education.

Inclusion in Science Education for Students With Disabilities

www.as.wvu.edu/~scidis/sitemap.html

This website has hundreds of ideas for accommodations and modifications for students with disabilities in inclusive science classrooms. The site provides information, strategies, organizations, resources, and books and videos associated with the following disabilities: AD/HD, learning disabilities, behavior disabilities, intellectual disabilities, communication disorders, motor disabilities, and sensory impairments.

Science Education for Students With Disabilities

www.sesd.info/aboutus.htm

This is the home of the Science Education for Students With Disabilities website, which exists to promote and advance the teaching of science and develop curricula and instructional materials for students with disabilities at all levels. This organization disseminates information concerning the development of science materials and strategies for accommodations for students with special needs; promotes science as a viable career option for students with disabilities; develops publications that deal with science for students with disabilities; stimulates research related to the general area of science education for students with disabilities; collaborates with other organizations with similar purposes; and utilizes and works with technologies and strategies that impact teachers and students with disabilities in the science learning environment.

The American Printing House for the Blind

1839 Frankford Avenue
PO Box 6085
Louisville, K 40206
(800) 223-1839
info@aph.org
www.aph.org

Science Products

Lancaster, PA
(610) 296-8111

Virtual Field Trips

American Museum of Natural History: National Center for Science Literacy, Education, and Technology

www.amhn.org

Association for Supervision and Curriculum Development

amachi@commatascd.org

Maintains a list of virtual field trips that educators can request via email.

Curriculum/Materials/Resources

Carolina Biological Supply (CBS)

2700 York Road
Burlington, NC 27215
(800) 334-5551

Excellent resource for K–6 teachers, such as Science Technology for Children materials.

Delta Science Modules

Delta Education Inc.
PO Box 915
Hudson, NH 03051-0915
(800) 258-1302

Delta distributes their own activities-oriented materials with a large supply of manipulatives.

Full Option Science System (FOSS) (Encyclopedia Britannia Educational Co., 1992)

Offers hands-on, lab-based K–6 structured curriculum around four themes: scientific reasoning, physical science, earth science, and life science. This program also includes Science Activities for the Visually Impaired (SAVI) and Science Enrichment Learning for Learners with Physical Handicaps (SELPH), activities-based science programs for students with disabilities. FOSS was developed for general education based on the SAVI/SELPH materials.

Mind Ware

(800) 999-0398
www.mindwareonline.com

"Brainy toys for kids of all ages"

Pro-Ed

8700 Shoal Creek Boulevard
Austin, TX 78757-6897
(800) 897-3202

www.proedinc.com
Raised-line paper.

Resources for Teaching Elementary School Science

National Science Resources Center
Washington, DC 20560
(202) 357-2555

This excellent public resource for teachers—with many summer workshops and a mailing list, Science for All Children (SAC; Cawley, Miller, Sentman, & Bennett, 1993)—addresses four interrelated themes and thinking processes—systems, change, structure, and relationship—designed for elementary-level children

SAVI/SELPH

Lawrence Hall of Science
The University of California at Berkeley
2547 8th Street
Berkeley, CA 97410

Science Activities for the Visually Impaired/Science Enrichment for the Learners With Physical Handicaps

Steck-Vaughn

PO Box 26105
Austin, TX 78755
(800) 531-5015

A variety of science curricula for students with disabilities.

References

Abruscato, J. (2000). *Teaching children science.* Boston: Allyn and Bacon.

American Association for the Advancement of Science. (1990a). *Benchmarks for science literacy.* New York: Oxford University Press.

American Association for the Advancement of Science. (1990b). *Science for all Americans.* New York: Oxford University Press.

Barber, R. H. (1998). *Science in the multicultural classroom.* Boston: Allyn and Bacon.

Bial, R. (2000). *A handful of dirt.* New York: Walker.

Brownell, M., & Thomas, C. W. (1998). Margo Mastropieri: Quality science instruction for students with disabilities. *Intervention in School and Clinic 34*(2), 118–122.

Carnine, D. W., Silbert, J., Kame'enui, E. J., & Tarver, S. (2004). *Direct instruction reading* (5th ed). Upper Saddle River, NJ: Pearson.

Cawley, J. F. (1994). Science for students with disabilities. *Remedial and Special Education, 15*(2), 67–71.

Choate, J. S. (2000). *Successful inclusive teaching: Proven ways to detect and correct special needs.* Boston: Allyn and Bacon.

Cohen, L. G., & Spenciner, L. J. (1998). *Assessment of children and youth.* New York: Addison Wesley Longman.

Conderman, G. (1998). How are we practicing inclusion? *Kappa Delta Pi Record, 34*(2), 52–55.

Conderman, G., & Koroglanian, C. (2002.) Writing test questions like a pro. *Intervention in School and Clinic, 38*(2), 83–87.

Conderman, G., & Pedersen, T. (2005, October). Mnemonics across the curriculum. Paper presented at the Illinois Council for Exceptional Children conference, Schaumburg, IL.

Cox, P. R., & Dykes, M. K. (2001). Effective classroom adaptations for students with vision impairments. *Teaching Exceptional Children, 33*(6), 68–74.

DiSarno, N., Schowalter, M., & Grassa, P. (2002). Classroom amplification to enhance student performance. *Teaching Exceptional Children, 34*(6), 20–26.

Dugger-Wadsworth, D. E., & Knight, D. (1999). Preparing the inclusion classroom for students with special physical and health needs. *Intervention in School and Clinic 34*(3), 170–175.

Fradd, S. H., & Lee, O. (1995). Science for all: A promise or a pipe dream for bilingual students. *The Bilingual Research Journal, 19*(2), 261–278.

Friend, M. (2006). Special education: *Contemporary perspectives for school professionals.* Boston: Pearson.

Friend, M., & Bursuck, W. D. (2006). *Including students with special needs: A practical guide for classroom teachers.* Boston: Pearson.

Goldberg, H., & Wagreich, P. (1989). Focus on integrating science and math. For a real lesson in science, students should conduct an experiment involving quantitative variables. *Science and Children, 26*(5), 22–24.

Hein, G. E., & Price, S. (1994). *Active assessment for active science.* Portsmouth, NH: Heinemann.

Hitchcock, C., Meyer, A., Rose, D., & Jackson, R. (2002). Providing new access to the general curriculum: Universal design for learning. *Teaching Exceptional Children 35*(2), 8–17.

Inclusion in Science Education for Students With Disabilities. (2005). Retrieved December 21, 2005, from www.as.wvu.edu/~scidis/

Jarrett, D. (1999). *The inclusive classroom: Mathematics and science instruction for students with disabilities.* Portland, OR: Northwest Regional Educational Laboratory.

Kame'enui, E. J., Carnine, D., Dixon, R., Simmons, D., & Coyne, M. (2002). *Effective teaching strategies that accommodate diverse learners.* Upper Saddle River, NJ: Merrill/Prentice Hall.

Karten, T. J. (2005). *Inclusion strategies that work: Research-based methods for the classroom.* Thousand Oaks, CA: Corwin Press.

Kellough, R. D. (1995). *Integrating mathematics and science: For kindergarten and primary children.* Englewood Cliffs, NJ: Merrill.

Kucera, T. J. (1993). *Teaching chemisty to students with disabilities.* Washington, DC: American Chemical Society.

Magg, J. W. (1999). *Behavior management.* San Diego: Singular.

Mastropieri, M., & Scruggs, T. (1994). Text verses hands-on science curriculum: Implications for students with disabilities. *Remedial and Special Education, 15*(2), 72–85.

Mastropieri, M., & Scruggs, T. (1995). Teaching science to students with disabilities in general education settings. *Teaching Exceptional Children, 27*(4), 10–13.

Mastropieri, M., & Scruggs, T. (2004). *The inclusive classroom: Strategies for effective instruction.* Upper Saddle River, NJ: Pearson.

Munk, D., Bruckert, J., Call, D., Stoehrmann, T., & Radandt, E. (1998). Strategies for enhancing the performance of students with LD in inclusive science classes. *Intervention in School and Clinic, 34*(2), 73–78.

National Research Council. (1996). *National science education standards.* Washington, DC: National Academy Press.

National Science Teachers Association. (2000). Nature of science. Retrieved December 8, 2005, from www.nsta.org/positionstatement&psid=22

National Science Teachers Association. (2002). Elementary science education. Retrieved December 8, 2005, from www.nsta.org/positionstatement&psid=8

National Science Teachers Association. (2004). Students with disabilities. Retrieved December 8, 2005, from www.nsta.org/positionstatement&psid=41

Neuman, D. B. (1992). *Experiences in science for young children.* Prospect Heights: Waveland Press.

Nolet, V., & McLaughlin, M. J. (2005). *Accessing the general curriculum: Including students with disabilities in standards-based reform.* Thousand Oaks, CA: Corwin Press.

Ormsbee, C. K., & Finson, K. D. (2000). Modifying science activities and materials to enhance instruction for students with learning and behavioral problems. *Intervention in School and Clinic, 36*(1), 10–21.

Pappas, C. C., Kiefer, B. Z., & Levstick, L. S. (1990). *An integrated language perspective in the elementary school: Theory into action.* New York: Longman.

Rakes, T. A., & Choate, J. S. (2000). Essential science: Relevant topics, process, and strategies. In J. S. Choate (Ed.), *Successful inclusive teaching: Proven ways to detect and correct special needs* (pp. 304–335). Boston: Allyn and Bacon.

Salend, S. (1998). Using an activities-based approach to teach science to students with disabilities. *Intervention in School and Clinic, 34*(2), 67–72,78.

Schumm, J., Vaughn, S., & Harris, J. (1997). Pyramid power for collaborative planning. *Teaching Exceptional Children, 29*(6), 62–66.

Short, D., & Echevarria, J. (2005). Teacher skills to support English language-learners. *Educational Leadership, 62*(4), 8–13.

Shymansky, J. A., Kyle, W. C., & Alport, F. (1990). A reassessment of the effects of inquiry-based science curricula of the 60's on student performance. *Journal of Research in Science Teaching, 27,* pp. 127–144.

Trowbridge, L. W., & Bybee, R. W. (1996). *Teaching secondary school science: Strategies for developing scientific literacy* (6th ed.). Englewood Cliffs, NJ: Prentice Hall.

Turnbull, R., Turnbull, A., Shank, M., & Smith, S. (2005). *Exceptional lives: Special education in today's schools* (5th edition). Upper Saddle River, NJ: Pearson.

Watson, S. (2004). Open the science doorway: Strategies and suggestions for incorporating English language learners into the science classroom. *Science Teacher, 71*(2), 32–35.

Weber, E. (1999). *Student assessment that works: A practical approach.* Boston: Allyn and Bacon.

Whitehead Nagda, A., & Bickel, C. (2000). *Tiger math: Learning to graph from a baby tiger.* New York: Henry Holt.

Wood, J. M. (1998). Adapting instruction to accommodate students in inclusive settings. Upper Saddle River, NJ: Merrill/Prentice Hall.

Wood, J. M. (2006). *Teaching students in inclusive settings: Adapting and accommodating instruction.* Upper Saddle River, NJ: Pearson.

Woods, C. S., & Conderman, G. (2005, Spring). Service learning and teacher education. *Academic Exchange Quarterly, 9*(1), 155.

chapter 11

Social Studies in the Inclusive Classroom

Ereka R. Williams

Objectives

After reading this chapter, students will be able to

- Define social studies.
- Identify the ten thematic strands for the social studies.
- Discuss the role of social studies in a balanced curriculum.
- Identify the major content areas situated within the social studies.
- Discuss the role of children's literature in the teaching of social studies.
- Identify several learner-centered ways to teach social studies to early-elementary-age students of varying abilities.
- Identify several national and international resources for the teaching of social studies in the elementary classroom.

Key Terms

National Council for the Social Studies

Social studies

Expanding Environments Approach

Theory of multiple intelligences

Culturally responsive pedagogy

Practical Application Vignette

Alejandro and Melanie are two teachers (general education and special education respectively) that coteach a second-grade classroom. They have recently been asked by their principal to take the lead on ensuring that the other second-grade teachers are meaningfully integrating social studies into their day-to-day curricula. The principal is concerned that the teachers in that area may ignore the social studies in their efforts to accomplish literacy and mathematics goals. Mel and Alejandro express concerns to their principal about their ability to get past their own lackluster experiences with social studies as K–12 students to accomplish this objective. While they are sincerely interested in bringing social studies into the classroom daily with their diverse classroom makeup (typically developing second graders as well as second graders with disabilities in the same room), they wonder if it would be asking too much to stray away from the basics. Also, they express concerns over the traditional approaches to teaching social studies, which typically left the subject area to be viewed as boring. Is there more to social studies than textbooks and maps? Is it possible to have a well-balanced curriculum without social studies? Is it necessary to address it deliberately in the early grades, when students have required, dedicated classes devoted to the subject area in middle and high school? Alejandro and Melanie have quite a few concerns related to this request.

At a time when classroom teachers feel as though there simply are not enough hours in the day, the thought of adding something else to do or re-designing their approach to an area of the curriculum may seem like a daunting, possibly even impossible, task. However, the questions that Alejandro and Melanie are addressing get to the root of some long-held discussions, concerns, and issues in the field of education as it relates to social studies. This chapter will clarify some core issues, topics, and questions related to the principal's request of Alejandro and Melanie and of elementary teachers every day in our classrooms.

Introduction to Social Studies

Alejandro and Melanie mention the historic notion of social studies as the "boring" subject. It is not uncommon for images of dense text books, filmstrips or videos, hanging maps, and globes to start circulating through one's mind when the mere mention of the term *social studies* comes up. While textbooks, maps, globes, film projectors (pre-1980s), and videos (1980s and beyond) encompass part of what is rightfully associated with social studies, they in no way fully encompass the depth and breadth of the subject we have come to call social studies.

Differences and disagreements in the field abound when it comes to a sole definition of the term *social studies.* Several well-noted academicians or scholars have summarized and defined social studies. Table 11.1 displays the summaries or definitions of several of those individuals.

The **National Council of Social Studies** (NCSS), the leading professional community of teachers, scholars, researchers, and educational professionals responsible for articulating standards

Table 11.1 ● Social Studies Definitions

Author(s)	Definition
Parker	"Civic efficacy is the readiness and willingness to assume citizenship responsibilities and the belief that one can make a difference" (2005, p. 5).
Savage & Armstrong	". . . the need for social studies instruction that helps learners develop attitudes and skills that will enable them to adapt and construct new knowledge necessary to cope with future challenges" (2000, p. 6).
Zarrillo	"Social studies is the study of people. Social studies should help students acquire knowledge, master the processes of learning and become active citizens" (2004, p. 4).

for **social studies** and setting the pace on matters associated with the social studies, adopted the following definition in 1993:

> *Social studies is the integrated study of the social sciences and humanities to promote civic competence. Within the school program, social studies provides coordinated, systematic study drawing upon such disciplines as anthropology, archaeology, economics, geography, history, law, philosophy, political science, psychology, religion, and sociology, as well as appropriate content from the humanities, mathematics, and natural sciences. The primary purpose of social studies is to help young people develop the ability to make informed and reasoned decisions for the public good as citizens of a culturally diverse, democratic society in an interdependent world* (NCSS Task Force on Standards for Teaching and Learning in the Social Studies, 1994)

The terms and/or phrases that tend to be consistent among the definitions include informed, citizenship, democracy, diversity, and decisions. The ultimate goal of a social studies curriculum is to develop the knowledge, skills, and attitudes necessary to be an informed, active participant in a diverse, democratic society.

In 1994, NCSS identified ten broad, distinct areas, or strands, that compose the social studies. These strands serve as the skeleton on which social studies rest, live, and breath. As an integrated whole, this body has the ability to create the "civic competence" that organization's definition stresses as the ultimate goal of social studies. These strands are (1) Culture, (2) Time, Continuity, and Change, (3) People, Places, and Environments, (4) Individual Development and Identity, (5) Individuals,

Groups, and Institutions, (6) Power, Authority, and Governance, (7) Production, Distribution, and Consumption, (8) Science Technology and Society, (9) Global Connections, and (10) Civic Ideals and Practices.

While the scope of the ten thematic strands ranges from kindergarten through twelfth grade, for our purposes we will examine what each strand offers by way of the young learner. For each of the ten strands there are broad questions/concepts that a young learner should conceptually explore as it relates to the strand. Table 11.2 connects the strand to the overarching questions it explores. The

Table 11.2 ● NCSS Ten Thematic Strands and Related Thematic Questions

Thematic Strand	Thematic Organizing Questions
Culture	What are common characteristics of different cultures?
	How do belief systems, such as religion or political ideals of the culture, influence the other parts of the culture?
	How does the culture change to accommodate different ideas and beliefs?
Time, Continuity, and Change	Who am I?
	What happened in the past?
	How am I connected to those in the past?
	How has the world changed, and how might it change in the future?
	How do our personal stories reflect varying points of view and inform contemporary ideas and actions?
People, Places, and Environments	Where are things located?
	Why are they located where they are?
	What patterns are reflected in the groupings of things?
	What do we mean by region?
Individual Development and Identity	How do people learn?
	Why do people behave as they do?
	What influences how people learn, perceive, and grow?
	How do people meet their basic needs in a variety of contexts?
Individuals, Groups, and Institutions	What is the role of institutions in this and other societies?
	How am I influenced by institutions? How do institutions change?
Power, Authority, and Governance	What is power? What forms does it take?
	Who holds it? How is it gained, used, and justified?
	How are governments created, structured, changed?
	How can an individual's rights be protected within the context of the majority rule?

(Continued)

Introduction to Social Studies

Table 11.2 ● *(Continued)*

Thematic Strand	Thematic Organizing Questions
Production, Distribution, and Consumption	What is to be produced? How is production to be organized?
	How are goods and services to be distributed?
	What is the most effective allocation of the factors of production (land, labor, capital, and management)?
Science, Technology, and Society	Is new technology always better than that which it will replace?
	What can we learn from the past about how new technologies result in broader social change, some of which is unanticipated?
	How can we preserve our fundamental values and beliefs in a world that is rapidly becoming one technology-linked village?
Global Connections	How do patterns and relationships within and among world cultures, such as economic competition and interdependence, political and military alliances, and others influence policy alternatives that have both national and global implications?
Civic Ideals and Practices	What is civic participation, and how can I be involved?
	How has the meaning of citizenship evolved?
	What is the balance between rights and responsibilities?
	What is the role of the citizen in the community and the nation, and as a member of the world community?

Source: *NCSS: Expectations in Excellence.* Retrieved September 16, 2006, from www.socialstudies.org/standards/

broad questions are meant to serve as guideposts for building a social studies curriculum supporting the thematic strand, but they are not exhaustive. You may be able to identify other overarching questions that connect the theme to the young learner.

As the NCSS description articulates, social studies calls for the examination of several content areas. It is not uncommon for many to associate its study with historical facts and geographic principles; however, there are several major content areas that drive the social studies curriculum. Major content areas enveloped within the social studies curriculum are detailed below:

1. Democratic citizenship—The study of civic life, how individuals decide or act in any way that affects others, and the rights/responsibilities of citizens of a democratic society.

2. History—A study of the past in which students learn how stories of the past are created, how these stories are created differently by different people, and how to build their own (Parker, 2005). It includes five processes identified from the *National Standards for History* (Zarrillo, 2004): chronological thinking, historical comprehension, historical analysis and interpretation, historical research capabilities, and historical issues: analysis and decision making.

3. Geography—A study of place, the spatial settings of people and places on Earth. It requires that the learner has the ability to read and make several types of maps, and should help learners understand how people and resources are distributed.

4. Economics—The study of the production, distribution, and consumption of goods. Learners examine issues surrounding supply versus demand and need versus want.

5. Global education—An area of international scope concerned with five areas: universal and cultural values and practices; global connections; contemporary worldwide concerns; conditions, origins, and past patterns of worldwide affairs; and alternative future directions in worldwide affairs.

6. Environmental education—Often embedded in science, in social studies this discipline can focus on how people influence changes in the environment and responsibility of citizens to preserve and protect the environment.

7. Anthropology—Study of physical and cultural characteristics of people.

8. Other social science areas (i.e., psychology and sociology)—Focus on the study of self and others—how people identify and organize themselves.

The field of social studies encompasses skills, concepts, and attitudes of these major areas. A quick review of the thematic strands and the related organizing questions evidence this broad range of categories embedded within the social studies curriculum.

Constructing Knowledge in Social Studies

Part of the challenge of our two teachers in the earlier vignette, Alejandro and Melanie, lies with the scope and sequence of social studies curriculum. The *scope* (which is the "what" of curriculum) and the *sequence* (which is the "when or in what order" of curriculum) is part of their struggle. What is the most coherent, developmentally appropriate delivery of social studies curricula in the early elementary classroom?

In the United States, social studies has traditionally taken a somewhat predetermined scope and sequence in the early grades. This sequence is defined as the **Expanding Environments Approach**. While Lucy Sprague Mitchell is acknowledged as the creator of this concept (Maxim, 2006), scholars in the field (Maxim, 2006; Zarrillo, 2004) credit Paul Hanna with the advocacy of this approach as a defining theory for the scope and sequence of social studies. The Expanding Environments Approach appears to support the early childhood theory that children at very young ages are very egocentric.

To effectively account for where they are developmentally, it is somewhat natural to start a social studies curriculum with the examination of one's self and to move further out from self-examination each year until a more global, external view of oneself and others is achieved. Each year, as the child grows or matures, the child explores new environments that continue to open the child's world from self, family, community, state, United States, and the world. Table 11.3 shows how the Expanding Environments Approach is specifically articulated in one state's (North Carolina) social studies scope and sequence.

Table 11.3 • Expanding Environments and One State's Social Studies Scope

Grade Level	Expanding Environments	NC Social Studies Curriculum
Kindergarten	Self & Family	Self & Families/Families Around the World
Grade 1	Family & School	Neighborhoods & Communities Around the World
Grade 2	Neighborhood & Community	Regional Studies: Local, State, United States, & World
Grade 3	Community	Citizenship: People Making a Difference
Grade 4	State or Region of US	North Carolina: Geography & History
Grade 5	United States and Close Neighbors	United States History, Canada, Mexico, & Central America

Source: Retrieved September 16, 2006, from www.ncpublicschools.org/curriculum/socialstudies/

Social Studies Process Skills

Along with identifying the ten thematic strands necessary to effectively teach the social studies curriculum, the NCSS identified specific skills that a learner would need in order to grasp the curriculum. The various subskills are aligned along three major skill areas that the learner would need to show proficiency and include a learner's ability to acquire information, organize and use information, and develop or build interpersonal relationships through social participation. Each of the major skill areas develop through deliberate, focused, and monitored experiences that are facilitated by the teacher(s). Each of the major skill areas also have the potential to present challenges to learners in the early elementary classroom given the various cultural, linguistic, and ability-driven differences that teachers address in a diverse setting. Tables 11.4, 11.5, and 11.6 outline the subskill areas and potential difficulties that may occur during instruction that includes the general skill or subskill. In addition to the potential difficulty, suggestions or strategies to consider for the skill area are offered as well. With any strategy or suggestion it is imperative that the teacher remembers that a "one size fits all" approach is not the premise behind the suggestion or strategy. Therefore, professional judgment and student-specific variables will often call for a variation of the strategies suggested.

Acquiring Information

Whether the learner is heading to the library to find a book on farms, dropping in a compact disc to look at a program about families, or listening to a audiotape of *Mufaro's Beautiful Daughters* in a listening center devoted to a current unit on families; the skills necessary to acquire information are essential. Throughout any typical day in the elementary classroom, the young learner must be able to acquire or access information for a variety of purposes. The ability to acquire information is essential to the acquisition of social studies content and other areas of the curriculum as well (see Table 11.4).

Table 11.4 ● Essential Skills for Social Studies With Differentiation Strategies

Acquiring Information		
Social Studies Skill	**Possible Difficulty**	**Differentiated Strategy**
Reading Skills a) comprehension b) vocabulary c) rate of reading	General challenges/problems associated with processing grade-level print material	● Establish clear purpose for reading ● Provide study guides ● Modify the length of the reading activity ● Have an audio recording to accompany the learner as he/she reads
Study Skills a) find information b) arrange information in usable form	Lack of organization Challenge or inability to coherently organize information	● Teach students how to identify/locate key topics/ideas ● Discuss/model how to create outlines and organizers
Reference and Information-Search Skills a) use of library b) special references c) maps, globes, graphics d) community resources	Challenge or inability to use resources in efficient ways Confusion/inability to navigate reference materials to gain information	● Teach uses of library ● Make certain student knows the purpose of the library for any library-related activity ● Teach student to consult media specialist for help ● Create/structure deliberate opportunities/activities that help students use materials/library
Technical Skills a) computer b) telephone & television information networks	Challenge or inability to use applications/software	● Explicitly teach applications/ software programs necessary to complete tasks ● Provide simplified guides for individual applications/software programs

Table 11.5 ● Essential Skills for Social Studies With Differentiation Strategies—Organizing

	Organizing and Using Information	
Social Studies Skill	**Possible Difficulty**	**Differentiated Strategy**
Thinking Skills a) classify information b) interpret information c) analyze information d) summarize information e) synthesize information f) evaluate information	Challenges associated with accessing and utilizing information in coherent, meaningful ways	• Explicitly teach information • Use graphic organizers to demonstrate how to sift through a body of information
Decision-Making Skills	Challenges with setting goals or setting unreasonable goals	• Teach students to assess situation • Assist students with setting realistic goals • Teach student how to identify information to make decision • Assist student with generating options, selecting the best option, and developing a plan
Metacognitive Skills	Challenges with determining whether adequate progress is being made with an assignment	• Teach self-evaluation skills • Create checklists for students to monitor their thinking/processing

Organizing Information

Whether it's a first grader preparing to share his family project with his classmates or a small group of second graders preparing to share their group project on their continent, our young learners need help to organize or arrange the information they have been gathering. How do we help young learners use and assemble the information they've acquired in coherent, meaningful ways? If our learners can not effectively and meaningfully use and organize the information they have read, collected, and gathered, it is not likely that they will comprehend social studies content (see Table 11.5).

Whether it's a group of kindergarteners expected to participate as good citizens during center activities or two second graders partnering to complete an in-class activity, there are multiple opportunities daily for our learners to demonstrate their ability to communicate with the peers and adults in their learning community. Their ability to effectively communicate and collaborate alone, regardless of subject or content area, is core to social studies, specifically as it relates to citizenship. However, when social studies content is explicitly taught, the performance of these skills can be observed and assessed as well (see Table 11.6).

Table 11.6 • Essential Skills for Social Studies With Differentiation Strategies—Social Skills

Interpersonal Relationships and Social Participation

Social Studies Skill	Possible Difficulty	Differentiated Strategy
Personal Skills		• Teach self-evaluation skills
Group Interaction Skills	Challenges with pragmatics, verbal, and nonverbal rules associated with communicating with others in small and large groups	• Teach interpersonal skills • Provide interpersonal skill checklist • Rehearse interpersonal skills with role play/simulations • Acknowledge the use of appropriate interpersonal skills in different situations
Social and Political Participation Skills	Challenges with oral delivery of content to an audience	• Provide student with ample time to prepare presentation • Provide different situations for oral presentations (formal/informal) • Create a nonthreatening environment to minimize peer criticism

Plural Perspectives

The field of social studies, particularly the area of history, has received criticism over the years for embracing a monolithic view of history—a view that is largely from the perspective of the dominant, western culture. Social studies textbooks of the past are frequently the subject of many research studies that examine the western interpretation of events in U.S. and world history. Professional organizations such as the National Association for Multicultural Education and Rethinking Schools have worked for decades to help the profession retool and redefine curricula and instruction to include the perspectives of ethnic minorities and women, whose voices have historically been absent or minimalized in historical accounts on the past. Zarrillo (2004) speaks of the *transformed social studies* curriculum that (a) reconsiders the scope of the curriculum, (b) expands the geographic boundaries of instruction, and (c) introduces learners to rich, diverse groups of people. In reconsidering the scope of the curriculum, a teacher and his or her colleagues must consider if their curricular units present one group's or the mainstream's perspective only. How can those units be retooled or redesigned to include the angle, ideas, or perspectives of other groups involved with the event or period of history? When exploring ways to expand the geographic boundaries of units, teachers must examine ways to have young learners do comparisons between their immediate world and the world beyond their reach. This exercise also encompasses Zarrillo's third transformation process of introducing diverse people to learners. Young learners should be given opportunities to explore the history, influences, and contributions of various ethnic groups, women, and other children throughout the curriculum.

This paradigm is more than the "holidays and heroes" approach to teaching social studies often found in schools and used to highlight a school or grade level's attempt to address diversity. While celebrating various cultures can be a fine stand-alone activity, it shows little to no evidence of an embedded attempt to include the voices of those other cultures or groups throughout the curriculum throughout the year.

Differentiating Instruction in Social Studies

Kelley and Dwayne are first-grade and special education resource teachers, respectively, and work together to teach 21 first graders, 4 of which have been identified with various disabilities. Kelley and Dwayne are planning a unit on families and wonder how they can accomplish the following:

- Include social studies content that is meaningful in meaningful ways
- Incorporate the library's extensive collection of classroom Big Books/picture books
- Accommodate for the differing learning styles and abilities of their students

What might Kelley and Dwayne need to consider for each? What resources should they explore? How can Kelley and Dwayne accomplish this task?

Latoya and Caroline are third-grade and special education resource teachers, respectively. They coteach a diverse group of 22 third graders that include learners from five different ethnic groups, 6 learners who have been identified with disabilities, and 2 learners who are English language learners (ELL). With this mix of background, ability, and linguistic/cultural diversity, they face a variety of concerns daily. As they prepare to teach their next unit on famous Americans, Latoya and Caroline are concerned that their learners may not connect to the unit personally since most of the grade-level teachers have identified a few Americans that appear to have so little in common with their students. Latoya and Caroline are spending time planning how to blend what their students present by way of diversity into their unit plans. What do Latoya and Caroline need to consider?

Each of the pairs above raise very valid concerns about the placement of social studies in the early elementary curriculum and the instructional delivery or options specifically related to social studies as a subject area. The following questions are only a few of the curriculum and instruction-based decisions classroom teachers must make everyday regarding social studies:

- How do I make this meaningful to my learners?
- How can I best utilize the resources available to me within and around the school and/or community?

- How do I accommodate and utilize the diversity that exists within my classroom (ethnic, cultural, linguistic, ability, etc.)?
- How can I incorporate different types of instruction that addresses the varying learning styles and interests of my students?

A quick glance over the list shows how these questions not only are applicable to the subject area of social studies but are fundamental questions for any teacher of any subject area or age group.

Learner and Social Studies

When determining how to approach the teaching of social studies, it is important to consider who exactly our learners are. Teachers must consider the pluralities/differences that exist within the classroom in terms of their learners' approaches to learning in the elementary classroom. Part of an elementary teacher's approach should rest with how the learner at this age approaches thinking and tasks. Woolfolk (2004) acknowledges two major theorists that affirm the young learner's approach to thinking, Piaget and Vygotsky. Piaget asserted that students in the early elementary group are concrete in their thinking and require hands-on learning. Vygotsky asserted that learning is a coconstructed, cultural process requiring the scaffolding or support of a more capable peer or adult in order for learning to occur. What do these theories spell for the teacher attempting to teach social studies in the early elementary classroom? What it spells for this teacher is the importance of remembering to use hands-on, active, engaging activities and/or lessons with the elementary learning.

One theory on learners' approaches to cognitive activities that has gained momentum and application in the field is Howard Gardner's **theory of multiple intelligences** (MI theory) (Woolfolk, 2004). Gardner's theory supports the notion that a learner's intelligence should be viewed in more than the typical two ways we view or assess intelligence, which are mainly verbal and mathematical. Gardner asserts that there are multiple ways to access what students know and how they process information. Therefore, teachers must organize and create learning opportunities that evidence this belief. Table 11.7 outlines the areas of intelligence Gardner identified and the description of each area (Woolfolk, 2004).

Table 11.7 ● Gardener's Theory of MI

MI Area	Description
Musical Intelligence	Rhythm, melodies, or tunes guide thinking/learning
Verbal/Linguistic Intelligence	Words are tools for thinking/learning
Naturalist Intelligence	Dimensions in nature guide thinking/learning
Bodily Kinesthetic Intelligence	Movement guides thinking/learning
Intrapersonal Intelligence	Knowledge of self guides thinking/learning
Interpersonal Intelligence	Exchanging ideas with or understanding others is significant to thinking/learning
Spatial Intelligence	Pictures and images guide thinking/learning
Logical/Mathematical Intelligence	Reasoning guides thinking/learning

Table 11.8 demonstrates a MI theoretical connection to social studies. Campbell (1997) published lesson design menus or a framework that gave insight into the Gardner theory and the classroom. Campbell's lesson menus are used below as a framework for considering how to implement Gardner's theories in the social studies classroom. In the far-right column are the special education areas that may be supported or challenged by the activities listed in the second column. An activity listed that may present an appropriate modification for a learner with a particular disability should be considered and integrated where appropriate. A challenge that may be presented should be viewed not as a roadblock but rather a point of introspection and examination by the coteachers of a learner with that particular disability, so as to determine the appropriate modification for the specific learner that may be challenged by a particular activity listed for the MI area. Another key issue for coteachers in the classroom to remember is that the activities listed in the table (which is not exhaus-

Table 11.8 ● Multiple Intelligences, Social Studies, and Exceptionalities

MI Area	Social Studies Connection (Campbell, 1997)	IDEA Category Possibly Requiring Modifications
Musical Intelligence	Integrating lessons with music from the country or time period being studied	Auditory Processing Modification
Verbal/Linguistic Intelligence	Analyzing the patterns and language in poetry used during a unit of families	Speech/Language Impairment Mental Retardation Traumatic Brain Injury
Naturalist Intelligence	Describe changes in a local environment after . . .	Mental Retardation
Bodily Kinesthetic Intelligence	Build or construct . . . Create a movement that . . .	Orthopedic Impairment Other Health Impairment
Intrapersonal Intelligence	Describe qualities you possess that will help you	Serious Emotional Disturbance Autism Multiple Disabilities
Interpersonal Intelligence	Participate in a service project to . . .	Specific Learning Disability Serious Emotional Disturbance
Spatial Intelligence	Map out a region . . .	Visual Impairment Mental Retardation
Logical/Mathematical Intelligence	Design and conduct . . .	Specific Learning Disability Mental Retardation
Auditory Intelligence	Listen and analyze a speech given by a political leader	Deafness Deaf-Blindness

tive), or any strategy, for that matter, that may be appropriate for one learner may be inappropriate for another learner. That is where understanding the individual learner, having a bank, or range, of activities, strategies, and/or modifications, and remembering the definition of special education—specially designed, individualized instruction—comes into focus.

If Piaget, Vygotsky, and Gardner are to drive how we attempt to view learning for social studies in the elementary classroom, the teacher must include varying activities and lessons that provide hands-on, concrete opportunities for students to actively construct what they know. Instruction in the classroom delivered through this combined model would make social studies come to life in the elementary classroom (see Table 11.8).

The Diverse Learner and Social Studies

Culturally responsive pedagogy is the term commonly used in the field (Banks, 2005; Gay, 2000; Ladson-Billings, 1998) today to address what is needed to teach learners of diverse backgrounds in ways that equip learners to advance and succeed in the mainstream without ignoring or disregarding the differences they bring to the classroom. Culturally responsive pedagogy requires the examination of practices in the classroom that teach to and about differences that are ethnic, cultural, religious, economic, geographic, and linguistic. Culturally relevant pedagogy permeates the curriculum and the instruction within a classroom.

A teacher who is making the attempt to teach in culturally responsive ways will consider how the types of texts, videos, books, field trips, and other materials used to teach content reflect the diversity that exists inside and outside of the classroom. Latoya and Caroline from the vignette at a minimum would want to consider ways to include literature and materials that reflect the ethnic diversity represented within those five ethnic groups in their classroom. While they are not limited to including in some way only those ethnic groups in their family unit, the inclusion of those would show a good-faith effort of the two to open the borders of their unit to include groups of people who are not in the majority or mainstream. The students of those groups as well as the students who do not identify with those groups stand to gain a great deal. It is a great example of the transformation of curriculum mentioned earlier in the section.

Culturally responsive practices also call for the revising of traditional approaches to delivery of instruction in the classroom. Understanding our students' differences means understanding that they may communicate in ways that are different than the mainstream and one another. Teachers must consider the multiple ways we communicate with students verbally and nonverbally within the classroom daily. Particularly when working with students of linguistically diverse backgrounds, it is imperative that classroom teachers remember to adjust their rates of speaking, tone, and expressions to accommodate the differences their students have. English language learners (ELL) are students for whom mainstream English is not the primary language. The literature (Woolfolk, 2004) shows that it takes at a minimum of three to five years to acquire a new language pragmatically. Add to the three-to-five-year learning curve the fact that so much of communication is nonverbal, and it is not difficult to see how these learners require some special consideration in the classroom. Cruz, Nutta, O'Brien, Feyton, and Govoni (2003) note that social studies may present particular challenges for the ELL student in comparison to other subjects primarily because social studies depends greatly on language and literacy skills, is often abstract, with higher order thinking skills, and often relies minimally on manipulatives and hands-on activities like science and math. When teaching social studies to the ELL student, teachers may want to consider some of the recommendations by the NCSS resource on teaching social studies to ELL students, which include

1. correctly pronouncing student's names;
2. sending letters and other communication home to families in their native language;
3. providing pictorial displays of class routines;
4. labeling items in a classroom in the languages of the ELL students and in English; and
5. continually checking for comprehension in ways that allow the ELL learner to demonstrate that she or he understands, because a learner may say "yes" to a yes/no question to avoid disagreement or embarrassment.

In addition there are potentially a great deal of positives related to the immigrant learner in the social studies classroom, from the presentation of a different perspective on topics to the cultural insight and practices that can be articulated between the child's culture and U.S. culture. Teachers of ELL students have resources available to them to help them teach the ELL learner just as the teachers of the students with disabilities do.

Lesson/Unit Planning and Social Studies

When deciding on what to teach in social studies, the planning process would resemble the process for any of the other subject areas, to a degree. An integrated, balanced curriculum in the elementary classroom would ultimately show evidence of the following: inclusion of major subject areas (mathematics, language arts, science, social studies, and the arts), which are linked thematically and tied to specific objectives. A range of lessons and activities would be organized around a central or unifying theme. Teachers vary in how they decide on which themes/activities they want to address with their students. However, in order for their curricular and instructional decisions to be defensible, they must show how their lessons are tied to standards. Often the state standards for a subject determine what will be covered in a classroom. Even in districts where the local school district has determined when certain objectives to be covered, the state's curriculum or objectives must be followed. The decision on how to cover the objectives and in what way then tends to rest on the grade level or individual teacher. Keep in mind that the Expanding Environments Approach and the National Council for Social Studies Thematic Strands mentioned earlier do tend to influence what occurs, but some modifications do to tend to make each state different, if only slightly. However, the pacing of the social studies objectives and determination of what is to be covered and when is dependent upon the politics and climate of the state, district, and school. Table 11.9 shows a typical sequence for the determination of objectives for a grade level. While Table 11.10 shows an almost reverse planning sequence that involves the grade level or teacher determining what they desire thematically FIRST and then following the chain to the standards to make the standards "fit" the theme. There is not "one" way to approach this; however, ultimately, the teacher must be able to explicitly connect the lesson/thematic unit to the standards.

Once a teacher has determined the district's expectations for social studies, then decisions can be made regarding the "how" of instruction. The "how" decisions for covering social studies in the classroom may be either a grade-level decision or an individual decision. In some schools, the teach-

Table 11.9 ● Standards to Classroom Sequence

National Standards

State Standards

District/Local Standards

School/Grade-Level Focus

Themes

Unit Plans

Social Studies Content/Lessons

Table 11.10 ● School Focus to Classroom Sequence

School/Grade-Level Focus

Themes

State Standards/National Standards/District/
   Local Standards

Unit Plans

Social Studies Content/Lessons

ers for an entire grade collaboratively decide on which themes will be covered and even plan their specific lessons as a group. In others, the grade level may decide on themes, but individual teachers determine their specific lessons. While in others, the decisions on themes, lessons, and activities are completely independent decisions made by the classroom teacher. The instructional planning process in elementary classrooms varies. However, once a grade level or teacher is ready to approach the "how" of instruction, several questions will need to be addressed:

1. Which theme(s) will best link the identified objectives together this quarter/semester/year?
2. Are there certain themes I want to specifically cover during certain seasons?
3. What kind of interests do children at this age typically have, and how can I use that to choose my themes and activities?
4. What resources available to me in my school, local library, community agencies, and community at large would support the themes I choose?
5. What specific content is needed to achieve this thematic unit?
6. What kind of activities will give my students multiple ways to connect to the content?

Once these questions have been addressed and decisions have been made, the teacher can then progress to determining which types of specific activities/lessons will be used to teach social studies content.

In determining the thematic strands for social studies, the NCSS also specifically addressed how the strands related to the young learner. Table 11.11 outlines the key questions a young learner should be able to address for each national standard. When integrated units are used in the classroom involving one or more of the specific strands below, the young learner column may serve as a way to gauge the degree to which social studies content within the unit is aligned to the national standards (see Table 11.11).

Literature and Social Studies

"Literature is simply the vehicle through which important social studies concepts are taught" (Obenchain & Morris, 2003, p. 98). One way to make social studies objectives and content connect to

Table 11.11 ● Thematic Strands and the Young Learner Connection

Thematic Strand	Examples of What a Young Learner's Experience May Address
Culture	Exploring likenesses and differences in school subjects such as language arts, mathematics, science, music, and art makes the study of culture appropriate
	Beginning to interact with other students who are alike and different and naturally want to know more about others
Time, Continuity, and Change	Experiencing sequencing to establish a sense of order and time
	Enjoy hearing stories of the recent past and of long ago
	Recognizing that individuals may hold different views about the past and to understand the linkages between human decisions and consequences
People, Places, and Environments	Drawing upon immediate personal experiences as a basis for exploring geographic concepts and skills
	Expressing interest in things distant and unfamiliar and have concern for the use and abuse of the physical environment
Individual Development and Identity	Observing siblings, looking at family photos, remembering past achievements, projecting oneself into the future, and comparing the patterns of behavior evident in people of different age groups
Individuals, Groups, and Institutions	Given opportunities to examine how various institutions affect their lives and influence their thinking
	Assisted in recognizing the tensions that occur when the goals, values, and principles of two or more institutions or groups conflict
Power, Authority, and Governance	Exploring their natural sense of fairness and order as they experience relationships with others
	Developing an increasingly comprehensive awareness of rights and responsibilities in specific contexts
Production, Distribution, and Consumption	Differentiating between wants and needs
	Exploring economic decisions as they compare their own economic experiences with those of others and consider the wider consequences of those decisions on groups, communities, the nation, and beyond
Science, Technology, and Society	Learning how technologies form systems and how their daily lives are intertwined with a host of technologies
	Constructing examples of how technologies such as the wheel and the transistor radio altered the course of history
Global Connections	Becoming aware of events on a global scale through exposure to various media and first-hand experiences
	Examining and exploring global connections and basic issues and concerns
Civic Ideals and Practices	Introduced to civic ideals and practices through activities such as helping to set classroom expectations, examining experiences in relation to ideals, and determining how to balance the needs of individuals and the group

Table 11.12 • Folktale Data Retrieval Chart

	Story 1	Story 2	Story 3
Shelter			
Clothing			
Food			
Rituals/Traditions			

learners is to utilize children's literature. Children's literature offers a range of fictional and nonfictional bridges to social studies content. Certain genres lend easily to this (historical fiction and informational texts for example), while others connect through a more guided instruction and focused inquiry (myths and legends, folktales). A read-aloud from a picture book may be a good way to introduce a new unit, while an in-depth study on various folktales from a particular region may provide the daily lessons for social studies, language arts, and the arts on a particular cultural group. For example, in Obenchain and Morris (2003), a folktale study is an opportunity to have learners read, collect, and evaluate data on a cultural group across folktales. Table 11.12 shows a data retrieval chart a learner or group of learners would use to examine the shelter, clothing, food, and traditions of a people in various stories. This activity could be used in a variety of ways by the teacher and students and involves social studies concepts and objectives as well as several objectives across content areas.

Literature from a variety of genres can be used in a variety of ways to introduce, teach, or culminate a unit that includes social studies. The Cooperative Children's Book Center, a noncirculating library at the University of Wisconsin, uses four criteria in the selection of "excellent" books that teach social studies curriculum:

1. the book has potential for constructing one or more of the 10 NCSS strands for children,
2. the book is interesting,
3. the book is accurate—free of misconceptions and stereotypes, and
4. in sum, the book presents a multicultural view of the world. (Krey, 1998, p. 17)

NCSS added a fifth and sixth criterion when deciding on which books to identify annually for their notable books lists, which were that (a) the book be of high literary quality and (b) the book have illustrations of photographs that directly support the text. NCSS annually publishes a list referred to as the Notable Books List. This list is an excellent resource of children's and adolescent literature that deliberately connects to the ten thematic strands for social studies. The list is organized by topic and then following a brief description on the book and why it is noteworthy, a targeted reader's level or age range, and the thematic strands explicitly represented in the book. When planning a unit involving social studies, a teacher could easily identify texts he or she can use to support instruction and have the thematic strand already identified:

- Folktales—Stories involving heroes/heroines that demonstrate how virtuous ways outweigh challenges

Differentiating Instruction in Social Studies

- Fables—Short tales that illustrate a moral
- Myths—Stories created by cultural groups to explain natural phenomena
- Legends—Hero or tall tales that demonstrate great bravery in fighting a battle or challenge of some sort
- Realistic/historical fiction—Realistic stories that capture historic events and are set in the past
- Nonfiction/informational texts—Factual information that describes a group of people, object, or event

Integrating Social Studies throughout the Curriculum

There is a cornucopia of methods, projects, approaches, and activities that incorporate social studies concepts in the elementary classroom. The possibilities and options are probably endless. When teaching social studies content to the young learner, it is important to remember where they are developmentally (concrete thinkers needing active engagement with others and materials) if we are attempting to identify the methods that will best connect to them. Each of the methods below are offered as just ideas or springboards for what can be used in a classroom; the list is not finite. The only thing that is definite is that it will take varied approaches to meaningfully teach social studies material in the elementary classroom.

Puppet theater/reader's theater—Unlike a full stage production, reader's theater allows students to engage in expressive retellings of historical events or social-studies-related material without having to devote time to creating props. Students can really delve into the literature and the cultural or historical significance of the piece you choose to use.

Role play—Gives students a concrete way to physically and cognitively assume and examine the perspective or viewpoint of an individual or group from a particular historical era or event. After reading on a particular event or period with children, give them a picture or visual representation of some sort and ask them to recreate the scene or event.

Classroom society/roles/leaders—In giving students responsibilities within the classroom for leadership and having the class provide input on rules and other decisions, the elementary teacher is giving students an opportunity to practice democracy daily. Assuming leadership roles, having a class discussion on a problem about trash on the floor, or deciding on whether snack time should be moved to after lunch instead of the morning via group vote—the young learner is concretely understanding what it takes to be an active citizen in a society.

Graphic organizers—A visual way for students to compare data, look for patterns, and draw conclusions. Students will initially need direction on how to construct and interpret organizers.

Field trips/virtual field trips—Create excellent opportunities for students to physically visit and learn about historically significant sites and groups. Virtual field trips give teachers the flexibility to visit or tour sites without leaving the classroom. Teachers can identify one or more websites that connect to their curriculum and have students tour or visit the site independently or whole class.

Webquest—Students are given several websites that are linked or connected around a theme with a problem or question to research, analyze, and draw conclusions on. The teacher takes

the guesswork out of locating relevant sites for collecting data needed for the inquiry-based activity by identifying sites in advance. Students work cooperatively to solve or research their issue/problem.

Inquiry-based activities—Student-directed learning centered around a question or dilemma of interest to students. Students generate the questions, formulate a hypothesis, collect and analyze data, and test the hypothesis.

Music—Music has the potential to engage learners by providing opportunities for them to use their listening skills to examine the experiences of different people.

Oral history—Organized/structured interviews with family members, community members, or others to gain perspective on a previous time period or significant event. Learners are naturally curious about others, and this activity gives them an opportunity to find out about their families, community, and the world in a time when they were much younger or not even born.

Primary sources—Pieces of art, documents, or artifacts produced during a particular time period being studied. They give students an opportunity to explore daily life and events from another period of time.

Timelines—Charts that show intervals between events and allow learners to "see" chronology. They can be created by students using paper, markers, pictures, or software.

Summary

It should be clear that social studies is in fact a necessary component of the balanced curriculum in an early elementary classroom. Social studies easily serves as the filter for other academic content areas and bridges the curriculum to the young learner in natural, thematic ways. A classroom that is culturally responsive, attuned to multiple intelligences, and accommodating of the various abilities and challenges young children face is a classroom in which the social studies will undoubtedly, naturally, seamlessly thrive.

Thinking It Through

1. Pick a theme you would like to address in your classroom. What children's books would you use to support that theme?

2. How will you incorporate democratic citizenship in your classroom?

3. Time is an important component of a social studies curriculum, yet many young children have a difficult time with this concept. Think of an activity that addresses the past, present, and future.

4. Name five things you would do to support diverse learners in your classroom.

5. How would you address holidays in your classroom?

Children's Literature in Social Studies

Adoff, A. (1991). *Hard to be six.* New York: Lothrop, Lee & Shepard.

Banish, R., & Jordan-Wong, J. (1992). *A forever family.* New York: HarperCollins.

Gavin, C. (1990). *Grandma's baseball.* New York: Crown.

Henkes, K. (1995) *Good-bye, Curtis.* New York: Greenwillow.

Johnson, A. (2005). *A sweet smell of roses.* New York: Simon and Schuster.

Johnson, P. B. (1997). *Farmer's market.* New York: Orchard.

Martin, J. B. (1996). *Grandmother Bryant's pocket.* Boston: Houghton Mifflin.

McMillan, B. (1996). *Jelly beans for sale.* New York: Scholastic.

Van Laan, N., (1996). *La boda: A Mexican wedding celebration.* Boston: Little, Brown.

Weatherford, C. B. (2005) *Freedom on the menu: The Greensboro sit-ins.* New York: Books for Young Readers.

Resources

Professional Organizations With Social Studies–Related Resources

National Council for Social Studies

www.socialstudies.org

The National Council for Social Studies, or NCSS, is an organization whose mission to provide "leadership, service, and support for all social studies educators" (elementary through college). NCSS is the largest association in the country devoted solely to social studies education—purposefully equipping its members and all teachers in general to work toward the "strengthening and advocating" of social studies. On this organization's site teachers can find unlimited resources by way of lesson plans, classroom teacher grants, and professional development opportunities locally, nationally, and abroad.

National Museum of American History

http://americanhistory.si.edu/

This museum opened to the public in 1964 as the National Museum of History and Technology and is dedicated to providing collections and scholarship related to our nation and its many peoples. Most notable is that the museum collects and preserves more than 3 million artifacts. The website offers online exhibitions, behind-the-scenes glimpses into collections, and an overview of museum programs and activities. With the virtual tour capabilities of the museum's website, Web quests and virtual field trips that involve any aspect of our nation's history just may be incomplete if this site is not included. From the original "Star-Spangled Banner" to Dorothy's ruby slippers from *The Wizard of Oz,* this museum has it.

Public Broadcast Television

www.pbs.org

Public Broadcast Station, or PBS, is a private, nonprofit media enterprise owned and operated by the nation's 349 public television stations. PBS uses noncommercial television, the Internet, and other media to deliver quality programs and education services that inform, inspire, and delight. For over thirty years, teachers have trusted PBS's quality programming and educational services. The PBS TeacherSource is the enterprise's teacher-related weblink. Through the teacher link, teachers can identify programming, videos, lesson plans, multimedia, professional development opportunities, and projects that support their delivery of social-studies-related subject matter.

Multicultural Pavilion

www.edchange.org

Multicultural Pavilion is part of the EDChange clearinghouse and is dedicated to diversity, equity, and justice in schools and society. EDChange lists describe their mission in the following way: "We *act* to shape schools and communities in which all people, regardless of race, gender, sexual orientation, class, (dis)ability, language, or religion, have equitable opportunities to achieve to their fullest." The Multicultural Pavilion has a host of lesson plans, enrichment activities, video reviews, team-building activities, etc., to support your efforts of teaching to and about diversity.

National Council for Economics Educators

www.ncee.net

The National Council on Economic Education (NCEE) is a nationwide network that promotes economic literacy with students and teachers. NCEE's mission "is to help students develop the real-life skills they need to succeed: to be able to think and choose responsibly as consumers, savers, investors, citizens, members of the workforce, and effective participants in a global economy." This organization provide teachers with tools such as lessons, materials, and other resources to teach economics and personal finance within the classroom and their lives.

National Council for History Education

www.garlandind.com/nche/

The National Council for History Education, or NCHE, is an organization devoted to promoting the importance of history in schools and in society. The Council, which is supported by the contributions of individuals and organizations, provides a network for all who teach history from kindergarten through graduate school. This organization has a variety of resources for anyone interested in included history content within a lesson or unit.

National Association for Multicultural Education

www.nameorg.org

The National Association for Multicultural Education, or NAME, is one of the field's leading professional organizations devoted to individuals and groups with an interest in multicultural education from all levels of education, different academic disciplines, and from diverse educational institutions and occupations. Geneva Gay, James Banks, Sonia Nieto, and others who are considered the foremothers and forefathers of culturally responsive movement were integral in the organization's beginnings. The organization's resources for the classroom teacher include lessons, curriculum guides, books, videos, hyperlinks, etc., that provide teachers a framework for restructuring or organizing their classroom curriculum and instruction in ways that are culturally responsive to learners.

Association for Supervision and Curriculum Development

www.ascd.org

The Association for Supervision and Curriculum Development, or ASCD, is of significance to teachers across the K–12 span. The organization's history rests in the ability to address all aspects of effective teaching and learning—such as professional development, educational leadership, and capacity building. ASCD offers broad, multiple perspectives—across all education professions—in reporting key policies and practices.

This organization's classroom teacher resources include online full-text articles that give teachers specific, detailed classroom application of strategies and ideas, lesson plans, guides, list-

servs, online professional development opportunities, and other resources that support the teacher of social studies.

Social Studies Content-Related Resources

National Archives and Records Administration

www.nara.gov/

This resource preserves and provides access to federal government records. Teaching with primary documents encourages a varied learning environment for teachers and students alike. This resource has an area called the digital classroom, which contains activities and resources connected to using the primary sources contained housed at the NARA and in general.

U.S. Department of Justice

www.usdoj.gov/kidspage

This resource is designed just for learners and provides information and activities related specifically to different aspects of justice, such as Internet crimes, drug prevention, and laws that protect citizen's rights. Students can navigate the site to find out how to fight crime, view the FBI's Ten Most Wanted list and read about the history of civil rights.

White House and White House for Kids

http://whitehouse.gov; http://whitehouse.gov/kids/

The first site gives a history and overview of the home of the United States President, past to present. The second site is the section of the White House's website exclusively for young learners. Students can contact their president, vice president, take a tour, or familiarize themselves with the president's pet.

Ben's Guide to U.S. Government for Kids

http://bensguide.gpo.gov

This resource provides learning tools for K–12 students, parents, and teachers. These resources address how our government works and uses primary source materials.

National Geographic Society

http://nationalgeographic.com

This resource is a long-time, well-documented resource on issues and topics related to geographic knowledge. The Society established educational and children's programs that focus on geographic literacy. They produce a periodical just for kids (which resembles the one for older, more mature readers) that covers a range of topics related to this goal. Also, this site has over 600 maps (printable) that can be used with classroom activities.

Blank Outline Maps of the World, Continents, Countries, and the U.S.

http://geography.about.com/science/geography/cs/blankoutline maps/index.htm

This classroom-ready resource links teachers to collections of blank and outline maps to print out for educational or personal use at home or in the classroom.

Women in World History

http://womeninworldhistory.com/resources.html

This resource provides the classroom teacher with a site is full of resources to assist with teaching about women's history in an American and global context. Teachers can find biographies, lessons, essays, book reviews, and other resources that can aid with the integration of women throughout the social studies curriculum.

References

Banks, J. (2005). *Cultural diversity and education: Foundations, curriculum, and teaching.* Boston: Pearson.

Berson, M. J., Cruz, B. C., Duplass, J. A., & Johnston, J. H. (2004). *Social studies on the Internet.* Upper Saddle River, NJ: Pearson.

Campbell, L. (1997). Variations on a theme: How teachers can interpret mi theory. *Educational Leadership, 55*(1), 14–19.

Cruz, B. C., Nutta, J. W., O'Brien, J., Feyten, C. M., & Govoni, J. M (2003). *Passport to learning: Teaching social studies to ESL students.* Silver Spring, MD: National Council for the Social Studies.

Gay, G. (2000). *Culturally responsive teaching: Theory, research, and practice.* New York: Teachers College Press.

Krey, D. M. (1998). *Children's literature in social studies: Teaching to the standards.* Silver Spring, MD: National Council for Social Studies.

Ladson-Billings, G. (1998). *Dreamkeepers: Successful teachers of African American students.* San Francisco: Jossey-Bass.

Laughlin, M. K., & Kardaleff, P. P. (1991). *Literature-based social studies: Children's books & activities to enrich the K–5 curriculum.* Phoenix: Oryx Press.

Lemlech, J. K. (2002). *Curriculum and instructional methods for the elementary and middle school.* Upper Saddle River, NJ: Pearson.

Lindquist, T. (1997). *Ways that work: Putting social studies standards into practice.* Portsmouth, NH: Heinemann.

Lindquist, T., & Selwyn, D. (2000). *Social studies at the center: Integrating kids, content, and literacy.* Portsmouth, NH: Heinemann.

Manning, M., Manning, G., & Long, R. (1997). *Theme immersion compendium for social studies teaching.* Portsmouth, NH: Heinemann.

Maxim, G. (2006). *Dynamic social studies for constructivist classrooms: Inspiring tomorrow's social scientists* (8th ed.). Upper Saddle River, NJ: Pearson.

National Council for the Social Studies (NCSS). (1994). *Expectations of excellence: Curriculum standards for social studies.* Retrieved October 4, 2006, from www.socialstudies.org/standards/

Obenchain, K. M., & Morris, R. V. (2003). *50 social studies strategies for K–8 classrooms.* Upper Saddle River, NJ: Pearson.

Polloway, E. A., Patton, J. R., & Serna, L. (2001). *Strategies for teaching learners with special needs.* Upper Saddle River, NJ: Merrill.

Parker, W. (2005). *Social studies in elementary education.* Upper Saddle River, NJ: Pearson.

Savage, T. V., & Armstrong, D. G. (2000). *Effective teaching in elementary social studies.* Upper Saddle River, NJ: Merrill.

Tompkins, G. E. (2004). *Literacy for the 21st century: Teaching reading and writing in grades 4 through 8.* Columbus: Pearson.

Woolfolk, A. (2004). *Educational psychology.* Boston: Allyn and Bacon.

Wyman, R. M. (2005). *America's history through young voices: Using primary sources in the K–12 social studies classroom.* Boston: Pearson.

Zarrillo, J. J. (2004). *Teaching elementary social studies.* Upper Saddle River, NJ: Pearson.

Integrating Art and Music in the Inclusive Classroom

Susannah Brown and Cathy Smilan

Objectives

After reading this chapter, students will be able to

- Understand basic concepts in Visual Art and Music Education.
- Understand concepts in Arts Integration.
- Understand how to apply these concepts through integration within an inclusive classroom at kindergarten-through-third-grade levels.

Key Terms

Arts
Arts discipline and art form
Arts integration
Creativity
Elements of Art
Principles of Design
Elements of Music

Practical Application Vignette

Bobby always wanted to wash his dried, chapped hands. A sweet, affable boy, he would comply with my requests to manipulate the clay. But after the first week of art class, it was very clear that Bobby preferred to clean the tools and work trays of his eager peers rather than complete his art tasks. I would sit with Bobby, guiding his hands over the textured surface, gently smoothing out the surface cracks and feeling the thickness of the vessel walls; his product exceeded expectations, yet the process seemed repellent to Bobby. Eventually, we agreed that he would glaze sample pots rather than hand-build his own, thus preserving his art education and his motivation to participate. It was not until years later, while conducting a workshop for Integrating Art for Students With Special Needs, that I was finally enlightened. Mr. Hector explained, "Every time you asked Bobby to put his hands in the clay it was as if you were putting mud in his eyes." Bobby is blind; he uses his fingertips to "see" the world.

Introduction to the Arts

Sometimes what we as teachers imagine as the perfect activity, a wonderful experience coupled with a unique learning opportunity, falls short of our expectations. The best intentions can go awry due to a teacher's lack of actual experience and situational application of well-learned theory. This chapter explores arts education theory and practice focused on students with special needs. It is our hope that this chapter will facilitate the development of arts integration concepts for classroom teachers and arts specialists alike, so that all children will be able to enhance their creativity, motivation, and perseverance through arts learning. Along with an overview of media and techniques in visual art, drama, and music, the chapter provides strategies for implementing physically, intellectually, and culturally sensitive curricular experiences that will help the K–3 student to learn in and through the arts.

Think of arts integration like a weaving where the design may repeat a pattern or be variable. Just as the warp and weft strings are integral parts of a woven whole, the arts disciplines are an integral part of the curriculum, and are valuable in all aspects of teaching and learning. Just as a weaver carefully selects materials that describe his or her artistic vision, the teacher selects the learning objectives and concepts for a lesson or unit of study. In weaving, the weft strings create the design by moving over and under the stationary warp strings. In arts integration, the weft strings are the disciplines within the unit of study, which are based upon research. The weft strings constantly change color and texture to create the weaving design. Imagine a similar process of change involving the arts disciplines integrated with other subjects of study. The color and texture of the arts influence every aspect of the arts integration weaving. Thus, the arts are the center of the woven design (Fowler, 1994).

With this philosophical approach in mind, think about the many ways you might integrate the arts in the curriculum. How one learns is as important as what one learns. Within art integration, the arts provide an avenue for learners to work, communicate, and develop new insights in the arts and other disciplines. The ability to see beyond the structure of a discipline into other disciplines leads to creative teaching and learning (Bigge & Shermis, 1992; Consortium of National Arts Education Associations, 1994).

Constructing Knowledge in the Arts

When the arts become integrated throughout the curriculum, they foster learning in and through other disciplines by expanding awareness and comprehension (Fowler, 1994). The **arts** are "culturally significant meaning, skillfully encoded in an affecting, sensuous medium" (Anderson, 1990, p. 238).

Feeling, emotion, and cognition are integral to this process. The arts "point to and help define meaning, truth, spirit, social values, religion, and other foundations of human culture" (Anderson, 1995, p. 10). Often the arts are described a specific **arts discipline and/or art form**, which includes Dance, Drama, Music, and Visual Art and encompasses a variety of forms involving philosophy, history, criticism, and production (Consortium of National Arts Education Associations, 1994; Getty Institute for the Arts, 1996).

Arts integration refers to an approach to teaching and learning in and through the arts as a way of understanding and transferring knowledge in other disciplines such as mathematics, science, language arts, and social studies. This approach often involves creative, imaginative, experimental, and purposive and collaboration interaction, which does not lose focus on the integrity of the arts and other disciplines (Krug & Cohen-Evron, 2000; Marshall, 2005; Roucher & Lovano-Kerr, 1995).

Smilan (2004) suggested that applying previously learned knowledge or skill sets to new content can be redefined in the arts as a dynamic interchange of competencies. Burton, Horowitz, and Abeles (1999) defined this relationship as interactive correspondence in which one discipline serves and influences another (as cited in Smilan, 2004). Thoughts and ideas form connections that create new thoughts and ideas. In an integrated curriculum, "connectedness" is emphasized. Each discipline (Math, Language Arts, Art, Music, etc.) is important, and the concepts learned in each discipline are linked within an arts integrated curriculum (Burton, Horowitz, & Abeles, 2000; Marshall, 2005).

Children who actively participate in artistic and musical activities experience and begin to think like musicians and visual artists. Active learning encourages children's critical thinking and artistic thinking processes. Acting and thinking like musicians and visual artists expand the child's repertoire of learning strategies to include thinking and responding musically, spatially, kinesthetically, and visually. Through an arts integrated curriculum, teachers and students can tap into the process of multimodal connections that include imagination and emotional expression. The arts often activate and inspire students to discover the joys of learning, the wonders of life, and the satisfaction of accomplishment. Students connect learning in various disciplines with arts learning, which provides a more cohesive curriculum that values the arts as another dimension of meaning and knowing. The arts connect many forms of knowing, making curriculum more comprehensive, cohesive, engaging, humanistic, and connected to our culture (Fowler, 1994).

Part of the reason for valuing the arts in an integrated curriculum lies with the concept of **creativity.** Creativity concerns inspired and new achievements that significantly change the way something is done (Csikszentmihalyi, Feldman, & Gardner, 1994). Creativity involves a willingness to try new and different things (Gardner, 1991, 1999). Based upon the ability to think independently and divergently, creativity may stem from critical thinking, analysis, and evaluation. Creativity can be expressed in human abilities to invent, see, and communicate new dimensions of meaning, using imaginative thought processes, creating individual visions of the world based upon past, present, and future (Fowler, 1994). Creativity is an important part of the learning process affected by the learning and psychological environment, materials used, social values, individual personality, abilities, and learner attitude. Within the learning environment, a joy of discovery should be cultivated, enabling further exploration, investigation, and inquiry (Brittain & Lowenfeld, 1987; Lowenfeld, 1968).

When considering an arts integrated curriculum, key terms from the arts discipline should be interwoven throughout the unit of study. For Visual Arts, a focus on the **elements of Art**, which includes the concepts of line, shape, form, color, value, space, and texture, should be considered. These Visual Art elements are the building blocks for describing, analyzing, creating, and evaluating Visual Art. Along with the elements of Art, the **principles of design** include, but are not limited to, balance (symmetry/asymmetry), pattern/repetition, emphasis, variety, and unity. The principles of design describe how the elements of Art are applied in an artwork.

For the discipline of Music, educators should focus on the **elements of music**, including but not limited to beat, rhythm, meter, tempo, repetition, tone, melody, pitch, harmony, texture, and accent. These Music elements are the building blocks for listening to, analyzing, composing, and performing music.

Making connections is a change in the dominant paradigm of thinking about the arts, the symbol systems account, which considers disciplines as discrete and different. Akin to making connections in and through arts integration, the interpretive account of thinking about the arts allows for multiple, transitional, and contextual development of meaning (Parsons, 1998). For example, through the study of the arts, "students gain a greater understanding of the whole; the sensory nature of the arts helps build bridges between verbal and nonverbal experiences" (The State of Florida, Department of State, 1996, pp. 229–230). Building bridges through curricular connections is part of arts integration (Fowler, 1994).

Arts Integration Practices

Learning in and through the arts can occur in different ways, from minimal integration to total arts infusion into the curriculum. There are many different terms, styles, and approaches used by educators to describe and define arts integration. Some of these terms are *fusion, correlation, co-equal integration, interdisciplinary, parallel instruction, and multidisciplinary* (Anderson, 1995; Krug & Cohen-Evron, 2000). The practice of arts integration is constantly evolving within schools. Educators planning an arts integrated unit often pull from a variety of approaches depending upon their needs, restraints, and instructional goals (Krug & Cohen-Evron, 2000). It is important to note that keeping the integrity of each art form is essential. The arts should not be marginalized in the curriculum. Meeting authentic arts goals as defined through national and state standards is crucial. Each possible discipline in an arts integrated approach has a body of knowledge for study and practice. An integrative curriculum can blur the boundaries between the disciplines, relating thoughts and ideas through pedagogical experiences (Irwin & Reynolds, 1995).

Before designing an arts integrated curriculum, educators should ask several questions, such as, What is the content? What is appropriate instruction? Who provides instruction? What strategies are implemented? and How is instruction assessed? Thus, the questions educators ask concerning integration address content, instruction, implementation, and assessment (Roucher & Lovano-Kerr, 1995). Arts integration practices vary just as students and educators have various teaching and learning needs.

Arts Process Skills

Inquiry-Based Learning and the Inclusive Classroom

Best practice in lesson plan development is to focus lesson content on the exploration of inquiry questions. The standards-based inquiries that are directed by a series of activities involving experiential, discovery learning must be predicated on the quest for information. This journey, although guided by the teacher through a set of learning episodes, is most beneficial when students are vested in the inquiry questions. An important part of pre-K and early elementary learning is the ability of the student to comprehend and articulate the skills that she or he is learning through the various learning episodes. Only by guiding our students toward acknowledging the learning goals of the experiential learning can we hope to develop the artistic and musical skills in children.

The arts offer opportunities for developing investigation through alternative means. Teaching concepts in and through the arts can offer learners the opportunities to find entry points into the curriculum as well as opportunities to successfully engage with collaborative, social learning and communication. Motivation to learn is thus fostered through intrinsic reward.

Research (Deasy, 2002; Fiske, 1999) suggests that learners with disabilities benefit greatly from the affective effects of learning in and through the arts. Involving students in arts-based learning allows them to be more engaged in classroom activities, and the experiential nature of the lessons often fosters task perseverance and, ultimately, successful learning. According to Catterall, Chapleau, and Iwanaga (1999), the arts affect human development by providing opportunities for different types of human interaction in the classroom. The interpersonal and intrapersonal interactions associated with collaborative arts learning, with dramatic, musical, or dance performance, develop communication skills of learners. Furthermore, use of arts-based teaching and learning strategies in the inclusive classroom guides students toward the development of empathy and tolerance for differences. The arts can be thought of as a continuum of the human experience. Similarly, the various needs of our nation's children are all a part of the continuum of the human experience. What better way than to celebrate and accommodate these various abilities than through participation in the arts processes.

Multicultural Art and Music Education

Incorporating multicultural experiences into the classroom can help students to make more connections with other people and the world around them. Arts-based lessons involving other peoples and cultures can help students to identify similarities and differences in physical and social attributes as well as broaden their musical and artistic experience. Honoring other cultures through art- and music-making activities can help to further our teachings of acceptance of others and of self. Multicultural arts education also affords the opportunity to invite community members, including parents and grandparents, to participate in the classroom and share the rituals, artifacts, music, and dance that are important parts of their heritage.

Integrating the Arts

Art Integration as Teaching Strategy

Arts integration, in and of itself, can be viewed as a strategy for teaching students of varying exceptionalities. Arts integration is the simultaneous teaching of complementary or parallel concepts through arts-based curriculum. In effective arts integration, concepts in an academic discipline are taught through an arts experience that is designed to authentically teach arts concepts while providing instruction in similar concepts in another discipline. Arts integrations are most successful when the lesson planners develop learning experiences that align with legitimate, overlapping objectives. While arts experiences that reinforce other academic lessons can be useful alternative forms of concept repetition, arts integrations for learners with disabilities are most effective when the other discipline concepts are initially explored through the arts experience. In this way, the student has the opportunity to explore and discover the academic ideas in a creative way. Arts integrated learning can help to motivate the learner to engage in the learning activity and to take ownership of the learning experience. In this way, the arts invite students to the academic drawing table. According to Eisner (1994), the arts allow learners to express multiple forms of knowing through various methods.

Addressing multiple intelligences through arts education. Integrating the arts into the curriculum allows for multiple entry points and addresses multiple styles of learning. Gardner (1993) identified eight discrete learning styles: linguistic, logical and mathematical, interpersonal, musical, spatial,

bodily kinesthetic, intrapersonal, and naturalistic. Wachowiak and Clements (2006) suggest that all of these intelligences have a place in the arts education curriculum. Through the oral and written discussion of the visual art and musical performances of others, or description of student self-created artwork or musical performances, children are learning through the linguistic intelligence. Through learning about and incorporating the elements of Art, including shape, form, line, and space through the organizational principles of design and the elements of Music, including rhythm, meter, tempo, and repetition, students are developing their logical mathematical intelligence.

Students develop interpersonal intelligence by learning about other cultures and the ideas of other individuals through the arts and artifacts of people. Musical and bodily kinesthetic intelligence is enhanced through experiences with listening and performing, including instrumental, vocal, and movement. Linking music with a specific time period or a visual artist's life is another way to address musical intelligence. For example, the artist Mondrian was inspired by jazz music. Also students can write songs about a musician's or visual artist's life. Students can use a well-known song and change the words to highlight art and music vocabulary. For example, the words to "Twinkle, Twinkle Little Star" can be changed to "line, shape, form, color, value, don't forget space, texture too" (Brown, 2006).

Again, spatial intelligence is developed in every visual arts experience, as well as musical experiences that focus on the concept of space and time (beat, rhythm, tempo). Oftentimes the arts are integrated with math and science to help students to create images, mental models, or other representations of more abstract scientific and mathematical concepts. These concrete representations are especially crucial to the identifying and redirecting misconceptions in young learners. Manipulatives, created in the arts classrooms, can be important visual aids and learning tools for the student with disabilities. Developmentally appropriate models of concepts are often required to illustrate these intangible ideas.

Penultimately, the intrapersonal intelligence is cultivated through the reflective and expressive component of art making. Students can create images and representations of themselves, of their feelings and imaginings. Once committed to an image, a sculpture, a song, or interpretive dance, these ideas, perceptions, and perspectives can be shared with others in the community. Art becomes an outward extension of the self. Through this sharing, empathy and understanding is developed.

Last, the naturalistic intelligence can be developed through a number of arts experiences. Students can learn about the environment through sketching field trips and observations. They can use materials and artifacts from the environment in artwork. For example, fallen pieces of bark or palms can be used to create assemblage or collage. Similarly, various fibrous roots and vines can be used to create handmade papers and weavings, respectively. Musical sound stories can be developed in response to an outdoor field trip. The sounds of nature can be replicated using a variety of musical instruments, and a melody can be performed by the students. Books that focus on nature can be illustrated by students and read along with performances of original musical compositions. The sounds of the book can be performed on musical instruments during the reading as well. Development of the naturalistic intelligence can be incorporated into lessons that encourage students to experience the world as a classroom, far beyond the confines of the school building. These experiences help to develop children's perceptual skills and add new schema to the mental sketchpad. See Table 12.1, as it gives some examples of how Visual Art, Music, multiple intelligences, and other disciplines can be linked in an inclusive setting.

Competencies Taught in an Arts-Based Curriculum

Art education in the twenty-first century is focused on teaching and learning in the areas of aesthetics, criticism, history, and production. Based on national goals and standards, teachers develop lessons using materials and art tools, and teach the techniques required for art and music. Teachers design a course of study leading to knowledge of the history of art and music, including a variety of artists, musicians, music, and art forms. The experiences designed for students include practice in producing a variety of two-dimensional and three-dimensional artworks and in performing on musi-

Table 12.1 ● Arts Linked With Disciplines in the Inclusive Classroom

Arts Objectives /Activities	Objectives for Students with Disabilities	Multiple Intelligences	Related Subject Areas Objectives
Creative Drama: Acting out an artwork or musical selection	Communication	Linguistic Interpersonal Intrapersonal	Language Arts—Write a play or story. Physical Education—Create a movement sequence.
Visual and musical storytelling	Independent and group learning	Logical/mathematical Sequential Interpersonal	Mathematics—Create a pattern sequence or predict what will be next in a pattern. Language Arts—Relate images and sounds to a children's story. Social Sciences/Multicultural—Relate to historical or current events.
Interpretation of nonprint cues in a group discussion about an artwork or musical selection from diverse cultures	Interdependent peer learning	Spatial/Visual Musical Interpersonal	Social Sciences/Multicultural—Use photographs from newspaper as discussion points. Share photographs of homes around the world or clothing style.
Perseverance while creating complex artwork or music	Behavior modification Stay on task Self-motivate Task completion	Musical Visual Intrapersonal	Language Arts—Write a story with a beginning, middle, and end. Science—Complete a series of experiments that, when information is combined, supports or disproves a hypothesis.
Creative and Critical Thinking when creating, analyzing, and evaluating artwork or music	Vary thinking and problem-solving abilities	Bodily kinesthetic Linguistic Mathematical Intrapersonal	Language Arts—compare and contrast two folk tales from different cultures. Physical Education—Compare and contrast different dance styles.

Table 12.1 • (Continued)

Arts Objectives /Activities	Objectives for Students with Disabilities	Multiple Intelligences	Related Subject Areas Objectives
Self-Expression when creating artwork or music	Communication of ideas, wants, and needs to others	Intrapersonal Interpersonal	Language Arts—Write stories. Mathematics—Create own word problems. Science—Hypothesize, predict. Physical Education—Create new games with new rules. Social Sciences—After reading about a current event students write what they think can happen next.
Understanding Ideas of others by learning about artwork and music from diverse cultures	Communication of ideas, wants, and needs Empathy	Naturalistic Visual Musical Linguistic	Science—Learn about environments around the world. How does this effect housing and clothing needs? Go outside and observe plants, animals, and insects live in the area. Take care of a pet.

cal instruments as well as vocally. Practice in describing and criticizing the artwork and music that is created by themselves and others is part of the curriculum. In the early childhood curriculum, it is particularly important to help students to develop confidence in their abilities to use various art mediums and musical instruments.

Young children must be encouraged to learn through discovery of materials and processes and to communicate their ideas through nonverbal and verbal expression. These skills, while important for all children, may be essential for learners with disabilities. Through the arts, students can describe who they are and what they believe. Through the arts, children can share their vision with the world and become a part of a larger community. Attributes, which are developed through arts education beyond the technical skills associated with creating products from various materials and performing on various instruments, are the following:

- Student self-expression
- Relationships between and among forms, objects, musical selections, and instruments

Competencies Taught in an Arts-Based Curriculum

- Communication of ideas of self and others
- Narrative storytelling through images and words, and performance through voice or instruments.
- Organizational skills
- Ability to visualize and perform from alternative perspectives
- Ability to sustain focus on parts or whole and to distinguish between part and whole
- Other academic skills and relationships
- Cultural awareness/global awareness
- Tolerance for differences of others
- Fine motor skills development
- The ability to imagine alternative solutions and vantage points

Differentiating Instruction in the Arts

The Arts as a Bridge in the Inclusive Classroom

Students need to express themselves and to be included in creative endeavors. Art can help students to bridge the often seemingly impassible curricular and social gaps. Through the arts, teachers can create more equitable learning situations through targeting the learning capabilities of their students. Vygotsky (1978) indicated that peer partnering is an effective method for social learning and extending the zone of proximal development. Collaborative learning opportunities afforded through the arts can target multiple accommodation strategies. For example, the experiential learning required for participation in the creation of a classroom mural or environmental sculpture, or the collaboration required for a vocal ensemble or theatrical production, relates to cooperative learning. Reader's theater, a strategy traditionally used in the elementary classroom, promotes the development of social skills, written, and oral communication, and creative expression.

Strategies for Teachers in Inclusive Classrooms

Teachers must be prepared to make whatever accommodations are necessary so that every student has an equal opportunity to participate in every arts experience. Teachers who wish to integrate the arts in the curriculum must be versed in differentiating instruction to facilitate learning at all different ability levels. Simultaneous, or concurrent, instruction is sometimes necessary so that similar projects, addressing the same art and music concepts, are provided to students of varying talents and abilities. Accommodations include using alternative instructional materials, utilizing peer tutoring, alternative assignments and assessments, alternative time frames and sequencing or scheduling of projects and events, variations in learning environments, equipment and tools, including adapted art tools such as thick-handled brushed and crayons, and use of special systems for communication and assistive technology devices.

For example, when teaching a student with a vision disability in the arts-integrated inclusive classroom, the teacher must make adjustments by focusing on auditory instruction or providing the child with braille text for any written components of the lesson. Children with vision impairment who retain some visual acuity may be accommodated with large-print text and given larger visual aids. Additionally, the teacher must be made aware that the child with the visual impairment may be sensitive to certain tactile sensations. When providing experiences in clay or other mediums that require the students' fingers to become immersed in a sticky substance such as glue, paper mache, or finger painting, the teacher must be aware that he or she is in effect compromising the very instrument by which the youngster "sees" or experiences the world.

The teacher must be sensitive to the materials presented to the child. Tactile, nonintrusive materials are most appropriate for the student who has a visual impairment. Drawing activities could be modified to include relief images; often two-dimensional exercises can be easily modified to relief or three-dimensional projects by layering of materials and collage. In this way, the student can participate in the art activity and meet the learning objectives of the lesson. Concerning a music lesson, the teacher can use the various tones from instruments to "illustrate" a bold line in a drawing. Perhaps a wavy line in an artwork can be translated into a flute melody that fluctuates along the musical scale.

For the child with a hearing impairment, the instructor must be sure to provide written or visual instruction in lieu of verbal, auditory direction. In an inclusive classroom in which there are students with multiple exceptionalities, one must be well prepared with a variety of instructional techniques. For example, concepts intrinsic to the visual arts and music, such as pattern, rhythm, and movement, can be illustrated through image as well as through sound waves and vibration to involve the senses of seeing, hearing, and touch.

For students with various specific learning disabilities, the educator must be able to help them to focus on the essential criteria of the assignment. Organization skills are often critical for students with disabilities. The teacher must accommodate the student by providing clear and concise steps and structures for each art and music lesson. The learning goals that make up the overall task, or art product, must be clearly defined for the learner. In developing step-by-step strategies, however, the arts integration educator must be careful not to thwart the creative development of the learner.

At the elementary level, there are often opportunities for structured lessons, which break down arts assignments into manageable components. This strategy can be very effective for students with disabilities, who are motivated by sequential successes with their projects. Art integration teachers must be careful, however, to guide the development of creativity in their students with all projects. Creativity can easily be compromised to rote learning episodes when step-by-step lessons are presented. Here, the educator must walk a fine line of breaking down the assignments into manageable sections, while maintaining the integrity of the students' individuality and encouraging divergent response.

Teachers integrating the arts can use strategies of Socratic questioning and think-aloud techniques, which require critical thinking and problem solving. By modeling thought process strategies for students, educators can assist learners to develop their own strategies for concept application. These strategies also assist learners in developing skills in perseverance. By relooking, rethinking, and reapplying, all students are given the opportunity to learn important skills that will serve them in the world outside of school.

Assessment in the Arts

Assessment is a broad concept, involving both measurement and evaluation. Measurement establishes individual or group characteristics, while evaluation is a combination of what is measured and information gathered in order to decide if what was observed is important and applicable to the learning objectives. The use of assessment may extend beyond measurement and evaluation. For example, in assessment, information is gathered for interpretation and synthesis of concepts. Then criteria and characteristics are named based upon what the information describes.

Informal, periodic review—formative assessment by student and teacher—must be planned into the learning experience. Assessment of learning and continued reference to learning objectives is critical to the efficacy of the lesson. In order for students to take ownership of their learning, they must be involved in the assessment process. Such involvement enhances student metacognitive skills and motivation. Feedback and acknowledgment of successes, both during and after the project, are essential. Appropriate assessment tools include oral and narrative reflection with the teacher and other students. This process can be facilitated by informal (formative) critiques of the ongoing art process, as well as summative critiques of the product. A show-and-tell experience of student work and/or performance would be an appropriate assessment strategy.

Examples of assessment may be a portfolio, performance, or a series of complex observations completed by the teacher (Oosterhof, 1996). Eisner (1994) has devised criteria that are appropriate to use in assessment. Assessment should reflect the nature of the tasks to be assessed, which in turn should reflect what students and teacher will be expected to do. The assessment should measure the process of problem formation and solving as well as the actual solution. Assessment should reflect the values to an intellectual community in the field of study. Group tasks and individual tasks should be included and related to the curriculum taught. Also, learners should be given the opportunity to demonstrate their knowledge in situations. This way, they are able to understand how something works as a whole rather than discrete parts. (Eisner, 1994).

Eisner's (1994) concept of multiple forms of assessment relate to Gardner's (1991, 1999) theory of multiple intelligences, in that students and teachers learn through a variety of methods. The multiple intelligences theory involves learning through kinesthetic, visual, logical, linguistic, musical, naturalistic, interpersonal, and intrapersonal activities (Gardner, 1991, 1999). Ideas for arts activities that can be assessed include expressive paintings in which children use color to communicate feelings in appropriate ways, and drawing from partner description, which encourages peer communication and appropriate socialization. Narrative drawings, which share stories, followed by oral presentation of the artwork in a "circle of friends" discussion can also promote this important social and communication development. Musical stories can be told using instruments in place of words. Choreographed narratives can be added to further develop kinesthetic learning and responses.

Also, assessment components for arts integration can take many forms including written work, arts production/performance, journals, observation, inquiry, discussion, and reflection, all of which are criteria and objective based. Students, teachers, administrators, and peers in either group can complete assessment. Assessment in arts integration should be continuous, embedded, and authentic (Glanz, 1999).

Assessment also involves standards and criteria. According to Eisner (1994) standards are not value statements; rather, standards propose particular outcomes as based in a specific condition or situation. Standards describe outcomes that are completed or are not completed. For example, either a student can list at least four design elements in visual art or he or she cannot. When judging the quality of learning outcomes, criteria come into play. Criteria can be a group of complex qualities used to appraise the value of a learning outcome. For example, judgments of the quality of a student drawing may be based upon either criteria derived from a portfolio of past drawings by the same student or, otherwise, specified criteria used to compare and contrast the student's drawing with another drawing perceived by the instructor as epitomizing the learning outcome. Teaching and learning benefit if arts criteria and standards are made explicit. By clearly stating the criteria and standards, the teacher enables the learner to motivate and assess his or her own learning (Beattie, 1997a, 1997b; Eisner, 1994; The State of Florida, Department of State, 1996).

Rubrics describe specifically what is expected, and can be developed by the educator collaboratively with learners. They include levels of performance and learning characteristics, and provide a guideline for learners and educators when assessing performance. Rubrics can assess performance in a variety of ways and include analytic scoring rubrics, which score parts or specific qualities of the product individually; holistic scoring rubrics, which assesses the product as a whole providing qualitative analysis of the student's achievement level; and modified holistic rubrics, which score the whole product and specific qualities of the product that exemplify the standard. Deciding which type of scoring rubric to use is dependent upon what is being assessed and why it is being assessed. For example, if a portfolio is viewed as a tool to contain a body of work demonstrating different knowledge areas, requiring individual grades, an analytic scoring rubric may be used. The assessment strategies, standards, scoring rubrics, and judging criteria should be made clear to all students. This way, learners become self-directed throughout the creation and assessment of their work (Beattie, 1997a).

Meeting authentic arts goals as defined through national, state, and local standards is an issue in the assessment of arts integration. The integrity of each art form should be reflected in all aspects of assessment (Roucher & Lovano-Kerr, 1995). The national standards provide general guidelines for what students should learn in kindergarten through grade twelve, while each state designed standards that express general learning goals based upon the national standards. Many school districts have requirements for arts learning as defined through district curriculum guidelines and grade-level expectations (Consortium of National Arts Education Associations, 1994).

In the field of arts education, advocates of arts standards claim that the description of what students should know and be able to demonstrate gives value to the arts within the educational context, thus student achievement in the arts is valued (Consortium of National Art Association, 1994; Day, 1998). Eisner (2001) claims that standards should allow educators to reflect upon the purposes of the field. Therefore, educators should look closely at their own teaching and students' work in order to strengthen programs of study. The spirit of the arts can infuse all areas of study by valuing the arts processes and giving direction to teaching practice, thereby becoming the center of schooling (Eisner, 2001).

Students must also be told how their work will be assessed. For learners with disabilities, teachers may plan alternative assessment strategies. For example, written responses may be replaced by oral narrative or visual cues for some students with specific learning disabilities. Practical visual representation or visual cue cards that explain the project or performance may serve as evidence of learning. Performance and more authentic assessment of art or music processes may replace a traditional written testing format for content knowledge. Another assessment tool that involves decision making and self-selection are the process-folio (Gardner, 1993) and portfolio. In developing a process-folio, students make selections of work at various stages of production including written or scribed reflections and images. This documentation is collected during the learning process, hence the name of the data collection system. Both the process-folio and the portfolio allow students to reflect upon their work based on the given assignment criteria and to strategize about edits and improvements. This helps to develop student motivation, evaluation skills, and perseverance.

Shared Responsibilities: Teachers and Paraprofessionals

Teachers may require the assistance of other adults from the school or extended community. Parents may be involved in the classroom with children with special needs. Other partners may include paraprofessional educators. Paraprofessionals often assist students in the inclusive classroom.

Students of varying disabilities may be accompanied by a nurse, interpreter, or other paraprofessional. This adult individual is in the classroom to assist the child in his or her learning endeavors. The paraprofessional may or may not have expertise in the arts, and may require additional instruction as to how to facilitate arts learning for the students to whom he or she have been charged.

What is the role of the paraprofessional in the classroom? The answer to this question is varied according to the student's needs. The educator must negotiate boundaries for the involvement of the paraprofessional in the arts integrated curriculum. In the busy arts integrated classroom, the teacher must be careful not to delegate too much of her or his teaching responsibilities to this other adult. The teacher is, of course, ultimately responsible for the arts learning of all of her or his students. Educators understand the importance of developing perseverance and creativity along with the arts concept learning of their students. Paraprofessionals may be inclined to assist the student more than is necessary in order to conform to a standard for the project, whether represented by the teacher or imagined by the paraprofessional (Guay, Marsh, & Boivin, 2003). When a paraprofessional is in attendance in the classroom, the educator may be required to restrict her or his involvement to allow the student to create the artwork or musical performance. For example, a technique for developing perseverance with students is to redirect their attention to the criteria established for any given lesson and encourage them to revisit their work. Oftentimes, the paraprofessional sees his or her task in the arts integrated lesson as that of assisting the child to complete the work in a manner consistent with the paraprofessional's criteria, other students' work, or teacher-created samples (Guay et al., 2003). This goal of convergent response can serve to stifle student creativity and perseverance and goes against the objectives of arts education curriculum.

In keeping with other accommodation strategies for learners with special needs, it is beneficial for the educator to make the steps and strategies for each lesson concise and visible for both the student with special needs and the paraprofessional educator. Each task and concept must be explicit and the student/adult expectations carefully negotiated and planned. Empowering the learner with the lesson expectations as well as techniques and procedures for achieving formative and summative goals are important components of the accommodation strategy.

Teachers serve all students and thus are required to understand the Individual Education Plans (IEP) of their students. This responsibility extends beyond the requirement to read and sign student IEPs. According to Villa and Thousand (2005), school administrators must take a leadership role to ensure that all general educators and educator specialists understand their legal responsibility to meet the needs of the diverse learners in their classrooms.

The Role of School Site Administration and Art Education for the Learner with Special Needs

Kluth, Villa, and Thousand (2002) emphatically stated, "Special education is not a program or a place, and inclusive schooling is not a policy that schools can dismiss outright" (p. 25). According to research (Kluth, Villa & Thousand, 2002), schools in which administrators take a leadership role in the policy and practice of the IDEA law have the most successful learning environments for all learners. Not surprisingly, they also found that administrative support and district mandate were imperative for sustaining a viable arts education curriculum for all students. Thus, the role of the on-site administrator and the district-level administration in inclusive arts education is paramount to its success.

Models that facilitate training, cooperative planning, and teaching coupled with budgets to support individualized instruction and materials must be a part of the arts education design. Just as students with disabilities need to be educated in an environment that does not isolate, educators need to avoid working in isolation in order to make the necessary accommodations for all students.

Since the law requires that schools and the school district provide whatever is needed for the child to have a successful learning experience, it is imperative for all teachers to understand what this means and where the resources can be found. This policy has implications for in-service professional development as well as preservice education. Direction for such curriculum and instruction may be found in alliance with the professionals involved with Very Special Arts (VSA).

Very Special Arts

VSA is an organization dedicated to the philosophy that the arts significantly enrich the lives of individuals with disabilities, allowing for full participation without judgment or restriction. VSA is an international nonprofit organization founded in 1974 by Ambassador Jean Kennedy Smith. VSA strives to link schools, universities, cultural organizations, and individuals with disabilities, helping to promote opportunities for all people to participate. Through the arts, individuals with disabilities may find alternative ways to express themselves communicate and participate with society. The arts, in effect, bridge stereotypes and lift exclusive barriers.

> For people with disabilities, the arts represent a world of resources and opportunities, providing an outlet for creative expression and unlimited possibilities for personal, academic, and professional success. And, because art is an infinite and unconditional field, people with disabilities are free to express themselves without physical, social, or attitudinal barriers. (VSA, 2006)

Programming and initiatives of VSA are guided by four essential principles:

- Every young person with a disability deserves access to high-quality arts learning experiences.
- All artists in schools and art educators should be prepared to include students with disabilities in their instruction.
- All children, youth, and adults with disabilities should have complete access to cultural facilities and activities.

- All individuals with disabilities who aspire to careers in the arts should have the opportunity to develop appropriate skills. (VSA, 2006, pp. 1–2)

Visual Art and Music Integration Lesson Planning

Learning in and through the arts requires the teacher to relate foundational concepts in each discipline. It is important for the teacher to become familiar with the national and state standards for each discipline. National Music content standards involve

- singing alone and with others,
- performing on instruments, improvising melodies, variations, and accompaniments,
- composing and arranging music,
- reading and notating music,
- listening to, analyzing, and describing music,
- evaluating music and music performances,
- understanding relationships between music and other disciplines, and
- understanding music in relation to history and culture. (National Association for Music Education, 2005)

Each of these content standards has specific achievement standards that explain what the student should know and be able to do.

Visual Art national content standards include

- understanding and applying media, techniques, and processes,
- using knowledge of structures and functions,
- choosing and evaluating subject matter, symbols, and ideas,
- understanding visual arts in relation to history and cultures,
- reflecting upon and assessing the characteristics and merits of artwork, and
- making connections between visual art and other disciplines (National Art Education Association, 2005).

Again, each of the content standards has specific achievement standards that explain what the student should know and be able to do. At state and local levels, standards are modeled after the national-level standards.

After becoming familiar with the standards for the disciplines that the teacher wishes to integrate, the teacher should link content standards to the topic or theme of study. When lesson planning, the teacher selects the subject matter for study from any discipline, such as measuring in Mathematics. Next, the teacher wishing to integrate Music and Visual Art with this topic looks through the standards and tries to relate concepts. For example, in Visual Art a paper-weaving project requires measurement, and in Music performing according to notation requires knowledge of measurement. So the teacher begins to plan a lesson that involves the concept of measuring as it is linked to a paper-weaving project where students use rulers to measure where the paper will be cut. Then the students create notation that is inspired by the artwork, such as a series of half and quarter notes. Next, the students can clap, sing, or perform on instruments the notation sequence that was composed by the group. Listing the standards from each discipline in the lesson plan is important in order to provide a clear foundation to important concepts in each discipline. Table 12.2 is sample lesson format that may help when integrating several disciplines. Table 12.3 illustrates how to use this format.

There are many arts integrated lessons that can be used as resources. One example integrates Music, Art, Language Arts, and Social Studies. A focus on jazz, blues, and Romare Bearden's artwork can be linked to children's literature and American culture. Students can create songs that become student-illustrated books. Another lesson idea integrates Art, Music, Science, and Mathematics through the study of Impressionist artwork. Students can study Monet's paintings that depict Chartres Cathedral at different times of day. Then students can describe and draw a tree or building

Table 12.2 • Sample Arts Integration Lesson Plan Format

Title of Lesson:

Subject:

Grade Level:

Time Required:

Instructional Objectives:
Students will . . . List as many as needed for the lesson.

National Standards:

Subject Matter Content:
Visual Arts Concepts and Vocabulary With Definitions
Music Concepts and Vocabulary With Definitions
Cooperating Discipline Concepts and Vocabulary With Definitions

Key Questions
List at least two key questions to ask students. Remember to address lower order questions (what, identify, acquiring knowledge) and higher order questions (how, application of knowledge).

Lesson Initiating Activity
How will you begin the lesson? Use attention-grabbing activities to motivate learning.

Core Activities
List what the teacher will do throughout the lesson.
List what the students will do throughout the lesson.
Be sure to include step-by-step instructions for Visual Art processes.

(Continued)

Differentiating Instruction in the Arts

Table 12.2   ●   *(Continued)*

Closure Activity

Explain how the lesson will end, including a review of concepts. Don't forget cleanup procedures.

ESOL, ESE, Gifted Strategies

List what strategies or accommodations that will be implemented throughout the lesson.

Materials and Equipment:

List all the materials and equipment that will be needed when teaching this lesson.

Assessment/Evaluation:

Design a rubric and explain how assessment will be conducted. For example, assessment can be conducted through teacher observation throughout the lesson, student self-assessment after completion of artwork and musical performance using a list of criteria, group critique at end of lesson, etc.

Follow-Up Activities:

List some ideas for you next step. This may be a homework assignment or something for students who finish early.

Self-Assessment:

Don't forget to assess your teaching after the lesson. Here are some points to consider, or you can write your own ideas on how you may self-assess the lesson plan.

Reflect upon the lesson with regard to the following items:

1. Effective assessment of prior knowledge of students was conducted.
2. Timely, sequential presentation and organization of materials were completed.
3. Students were involved in pre-activity task, brainstorming, and/or guided practice session.
4. Teacher demonstrated Visual Art technique or process (for example, painting technique of blending). Teacher demonstrated Music performance (for example, clapping a notation sequence).
5. Effective and clear communication of procedures was evident (for example, step-by-step or how-to directions and expectations during class).
6. Teacher demonstrated the ability to assist learners with formalistic (design elements and principles of Visual Art and elements of Music) as well as contextual (social and cultural) issues.
7. Effective cleanup and closure procedures were used.

References/Bibliography:

Don't forget to list the resources you used when creating the lesson plan. This is particularly important when sharing the lesson with other teachers.

Table 12.3 ● Sample Arts Integration Lesson

Fall Season and Patterns/Texture

Kindergarten–Third Grade

Length of Lesson: 50 minutes

Instructional Objectives

Students will:

- Listen to the teacher review the concepts of the design principles of pattern, repetition, and balance and how this relates to Visual Art and Music.
- Develop fine motor skills and craftsmanship, utilizing a sense of pressure while grating colored chalk across a variety of textures such as screen and sandpaper.
- Create a sound sequence for a fall story using objects such as crackling leaves, manual egg beaters, triangle, and drums.
- Learn about the fall season.
- Demonstrate understanding of the concepts through group discussion and evaluation of the finished artwork and musical composition.

  Visual Art National Standards:
  1. Understanding and applying media, techniques, and processes.
  5. Reflecting upon and assessing the characteristics and merits of their work and the work of others.

  Music National Standards:
  3. Improvising melodies, variations, and accompaniments.
  6. Listening to, analyzing, and describing music.

  Science National Standards:
  - Content Standard C: Life Science—Life cycles of organisms
  - Content Standard D: Earth and Space Science—Changes in Earth and Sky

Subject Matter

Visual Art

- Pattern—Repeated shapes, color, lines, etc., to create a sequence.
- Texture—How something feels to the touch or appears to be bumpy, rough, smooth, etc.

Music

- Pattern—Repeated sounds on instruments or through voice to create a sequence.
- Texture—The relationship between sound and physical touch achieved through a variety of instruments and variations of voice.

Science

- Leaf—Grown from a stem of a plant, usually green, but can be other colors.
- Fall season—Changes in weather occur due to the Earth's movement in outer space. This results in changes for organisms, such as plants (change in leaf color and eventual dropping to ground).

(Continued)

Differentiating Instruction in the Arts

Table 12.3 ● *(Continued)*

Key Questions: What is repetition? What is pattern? How will you be using the idea of pattern or repetition in your artwork and music? What happens when you press the chalk harder or more softly on the surface of the screen or sandpaper? What type of sound do you think dry leaves will make when I crush them with my hands? (You can ask this question about predicting sound from any object or instrument.) How do you think pattern is shown in this artwork or music? Is pattern created through the color, or by the placement of the leaves on the page? Can you touch the color that is repeated? Which sound do you think was repeated the most? Can you make the sound that was repeated the most in our composition? Explain what happens during the fall season to the plants and environment?

Lesson Initiating Activity: An initial review of plant parts will be conducted having students demonstrate their knowledge of plant parts (stems, leaves, veins) through touching and speaking the names.—5 minutes

Teacher will show an example of the project and introduce the concept of silhouette.

Teacher will review the design principles of repetition and pattern utilizing the sample artwork and musical selections as examples of those concepts.—5 minutes

Core Activities: Students will receive and implement step-by-step instruction on the process of creating the leaf silhouette and will be given time to explore the different effects achieved from using screen and sandpaper. The student will create a fall sound sequence.—30 minutes

Steps:

1. Using proper classroom behavior, take a brush from the bowl of watered down glue and evenly cover your entire piece of black construction paper. (Remind them not to over apply the watered down glue.)
2. Place the leaves and stems onto the construction paper to show repetition and pattern.
3. Use sandpaper or screen to scrape chalk over your picture. You may change around and use all three tools. Please be sure to use at least three different colors of chalk. Cover your entire paper with chalk dust.
4. Once students are finished applying the chalk, they remove the leaves and stems, leaving a silhouette shape.
5. Students talk about the fall season and the different sounds that you can hear during this season. A list of fall descriptions, such as cool, crisp wind and crunching leaves, is placed on the board or chart paper.
6. The teacher shows an object or instrument and asks students to predict what sound it will make. Students experiment making sounds with objects and instruments. Each sound is discovered through inquiry and personal experimentation.
7. Students create musical sounds to represent the fall season. Then the sounds are composed into a pattern. The teacher may include words such as *leaves crunching, cool wind, rustling,* and *crisp air*.
8. Once the group decides on the sequence of sounds, the sequence is performed.

Table 12.3 ● *(Continued)*

Closure Activity: Students discuss individual artwork and the group musical composition concerning pattern and repetition. A review of concepts for Visual Art, Music, and Science is conducted by questioning students about the fall season, pattern, and repetition.— 5 minutes

For cleanup, the students will be instructed to put their individual artwork in the drying rack, and one student in each group is chosen to place the brushes in the sink. Another student collects the chalk. Two other students collect the remaining supplies.— 5 minutes

ESOL, ESE, Gifted Strategies:

Strategies for diverse learners include using visuals of the completed artwork, tactile objects during discussion and music composition, and teacher modeling. Peer helpers are assigned as needed. Adult assistance is given as needed.

Materials and Equipment:

- Colored drawing chalk
- Large-size paint brushes
- School glue/watered down
- Construction paper—varying dark colors
- Screen squares with taped borders
- Sandpaper
- Paper towels

Assessment/Evaluation:

Satisfactory performance includes discussing fall concepts, creating artwork following directions, participating in musical performance, discussing pattern and repetition in artwork and musical performance, and cleanup.

The following criteria are considered for the artwork:

   Overlapping of leaves on paper

   Pattern created using leaf shapes

   Repetition of leaf shapes

   Use of chalk to create a silhouette

The following criteria are considered for the musical performance:

   Using a variety of instruments or objects to create sound

   Creating a pattern of repeated sound

   Able to perform musical sequence

Follow-Up Activities:

This lesson is an extension of a previous science lesson on plant parts. After an initial instruction on stems, leafs, and veins, students used leaves to create an artwork and inspire a musical composition. Further study about plants during different seasons could be conducted following this lesson.

Students could use fall descriptive words and write a story. Handmade books can be made using the artwork as the cover.

(Continued)

Differentiating Instruction in the Arts

Table 12.3 ● *(Continued)*

Self-Assessment:

1. Were clear directions about the creation of the artwork and musical composition given?
2. Was cleanup efficient and effective?
3. Were all students able to perform the musical sequence or complete the artwork?

References/Bibliography:

Crayola.com for art lesson resources

on the school campus at different times of the day by keeping a journal or sketchbook for a period of time. A link can be made to several familiar children's songs that describe different times of day, such as "Hickory, Dickory, Dock," "Wee Willy Winkee," and "Are You Sleeping, Brother John." Weather patterns also can inspire different artworks and relate to children's songs, such as "Rain, Rain, Go Away." Concerning Mathematics and the concept of pattern and sequencing, a lesson can be taught integrating Music and Art by pattern printmaking on grids with simple stamp shapes (circle, square, triangles) and pattern sequencing with rhythm instruments and voice.

Potential Difficulties and Differentiated Strategies Within Arts Integration

A variety of strategies may be used within the arts integrated curriculum (see Tables 12.4 and 12.5). It is important to provide an open, relaxed environment that encourages students to explore and be creative. When students are enjoying the learning experience, they often forget about being fearful of new experiences. Using a rich vocabulary for art and music paints word pictures and provides clear details. It is often necessary to describe and demonstrate art materials, instruments, artwork, and musical selections in order to create connections between what is known and what is being learned. When adapting lessons for students with special needs, it is important to consider the learning setting, or how the desks, tables, seats, and visuals are arranged. The educator may need to change the environment or use of space through the use of carrels, centers, or carpet squares or change the lighting (dimmer or brighter).

Classroom arrangement for Music and Visual Art activities should consider not only the needs of students during the activity, but also the needs of students during initial motivation and cleanup periods. In general, teachers should arrange desks in groups to provide large work spaces for Visual Arts activities. Often, large paper is used with young students, and the traditional small individual desks are not large enough to accommodate the larger papers. If this is a problem in the classroom, try working directly on the floor area, or use an outdoor space, weather permitting. If working outdoors, remember to give students something to secure the paper—either masking tape or heavy objects—in case of windy conditions. Cover work areas with newspapers or plastic sheeting when working with media that might get messy. Remember that young students will also need to wear a smock or old T-shirt over their clothes. Most art supplies are grouped together on a tray or portable container and can be easily placed on each group table.

Table 12.4 • Differentiated Strategies for Art

Art Skill Area	Potential Difficulty	Differentiated Strategy
Drawing shapes (squares, triangles, circle, rectangle, etc.) Using shapes to draw people, animals, and objects	Comprehension of shapes Physical/motor impairment	Assist/partial assist. Repeated demonstration using a variety of examples. Play "I Spy" shapes in the classroom. Trace shapes using hand motions (large motor skills). Use string to make shapes on the table. On a large piece of paper draw shapes repeatedly.
Painting shapes Mixing primary colors to make secondary colors	Comprehension of colors Physical/motor impairment	Assist/partial assist. Use large brushes to paint with thick tempera paint on large paper. Demonstrate use of brush and color mixing. Tell a story or read a story about color mixing (e.g., *Mouse Paint* by Ellen Stoll Walsh).
Sculpting three-dimensional forms	Physical/motor impairment Comprehension of forms	Bring in a variety of everyday objects to show how shapes become three dimensional forms. Use a variety of materials: Soft Play-doh, flour/salt clay, ceramic clay, oil based clay, and model magic.
Cutting, tearing, folding, or otherwise creating using paper	Physical/motor impairment	Use four-hole scissors, loop scissors, spring return scissors, or other modified products. Use a variety of papers: easy-to-tear papers such as tracing paper and newsprint; stiff papers such as construction paper, bogus paper, and manila paper. Precut shapes. Die cut shapes. Use glue stick to adhere papers.

(Continued)

Differentiating Instruction in the Arts

Table 12.4 ● *(Continued)*

Art Skill Area	Potential Difficulty	Differentiated Strategy
Printmaking	Physical/motor impairment Comprehension of reversed images from printing plate	Use liquid glue to create a relief printing plate. Use Styrofoam trays and have students press objects into the trays to create a printing plate.
Pattern Recognition and Development	Physical/motor impairment Comprehension of the pattern elements (shapes, colors)	Demonstrate completed and uncompleted pattern sequences. Use actual objects and visuals that can be physically arranged (manipulatives). Use pieces of construction paper cut into shapes and move them to create pattern sequences. Provide a large grid so students can print in each grid square. Use large contrasting shapes and colors.
Views, Analyzes, and Discusses Artwork Art Criticism Art History	Cognitive Language	Use puppets, props, and costumes related to the artwork. Discuss one element of art at a time (e.g., Look at the different types of lines). Use a piece of acetate over the artwork, and draw on the acetate to visually direct students. Have students create movement sequences that relate to the artwork (e.g., move like the wind in Van Gogh's Starry *Night).* Read children's books that focus on artists' lives, such as the *Getting to Know the World's Greatest Artists* series by Mike Venial. Share pictures of artists at work in their studio. Use timelines with pictures illustrating events.

Table 12.4 • *(Continued)*

Art Skill Area	Potential Difficulty	Differentiated Strategy
Aesthetics	Cognitive Language	Have students bring in objects that they consider to be art and not art. Make a list of qualities described by the children. Keep a chart of art questions asked by students. Teachers ask questions about what makes an artwork beautiful or ugly. Can an ugly work be art? Socratic questioning.

Table 12.5 • Differentiated Strategies for Music

Music Skill Area	Potential Difficulty	Differentiated Strategy
Sings alone and with others	Physical/motor impairment Comprehension of language	Tell musical stories using a variety of vocal sounds (car sounds, animal sounds, crashing sounds). Emphasize known words. Use visual cue cards. Use puppets, dolls, or stuffed animals as singing partners. Sing and perform with instruments familiar children's songs.
Performs on a variety of instruments	Physical/motor impairment Pattern recognition	Demonstrate performance. Assist/partial assist. Listen to everyday sounds and identify how they occur (e.g., Door creaks when opened, shoes scuff along the floor). Use full body movement and large motor skill ability to begin. Use visual cue cards or body language to identify when to perform. Create or find already made instruments.

(Continued)

Differentiating Instruction in the Arts

Table 12.5 ● *(Continued)*

Music Skill Area	Potential Difficulty	Differentiated Strategy
Reads and notates music	Visual impairment	Use large-format notation.
	Comprehension of notation	Use physical full body motion to determine beat, tempo, etc.
		Use flash cards of notation. Have students arrange cards in a sequence and perform by clapping or using an instrument.
		Repetition and practice.
Improvises	Comprehension of musical concepts	Immerse students into a variety of musical styles or genres.
		Provide opportunities to sing and play instruments in variety of settings, not just during music class.
		Model and demonstrate the process.
		Have students make up a new verse in a well-known song.
		Use props or toys to inspire a song.
		Teacher plays a part of a composition, and students respond using a similar tempo.
Composes and arranges music	Comprehension of musical concepts	Use flash cards of notes to arrange in a desired order. Have large notes cut out with Velcro on back for students to stick on a large staff.
		Have the teacher start with a verse of a song and have students finish the song.
		Have students compose a song to a familiar children's story, such as *Jack and the Beanstalk*.
		Use an artwork to inspire a composition.

Table 12.5 • *(Continued)*

Music Skill Area	Potential Difficulty	Differentiated Strategy
Listens to, analyzes, and describes music	Comprehension	Share a variety of genres, such as folk, patriotic, spiritual, jazz, Renaissance, etc. Share songs from a variety of cultures.
		Use musical terms to describe a familiar song.
		Have students identify musical forms after listening to a short recorded sample, ABA, AABA.
		Compare and contrast two selections concerning rhythm and tempo.
		Have students respond to the selection by physically moving.
		Identify the various instruments used in a selection.
Evaluates music and performances	Comprehension	Have students move in response to musical characteristics.
		Have students list three important criteria for evaluating music performances. Make a list on the board and have students think to themselves and share with another classmate their ideas about the characteristics.
		Name a favorite song and explain why it the student's favorite.
		Use happy face/frowning face cards for each student to identify whether they like or dislike the musical selection played. Talk about why.
		Have a variety of emotion face cards (happy, sad, angry, and bored), and have students identify what emotion they feel when listening to a musical selection. Discuss why.

Differentiating Instruction in the Arts

When considering the work space for music activities, teachers may wish to leave a large space open and have students sit on the floor. Another solution may be to arrange individual chairs in a slight curve similar to an orchestra seating area. Group musical instruments either together or be creative and group in sequence for the activity. Musical instruments are expensive, so consider making instruments or having students make them. Also, household objects and found objects can make musical sounds thus becoming instruments.

Creativity is key when arranging your room for the Art and Music activity. Perhaps your room will be transformed into a cave, where students will explore cave art and sounds on primitive instruments. Will your room become an ocean? Children can make paper fish to hang from the ceiling, and ocean sounds can be explored.

Another factor in designing Art and Music activities involves the amount of time and materials used. For example, you may need to give more or less time to explore a new media or instrument or change the number of things to be learned in a lesson (reduce or increase). Sometimes a change of pace is needed: Either a concept needs to be repeated, or the group is ready to move on to the next concept. In all arts integration activities, the educator and students must have clear objectives or outcomes. It helps if the objectives are life centered or connected to student interests. A variety of teaching strategies benefit all students learning in and through the arts. Modeling, demonstration, examples, descriptive feedback, and scaffolding (building learning from prior learning) are some examples. You may need to organize lesson in whole-part-whole fashion to help learners accomplish the goal. Sometimes peer tutoring, grouping, and other structure changes may be the key in advancing learning. Finally, allow students to demonstrate what they know in a variety of ways. Don't be afraid if this means exemptions to a specific part of the project or performance or substituting another arts activity, which is just as meaningful for the student as an accommodation (Cornett, 2003).

For more examples of potential difficulties and differentiated strategies for Art, see Table 12.4. For music examples, see Table 12.5. Also, for examples of modifications or accommodations in teaching art and music skills and concepts for specific IDEA disability categories, see Table 12.6.

Table 12.6 • Disability Modifications in Accordance With IDEA for the Arts

Art and Music		
IDEA Disability Category	Concept	Accommodation/Modification
Autism	Drawing a person using shapes	Provide shape cutouts for child to arrange and rearrange.
	Singing specific lyrics	Demonstrate both art and music skills.
		Allow time to practice.
		Use a chart or pocket chart to write the words large enough for all to see.
		Explore singing voice with nonsense syllables, such as "la, ti, tah."
		Sing a line and have students echo.

Table 12.6 ● *(Continued)*

Art and Music		
IDEA Disability Category	**Concept**	**Accommodation/Modification**
Deaf-Blindness	Creating collage and sculpture—texture Experiencing sound vibration—texture	Assist/partial assist. Use a variety of textural papers and objects to create a collage. Sculpt using a variety of media, modeling clay, clay, model magic, and paper mache. Tactile communication working directly with the media. Use sound vibration to stimulate a musical texture. Different textural surfaces translate into different sounds and vibrations. Encourage directly working with a variety of instruments, rhythm, beat, and tempo.
Hearing Impairment	Viewing, performing, analyzing, interpreting, and evaluating artwork and musical performances	Provide visuals representing the project directions. Have student write or draw their answers as well as discuss. Keep a written chart of all student responses to questions. If applicable, use microphones and speakers that amplify sound. Use technology that visually represents sound waves of voice or instruments. Represent the sound from various instruments in a visual format by drawing various line types. Wavy lines can represent an undulating pattern of a harp. Emphasize tactile sense while playing with instruments.

(Continued)

Differentiating Instruction in the Arts

Table 12.6 ● *(Continued)*

Art and Music		
IDEA Disability Category	Concept	Accommodation/Modification
Mental Retardation	Creating a group mural Singing and performing with others	Assist/partial assist. Assign a peer tutor. Provide step-by-step instructions for art making project. Allow for success at each stage. Emphasis on playing one note at a time or singing one word at a time. Sing and perform familiar children's songs.
Orthopedic Impairment	Sculpting with clay Playing a variety of instruments	Assist/partial assist. Provide materials that are easily formed. Substitute model magic. Allow for other types of sculpture, for example, additive sculpture with found objects such as Louise Nevelson's sculptures. Experiment with different instruments, having students choose one with which they are comfortable playing. Use adaptive tools in both art and music depending upon student needs (e.g., brushes that attach to wrists or a mouth piece, straps for holding instruments). Use technology that accommodates for the specific disability, such as specialized keyboards that create music.
Speech or Language Impairment	Creating artwork Discussing artwork Performing on instruments Singing alone and with others.	Visual art production in any media and performance on instruments are excellent ways to communicate ideas and thoughts. When discussing artwork, allow students to write or draw answers to the questions. When singing provide the alternative of playing an instrument or conducting.

Table 12.6 ● *(Continued)*

Art and Music		
IDEA Disability Category	**Concept**	**Accommodation/Modification**
Visual Impairment	Viewing and discussing artwork Listening to, analyzing a variety of musical selections.	Provide large-format artworks and individual prints of artworks for students to use at their desks. Use drawing and painting implements that provide contrast such as a black marker on white paper. Use magnifying screens and technology to accommodate needs. Verbally describe the artwork—paint a picture with words. Sculpt or use other tactile media for creation of artwork. Musical performance is an excellent way for students to communicate. Students can listen to a variety of musical selections and use the teacher's verbal directions to answer questions. Physically model the correct hand positions, etc., for a variety of instruments.
Deafness	Creating artwork in any media Viewing and discussing artwork Listening to and analyzing musical selections Playing musical instruments	The creation of artwork is an excellent means of communication. Give visual cues for directions of project. Model/demonstrate project steps. Allow for written response. Write on a chart the student responses. Similar to hearing impairment: Use technology that visually represents sound vibrations of voice or instruments. Represent the sound from various instruments in a visual format by drawing various line types. Emphasize tactile sense while playing instruments.

(Continued)

Differentiating Instruction in the Arts

Table 12.6 ● *(Continued)*

	Art and Music	
IDEA Disability Category	**Concept**	**Accommodation/Modification**
Emotional Disturbance	Drawing with a variety of media Improvising Performing on instruments	Begin the art project or musical performance with "practice exercises" that allow the student to become comfortable with a new skill. Progress in stages and allow for success at each stage. Use full body movements to start work, such as drawing circles in the air with full arm movements and exaggerated movements to describe how to play specific instruments. Provide an area where the student can work alone, such as carousel with headphones and a tape player/keyboard. Have student work in groups such as making murals and drumming circles.
Learning Disability	Researching artists and musicians from a variety of cultures Singing while responding to the cues of a conductor	Use visuals, props, puppets, charts, and other aids to assist learning. Plan activities to move from simple to complex. Use clear step-by-step directions allowing for success at each step. Work in groups on murals about artists and musicians.
Multiple Disabilities	Creating artwork using a variety of media Reading music and notation	Depending upon the specific disabilities various accommodations are made. For example, mental retardation and orthopedic impairment may require specialized tools and musical instruments. The use of technology may be necessary, such as keyboards that simulate various sounds and software that allows students to create graphic art. Musical notation may have to be in large format or in braille for those students with visual impairment.

Table 12.6 ● *(Continued)*

	Art and Music	
IDEA Disability Category	Concept	Accommodation/Modification
Other Health Impairment	Creating artwork Performance on instruments Singing alone and with others	At all times materials used for making artwork should be nontoxic. Be aware that clay used to make ceramics creates dust when dry. Clean up with water and sponges/towels are needed. Keeping a clean work area is vital to health of all students. Provide areas where students can work alone and work quietly, such as a center with headphones/keyboards/tape player and art supplies for individual work. When working in groups provide an option to work alone.
Traumatic Brain Injury	Creating of artwork Composing	Depending upon the specific disabilities various accommodations are made. For example, for students with speech impairments allow them to work with musical instruments on rhythmic activities, or use unison choral speaking and character role-playing. Group work may relax students lessening fears of trying new skills. Move the lesson in slow increments to increase concentration. Model the composing skills and allow time to practice.

Summary

Arts integration in the inclusive classroom allows all students to apply and demonstrate their understanding through unique avenues of expression. As a teaching strategy, arts integration focuses on teaching for connections that involved authentic arts concepts as aligned with concepts in other disciplines. Arts standards and benchmarks that legitimately overlap the standards and benchmarks of other disciplines can be a starting point for lesson planning. Teaching and learning through the arts has been the central theme of this chapter. Often the arts activity is the motivation or engaging activity for all students. There is great value in allowing for the creative expression of knowledge for all children. When planning arts integrated lessons in the inclusive classroom, we hope the information presented in this chapter will guide your decision making for the success of all students in your classroom.

Thinking It Through

1. What are the qualities of an arts integrated curriculum?

2. Describe a lesson activity that relates to the theory of multiple intelligences and the arts that accommodates all learners.

3. How could a classroom be arranged to meet the needs of all students for a visual art activity that involves painting with tempera? Or for a music activity that involved using a variety of percussion instruments?

4. Describe an integrated visual art activity that accommodates a child with a specific disability. Use Table 12.6 to guide your answer.

5. Describe an integrated music activity that accommodates a child with a specific disability. Use Table 12.6 in the chapter to guide your answer.

Children's Literature in the Arts

Alcron, J. (1991). *Rembrandt's beret.* New York: Tambourine.

Aliki. (1968). *Hush, little baby.* Upper Saddle River, NJ: Prentice Hall.

Aliki. (1974). *Go tell Aunt Rhody.* New York: Macmillan.

Andrews-Goebel, N. (2002). *The pot that Juan built.* New York: Lee & Low Books.

Anholt, L. (1994). *Camille and the sunflowers.* Hauppauge, NY: Barron's Educational Series.

Baker, A. (1994a). *Brown rabbit's shape book.* New York: Larouse Kingfisher.

Baker, A. (1994b). *White rabbit's color book.* New York: Larouse Kingfisher.

Burns, M. (1994). *The greedy triangle.* New York: Scholastic.

Bush, T. (1995). *Grunt, the primitive cave boy.* New York: Crown.

Carle, E. (1984). *The mixed-up chameleon.* New York: Crowell.

Emberly, E. (1991). *Ed Emberly's drawing book: Make a world.* Boston: Little, Brown.

Harfield, C. (2002). *Me and Uncle Romie.* New York: Dial Books for Young Readers.

Le Tord, B. (1999). *A Bird or two: A story about Henri Matisse.* Grand Rapids, MI: Eerdmans Books for Young Readers.

Ringgold, F. (2002). *Cassie's word quilt.* New York: Alfred A. Knopf.

Venzia, M. (1988–1991). Getting to Know the World's Greatest Artists Series: *Picasso; Rembrandt; van Gogh; da Vinci; Mary Cassatt; Edward Hopper; Monet; Botticelli; Goya; Paul Klee; Michelangelo.* Chicago: Children's Press.

Further Reading

Selected Children's Literature Connected to Art and Music Concepts

Alcron, J. (1991). *Rembrandt's beret.* New York: Tambourine.

Aliki. (1968). *Hush, little baby.* Upper Saddle River, NJ: Prentice Hall.

Aliki. (1974). *Go tell Aunt Rhody.* New York: MacMillan.

Anholt, L. (1994). *Camille and the sunflowers.* Hauppauge, NY: Barron's Educational Series.

Baker, A. (1994a). *Brown rabbit's shape book.* New York: Larouse Kingfisher.

Baker, A. (1994b). *White rabbit's color book.* New York: Larouse Kingfisher.

Burns, M. (1994). *The greedy triangle.* New York: Scholastic.

Bush, T. (1995). *Grunt, the primitive cave boy.* New York: Crown.

Carle, E. (1974). *My very first book of colors.* New York: Crowell.

Carle, E. (1984). *The mixed-up chameleon.* New York: Crowell.

Carle, E. (1996). *I see a song.* New York: Scholastic.

Cole, J., & Calmenson, S. (1991). *The eensy weentsy spider: Findgerplays and action rhymes.* New York: Mulberry.

Emberly, E. (1991). *Ed Emberly's drawing book: Make a world.* Boston: Little, Brown.

Glazer, P. (1980). *Do your ears hang low? Fifty more musical fingerplays.* New York: Doubleday.

Venzia, M. (1988–1991). Getting to Know the World's Greatest Artists Series: *Picasso; Rembrandt; van Gogh; da Vinci; Mary Cassatt; Edward Hopper; Monet; Botticelli; Goya; Paul Klee; Michelangelo.* Chicago: Children's Press.

Selected Teacher Resources

Fiarotta, N. (1995). *Music crafts for kids: The how-to book of music discovery.* New York: Sterling.

Hopkin, B. (1995). *Making simple musical instruments.* Asheville, NC: Lark.

Jensen, E. (2001). *Arts with the brain in mind.* Alexandria, VA: Association for Supervision and Curriculum Development.

Mitchell, L. (1991). *One, two, three-echo me! Ready-to-use songs, games, and activities to help children sing in tune.* West Nyack, NY: Parker.

Sadie, S. (Ed.). (2001). *New Grove dictionary of music and musicians.* New York: Grove.

Terzian, A. (1993). *The kids' multicultural art book: Art & craft experiences from around the world.* Charlotte, VT: Williamson.

Resources

www.artsedge.kennedy-centr.org
www.vsarts.org/
www.naea-reston.org/
http://aep-arts.org/
www.newhorizons.org/spneeds/front_spneeds.html

www.artsednet.getty.edu
www.menc.org
www.nasaa-arts.org
www.arts.endow.gov
http://pzweb.harvard.edu

References

Anderson, R. L. (1990). *Calliope's sisters: A comparative study of philosophies of art.* Englewood Cliffs, NJ: Prentice Hall.

Anderson, T. (1995). Toward a cross-cultural approach to art criticism. *Studies in Art Education, 36*(4), 198–209.

Anderson, T., & Milbrandt, M. K. (2005). *Art for life: Authentic instruction in art.* New York: McGraw-Hill.

Beattie, D. K. (1997a). *Assessment in art education.* Worcester, MA: Davis.

Beattie, D. K. (1997b). Visual arts criteria, objectives, and standards: A revisit. *Studies in Art Education, 38*(4), 217–231.

Bigge, M. L., & Shermis, S. S. (1992). *Learning theories for teachers* (5th ed.). New York: Harper Collins.

Brittain, W. L., & Lowenfeld, V. (1997). *Creative and mental growth.* New York: Macmillan.

Brown, S. (2006, Summer). Multiple intelligences in the art room. *NAEA Advisory.* Reston, VA: National Art Education Association.

Burton, J. M., Horowitz, R., & Abeles, H. (1999). Learning in and through the arts: Curriculum implications. In E. B. Fiske (Ed.), *Champions of change: The impact of the arts on learning* (pp. 35–46). The Arts Education Partnership, The President's Committee on the Arts and Humanities. Funded by the GE Fund and the John D. & Catherine T. MacArthur Foundation, New York.

Burton, J., Horowitz, R., & Abeles, H. (2000). Learning in and through the arts: The question of transfer. *Studies in Art Education, 41*(3), 228–257.

Catterall, J., Chapleau, R., & Iwanaga, J. (1999). *Involvement in the arts and human development: General involvement and intensive involvement in music and theater arts.* The Imagination Project at UCLA Graduate School of Education and Information Studies, University of California at Los Angeles.

Consortium of National Arts Education Associations. (1994). *Dance, music, theatre, visual arts: What every young American should know and be able to do in the arts: National standards for arts education.* Reston, VA: Music Educators National Conference.

Cornett, C. (2003). *Creating meaning through literature and the arts.* Upper Saddle River, NJ: Merrill Prentice Hall.

Csikszentmihalyi, M., Feldman, D., & Gardner, H. (1994). *Changing the world: A framework for the study of creativity.* Westport, CT: Praeger.

Day, M. (1998). Art education: Essential for a balanced education. *Bulletin, 82*(597), 1–7.

Deasy, R. J. (2002). *Critical links: Learning in the arts and student academic and social development.* Washington, DC: Arts Education Partnership.

Dissanayake, E. (1992). *Homoaesthetics: Where art comes from and why.* New York: A Division of Macmillan.

Eisner, E. (1994). *The educational imagination on the design and evaluation of school programs* (3rd ed.). New York: Macmillan College.

Eisner, E. (2001). Should we create new aims for art education? *Art Education, 54*(5), 6–10.

Feldman, E. (1994). *Practical art criticism.* Englewood Cliffs, NJ: Prentice Hall.

Fiske, E. (Ed.). (1999). *Champions of change: The impact of the arts on learning.* Washington, DC: The Arts Education Partnership and the President's Committee on the Arts and the Humanities. Retrieved September 29, 2006, from http://www.artsedge.kennedy-center.org/champions/.

Fowler, C. (1994). *Strong arts, strong schools: The promising potential and shortsighted disregard of the arts in American schooling.* New York: Oxford University Press.

Gardner, H. (1991). *The unschooled mind: How children think & how schools should teach.* New York: Basic Books.

Gardner, H. (1993). *Multiple intelligences: The theory in practice.* New York: Basic Books.

Gardner, H. (1999). *Intelligence reframed: Multiple intelligences for the 21st century.* New York: Basic Books.

Getty Institute for the Arts. (1996). *What is discipline-based art education?* Retrieved August 17, 2006, from http://artsednet.getty/ArtsEdNet/advocacy

Glanz, J. (1999). Action research. *Journal of Staff Development, 20*(3), 10–13.

Guay, F., Marsh, H.W., & Boivin, M. (2003). Academic self-concept and academic achievement: A developmental perspective on their causal ordering. *Journal of Educational Psychology, 95*(1), 124–136.

Hagaman, S. (1990). The community of inquiry: An approach to collaborative learning. *Studies in Art Education, 31*(3), 149–157.

Irwin, R. L., & Reynolds, J. K. (1995). Integration as a strategy for teaching the arts as disciplines. *Arts Education Policy Review, 96*(4), 13–19.

Kluth, P., Villa, R.A., & Thousand, J.S. (2002). "Our school doesn't offer inclusion" and other legal blunders. *Educational Leadership, 59*(4), 24–30.

Krug, D., & Cohen-Evron, N. (2000). Curriculum integration positions and practices in art education. *Studies in Art Education, 41*(3), 258–275.

Lowenfeld, V. (1968). *Viktor Lowenfeld speaks on art and creativity.* Reston, VA: National Art Education Association.

Marshall, J. (2005). Connecting art, learning, and creativity: A case for curriculum integration. *Studies in Art Education, 46*(3), 227–241.

National Association for Music Education (NAME). (2005). Retrieved September 29, 2006, from www.menc.org.

Oosterhof, A. (1996). *Developing and using classroom assessments.* Englewood Cliffs, NJ: Prentice Hall.

Parsons, M. (1998). Integrated curriculum and our paradigm of cognition in the arts. *Studies in Art Education, 39*(2), 103–116.

Roucher, N., & Lovano-Kerr, J. (1995). Can the arts maintain integrity in interdisciplinary learning. *Arts Education Policy Review, 96*(4), 20–25.

Smilan, C. (2004). *The impact of art integration as an intervention to assist learners' visual perception and concept understanding in elementary science.* Unpublished doctoral dissertation, Florida Atlantic University, Boca Raton, FL.

State of Florida, Department of State. (1996). *Florida curriculum framework, the arts: Pre-K–12 sunshine state standards and instructional practices.* Tallahassee, FL: Author.

Very Special Arts. (2006). Retrieved November 9, 2006 from www.vsarts.org/X696.xml

Villa, R., & Thousand, J., (Eds.). (2005). *Creating an inclusive school.* Alexandria, VA: Association for Supervision and Curriculum Development.

Vygotsky, L.S. (1978). *Mind and society: The development of higher mental processes.* Cambridge, MA: Harvard University Press.

Wachowiak, F., & Clements, R. (2006). *Emphasis arts: A qualitative art program for elementary and middle schools.* Boston: Allyn and Bacon.

Index

A

ABC or word center, 247
Able-Boone, H., 8, 20, 22, 24
Abruscato, J., 310, 331–38, 340, 341
Academic-behavior connection, 138–39
Accommodations, 94
    assessment, 329–30
    in science, 324
Active learning, 73
Activity-based approach, to science, 321
Adams, A., 20, 21, 24
Adams, M., 235, 239
Adams, R.S., 101
Adaptations, curricular, 57
Addition, 289, 291–94
Advance organizers, 323
Allen, K.E., 6, 9
Allington, R.L., 194
Alphabetic principle, 208
Alphabet inventory, 210, 212
American Speech-Language Hearing
    Association (ASHA), 190
Americans with Disabilities Act
    (ADA), 10
America's Children: Key National
    Indicators of Well-being, 55
Amputations, 40
Analytic cycle, initiating, 206–7
Anchored instruction, 70, 79–80
Anderson, J.R., 282
Anderson, R.L., 373
Anderson, T., 373, 374
Anecdotal records, 270
Angeles Baseline Quiet Divider, 111
Antia, S.D., 7
Art, elements of, 374
Art and music, in inclusive classroom,
    372–404
    assessment in, 381–84

as bridge in, 380
competencies taught in, 377, 379–80
constructing knowledge in, 374–75
differentiating instruction in,
    380–403, 393–97
disability modifications, 398–403
integrating, 374–75, 376–77,
    376–80, 392
lesson planning, 386–87
multicultural education, 375–76
practical application vignette, 372
process skills, 375–76
sample integrated lesson plan format,
    387–92
school administrator, role of, 385
shared responsibilities and, 384
very special arts, 385–86
Arts, 373
    discipline, 373
    form, 373
    integration, 373
Ashbaker, B., 169, 170, 173
Asperger's disorder, 111
Assessment, 22, 65
    accommodations, 329–30
    in arts, 381–84
    environmental, 98
    functional behavior, 147–49
    performance-based, 327–28
    of student-teacher relationship, 160
    teacher-family, 142
    writing, 270–73
Assistive technology, 5
Association for Childhood Education
    (ACEI), 100
    position on play, 100
At risk children, 35
Attention, tennis balls and, 109
Attwood, T., 179
Atwater, J.B., 16

Au, K., 168
Audience, in writing, 248–49
Auditory environment, 107–11
Authentic writing, 244–45
Autism Network, 161
Autism spectrum disorders (ASD), 38,
    110, 111
    behavior, 133
    instruction and, 199
    writing instruction, 261

B

Bailey, D.B., 6, 7, 8, 16
Ball, D.L., 280, 281, 282
Banks, J., 361
Barber, R.H., 315
Barriers, 105
Barrows, H.S., 79
Bauwens, J., 173, 174, 176, 177
Beach Center on Families and
    Disability, 166
Bear, D., 225
Beattie, D.K., 383
Beckman, P.J., 7
Behavior
    challenging, 129, 130–39
    disabilities and, 133–35
    engaging parents and, 141
    grouping, 140
    preventing problem, 139–46
    prosocial skills, teaching, 141–44
    routines and, 140
    scheduling, 139–40
    self-assessment, 146
    social skills, teaching, 144–45
    supportive classroom environment
        and, 139–41
    transitions and, 140–41
Behavioral supports, in classroom,
    129–55

Behavioral supports, in classroom
(*cont.*)
challenging behaviors and, 130–39,
147–49
discipline and IDEA, 150–51
practical application vignette, 129
preventing behavior, 139–46
Behl, D., 164
Beilin, H., 63
Beninghof, A.M., 122
Berk, L.E., 132
Bial, R., 315
Biddle, B., 101
Bigge, M.L., 373
Blasé, J., 171, 172
Blended education, rationale for, 2–26
inclusion, 2–19
practical application vignette, 2
teacher preparation, 19–25
Blended service delivery, rationale for,
5–8
Blended teacher preparation, rationale
for, 19–25
common core of knowledge and
skills, 21–22
composition of programs, 24–25
content standards for educators,
22–23
course content, 20–21
Blending, 192, 223
Blindness, 41
instruction for, 203
writing and, 266
Board of Education v. *Rowley,* 9
Bodrova, E., 241
Bone tuberculosis, 40
Borko, H., 281, 282
Bos, C.S., 22, 24
Boulerice, B., 132
Bowen, C., 189
Boyett, S., 113, 114
Bradley, R., 11
Bredekamp, S., 16, 17, 18, 21, 74, 75,
130
Brendefur, J.L., 280, 287
Brewer, J.A., 122, 164
Brewer, W., 282
Bricker, D.D., 4, 6, 7, 8

Brittain, W.L., 374
Bronfrenbrenner, U., 43
Brooks, J.G., 65, 85
Brooks, M.G., 65, 85
Brophy, J.E., 115, 117
Brown, C.A., 279, 285
Brown, K.J., 236, 237
Brown, S., 138, 139, 377
Brownell, K., 2, 19
Brownell, M., 20, 21, 24, 321
Brown v. *Board of Education,* 9
Bruder, M.B., 7, 8, 20, 24
Bruner, J.S., 73, 84
Burns, 40
Burns, M.S., 224
Burrell, L., 164
Bursuck, W.D., 5, 7, 13, 19
Burton, C., 21
Burton, J.M., 373
Bush, George W., 131
Buyusse, V., 6, 7, 8, 20, 22, 24

C

Calkins, L., 254
Camine, D.W., 323, 324
Campbell, L., 360
Campbell-Whatley, G.D., 168
Canter, L., 115, 116
Canter, M., 116
Cappellini, M., 7
Carpenter, T.P., 284, 288, 291
Carta, J.J., 16
Carter, M., 75
Catlett, C., 20, 24
Cawley, J.F., 320
Centers for Disease Control (CDC), 19
Cerebral palsy, 40
Chall, J., 198, 204, 235
Challenging behaviors, 129
academic-behavior connection,
138–39
biological causes, 130–35
environmental causes, 135–37
functional behavior assessment,
147–49
managing all students, 149
position statement on interventions
for, 152–53

positive support, 147
reasons for, 130–39
sociocultural causes, 137–38
Chandler, L.K., 4, 7, 8, 25
Charles, C.M., 57, 115
Chess, S., 132
Children with disabilities
benefits of inclusion, 7, 8
toy selection for, 165
Chissom, J., 171, 172
Choate, J.S., 322
Christie, J., 238, 271
Circle of Friends, 161
Circle of Inclusion Project, 96
Civil rights legislation, 9–10
Clark, R., 112
Classroom
acoustics, 107
inclusive, 92–126
positive behavioral supports in,
129–55
rules, 116–17
Classroom organization, 100–104
room format, 102–4
seating arrangements, 101–2
Clay, M., 193, 198, 206, 208, 213, 221,
236, 239, 241, 242, 243
Clayton, M.K., 110, 113
Clements, D.H., 72, 73
Climate, creating, 129
Clubfoot, 40
Cluster seating arrangements, 102
Cobb, P., 67, 68, 73, 285
Cognitive development, 136
Erikson's stages of, 136
Cohen, D.K., 280
Cohen, L.G., 328
Colarusso, R., 35
Cold reason, myth of, 69
Cole, P., 70
Colker, L., 7
Collaboration, 173–78
characteristics of, 95–96, 174, 175
definition, 173
interpersonal, 95
in K-3 inclusive classroom, 97
models, 175–77
parent-professional, 169

trust, 177–78
Collaborative planning, 94–96
Collaborative team, 92
Combs, M., 236, 240
Common core of knowledge and skills, 21–22
Communication, 161
  in classroom instruction, 287
  contributive, 287
  disorders, 41
  instructive, 287
  reflective, 287
  unidirectional, 287
Communicative ethics, 69
A Comprehensive Guide for Practical Application in Early Intervention/Early Childhood Special Education, 18
Comprehensive literacy instruction, 197
Concepts about print (CAP), 197, 208, 221–22
  observation form, 211
  writing and, 238–39
Conderman, G., 323, 328
Conn-Powers, M., 105
Consistency, in inclusive classroom, 99
Consortium of National Arts Education Associations, 373, 383
Constantine, L.L., 166
Constructionism, 69
Constructivism, 62–87
  activities, 85–87
  anchored instruction, 79–80
  classroom examples, 80–82
  components of, 64–69, 65
  constructionism, 69
  content area methods, 77–78
  critical, 68–69
  cultural, 68
  definition, 62, 71–72
  Developmentally Appropriate Practice, 74–76
  differentiated instruction, 76–77
  explicit instruction, 78
  implicit *versus* explicit instruction, 72–74
  misconceptions, 73–74

objectives, 65
pedagogies and, 74–80
practical application vignette, 62
problem-based learning, 78–79
psychological, 63, 72
radical, 66–67
social, 67–68
theoretical views on application, 69–72
traditional transmission perspective *versus,* 81
trivial, 66
types of, 66
Content area methods, 77–78
Content enhancements, 323
Content standards, for educators, 22–23
Conventional spelling, 244
Conventions of print, writing and, 239–40
Cook, L., 19, 95, 97, 174
Cook, R.E., 120
Cooney, T.J., 287
Cooperative learning, 73
Cooter, R.B., 197
Copple, C., 16, 17, 18, 74, 75
Council for Exceptional Children (CEC), 3, 4, 5, 6, 14, 17, 19, 130
Course content, 20–21
Cowdery, G.E., 6, 9
Cox, P.R., 330, 332
Cramer, M.M., 172
Creativity, 373
Critical constructivism, 68–69
Cross, A.F., 105
Cross-age tutoring, 163
Cruz, B.C., 361
Csikszentmihalyi, M., 374
Cuban, L., 280
Cultural constructivism, 68
Cultural diversity, 114, 178
Culturally Appropriate Practice, 16
Culturally responsive pedagogy, 361
Cultural view, of disabilities, 54
Cunningham, P.M., 225, 247
Curran, M., 114
Curriculum, 55–58
  activities and experiences, 57
  adaptations, 57

critiquing, 58
data collection and use, 57–58
environment and, 57
equitable, 105, 106
flexible, 106
instructional methods, 56–57
integrating science through, 315–20
integrating social studies through, 366–67
integrating writing through, 240–47
literacy, developing, 240–41
national, state, and district-mandated content, 56
philosophical framework, 56
scope and sequence, 56
success-oriented, 106
Curtis, D., 75

D
Dahlquist, C.M., 4, 7
Daniel R.R. v. *State Board of Education,* 9
Data collection, 57–58
Davis, B., 77, 78
Deaf-blindness (DB), 39
  behavior, 133
  instruction and, 199
  writing instruction, 261
Deafness, 39
  behavior, 133
  instruction and, 199–200
  writing instruction, 262
Deasy, R.J., 375
Delpit, L., 78, 195
Descriptive writing, 251
Design, principles of, 374
Design for All Children, 106
Dettmer, P., 166
Developing literacy, 240–41
Development
  learning and, 75
  social, 163–64
Developmental delay, 35, 38, 131
  examples of, 33, 34
Developmentally Appropriate Practice (DAP), 16–17, 22, 56, 74–76
  NAEYC position statement regarding, 17

Developmentally Appropriate Practice in Early Childhood Programs, 16
Dewey, J., 63, 164
Dialogic reading, 220–21
Diamond, K.E., 6, 7, 8
Diaz, C.F., 114
Dictation, 273
Differentiated instruction, 76–77
Dinnebeil, L.A., 18, 20
Directionality, in writing, 242
Disabilities
    behavior and, 133–35
    definition, 34
    diversity and, 54
    high-incidence, 41–42
    low-incidence, 41–42
    multiple, 40
Disabilities Improvement Act of 2004, 35
Disability-first language, 12
DiSarno, N., 337
Discipline, IDEA and, 150–52
Discourse, 287
Diversity
    cultural, 114, 178
    disabilities and, 54
    increase in, 55
    linguistic, 178
Division, 295, 296–98
Division for Early Childhood (DEC), 3, 8, 17–19, 18, 21, 22, 130
    core content standards for, 23
Doering, K., 7, 8
Dolch, E.W., 214, 215
Dolch Word-First Word List, 215
Dole, J.A., 217
Donato, R., 167
Doorlag, D., 42
Dover, W., 171
Doyle, W., 101
Drafting, 250, 253
Drascow, E., 11, 45
Driver, R., 84
Duffy, G.G., 206, 217
DuFour, R.P., 173
Dugan, E., 7, 8, 25

Dugger-Wadsworth, D.E., 334
Dyke, N., 166
Dyson, A.H., 250

E
Early, D.M., 8, 21
Early childhood, websites about, 15
Early intervening services, 13
Early literacy, in inclusive classroom, 186–229
    constructing knowledge in reading, 187–93
    differentiating instruction in reading, 197–215
    evaluating information, 215–28
    literacy instruction, 195–97
    practical application vignette, 186
    reading process skills, 193–95
Early writing, in inclusive classroom, 234–76
Easley, J., 84
Ecken, L., 159
Economic Opportunity Education Act, 9
Editing, 253–54
Education for All Handicapped Children Act, 9, 10–12
    free and appropriate public education, 11
    individualized education plan, 11
    least restrictive environment, 11
Education of the Handicapped Act Amendments of 1986, 35
Educators
    content standards for, 22–23
    culturally competent, 167–69
Edwards, B., 77, 78
Eggbeer, L., 22
Ehri, L., 239
Eisner, E., 376, 382, 383
Elementary education, science, 313–14
Elements of art, 374
Elkonin, D.B., 224
Elkonin boxes, 225
Elliott, D., 176

Emergent literacy, 187
    writing and, 236–37
Emergent readers, characteristics of, 274
Emergent writers, characteristics of, 274
Emergent writing, 243
    checklist, 271
Emmer, E.T., 115
Emotional disturbance (ED), 39
    behavior, 133
    instruction and, 200
    writing instruction, 262
English language learners (ELL), 19, 361
    developmental delay and, 38
Environmental assessment, 96, 98
Environments
    auditory, 107–11
    curriculum and, 57
    designing, 104–7
    inclusive, 43
    least restrictive, 42–44
    natural, 42–44
    physical, assessing, 96
    positive visual, creating, 111–12
    social-emotional development and, 135–37
    supportive classroom, 139–41
Equilibration, 63
Equitable curriculum, 105, 106
Equity, 279
Erikson, E., 136
    stages of development, 136
Ernest, P., 64, 71
Erwin, E., 55
Ethics, communicative, 69
Evans, S.S., 101
Evans, W.H., 101
Everston, C., 115
Exceptional needs, 34–35
Exceptional needs, young children with, 33–58
    practical application vignettes, 33–34
Expanding environments approach, 353, 354

Explicit instruction, 72–74, 78
Expressive language, 187, 188–89

F
Fader, L., 3
Faigley, L., 253
Families
    benefits of inclusion for, 7, 8
    changing roles of, 55
    characteristics of, 166
Family participation, in learning
        environment, 43
Family systems, 164–69
Fathers, involvement of, 168
Federal laws
    civil rights legislation, 9–10
    Education for All Handicapped
        Children Act, 10–12
    Head Start legislation, 9
    supporting inclusion, 8–14
    Individuals with Disabilities
        Education Act, 12–14
    landmark legislation, 10
    No Child Left Behind, 13
    Rehabilitation Act, 10
Federal Register, 14
Fenichel, E.S., 22
Fennema, E., 279, 281, 284, 287
Ferreiro, E., 242
Fiechtl, B., 22, 24
Fiedler, C.R., 38
Fitzpatrick, J., 223
Flanagan, D.P., 159, 168
Fletcher, R., 248
Flexibility principle, 242
Flexible curriculum, 106
Floyd, L., 171, 172
Flynn, L., 120
Foley, T., 104
Forton, M.B., 110, 113
Fosnot, C.T., 83
Fountas, I., 204, 218, 220, 224, 225,
        239, 245, 257, 260, 268, 273
Fowler, C., 372, 373, 374
Fractures, 40
Fradd, S.H., 321

Fraser, B., 57
Frazeur Cross, A., 8, 20
Frechtling, J.A., 281
Free and appropriate public education
        (FAPE), 11, 150
Frelow, V.S., 21
French, N.K., 171, 172, 173
Friend, M., 5, 7, 13, 19, 95, 97, 174,
        323, 325, 327, 328, 333
Friendships, 161–63
Frith, G.H., 172
Frost, J.L., 44, 56
Fry, E., 214
Frykholm, J.A., 280
Functional behavior assessment (FBA),
        147–49

G
Gable, R.A., 101
Gale, J.E., 71
Gallagher, J.J., 9
Gallagher, S.A., 78, 79
Gambrell, L., 197
Ganske, K., 212
Gardner, H., 374, 376, 382, 383
Garfield, J.B., 84
Garfield Reading Survey, 213
Gartin, B.C., 45
Gartner, A., 177
Gay, G., 361
Gee, J.P., 194
Gender, behavior and, 131–32
Generative principle, of words, 205
Genishi, C., 187, 189, 190, 228
Genres, 249, 251–52
Geometry, 299–300
Gergen, K.J., 62, 69
Gerlach, K., 170, 173
Getty Institute for the Arts, 373
Giabcobbe, M.E., 268
Gipe, J.P., 206, 215, 217
Glasgow, N.A., 94
Glickman, C.D., 171
Glosemeyer, R., 107
Goldberg, H., 319
Goldstein, H., 4

Good, T.L., 117
Goodman, K, 186, 193
Goodman, Y., 198
Gordon, S.P., 171
Goudvis, A., 226, 228
Gough, P.B., 193, 195
Graphic principles, 221
Graphophonic relationships, 210
Graves, D., 250, 254
Greenspan, S.I., 132
Griffin, P., 224
Grisham-Brown, J., 4, 9
Grossman, P., 281, 282
Grouping, for behavior, 140
Grouws, D.A., 281
Gruender, C.D., 63, 72
Guided reading, 219
Guided writing, 259, 268–69
Gunderson, S., 274
Guralnick, M.J., 3, 4, 5, 6, 7, 8, 9, 10
Gutierrez, S., 7, 161

H
Habermas, Jurgen, 68
Hall, T., 76, 78
Hallahan, D.P., 38
Halliday, M.A.K., 187, 194, 228
Hamilton, S.L., 7, 8
Hanline, M.F., 21
Hanson, M.J., 7, 161
Hard control, myth of, 69
Harden, P.W., 132
Hardy, M.D., 67
Hargrave, A.C., 220
Harris, K.C., 22
Harry, B., 167
Harste, J., 235, 238, 274
Hartwig, E.P., 150
Harvey, S., 226, 228
Head Start
    legislation, 9
    program, 10
Healy, A., 165
Hearing impairment (HI), 39
    behavior, 134
    instruction and, 200

Hearing impairment (HI) (*cont.*)
 writing instruction, 263
Heath, S., 187
Hein, G.E., 328
Hemmeter, M.L., 4, 8, 9, 18, 19, 42
Hendry, G.D., 87
Henley, M., 117
Hennger, M.L., 120
Heward, W.L., 164, 167
Heylighen, F., 63, 71
Hickman, J., 194
Hiebert, E.H., 77, 186
Hiebert, J., 279, 281, 282, 283, 284,
 286
Higgins Hains, A., 21
High-incidence disabilities, 41–42
Hirose-Hatae, A., 7, 8
Hitchcock, C., 324
Holcombe, A., 19
Holdoway, D., 237
Holistic theory, 196
Hollands, C., 161
Home language, respecting, 168
Honebein, P., 71
Honig v. *Doe,* 150
Hoover, J.H., 172
Hoover, W.A., 72, 73, 74
Hopfengardener Warren, S., 14
Horn, E., 7, 8
Hourcade, J.J., 173, 174, 176, 177
Howard, M., 192
Howard, V.F., 169
Hoy, W.K., 177
Hulce, E., 107
Hulit, L., 192
Hunt, P., 2, 4, 7, 8
Hunter, D., 7, 8
Hutter-Pishgahi, L., 8, 20
Hyson, M., 4, 22, 23, 25
Hyten, C., 177

I
IDEAdata.org, 3
Implicit instruction, 72–74
Inclusion
 benefits of, 6–8
 definition of, 2–5
 federal laws supporting, 8–14

models, 19
national organizations' support for,
 14–19
rationale for, 5–8
research, 6
websites about, 15
*Inclusion in Science Education for
 Students with Disabilities,* 325
Inclusive classroom
 art and music in, 372–404
 auditory environment, 107–11
 collaborative planning for
  organization, 94–96
 consistency in, 99
 cultural diversity, 114
 definition, 92–94
 design for all children, 94
 early literacy in, 186–229
 early writing in, 234–76
 environments, designing, 104–7
 fitting children's bodies into, 110
 K-3 children in, 96–100
 mathematics in, 279–306
 optimizing, 112–14
 organization check, 113
 organizing areas within, 100–104
 organizing for grades K-3, 92–126
 physical environment, 96
 playground/recess, 119–22
 positive visual environment, creating,
  111–12
 practical application vignette, 92
 reducing noise in, 108
 rules and routines, developing,
  114–19
 scheduling in, 123–25
 science in, 310–245
 social studies in, 349–70
 support in, 99
 universal design, 94
Inclusive environments, 43
Independent reading, 219–20
Independent writing, 260, 269–70
Individual education plan (IEP), 11,
 150
 arts and, 384
 components of, 45–46
 sample, 47–54

team, 45–46
Individually Appropriate Practice
 (IAP), 16, 18, 22
Individuals with Disabilities Education
 Act (IDEA), 12–14, 131
 of 2004, 35, 44
 amendments of 1997, 38
 collaboration and, 176
 differentiating instruction across,
  199–203, 261–66
 disability modifications for arts,
  398–403
 discipline and, 150–52
 English language learners and, 38
 least restrictive environment and, 44
 provisions of, 14
Infants
 brain development, 130
 early intervention for, 12
Inferring, in reading, 227
Informational writing, 251
Inhelder, B., 63
Inquiry-based learning, 375
Instruction
 anchored, 70, 79–80
 differentiated, 76–77
 differentiating across IDEA,
  199–203
 explicit, 72–74, 78
 implicit, 72–74
 literacy, 206
 mathematics, 285–87
 peer-mediated, 323
 reading, 197–215
 science, 320–27
 simple and intuitive, 106
 writing, 256–73
Instructional methods, 56–57
Integration, 5
Interactive theory, 196–97
Interactive writing, 252, 258–59, 260,
 267–69
Intuitive learning, 73
Invented developmental spelling, 239
Invented spelling, 243
Invernizzi, M., 225
Irwin, R.L., 375
Isenberg, J.P., 100

J

Janko, S., 4
Jarrett, D., 315, 326, 327
Jewett, F., 76
Johnson, K.L., 138, 139
Johnson, L.J., 176, 177
Johnson, L.M., 167
Jonassen, D., 70
Jones, F.H., 101, 103
Jones, L.V., 159
Jones, V., 159
Jonson, K.F., 94
Joram, E., 298
Joseph, G., 18
Journals, 251

K

Kagan, S.L., 21
Kalkowski, P., 162
Kame'enui, E.J., 322, 324
Kamii, C., 293
Kamps, D., 7, 8, 25
Karp, N., 20
Karten, T.J., 320
Kauffman, J.M., 38
Kazmarek, L., 4
Kea, C.D., 168
Kear, D., 213
Kearsley, G., 79
Keene, E.O., 218, 226
Keesee, P.D., 165
Kellough, R.D., 315
Kicks, C.D., 94
Kieff, J., 164
Kilgo, J.L., 20, 24
Kirby, P.C., 171, 172
Kleff, J., 120
Klein, M.D., 22, 120
Kluth, P., 110
Knapp, M.S., 280
Knight, W., 102
Knowledge, 66
Konold, C., 283, 284
Korinek, L., 174, 176, 177
Krey, D.M., 365
Kronowitz, E.L., 94
Krug, D., 373, 374
Kucera, T.J., 325

L

Ladson-Billings, G., 361
Lamorey, S., 7, 8
Lampert, ., 279, 287
Language
    disability-first, 12
    disorders, 42
    expressive, 187, 188–89
    home, respecting, 168
    impairment, 41
    learning, 187, 190–93
    oral, 189
    person-first, 10, 11, 12, 13
    receptive, 187, 188–89
Language experience approach (LEA),
        221, 258
Language learning, supporting, 190
LaRocque, M., 138, 139
Lead State Agencies, 35, 36–37
Learning
    active, 73
    cooperative, 73
    development and, 75
    inquiry-based, 375
    intuitive, 73
    mathematics, 279–81
    problem-based, 70, 78–79
    styles, 19
Learning disabilities (LD), 41
Learning or behavioral characteristics,
        38–41
    autism, 38
    deaf-blindness (DB), 39
    deafness, 39
    emotional disturbance, 39
    hearing impairment, 39
    mental retardation, 39–40
    multiple disabilities, 40
    orthopedic impairment, 40
    other health impairment, 40
    specific learning disability, 40–41
    speech or language impairment, 41
    traumatic brain injury, 41
    visual impairment, including
        blindness, 41
Least restrictive environment (LRE),
        11, 42–44
    definition, 44

strengthening, 13
Leiber, J., 8
Letter and word study, 245–47
Letters, 251
Levin, J., 114
Levine, L.M., 7
Lewis, R., 42
Lindsey, J.D., 172
Linguistic diversity, 178
Lipsky, D.K., 177
Literacy. *See also* Reading
    analytic cycle, 206–7
    concepts about prints, 211
    development, 75, 240–41
    emergent, 187
    gathering information, 207–8
    holistic theory, 196
    hypotheses, generating, 217–18
    instruction, 195–97
    interactive theory, 196–97
    interests and attitude surveys,
        212–14
    principles of learning, 204–6
    retellings, 213–14
    running record, 213, 214
    sight vocabulary, 214
    skills-based theory, 195–96
    teaching, 218
    transactional theory, 197
Local educational agency (LEA), 45,
        131, 151
Lomax, R., 238
Lonigan, C.J., 195, 220, 221
Lord, T.R., 65
Low birth weight, 130
Lowenfeld, V., 374
Low-incidence disabilities, 41–42
Lue, M.S., 179
Lutzer, C., 4
Lynch, K., 20, 24

M

Ma, L., 281, 282
Magg, J.W., 321
Maier, J., 2, 4, 7
Mainstreaming, 5
Malloch, I., 208
Malloch, J., 208

Mallory, B., 16
Manifestation determination, 150
Manipulatives, mathematics, 303
Mann, D., 164
Marshall, J., 373
Martin, C.G., 19
Mason, C., 105, 106
Masonheimer, P., 238
Massachusetts IEP form, 47–54
Mastropieri, M.A., 7, 8, 41, 42, 172,
    319, 320, 321, 322, 325, 327, 331,
    336, 340
Mathematics, in inclusive classroom,
    279–306
  addition and subtraction, 289,
    291–94
  beliefs and knowledge, 285
  constructing knowledge in, 281–82,
    287–98
  differentiating instruction in,
    285–87
  discourse, 286–87
  functional perspective of
    understanding, 284–85
  geometry, 299–300
  learning and teaching, 279–81
  manipulatives and games, 303
  multiplication and division, 294–98
  number, idea of, 288–91
  probabilistic and statistical thinking,
    301–3
  process skills, 282–85
  science and, 319
  shape, 300–301
  structural perspective of
    understanding, 282–84
  students' ideas of measurement,
    298–301
Maude, S., 4, 8, 25
Maxim, G., 353
Mazzoni, S., 197
McCarrier, A., 247, 260, 267
McCollum, J., 4, 12, 24
McDiarmid, G.W., 280, 281, 282
McDonnell, A.P., 2, 19
McEvoy, M.A., 5, 7, 8
McGee, L., 238
McGreal, T., 57

McGregor, G., 6, 8, 22, 24
McGuire, J.M., 104
McKenna, M., 213
McKenney, M., 176
McLaughlin, M.J., 14, 177
McLaughlin, V.L., 6, 7
McLean, M.D., 8, 16, 18, 42
McNary, S.J., 94
McWilliam, R.A., 7, 8, 43
Measurement, 298–99
Mental retardation (MR), 39–40, 41
  behavior, 134
  instruction and, 201
  writing instruction, 263
Mercer, A.R., 117, 123
Mercer, C.D., 117, 123
Metacognition, 71
Mewborn, D.S., 280, 281, 282
Meyer, D.J., 178
Miller, D., 226, 228
Miller, P.S., 3, 6, 18, 20, 22, 24, 25
Mills v. *the Washington, DC, Board of*
    Education, 9
Mnemonics, 323
Modeling, 145
Modifications, 94
  in science, 324, 328–41
Montessori, M., 99
Morgan, J., 169, 170, 173
Morgan, M., 7
Morpheme, 191
Morphology, 191
Morrison, R.S., 164
Mortweet, S.L., 6, 7, 25
Moustafa, M., 214
Mueller, P.H., 172
Multicultural education, 375–76
Multiple disabilities, 40
  behavior, 134
  instruction and, 201
  writing instruction, 264
Multiple intelligences (MI), 359, 360
Multiplication, 294–96
Multisensory instructional strategies, 5
Munk, D., 20, 24, 325
Murdock, N.L., 45
Murphy, E., 63
Murphy, J., 57

Murray, W.S., 248
Music, elements of, 374

N
Narrative writing, 251
National Assessment of Educational
    Progress (NAEP), 327
National Association for the Education
    of Young Children (NAEYC), 3,
    14, 21, 35, 74, 75, 130
  core content standards for, 23
  Developmentally Appropriate
    Practice, 16–17
  support for inclusion, 14, 16
  terminology, 35
National Association of Nursery
    Education (NANE), 14
National Board for Professional
    Teaching Standards, 22
  core content standards for, 23
National Center for Early Development
    and Learning, 21, 160
National Center for Education Statistics
    (NCES), 3, 19, 279
National Coalition for Parent
    Involvement in Education
    (NCPIE), 168
National Council for Social Studies
    (NCSS), 350, 352
National Council for Teachers of
    Mathematics (NCTM), 56, 279,
    281, 286, 287
National Council of Social Studies
    (NCSS), 349
National Dissemination Center for
    Children with Disabilities, 38
National Education Goals Panel, 150
National Longitudinal Survey of
    Children and Youth, 132
National Reading Panel, 77
National Research Council (NRC), 75,
    76, 311
National Science Teachers Association
    (NSTA), 311, 313, 314, 326
Nations, S., 113, 114
Natural environment, 12, 42–44
Neuman, D.B., 315
Neuman, S., 238

Newmann, F.M., 281, 284
New York Longitudinal Study, 132
New Zealand Staff Ministry of
    Education, 257, 273, 274
No Child Left Behind (NCLB), 13, 93,
    324
Nolan, J., 114
Nolet, V., 323, 324, 328
Nord, C.W., 169
Notational systems, 293

O

Obenchain, K.M., 363, 365
Oberti v. *Board of Education,* 6, 10
Odom, S.L., 2, 3, 4, 5, 6, 7, 8, 16, 25, 43
Online Asperger's Syndrome
    Information and Support (OASIS),
    162
Oosterhof, A., 382
Optimizing, 112–14
Oral language, 189
    checklist, 207, 208
Oral presentations, 220–22
Organization
    in classroom, 100–104
    collaborative planning for, 94–96
    for grades K-3, 92–126
Orkwis, R., 105, 106
Ormsbee, C.K., 325
O'Rourke, C., 35
Orthographic knowledge, 222–24
Orthopedic impairment (OI), 40
    behavior, 134
    instruction and, 201
    writing instruction, 264
Ortiz, S.O., 159, 168
Ostrosky, M., 18
Other health impairments (OHI), 40
    behavior, 134
    instruction and, 202
    writing instruction, 265

P

Pajares, M.F., 285
Paley, V.G., 80, 81
Pappas, C.C., 235, 315
Paradigm shift, 65
Paraeducators, 158, 169–73

classroom application tips for,
    172–73
principles *versus* preferences, 170
supervision, 170–72
PARC v. *Pennsylvania,* 9
Parent-professional collaboration, 169
Parents, engaging, 141
Parker, W., 350, 352
Parsons, M., 374
Patton, J.E., 102
Patton, J.R., 123, 124
Pearpoint, J., 161
Pearson, P.D., 217
Peck, C.A., 6, 8
Peer
    mentors, 162
    relationships, 160
    tutoring, 163
Peer-mediated instruction, 323
Pelco, A., 132
Pereira, L., 161
Performance-based assessments, in
    science, 327–28
Perkins, D., 67, 68, 281
Perlmutter, J., 164
Personal spaces, 100
Person-first language, 10, 13
    disability-first language *versus,* 12
Persuasive writing, 252
Phillips, D.A., 130, 131
Phillips, D.C., 62, 74
Phonemes, 191
Phonemic awareness, 238–39
Phonics, 195, 224–25
Phonograms, 195
Phonological awareness, 191, 192, 223,
    273
    inventory, 208, 209–10
Phonology, 191
Physical environment, 96
Piaget, J., 63, 66, 72, 76, 161
Pianta, R.C., 159
Pickett, A.L., 170, 173
Pinchot, G., 173
Pinnell, G.S., 204, 218, 220, 224, 225,
    239, 245, 257, 260, 268, 273
Planned participation, 4
Planning pyramid, 324, 326

Play, ACEI position on, 100
Playground/recess, 119–22
    layout, 121
    materials, 120
    rules, 122
    safety issues, 120–22
    social skills and interactions, 122
Play space, 93, 100
Poetry writing, 252
Poliomyelitis, 40
Polloway, E., 123, 124
Positive behavior support (PBS), 147
Pragmatics, 192–93
Praisner, C.L., 8
Pregnancy complications, behavior and,
    130–31
Pretti-Frontczak, K., 4, 9
Prewriting, 248
Prigge, D.J., 172
Primary settings, 44
Probability, 301
Problem-based learning (PBL), 70,
    78–79
Process skills, 313
Professionalism, 22
Programs, composition of, 24–25
Prosocial skills, teaching, 141–44
Psychological constructivism, 63, 72
Public schools, children with special
    needs in, 34–35
Publishing, 254–55
Pugach, M.C., 176, 177
Putnam, R.T., 281, 282

Q

Questioning, in reading, 226–27
Quill, K.A., 110
Quisenberry, N., 100

R

Radical constructivism, 66–67
Radziewicz, C., 91, 94
Rakes, T.A., 327
Raphael, T.E., 77
Rea, P.J., 6, 7
Reading
    affective processes, 192–93
    aloud, 218

Reading (*cont.*)
  cognitive processes, 192
  constructing knowledge in, 187–93
  definition, 198, 204
  determining importance of, 227
  development stages, 198, 204
  dialogic, 220–21
  emerging processes, 193–94
  guided, 219
  independent, 219–20
  inferring in, 227
  instructional activities, 220
  language experience approach, 221
  language learning, 187, 190–93
  meaning making with texts, 226–27
  oral language, centrality of, 187
  orthographic knowledge, 222–24
  phonics, 224–25
  process skills, 193–95
  questioning technique, 226–27
  shared, 218–19
  sociocultural processes, 193
  synthesizing information, 227–28
  types, 218–20
  understanding, 228
  visualization, 227
  word recognition, 225
Reading-writing connection, 273–74
Receptive language, 187, 188–89
Reed-Victor, E., 132
Referral, 45
Rehabilitation Act (RA), 10
  Section 504, 10
Reifel, S., 44, 56
Reinforcement, 144
Related services, 12
Relationships, in and outside of
      classroom, 157–81
  collaboration in, 173–78
  communication, 161
  family systems, 164–69
  friendships, 161–63
  paraeducators, 169–73
  peer, 160
  practical application vignettes, 157
  social development, 163–64
  special issues, 178
  students with disabilities, 163

  student-teacher, 159–60
Research, on inclusion, 6
Retellings, 213–14
  prompts, 215
Reusch, G.M., 150
Reutzel, D.R., 197
Reverberation time, 107, 108
Revising, 253
Rhyme, 223
Richardson, V., 280
Richardson-Gibbs, A.M., 120
Robinson, T.R., 45
Rokeach, M., 285
Rombert, T.A., 279, 283, 284
Room format, 102–4
Rose, R., 172
Rosenblatt, L.M., 198
Ross, G., 73
Roucher, N., 373, 375, 383
Rous, B., 4
Routines
  for behavior, 140
  developing, 117–19
Royer, J., 7, 8, 25
Rubrics, 383
Rule, S., 22, 24
Rules, developing, 114–17
  outside classroom, 117
  playground, 122
  teaching classroom, 116–17
Running record, 213, 214

S

Safety, on playground, 120–22
Sage, D.D., 177
Salend, S., 325
Salisbury, C.L., 5, 6, 7, 8, 22, 24
Saloman, G., 67, 68
Sandall, S.R., 3, 4, 8, 18, 19, 42
Sanford, J., 115
Savage, T.V., 350
Scaffolding, 22
Scheduling, 123–25
  behavior and, 139–40
Schema, 282
  developing, 237–38
Schifter, D., 86
Schoenfeld, A.H., 285

Schofield, P.F., 14
Schroeder, C., 19
Schumm, J., 324
Schunk, D.H., 74, 76, 77
Schwartz, I.S., 3, 4, 8, 16
Science, in inclusive classroom,
      310–245
  constructing knowledge in, 313–15
  definition, 310–11
  differentiating instruction in, 320–27
  elementary level, 313–14
  integrating through curriculum,
      315–20
  national standards, 311
  nature of, 311–13
  performance-based assessments in,
      327–28
  practical application vignette, 310
  process skills, 315, 316–18
  resources, 343–45
  sample activities, 328–41
  standard themes, 314–15
  universal design, 325
Scott, R., 105, 106
Scott, S.S., 104
Scott-Little, C., 21
Scruggs, T.E., 7, 8, 41, 42, 172
Seating arrangements, 101–2
  cluster, 102
Section 504, 10
Seep, B., 107
Segmenting, 223–24
Self-assessments
  behavior, 146
  writing, 271
Self-education checklist, 171
Self-reflection, 68
Semantics, 191–92
Senechal, M., 220
Service delivery options, 42–44
  natural/least restrictive environment,
      42–44
Service providers, benefits of inclusion,
      7, 8
Shanklin, N.K., 237
Shape, in mathematics, 300–301
Shared preparation, 25
Shared reading, 218–19

Shared space, 100
Shared writing, 257, 258, 260
Shea, T., 115
Shonkoff, J.P., 130, 131
Short, D., 325
Shulman, L., 281, 284
Shuman, J.J., 22, 24
Shymansky, J.A., 321
Siblings, 178
Sibshops, 178
Sight vocabulary, 214
Signal-to-Noise ratio, 108
Silliman, E.R., 195
Simon, M.A., 282
Simple and intuitive instruction, 106
Simpson, R.L., 38
Sindelar, P., 20, 21, 24
Situated Learning and Cognitive
    Flexibility Theory, 79
Skills-based theory, 195–96
Skillstreaming the Elementary School
    Child, 143
Smalley, B.S., 179
Smilan, C., 373
Smith, B.J., 11, 18, 19
Smith, D.D., 44
Smith, F., 186, 193, 253
Smith, J.P., 283
Smith, T.E.C., 123, 124
Snell, J., 102
Snow, C.E., 235
Snow, M.A., 75
Social constructivism, 67–68
Social development, 163–64
Social-emotional development, 135–37
Social interactions, on playground, 122
Social skills, 143
    difficulties with, 144
    on playground, 122
    teaching, 144–45
Social Skills Rating System (SSRS),
    143
Social studies, in inclusive class-
    room, 349–70
    constructing knowledge in, 353
    content areas, 352–53
    definitions, 350
    essential skills for, 355–57

expanding environments approach,
    353, 354
integrating through curriculum,
    366–67
learner and, 359–61
lesson/unit planning, 362–63
literature and, 363, 365–66
organizing information, 356
plural perspectives, 357–59
practical application vignette, 349
process skills, 354, 356–66
resources, 368–70
standards, 363
thematic strands, 351–52, 364
transformed, 357
Soto, G., 2, 4, 7, 8
Sowder, J.T., 280
Spandel, V., 255
Special education
    definition of, 12
    websites about, 15
Special needs, 34
Specific learning disability, 40–41
    behavior, 134
    instruction and, 202
    writing instruction, 265
Speech, 42
Speech or language impairment, 41
    behavior, 134
    instruction and, 202
    writing instruction, 265
Spelling
    conventional, 244
    invented, 239, 243
Stacey, S., 6, 7, 8
Stainback, S., 177
Stainback, W., 177
Standardized testing, 84
Stanovich, K., 225
State of Florida, Department of State,
    374, 383
Statistics, 302–3
Stayton, V.D., 6, 18, 20, 22, 24, 25
Steffe, L.P., 63, 71, 73, 287
Steier, F., 69
Stepien, W.J., 78, 79
Stigler, J., 279, 281
Stoecklin, V.L., 106

Stoneman, Z., 6, 7, 8
Stormont, M., 159
Strain, P.S., 16
Strickland, D.S., 187, 212
Students, managing, 149
Student-teacher relationships, 159–60
    assessing, 160
Student-Teacher Relationship Scale
    (STRS), 159
Study guides, 323
Subtraction, 289, 291–94
Success-oriented curriculum, 106
Sulzby, E., 186, 193, 198, 235, 236,
    243, 244, 271
Supervision, of paraeducators, 170–72
Supportive classroom environment,
    139–41
Syllabication, 223
Syntax, 192

T
Tabula rasa, 72
Tate, W.F., 286
Taylor, D., 187
Taylor, P.C., 67, 68, 69
Taylor, R.C., 11
Teacher, constructivist, 85
Teacher/family assessment, 142
Teaching
    art integration strategy, 376–77,
        378–79
    mathematics, 279–81
Teale, W., 186, 187, 198
Technology, assistive, 5
Temperament, behavior and, 131–32
Testing, standardized, 84
Theory of multiple intelligences (MI).
    See Multiple intelligences (MI)
Thomas, A., 132
Thompson, A.G., 280
Tiegerman-Farber, E., 91, 94
Tippins, D., 82
Tobin, K., 82
Toddlers, early intervention for, 12
Tomlinson-Clarke, S., 114
Tomlison, C.A., 140
Tompkins, G.E., 248, 249, 250, 252,
    254

Topic selection, writing, 248
Toys, selecting, 165
Transactional theory, 197
Transitions, behavior and, 140–41
Traub, E.K., 8, 20, 105
Traumatic brain injury (TBI), 41
  behavior, 135
  instruction and, 203
  writing instruction, 266
Treiman, R., 193
Tremblay, R.E., 132
Trivial constructivism, 66
Trowbridge, L.W., 325
Trust, 177–78
Tschannen-Moran, M., 177
Tulviste, P., 64
Tunmer, W.E., 193, 195
Turnbull, A.P., 43, 55, 161, 166, 174, 327, 330
Turnbull, H.R., 6, 43, 55, 166, 174, 327, 330
Tutoring
  cross-age, 163
  peer, 163

U
United States Consumer Products Safety Commission (USCPSC), 120–21
Universal design for learning (UDL), 324
Universal design (UD), 94, 104, 105, 106
  in science, 325
U.S. Department of Education, 24, 150, 176
  Office of Special Education and Rehabilitative Programs, 44
Utley, C.A., 6, 7, 25

V
Vadasy, P.F., 178
VanLaarhoven, T., 20, 24
Vaughn, S., 22, 24
Venn, M.L., 19
Vernon, L.J., 176, 177
Verstegen, D.A., 177

Very special arts (VSA), 385–86
Viability, 67
Vico, Giambattista, 63
Villa, J., 7
Vincent, L.J., 3
Virginia Department of Education, 170, 173
Visual impairments, 41
  behavior, 135
  instruction and, 203
  writing instruction, 266
Visualization, 227
Visuals, 323
Vocabulary, 191
  sight, 214
von Glasserfeld, E., 63, 64, 67, 71
Vosniadou, S., 68
Vygotsky, L.S., 42, 62, 63, 64, 72, 73

W
Walberg, H., 57
Walker, D., 6, 7, 25
Walker, J., 115
Walsh, S., 4, 11
Walther-Thomas, C., 6, 7, 174, 176, 177
Watson, D., 198
Watson, M., 159
Watson, S., 325
Weaver, C., 196
Weber, C., 164
Weber, E., 320
Weil, M., 57
Weinstein, C., 114
Welch, M., 173
Wellhousen, K., 120
Werts, M.G., 172
Wertsch, J.V., 64
Wesley, P.W., 8, 20, 22, 24
West, J., 169
Whitechurch, G.G., 166
Whitehurst, G.J., 195, 220, 221
Wickstrom Kane, S., 4
Wilkinson, L.C., 195
Willis, B.F., 169
Willis, S., 174
Wilson, B., 70
Windschilt, M., 85

Winton, P.J., 4, 8, 20, 21, 25
Wolery, M., 2, 4, 8, 16, 19, 25
Wolery, R.A., 8
Wong, H.K., 101
Wong, R.T., 101
Wood, D., 73
Wood, J.M., 324, 328
Wood, T., 68, 284
Woods, C.S., 319
Woolfolk, A., 359, 361
Word center, 247
Word recognition, 225
Word walls, 247
Wortham, S., 44, 56
Writing, 234–76
  assessment in, 270–73
  authentic, 244–45
  concepts about print, 238–39
  constructing knowledge in, 235–36
  criteria for quality, 272
  descriptive, 251
  developing schema, 237–38
  differentiating instruction in, 257–73
  directionality in, 242
  early attempts at, 242–44
  emergent, 236–37, 243
  genres, 249, 251–52
  guided, 259, 268–69
  independent, 260, 269–70
  informational, 251
  instruction, 256–57
  integrating through curriculum, 240–47
  interactive, 252, 258–59, 260, 267–69
  journals and letters, 251
  letter and word study, 245–47
  meaningful opportunities in, 245
  narrative, 251
  origins of, 235–36
  persuasive, 252
  poetry, 252
  practical application vignette, 234
  process skills, 236–40
  reading-writing connection, 273–74
  shared, 257, 258, 260
  traits of, 255–56

workshop, 259, 268–69
written language principles, 241–42
Writing process, 248–57
    audience, 248–49
    drafting, 250, 253
    editing, 253–54
    form, 249–50
    organization, 250
    prewriting, 248
    publishing, 254–55
    purpose, 248
    revising, 253
    topic selection, 248
    younger children and, 248, 249

Y
Yackel, E., 68
Yeatts, D.E., 177
Yell, M.L., 11, 45
Yopp, H., 223, 224
Young children with exceptional needs,
    33–58
    changing needs of, 55
    curricular implications, 5558
    development delay, 35, 38
    disabilities and diversity, 54
    family roles, 55
    high- and low-incidence disabilities,
        41–42

IEP team, 45–54
learning or behavioral characteristics,
    38–41
in public schools, 34–35
referral, 45
service delivery options, 42–44

Z
Zahotik, J.A., 72, 83, 84
Zarrillo, J.J., 350, 352, 353, 357
Zeichner, K., 280
Zimmerman, S., 218, 226
Zone of proximal development (ZPD),
    64